The Blackwell Guide to Recorded Jazz

The Blackwell Guide to
Recorded Jazz

Second Edition

Edited by

Barry Kernfeld

BLACKWELL
Reference

First published 1995

Blackwell Publishers Inc.
238 Main Street
Cambridge, Massachusetts 02142, USA

Blackwell Publishers Ltd
108 Cowley Road
Oxford OX4 1JF
UK

Library of Congress Cataloging in Publication Data

The Blackwell guide to recorded jazz/edited by Barry Kernfeld. –
2nd ed.
p. cm.
Includes discographies and indexes.
1. Jazz–Discography. I. Kernfeld, Barry Dean.
II. Title: Recorded jazz.
ML 156.4.J3B66 1995
016. 78165′026′6–dc20 95-762
CIP
MN

ISBN 0-631-195521
ISBN 0-631-200754

British Library Cataloguing in Publication Data

A CIP catalogue record for this book is available from the British Library.

Typeset in Palatino on 10/12pt by Acorn Bookwork, Salisbury, Wilts
Printed in Great Britain by TJ Press (Padstow) Ltd, Cornwall

This book is printed on acid-free paper

Contents

Contributors

JAMES LINCOLN COLLIER is an author whose publications include the history *The Making of Jazz* (1978), biographies of Louis Armstrong (1983), Duke Ellington (1987) and Benny Goodman (1989), the leading article, 'Jazz', in *The New Grove Dictionary of Jazz* (1988) and the essay collection *Jazz: the American Theme Song* (1993).

DIGBY FAIRWEATHER maintains several careers in the music: as a cornet player he was named the BBC Jazz Society's Musician of the Year in 1979, and he is today more active than ever. With Ian Carr and Brian Priestley he wrote *Jazz: the Essential Companion* (1987), and is a regular broadcaster for BBC Radio 2.

MARK GARDNER is a veteran interviewer and discographer of bop and hard-bop musicians. From 1962 until their demise his work appeared regularly in *Discographical Forum* and *Jazz Monthly*, and he continues to write for *Jazz Journal*. He is a prolific writer of liner notes, contributed extensively to *The New Grove Dictionary of Jazz* and is the author of *Jam Session* (1984).

MARK GILBERT has been deputy editor of *Jazz Journal International* since 1980 and has written about jazz for *Melody Maker*, the *Daily Mail* and *The Stage* as well as contributing to *The New Grove Dictionary of Jazz*. He is also contemporary jazz consultant for MC Europe, the cable radio company, and a musician and music teacher.

MIKE HAZELDINE managed tours for New Orleans musicians and produced and distributed some historic recordings during the 1960s. He has organized two Duke Ellington International Conferences and put together wide-ranging jazz concerts for various theatres. He contributed to *The New Grove Dictionary of Jazz* and is currently editor of *New Orleans Music*. He is the author of the bio-discography *Bill Russell's American Music* (1993) and co-author with Barry Martyn of *The New Orleans Style* (1994).

EKKEHARD JOST is professor of musicology at the University of Giessen in Germany and he plays baritone saxophone. His publications include *Free Jazz* (1974), *Sozialgeschichte des Jazz in den USA* (1982), *Jazzmusiker: Materialien zur Soziologie der afro-amerikanischen Musik* (1982) and *Europas Jazz, 1960–1980* (1987).

BARRY KERNFELD is an independent scholar. He is the editor of *The New Grove Dictionary of Jazz* (1988), the author of *What to Listen For in Jazz* (1995) and a contributor to *The New Harvard Dictionary of Music* (1986), *Encyclopedia of New York City* (1995) and *American National Biography* (forthcoming).

Preface and Acknowledgements

The first edition of *The Blackwell Guide to Recorded Jazz* was published in 1991, again with an updated CD supplement in 1992, and again in German translation in 1993. Since then, friends unfamiliar with jazz, noticing these three books on the shelf, have asked, 'What is the purpose of the *Guide*?', to which I reply, 'To direct listeners to good tunes'. Our extensively revised second edition has the same aim: get the book, go to record stores, buy some CDs in a style that you like (or might like), and enjoy them. For many listeners, no further introduction should be necessary.

More formally, the foremost aim of this new edition of *The Blackwell Guide to Recorded Jazz* is to suggest a starter collection as a means for newcomers to gain a grasp of this wonderful music. There are about 230 selections in the book, depending on how you wish to count double and boxed-CD sets. These selections are – within particular eras, styles and instrumental genres – among the best of jazz. But it must be said at the start that they should not be construed as embracing *all* the best of this vast and ever-expanding music.

The new *Guide* edition differs from its predecessor in two significant ways. First, listings of issued recordings have been drastically abridged, the editor having realized that such discographical detail is misplaced in a book such as this. With few exceptions (detailed in the text), the focus is on the principal selection only and on compact discs only. Second, having thereby gained a considerable amount of room by deleting long lists of LPs and tapes, we have nearly doubled the number of selections in the book. The original *Guide* explicitly focused on the first and best of jazz and consequently was heavily weighted toward the genre's formative decades. The new *Guide* supplements this core collection with selections from some of the most creative continuations of extant traditions. Consequently it covers recent decades in considerably greater proportion. As before, the text focuses on the music itself rather than on technological matters, although occasionally we have addressed questions of recording fidelity or presentation when these are relevant to our approach.

Like the weather, the availability of compact discs is a subject much less suited to a book than to a newspaper, so quickly does it change.

This volatility reinforced our decision to focus on a concise collection of great recordings, because the majority of these have remained available in one format or another more or less permanently (in so far as permanence is possible in the recording marketplace). However, we have occasionally left in a discontinued item listed in the first edition (for example, Ella Fitzgerald's session at the 1964 Antibes–Juan-les-Pins festival), on the theory that such a great album eventually *must* be reissued; this is not just wishful thinking, given the extent to which our former selections on LP are now on CD, as a comparison of the first and second editions would indicate.

The Blackwell Guide to Recorded Jazz is one in a series of Blackwell Guides, and in particular we have taken account of the coverage of boogie-woogie pianists, blues shouters and classic blues singers in *The Blackwell Guide to Blues Records*, edited by Paul Oliver. These musicians are intimately tied to jazz, but there seemed no point in retracing the same ground. Accordingly, the jazz guide defers to the blues guide in these areas.

We have endeavoured to write in plain English (using English spelling and punctuation) but making use of a hybrid style that reflects both the international authorship (English, American and German) and the Americanisms that dominate jazz literature. We avoid jazz jargon whenever possible; those few terms which are absolutely essential are explained parenthetically at their first appearance. A small proportion of the text presumes a rudimentary knowledge of music (for example, the identification of an instrument, a minor key blues progression or a syncopated rhythmic pattern). One such item requires systematic explanation: in descriptions of the form of a piece, upper-case italic letters refer to themes, while lower-case italics refer to sections of a single theme.

The discographies were prepared by Mark Gardner, Howard Rye and Barry Kernfeld. Tracks are listed in chronological order where known; otherwise we simply list tracks in the order that they appear on the CD. In addition to the recorded documents themselves, we have consulted for one reason or another the majority of the general and specialist discographies and catalogues available. It is impossible to list these sources in a non-academic book such as this; instead a blanket acknowledgement of our indebtedness to jazz discographers and an expression of our gratitude must suffice.

Few record stores carry large inventories of jazz recordings, and even fewer record stores carry inventories that span all of the styles surveyed in this *Guide*. To find what one wants, a listener with catholic tastes often has to shop around. Such a listener may find it useful to know that Bill Hery has compiled a worldwide list of jazz record stores for the NCSA Mosaic online computer network.

To call up the list directly, use command
http://www/nwv.edu/jazz/lists/stores.html

To get to the list screen-by-screen from the main menu: (click) Starting Points, (click) World Wide Web info, (click) information by subject, (click) music, (click) other interesting links, (click) jazz, (click) HAUNT'S archive or rec. music. bluenote club discussion, (click) list of jazz clubs, hotlines, and record stores around the world, (click) jazz music stores around the world.

This book owes its existence to the late Peter Clayton, who created its original plan, saw it through the normal stages of proposal and approval at the publisher, and commissioned chapters from contributors before ill-health forced him to withdraw from the project. The book has changed dramatically since then, but three of the contributors and a number of their selections remain as Peter had planned. I offer my thanks to Peter for having cut through so much of the red tape, and I regret that he could not share more in the rewards of completing the project.

I am also deeply grateful to Alyn Shipton, Reference Publisher at Basil Blackwell, for asking me to edit the book after Peter determined he could not continue. Alyn's penetrating suggestions and criticisms, stemming both from his regular duties as a publisher and from his intense involvement with jazz, have substantially improved the quality of the volume. And it was a delight and privilege to be involved once again with the book's managing editor, Caroline Richmond. Having spent four years working together on a jazz dictionary, we long ago arrived at an easy manner of communicating and a virtually telepathic agreement on matters of style and substance.

It goes without saying that my thanks are due to the six contributors, all of whom took time away from busy schedules to do their part.

For this new edition, I also wish to thank Roger W. Jordan, copy-editor, and Josh Ferko and his employees at Arboria Records in State College, PA, for helping to procure some of our selections and for calling my attention to Eddie Palmieri's disc Palmas, which would have been a shame to miss. I am deeply grateful to Acorn Bookwork for typesetting with great accuracy when, owing to circumstances beyond our control, it became necessary to set the entire second edition anew, rather than merely inserting revisions into the first edition.

The acknowledgements end with loving thanks to my wife and 'patron', Sally McMurry, whose flourishing career as Associate Professor of History at the Pennsylvania State University allows me to indulge in a career as a freelance jazz scholar.

Barry Kernfeld
State College, Pennsylvania

Discographical Abbreviations

arr	arranger
as	alto saxophone
bar	baritone saxophone
bb	brass bass
bj	banjo
bsx	bass saxophone
c	cornet
cl	clarinet
d	drums
elb	electric bass guitar
elg	electric guitar
elp	electric piano
fl	flute
g	guitar
kbd	keyboard
org	organ
p	piano
per	percussion
sb	string bass
ss	soprano saxophone
syn	synthesizer
tb	trombone
tpt	trumpet
ts	tenor saxophone
v	vocal
vb	vibraphone/vibraharp
vln	violin
wbd	washboard

The personnel and instrumentation on a jazz disc routinely changes several times if not on every track. We have sometimes used the words 'omit' and 'add' to indicate these changes rather than to spell out the personnel and instrumentation in full each time.

Principal Selections

CHAPTER 1

The First Hot Bands

James Lincoln Collier

It is generally accepted that jazz first developed in New Orleans in the early years of the century, and that all jazz has evolved from the version that was created there. It was an outgrowth or variant of ragtime, differing mainly in a certain rhythmic feel which has come to be called 'swing'. In addition, elements of the blues were added, especially the inflection of notes through the use of pitch bends, mutes of various kinds, and throat-tones to roughen the sound.

This New Orleans music was played by many different combinations of instruments. In the honky-tonks of the New Orleans brothel district, bands were likely to be small, consisting of one or two brass or reed instruments accompanied by one or two rhythm instruments. The new style also found its way into music of the larger marching or brass bands of the city. But in time there developed a jazz dance band of cornet, trombone and clarinet over a rhythm section, which in its fullest form comprised string bass, guitar, drums and piano – although in many if not most instances not all of these rhythm instruments would be present. At times a violin would be added to double the lead. Later, after about World War I, tuba and banjo were usually substituted for string bass and guitar.

The classic New Orleans band played an ensemble music that was frequently interrupted by short solo 'breaks' which were usually two bars in length, but could be longer or shorter. Full-dress solos were relatively rare, and when they did occur they were not improvised, but fairly formal statements of a theme. In the ensemble the cornet played a comparatively simple melody in the middle register, the clarinet wove rising and falling lines through the melody or shrilled on top in imitation of marching fifes, and the trombone provided a bass line, as well as making connecting links between phrases of the melody, often through the use of slurs.

This fairly rigid system of the classic New Orleans style obviously owes a great deal to the band marches which were so popular in America in the years around the turn of the century. It was in place by 1915, certainly, and probably at least eight years earlier. We cannot be sure precisely who developed jazz out of previous forms. Clearly the racially-mixed, French-speaking creoles, many of them descended from refugees from Haiti a hundred years earlier, played a major role. For a variety of reasons these Haitians had held on to residues of African culture more than had American-born blacks, and appear to have carried with them elements of African rhythm that they eventually used in the making of jazz. However, mainstream blacks were certainly involved, and it is likely that white musicians, many of them of Sicilian descent, and Latin American musicians also made contributions. Jazz began to spread out from New Orleans by 1907 or perhaps earlier, carried especially to the West Coast, and then Chicago, by musicians from New Orleans adept at it. These bands played in a variety of situations, but many worked in the dance halls and saloons of the vice districts that were a feature of American cities at that time. Associations with the brothels discredited the music in the eyes of many Americans; none the less, it rapidly attracted a nationwide audience, and, with the astounding success of the records of the Original Dixieland Jazz Band in 1917, New Orleans jazz became an important part of American popular music, played for listening as well as dancing. The music was simply called jazz; but as other forms arose, it began to be referred to as 'New Orleans jazz', 'New Orleans' and eventually 'dixieland', after the group which had first made it famous. In time it was supplanted by big dance bands playing arranged music, and then other forms; but dixieland has continued to attract an audience worldwide, and must be honoured as the seminal form of the music.

* * *

Original Dixieland Jazz Band: *The Complete Original Dixieland Jazz Band (1917–1921)*

In 1915, as part of the diaspora from New Orleans, some white New Orleans musicians were brought to Chicago to play in the city's clubs and dance halls. Two of these groups were led by drummer Johnny Stein and trombonist Tom Brown. After some switching of personnel the Stein group, without Stein and now called the Original Dixieland Jazz Band, was brought east. In January 1917 it opened at a famous restaurant in New York called Reisenweber's, where it quickly became something of a popular sensation. Reisenweber's was one of the lobster palaces catering to middle-class New Yorkers and tourists. The introduction of jazz to such a locale signalled that it was now acceptable to mainstream Americans. The group's Victor records made that year and after were best-sellers and were important in making jazz a national phenomenon. Its first hit paired *Barnyard Blues* (better known as *Livery Stable Blues*) and *At the Jazz Band Ball*. Besides these, perhaps the best known of the Victor Original Dixieland Jazz Band sides were *Bluin' the Blues, Ostrich Walk, Sensation Rag, Clarinet Marmalade, Fidgety Feet* and *Tiger Rag*, which became virtually the theme song for early jazz. The first records used the variant spelling 'Jass', but 'Jazz' quickly became standard.

Because there was little true improvising, early jazz musicians were not as individually distinctive as later jazz musicians would be. LaRocca played a bright, relatively simple, punchy line, with the notes sharply attacked, and the tone clean and muscular. Shields frequently began his figures on a high note, which he would then let fall off in a descending slur which would break into a downward cascade. His tone was somewhat shrill in the upper register, as was generally the case with early New Orleans players, but was liquid and clean in the mid-range. Edwards played almost invariably in the mid to low range, to stay out of the way of the other instruments. As was typical of New Orleans trombonists, he introduced a great many slurs; the slide trombone had only recently supplanted the valve trombone in general use in popular music, and trombonists were, at the period, over-using the potential for slurs. None of these musicians developed along with the music to become important individual soloists. In 1936 the group was reassembled to make a documentary film and to re-create its earlier performances on record. The musicians played in much the same manner as they had in 1917, although with an inevitable loosening of the rhythm.

The tunes made famous by the Original Dixieland Jazz Band were typical of New Orleans jazz vehicles, usually consisting of two, three or even more strains, like the rags and marches from which they were derived. The strains often modulated to another key, usually up a fourth. The famous *Tiger Rag*, for example, consists of strains in B flat, E flat and A flat. Some strains were linked by interludes, as in *Clarinet Marmalade Blues*. At times its music, and that of other New Orleans bands, was not melodic, but consisted of collections of devices rather arbitrarily strung together: slurs, growls, sudden outbursts of drumming. Particularly important was the break, where the band ceased briefly – usually for two measures – in order to allow one instrument to parade alone. These breaks were often comical in intent: early jazz had one foot in vaudeville, and there were always elements of humour in the music, for example, the imitation of the whinnying horse and the crowing rooster in *Barnyard Blues* and the trombone's downward octave plop, meant to imitate the roar of the tiger, in the last strain of *Tiger Rag*.

The Original Dixieland Jazz Band has never been considered a truly great jazz band. But it was a good one, which played with verve and infectious swing, and, considering that the musicians were mostly untutored, with surprising accuracy and good intonation. It may have been typical of the New Orleans bands of the day, though we have no idea how typical, because it was in any case the first jazz band to record. As the first to have not only national, but – through its work in London in 1919 – international success, it played a seminal role in teaching the world about this exciting new music, and became the early model for thousands of young musicians who were attempting to play it, among them Bix Beiderbecke and Benny Goodman.

CD

***The Complete Original Dixieland Jazz Band (1917–1921)*, Bluebird CD 61098 (USA) and RCA PD 90026 (France)**

Nick LaRocca (c), Eddie Edwards (tb), Larry Shields (cl), Henry Ragas (p), Tony Sbarbaro (d)

New York	26 Feb 1917	**Livery Stable Blues**
		Dixie Jass Band One-Step
	18 March 1918	**At the Jazz Band Ball**
		Ostrich Walk
	25 March 1918	**Skeleton Jangle**
		Tiger Rag
	25 June 1918	**Bluin' the Blues**
		Fidgety Feet
		Sensation Rag
	17 July 1918	**Mournin' Blues**
		Clarinet Marmalade Blues
		Lazy Daddy
add Benny Krueger (as); J. Russel Robinson (p) replaces Ragas		
	1 Dec 1920	**Margie**
	4 Dec 1920	**Palesteena**
	30 Dec 1920	**Broadway Rose**
add Clifford Cairns, Eddie King, band (v)		**Sweet Mamma**
omit (v)	28 Jan 1921	**Home Again Blues**
		Crazy Blues
Frank Signorelli (p) replaces Robinson		
	3 May 1921	**Jazz Me Blues**
add Al Bernard (v)		
	25 May 1921	**St Louis Blues**
		Royal Garden Blues
	7 June 1921	**Dangerous Blues**

omit Bernard and Sbarbaro

1 Dec 1921 **Bow Wow Blues**

* * *

New Orleans Rhythm Kings: *New Orleans Rhythm Kings and Jelly Roll Morton*

The success of the Stein and Brown bands in Chicago, followed by the national celebrity of the Original Dixieland Jazz Band, led cabaret and dance-hall managers to search for similar New Orleans groups. Over the years after 1917 more New Orleans musicians, both singly and in groups, began to move northward, encouraged to do so in no little part by the pay scale, which was substantially higher in places such as New York, Chicago and San Francisco than it was in New Orleans. In the years after about 1916 or so, Chicago in particular came to be seen as the centre of jazz activity, supplanting New Orleans, in considerable measure because most of the best New Orleans musicians had come north. Even in New York, through much of the 1920s, it was recognized that the western musicians in Chicago were playing a hotter, stronger version of jazz than was to be heard in the East.

One of the most influential of the New Orleans bands to arrive in Chicago was the group that came to be called the New Orleans Rhythm Kings, although its initial recordings were issued as by the Friar's Society Orchestra, after the Friar's Inn, where the band was playing. This group was not brought intact from New Orleans, as some of the earlier groups had been, but was put together piecemeal out of combinations of New Orleans musicians who had drifted north, with midwesterners who, by the early 1920s, were playing the new music. The group which made the first and very influential recordings included four New Orleanians: Paul Mares, cornet; George Brunies, trombone; Leon Roppolo, clarinet; and Steve Brown, bass. To them were added midwesterners Jack Pettis, saxophones; Elmer Schoebel, piano; Lou Black, banjo; and Frank Snyder, drums. Through the relatively brief career of the group the personnel shifted as saxophonists came and went, and changes were made to the rhythm section. For a period Ben Pollack, considered by other musicians to be one of the finest drummers of the time, was in the band. But the key figures were the front line of Mares, Brunies and Roppolo, who were on all of the early, influential cuts. (George Brunies later changed his 13-letter name to Georg Brunis on the advice of a numerologist.)

Like the ODJB, the New Orleans Rhythm Kings was a typical New

Orleans group, playing the classic contrapuntal style with cornet lead, clarinet weaving upwards and downwards through the melody in the flute or fife-like marching band style, and the trombone providing connecting links. The saxophones that appear on some of these sides were a concession to a fad for the instrument: in 1919 the Art Hickman band, a jazz-based dance group which featured a saxophone duet, had become widely popular, and the saxophone had become, during the early 1920s, a vogue instrument.

As was the case with the Original Dixieland Jazz Band, the New Orleans Rhythm Kings did not improvise, in the main, but played set-pieces with carefully worked out parts, which they might embellish or vary to some extent in the course of playing. This was true even of the solos: George Brunies plays his famous solo on *Tin Roof Blues* more or less the same on three takes of the tune, and he continued to play it thus for the remainder of his career. This was still primarily an ensemble jazz band in the old New Orleans style, with the solos scattered sparsely through the performance and meant mainly to provide variety rather than to act, as happened a few years later, as the central point of the music. On *Eccentric*, for example, the solos consist of sets of two-bar breaks by clarinet, trumpet and trombone for a total of 22 bars; the rest of the cut is played by the ensemble.

The band performs with less of the hokum that had helped to make the Original Dixieland Jazz Band famous, and there is nothing like the obvious horseplay of that group's *Livery Stable Blues*. But touches of comedy remain in, for example, some of the breaks on *Eccentric*.

The New Orleans Rhythm Kings is clearly a superior jazz band to its predecessor. Paul Mares's breaks on *Bugle Call Blues* are played with the plunger mute, a device believed to have been developed by King Oliver, and employ mainly quarter, rather than eighth, notes, a characteristic of Oliver's style. Taken as a whole, the New Orleans Rhythm Kings plays with a looser, more supple swing than the Original Dixieland Jazz Band, as is evident in the very driving lead of Mares on the aforementioned *Bugle Call Blues*. Note also on the last ride-out chorus of this piece the drum 'backbeat' (accents on the second and fourth beats), a device which would become a cliché in jazz playing, providing here the classic rocking two-beat swing.

Although Mares and Brunies were influential as far as the young jazz players in Chicago and elsewhere were concerned, the most admired member of the group was clarinettist Leon Roppolo. To some extent this was owing to his early madness and death, which cast a romantic aura around him, but there is no denying the liquid quality of his tone, evident in the breaks on *Eccentric*, and the easy swing he achieved. His playing is less shrill than that of many of the early jazz clarinettists, especially in the upper register.

Just as the Original Dixieland Jazz Band brought into the repertory a number of classic tunes, such as *Tiger Rag* and *Clarinet Marmalade*, so too the New Orleans Rhythm Kings added at least three famous ones – *Bugle Call Blues* (better known as *Bugle Call Rag*), *Farewell Blues* and *Tin Roof Blues*, possibly the most frequently played of any of the New Orleans pieces. The band's music director, Elmer Schoebel, wrote some of these, including *Farewell Blues*, but others were put together out of musical oddments familiar to many players. But they have remained classics.

(A footnote to this collection: during the course of extensive interviews with Tom Thibeau, a Connecticut businessman who had been a professional pianist in Chicago, the latter explained that Kyle Pierce had sent him as a substitute for the session of 17 July 1922, a session attributed to Pierce and Jelly Roll Morton. Thibeau definitely identified himself as the soloist on *Marguerite* and also claimed to be on *Sobbin' Blues*. He did not remember Morton being on the date, though no one challenges Morton's presence on *Mr Jelly Lord* and two tracks from the next day).

CD

New Orleans Rhythm Kings and Jelly Roll Morton **Milestone MCD-47020-2 (USA)**

(Friar's Society Orchestra:) Paul Mares (tpt), George Brunies (tb), Leon Roppolo (cl), Jack Pettis (C-melody sax, ts), Elmer Schoebel (p), Lou Black (bj) Steve Brown (sb), Frank Snyder (d)

Richmond, IN	29 Aug 1922	**Eccentric**
		Farewell Blues
		Discontented Blues
		Bugle Call Blues
	30 Aug 1922	**Panama**
		Tiger Rag
		Livery Stable Blues
		Oriental

Mares (tpt), Brunies (tb), Roppolo (cl), Mel Stitzel (p), Ben Pollack (d)

	12 March 1922	**Sweet Lovin' Man**
		That's a Plenty (take A)
		Shimmeshawabble
		Weary Blues
	13 March 1922	**Da Da Strain**
		Wolverine Blues (take B)
		Maple Leaf Rag
		Tin Roof Blues (take B)

Mares (tpt), Brunies (tb), Roppolo (cl), Pettis (C-melody sax), Glenn Scoville (as, ts), Don Murray (cl, ts), Tom Thibeau (p), Bob Gillette (bj), Chink Martin (bb), Pollack (d)

	17 July 1923	**Sobbin' Blues**
		Marguerite
also incl. Thibeau ?		**Angry**
		Clarinet Marmalade
		Clarinet Marmalade (take A)
Jelly Roll Morton replaces ? (p)		**Mr Jelly Lord** (take A)
		Mr Jelly Lord (take C)
	18 July 1923	**London Blues**
		Milenberg Joys
		Milenberg Joys (take C)
Kyle Pierce (p) replaces Morton		**Mad**

* * *

King Oliver: *Louis Armstrong and King Oliver*

By 1920, with the enormous success of the Original Dixieland Jazz Band and its imitators, New Orleans jazz had become a national fad. Everywhere young musicians were attempting to learn the new music, and they were looking to established New Orleans players to provide a lead. One effect of the vogue for jazz was to draw out of New Orleans many of the best musicians. Among these was King Oliver, who from about 1919 was playing in Chicago with his Creole Jazz Band. The group very quickly became the primary model for the jazz musicians of Chicago and, as its first records appeared, elsewhere.

The personnel of the group shifted over time, as was generally the case with early jazz bands, but most of its recordings were made with Oliver, cornet; Honore Dutrey, trombone; Johnny Dodds, clarinet; Baby Dodds, drums; Bill Johnson, banjo; Lil Hardin, piano; and, at times, various saxophone players. And in 1922 Oliver added Louis Armstrong on second cornet. All the recordings of this important early Oliver group were made in 1923 for four different companies: Gennett, Paramount, Okeh and Columbia. The Gennett and Okeh series are longer, and are considered the heart of Oliver's recordings.

Like most New Orleans bands, the group worked out its music in advance, even including the solos – as is indicated, for example, by the different masters of *Riverside Blues*, which contain virtually identical solos by Armstrong. Rhythmically, the group achieves an easy two-beat rock, somewhat different from the four-beat swing that would evolve during the 1920s. Oliver did not want a frantic, hard-driving band. He believed in a controlled, well-organized performance which swung but did not press. As a consequence the three main melody instruments work at keeping their lines distinct and clean; it is this ensemble sound for which we listen in the work of this band. This is also dance music, as was most early jazz. Tempos are necessarily moderate, in the range of 140 to 190 beats per minute. The music is not without flaws: structurally there is a tendency for the pieces simply to alternate two strains, an acceptable practice for dancing, but too predictable for music meant to be listened to. The saxophones add nothing, and at times simply muddy the sound.

Paradoxically, the band's best-known tune was a solo feature for Oliver, employing his specialty, mutes. This was *Dippermouth Blues*, known in some later versions as *Sugar Foot Stomp*. Oliver's solo shows the deep influence of the blues on early jazz. The opening note is the blue third slurring down to the tonic and shaded by the opening and closing of the plunger mute. It bears an uncanny resemblance to the whine of a blues guitar, especially one played with a bottleneck, as it was undoubtedly meant to do. We can also hear in this solo the way that Oliver has placed the notes around the beat, rather than on them, an important characteristic of jazz. Indeed, in many cases it is actually difficult to determine where the notes come, so ambiguous are they.

Although it was not realized at the time, in retrospect we see *Chimes Blues* and *Froggie Moore* are equally important, for they contain Louis Armstrong's first two recorded solos. *Chimes Blues* is so thoroughly worked out that the musicians could have been reading it from written scores, and it is characterized by the easy rock that the band frequently achieved. Typically, Armstrong's solo is played straight, presumably on Oliver's instructions. One of Oliver's trademarks was the use of figures which displace accents from their normal spots, thus contradicting the prevailing metre. The main figure in Armstrong's solo is one of this type, and it confuses Armstrong, so that he turns the beat around in the middle of the solo and has to take a quick skip to find his place again.

Armstrong's solo on *Froggie Moore*, a Jelly Roll Morton tune, can be considered the first important recorded jazz solo. (However, it is only partially a 'solo' as other winds continue to play a reduced role.) From the moment Armstrong enters we feel a difference in the rhythm from the way the rest of the band is playing. Through a use of terminal vibrato (a vibrato increasing in intensity during a held note), shifting accents, uneven division of the beat and placement of his notes around the beat, rather than on it, Armstrong defines what would come to be called 'swing'.

At the time, however, Oliver, and not Armstrong, was seen by other musicians as the key figure in the group. One device that impressed them was the use of duet breaks featuring the two cornets, who appeared to improvise a break together spontaneously in correct harmony. In fact, according to Armstrong, at an appropriate moment ahead of time Oliver would play for Armstrong the figure he intended to use; it would be no problem for a trained musician to improvise a harmony to the line. These duet breaks appear on a number of the Creole Jazz Band cuts, especially *Snake Rag*, in which they are featured.

The Creole Jazz Band is considered by many jazz authorities to be the most influential of the early jazz bands. By 1922 young musicians, including many white ones, were visiting Lincoln Gardens to hear the group. In fact, in time the management began putting on special 'for whites only' musical nights for the benefit of white musicians when they came off their jobs. Musicians were also buying the records as they came out. By the mid-1920s King Oliver was well known not merely to jazz musicians and fans, but to the wider audience for hot dance music. In 1924 a show business newspaper could say, 'King Oliver, Negro jazz trumpeter, is the "hottest" jazz musician of his kind in the business. He has set the pace which all the jazz cornetists with the crack bands follow' (Abel Green in *The Clipper*, 10 April 1924, 14).

The reissue on Milestone also contains some cuts by a group called the Red Onion Jazz Babies. By the mid-1920s a black composer named Clarence Williams, a New Orleanian, was in New York, building what would become a small musical empire. Williams was, among other things, organizing recording sessions for various companies, employing New Orleans players when he could. He frequently used Louis Armstrong, who was working with the Fletcher Henderson band in New York, as well as the brilliant but bristly New Orleans clarinet and soprano saxophone player Sidney Bechet. These two giants of early jazz appear together on several of these items. The most important is *Cake Walking Babies (from Home)*, a blazing hot version of the tune which Bechet dominates, in part because he was over-recorded. This is not the disciplined ensemble work of the Oliver group, but it may have been more representative of the way jazz was played in New Orleans honky-tonks.

CD

***Louis Armstrong and King Oliver* Milestone MCD-47017-2 (USA)**

King Oliver, Louis Armstrong (c), Honore Dutrey (tb), Johnny Dodds (cl), Lil Hardin (p), Bill Johnson (bj), Baby Dodds (d)

Richmond, IN	5 April 1923	**Just Gone**
		Canal Street Blues
		Mandy Lee Blues

		I'm Going Away to Wear You off my Mind
		Chimes Blues
	6 April 1923	**Weather Bird Rag**
add Johnson (v break)		**Dippermouth Blues**
omit (v break)		**Froggie Moore**
		Snake Rag

add Stump Evans (C-melody sax); Johnny St Cyr (bj) replaces Johnson

	5 Oct 1923	**Alligator Hop**
		Zulu's Ball
		Working Man's Blues
		Krooked Blues

Oliver (c), Armstrong (c, slide whistle), Dutrey (tb), Johnny Dodds (cl), Hardin (p), Charlie Jackson (brass bass), Baby Dodds (d)

Chicago	c.24 Dec 1923	**Mabel's Dream** (take 1)
		Mabel's Dream (take 2)
		The Southern Stomps (take 1)
		The Southern Stomps (take 2)
		Riverside Blues

(Alberta Hunter and the Red Onion Jazz Babies:) Louis Armstrong (c), Aaron Thompson (tb), Buster Bailey (cl), Lil Armstrong (p), Buddy Christian (bj), Hunter (v)

New York	8 Nov 1924	**Texas Moaner Blues**
(Red Onion Jazz Babies:) omit Hunter		**Of All the Wrongs You Done to Me**
	26 Nov 1924	**Terrible Blues**
		Santa Claus Blues

(Hunter and Red Onion Jazz Babies:) Louis Armstrong (c), Charlie Irvis (tb), Sidney Bechet (cl, ss), Lil Armstrong (p), Christian (bj), Hunter (v)

	22 Dec 1924	**Nobody Knows the Way I Feel 'dis Mornin'**
		Early Every Morn

(Red Onion Jazz Babies:) Eva Taylor (v) replaces Hunter; add Clarence Todd (v)

		Cake Walking Babies (from Home)

* * *

Original Memphis Five: *Original Memphis Five Groups*

Of all the groups that set out to imitate the Original Dixieland Jazz Band, far and away the most successful was the one generally known as the Original Memphis Five, which actually made its first recording as a substitute for the ODJB. Primarily a recording band, it made dozens of discs under that name and dozens more under a variety of pseudonyms, among them the Cotton Pickers, Jazz-bo's Carolina Serenaders and Ladd's Black Aces, for records aimed at the market for black groups. The personnel shifted frequently, but was built around Phil Napoleon, cornet; Jimmy Lytell, clarinet; either Miff Mole or Charlie Panelli, trombone; Jack Roth, drums; and Frank Signorelli, piano. Other musicians who recorded with the group included pianist (and comic) Jimmy Durante; the obscure clarinettist Doc Behrendson, a major influence on Benny Goodman; drummer Ray Bauduc, a star with Bob Crosby's orchestra in the swing band era; and bigger names such as Red Nichols and the Dorsey brothers.

Initially the band frankly imitated the Original Dixieland Jazz Band – in fact, its first recordings were issued under that name. On *Aunt Hagar's Children Blues*, recorded in 1921 under the pseudonym Ladd's Black Aces, trombonist Moe Gappell sounds like Eddie Edwards. The clarinettist is Behrendson, a New Orleanian who played a simpler, more direct style than Shields, with fewer of the saw-toothed figures. There appears to be some collective improvisation, but for the most part the ensemble passages are worked out, as was the case generally with these early dixieland bands. *Shake it and Break it*, from the same recording session, features a number of typical New Orleans breaks.

However, the Original Memphis Five generally employed skilled professionals, more proficient than the New Orleanians as a general rule and more musically sophisticated. Mole would quickly establish himself as the most influential jazz trombonist of the mid-1920s, vastly admired for his brilliant technique; the others were, if not on Mole's level, none the less excellent musicians. As a consequence, even on the aforementioned *Shake it and Break it*, the playing is very clean, almost precise, and there are bits of arranged passages scattered through the dixieland ensemble. The tendency toward arrangement appears again in *I wish I could shimmy like my sister Kate*, recorded in 1922 under another pseudonym, the Cotton Pickers. By the time of *How come you do me like you do?*, recorded in 1924 under the name of the Original Memphis Five, there are a considerable number of arranged passages. The tune also features an improvised duet with clarinettist Lytell taking the lead while cornetist Napoleon, using a wa-wa mute, weaves a line around it, a very novel device for the time. *Meanest Blues*, from 1925, presents a harmonized line for trumpet and clarinet.

This was the period when the dixieland ensemble was giving way to the big band playing from arrangements and featuring improvised solos, which were relatively rare in jazz before 1924. Using a mute and featuring squeezed half-valve effects, Napoleon plays an improvised solo in *Got to Cool My Doggies Now* from that year, 1924. On the same track Mole demonstrates his already considerable technique in a break.

The weakness of the Original Memphis Five, as was the case with most of the early non-New Orleanian groups, was a rhythmic feel, derived from ragtime, that still was somewhat stiff by comparison with the more rocking swing of the New Orleanians. However by 1925 the group was playing with a looser beat, and by the later years of the 1920s it was able to swing as well as all but the best of jazz musicians.

The Original Memphis Five, in its many guises, recorded some 400 sides, and, because these records sold well, it was one of the most generally influential jazz bands of the time with jazz fans and the dance-band audience. To many Americans in the mid-1920s this, more than the Oliver or Armstrong sound, was what jazz was all about.

CD

Original Memphis Five Groups **Village VILCD016-2 (Germany)**

(Ladd's Black Aces:) Phil Napoleon (tpt), Moe Gappell (tb), Doc Behrendson (cl), Jimmy Durante (p), Jack Roth (d)

New York	Aug 1921	**Aunt Hagar's Children Blues**
		Shake it and Break it

(Cotton Pickers:) Napoleon (tpt), Miff Mole (tb), Jimmy Lytell (cl), Frank Signorelli (p), John Cali (bj), John Helleberg (bb), Roth (d)

	Sept 1922	**I wish I could shimmy like my sister Kate**
		Got to Cool My Doggies Now

(Southland Six:) Napoleon (tpt), Charlie Panelli (tb), Lytell (cl), Signorelli (p), Ray Kitchingman (bj), Roth (d)

	2 Dec 1922	**Runnin' Wild**
		Ivy (Cling to me)

(Original Memphis Five:) omit Kitchingman

	late Jan 1923	**Loose Feet**
		Aggravatin' Papa
		The Great White Way Blues
		Four O'Clock Blues
	22 Sept 1923	**The Jelly-Roll Blues**
		A Bunch of Blues
	1 Oct 1924	**How come you do me like you do?**
		The Meanest Blues

(Cotton Pickers:) Napoleon (tpt), Miff Mole (tb), Chuck Miller (cl), Frank Trumbauer (C-melody sax), Rube Bloom (p), John Cali (bj), Joe Tarto (bb), Harry Lottman (d)

	4 Dec 1924	**Prince of Wails**
	6 Dec 1924	**Jimtown Blues**

9 April 1925	**Those Panama Mamas**
	Down and Out Blues

(Original Memphis Five:) Napoleon, Mole, Lytell, Signorelli, Roth

25 Sept 1925	**Indiana Stomp**

* * *

Jelly Roll Morton: *Jelly Roll Morton, 1923/24; The Pearls*

Jelly Roll Morton was one of the most fascinating characters in jazz history. A braggart who fancied himself a pool shark and pimp, he was nevertheless a brilliant musician, one of the three or four greatest of the early jazz pioneers. Born in New Orleans, where he served his apprenticeship, he followed the migration of jazz out of the South to the West Coast, and eventually to Chicago. By the early 1920s it was clear that he was one of the pre-eminent pianists in jazz, playing in an individual style he had manufactured for himself, with blues as the important element. Eventually Morton's supremacy would be challenged by Earl Hines, the stride players such as Fats Waller, and the swing players who followed. But in the early 1920s he was dominant. He began his recording career in 1923 with some band sides, but the most important recordings he made during these first years were a series of piano solos, among them his classics *Wolverine Blues, The Pearls, Kansas City Stomp* and *King Porter* (which would be a hit during the swing period in a Benny Goodman version arranged by Fletcher Henderson).

Morton's piano pieces, like much jazz of the time, were based on rags. They all have two or more strains, usually with transitional interludes between them, as had rags and the marches from which they were derived. For example, *Wolverine Blues* has an interlude modulating up a fourth. The first two choruses of the following strain are particularly interesting: the first chorus is played in whole notes with no rhythmic accompaniment and comes as close to being arhythmic as anything in early jazz; the second is a fancy variation on the same theme using trills and ornaments of various kinds, typical of ragtime playing. The right-hand figures in the opening strain of *Grandpa's Spells* are pure ragtime.

However, we must remain aware that Morton undergirds his music with a four beat, instead of the two beat that was almost invariable in ragtime. This shift was crucial in making the jump from ragtime to jazz – indeed it may have been the single critical change. Morton claimed that he was the first to employ this device, and it is even possible that he is correct. For another thing, Morton had grown up hearing the blues and utilized them more in his playing than did the stride players of the Northeast: note the seventh chord which ends *New Orleans Joys*, a characteristic blues device, and the eccentric 'tone clusters' in the second strain of *Grandpa's Spells*, which suggest the microtonality of blue notes. Finally, Morton believed that the piano ought to imitate a band, and he used trills to suggest woodwind and in particular trombonistic figures in the bass, very evident in *New Orleans Joys*.

Had Jelly Roll Morton recorded nothing but his piano solos, especially this early series, he would have had a secure place in jazz history. However, during the years when he was at his peak of fame and influence, he worked and recorded primarily with a classic New Orleans jazz band, utilizing the standard cornet–trombone–clarinet front line with a rhythm section, known as Jelly Roll Morton's Red Hot Peppers. Many of the numbers played by this group were improvised in the ordinary manner of New Orleans ensembles, but, for recording, Morton usually made careful arrangements of the tunes, guided the musicians and rehearsed them in advance. His arrangements are often quite elaborate and are true compositions, in the sense that Duke Ellington's arrangements are usually thought of as compositions. From this point of view, Morton can be considered the first significant jazz composer.

The care with which Morton went about presenting his music is evident in the attention to detail. Individual brass and reed melodies are accompanied by riffs, introduced by propelling figures and carefully taken out with other figures. Many of these solos are not freely improvised, but were worked out in advance or guided by Morton, as, for example, the clarinet solo which precedes the piano solo on *Black Bottom Stomp*. For *Sidewalk Blues* Morton brought into the studio two extra clarinets just to play one chorus of a clarinet trio. Nothing was left to chance.

Particularly striking is the variety Morton brings to his music with this limited orchestra, frequently using the most basic materials. *Sidewalk Blues*, for example, opens with the honking of an auto horn and some patter; there are brief breaks by the horns in sequence to provide an introduction. There follows a cornet melody accompanied by the band's backbeat rhythm, a second blues chorus of collective playing and a clarinet solo with the same backbeat rhythm. An interlude built on a descending scale leads from the blues into a harmonized dirge, during the middle of which the raucous auto horn suddenly intrudes. As the new second strain concludes and repeats there is more collective playing, then the clarinet trio and a last jammed ensemble, this time with a plunger mute in the trumpet. To close, we have the auto horn again and a final bit of patter. This constant shifting of tone colour, key, theme and orchestration is basic to Morton's method. The introduction of the auto horn in the middle of the recording is particularly felicitous, for it integrates into the piece what in other hands would have been simple hokum, making it a genuine thread in the composition – no different from the mechanical sounds woven into pieces by the avant-garde composers of the same period.

In these sides Morton carried the New Orleans style a step further; they were certainly New Orleans in feeling, but, inventing new devices and drawing others from around him, Morton raised the older form to a new level of musical sophistication. In fact, the Jelly Roll Morton Hot Peppers sides brought the New Orleans style – which was then dying – to an apogee.

In 1939 Morton was in obscurity, forgotten by a new generation of jazz fans and many of the older ones as well. However, as a historical interest in jazz began to assert itself, he found his way back to the studio that same year with a band drawn from some of the best of the musicians working both in the old style and in the more modern, swing manner. These recordings are basically in the mode that he had established for himself 15 years earlier. The ensemble work is not improvised but generally worked out, with arranged passages that may actually have been scored, as, for example, the figures behind Sidney Bechet's solo on *I Thought I Heard Buddy Bolden Say* and again behind the trombone lead on *Winin' Boy*. On this latter passage Bechet is given an obbligato against the lead; typically he plays too loud for a proper balance. The trombone line, too, is executed in a modern swing band style that is not entirely in keeping with the general New Orleans tone of these recordings. Morton sings the famous words on both these cuts. His voice has lost some of its old power and confidence, and he suffers from intonation problems, particularly on *Winin' Boy*. But, taken all in all, they show that he was still capable of putting together first-rate jazz performances.

CD

***Jelly Roll Morton, 1923/24* Milestone MCD-47018-2 (USA)**

Bernie Young (c), unknown (tb), Wilson Townes (cl), Jelly Roll Morton (p), Jasper Taylor (woodblocks)

Chicago	June 1923	**Big Foot Ham** (take 2) **Muddy Water Blues**

Morton (p)

Richmond, IN	17 July 1923	**King Porter – a Stomp** [*sic*] **New Orleans (Blues)** [*sic*] **Joys** **New Orleans (Blues)** [*sic*] **Joys** (take A)
	18 July 1923	**Grandpa's Spells** **Kansas City Stomp**

		Wolverine Blues
		The Pearls (a Stomp)

'Memphis' (comb), Jack Russell (kazoo), Boyd Senter (cl), Morton (p)

Chicago	*c.*April 1924	**Mr Jelly Lord** (take 3)

Morton (p)

		Thirty-Fifth Street Blues
		Mamanita
	9 June 1924	**Tia Juana**
		Shreveport Stomps
		Mamamita
		Jelly Roll Blues
		Big Foot Ham
		Bucktown Blues
		Tom Cat Blues
		Stratford Hunch
		Perfect Rag
Chicago	late June 1924	**Froggie Moore (Frog-i-more)**
		London Blues

King Oliver (c), Morton (p)

	*c.*Dec 1924	**King Porter**
		Tom Cat

Ray Bowling (tpt), 4 unknown (tb, as, ts, bj), Morton (p), Clay Jefferson (d)

Richmond, IN	23 Feb 1926	**Mr Jelly Lord**

CD

***The Pearls*, Bluebird 6588-2 RB (USA) and RCA ND 86588 (Europe)** (takes not identified)

George Mitchell (c), Kid Ory (tb), Omer Simeon (cl), Morton (p), Johnny St Cyr (bj), John Lindsay (sb), Andrew Hilaire (d)

Chicago	15 Sept 1926	**Black Bottom Stomp**
		Smoke-House Blues
		The Chant

add Morton, St Cyr (dialogue), Barney Bigard, Darnell Howard (cl), Marty Bloom (sound effects)

	21 Sept 1926	**Sidewalk Blues**
		Dead Man Blues

add Simeon (bass cl); omit Bigard, Howard		**Steamboat Stomp**

omit (dialogue), omit (bass cl); add St Cyr (g)

	16 Dec 1926	**Grandpa's Spells**
		Original Jelly-Roll Blues

add Morton (v)		**Doctor Jazz**
omit (v)		**Cannon Ball Blues**

Mitchell (c), Gerald Reeves (tb), Johnny Dodds (cl), Stump Evans (as), Morton (p), Bud Scott (g), Quinn Wilson (bb), Baby Dodds (d)

	10 June 1927	**The Pearls**
Johnny Dodds (cl), Morton (p), Baby Dodds(d)		**Wolverine Blues** **Mr Jelly Lord**

Ward Pinkett (tpt), Geechie Fields (tb), Simeon (cl), Morton (p), Lee Blair (bj), Bill Benford (bb), Tommy Benford (d)

New York	11 June 1928	**Georgia Swing** **Kansas City Stomps**
Simeon (cl), Morton (p), Benford (d)		**Shreveport**
add Fields (tb)		**Mournful Serenade**

Ed Anderson, Edwin Swayze (tpt), William Kato (tb), Russell Procope (cl, as), Paul Barnes (ss), Joe Garland (ts), Morton (p), Blair (g), William 'Bass' Moore (bb), Manzie Johnson (d)

	6 Dec 1928	**Red Hot Pepper** **Deep Creek**

Morton (p)

Camden, NJ	8 July 1929	**Freakish**

Boyd 'Red' Rosser, Walter Briscoe (tpt), Charlie Irvis (tb), George Baquet (cl), Barnes (ss), Joe Thomas (as), Foots Thomas (ts), Morton (p), Barney Alexander (bj), Harry Prather (bb), William Laws (d)

	12 July 1929	**Tank Town Bump**

Sidney De Paris (tpt), Claude Jones (tb), Albert Nicholas (cl), Sidney Bechet (ss), Happy Caldwell (ts), Morton (p, v), Lawrence Lucie (g), Wellman Braud (sb), Zutty Singleton (d)

New York	14 Sept 1939	**I Thought I Heard Buddy Bolden Say** **Winin' Boy Blues**

Other CDs

plus additional tracks:

The Jelly Roll Morton Centennial: His Complete Victor Recordings, Bluebird 2361-2 RB (USA) and Bluebird ND 82361 (Europe)

* * *

Louis Armstrong: *The Hot Fives and Hot Sevens, vols. 1–3*; *Louis Armstrong and Earl Hines, vol. 4*

Louis Armstrong is considered by the majority of jazz critics to be one of the most profoundly influential of all jazz musicians. Others, especially Charlie Parker and John Coltrane, drastically reshaped the music by their example, but Armstrong established its course in the early days. When he came to prominence, jazz was an ensemble music; within five years he had turned it into a soloist's art. The first important soloist in jazz was Sidney Bechet, who initially was ahead of Armstrong. But Armstrong, through genius and greater exposure, was the player who most captured other musicians' imaginations. Armstrong served his apprenticeship in New Orleans, came to Chicago to work with Oliver's Creole Jazz Band, and then went to New York as the jazz specialist in Fletcher Henderson's orchestra. With Henderson's group he had the opportunity to solo frequently, and it quickly became clear that he was a special talent. In 1925 he returned to Chicago, where he began to record under his own name the series generally known as the Hot Fives, although that included varying combinations of musicians.

The Hot Fives are critical to jazz history. Listening to them chronologically reveals two things. The first is the development of Armstrong's style. At first rather sunny and happy-go-lucky, it deepens emotionally as the series goes on, until we reach the climactic moments in the deeply sad *Tight Like This* and *West End Blues*. The second tendency through these recordings is the emergence of Armstrong as a soloist. In the earlier sides he functions primarily as the cornet lead in a classic New Orleans ensemble. As it became clear to the record producers that Armstrong was the draw, and the other members of the group only a supporting cast, Louis was brought more and more to the front, both as a singer and a jazz soloist, until by the end of the series he was taking a good half of many of these recordings for himself. From this moment on it was the jazz solo, not the ensemble, that mattered, and by 1928, when the last of the Hot Fives was made, the old New Orleans style was moribund.

The personnel for the first of the Hot Fives was Armstrong, cornet; Johnny Dodds, clarinet; Kid Ory, trombone; Johnny St Cyr, banjo; and Armstrong's wife, Lil, piano. As time went on the New Orleans musicians were replaced by others, most notably pianist Earl Hines and drummer Zutty Singleton, and Armstrong himself switched from cornet to trumpet in the midst of the series.

The first important issue is *Heebie Jeebies*, a novelty tune with an aimless lyric. It was not Armstrong's first vocal recording, but it was the first one to attract attention. In particular, Armstrong, rather than sticking to the lyric, sang in nonsense syllables ('scat singing') during the second half of the chorus, and the novelty of the scatted vocal helped to make the record a big hit for that time, selling perhaps 40,000 copies fairly quickly. (There is a legend that Armstrong dropped the lyric sheet halfway through the vocal and was forced to scat the rest, but as the switch to scatting takes place at a natural division in the song, the tale is open to question.)

Immediately after *Heebie Jeebies* was cut, the band made *Cornet Chop Suey*, a tune conceived as a feature for Armstrong. The high point of the recording is a 16-bar stop-time chorus which amounts to a series of breaks exhibiting many of the devices intrinsic to his style. Note that he never proceeds for very long in one direction, but is constantly turning the line back on itself. Note also the great rhythmic variety, with many rhythmically indefinable figures regularly mixed in. *Cornet Chop Suey* astonished musicians, and fans, and was learned and imitated by trumpet players all over the country.

Another recording which excited the musicians was *Big Butter and Egg Man*, a tune that Armstrong played and sang at the Sunset Café, where he was then appearing. The solo is taken in an easier, less impassioned mood than was usual with Armstrong, and consists of a series of related figures each of which is by itself a melodic gem. By now Armstrong had grown confident of his power and was ready for what would come. From this point on the masterpieces followed in what seemed an unending stream.

It is impossible to touch on more than a few in a short space. Of particular importance is *Hotter Than That*, considered by some critics Armstrong's finest fast number from this period. He plays it with a breakneck dash and confidence, beginning with a fiery eight-bar introduction which leaps directly into what is putatively a New Orleans ensemble, but is in reality a solo with accompanying musicians. Note especially the figure which begins in the second bar; a less imaginative musician would have finished it off logically in the next bar, but Armstrong unwinds out of it a related extension which carries it further. *Hotter Than That* also contained a scatted vocal featuring a series of notes in a polyrhythmic passage of two against three over the ordinary $\frac{4}{4}$ time, today a cliché, but fresh and exciting when Armstrong first spun it out.

By 1928 the pretence that this was a New Orleans ensemble had been dropped. Don Redman was brought in to work out arrangements, using for the most part journeyman musicians, and the recordings were now showcases for Armstrong. Among the best known of these is *Muggles*. It opens as a slow blues, and then Armstrong leaps in with a break to double the tempo up, a masterful example of an ambiguous tempo finally resolving to the new time. He follows this with a solo built around a reiterated tonic, which he fills in with rapid phrases, always returning to the repeated note as a point of reference.

Even more celebrated than *Muggles* is *Tight Like This*. The high point is the final passage in which Armstrong plays a sequence of passionate figures running up and down the instrument, ending with a series of high notes which finally winds down to a melancholy conclusion.

The best known of Armstrong's recordings is *West End Blues*, considered by some critics to be the greatest of all jazz recordings. It opens with a famous elaborate cadenza introduction, which falls, rises and falls, followed by a very simple blues chorus, which grows more complex as it proceeds. There are solos by other instruments and a moody, introspective scat chorus by Armstrong. Then comes the great final chorus. Armstrong opens it with a long held note, then breaks into a succession of falling figures which finally wind down into a mood of quiet resignation; there is a brief piano interlude, and a quiet ending by Armstrong. *West End Blues* is a masterpiece of construction, a complete, if small, drama with a beginning, a middle and an end. It is filled with movement and variety, but proceeds relentlessly to the climactic last chorus and then the quiet denouement, so that the piece does not merely end, as so many jazz performances do, but finishes.

Although Armstrong came in the end to dominate the Hot Fives, the personnel included a number of the best jazz musicians of the day, among them trombonist Kid Ory, who was possibly the best of those playing in the old, slurred style, and clarinettist Johnny Dodds. Dodds has always been seen as a particularly fine player of the blues. In *Gut Bucket Blues* he executes a much more imaginative obbligato over the cornet lead than was typical of the New Orleans players, filled with high-register splashes and rising and falling lines. His solo on the piece again employs held notes in the upper register which slur downwards to produce the smeary effect characteristic of the early blues.

Yet another musician who made important contributions to this series was Earl Hines, who, unlike the stride pianists, had heard a lot of blues as a youth and played in a less pianistic style, using octaves and single-finger runs in the right hand, and jagged, broken figures in the left hand. His best-known piece with Armstrong is *Weather Bird*, a duet which, while not strictly one of the Hot Fives, is usually classified with the series. In Hines's solo which follows the opening chorus we hear all of these devices: the right-hand octaves, the irregular bass patterns, and passages where right and left hand even appear to be quarrelling with each other.

But regardless of the virtues of the other players, it was Louis Armstrong who mattered. The Hot Five series is at the heart of any study of jazz, playing a role in jazz history akin to that of the masterpieces of Bach in classical music.

CDs

***The Hot Fives and Hot Sevens*, vol. 1–3, *Louis Armstrong and Earl Hines*, vol. 4, Columbia Jazz Masterpieces CK 44049, CK 44253, CK 44422, CK 45142 (USA) and CBS Jazz Masterpieces 460821-2, 463052-2, 465189-2, 466308-2 (Europe)**

Louis Armstrong (c), Kid Ory (tb), Johnny Dodds (cl), Lil Armstrong (p), Johnny St Cyr (bj)

Chicago	12 Nov 1925	**My Heart** **Yes! I'm in the Barrel**
add Louis Armstrong (speech)		**Gut Bucket Blues**
omit (speech); add Dodds (as)	22 Feb 1926	**Come Back, Sweet Papa**
add Louis and Lil Armstrong (v)	26 Feb 1926	**Georgia Grind**
omit Lil Armstrong (v)		**Heebie Jeebies**
omit (v)		**Cornet Chop Suey** **Oriental Strut** **You're Next** **Muskrat Ramble**
add Louis Armstrong (v); Dodds (as, not cl)	16 June 1926	**Don't Forget to Mess Around**
Dodds (cl, not as)		**I'm Gonna Gitcha** **Dropping Shucks**
omit (v); add Louis Armstrong (slide whistle)		**Whosit**
omit (slide whistle); add Louis and Lil Armstrong, Clarence Babcock (speech)	23 June 1926	**The King of the Zulus**
omit (speech); add Louis Armstrong (v)		**Big Fat Ma and Skinny Pa** **Lonesome Blues**
omit (v)		**Sweet Little Papa**
	16 Nov 1926	**Jazz Lips**
add Louis Armstrong (v)		**Skid-dat-de-dat**
add May Alix (v)		**Big Butter and Egg Man**
omit Armstrong (v)		**Sunset Cafe Stomp**

Louis Armstrong (v) replaces Alix; probably Henry Clark (tb) replaces Ory
27 Nov 1926 — **You Made Me Love You**
Irish Black Bottom

Louis Armstrong (c), John Thomas (tb), Johnny Dodds (cl), Lil Armstrong (p), St Cyr (bj), Pete Briggs (bb), Baby Dodds (d)
7 May 1927 — **Willie the Weeper**
Wild Man Blues

Armstrong, Bill Wilson (c), Honore Dutrey (tb), Boyd Atkins (cl, ss, as), Joe Walker (as, bar), Albert Washington (ts), Earl Hines (p), Rip Bassett (bj, g), Briggs (bb), Tubby Hall (d), Carroll Dickerson (director)
9 May 1927 — **Chicago Breakdown**

*as **Willie the Weeper*** — 10 May 1927 — **Alligator Crawl**
Potato Head Blues
11 May 1927 — **Melancholy Blues**
Weary Blues
Twelfth Street Rag

add Louis Armstrong (v)
13 May 1927 — **Keyhole Blues**
S.O.L. Blues
14 May 1927 — **Gully Low Blues**

add Lil Armstrong (v) — **That's When I'll Come Back to You**

Louis Armstrong (c, v), Ory (tb), Johnny Dodds (cl), Lil Armstrong (p), St Cyr (bj, g)
2 Sept 1927 — **Put 'em Down Blues**

omit (v) — **Ory's Creole Trombone**

add Louis Armstrong (v)
6 Sept 1927 — **The Last Time**

omit (v) — 9 Dec 1927 — **Struttin' with Some Barbecue**
Got No Blues
10 Dec 1927 — **Once in a While**

add Louis Armstrong (v), Lonnie Johnson (g); St Cyr (bj, not g)
I'm not Rough
13 Dec 1927 — **Hotter Than That**

omit (v) — **Savoy Blues**

Armstrong (tpt), Fred Robinson (tb), Jimmy Strong (cl, ts), Earl Hines (p), Mancy Carr (bj), Zutty Singleton (d)
27 June 1928 — **Fireworks**
Skip the Gutter

add Armstrong, Hines (v)		**A Monday Date**
omit (v)	28 June 1928	**Don't Jive Me**
add Armstrong (v)		**West End Blues** **Sugar Foot Strut**
omit (v)	29 June 1928	**Two Deuces**
add Armstrong, Hines, Carr (v)		**Squeeze Me**
as **Fireworks**, *but Strong (cl)*		**Knee Drops**

(Dickerson:) Armstrong, Homer Hobson (tpt), Robinson (tb), Bert Curry, Crawford Wethington (as), Strong (cl, ts), Hines (p), Carr (bj), Briggs (bb), Singleton (d)

	5 July 1928	**Symphonic Raps** **Savoyageurs' Stomp**

as **Fireworks**, *but add Hines (celeste)*

	4 Dec 1928	**No (No, Papa, No)**
add Armstrong, Hines, Carr (v)		**Basin Street Blues**

Armstrong (tpt, v), Robinson (tb), Don Redman (cl, as), Hines (p), Dave Wilborn (bj), Singleton (d)

	5 Dec 1928	**No One Else But You** (arr Redman) **Beau Koo Jack** (arr Alex Hill) **Save it, Pretty Mama** (arr Redman)
Armstrong (tpt), Hines (p)		**Weather Bird**
as **Fireworks**	7 Dec 1928	**Muggles**

add Armstrong (speech), Redman (cl, as), Strong (cl, ts)

	12 Dec 1928	**Heah Me Talkin' to Ya**
omit (speech), but Armstrong (v)		**St James Infirmary**
omit (v), but Armstrong, Redman, Hines (speech)		**Tight Like This**

* * *

Johnny Dodds: *Johnny Dodds, 1926–1928*

Johnny Dodds, almost from the moment he opened with the Creole Jazz Band at Lincoln Gardens, was seen as the quintessential New Orleans clarinettist. With the Creole orchestra he was featured more than anybody, except Oliver, playing brief breaks on almost every one of the band's recordings and extended solos on many of them. He then became the primary clarinettist for Armstrong's critically important and widely admired Hot Five series. He thus achieved greater exposure on important recordings than any of the New Orleans clarinettists, if we except Shields with the best-selling Original Dixieland Jazz Band. The sound of Dodds's clarinet came to be almost intrinsic to New Orleans jazz.

Dodds, like many New Orleans clarinettists, studied with Lorenzo Tio Jr, and, like many of the clarinettists with some formal training, his playing is replete with long passages of fairly evenly played notes. However, Dodds proved by nature to be a more driving, fiery player than clarinettists more in the creole tradition, such as Jimmie Noone and Barney Bigard, and it was this relentless forward motion, more than anything, that attracted so many jazz fans, both then and now.

Johnny Dodds left Oliver along with some of the other regulars in a fight over money. He quickly took over a band at Kelly's Stables, which he led for six years and which gave him yet more exposure, at least to the musicians and jazz fans haunting Chicago's night spots. This regular job made him available for a lot of freelance recordings, among them the Hot Fives. In addition, between 1926 and 1929 he made a long series of recordings under his own name – including sessions by the Black Bottom Stompers – and as a member of the New Orleans Wanderers, the New Orleans Bootblacks, and the Chicago Footwarmers. Some of these are with standard dixieland instrumentation, some are duets or trios featuring Dodds and some are quartets with two horns and rhythm. These Dodds sides, with cornetist George Mitchell or Natty Dominique, have always held a special place in the hearts of followers of New Orleans jazz.

A good example of Dodds's hot style is on the up-tempo *Grandma's Ball* with Dominique on cornet. Dodds is almost constantly in motion, barely pausing to breathe as he rolls long chains of eighth notes up and down through the cornet line. This busy, swirling style was typical of Dodds on fast passages. On the blues, however, he adopted a different course. He plays the introduction to the minor-key opening strain of *Perdido Street Blues* with a sequence of glissandos – long, deep swoops which have always been characteristic of blues playing. In his solo on the major-key strain he uses the fast terminal vibrato that was a staple part of the New Orleans style on long held notes, suddenly interrupting them, usually to cascade downwards in a shower of fast notes. This practice of breaking off a held note in the upper register in a downward plunge was a standard New Orleans clarinet device, evident on recordings in the playing of Larry Shields on the earliest of the Original Dixieland Jazz Band's sides.

Dodds was certainly the prototype New Orleans musician, and the style he chose for his recordings reflects this. *Gate Mouth* is played almost entirely by the whole ensemble, except for a brief saxophone solo and characteristic breaks, including one trio break in the last chorus. The piece is stitched together with long slurs by Ory's trombone, and features a spare lead by Mitchell, who at times uses the plunger mute very much in the Oliver manner.

But the most highly regarded of Dodds's sides are the quartets issued as the first of the sessions by the Chicago Footwarmers, which had cornet, piano, washboard and the leader's clarinet. Such groups frequently worked in the honky-tonks of New Orleans, where the music would be tough and hot. Typical is the up-tempo *Ballin' a Jack*, on which cornetist Dominique uses the plunger mute when he re-enters after Dodds's solo. In a small group of this kind, where there is less aural competition, a clarinettist is able to use the lower register in a more normal fashion, and even on the ensembles we hear Dodds playing extended figures which frequently move into the mid-range, or below.

These recordings were popular at the time they were issued and continued to be important to later generations of fans of New Orleans music. As a consequence it was Dodds's manner of playing on which much of the New Orleans revival was based. His influence on jazz clarinet playing was immense.

CD

***Johnny Dodds, 1926–1928*, JSP CD 319 (UK)**

(New Orleans Wanderers:) George Mitchell (c), Kid Ory (tb), Johnny Dodds (cl), Lil Armstrong (p), Johnny St Cyr (bj)

Chicago	13 July 1926	**Perdido Street Blues**
add Joe Clark (as)		**Gate Mouth**
add St Cyr (speech)		**Too Tight**
omit (speech)		**Papa Dip**
(New Orleans Bootblacks:) as ***Gate Mouth***		
	14 July 1926	**Mixed Salad**
		I Can't Say
		Flat Foot
		Mad Dog

(Johnny Dodds's Black Bottom Stompers:) Mitchell, Natty Dominique (c), John Thomas (tb), Johnny Dodds (cl), Charlie Alexander (p), Bud Scott (bj), Baby Dodds (d)

	8 Oct 1927	**Come on and Stomp, Stomp, Stomp**
add unknown (v)		**After You've Gone**
omit (v)		**After You've Gone** **Joe Turner Blues** **When Erastus Plays his Old Kazoo**

(Chicago Footwarmers:) Dominique (c), Johnny Dodds (cl), Jimmy Blythe (p), Baby Dodds (washboard)

	3 Dec 1927	**Ballin' a Jack** **Grandma's Ball**
	15 Dec 1927	**My Baby** **Oriental Man**
add Ory (tb), Bill Johnson (sb)	2 July 1928	**Get 'em Again Blues** **Brush Stomp** **My Girl**
Honore Dutrey (tb) replaces Ory	4 July 1928	**Sweep 'em Clean** **Lady Love** **Brown Bottom Bess**

Other CDs

plus additional tracks:
Johnny Dodds 1926, Classics 589; . . . *1927–1928*, Classics 617 (France)

* * *

Jimmie Noone: *Apex Blues*

There has been some tendency on the part of jazz scholars to separate out from the New Orleans clarinets a school of creole clarinettists. Actually, the term 'creole' is subject to some confusion. What is really meant is a New Orleans subculture of mixed-blood people, who descended from the French-speaking old settlers of New Orleans and elsewhere in the Caribbean. Musically, their interests lay in the so-called French Opera House and in classical music generally, and they studied 'legitimate' technique. The consequence was that the creole clarinettists tended to approach jazz music in a somewhat classically oriented manner. They tended to use a purer sound, eschewing to an extent the bent notes and growls common in the playing of the black clarinettists; they played their eighth notes more evenly, instead of emphasizing the first of pairs of putative eighths; and their intonation was often better than that of self-taught clarinettists.

Jimmie Noone studied at least briefly with the creole Sidney Bechet and perhaps more formally with Lorenzo Tio Jr, a classically trained Mexican player who taught many of the New Orleanian clarinettists. He was thus given early in his career a symphonic approach to the instrument. He was one of the musicians who began drifting away from New Orleans around the time of World War I, and he eventually landed with one of the early versions of the famous Creole Jazz Band – whose members were not, in the main, creoles. With this group Noone made a few recordings in 1923 which show him playing with the liquid sound and more evenly played eighth notes characteristic of the creole style.

At about this time, Noone began to study with a classical clarinettist, Franz Schoepp, a remarkable man who not only taught many of the reed players with the Chicago Symphony Orchestra but, probably out of social conscience, worked with immigrant and black youngsters, among them Benny Goodman, Buster Bailey and Noone. Schoepp gave Noone one of the best foundations of any clarinettists in jazz of the time, and it is no accident that Noone and Goodman were the most technically proficient players in the music.

With this background, in 1928, and with a band he was leading at the Apex Club, Noone made the series of recordings that has given him his place in jazz history. The personnel was Joe Poston, alto saxophone; Bud Scott, banjo; Johnny Wells, drums; and Earl Hines, piano. Hines was about to become, as a consequence of his work with Armstrong's Hot Fives and a series of solo performances he would make later that same year for QRS, a major figure in jazz. Poston was never highly regarded, but he played the lead lines accurately and with considerable swing, and made an excellent foil for Noone.

Noone, however, is the important figure on these sessions. The best known of the Apex Club Orchestra's cuts is *I Know That You Know*. The tune is somewhat idiosyncratic in its avoidance of the tonic for much of its length. After an opening statement of the melody, Noone takes a full chorus, utilizing long passages of relatively even eighth notes which rise and fall through the chord changes. This is followed by a solo by Earl Hines in his typically choppy style with the broken bass line, which is neither true stride nor simple chording, but a mix of both. Then, after an ensemble chorus built on a repeated riff, Noone returns with a low-register chorus again consisting principally of fast eighth notes. In the final chorus Noone breaks out into driving upper-register quarter notes which contrast with the general tenor of the rest of his playing on this recording; just after the middle of this chorus, he executes a sequence of descending eighths as precisely as a symphonic musician would.

Another of the best of this series is *Sweet Sue – Just You*. It is taken at a very slow, almost lugubrious tempo. The whole second chorus is played straight by the alto saxophone and clarinet in harmony, the interest being supplied by Hines's highly rhythmic right hand behind the horns. For the last chorus Noone plays a series of long, looping, rubato figures over the melody by Poston. This kind of easy, measured delivery was typical of the New Orleans creole style, which contrasted with the far hotter manner of a clarinettist like Johnny Dodds.

The contrast is even more marked in Noone's approach to the blues. In *Apex Blues*, which employs a very simple riff as a theme, Noone plays far fewer of the bent notes that were typical of the standard blues style, and entirely avoids the rasps and throat-tones that were almost a *sine qua non* of the blues. Note how evenly played are his eighth notes, especially in the liquid, low-register ending to his first solo chorus. But Noone did not entirely dismiss the characteristic traits of the blues: he leads into the down beat of the last chorus of the recording with a long high note which rises in pitch and then drops off again, one of those twisted notes that give the blues much of their emotional force.

A Monday Date again shows the band in its hot, driving mode. The tune was written by Hines, and his solo evinces all the trademarks of his style: the choppy bass figures, the octaves, the tremolos in the right hand. Noone, particularly in the last choruses, demonstrates a characteristic of the creole style, a tendency to play scalar runs rather than the saw-toothed half-step up, step down, pattern more typical of jazz clarinet playing. (Note that the first clarinet solo chorus, after the piano solo, is by Joe Poston.)

Noone's Apex Club Orchestra is in format a long way from the standard New Orleans dixieland band, but it carries with it a certain easy, relaxed swing that was typical of the best New Orleans bands. These recordings by the Apex Club Orchestra are among the finest small-group recordings in jazz. Noone influenced a whole school of clarinettists, among them Buster Bailey with Fletcher Henderson, and Barney Bigard with Duke Ellington. Contrary to what has often been said, he did not directly influence Benny Goodman, whose style was forming before he heard Noone. But Goodman did employ devices which Noone featured, such as the fast, low-register passages; and Goodman's quartet version of *Sweet Sue – Just You* is taken at the same kind of deliberate tempo as Noone's.

CD

***Apex Blues*, Decca GRD-633 (USA)**

Jimmie Noone (cl), Joe Poston (cl, as), Earl Hines (p), Bud Scott (bj), Johnny Wells (d)

Chicago	16 May 1928	**I Know That You Know**
		Sweet Sue – Just You
add Noone, Poston (v)		**Four or Five Times**
omit (v)		**Every Evening (I Miss You)**
add Noone, Poston (v)	14 June 1928	**Ready for the River**
omit (v)		**Forevermore**
add Lawson Buford (bb)		
	23 Aug 1928	**Apex Blues**
		A Monday Date (My Monday Date)
		Blues my Naughty Sweetie Gives to Me
	25 Aug 1928	**Oh, Sister! Ain't That Hot?**
		King Joe
		Sweet Lorraine (take B)

George Mitchell (c), Fayette Williams (tb), Noone (cl, v), Poston (as, v), Alex Hill (p), Junie Cobb (bj, v), Bill Newton (bb), Wells (d)

	27 Dec 1928	**It's Tight Like That** (take A)
omit Mitchell, Williams (v)		
	26 Feb 1929	**Chicago Rhythm**

add Mitchell, ?Williams, May Alix (v); Zinky Cohn (p) replaces Hill

	11 July 1929	**My daddy rocks me**
omit (v)	18 July 1929	**Off Time**

Noone, Poston, Cohn, Wilbur Gorham (bj), Newton, Wells

	3 Feb 1930	**El Rado Scuffle**
		Deep Trouble
Eddie Pollack (cl) replaces Poston		
	1 July 1930	**So Sweet**
*as **So Sweet**, but Pollack (as)*		**San** (take B)

* * *

Bix Beiderbecke: *Bix Beiderbecke, vol. 1: Singin' the Blues*

Bix Beiderbecke is generally considered to be the most significant jazz musician, after Louis Armstrong, from the 1920s period. Like Armstrong, he astonished musicians and jazz fans with the clarity of his bell-like cornet sound, the freshness of his conception and the intensity of his feeling. A whole school of players, both black and white, followed in his path, providing an alternative approach to jazz playing that differed significantly from Armstrong's. Where Armstrong was broad in his conception, Beiderbecke hewed to a narrow spectrum; where Armstrong employed the whole range of his instrument, Beiderbecke played mainly in the middle register; where Armstrong was at times ornate, even showy, Beiderbecke was consistently modest. Few deny that Armstrong was, finally, the greater musician, in part because of his more sweeping, romantic approach, but Beiderbecke was not far behind.

Like many of the jazz players of the day, Beiderbecke was self-taught. His first important recordings were made with the Wolverines, a dixieland group typical of the time. He moved on to work with the large dance orchestras of Jean Goldkette and Paul Whiteman, with whom he was the star soloist. Unhappily, he suffered from alcoholism, and died from the effects in 1931.

Despite the excellence of the solos he made with Whiteman, Beiderbecke's best-known recordings were a series he made from 1924 to 1928 with pick-up groups under his own name, with others under pseudonyms such as Sioux City Six and the Chicago Loopers, and with yet others under the leadership of Frankie Trumbauer. The sessions were rather haphazardly put together. The personnel was usually drawn from the bands Beiderbecke happened to be working with at the moment, and owed as much to friendship as to musical skill. Some of the men on these dates were excellent jazz musicians, some were merely adequate. As a consequence, the accompaniment is less good than it might have been had Beiderbecke taken firm charge of the musical aspects of the sessions.

The most important of these players was C-melody saxophonist Frankie Trumbauer, known as Tram. Trumbauer was not a great improvising jazz player, but a skilled technician who often worked out his solos in advance, and was much admired by other musicians of the day. He undoubtedly helped to give Bix the thoughtful approach to improvising that was characteristic of his playing. The partnership produced some of Bix's finest work.

One of Beiderbecke's best-known solos is on *Royal Garden Blues* (on vol. 2 of the series); this opens with a rising and falling line built on triplets, which is then repeated. This deliberateness carries over to his often very subtle, but thoughtful placement of notes around the beat, as, for example, the opening quarter notes to his solo on *Way Down Yonder in New Orleans,* which are placed slightly differently against the beat each time. Again, in bars 9 and 10 of this chorus he plays a variation of the same idea.

Beiderbecke's masterpieces are *I'm Coming, Virginia* and especially *Singin' the Blues,* which was learned by young musicians all over the United States: Fletcher Henderson had the entire piece orchestrated for his band, with Rex Steward playing Beiderbecke's famous chorus. Beiderbecke thought more deeply about improvising methods than did many other jazz musicians. In particular, he devised the concept of the 'correlated chorus', in which, let us say, two bars of a given idea are followed by two or more of a related one, after which the whole four-bar segment is re-examined in the following four bars. We can see this method at work in the opening part of his solo on *Singin' the Blues,* in which the second figure is a reflection of the first, and the following one re-examines the previous two; the four bars which follow amplify what has gone on before. His *I'm Coming, Virginia* is not so precisely worked out, but figures are constantly related to each other. Many of them are built around alternations of notes a third apart and feature sudden reversals of direction. But Beiderbecke was capable of less introspective, more driving work. In the ride-out chorus of *Goose Pimples* (also on vol. 2) he plays one hard, hot figure three times, slightly varied, and then suddenly twists it into a new shape and stretches it out to twice its length.

Bix was also admired at the time for his piano playing, in particular a group of rambling compositions which drew from modernists such as Debussy and Ravel. Bix played these differently at each performance, but he recorded one, *In a Mist,* which thus took on a comparatively fixed form and became quite celebrated: he once played it at Carnegie Hall. Today we tend to see these pieces as pastiches; it is his cornet playing that matters.

CD

***Bix Beiderbecke, vol. 1: Singin' the Blues,* Columbia Jazz Masterpieces CK 45450 (USA) and CBS Jazz Masterpieces 466309-2 (Europe)**

(Frankie Trumbauer:) Bix Beiderbecke (c), Bill Rank (tb), Jimmy Dorsey (cl, as), Trumbauer (C-melody sax), Paul Mertz (p), Eddie Lang (bj, g), Chauncey Morehouse (d)

New York	4 Feb 1927	**Trumbology** (arr Mertz)
add Doc Ryker (as)		**Clarinet Marmalade**
		Singin' the Blues

Don Murray (cl, bar) replaces Dorsey, Itzy Riskin (p) replaces Mertz

9 May 1927	**Ostrich Walk** (arr Bill Challis)
	Riverboat Shuffle (arr Challis)
13 May 1927	**I'm Coming, Virginia** (arr Riskin)
	'Way Down Yonder in New Orleans (arr Murray)

(Trumbauer:) Beiderbecke (c, p), Trumbauer (C-melody sax), Lang (g)

For No Reason at All in C

(Trumbauer:) Beiderbecke (c), Rank (tb), Murray (cl, bar), Ryker (as), Trumbauer (C-melody sax), Adrian Rollini (bass sax), Riskin (p), Lang (g), Morehouse (d)

25 Aug 1927	**Three Blind Mice** (arr Trumbauer, Murray)

add Seger Ellis (v)

Blue River
There's a Cradle in Caroline

(Beiderbecke:) Beiderbecke (p)

9 Sept 1927	**In a Mist**

(Trumbauer:) Beiderbecke (c, p), Trumbauer (C-melody sax), Lang (g)

17 Sept 1927	**Wringin' and Twistin'**

(Trumbauer:) Beiderbecke (c), Rank (tb), Murray (cl, bar), Bobby Davis (as), Trumbauer (C-melody sax), Rollini (bass sax), Joe Venuti (vln), Frank Signorelli (p), Lang (g), Morehouse (d)

28 Sept 1927	**Humpty Dumpty** (arr Fud Livingston)
	Krazy Kat (arr Murray)
	Baltimore

(Broadway Bell Hops:) Beiderbecke (c), Hymie Farberman (tpt), Rank (tb), Murray (cl), Davis (as), Trumbauer (C-melody sax), Venuti (vln), Signorelli (p), John Cali (bj), Joe Tarto (bb), Vic Berton (d), Irving Kaufman (v)

29 Sept 1927	**There Ain't No Land Like Dixieland**
	There's a Cradle in Caroline

(Trumbauer:) as **Humpty Dumpty**, *but Lang (bj) and add Sylvester Ahola (tpt), Kaufman (v)*

30 Sept 1927	**Just an Hour of Love**
	I'm Wonderin' Who

Other CDs

same contents, except *In a Mist* omitted:

Bix Beiderbecke and Frankie Trumbauer, JSP CD 316 (UK)

* * *

Red Nichols: *Rhythm of the Day*

Red Nichols had the misfortune to become a jazz star playing in a style similar to Bix Beiderbecke's at a time when Beiderbecke was little known. When it became apparent that Beiderbecke was the greater of the two men, there was a tendency on the part of romantically inclined jazz fans to see Nichols as a usurper who built a major reputation in jazz, and the dance-band world in general, on the work of another man. Making matters worse, in the years after World War II Nichols had some popularity with a rather slick dixieland band which featured his own technically adroit, but somewhat empty playing, and this did not add to his reputation as a great jazz musician. None the less, in the 1920s he was one of the best cornetists in jazz, a player with a bell-like tone, exceptionally clean execution and a good, if not great, conception. He deserves more consideration than he has received from jazz critics.

In 1926 Nichols began to record with a group under his own name, which at times included Miff Mole and Jimmy Dorsey, both also among the technically most proficient musicians in jazz, and both capable of excellent hot playing. Given the high quality of this front line, it is hardly surprising that this early Nichols group rapidly became vastly admired by both jazz musicians and closer observers of dance-band music. Over the next several years Nichols made scores of recordings with various combinations, some using arrangements, others primarily improvising in the dixieland style. Although Nichols's groups were generally known as Red Nichols and his Five Pennies, the band recorded under a number of pseudonyms.

The first of his recordings were basically in the older, dixieland mode, and contained a good deal of ensemble jamming. However, Nichols's players were musically more sophisticated than most of the early jazzmen, and this shows in the little arranged passages found throughout the cuts, and in the use of unusual instruments, such as the mellophone and timpani, the latter of which the group's primary drummer, Vic Berton, was trained to play.

All these tendencies may be noted in *Boneyard Shuffle* (1926), which has little arranged passages, a solo by guitarist Eddie Lang and timpani splashed in here and there. The solos on the old New Orleans tune *Buddy's Habits* are particularly fine. The playing of these white New Yorkers was much more clipped than was the case with the New Orleans players – Mole in particular used a more staccato manner than any other important trombone player in jazz. Nichols's solo on *Buddy's Habits* is replete with devices associated with Beiderbecke, which can be heard clearly in his opening break, in bars 3 and 4 and in the break at mid-chorus. Nichols's debt to Beiderbecke, which he readily admitted, is also obvious – for example, in the upward rip he plays going into the middle of his solo on *Alabama Stomp*. But, as this solo shows, his ringing tone was his own and can stand comparison with Beiderbecke's sound. This recording also features a fine solo by Miff Mole in his bright, clipped style, which had become firmer and more confident since the days of the Original Memphis Five; by now Mole was, perhaps, the most admired trombone player among jazz musicians. *Alabama Stomp* ends with a quick splash of timpani played by Berton.

One of the best in this series is *Hurricane*. It is essentially a string of solos, with relatively brief ensemble passages to open and close the cut. Particularly under the influence of Armstrong, jazz was rapidly becoming a soloist's music. The dixieland style was already being pushed aside by the big bands when *Hurricane* was made, and when dixieland was later revived it took this form, with ensembles limited in the main to opening and closing choruses and the rest of the space given over to solos. Furthermore, the careful assignment of roles to cornet, clarinet and trombone was breaking down. For example, in the final ensemble, although Mole stays out of the upper register, he is not playing the slurs that had been typical of the dixieland style, but rather extended passages of eighth notes, to produce a more truly contrapuntal effect than had been typical of the form.

By the late 1920s it was apparent that the popularity of the improvising dixieland ensemble was rapidly waning: the public preference was now for the big 10- or 12-piece hot dance band playing arranged music, with a good deal of jazz soloing throughout. Nichols added musicians and made the change, and his later recordings continue to offer first-rate jazz, including solos by himself and premier jazz players such as Benny Goodman, Jack Teagarden and many others. This tendency was already apparent in the 1927 recording *Cornfed*, which has brief arranged passages – probably *ad hoc* arrangements worked out in the studio – and the solos in many cases cut back to four or eight bars.

Red Nichols today is seen as a minor figure in jazz, but in fact the influence of his groups was substantial during the late 1920s. Many of the musicians who would become important figures in the swing-band movement a decade later served apprenticeship with Nichols, and this lighter, more precise style came to be an important element in jazz of the swing era.

CD

***Rhythm of the Day*, ASV Living Era CD AJA 5025 (UK)**

(Ross Gorman and his Earl Carroll Orchestra:) Red Nichols, Donald Lindley, James Kozak (tpt), Miff Mole (tb), Gorman (cl, as, bar), Alfie Evans (cl, as, vln), Harold Noble (cl, as, ts), Billy McGill (cl, ts), Barney Acqueline (bass sax), Nick Koupoukis (fl,

piccolo), Jack Harris, Saul Sharrow (vln), Milton Susskind, Edgar Fairchild (p), Dick McDonough (bj), Tony Colicchio (g), David Grupp (d)

New York	29 Oct 1925	**Rhythm of the Day**

Nichols (tpt), Mole (tb), Jimmy Dorsey (cl, as), Arthur Schutt (p), Eddie Lang (g), Vic Berton (d, timpani)

	20 Dec 1926	**Buddy's Habits**
		Boneyard Shuffle
	12 Jan 1927	**Alabama Stomp**
		Hurricane

(Mole:) omit Dorsey; McDonough (bj, g) replaces Lang

	26 Jan 1927	**Alexander's Ragtime Band**

Nichols, Mole, Dorsey, Adrian Rollini (bass sax), Schutt, Lang, Berton

	20 June 1927	**Cornfed**
	25 June 1927	**Mean Dog Blues**

Nichols, Leo McConville, Manny Klein (tpt), Mole (tb), Pee Wee Russell (cl), Fud Livingston (cl, ts), Rollini (bass sax), Lennie Hayton (p, celeste, arr), McDonough (g), Berton (d)

	15 Aug 1927	**Riverboat Shuffle**
		Eccentric
omit McConville, Klein		**Feelin' No Pain**

(Mole:) Nichols, Mole, Russell, Livingston, Rollini, Schutt, McDonough, Lang, Berton

	30 Aug 1927	**Original Dixieland One-Step**
	1 Sept 1927	**Honolulu Blues**

Nichols, McConville, Klein (tpt), Mole (tb), Dudley Fosdick (mellophone), Dorsey (cl, as), Livingston (cl, ts), Murray Kellner (vln), Schutt (p), Carl Kress (g), Art Miller (sb), Berton (d)

	28 May 1928	**There'll Come a Time**

Nichols, McConville, Mole, Fosdick, Livingston, Schutt, Kress, Chauncey Morehouse (d, vb, v)

	21 June 1928	**Harlem Twist**

Nichols, Klein, Mole, Fosdick, Livingston, Benny Goodman (cl, as), Rollini, Hayton, Kress, Berton

	16 Feb 1929	**Alice Blue Gown**

Nichols, Ruby Weinstein, Charlie Teagarden, Wingy Manone (tpt), Glenn Miller (tb), Goodman (cl, bar), Babe Russin (ts), Jack Russin (p), Miller (sb), Gene Krupa (d)

	10 Dec 1930	**Corrinne Corrina**

Nichols, Dorsey, Joe Venuti (vln), Fulton McGrath (p), Lang, Berton

	16 Sept 1931	**Oh! Peter (You're so Nice)**

Nichols, Johnny Davis (tpt), Will Bradley (tb), Dorsey (cl, as), Babe Russin (ts), Jack Russin (p), Tony Starr (bj), Artie Bernstein (sb), Victor Engle (d)

2 Dec 1931 **Waiting for the Evening Mail**

Nichols, Dorsey, Babe Russin, McGrath, McDonough, Bernstein, Engle

18 Feb 1932 **Sweet Sue, Just You**

* * *

Joe Venuti and Eddie Lang: *Jazz Classics in Digital Stereo: Joe Venuti/Eddie Lang*

The earliest true New Orleans jazz bands frequently included a violin, which roughly doubled the lead with the cornet. It owed its presence, for one reason, to the fact that it was one of the basic instruments in dance bands, and was therefore carried over into the early jazz bands. For another, violinists were generally trained to read music and could therefore teach the new tunes to the wind players, who were often non-readers. However, as the jazz band developed in New Orleans and elsewhere, the violin, unable to match the volume of the horns, began to drop out. One of the few early players to make a specialty of the instrument was Joe Venuti. He became well known to the dance-band public for the long series of recordings he made with a schoolboy friend, guitarist Eddie Lang, who had also started as a violinist. They worked together as a duo and in small groups.

Duets can put a considerable burden on both the rhythm player and the melody instrument, and the musicians are likely to be unnerved by the responsibility of carrying the whole load. But Venuti and Lang flew through theirs with vigour and aplomb. A fine example of their skill with the form is *Stringing the Blues*, a thinly disguised version of *Tiger Rag*. Both musicians play continuously throughout the cut. Venuti's playing is typically flamboyant and heedless, without frills. He bows double-stops (two notes simultaneously) only rarely and then mainly to accentuate the line during the breaks the piece provides. Lang, who must supply both the harmonies and the ground beat, perforce plays full chords constantly. So impeccable is his time that he holds the beat almost exactly from beginning to end.

But, typically, Lang was a single-string soloist, using chords only infrequently. A fine example of this style is *Eddie's Twister*, an original composition. An important strain in jazz of the period was the attempt to marry classical music with jazz. *Eddie's Twister* is by no means classical music, but its advanced harmonies and somewhat formal quality reflect Lang's early training as a violinist playing the classical repertory, as well as the devices from classical music which arrangers such as Bill Challis and Ferde Grofé were bringing to jazz.

Lang was seen as cool-headed and businesslike by his colleagues, but Venuti was the reverse – hot-headed, earthy, and a notorious practical joker around whom anecdotes clustered. Another musician who recorded with Venuti and Lang frequently, Adrian Rollini, was quixotic. Given these temperaments it is not surprising that there is a comic, or even fey, quality to some of their recordings. In part this was to enhance audience appeal in a day when having fun was the spirit of the time; but it also suggests the attitude of first-rate musicians throwing together in the studio something light for their own pleasure. *Put and Take*, which is credited to Venuti, but is in reality just improvising on three unrelated strains strung together for no apparent reason, is certainly that.

Lang and Venuti play excellent and wholly typical solos, and Rollini is featured on bass saxophone and hot fountain pen (a small clarinet with a limited range), one of the home-made instruments he liked to devise. Rollini was an excellent musician with a rather precise conception, good intonation, a crisp attack and a considerable ability to swing. Besides the bass saxophone and the home-made instruments, Rollini, who had trained as a pianist as a boy, played vibraphone, then a rare instrument. Had he chosen to take up one of the more standard instruments, for example, alto saxophone, he would today have a major reputation.

The small Venuti–Lang combinations were popular with jazz fans and with the general public. However, in retrospect it was a recording session with a somewhat larger group which appears more significant. Issued in 1931 as by Venuti–Lang and their All-Star Orchestra, it included trombonist Jack Teagarden, clarinettist Benny Goodman, and Teagarden's brother Charlie playing trumpet. Goodman, Jack Teagarden, Lang and Venuti were perhaps the best jazz musicians on their respective instruments at that moment, and the others were above average. The results were felicitous.

The BBC anthology includes one of the four tracks from the session, *Beale Street Blues*. It opens with a carefully thought-out introduction by Venuti and Lang in sequence. Charlie Teagarden leads a quiet, relaxed ensemble; in later years the trumpeter could be rather mechanical in approach, but here he strikes a note of ease. Jack Teagarden then sings the famous lyric, accompanied by Goodman, always excellent at accompanying singers. At times he plays no more than a single, unobtrusive note which acts like a finger pointing briefly at Teagarden's musical phrase. Taken altogether, *Beale Street Blues* is a relaxed, almost tender performance. Even the usually impassioned Venuti catches the easy-going mood. This session with these jazz giants is one of the little gems from the period.

CD

***Jazz Classics in Digital Stereo: Joe Venuti/Eddie Lang*, BBC CD 644 (UK)**

(Venuti:) Joe Venuti (vln), Eddie Lang (g)
New York 29 Sept 1926 **Stringing the Blues**

(Red Nichols:) Nichols (c), Miff Mole (tb), Jimmy Dorsey (cl, as), Venuti (vln), Arthur Schutt (p), Lang (g), Vic Berton (d)
3 March 1927 **Bugle Call Rag**

(Lang:) Schutt (p), Lang (g)
1 April 1927 **Eddie's Twister**

(Frankie Trumbauer:) Bix Beiderbecke (c), Bill Rank (tb), Trumbauer (C-melody sax), Don Murray (cl, bar), Bobby Davis (as), Adrian Rollini (bass sax), Venuti (vln), Frank Signorelli (p), Lang (g), Chauncey Morehouse (d)
28 Sept 1927 **Krazy Kat**

(Venuti:) Murray (cl, bar), Venuti (vln), Signorelli (p), Lang (g), ?Justin Ring (cymbal)
15 Nov 1927 **Four String Joe**

(Red McKenzie:) Venuti (vln), Lang (g), Eddie Condon (bj), McKenzie (comb, v)
28 May 1928 **My Baby Came Home**

(Venuti:) Dorsey (cl, as, bar), Venuti (vln), Rube Bloom (p, v), Lang (g), Paul Graselli (d)
27 Sept 1928 **Sensation**

(Blind Willie Dunn:) Signorelli (p), Lang (g), Ring (chimes)
5 Nov 1928 **Church Street Sobbin' Blues**

(Lang:) Leo McConville (tpt), Tommy Dorsey (tb), Jimmy Dorsey (cl, as), Schutt (p), Lang (g), Joe Tarto (sb), Stan King (d)
22 May 1929 **Hot Heels**

(Trumbauer:) Charlie Margulis (tpt), Andy Secrest (c), Bill Rank (tb), Charles Strickfaden (as), Trumbauer (C-melody sax), Izzy Friedman (cl, ts), Min Leibrook (bass sax), Venuti (vln), Lennie Hayton (p), Lang (g), George Marsh (d)
22 May 1929 **Shivery Stomp**

(Venuti:) Trumbauer (bassoon), Venuti (vln), Hayton (p), Lang (g)
18 Oct 1929 **Runnin' Ragged (Bamboozlin' the Bassoon)**

(Venuti:) Rollini (bass sax, hot fountain pen), Venuti (vln), Itzy Riskin (p), Lang (g)
7 May 1930 **Put and Take**

(Venuti:) Pete Pumiglio (cl, bar), Venuti (vln), Signorelli (p), Lang (g)
7 Oct 1930 **The Wild Dog**

(Nichols:) Nichols (tpt), Jimmy Dorsey (cl, as), Venuti (vln), Fulton McGrath (p), Eddie Lang (g), Vic Berton (d)
16 Sept 1931 **Oh! Peter (You're so Nice)**

(Venuti–Lang:) Charlie Teagarden (tpt), Jack Teagarden (tb), Benny Goodman (cl), Venuti (vln), Signorelli (p), Lang (g), Ward Lay (sb), Neil Marshall (d)
22 Oct 1931 **Beale Street Blues**

(Venuti:) Jimmy Dorsey (tpt, cl, as), Rollini (vb, sound effects), Venuti (vln, sb), Phil Wall (p), Dick McDonough (g), unknown (kazoo)
8 May 1933 **Vibraphonia**

* * *

Eddie Condon: *Eddie Condon, 1927–1938*

The presence in Chicago of some of the best of the New Orleans bands, both black and white, for long stays – especially after 1920 – worked as a training school for young white musicians, many of them still adolescents, who were being drawn to the new jazz music. These youngsters spent as much time as they could listening to King Oliver at the Lincoln Gardens and the Plantation Café, the New Orleans Rhythm Kings at Friar's Inn, Louis Armstrong at the Dreamland Café and the Sunset Café, Jimmie Noone at the Apex Club, and others elsewhere. They set out frankly to copy their heroes: Muggsy Spanier followed Oliver; Gene Krupa, Baby Dodds; the clarinettists, Johnny Dodds, Noone and Leon Roppolo; and everybody, Armstrong.

The core of this cadre of young white musicians was a group who were attending Chicago's Austin High School, including cornetist Jimmy McPartland, his brother, guitarist Dick McPartland, bassist Jim Lanigan and clarinettist Frank Teschemacher. They jammed together after school, began to play at local dances and attracted like-minded youngsters, among them tenor saxophonist Bud Freeman, pianist Joe Sullivan, drummers Krupa and Dave Tough, clarinettist Benny Goodman and eventually others from the Midwest outside Chicago, such as drummer George Wettling, cornetist Wild Bill Davison, clarinettist Pee Wee Russell and banjoist Eddie Condon, an outgoing, witty Irishman who eventually became the catalyst for the group. These musicians developed a way of playing that came to be called 'Chicago style'. Their music grew directly out of the New Orleans style and can best be seen as a sub-genre of dixieland. It tended to be more impassioned, less relaxed, than the dixieland of Oliver and Noone. By the late 1920s it was attracting many followers.

Probably the most important of the recordings from this sub-genre are four cuts made in Chicago in December 1927: *Sugar, China Boy, Nobody's Sweetheart* and *Liza* (not George Gershwin's *Liza*, but a tune written by Condon). The sides were issued as by McKenzie and Condon's Chicagoans, the first leader being Red McKenzie, a rough singer and comb player who had made a public reputation with novelty groups, the best known of which was the Mound City Blue Blowers. He had, however, little to do with these recordings, which set the mould for the Chicago style. There is a tenor saxophone instead of a trombone. There are substantially more arranged passages than was customary in the New Orleans system. Following the first chorus of *Sugar* and in the opening chorus of the other three titles, Teschemacher and Freeman mainly play harmonies parallel to the cornet lead, rather than creating the opposite motion usual with the dixieland clarinet and trombone. There is a good deal more soloing than took place in New Orleans music. And the final 'ride-out' chorus was raised a notch in intensity, which was not always the case with the New Orleans bands.

Not all of this music was intense: some of the slower numbers, such as *Sugar*, are relatively relaxed, but even this title picks up steam at the end. More typical is the thoroughly hot *China Boy*. It was this recording which especially excited young listeners at the time. Issued at the moment when Duke Ellington was beginning to attract serious attention, when Louis Armstrong was in the midst of making the great Hot Five series and when Bix Beiderbecke was producing some of his most important recordings, *China Boy* offered something different – a way of playing that was at a considerable remove from the expressionistic colouring of Ellington, the sweeping conception of Armstrong or the carefully carved sculptures of Bix. This was heedless, hot playing, full speed ahead and damn the torpedoes.

The solos were not meant to be thoughtful. Sullivan, clearly influenced by Earl Hines, plays driving, rhythmic piano, and there is a rough and equally driving solo by Freeman, who inflects his lines with growls and swirls more expressive of heated passion than of cogitation. Teschemacher is generally regarded as the quintessential Chicago player. *China Boy* shows him using a broad vibrato, a shrill whining timbre as well as vocalized tones, descending saw-toothed figures, a division of the beat into more equal eighth notes than was customary with players like Goodman or Armstrong, and a very hot approach to playing. Despite questionable intonation and many blatant clinkers (for example, the wrong note repeated five times in the last part of his solo), he was much admired by the musicians who worked with him, some of whom said that he would have proved to be one of the great clarinettists in jazz had he not been killed in an automobile accident in 1932.

Like most of the geographic definitions that were popular in early jazz writing, the term 'Chicago' was a loose one. Many of the musicians associated with the school were from elsewhere, and some did not even work much in Chicago during the period. A case in point is Jack Teagarden, who was born and raised in the Southwest, where he acquired his early musical experience, and was based in New York during the heyday of the Chicago style. But his classic *Makin' Friends* was recorded under Condon's name and included many of the Chicagoans. The high point of the recording is the concluding minor-key passage for trombone. Teagarden here uses a stunt he made into a feature: removing the bell of the trombone, he slips an ordinary water glass over the open end of the slide and proceeds to play. It is a trick which requires some practice, for the slide positions are completely altered, but it produces a cold, smoky sound eminently suitable for the minor mode.

Another of the best-known recordings from the Chicago school was *The Eel,* written by Bud Freeman and used by him as a set-piece to display his virtuosity. It is built around strings of eighth notes. Freeman races through the idiosyncratic melody, then improvises a hot solo on it. After an ensemble interlude he improvises two more choruses on the blues. Other members of the band also solo on the blues, and then Freeman plays the theme again for a finale. Freeman handles the fast passages adroitly and swings hard in the typical Chicago helter-skelter style on the improvised passages. The recording was something of a *tour de force* and gave Freeman the start of his reputation with jazz musicians and fans.

CD

***Eddie Condon, 1927–1938*, Classics 742 (France)**

(McKenzie and Condon's Chicagoans:) Jimmy McPartland (c), Frank Teschemacher (cl), Bud Freeman (ts), Joe Sullivan (p), Eddie Condon (bj), Jim Lanigan (bb, sb), Gene Krupa (d)

Chicago	8 Dec 1927	**Sugar**
		China Boy
	16 Dec 1927	**Nobody's Sweetheart**
		Liza

(Condon:) Teschemacher (cl), Sullivan (p), Condon (bj), Krupa (d)

New York	28 July 1928	**Oh! Baby**
omit (v)		**Indiana**

McPartland (c), Jack Teagarden (tb), Mezz Mezzrow (cl), Sullivan (p), Condon (bj, v), Art Miller (sb), Johnny Power (d)

	30 Oct 1928	**I'm Sorry I Made You Cry**

add Mezzrow (speech), Teagarden (v) replaces Condon (v)

Makin' Friends

Leonard Davis (tpt), Teagarden (tb, v), Mezzrow (cl), Happy Caldwell (ts), Sullivan (p), Condon (bj), George Stafford (d)

8 Feb 1929 — **I'm Gonna Stomp, Mr Henry Lee** (take 1)
That's a Serious Thing (take 2)

Max Kaminsky (tpt), Floyd O'Brien (tb), Pee Wee Russell (cl), Freeman (ts), Alex Hill (p), Condon (bj), Artie Bernstein (sb), Sid Catlett (d)

21 Oct 1933 — **The Eel**
Tennessee Twilight (take A)
Madame Dynamite (take A)
Home Cooking

Joe Sullivan (p) replaces Hill

17 Nov 1933 — **The Eel**
Home Cooking

Bobby Hackett (c), Georg Brunis (tb), Russell (cl), Freeman (ts), Jess Stacy (p), Condon (g), Artie Shapiro (sb), George Wettling (d)

17 Jan 1938 — **Love is just around the corner**
Beat to the Socks
Carnegie Drag
Ja Da

Teagarden (tb) replaces Brunis

30 April 1938 — **Embraceable You**
Meet Me Tonight in Dreamland

* * *

Sidney Bechet: *The Victor Sessions, Master Takes, 1932–43*

A substantial number of the first generation of jazz musicians, and some of the best of them, were creoles, and it may have been these musicians who were largely responsible for giving jazz its shape, although that is by no means certain. The most highly regarded of them in the early days was Sidney Bechet.

Bechet was originally a clarinettist. He studied to an extent with Lorenzo Tio Jr and others, but was basically self-taught. Early in the 1920s he took up the soprano saxophone, then more in use than it would be later on. Although he continued to play clarinet throughout his career and made some excellent recordings with it, including his moving blues *Blue Horizon*, he is thought of primarily as a soprano saxophonist. He was a ferocious player who tended to dominate any musical circumstance he was in. He liked to work out figures and practise them, and as a result his solos tend to be more regular and patterned than is frequently the case in jazz. Most important in his playing, however, is the characteristic drive, the sharply attacked notes followed by slurs, and the pronounced terminal vibrato.

All these effects can be heard on *Maple Leaf Rag*, recorded in 1932. The tune, of course, is the most famous of all rags, intended by its composer, Scott Joplin, to be played with delicacy at a moderate speed. Bechet instead takes it at a breath-taking tempo, roaring through at a mad dash which leaves the other musicians sitting in the dust. Aside from a brief piano solo, Bechet carries the whole piece, flinging patches of phrases out with abandon one after the other. We are now a long way from the New Orleans format, despite the fact that Bechet and trumpeter Tommy Ladnier, who worked with Bechet frequently, are both New Orleanians. Armstrong had just finished refashioning jazz as a soloist's music, and this is a solo *par excellence* – one of the rare examples in jazz where one player solos for virtually the full length of a three-minute 78 rpm record.

Sweetie Dear was recorded at the same session as *Maple Leaf Rag*, and the two were issued as a coupling. It is one of the great couplings in jazz. Bechet was in superb form that day. He plays clarinet here, and with the softer instrument does not dominate the music as he did on *Maple Leaf Rag* – trumpeter Ladnier just manages to stay on top of things. The piece ends with a series of riffs, again typical of Bechet, who, however impassioned he might be, liked a certain orderliness in what he played. These riffs signal, if nothing else had, that the New Orleans style was gone, or was at least going.

Bechet liked to play 'oriental' set-pieces – supposed oriental music was popular with the American public in the teens and 1920s. *Egyptian Fantasy* is one of these, a piece with a slightly spooky theme in a minor key, opening out into a second strain in the major. On this and on *Wild Man Blues*, a tune originally cut by Armstrong as part of the Hot Five series, Bechet reverts to his first instrument, the clarinet. Although Bechet was a creole, his approach was closer to that of Dodds than Noone. It is true that this clarinet sound has the liquid, fluid quality associated with creole players, and it is also true that Bechet uses a narrower vibrato on clarinet than on soprano saxophone. But where Noone tended to use a clear, clean, more 'legitimate' tone throughout, Bechet's sound is enormously varied – at times liquid, at times shrill, at times even capturing some of the quality of a cornet played with a plunger mute.

Bechet occasionally played both soprano and clarinet on the same recording. He does that on *Texas Moaner Blues*, a tune he had originally cut in 1924 under Clarence Williams's leadership, with Louis Armstrong on cornet. Allowing for the way the music had developed, it is classic New Orleans blues, played much the way it would have been for the whores and their customers to dance the slow-drag in the New Orleans honky-tonks. Bechet switches to the soprano midway through, at the unprepared modulation to a new key; his playing on the saxophone is stronger, less delicate than it sometimes is on the clarinet. This recording includes trumpeter Charlie Shavers, usually associated with bravura big-band playing, but here working in the narrower, more perfervid blues style.

One other cut of interest is the famous one-man band version of *The Sheik of Araby*, on which Bechet plays all the instruments – clarinet, soprano and tenor saxophones, bass and drums. It is not great jazz, but it is a technical triumph of sorts at a time before tape recording.

CD

***The Victor Sessions, Master Takes, 1932–43*, Bluebird 3 2402-2-RB (USA)**

(New Orleans Feetwarmers:) Tommy Ladnier (tpt), Teddy Nixon (tb), Sidney Bechet (cl), Hank Duncan (p), Wilson Myers (sb), Morris Morland (d)

New York	15 Sept 1932	**Sweetie Dear**
add Bechet (ss), Myers (v)		**I want you tonight**
omit (cl), (v)		**I've found a new baby**
add Bill Maxey (v)		**Lay Your Racket**
omit (v)		**Maple Leaf Rag**
add Maxey (v)		**Shag**

(Ladnier:) Ladnier (tpt), Bechet (cl, ss), Mezz Mezzrow (ts), Cliff Jackson (p), Teddy Bunn (g), Elmer James (sb), Manzie Johnson (d)

	28 Sept 1938	**Ja-Da**
as ***Ja-Da****, but Mezzrow (cl)*		**Really the Blues**
as ***Ja-Da****, but Bechet (cl)*		**When You and I Were Young, Maggie**
as ***Ja-Da***		**Weary Blues**

(Jelly Roll Morton:) Sidney De Paris (tpt), Claude Jones (tb, preaching), Albert Nicholas (cl), Bechet (ss), Happy Caldwell (ts), Morton (p), Lawrence Lucie (g), Wellman Braud (sb), Zutty Singleton (d)

	14 Sept 1939	**Oh, Didn't He Ramble**

omit (preaching)		**High Society**
add Morton (v)		**I Thought I Heard Buddy Bolden Say** **Winin' Boy Blues**

(New Orleans Feetwarmers:) Bechet (ss), Sonny White (p), Charlie Howard (elg), Myers (sb), Kenny Clarke (d)

	5 Feb 1940	**Indian Summer**
as **Indian Summer***, but Bechet (cl)*		**One O'Clock Jump**
as **Indian Summer***; add Myers (v)*		**Preachin' Blues**
as **Indian Summer***, but Bechet (cl, v)*		**Sidney's Blues**

(Bechet:) De Paris (tpt), Sandy Williams (tb), Bechet (ss), Jackson (p), Bernard Addison (g), Braud (sb), Sid Catlett (d)

	4 June 1940	**Shake it and Break it** **Old Man Blues**
as **Old Man Blues***, but Bechet (cl)*		**Wild Man Blues**
add Bechet (ss)		**Nobody knows the way I feel dis' mornin'**
Bechet (ss, v), Jackson, Braud, Catlett		**Make me a pallet on the floor**

(Henry Levine:) Levine (tpt), Jack Epstein (tb), Alfie Evans (cl), Bechet (ss), Rudolph Adler (ts), Mario Janarro (p), Tony Colucci (g), Harry Patent (sb), Nat Levine (d), Frank Marks (arr)

	28 July 1940	**Shake it and Break it** **St Louis Blues**

Bechet (cl), Earl Hines (p), Baby Dodds (d)

	6 Sept 1940	**Blues in Thirds**

Rex Stewart (c), Bechet (ss), Hines (p), John Lindsay (sb), Dodds (d), Herb Jeffries (v)

		Blue for You, Johnny
omit (v)		**Ain't Misbehavin'**
add Bechet (cl)		**Save it, Pretty Mama**
omit (cl)		**Stompy Jones**

(Henry Levine:) Levine (tpt), Epstein (tb), Evans (cl), Bechet (ss), Adler (ts), Janarro (p), Colucci (g), Patent (sb), Nat Levine (d)

	11 Nov 1940	**Muskrat Ramble** (arr Marks)

Henry 'Red' Allen (tpt), J. C. Higginbotham (tb), Bechet (cl), James Tolliver (p), Braud (sb), J. C. Heard (d)

	8 Jan 1941	**Coal Black Shine**
		Egyptian Fantasy
as **Coal Black Shine**, *but Bechet (ss)*		**Baby, won't you please come home?**
		Slippin' and Slidin'

Bechet (cl, ss, ts, p, sb, d)

	18 April 1941	**The Sheik of Araby**
		Blues of Bechet

Gus Aiken (tpt), Williams (tb), Bechet (ss), Lem Johnson (ts), Jackson (p), Myers (sb), Arthur Herbert (d)

	28 April 1941	**Swing Parade**
		I know that you know
		When it's Sleepy Time Down South
		I ain't gonna give nobody none o' this jelly roll

Charlie Shavers (tpt), Bechet (ss), Willie 'the Lion' Smith (p), Everett Barksdale (elg), Braud (sb), Johnson (d)

	13 Sept 1941	**I'm coming, Virginia**
		Limehouse Blues
		Georgia Cabin
add Bechet (cl)		**Texas Moaner**
Bechet (ss), Smith (p), Barksdale (elg)		**Strange Fruit**
		You're the Limit

Henry Goodwin (tpt), Vic Dickenson (tb, v), Bechet (ss), Don Donaldson (p), Ernest Williamson (sb), Johnson (d), group (v)

	14 Oct 1941	**Rip Up the Joint**
omit group (v)		**Suey**
omit Dickenson (v)		**Blues in the Air**
		The Mooche
add Goodwin and group (v)		**Laughin' in Rhythm**

as **I'm coming, Virginia**, *but Catlett (d) replaces Johnson*

	24 Oct 1941	**12th Street Rag**
		Mood Indigo
		Rose Room
		Oh! Lady, Be Good!
		What is this thing called love?

Dickenson (tb), Bechet (ss), Donaldson (p), Myers (sb), Wilbert Kirk (d)

8 Dec 1943	**After You've Gone**
	Bugle Call Rag
	Ole Miss Blues
	St Louis Blues

Other CDs

same contents:

Sidney Bechet 1932–1943: The Bluebird Sessions, Bluebird ND 90317 (Europe)

* * *

Billy Banks: *The Henry Allen Collection, vol. 1, 1932*

The series of recordings issued under the name of Billy Banks and his Orchestra, The Rhythmakers and Jack Bland and the Rhythmakers holds a special place in the history of jazz. They are perhaps the hottest jazz recordings ever made – if we define hot as meaning music played with perfervid, reckless abandon. Billy Banks was a singer and general entertainer of no great talent who specialized in falsetto, a device employed commonly by black entertainers. The recordings were meant to feature his singing, but so hot were the instrumental sections that the singing is today seen as merely an intrusion. These groups included some of the finest jazz players of the day, both black and white, and are among the earliest important bands to mix racially in the recording studios. Among the musicians were trumpeter Henry 'Red' Allen, who also sings on some of the items, pianist Fats Waller, clarinettist and tenor saxophonist Pee Wee Russell, pianist Joe Sullivan, banjoist Eddie Condon and even trombonist Tommy Dorsey. Drummer Zutty Singleton is on all but the first session, which has Gene Krupa, and Singleton's New Orleans compatriots Al Morgan and Pops Foster are on bass. Perhaps the least known among the other participants was guitarist Jack Bland, who became the nominal leader on a few tracks made without Banks.

These cuts were recorded in 1932, at a time when the New Orleans style was virtually dead and the big bands were taking over. They are not classic New Orleans jazz – among other things, most of them have no trombone. But Allen and the aforementioned rhythm players were New Orleanians, and Russell, Sullivan and some of the other supporting cast had been weaned on New Orleans music. This is what came to be called Chicago style – hot, driving playing with the New Orleans flavour, filled with the blues and unconcerned with form.

The playing here is rhythmic, not melodic. The musicians again and again resort to the simplest of phrases, frequently repeating a two- or three-note figure several times with slightly varied rhythm. In many instances the music becomes even more basic, as, for example, when clarinettist Russell repeats a single note several times after the break in the fifth chorus of *Bugle Call Rag*. If that were not basic enough, at times the players hold one note for long stretches, varying it in pitch and intensity as it goes along: Tommy Dorsey holds a single note, with very broad lip vibrato, for over half his solo on *Who Stole the Lock?*, and Russell plays almost the entire last 16 bars of *Bugle Call Rag* on a held note. Even Fats Waller, ordinarily a very busy player, catches the mood: his introduction to *Mean Old Bed Bug Blues* is atypically sparse and punchy.

Among the occasional solos on these recordings, Russell plays tenor sax on *I Would Do Anything for You*, *Mean Old Bed Bug Blues* and *Yellow Dog Blues*; he frequently worked in saxophone sections of commercial dance bands, but his recorded solos on the instrument are very rare. The solo offerings are outnumbered by a lot of hard-driving ensemble playing, with Allen banging away at the top of his range and the clarinet and tenor saxophone swirling along in his wake.

In addition, the pieces are built on the simplest of material. About half are blues, and the rest are pop tunes or comic material (such as *Yes, Suh!* and *Who Stole the Lock?*) on the most basic chord changes. The Rhythmaker sides do not call for extended musical analysis. They are simply superb jazz at its hottest, made by some of the finest players of the day. If the New Orleans format was gone, there remained the lusty, heedless swing of that good-time city.

There is a bizarre footnote to these recordings: Billy Banks ended his career as an entertainer in Tokyo, where he was discovered by *Life* magazine, and where he died in 1967.

CD

***The Henry Allen Collection, vol. 1, 1932*, Collector's Classics COCD1 (Denmark)**

(Billy Banks and his Orchestra:) Henry Allen (tpt), Pee Wee Russell (cl, ts), Joe Sullivan (p), Eddie Condon (bj), Jack Bland (g), Al Morgan (sb), Gene Krupa (d)

New York	18 April 1932	**Bugle Call Rag**
add Allen (v)		**Oh Peter** (take 2)

Banks (v) replaces Allen (v) — **Margie**

*as **Margie**, but Zutty Singleton (d) replaces Krupa*

23 May 1932

Oh Peter (take 4)
Spider Crawl
Who's Sorry Now?
Take it Slow and Easy
Bald-headed Mama

(The Rhythmakers:) Allen (tpt), Jimmy Lord (cl), Russell (ts), Fats Waller (p), Condon (bj), Bland (g), Pops Foster (sb), Singleton (d), Banks (v)

26 July 1932

I Would Do Anything for You (takes 1–2)

add second (v), probably Waller — **Mean Old Bed Bug Blues** (takes 1–2)

omit second (v) — **Yellow Dog Blues** (takes 2–3)

add band (v) — **Yes, Suh!** (take 1)

(Jack Bland and his Rhythmakers:) Allen (tpt, v), Tommy Dorsey (tb), Russell (cl), Happy Caldwell (ts), Frank Froeba (p), Condon (bj), Bland (g), Foster (sb), Singleton (d), band (v)

8 Oct 1932

Who Stole the Lock? (take 2)

omit Allen and band (v); add Chick Bullock (v) — **A Shine on Your Shoes** (take 1)
It's gonna be you

Allen (v) replaces Bullock — **Someone stole Gabriel's horn** (take 1)

CHAPTER 2

Solo Stride and Swing Piano

Barry Kernfeld

At the same time that the hot combos and the big bands developed, pianists began to stake out a separate realm of unaccompanied playing. From time to time solo guitarists offered a challenge to the pianists, and since the 1970s other possibilities have emerged, as in the extended unaccompanied musings of tenor saxophonist Sonny Rollins and the many solo free jazz concerts and albums on just about any instrument imaginable. But as jazz ends its first century, the piano has remained dominant for a straightforward reason: a pianist could outdo anyone else in the ability to produce single-handedly the explicit beat, bass, chords and melody essential to so many styles of jazz. Only the Hammond B-3 organ, with its bass pedals and two keyboards, might have offered jazz a more versatile solo instrument, but in practice this machine has rarely appeared in settings smaller than a trio. The wide variety of electronic keyboards available in the 1990s has now seriously begun to challenge the supremacy of the piano, but an assessment of their role remains speculative.

As an introduction to the field, this chapter surveys three of the pianists who created the unaccompanied stride and swing styles – James P. Johnson, Fats Waller and Earl Hines – two who carried these styles to extremes – Art Tatum and Thelonious Monk – and three who have sustained these styles in recent decades – Ralph Sutton, Dave McKenna and Marcus Roberts. Jelly Roll Morton's solo playing has been discussed in chapter 1. Other formidable pianists working in this tradition are present in this book for their crucial contributions to groups – Joe Sullivan in various rhythm sections with Eddie Condon; Teddy Wilson with Benny Goodman and Billie Holiday; Nat 'King' Cole and Erroll Garner leading trios; Count Basie leading combos and his big band; Duke Ellington leading his big band – but it should be noted that Sullivan, Wilson and Garner also made fine unaccompanied recordings, and there is a good dose of stride and swing soloing in the midst of Basie and Ellington's band work.

(The equally important early piano style of boogie-woogie has no proper representation here, simply because it receives a full chapter of its own in a companion volume in this series, *The Blackwell Guide to Blues Records*, ed. Paul Oliver, Oxford, 1989.)

* * *

James P. Johnson: *From Ragtime to Jazz*

At the end of World War I James P. Johnson, Luckey Roberts and Willie 'the Lion' Smith were at the centre of an informal group of Harlem-based stride pianists. They were soon joined by Fats Waller, who became Johnson's protégé after he had learnt Johnson's *Carolina Shout* by copying the action of the version recorded on a piano roll. Whereas he had begun to make such rolls while still playing in a ragtime style, Johnson was immersed in the jazzy stride style by the time of his recording the earliest discs in the CBS collection, which date from 1921. Easiest to hear, and thus most readily identified with the style, is the recurring motion of the left hand. Spread apart, the hand would 'stride' repeatedly back and forth between an interval (comprising a bass note in the little finger and another note above in the thumb) in the lower register and a chord (comprising several notes) in the middle register. This method of using the left hand comes directly from ragtime, but differs subtly in the use of intervals (generally tenths) rather than single bass notes, and in the practice of striking those intervals top to bottom ('backward tenths'), with the thumb hitting slightly before the little finger, so as to impart a special rhythmic drive.

There is more to stride than just this motion. Broadly speaking, Johnson developed a virtuoso, percussive, swinging adaptation of ragtime piano forms and figurations. In some ways his work represents an orchestral and formal approach which stands in opposition to the folk-like boogie-woogie blues style. (This view is supported indirectly by his personal goals: he aspired to write symphonies and the like.) He had a formidable classical technique, enabling him to present sophisticated accompaniments while negotiating twisted right-hand figures effortlessly. His use of harmony, though tinged by the blues, is generally straightforward, following the fundamental progressions of Western art music, as did ragtime. And the crucial early pieces, *The Harlem Strut*, *Keep off the Grass* and *Carolina Shout*, all his own compositions, follow typical ragtime structures in presenting several distinct 16-bar themes symmetrically divided into eight-bar antecedent and consequent phrases: Johnson states an idea, it continues without resolving, he restates the idea, and a varied continuation resolves it. (The second theme of *Keep off the Grass* is 32 bars long, rather than 16).

Yet for Johnson, more than for any of the other leading stride players, classification as an orchestral rather than a folk-like pianist may be misleading. The overall sensation of these performances is one of percussive attack. He strikes the piano as if it were a drum set. *The Harlem Strut* is nearly a perpetual motion piece, and *Keep off the Grass* is only slightly less frenetic. *Carolina Shout* is more relaxed, but this is on account of the slower tempo rather than any change in approach. Regularly in these pieces, Johnson imparts a feeling of swing in his right hand through the subtle differentiation of duration (making the notes alternately a bit longer and a bit shorter) and articulation (the manner in which he strikes those notes). His striding left hand is never continuous. Following ragtime composers like Scott Joplin and such jazzy ragtime pianists as Eubie Blake, Johnson erratically but purposefully breaks up the pattern, inserting successive bass notes or successive chords. These jerky off-beat accents, which became a universal part of stride playing, supply great energy to the performances. (This is most readily heard on a later recording, *Toddlin'*.) Both *The Harlem Shout* and *Carolina Shout* have sequences of stabbing alternations as the hands rock between beats and off-beats. In both *Keep off the Grass* and *Carolina Shout*, and on many of the later recordings, he smashes two adjacent pitches simultaneously; on pieces such as *Weeping Blues* and *Worried and Lonesome Blues* this device might be interpreted as a simulation of blue notes (which the piano cannot produce literally), but in the many instances on non-blues tracks Johnson can only be described as obscuring pitch in favour of accentuation. It is revealing that when he includes a popular song, *If Dreams Come True*, among his solo recordings of 1939, he obliterates the melody, first in a stream of smashing dissonances and next with florid ornamentation; he then discards it in favour of another perpetual motion figure and a cascading riff; when the melody returns, again in a rhythmically charged form, it gives way to other essentially rhythmic ideas. Another piece, *Riffs*, recorded a decade earlier (1929), carries these various rhythmic tendencies still further, offering a zany demonstration of unpredictable accentuation. At one climactic point Johnson drops in sparkling trebly off-beat chords, and at another he moves fleetingly into a stride waltz, repeating oom pah pahs.

This anthology focuses on Johnson's greatest contribution to jazz, his exuberant stride performances, but he was a great musician in other genres as well. He accompanied blues and vaudeville singers, including Bessie Smith and Ethel Waters, and during a long career in musical theatre he composed many popular songs, among them *The Charleston*, *Old Fashioned Love* and *If I Could Be with You One Hour Tonight*. To a lesser extent these talents find expression in this collection. *All That I Had is Gone* (1927) explores other approaches in addition to stride, including a bass movement reminiscent of boogie-woogie and an elegant passage of interweaving independent lines. The appropriately titled *Feelin' Blue* (1929) follows stride techniques, but the performance is emotionally introspective. (By contrast, the inappropriately titled *Snowy Morning Blues*, from 1927, is cheery and not a blues.) Finally, there are two vaudeville dialogues recorded with Clarence Williams in 1930. The jokes quickly grow tiresome, but they are supported and framed by more fine examples of stride playing, especially at the end of *I've Found a New Baby*. I can scarcely hear the two pianos which are ostensibly present on these two tracks with Williams. The lower lines are clear throughout, as if one man were playing, and the upper ones are only a bit muddy. Did Williams understand that he was not a pianist of Johnson's stature, and hold back, staying out of the way?

CD

***From Ragtime to Jazz*, CBS 465651-2 (Europe)**

James P. Johnson (p)

New York	Aug 1921	**The Harlem Strut**
	18 Oct 1921	**Keep off the Grass**
		Carolina Shout
	28 June 1923	**Weeping Blues**
		Worried and Lonesome Blues
	8 Aug 1923	**Scouting Around**
		Toddlin'
	25 Feb 1927	**All That I Had is Gone**
		Snowy Morning Blues
	29 Jan 1929	**Riffs**
		Feelin' Blue

Johnson and Clarence Williams (p)

New York	31 Jan 1930	**How Could I be Blue?**
		I've Found a New Baby

Johnson

New York	14 June 1939	**If Dreams Come True**
		Fascination
		A-Flat Dream
		The Mule Walk
		Lonesome Reverie
		Blueberry Rhyme

* * *

Fats Waller: *Turn on the Heat: the Fats Waller Piano Solos*

Fats Waller wore many hats, as composer, songwriter, pianist, organist, bandleader, singer and entertainer in diverse combinations for musical theatre, popular music and jazz. The Bluebird CD gathers together his finest unaccompanied jazz piano recordings. Two tracks are not solos, but duets with Bennie Payne. Unlike the collaborations between James P. Johnson and Clarence Williams, or Waller's duets with Johnson in 1928, or Waller's big band battle with his second pianist Hank Duncan in a 1935 version of *I Got Rhythm*, these are ponderous performances, with numerous clashes over harmony, melody and rhythm.

Having studied with Johnson, Waller thoroughly absorbed and extended the latter's left-hand stride technique, the backbone of these recordings. His version of Johnson's *Carolina Shout*, recorded in 1941, keeps close to the original. Among Waller's own compositions here, *Valentine Stomp* and *Smashing Thirds* (both from 1929) imitate Johnson's percussive stride style. *Smashing Thirds* is based on 16-bar themes in different keys, in the pattern *AABABBBA*, and there are the usual introductory and transitional passages. (Unusually, ascending and descending scales in block chords extend the first *B* to 24 bars). As Johnson might do, Waller composes a rhythmic melody and moves it up an octave, and then up another, in successive presentations of the first theme. There are moments of chordal accompaniment in the first two *A*s and a syncopated walking bass line during the third, but stride techniques predominate, with Johnson-like rhythmic surprises in the second half of the piece.

In this collection of recordings, when Waller leaves Johnson's approach behind the result is not for the better. *Clothes Line Ballet* (1934) is a frivolous pastiche, presenting in sequence a trill; four bars of slow quasi-blues juxtaposed with four of fast riffs and stride; a sentimental light romantic ballad played chordally in free rhythm; a 32-bar *aaba* riff theme; and the quasi-blues.

On his best-known stride composition, *Handful of Keys* (1929), as well as on *Gladyse* (1929), *African Ripples*, *Alligator Crawl* and *Viper's Drag* (all from 1934), he finds a happy medium between innovation and tradition. All have two strongly contrasting themes, but with the exception of the second one in *Handful of Keys* each theme is based on *aaba* popular song form rather than on antecedent and consequent ragtime phrases; this is hardly surprising, given Waller's other activities. There are also contrasts in volume (most dramatically in *Gladyse* and *Viper's Drag*), tempo (*Viper's Drag*) and in the manner of accompaniment. In *Gladyse* and *African Ripples* we can hear Waller working out versions of the same piece. A dancing motif (which also recurs in *Valentine Stomp*) is supported in the first theme by smooth, gentle swing chords, with one note oscillating up and down. Cleverly and deceptively, this chordal motion also serves as the introduction, eliding with the theme proper so that its first appearance and its return is not 16, but 18 (in *Gladyse*) or 20 (in *African Ripples*) bars long. As this theme recurs, Waller increases the intensity by replacing the legato chords with a stride motion. Both pieces also use a four-bar transition to the new key of their 32-bar *B* themes, and leave the latter with an abrupt plonk, but here the relationship ends. In *Gladyse*, the earlier version, conventional stride predominates, supporting a heavily syncopated melody and then a return of the dancing motif. In *African Ripples* Waller invents a tuneful melody and loosens up the rhythm, playing at a free and generally slow tempo.

The Bluebird collection includes the 12-bar blues *Numb Fumblin'* and *My Feelin's Are Hurt* (both from 1929). These are delicate, elegant performances, stressing musicality rather than the emotional depth of the blues. This playing serves as a reminder that Waller may have learned as much from Willie 'the Lion' Smith as from Johnson. (Later, in 1939, Smith recorded his own series of solos, bringing together stride and French impressionism.) In the last chorus of *Numb Fumblin'* is one of Waller's great moments, as a breathlessly cascading 10-bar-long high register line moves in and out of phase with the stride bass.

Waller also interprets popular songs. Sessions from 1929 include routine readings (routine, at least, if you are Fats Waller!) of his and others' songs, with a regular stride motion accompanying fairly straightforward presentations of tunes. Representative are his own *Sweet Savannah Sue* and *Ain't Misbehavin'*. With the exception of *Rockin' Chair* (1941), in later years he took more liberties. In *Keepin' out of Mischief Now* and *Star Dust* (both from 1937) a good deal of pianistic filigree ornaments the melody. Both also include choruses of block chords, shouting and whispering above a rolling bass line. In *Basin Street Blues* (1937), taken at a bouncy tempo, unusually Waller pays little attention to melody and instead concentrates on rhythmic bass lines and chords. *Tea for Two* (1937) and *Honeysuckle Rose* (1941) are playful. The former begins with overly dramatic comical pauses throughout the opening statement of the tune, while the latter is completely fragmented, demonstrating how this familiar melody by Waller may be phrased, ornamented and harmonized in styles ranging from furiously paced stride to a romantic waltz. In a thoughtful rendition of *I Ain't Got Nobody* (1937) the opening phrases include a striking contrapuntal line in the middle register, more prominent than the melody; later, blues passages dissolve as Waller gracefully suspends a tinkling motif against a decelerating stride accompaniment. *Ring Dem Bells* (1941) is Waller's most radical recasting of existing material, his stark moody rendition standing in sharp contrast to high-spirited versions by Duke Ellington (1930) and subsequent remakes by, among others, Lionel Hampton (1938) and Andy Kirk (earlier in 1941). This performance suggests that Waller was dramatically furthering his creativity as a pianist during the last years of his life.

CD

***Turn on the Heat: the Fats Waller Piano Solos*, Bluebird 2482-2-RB (USA), ND 82482(2) (Europe)**

Fats Waller (p)

Camden, NJ	16 Feb 1927	**Blue Black Bottom Stomp**
New York	1 March 1929	**Handful of Keys**
		Numb Fumblin'
Camden, NJ	2 Aug 1929	**Ain't Misbehavin'**
		Sweet Savannah Sue
		I've Got a Feeling I'm Falling (take 1)
		I've Got a Feeling I'm Falling (take 2)
		Love Me or Leave Me (take 1)
		Gladyse (take 1)
		Valentine Stomp (take 1)
		Valentine Stomp (take 2)
	29 Aug 1929	**Waiting at the End of the Road** (take 1)
		Baby, oh! Where Can You Be? (take 1)
New York	11 Sept 1929	**Goin' About** (take 1)
		Goin' About (take 2)
		My Feelin's Are Hurt
	24 Sept 1929	**Smashing Thirds**
	4 Dec 1929	**My Fate is in your Hands**
		Turn on the Heat
Waller and Bennie Payne (p)		
	21 March 1930	**St Louis Blues**
		After You've Gone
Waller	16 Nov 1934	**African Ripples**
		Clothes Line Ballet
		Alligator Crawl
		Viper's Drag
	11 June 1937	**Keepin' out of Mischief Now**
		Star Dust
		Basin Street Blues
		Tea for Two
		I Ain't Got Nobody
	13 May 1941	**Georgia on my Mind**
		Rockin' Chair
		Carolina Shout (take 1)
		Carolina Shout (take 2)
		Honeysuckle Rose
		Ring Dem Bells

Other CDs

not incl. session of 13 May 1941:

Piano Masterworks, vol. 1, 1922–1929, Hot 'N Sweet FDC 5106, *vol. 2, 1929–1943*, FDC 5113 (France)

* * *

Earl Hines: *Special Earl Hines, 1928–1965*

A few days after recording the competitive duo *Weather Bird* with Louis Armstrong in December 1928, Earl Hines began recording under his own name by performing as a soloist for three remarkable sessions of piano rolls and discs. These had little effect on his studio career, which included only the occasional solo recording between 1929 and 1956, and evidently none whatsoever on his performing career. In 1964 David Himmelstein and Dan Morgenstern 'discovered that Hines had never played a concert as a featured pianist' and invited him to the Little Theater in New York (Morgenstern, 'Today's Life with Fatha Hines', *Down Beat*, xxxii, 26 Aug 1965, 25). His three concerts there were a rousing success, and for the remainder of his life Hines interspersed solo performances and recordings among his activities leading groups.

The CD **Special Earl Hines** is a tastefully expanded, artfully remastered edition of the album **Paris Session**, dating from a European tour in 1965, by which time James P. Johnson, Fats Waller, and Art Tatum were all dead. Added are extra takes of *Rose Room* from that same session, three titles from a less significant trio session in 1954, and the four titles surviving from his sessions for the OKeh label in December 1928.

The magnificent early recordings are based in the stride style, and on *Caution Blues* (also known as *Blues in Thirds*) Hines shows that he shared with Waller a focus on technical exploration, rather than blues emotion. But Hines was, by comparison with Waller, less delicate and far more adventuresome, with a predilection for sudden flights of pianistic fancy. As if to demonstrate his ability to operate on two channels at once, he explores the melody of *I Ain't Got Nobody* with great freedom and in a manner almost completely divorced from the calmness and detachment of his striding accompaniment, though for brief phrases he cannot contain himself and that accompaniment too breaks out into exuberant swing. *Fifty-Seven Varieties* is early Hines at his zaniest.

By the 1960s Hines was a veteran of continuous work in bands ranging stylistically from traditional jazz to bop, and all essential elements of his piano style were fully formed. He was consequently puzzled and a bit irritated by the hoopla surrounding his 'rediscovery'. Yet the late period piano work deserves to be singled out, because these tracks strike a fine balance between control and impetuosity which his earlier recordings as a bandleader cannot match, and because one gets nothing but Hines, who after all is a greater soloist than most of the sidemen on his decades of studio recordings as a leader. Moreover, Hines resists the temptation to pull out his most blatant applause-seeking tricks, such as the droning right-hand tremolo (which, even if amazing for his technique and endurance, is a bit crass). He does sing one chorus of *I Can't Give You Anything but Love* in a pleasant, laid back, but unremarkable voice resembling Doc Cheatham's; his radical recasting of the melody, especially in the substitution of repeated pitches for moving lines, is indebted to Louis Armstrong's famous version.

All the tunes are based on 32-bar popular song forms, including Hines's own composition *Sixty-Five Faubourg* (named after the address of Hugues Panassié who produced the session). He had co-written *Second Balcony Jump* during his years leading big bands. *Blue Because of You,* written by Hines's secretary Charlie Carpenter, his valet Louis Dunlap, and his bassist Quinn Wilson, was first recorded by his big band in March 1934 as *Blue;* general discographies have mistakenly confused this early rendition with a different song, *Blue (and Broken-hearted).* It might also be noted that Hines claims co-composer credit on reissues of this 1965 piano version of *Blue Because of You.* All the rest are familiar tunes by others, and Hines spends little time stating their melodies plainly. But he spends time building recognizable paraphrases, and regularly during his inspired improvisations he returns to fragments of tunes; the wildest instance occurs in *Somebody Loves Me,* where the ascending motif expressing the title words precedes and follows an upwardly screaming treble flourish at the beginning of the fourth 32-bar chorus.

A tremendous sense of swing permeates these performances. In achieving it, Hines subscribes to no fixed method. From one moment to the next we hear a walking bass and a running melody, stabbing off-beat single-note and chordal punctuations, a two-beat, a bit of stride, the hands locked together in block chords, the fingers chasing one another in octaves, a burst of classically inspired arpeggiation. Somehow amidst this seeming discontinuity there are always enough pounding bass notes and well-placed chordal attacks to keep the implicit beat at least firmly in place on such relaxed tunes as *I Cover the Waterfront* and *Blue Because of You,* if not positively charging ahead on such as *I Surrender Dear* and *Sweet Sue.* On better than half the LP, in pieces taken at medium to fast tempos, we can hear Hines's shoe making a metronomic click. Though by no means essential, I wonder if this little sound doesn't provide a useful anchor, as if a drummer were tapping out the beat lightly on a closed hi hat cymbal. Hines was not yet accustomed to playing without the support of bass and drums (although, of course, the results were already quite spectacular), and so he might have been using his shoe as a drumstick. (He also grunts along with some of his playing, contributing to the ambience of the session albeit in a less directly musical way.) On this album, the only exceptions to Hines's argument that solo piano playing ought to swing are the jarring yet still tasteful introduction to *I Cover the Waterfront*, the rhapsodic opening statement and ending of *A Pretty Girl is Like a Melody*, the extended out of tempo ending to *Blue Because of You* and the second *a* section of the fourth 32-bar *aaba* chorus of *Sweet Sue*, where the tempo (by my reckoning, at least) temporarily disintegrates under the force of Hines's torrent of accentuations.

CD

***Special Earl Hines, 1928–1965*, (EMI) Jazz Time 253 624-2 (France)**

Earl Hines (p)

Chicago	9 Dec 1928	**Caution Blues**
		A Monday Date
	12 Dec 1928	**I Ain't Got Nobody**
		Fifty-Seven Varieties

Hines (p), Paul Binnings (sb), Hank Mild (d)

Los Angeles	19 July 1954	**Nice Work if You Can Get it**
		If I Had You
		Humoresque

*Hines (p and *v)*

Paris	27 May 1965	**I Surrender Dear**
		I Cover the Waterfront
		Second Balcony Jump
		A Pretty Girl is Like a Melody
		I Can't Give You Anything but Love (*v)
		Blue Because of You
		Somebody Loves Me
		Sixty-Five Faubourg
		On the Sunny Side of the Street
		Sweet Sue
		Rose Room (take 1)
		Rose Room (take 2)
		Rose Room (take 3)

* * *

Art Tatum: *Art Tatum Solos 1940*

Appreciation of Art Tatum, the most technically gifted of all jazz pianists, tends to run into either/ors, ifs and buts. First comes the problem of the legendary Tatum and the available Tatum. The legendary Tatum –

one of jazz's most astounding improvisers, a man who at a party would spend hours disintegrating and reconstructing American popular songs – remains, well, mostly legendary. Only glimpses are available, mainly on very low fidelity recordings which require a considerable amount of wishful thinking to bring you to the party. The available Tatum – who recorded prolifically for major labels in good studios – was a more cautious man, who by no means avoided improvisation, but whose recorded legacy does not provide the wildly imaginative playing to which his respected colleagues testified again and again in interviews.

Listening to the studio recordings, one encounters the next roadblock, combo performances. The need for Tatum and his fellow players to be in some sort of agreement about rhythm and harmony undercut his fondness for varying the tempo and reharmonizing a chord progression without a moment's notice, and his busy style could get in the way of the others. This is especially a problem in his trios with Slam Stewart (whose own solos with Tatum, in his invariable style of humming while bowing the string bass, are not the best of his career and quickly wear thin). In his uncharacteristic combo sessions with blues shouter Joe Turner and in his mid-1950s albums with all star swing musicians this is less of a problem, but still the chemistry is not always right.

Among Tatum's unaccompanied studio recordings, again a problem appears. On late recordings for Capitol and for Norman Granz's labels Clef and Verve, the dazzle and flash of his early solos have given way to a deeper musicality on some titles, but more often have yielded to dullness and a lack of swing. And so there remain the dazzle and flash: the Decca solo recordings which many have criticized for shallowness. These sides are wonderful. Listen to *Get Happy*. How could anyone play the piano that well? And the examples of jazzing the classics are not offensive. Usually the idea is insipid and the results appalling, but by proceeding from such lightweight fare as Jules Massenet's *Elegie* and Antonin Dvořák's *Humoresque*, Tatum could scarcely do them terrible damage. Actually, this material is improved considerably by his arrangements, especially in the adaptation of *Humoresque* to Fats Waller's stride style.

For a jazz musician of his era, Tatum has an unusual conception of rhythm, in that for considerable stretches he plays out of tempo. Flexibly slow rhapsodic passages, interrupted by swoops up and down the keyboard, come directly from European romantic piano music and feed directly into the jazzy cocktail piano style which he inspired. But Tatum also has a manner of hurtling quickly through a melody, as in the opening statement of *Emaline*. This sensation of speed uncoupled from tempo seems more directly in the jazz tradition, but it had no direct impact; only later, separately, did free-jazz musicians develop the concept of rhythmic 'energy' freed from the beat.

Tatum also plays in jazz time, sometimes from the start, but at other times in the middle of a piece, the steady beat providing a structural contrast to the rhapsodic sections. On *Sweet Lorraine* sweeping bursts interrupt a stride motion, but the implicit beat remains steady and the performance swings wonderfully. On *Indiana,* also taken at a relaxed swing tempo, there is less stride motion and more of Tatum's left hand slithering through his chromatically coloured version of the tune's harmonies. *Get Happy* is also steady, but frantic; left-hand drones and trills alternate with a rapid stride motion. *Tiger Rag* is positively hysterical. If this is too fast for good taste, forget taste and marvel at technique. In a continuous outburst – as in the discontinuous swoops which ornament other performances – he shows an extraordinary touch, bringing out lines in either hand at lightning speed with great clarity. He effectively imitates the tailgate trombone plops in the 'hold that tiger' strain of the piece and then, for a breathless last chorus, moves into the fastest possible stride version.

The other great achievement of Tatum's playing is subtle – indeed well beyond the scope of this book; his ability to reharmonize songs can be demonstrated only through elaborate music examples. But perhaps a couple of the more blatant occurrences will provide some insight into this. In the late 1950s and early 1960s the notion of playing 'outside' came into jazz improvisation, especially through the work of Eric Dolphy, who intentionally emphasized pitches which were not in accord with the accompanying harmonies. Tatum was already a master at it. In the last chorus of *Indiana* he breaks out of the key on the first three phrases, then each time works his way back in. The same thing happens at the start of the second and third stride choruses of *Emaline,* where Tatum, having hurtled through the theme, now momentarily hurtles out of the key.

CD

***Art Tatum Solos 1940*, MCA MCAD 42327 (USA)**

Art Tatum (p)

Los Angeles	22 Feb 1940	**Elegie**
		Humoresque
		Sweet Lorraine
		Get Happy
		Lullaby of the Leaves
		Tiger Rag
		Sweet Emaline, my Gal (take A)
		Sweet Emaline, my Gal (take B)
		Emaline
		Moonglow

	Love Me
	Cocktails for Two
26 July 1940	**St Louis Blues**
	Begin the Beguine
	Rosetta
	Indiana

Other CDs

plus additional tracks:
Complete Brunswick & Decca Recordings, 1932–1941, Affinity AFS 1035-3 (UK)

* * *

Thelonious Monk: *Solo Monk*

Why place Thelonious Monk in the midst of stride and swing pianists? He was, after all, one of the most important bop musicians and most of his recordings were made with bop groups (see chapter 7). As a composer and improviser he contributed new melodic shapes, which in turn grew out of his untraditional notions of rhythmic placement, accentuation, piano voicings (how individual chords might be expressed at the keyboard) and harmonic progressions (how chords follow one another). All of these elements were incorporated into definitive bop recordings. At the same time, Monk remained a traditional melodist, above all in the very fact of his preference for repeating memorable tunes rather than spinning out ever-changing complex lines. On the album **Solo Monk** this concern comes to the fore, as do other features which show his fondness for earlier jazz styles.

The album de-emphasizes Monk's great bop writing. There are two blues based on repeated figures: the theme of *North of the Sunset* takes up a jagged boppish motif better known from his composition *Well You Needn't*, and *Monk's Point* uses adjacent pitches which are attacked and released in such a way as to simulate a blue note. There are two ballads, *Ruby, my Dear* and *Ask Me Now*, the latter belonging to neither his best-known nor his most distinctive work. The remaining eight tracks are popular songs. While this in itself marks some diversion from his usual approach, still more important is the way in which he treats the material. Bop performers frequently use the structures of pop songs as a basis for improvisation, downplaying, ignoring or rewriting the melodies. Here Monk doesn't merely borrow structures, he plays the songs themselves. Captivated by their melodies, he can hardly bear to move away from them. Characteristically, he ornaments a melody only a bit and slightly displaces its relation to the beat; for a clear example, listen to the first phrase of *Dinah,* beginning on beat 1 at the start and on beat 2 at its repetition eight bars later. He never improvises for long before returning to the tune, and showy pianistic gestures (the cascading and climbing runs at the end of *I Surrender Dear*) are rare. This is true not only of the pop songs, but also of his own ballads. *Ruby, my Dear* is essentially a meditation on his theme, the second half of which he repeats over and over again.

To help bring out these melodies, Monk plays mainly at slow (and sometimes elastic) tempos, and he never goes beyond a relaxed walking pace. By avoiding speedy performances and the temptation to go into double time, he takes up a rhythmic conception that harks back to the earliest southern traditions in jazz. In an equally strong way he invites comparison with the Harlem-based pianists and their followers. Steady stride rhythms crop up throughout the album, from the delightful and straightforward readings of *Dinah, I'm Confessin'* and *These Foolish Things* to the two blues, which would exemplify his bop playing were it not for his breaking into a stride motion as he begins to improvise. There are also moments of old-fashioned tremolos (a trademark of Earl Hines's playing) in several wry endings to tunes and in the last statement of the melody of *Sweet and Lovely*.

Other aspects of Monk's playing invariably stand apart from established styles, old or new. He prefers stark, dissonant, colourful combinations of pitches. A typical example occurs in *Sweet and Lovely*. Without disrupting the melody, he reharmonizes the first phrase so that the accompaniment slithers downwards in parallel minor sevenths (moving step-by-step from B flat with an A flat above, down to C with a B flat above). The touch of his right hand is hard and crisp, producing a bell-like sound; paradoxically, he likes to obscure this clarity by striking clusters of notes, which may, through his use of the foot pedal, ring on in an echoing mass of sound. Fine examples occur in his deliberate and freely metred version of *I Should Care,* where dense chords alternate with stark individual pitches, and overlapping sounds break into silence as he releases the pedal; and in the high-pitched thicket of notes which he punches out just before the end of *Ask Me Now*. In these respects his playing was intensely personal and has scarcely been imitated successfully.

CD

***Solo Monk,* Columbia Jazz Masterpieces CK 47854 (USA) and 471248-2 (Europe)**

Thelonious Monk (p)

Los Angeles	31 Oct 1964	**I Surrender Dear**
		Sweet and Lovely

		Everything Happens to Me
		I Should Care
		North of the Sunset
	11 Nov 1964	**These Foolish Things**
		I Hadn't Anyone Till You
		Dinah
		I'm Confessin'
		Monk's Point
New York	23 Feb 1965	**Ask Me Now**
	2 March 1965	**Ruby, my Dear**
		Introspection

* * *

Ralph Sutton: *Ralph Sutton at the Café des Copains*

Born in 1922 and still active seven decades later, Ralph Sutton is a survivor and a keeper of the flame within the specialized field of unaccompanied stride and swing piano playing. He is old enough to have learned his craft while Fats Waller's career was flourishing (Sutton joined Jack Teagarden's band in 1941 and Waller died in 1943), and in so far as he fits into a niche within this little field, Waller's playing would be the model: a refined, delicate style; clarity of tone; and a devotion to popular song melodies, from which elaborate improvised melodies and countermelodies emerge, always with periodic returns to the familiar theme. Perhaps the most fundamental difference is rhythmic. On this collection recorded in the mid-1980s, Sutton frequently uses unmetred introductions as a device for rhythmic contrast, but once the tune proper is under way, his left-hand pattern is less varied than Waller's and his right-hand work more persistently tied to a steady beat. Although he invites us to remember Waller (*Christopher Columbus*, without the lyrics), James P. Johnson (elaborating Johnson's gentle *Snowy Morning Blues*) and Earl Hines (*You Can Depend on Me*), Sutton shows no interest in Johnson's percussive violence or Hines's zaniness (compare Hines's wild version of *Sweet Sue*, made in 1965, with Sutton's stable reading).

Sutton's career has taken a different shape from that of these prominent colleagues. Evidently the jazz life has been kind to him. Like Hines, and unlike Waller and Johnson, he has lived to see his biography published (in 1975); unlike Hines, he gained opportunities to take a further step forward after this event. Since the 1980s he has recorded a large number of superlative solo and duo albums, among which this collection is representative. John Norris's CD pamphlet notes explain the circumstances of recording. With Sutton having reached a period of complete maturity and professional polish, and with the producer having had the opportunity to select the finest tracks from a period spanning half a decade, the results are consistently fine, and it seems almost foolish to try to point out the best tracks, though the honours might go to *Russian Lullaby*. The sound too is gorgeous, with Norris the producer having captured Sutton's ability to coax beauty out of the high quality piano at the Café des Copains. Somewhat like the proverbial tree falling in the forest, this sound was evidently scarcely heard, if the polite little smatterings of applause are any indication of who was listening during these several years of performance. Of course that too is a part of Sutton's jazz life. Fortunately with this document he can widen his audience from handfuls to thousands.

CD

***Ralph Sutton at Café des Copains*, Sackville CD 2-2019 (Canada)**

Ralph Sutton (p)

Toronto	1 June 1983	**Exactly like You**
	7 Feb 1984	**Laugh Clown Laugh**
		You Can Depend on Me
		Snowy Morning Blues
		St Louis Blues
		My Blue Heaven
	8 Feb 1985	**Russian Lullaby**
		Christopher Columbus
	28 Jan 1987	**Poor Butterfly**
		Sweet Sue
		This is All I Ask
		Somebody Stole My Gal

* * *

Dave McKenna: *My Friend the Piano*

Eight years younger than Sutton, Dave McKenna evidently grew up with an ear focused on the sound of the pioneer Jimmy Blanton (see chapter 3) and subsequent string bassists playing in late swing and early bop styles, from whom he developed a technique for unaccompanied playing that differs substantially from that of his famous predecessors. He favours walking bass lines that often extend into the lowest range of the piano. His overall style is firmly based in swing in his consistent devotion to melody and to the standard repertory of American popular song, of which his knowledge is encyclopedic and from which he weaves together the sorts of programmatically connected medleys heard on **My Friend the Piano**. Yet bop just as much as swing influences that relentless left hand, which serves in effect as a surrogate string bass.

The opening track *Margie* is characteristic. First he lays out the melody lovingly from start to finish, with improvised ornamentation, though never so much as to submerge the identity of the original tune. The steady, roaring bass then begins its walk, and as McKenna improvises melodies high above this improvised bass, subtle little snippets of accompanying chords gradually work their way into the middle of the instrument, as if he had suddenly grown a third hand. For the final time through the theme, he brings the piece to a climax by slowing down the tempo. (The freedom to create this sort of rhythmic jolt, without having to worry about messing up other instrumentalists, is one of the luxuries of unaccompanied playing.)

McKenna is by no means dogmatic in his approach. He draws from the stride tradition to provide textural contrast in the *Summer* and *Always* medleys, the latter moving from the oom-pah stride of *It's Always You*, to the oom-pah-pah swing waltz *Always*, to his walking bass and improvising treble style for *This is Always*. A Latin-flavoured pattern provides a framework for *Key Largo*. And indeed he is at his finest on ballads like *Only Trust Your Heart* and *Slowly*, and the relaxed slow blues *Baby, Baby, All the Time* (among these erudite piano soloists, McKenna is one of the most convincing blues players), when the stark contrast of treble and bass gives way to a fuller, more homogeneous sound in which chords are at the heart of the pianistic texture, hence affording an explicit forum for his lush harmonic thought.

CD

***My Friend the Piano*, Concord CCD-4313 (USA)**

Dave McKenna (p)
Rancho Bernardo, CA   Aug 1986

Margie
Only Trust Your Heart
Mean to Me
Slowly
You're Driving Me Crazy
Key Largo
Soon Medley:
  Soon (Rodgers & Hart)
  Soon (Gershwins)

Summer Medley:
Guess I'll go back home this summer
Indian Summer
Baby, Baby, All the Time
Always Medley:
It's Always You
Always
This is Always

* * *

Marcus Roberts: *Alone with Three Giants*

Having served as trumpeter Wynton Marsalis's pianist for five years in the 1980s and then as Marsalis's successor leading the Lincoln Center Jazz Orchestra in the mid-1990s, pianist Marcus Roberts has figured prominently in a movement of historical rediscovery that has taken on great strength in jazz. Founded on bop and its related styles, the movement is discussed later in the book under the heading of the bop revival (chapter 16), but some participants, including notably Marsalis and Roberts, have interests extending back through swing to early jazz and the origins of jazz. As such their contributions to the bop revival fall under a still broader category, jazz neo-classicism. The movement has been a mixed bag, offering at best a devoted and loving effort to assure that the creators of jazz get their due, and at worst both a gross over-assessment of the significance of the neo-classicists and a repressive musical correctness allowing no room for contemporaries working in free jazz and fusion.

Among its happiest results is Roberts's disc **Alone with Three Giants**, a collection of unaccompanied piano solos offered as a tribute to the compositions and piano styles of Jelly Roll Morton (three tracks, detailed on the disc notes), Duke Ellington (and assorted collaborators, including Bubber Miley and Ben Webster; six tracks) and Thelonious Monk (this last group of six tracks presented with at least as much emphasis on Monk's adaptation of stride piano, as on Monk's forward-looking contributions to bop). Roberts is fabulously gifted. Having mastered bop piano technique, with its necessarily sparse left-hand style, he has gained an equal mastery of the quite different two-handed blues, stride and swing piano styles discussed earlier in this chapter (and also in chapter 1, in the essay on Morton). Within these diverse traditions, he exhibits great versatility. He is capable of radically transforming pieces, as he might do for example when interpreting James J. Johnson's stride test piece *Carolina Shout* in live performance. But on

Alone with Three Giants he selects an approach that remains rather faithful to the original recordings. Of course this is jazz, and a comparison to these originals will quickly confirm that Roberts has allowed himself plenty of room for discreet, reflective and sensitive improvisation, without any displays of flashy technique.

Roberts's best evokes the spirit of Monk during a segment of *Misterioso* when he reiterates, with subtle rhythmic and harmonic variation, a weird, syncopated right-hand chord, set against steady blues chords in the left. In general he remains furthest from Monk, not because of any personal deficiency, but because Monk's piano playing is so extraordinarily individual that no-one has ever come close to sounding like him. Roberts's versions of Morton's swinging ragtime piano sound entirely authentic. He seems closest in spirit to Ellington, and the ballads *Solitude* and *I got it bad* are particularly beautiful and swinging, in a quiet way.

CD

***Alone with Three Giants*, Novus 3109-2-N (USA)**

Marcus Roberts (p)

New Orleans	3 June 1990	**Trinkle, Trinkle**
	4–5 June 1990	**Mood Indigo**
		Solitude
		I got it bad
		Misterioso
		Pannonica
		New Orleans Blues
		Prelude to a Kiss
		Shout 'em Aunt Tillie
		Monk's Mood
		In Walked Bud
		Crepuscule with Nellie
Bronxville, NY	22 Sept 1990	**Jungle Blues**
		Black and Tan Fantasy
		The Crave

CHAPTER 3

Big Bands to the Mid-1950s

Barry Kernfeld
(and James Lincoln Collier on Benny Goodman)

The leaders of the first important jazz big bands were pragmatic men. They established their orchestras somewhat haphazardly during the mid-1920s, expanding their small groups into big bands more to meet the demands of nightclub and dance-hall operators than from any inner musical impulse towards a new jazz style suitable for large ensembles. It was the 'jazz age'. Audiences were big. Music often had to fill vast spaces, without the aid of amplification. So each man augmented his number of instrumentalists, adding brass and reeds. But quickly a new music resulted. While drawing in many ways from that of the hot bands, it now treated brass and reeds not only as individuals, but also as members of a section; and when, a few years later, the brass split into two sub-sections, the big band had settled into its long-lived form: trumpets, trombones, reeds (saxophones and clarinets) and rhythm section (piano; banjo or guitar; tuba or string bass; drums). These developments immediately afforded a special status to the composer or arranger who could feature and combine the four sections in the most imaginative ways.

The idea of sections (but with a string section prominent) and the importance of a good writer had already made their mark in popular dance music, beginning at the end of the 1910s, and jazz-orientated leaders had not missed noting how much money this approach generated, above all when the baton was in Paul Whiteman's hand. Less than a decade later, though, the new idea of blending gutsy jazz with dignified control had proved so successful that the much tamer 'symphonic jazz' of Whiteman had fallen out of fashion. It was no longer enough just to hire a few hot soloists – whole bands were beginning to learn how to swing. Soon big-band jazz would reach its widest audience, as American popular music and jazz temporarily merged into one, blurring distinctions among dance big bands, swing big bands and jazz big bands.

This chapter surveys the most innovative and creative jazz big bands from the 1920s into the mid-1950s, a period governed by the principle of brass and reed sections. Additionally, Bob Crosby's big band figures in chapter 5 within the context of its consolidation of dixieland and swing in the 1930s, Machito's orchestra in chapter 12, within the context of his contribution to the emergence of a distinct Latin jazz style in the 1940s, and Gillespie's United Nation Superband in the same chapter, within the context of a resurgence of Afro-Cuban jazz in the late 1980s to 1990s. The story continues in chapter 14, which introduces Gil Evans's orchestral collaborations with Miles Davis in the late 1950s and a few of the most creative manifestations of the central big band tradition from the 1960s onwards. A different sort of big band, organized along principles of free jazz playing, is covered in chapters 17 and 19.

* * *

Fletcher Henderson: *The Chronological Fletcher Henderson and His Orchestra, 1924–1925; The Chronological Fletcher Henderson and His Orchestra, 1932–1934*

Fletcher Henderson's orchestra was at the vanguard of the jazz scene in New York, helping to develop a stylistic vocabulary for big bands at two crucial points: when such bands began to form, and later, just before big-band swing became the popular music of its day. Among the many and varied reissues of Henderson's prolific recordings, the series on the Decca/MCA label had covered these points in the decade that it spanned, but there is no evidence yet that these now obsolete LPs will reappear on CD on GRP's label Decca Jazz. Fortunately the French label Classics includes two volumes covering roughly the same ground. At the time of the first recording late in 1924, principles of big band arranging were emerging and the group's new featured soloist Louis Armstrong was helping transform the ensemble from a dance band to a jazz band (on record more so than in live performance, where dancing remained its focus of attention). Unfortunately this Classics volume begins just after the group recorded its single most important track, *Copenhagen*, on 30 October 1924, and listeners must seek this out on the previous volume of the Classics series, or elsewhere. (*Copenhagen* figures on many anthologies; finding it is not a great problem.) At the time of the last, September 1934, Henderson's drastically changed group was two months from disbanding, and in the next year their music, a good deal of it arranged by Henderson himself, would provide crucial material for Benny Goodman's big band. Happily this volume in the Classics series offers a much better selection of tracks than had been available on Decca.

This collection presents an orchestra that remained indebted to early jazz traditions, both black and white, well into the 1930s, to some extent in its repertory (the first track, *Eccentric*, is a dixieland classic) and more so in its rhythmic style. But ultimately the music moved far from its New Orleans basis under the guidance of Henderson's arrangers, among whom Don Redman was initially pre-eminent (although the arrangements remain unattributed for the majority of tracks on the early volume). These arrangers developed effective ways to utilize groups of wind instruments (initially four brass and three reeds), by replacing collective improvisation with rehearsed lines. *I'll take her back if she wants to come back* is characteristic of the band's blend of hot and sweet playing: for an introduction, a fanfare from the full ensemble. Then saxophones offer a sweetly harmonized rendition of the tune, with muted brass interjected between phrases of the melody; tenor saxes and brass play together; the sweetly harmonized reeds return, but with clarinet replacing one of the saxes; a friskier last chorus ends the piece. The uncredited arrangement of *I'll see you in my dreams* features a complicated and swinging muted brass obbligato that dances around tenor saxophonist Coleman Hawkins's squawking melodic statement. *Alabamy Bound* is Redman's reworking of *Cake Walking Babies from Home*, which Armstrong and Sidney Bechet had recorded a couple of months earlier; the nicest touch of the arranger's hand involves wa-wa-like sounds in the saxophones set against Charlie Green's trombone solo. The unattributed *Money Blues* anticipates the future of big band arrangements, by offering blues choruses of repeated brass riffs, the first riff in accompaniment to Buster Bailey's clarinet solo and the second standing alone, thus serving as melody. *Sugar Foot Stomp* is Redman's reworking of King Oliver's *Dippermouth Blues*, and by way of summarizing the old and new, it features densely packed and pleasantly chaotic dixieland-style collective improvisations that alternate with arranged chordal passages towards the end.

In organizing the orchestra, Redman was particularly fond of trios – trumpet trios, saxophone trios, clarinet trios – which may be heard throughout the early recordings. For the most part this was simply a matter of using what instruments he had. The band kept three trumpeters (at first, to be precise, two plus Armstrong's cornet). The saxophone trio grew as the saxophone section grew, but, oddly, the clarinet trio persisted as a stylistic device long after its sound had become old fashioned and Redman had left the orchestra. It pops out in one of the most unlikely places, the last chorus of *Down South Camp Meetin'* (1934), which in all other respects is one of the archetypal recordings of big-band swing. Composed by Henderson, *Down South Camp Meetin'* became one of the arrangements on which Goodman built his successful orchestra when Henderson's group failed and the leader was hired by Goodman. Nearly everything has a compelling energy: the driving four beat; the tight sax and brass riffs, traded back and forth; trumpeter Henry 'Red' Allen's solo, over sax chords and riffs; the fancier sax line, taken up by the brass in the following chorus. Only the anachronistic clarinet trio takes the steam out of the performance, although perhaps this is because of sloppy playing at the end rather than because of the clarinet trio *per se*.

Although Henderson's rhythm section was never the best of its day, these two volumes provide a tidy summary of the development of jazz rhythm sections over the decade. In the 1920s the beat is crisp and clipped, carried by the banjo playing on all four beats and the tuba playing a two-beat on beats 1 and 3. (Exceptionally, tubaist Ralph Escudero plays a four-beat – i.e., he sounds a note on each beat – to add to the density of the last portion of *Sugar Foot Stomp*.) The piano seems to support the banjo, though it can scarcely be heard apart from solo passages. Drummer Kaiser Marshall has little responsibility for keeping time. He may occasionally maintain some steady drum clicks or ornamental accents, and during *When You Do What You Do* he maintains a steady backbeat rhythm on the cymbal during Armstrong's solo. At other times seemingly he does not play at all.

By contrast the sessions from 1932–4 offer a nearly full-blown conception of swing rhythm. The brass and reed sections fluidly toss riffs back and forth on such titles as *Honeysuckle Rose* (in an arrangement borrowed five years later for Count Basie's first big band recording as a leader), *New King Porter Stomp* (based on Jelly Roll Morton's tune and later popularized by Goodman), and *Wrappin' It Up* (another of Goodman's borrowings). John Kirby's string bass has replaced Escudero's tuba, and it is now set against steady chords from the smooth rhythm guitar (not banjo) and a more prominently recorded piano, all underpinned by Walter Johnson's soft, slightly stiff cymbal patterns. The remaining link to past styles is the bass playing of Elmer James, who replaced Kirby for the sessions of September 1934. He has a hard attack that regularly crosses over into New Orleans 'slap-bass' technique, but apparently he could not quite handle fast tempos. On *Limehouse Blues* and *Happy as the Day is Long*, James steadfastly maintains a two-beat against the ensemble's furious four-beat, thus preventing the volcanic energy of these pieces from completely erupting. A comparison with Al Morgan's or Pops Foster's playing on the Rhythmakers sides (discussed in chapter 1) will show what might be done on pieces like these.

Henderson's soloists are always prominent. The reeds are less than distinguished, including even Coleman Hawkins, who despite his importance in establishing the tenor saxophone as a solo instrument in jazz, was for a long time improvising extremely awkward solos on that instrument. (His bass saxophone playing on *Hocus Pocus* seems much better suited to the band's clipped style.) Only in his last year with Henderson, before leaving for Europe in 1934, did Hawkins's improvisatory style finally begin to come to maturity. His solo on *It's the Talk of the Town* is often regarded as foreshadowing his famous version of *Body and Soul* from 1939 (discussed in chapter 4).

If the reed soloists are sometimes only passable, the brass are always glorious. Armstrong offered definitive examples of melodic creativity and swing, including his cornet solos on *Mandy Make Up Your Mind, I'll See You in My Dreams* and *Sugar Foot Stomp*. Apart from Armstrong's contribution, there are some long-standing questions of attribution involving Henderson's brass players. But it should be remembered that in many instances the brassmen were filling established roles rather than trying to express their individuality. It would be easy to get hung up trying to distinguish each one and to miss the point of how great all these players are. Early examples include trumpeter Joe Smith's pretty solo after the introduction to *Wha-cha-call-'em Blues* and trombonist Charlie Green's rollicking solo before the end. Later, in the span of the second Classics volume, it becomes unwieldy to list the best solos of trumpeters Bobby Stark, Henry 'Red' Allen, Irving 'Mouse' Randolph, cornetist Rex Stewart, and trombonists J. C. Higginbotham, Sandy Williams, Dicky Wells, Claude Jones, and Keg Johnson, because there are too many. And Allen's delightful singing on *Nagasaki* is not to be missed. Henderson's bands were never the tightest of their era, but they outclassed much of the competition in terms of individual creativity.

CD

***The Chronological Fletcher Henderson and His Orchestra, 1924–1925*, Classics 633 (France)**

Elmer Chambers, Howard Scott (tpt), Louis Armstrong (c), Charlie Green (tb), Buster Bailey (cl, as, ss), Don Redman (as, cl), Coleman Hawkins (ts, cl), Fletcher Henderson (p), Charlie Dixon (bj), Ralph Escudero (bb), Kaiser Marshall (d)

New York	early Dec 1924	**Prince of Wails** (take 1)
		Mandy Make Up Your Mind (take 1)
omit (ss)	mid-Jan 1925	**I'll see you in my dreams** (take 1)

Why couldn't it be poor little me? (take 2)

add Hawkins (C-melody sax)
23 Jan 1925 **Bye and Bye**
Play Me Slow (take 3)

omit (C-melody sax); add train whistles
2–6 Feb 1925 **Alabamy Bound** (take 2) (arr Redman)

omit train whistles **Swanee Butterfly** (take 1)

add Hawkins (c-melody sax) **Poplar Street Blues**
12th Street Blues

add unknown (ukulele) **Me Neenyah** [*sic*] **(My Little One)**

Chambers, Joe Smith (tpt), Armstrong (c), Green (tb), Bailey, Redman (as, cl), Hawkins (ts, cl, bass sax), Henderson (p), Dixon (bj), Escudero (bb), Marshall (d)
18 April 1925 **Memphis Bound**

omit (bass sax) **When You Do What You Do**
19 May 1925 **I'll take her back if she wants to come back**
Money Blues (take 1)

add ?Redman (v break), Hawkins (cl)
29 May 1925 **Sugar Foot Stomp** (arr Redman)

omit (v break) **What-cha-call-'em Blues** (arr Redman)

Armstrong (c), Billy Jones (v), plus unknown personnel, possibly involving members of Henderson's orchestra
7 Aug 1925 **I Miss My Swiss** (arr Redman)

omit (v) **Alone at Last** (arr Redman)

Chambers, Smith (tpt), Armstrong (c), Green (tb), Bailey, Redman (as, cl), Hawkins, (ts, cl), Henderson (p), Dixon (bj), Escudero (bb), Marshall (d)
21 Oct 1925 **T N T** (arr Redman)

add Hawkins (bass sax) **Carolina Stomp**

as ***TNT****, but Russell Smith (tpt) replaces Armstrong; Hawkins (cl, C-melody sax, ts)*
16 Nov 1925 **Sleepy Time Gal** (take 2)

add Redman (v) **Then I'll Be Happy** (take 1) (arr Redman)

***The Chronological Fletcher Henderson and His Orchestra, 1932–1934*, Classics 535 (France)**

Russell Smith, Bobby Stark (tpt), Rex Stewart (c), J. C. Higginbotham, Sandy Williams (tb), Russell Procope, Hilton Jefferson (as), Hawkins (ts), Henderson (p), Freddy White (g), John Kirby (aluminum sb), Walter Johnson (d)

New York	9 Dec 1932	**Honeysuckle Rose** (arr Henderson ?and Claude Hopkins)
		New King Porter Stomp (arr Henderson)
add Katherine Handy (v)		**Underneath the Harlem Moon** (arr Henderson)

Smith, Stark, Henry 'Red' Allen (tpt), Dicky Wells (tb), Procope, Jefferson (as, cl), Hawkins (ts, cl), Henderson (p), Bernard Addison (g), Kirby (sb), Johnson (d)

	18 Aug 1933	**Yeah Man!** (take 1) (arr Horace Henderson)
		King Porter's Stomp (take 1) (arr Fletcher Henderson)
add Williams (tb)		**Queer Notions** (arr Horace Henderson)
		Can You Take It? (take 1) (arr Fletcher Henderson)

Claude Jones (tb) replaces Williams; Horace Henderson (p) replaces Fletcher

	22 Sept 1933	**Queer Notions** (arr Horace Henderson)
		It's the Talk of the Town (arr Fletcher Henderson)
		Night Life (arr Will Hudson)
add Allen (v), unknown (vb)		**Nagasaki** (arr Horace Henderson)

Smith, Joe Thomas, Allen (tpt), Jones, Keg Johnson (tb), Procope, Jefferson (as, cl), Hawkins (ts), Fletcher Henderson (p), Addison (g), Kirby (sb), Johnson (d)

	6 March 1934	**Hocus Pocus** (take 1) (arr Hudson)
		Phantom Fantasie (take 2)
add Charles Holland (v)		**Harlem Madness** (arr Fletcher Henderson)
omit (v)		**Tidal Wave** (arr Russ Morgan)

Smith, Irving 'Mouse' Randolph, Allen (tpt), Jones, Johnson (tb), Bailey (cl), Procope, Jefferson (as), Ben Webster (ts), Henderson (p), Lawrence Lucie (g), Elmer James (sb), Johnson (d)

11 Sept 1934 — **Limehouse Blues** (arr Benny Carter)

Horace Henderson (p) replaces Fletcher Henderson (p)

Shanghai Shuffle (arr Fletcher Henderson)
Big John's Special (arr Horace Henderson)
Happy as the Day is Long (arr Carter)

as ***Limehouse Blues****, but Procope, Jefferson (as, cl)*
12 Sept 1934 — **Tidal Wave** (arr Morgan)
Down South Camp Meetin' (arr Fletcher Henderson)

as ***Shanghai Shuffle*** — **Wrappin' it up** (arr Fletcher Henderson)
Memphis Blues (arr Fletcher Henderson)

* * *

Duke Ellington: *Early Ellington; The Blanton–Webster Band; Ellington at Newport*

In 1924, while Henderson was working at the Roseland Ballroom and, owing to Louis Armstrong's presence in the band, almost immediately making a huge impact, Duke Ellington settled in a couple of blocks away at the Kentucky Club. There, somewhat more gradually, he organized what would soon become, and remain, the greatest of the big bands. His orchestra's rich and substantial legacy of recordings spanned a half century, and the selections here are drawn from his two best series of studio sessions and from a celebrated live appearance. The first collection captures the band while it was playing at the Cotton Club and traces its growth into the mid-1930s. The second dates from the early 1940s, when the swing era was in full bloom. The third was recorded in performance at the Newport Jazz Festival in 1956.

From the start of its tenure at the Cotton Club, Ellington's then ten-piece big band was not, like Henderson's, playing mainly for patrons to dance to. Instead the group supplied music for shows, and out of these shows there developed an unforgettable style of pseudo-Africana known as 'jungle music'. The pivotal figure in this new style was trumpeter Bubber Miley, who may be heard on these early Victor recordings playing in a distinctive 'growl-and-plunger' blues style: it involved a vocal growl to intensify the instrument's tone, and a toilet plunger mute to achieve wa-wa effects.

Miley's manner of using this technique yielded the first of the extraordinary sounds that helped make Ellington's orchestra so special, and it spread into the band's performances in other ways. Tricky Sam Nanton transferred the technique directly to the trombone, and using it he remained one of the orchestra's principal soloists for many years. Nanton may be heard, for example, on *Black and Tan Fantasie,* between Ellington's nimble stride piano solo and Miley's striking, stuttering return. Fleetingly, Adelaide Hall duplicated Miley as well. After Ellington heard her impromptu imitation, he organized *Creole Love Call,* on which the first 'instrument' is Hall's voice. (Hall's other piece in this collection, *The Blues I Love to Sing,* is unimportant, yet interesting, if only to remind us of how far her normal vaudeville voice was from this marvellous and freakish blues sound.) Later, when Miley left the band, his successors were expected to adopt some version of the growl-and-plunger approach. It is worth noting that there has been some dispute over the identity of the soloist who begins and ends *The Mooche.* Apparently Miley was absent, and at the session of 30 October 1928 Freddie Jenkins was in his chair. Whoever the soloist is, if it is not Miley, he is imitating Miley.

There were other elements to jungle music, though none as essential as Miley's contribution. These include a heightened emphasis on minor harmonies, as in the opening strains of *Black and Tan Fantasie, East St Louis Toodle-oo* and *The Mooche;* Harry Carney's dark, cutting baritone saxophone, which leads his section mates from below on *East St Louis Toodle-oo;* and such 'exotic' sounds as the mysterious chord that ends *Creole Love Call,* the clarinet trio's harmonized descent from a screaming chord on *The Mooche* and, also on *The .Mooche,* the combination of Barney Bigard's low-register clarinet and Sonny Greer's temple blocks (a 'clip-clop' sound). The blocks, incidentally, were but one of the vast array of items found in Greer's drum kit, which he designed to contribute visually as well as aurally to the jungle shows.

Separate from these features, but equally crucial to the band's early success, was Wellman Braud's string bass playing, which the Victor engineers recorded extremely well. Braud took two approaches, neither of which proved to be the preferred manner of bop bassists, but none the less in his hands the results were impressive. On *Black and Tan Fantasie* he bows the instrument, which ends up sounding much like a tuba, though slightly smoother. On *Washington Wobble* he plucks it, using the hot and driving slap-bass technique associated with New Orleans players (of which Braud was one). His solo bass breaks on *Black Beauty* foreshadow later developments, discussed below.

On the earliest of these pieces, Ellington and his men were still feeling their way towards a command of formal elements, so that all these marvels would hang together. *Creole Love Call* ducks the issue by presenting the jungle sounds over a beautifully expressed but utterly simple blues riff, which passes through the orchestra. But both *Black and Tan Fantasie* and *East St Louis Toodle-oo* attempt to juxtapose greatly varied themes. While in principle this need not be a drawback, in these instances the juxtapositions are jolting. With *The Mooche,* Ellington achieved for the first of many times a perfect balance between composition and improvisation, ensemble and individual, repetition and contrast. This piece rewards listening not only for all of the details already mentioned, but also for its formal gracefulness and logic. And it introduces yet another mainstay of the orchestra, Johnny Hodges, here playing alto saxophone in a dialogue with the Mileyesque trumpeter.

As the 1930s arrived, the band was gradually growing in size, its long stand at the Cotton Club was coming to an end and the 'jungle' star, Miley, had been gone for over a year – Cootie Williams having taken over that chair. All three pieces from the decade's beginning – *Ring dem Bells, Old Man Blues* and *Mood Indigo* – exemplify strong, well-conceived, satisfying big-band compositions. The last, *Mood Indigo,* is another landmark in the band's history, as a muted trumpet, muted trombone and clarinet present a deliberate, velvety, sad theme in phrases of magically inspired orchestration and harmony. The anthology closes in 1934 with *Solitude,* which marries the feeling and orchestration of *Mood Indigo* to one of the most complex popular ballad melodies in the jazz repertory.

The next and even greater burst of masterpieces came in the years 1940–42. These have been comprehensively reissued in a large anthology, **The Blanton–Webster Band**. At this point the band had 15 musicians, including cornetist Rex Stewart (whose mid-1930s achievements should not be missed, although with these two collections they fall between the cracks), as well as Williams, Nanton, Bigard, Hodges, Carney and Greer. Alongside them were string bassist Jimmy Blanton and tenor saxophonist Ben Webster. In the less than two years that Blanton remained a member, before succumbing to tuberculosis, he set new standards for the jazz bass, not only by filling roles that would previously have been given to a more conventionally melodic instrument, but more importantly by combining for the first time a fullness of tone, an ability to sustain pizzicato notes, a firmness of rhythm, an assured command of harmonically correct bass lines and a tuneful manner of executing those lines. Webster, no longer the halting voice heard on Henderson's big-band sides from 1934, had become one of the music's greatest soloists. A serious rival to Coleman Hawkins and Lester Young, he combined the former's intensity and arabesques with the latter's gentleness and melodiousness.

By 1940, long-term show work was years in the past, and it was touring that supported and would continue to support Ellington for the remainder of his career. But the jungle-music style had not died along with the shows. In fact, it reached its highest peak in *Ko-Ko,* a moody, seething piece. *Ko-Ko* begins with Carney's baritone sax and Greer's tom-tom droning together against a trombone riff. The body of the piece is a progression of increasingly urgent minor-key blues choruses. First, ascending saxophone chords and du-wah plunger-muted brass support Nanton's 'ya-ya' mute and plunger solo. Nanton yields to weird, atonal flourishes from Ellington's piano, and then the brass take over the sax riff, building to a series of breaks for Blanton's solo bass, and then to a climactic full ensemble chorus.

Concerto for Cootie was a feature for Williams at a time when he was about to end his lengthy first stay with Ellington. (He rejoined in the 1960s and 1970s.) If the melody seems familiar it may be because it reached a wider audience three years later, when it was regularized and popularized, with lyrics, as *Do Nothin' Till You Hear from Me*. The complex original composition, recorded shortly after *Ko-Ko* in March 1940, is noteworthy above all as a study in jazz trumpet timbres and effects. The introduction has Williams using his plunger, pressed tightly over a small straight mute. He plays the first theme (unusually, ten bars long, not eight or 12) with the plunger partially open, but on the theme's repetitions he pushes it back in tightly. Initially, on held notes, he adds a rapid, quivering effect that lies somewhere between vibrato and a 'shake' (a trill between non-adjacent pitches), and for the contrasting section of the first theme he adds a growl. Then, as Ellington moves the piece into a new key, presenting a bright new theme, Williams plays mainly with an open tone, though he also squeezes out notes in expressive upward glides. The first theme, with its characteristic timbres, returns to end the number.

Having once absorbed Williams's achievement, the listener might focus on Blanton. Regularly the bassist leaves aside a conventional walking rhythm to participate instead as a companion to the brass and reeds. He plays along exactly with their arranged lines and riffs, and he adds a little solo that bridges the movement from the bright second theme back to the first.

Shortly after recording these two demonstrations of big-band jazz as a high art, Ellington's orchestra showed that it was also a force to be reckoned with for earthy jazz. Certain artistic elements of *Cotton Tail* should not be missed, especially the careful way in which Ben Webster crafts his solo to build in intensity and to interlock with the brass punches, and also the virtuosic sax chorus he wrote. But the real point of the piece is its tremendous, toe-tapping swing, in which Blanton and Greer play no small part.

Never No Lament, recorded at the same session as *Cotton Tail*, started life earlier, as a counter-melody to a piece Ellington had recorded in 1938, *I Let a Song Go out of my Heart*. By 1940 it had taken on a life of its own, and, as with *Concerto for Cootie*, the instrumental *Never No Lament* was popularized and rereleased with lyrics a couple of years later, under the new title *Don't Get Around Much Any More*. The highlight of the 1940 Victor recording is Johnny Hodges's luscious alto saxophone chorus, in which he gently paraphrases the melody.

Harlem Air Shaft is yet another brilliantly orchestrated piece. It dances between swinging simplicity and arty complexity, both in its form and its accompanimental figures. Deceptively, the theme sounds as if it is a blues, but it breaks off after eight bars, which then prove to be the first eight of a standard 32-bar *aaba* song form (not a 12-bar blues). As often in Ellington's music, the accompanimental figures seek a balance between repeated riffs and arranged lines. These figures introduce and support a succession of greatly contrasting solos that typify the band's personalities: Nanton, presenting his du-wah effects with mute and plunger; alternately Williams, dominating with his open trumpet sound while Greer's drums kick him along, and Bigard, weaving his clarinet around reed riffs; Williams again, now muted and almost underneath the quiet ensemble; and finally Bigard, wailing away in his highest register.

These marvels, from *Ko-Ko* through *Harlem Air Shaft*, had been recorded in the space of four and a half months. The band's prolific sessions for Victor continued, and if, understandably, neither this orchestra nor any other ever matched this flurry of big-band jazz masterpieces, there would still be plenty of outstanding sides, of which the most important from the Blanton–Webster period are *In a Mellotone*, *Take the 'A' Train* and *Perdido*, the last dating from January 1942, not long after Blanton's illness had forced him to resign. On all three of these, Carney's rollicking baritone sax takes charge of laying out the melody, either with the section, or alone. These melodies are catchy, and the harmonies of *Take the 'A' Train* and *Perdido* made both of these into perennial jam session favourites. But, as usual with Ellington's recordings, casual jamming is not the point of the originals, which pay great attention to detail – as, for example, in the ornate, harmonized trombone lines that serve as a commentary on the melody of *In a Mellotone*. The memorable ensemble writing in *Take the 'A' Train* includes a transitional passage that momentarily moves into a waltz rhythm and – towards the end of Ray Nance's widely imitated trumpet solo – a fleeting, dissonant pyramid of sound that announces the melody's return. *Take the 'A' Train* caused Ellington some good-humoured grief in later years, because it became closely associated with him, probably more so than any other piece. But – as he was quick to point out – he did not write it. It is the work of Billy Strayhorn, a quiet, devoted man who from 1939 until his death in 1967 served as Ellington's second pianist and associate arranger and composer.

The third selection, **Ellington at Newport**, marked the beginning of a period of renewed interest in the orchestra, at a time when the bop style and its derivatives were beginning to grow stale and free jazz was about to be born. The reason was *Diminuendo in Blue* and *Crescendo in Blue*. This coupling is one of Ellington's most successful art works, the titles' simple programme (start loud, get softer, then grow loud again) forming an underpinning for elaborate, beautifully orchestrated motivic work. At the same time, this pair of pieces presents the sort of blues that can make you jump out of your seat. *Diminuendo in Blue* and *Crescendo in Blue* date back to 1937, when the orchestra recorded an unperfected version that was not immediately issued. Further versions survive from the mid-1940s, but the missing ingredient was added only after tenor saxophonist Paul Gonsalves joined Ellington in 1950. The following year the band performed *Diminuendo in Blue* and *Crescendo in Blue* at Birdland in New York in a version preserved on a broadcast recording, and Gonsalves took a long solo linking the two. It finds him playing with somewhat of a rhythm and blues simplicity, but mainly features a wild style, in which Gonsalves does to swing what Eric Dolphy would do to bop a decade later: playing 'outside' – stretching or contradicting the underlying chord progression.

Now, five years later at the Newport Jazz Festival in July 1956, Ellington again called for the linked pieces and Gonsalves once again took a long solo, playing in a highly emotive rhythm and blues style that whipped the audience into a frenzy of excitement. Gonsalves himself came to regret this performance: the piece grew tiresome as the orchestra was obliged to repeat it every night, owing to its (and Gonsalves's) new-found popularity; and Gonsalves's solo – renowned as much for length as for substance – was musically far less impressive than his playing 'outside' or his finest improvisations on ballads. None the less, the performance is perhaps the single finest document of jazz's raw vitality, ritualistically linking musician and audience. Regrettably the CD reissue has replaced George Avakian's original LP liner notes, which identified the soloists on this title and those that follow, and – more importantly – which described what it was like to be at this historic event.

Ellington's segment of the festival had begun with a *Newport Jazz Festival Suite*, one of his many (and largely unsuccessful) attempts to create new extended works during the last three decades of his life. Although the three-part suite lacks the coherence and breadth of *Diminuendo and Crescendo in Blue* (this title having been unified along with its performance), the individual parts are rewarding, particularly the second, *The*

Blues to Be There, with its beautiful melodies and an outstanding solo from clarinettist Russell Procope. According to discographies, the version of the suite performed at the festival was unacceptable, and it was recorded again two days later in New York and evidently spliced into the master tape as if it were the original. **Ellington at Newport** also includes *Jeep's Blues*, which alto saxophonist Johnny Hodges (nicknamed 'Jeep') had first recorded under his own leadership in 1938. This is yet another sensuous performance, beginning as a full-blown striptease tune and then becoming subdued.

These three collections include neither such landmarks as singer Ivie Anderson's rendition of *It Don't Mean a Thing if it Ain't Got That Swing* (recorded in 1932) and Mary Lou Williams's tremendously exciting arrangement of *Blue Skies*, titled *Trumpets No End* (recorded in 1946), nor the dozens of 'lesser' masterpieces which might head the list were we listening to any other big band. Indeed, while making sure not to miss Count Basie's big band of 1937–8, one might take a different route into big-band jazz from the approach detailed in this chapter: just go out and buy 15 or 20 Duke Ellington collections.

CD

***Early Ellington*, Bluebird 6852-2 RB (USA) and RCA Bluebird ND 86852 (Europe)**

Bubber Miley, Louis Metcalf (tpt), Tricky Sam Nanton (tb), Otto Hardwick (ss, as, bar), Harry Carney (cl, as, bar), Rudy Jackson (cl, ts), Duke Ellington (p), Fred Guy (bj), Wellman Braud (sb), Sonny Greer (d), Adelaide Hall (v)

Camden, NJ	26 Oct 1927	**Creole Love Call**
		The Blues I Love to Sing (take 2)
omit (v)		**Black and Tan Fantasie**
		Washington Wobble
New York	19 Dec 1927	**East St Louis Toodle-oo** (take 2)

Arthur Whetsol (tpt) replaces Metcalf, Barney Bigard (cl, ts) replaces Jackson

	26 March 1928	**Black Beauty**

Whetsol, Freddie Jenkins (tpt), Nanton (tb), Johnny Hodges (cl, ss, as), Carney (cl, as, bar), Bigard (cl, ts), Ellington (p), Guy (bj), Braud (bb), Greer (d)

	30 Oct 1928	**The Mooche**

add Miley (tpt); Braud (sb, not bb)

	16 Jan 1929	**Flaming Youth** (take 2)
		Saturday Night Function

Cootie Williams (tpt) replaces Miley

	3 May 1929	**Cotton Club Stomp**

add Williams (v), Juan Tizol (valve tb), Charlie Barnet (chimes)

Hollywood	20 Aug 1930	**Ring dem Bells** (take 3)

omit (v) and (chimes)

	26 Aug 1930	**Old Man Blues** (take 6)
New York	10 Dec 1930	**Mood Indigo**
	16 Jan 1931	**Rockin' in Rhythm** (take 1)
Camden, NJ	11 June 1931	**Creole Rhapsody**
	16 June 1931	**Echoes of the Jungle**

add Louis Bacon (tpt); Lawrence Brown (tb) replaces Tizol; add Harwick (cl, as, bass sax)

Chicago	4 Dec 1933	**Daybreak Express**
	9 Jan 1934	**Delta Serenade**
		Stompy Jones

add Tizol (valve tb)

	10 Jan 1934	**Solitude**

CD

***The Blanton–Webster Band*, Bluebird 5659-2 RB (USA) and PD 85659 (Europe)**

Wallace Jones, Williams (tpt), Rex Stewart (c), Nanton, Brown (tb), Tizol (valve tb), Bigard (cl), Hodges (cl, ss, as), Carney (cl, as, bar), Hardwick (as, bass sax), Ben Webster (ts), Guy (g), Ellington (p), Jimmy Blanton (sb), Greer (d), Herb Jeffries (v)

Chicago	6 March 1940	**You, You Darlin'**
omit (v)		**Jack the Bear**
		Ko-Ko
		Morning Glory
add Ivie Anderson (v)		**So Far, So Good**
omit (v)	15 March 1940	**Conga Brava**
		Concerto for Cootie (Do Nothin' Till You Hear from Me)
add Anderson (v)		**Me and You**

omit (v)

Hollywood	4 May 1940	**Cotton Tail**
		Never No Lament (Don't Get Around Much Any More)
Chicago	28 May 1940	**Dusk**
		Bojangles (A Portrait of Bill Robinson)
		A Portrait of Bert Williams
		Blue Goose
New York	22 July 1940	**Harlem Air Shaft (Rumpus in Richmond)**

add Anderson (v)			At a Dixie Roadside Diner
omit (v)			All too Soon
			Rumpus in Richmond (Brasserie)
		24 July 1940	My Greatest Mistake
			Sepia Panorama (Night House)
add Jeffries (v)			
	Chicago	5 Sept 1940	There Shall Be No Night
omit (v)			In a Mellotone
add Anderson (v)			Five O'Clock Whistle
omit (v)		17 Oct 1940	Warm Valley
			The Flaming Sword
		28 Oct 1940	Across the Track Blues
			Chloe (Song of the Swamp)
add Jeffries (v)			I Never Felt This Way Before
Ray Nance (tpt, vln) replaces Williams			
		28 Dec 1940	Sidewalks of New York
Billy Strayhorn (p) replaces Ellington; add Jeffries (v)			
			Flamingo
Ellington (p) replaces Strayhorn			The Girl in my Dreams Tries to Look Like You
omit (v)			
	Hollywood	15 Feb 1941	Take the 'A' Train
			Jumpin' Punkins
			John Hardy's Wife
			Blue Serge
Strayhorn (p) replaces Ellington			After All
Ellington (p) replaces Strayhorn			
		5 June 1941	Bakiff
			Are You Sticking?
			Just a-Settin' and a-Rockin'
			The Giddybug Gallop
add Anderson (v)			
		26 June 1941	Chocolate Shake
			I Got it Bad and That Ain't Good
omit (v)		2 July 1941	Clementine

add Jeffries (v)		**The Brown Skin Gal (in the Calico Gown)**
		Jump for Joy
omit (v)		**Moon over Cuba (Puerto Rican Gal)**
	26 Sept 1941	**Five O'Clock Drag**

Strayhorn (p) replaces Ellington; add Anderson (v)

		Rocks in my Bed

Ellington (p) replaces Strayhorn, Nance (v) replaces Anderson

		Bli-Blip

Strayhorn (p) replaces Ellington, Junior Raglin (sb) replaces Blanton; omit (v)

	2 Dec 1941	**Chelsea Bridge**
Ellington (p) replaces Strayhorn		**Raincheck**

Strayhorn (p) replaces Ellington; add Jeffries (v)

		What Good Would it Do?
Ellington (p) replaces Strayhorn		**I Don't Know What Kind of Blues I Got**

omit (v)

Chicago	21 Jan 1942	**Perdido**
		The 'C' Jam Blues
		Moon Mist (Atmosphere)
New York	26 Feb 1942	**What Am I Here For?**
add Anderson (v)		**I Don't Mind**
omit (v)		**Someone (You've Got my Heart)**

Strayhorn (p) replaces Ellington; add Jeffries (v)

Hollywood	26 June 1942	**My Little Brown Book**

Ellington (p) replaces Strayhorn; omit (v)

		Main Stem (Altitude)
Strayhorn (p) replaces Ellington		**Johnny Come Lately**

Chauncy Haughton (cl) replaces Bigard, Ellington (p) replaces Strayhorn; add Anderson (v)

Chicago	28 July 1942	**Hayfoot, Strawfoot**
omit (v)		**Sentimental Lady (Someone)**
add Nance (v)		**A Slip of the Lip (Me and my Wig)**
omit (v)		**Sherman Shuffle (Fussy Puss)**

CD

***Ellington at Newport*, Columbia Jazz Masterpieces CK-40587 (USA) and 450986-2 (Europe)**

Cat Anderson, Willie Cook, Ray Nance, Clark Terry (tpt), Quentin Jackson, John Sanders, Britt Woodman (tb), Jimmy Hamilton (cl, ts), Russell Procope (as, cl), Hodges (as), Paul Gonsalves (ts), Carney (bar), Ellington (p), Jimmy Woode (sb), Sam Woodyard (d)

Newport, RI	7 July 1956	**Diminuendo and Crescendo in Blue**
		Jeep's Blues
New York	9 July 1956	**Festival Suite:**
		Festival Junction
		Blues to Be There
		Newport Up

* * *

Bennie Moten: *Bennie Moten's Kansas City Orchestra: Basie's Beginnings*; Count Basie: *The Complete Decca Recordings*; *April in Paris*

While New York served as the base of operations for two of the three most innovative jazz big bands – those of Duke Ellington and Fletcher Henderson – the third, Count Basie's, developed gradually out of territory bands based in southwestern and midwestern states. In the late 1920s the principal rivals were Walter Page's Blue Devils and Bennie Moten's Kansas City Orchestra. Moten settled the contest by raiding Page's ranks. By the time of the 1929 sessions for Victor, he had hired Basie. (He had also hired two past Blue Devils and future Basie sidemen: trombonist, guitarist and arranger Eddie Durham and saxophonist Jack Washington.) By the 1930 recordings, he had acquired trumpeter Hot Lips Page (no relation to Walter or to Vernon Page, the tuba player on these sessions) and singer Jimmy Rushing. Finally, by 1932 he had hired Walter himself, whose string bass replaced the tuba.

These recordings look forward not only to future affiliations under Basie's name, but also to aspects of Basie's future style, most notably through Rushing's blues singing, the role played by Hot Lips Page, and the interlocking sectional riffs and relaxed swing of the 1932 session. They also point, in two unusually successful formal designs and in some details of arranging, in directions Basie would never pursue. But the main attraction of Moten's recordings is their sheer delightfulness, in which old-fashioned and simple elements play just as big a role as forward-looking and complex ones. I have even come to love the quirky bits: Buster Moten's hot accordion, with a tone like a thin version of a calliope on a merry-go-round; clarinettist Woodie Walder's violently clipped notes; Rushing's vaudeville style, with a heavy, fast vibrato, on the non-blues numbers. (Incidentally, Buster Moten should not be confused with band leader Bennie, who may have been Buster's brother or uncle.)

On the sessions from 1929 and 1930, the rhythm section is like a gracefully dancing fat man, somehow chunky and light at the same time, the tuba and bass drum's two beat rocking back and forth against the banjo and cymbal, with Basie's striding left hand supporting them all. (*When I'm Alone* has a tuba four beat rollicking through much of it.)

The best of the soloists are Hot Lips Page, Basie and Rushing. Page is by far the most consistent and mature instrumentalist in the band, creating unhurried, swinging lines. He plays mainly muted, bluesy wa-wa melodies (as does the lesser-known trumpeter Booker Washington at the opening sessions, on *The Jones Law Blues* and *New Vine Street Blues*). Basie at the time remained strongly under the influence of the busy stride piano style he had learned in New York, as heard on *Small Black* (some issues present a composite of two takes, spliced together to extend the piano solo) and also on *Rit-Dit-Ray*. Rushing's voice is slightly thinner than it would become, but at the time of this date he was already a great blues shouter, in touch with the inflections, urgency and emotion of down-home blues singing and yet comfortable with its translation into jazz. When he sings 'Good morning blues, blues how do you do?' and 'Sent for you yesterday, baby here you come today' in his two choruses on *That Too, Do*, everything that would be heard in Basie's orchestra is already in place.

Two unusual formal designs work well. *The Jones Law Blues* is made of three parts: a 'jungle-style' section built almost entirely on two minor chords; 12-bar blues solos by alto saxophonist Harlan Leonard and trombonist Thamon Hayes, each followed by a four-bar interlude; and a 16-bar spiritual, with a chord progression resembling that of *When the Saints Go Marching in*. The parts then repeat in reverse order, with the four-bar interlude preceding Basie's florid blues solo. *That Too, Do* is a 12-bar blues, but each of the first two choruses are followed by an eight-bar contrasting section, for Buster Moten's accordion solo and then for Basie.

There are also many clever touches of the arranger's hand. *Won't You be my Baby?* includes imitation between Hayes's trombone and the other brass (following Rushing's vocal), and the surprising sound of a vibraphone on the last note of the piece. *Oh! Eddie* has a similar imitation between accordion and brass (after Basie's solo); this leads to a single line chopped into pieces and divided between the saxophones and the brass, and then to the tremendous ending, which tosses about a three-beat figure played by the full ensemble (twice), then piano, reeds, brass, tuba, reeds again and full ensemble once more. *That Too, Do* uses the baritone sax as a bass instrument, playing an ostinato line against the rhythm section at the introduction and the ending; and Rushing makes his voice a part of the band's punctuation of Hot Lips Page's stop-time blues chorus.

The session in 1932 followed numerous changes in personnel, and it was made in the midst of a debilitating tour east and back home, by the end of which the band had begun to disintegrate. In spite of these circumstances the first three of ten titles recorded that day are marvels of big band swing, setting the model for the rhythm, riff and solo style of Basie's future group. *Toby, Moten Swing* and *The Blue Room* focus on riffs, which alternate with, support and sometimes bury the soloists, this last effect being not necessarily a fault, since the good, but less than consistently outstanding, quality of the soloists (excepting trumpeter Page) is one thing that *does* separate Moten's band from Basie's. Driven by Walter Page's four-beat string bass lines, the rhythm section is clean and flowing even at the very rapid tempo of *Toby*, and the saxophones are equally comfortable with their florid riffs set against brass punches. There is an incredible kick, another of the great moments in jazz, when, after Basie's stride piano solo on *Toby*, Page's bass and the riffs re-enter. Other exhilarating moments include, on *The Blue Room*, the smooth swing supporting Hot Lips Page's solo, with Basie's piano plinking away, and the co-ordinated effect of riffs and a strong cymbal backbeat at the end.

Basie did not record again for nearly four years, during which a pool of a few dozen musicians formed and re-formed under several leaders before crystallizing, a year after Moten's death in 1935, into a band which under Basie's leadership presented the Kansas City jazz style in its fullest glory. Because the myriad issues of Basie's recordings present *ad hoc* small combo sessions together with the regular work of the big band, and because Basie's style transferred effortlessly from one size of group to the other, it seems best to break the pattern of the book and discuss both together in this chapter. (Other swing combos, some including Basie's sidemen, appear in subsequent chapters.)

After signing a disadvantageous contract with Decca, Basie brought an instrumental quintet, plus Rushing, into a Vocalion studio in November 1936 to record under the conveniently anonymous pseudonym Jones–Smith Inc. The former was drummer Jo Jones, who, with Basie and Page, made up the rhythm section. The latter was trumpeter Carl Smith (substituting for Buck Clayton), who was joined in the front line by the big band's star soloist, tenor saxophonist Lester Young (yet another former member of Page's Blue Devils). Holding nothing back, the big band then made a string of great recordings for Decca from 1937 to February 1939; towards the end were a few less significant combo sessions. By the end of the decade the compositional weight of the group's performances had switched from an emphasis on improvised solos and casually made (though spectacularly played) riffs to a less successful emphasis on formal arrangement.

On these recordings Basie's groups carry the rhythm, riff and solo style developed under Moten to its highest possible level. The orchestra's *Swingin' at the Daisy Chain* represents a distinctive tune type, an *aaba* form with the *a* section built on top of a bass line that repeatedly walks down through a portion of a minor scale. But, otherwise, the formal bases of these performances are not meant to be interesting in themselves, since they draw their life from a flexible simplicity. Invariably the best tracks are built on conventional pop song forms and blues progressions.

The rhythm section is the best of its era, its understated approach generating tremendous propulsion and swing. Occasionally – as in his solo on *Swingin' the Blues* – Jones shows his command of the extroverted school of swing drumming. Still less often he goes in for special effects, as in the phrases played on temple blocks at the end of Clayton's muted wa-wa solo on *Swingin' at the Daisy Chain*. In the main he is a subtle drummer, concentrating on coaxing a metronomical, dancing beat from his cymbals. It is Jones's sensitive musicality that allows this band to produce many shades of volume, with sudden shifts from a roar to softness, and with endings that gradually fade away. Page is the same steady bass player he had been all along. He is supported beat by beat by guitarist Freddie Green, whose strumming, more felt than heard, comes through fairly clearly at the start of *Swingin' the Blues*. Repeatedly, Basie begins tunes alone; indeed, this was one of his most important functions, for he was acclaimed for his ability always to set the perfect tempo. As an accompanist he still provides moments of stride playing, as he had done with Moten, but now, four years later, he prefers to drop intermittent chordal accents into the rhythmic flow set up by the other three men. He carries this restraint to such an extent that, on some performances what might be construed as a piano solo is actually just a rhythmic groove focusing on the beat, not on making a melody.

The riffs work well enough in the combo performances, but no individual instrument can match the sectional riffing in the big band. *One O'Clock Jump* exemplifies this approach, in which repeated tidbits of swinging melody either serve as accompanimental figures or interlock with other tidbits to form themes in and of themselves. It beings with Basie's boogie-woogie piano setting the tempo, with firm but quiet support from the rhythm section. After two choruses of blues, an abrupt change of key marks the beginning of the riffs. These have been carefully chosen to provide timbral contrast to the soloist: muted brass against Herschel Evans's tenor sax, saxes against trombonist George Hunt, biting brass against Young's tenor sax, saxes against trumpeter Clayton. Basie sets up the rhythmic groove once again, to place in relief the final three blues choruses of band riffs, in which trombone and trumpet punctuations repeat against a saxophone part that changes with each new chorus. The equally famous *Jumpin' at the Woodside,* which finds Young at the top of his form, shows how the band applied the same approach to a popular song form rather than blues. Typically, the musicians invent an outstanding series of riffs which change chorus by chorus, but this effort is concentrated on the *a* sections of the *aaba* structure. They do not bother to come up with riffs for the *b* sections, but instead give these over for contrast to a soloist alone with the rhythm. Then, at the end, the riffs continue to keep up the level of excitement; during the second half of the first chorus of Herschel Evans's clarinet solo this last section of the piece includes as one of the trombone riffs a startlingly violent upward gliss, like an elephant trumpeting.

With this rhythmic, riffing support, a stream of star instrumentalists, and Rushing, walk up to the microphone. The most original and creative is Lester Young. Apart from noting that in its upper range his clarinet tone on *Blue and Sentimental* and *Texas Shuffle* is screechy (as is Evans's clarinet on *Jumpin' at the Woodside*), there is not much point in citing his best solos. As a tenor saxophonist he is consistently great. His soft, vibratoless sound and tunefully melodic approach offered the first significant alternative to Coleman Hawkins's conception of the instrument. An endlessly imaginative improviser, Young – just like the rhythm section – swings madly in a subtle way. With the aim of propelling the rhythm forward, at times he simplifies his melodies, perhaps oscillating between two notes, or changing the timbre of one, or starting emphatically and unexpectedly right on a down beat; towards that same goal, he made complex, asymmetrical melodies, weaving his lines through conventional phrase divisions with a fluency that few other soloists have ever matched. (Many players did, though, copy his patented use of false fingerings to alter a note's timbre, heard for example at his entrance on *Jumpin' at the Woodside.*)

By reputation Young engaged in battles with Herschel Evans, a player influenced by Hawkins. But on these recordings there are none of the phrase-by-phrase confrontations which would appear in later battles of the tenors in bop and hard bop (see chapter 7). For example, Evans is the only tenor soloist on *Swingin' at the Daisy Chain, Sent for You Yesterday* and *Texas Shuffle.* He plays separately from and before Young on *One O'Clock Jump, John's Idea* and *Doggin' Around,* separately from and after him on *Swingin' the Blues.* Moreover, on his ballad feature, *Blue and Sentimental*, Evans shows an individual sound falling between that of Hawkins and Young in his use of a slow, soft vibrato and a tone which is gentle but still has a slight edge. Nor – during Evans's last illness – were there immediate head-to-head battles with his temporary replacement Chu Berry, who plays before the trumpet solo on *Lady be Good* (Young follows trumpeter Shad Collins), or – after Evans's death early in 1939 – with his replacement Buddy Tate.

With the strong tenors, there is little room left for baritone saxophonist Jack Washington. Among his infrequent but excellent solos, the best is *Topsy*.

Earle Warren, an accomplished lead alto saxophonist, takes occasional undistinguished solos. (Not even Young dared try to improvise to the *b* section of *Cherokee*, which is omitted altogether during the second half of this two-part, six-minute performance; at the time of Basie's recording, Charlie Parker was just beginning to work out the definitive route through that labyrinth.)

In the trumpet section, the principals are Buck Clayton and Harry 'Sweets' Edison (who joined in 1938). Like their predecessor Hot Lips Page, both are polished, tuneful, bluesy, swinging improvisers, and both are fluent in the use of mutes, though they do not use these in the 'jungle style' that Page borrowed from Ellington's band. This is most evident in *Blues in the Dark*, where Clayton chooses not to join in with the growling, wa-wa trombones in the minor-key strain that precedes and follows Rushing's blues choruses, but instead plays with his typically delicate muted sound; the beginning of *Topsy* provides a similar example, though here Clayton aims for a tone that is a little bit nastier. Neither Clayton's nor Edison's playing could be mistaken for the overly ambitious work of trumpeter Bobby Moore, who hits quite a few clinkers on *Out the Window*. They play in a manner less clipped than Shad Collins's muted work on *Lady be Good*, though there is less obvious difference in Collins's solo on the preceding combo date, *You Can Depend on Me*. And distinguishing between the two principals, Clayton and Edison, is not a simple matter. I would only be copying from the definitive source (Chris Sheridan: *Count Basie: a Bio-discography*, New York, 1986) if I pretended to be able to do so. Even more than with the tenor saxes, Basie avoids setting up Clayton and Edison in head-to-head confrontations. According to Sheridan, on *Sent for You Yesterday* Clayton's muted trumpet embroiders Rushing's singing, while Edison's open sound follows Rushing's last blues verse; on *Swingin' the Blues* Clayton's muted solo follows Young, and after the interlude Edison's open and closed wa-wa solo follows Evans.

The band's trombonists soloed infrequently until mid-1938, when Dicky Wells replaced Eddie Durham, whose brass work was less prominent than his solo guitar playing and far less important than his arranging. Benny Morton had been in the band since September 1937, but he had few solos on studio recordings; presumably Basie found Morton's approach (as heard on *Out the Window*, from his first date with the band) somewhat old-fashioned and kept him out of the spotlight. Morton improvises nimbly on *Shorty George*, recorded in November 1938, and a few months after that was given the unpleasant assignment of being the only man in the band to try to solo over the *b* section of *Cherokee*, near the start of part 1. Wells, a widely acclaimed player, is not a personal favourite of mine. I find his tone cloying and his approach heavy-handed, as, for example, when he solos after Morton in *Cherokee*, on the comparatively easy *a* section of the theme. One of the most compelling arguments for following the band past the period of the tracks discussed here is the opportunity to hear the dry, witty, vibratoless trombone playing of Vic Dickenson, who joined in February 1940 and left with Lester Young at the end of that same year.

Alongside Rushing (whose talent and approach to the blues are unchanged, except for an even bigger sound than before), Young, Evans, Clayton and Edison, the other star is Basie, though he is erratic. Sometimes he falls back into thoughtless patterns, with a strong emphasis on sing-song, four-square, on-the-beat, right-hand figures, grating against the rhythm section's gliding swing. Sometimes he plays traditional stride and boogie-woogie figures. When he wished, he could bring forth one of the most original jazz piano styles, playing exceedingly sparse, perfectly placed progressions of riff-like motifs.

A third landmark in Basie's career came when, after the declining big-band business forced him to lead an octet from 1950 to 1951, he founded a new big band. Until roughly the late 1960s the group always had many fine soloists, and included on the album **April in Paris,** from the years 1955–6, are trumpeters Thad Jones and Joe Newman, trombonists Henry Coker, Benny Powell and Bill Hughes, tenor saxophonist Frank Foster, saxophonist and flautist Frank Wess (who, despite the liner notes on the original issue, plays alto, not tenor, sax on *Magic*) and of course Basie. But the main reason to listen to the band lies elsewhere, in its well-rehearsed and swinging execution of a single concept: melodies harmonized in block chords. Often these melodies build from riff-like patterns which repeat sequentially at different pitches. This sound pervades the album, and it would be misleading to pay too much attention to the individual arranging styles of Wild Bill Davis (on the title tune), Frank Foster (who as a composer does deserve special praise for contributing *Shiny Stockings* to the repertory), Ernie Wilkins, Neal Hefti and Freddie Green.

In playing in this manner, the group shows the same sensitivity to many shades of volume found in the earlier band, but on average this is more of a powerhouse ensemble than before. Regularly there are grand climaxes, headed by a screaming lead trumpet and by Sonny Payne's exuberant drum kicks; adding to the excitement are perfectly co-ordinated shakes (slow, wide trills between two notes). Rather than citing examples of all this, it seems more efficient to mention the exception: on Wilkins's arrangement of *Sweetie Cakes* the richly harmonized saxophone theme is not just in block chords, but instead moves through contrapuntal lines, with a prominent part for the baritone sax and with moments of unison playing. (The album also has a sextet performance, *Midgets*, featuring Newman's tightly muted trumpet alongside Wess's pure-toned flute.)

None of the soloists from this era had the same stature among their contemporaries as did the late 1930s soloists in their era, excepting Basie and an intermittent sideman, tenor saxophonist Eddie 'Lockjaw' Davis. But the group deserves consideration alongside Basie's earlier efforts for its single-minded achievement of a level of ensemble cohesiveness which has never been surpassed.

CD

***Bennie Moten's Kansas City Orchestra: Basie's Beginnings*, Bluebird 9768-2 RB (USA) and RCA ND 90403 (Europe)**

Ed Lewis, Booker Washington (tpt), Eddie Durham, Thamon Hayes (tb), Harlan Leonard (cl, ss, as), Woodie 'Hots' Walder (cl, ts), Jack Washington (cl, ss, bar), Count Basie (p), Buster Moten (accordion), Leroy Berry (bj), Vernon Page (bb), Mack Washington (d)

Chicago	23 Oct 1929	**The Jones Law Blues** (take 3)
add Durham (g)		**Small Black** (take 2) **Every Day Blues**
omit (g), add Mack Washington (v)		
	24 Oct 1929	**Rit-Dit-Ray** (take 2)
add Durham (g), omit (v)		**New Vine Street Blues** (arr Durham) **Sweetheart of Yesterday** (arr Bennie Moten)

Lewis, Booker Washington, Hot Lips Page (tpt), Durham, Hayes (tb), Leonard (cl, ss, as), Walder (cl, ts), Jack Washington (cl, ss, bar), Basie (p), Buster Moten (accordion), Berry (bj), Vernon Page (bb), Mack Washington (d, vb) Jimmy Rushing (v)

Kansas City	27 Oct 1930	**Won't You be my Baby?**
omit (vb) and (v)		
	28 Oct 1930	**Oh! Eddie** (arr Durham)

add Durham (g), Rushing (v), Buster or Bennie Moten (p solo)
That Too, Do (arr Basie and Durham; take 2)

omit (g) and (v), Buster Moten (accordion only)
29 Oct 1930 **The Count**

add Durham (g), Mack Washington (vb), Rushing (v)
Liza Lee (arr Basie and Durham; take 1)

as ***That Too, Do****, but Buster or Bennie Moten (second p)*
30 Oct 1930 **When I'm Alone**

omit (second p) and (v) **New Moten Stomp** (arr Basie and Durham)

omit (g), add Basie (v)
31 Oct 1930 **Somebody Stole my Gal**

omit Basie (v), add Rushing (v) **Now that I Need You**

Joe Keyes, Hot Lips Page, Dee Stewart (tpt), Durham (tb, g), Dan Minor (tb), Eddie Barefield (cl, as), Ben Webster (ts), Jack Washington (as, bar), Basie (p), Berry (g), Walter Page (sb), Mack Washington (d)
Camden, NJ 13 Dec 1932 **Toby** (arr Barefield)
Moten Swing (arr Basie and Durham)

as ***Toby****, but Durham (tb)* **The Blue Room** (arr ?Barefield)

as ***Toby****, but add Rushing (v)* **New Orleans**

as ***Toby****, but Durham (tb)* **Milenberg Joys** (arr ?Durham)
Lafayette (arr Durham)
Prince of Wails (arr Durham)

CD

***The Complete Decca Recordings*, Decca Jazz GRD-3-611 (USA)**

Buck Clayton, Joe Keyes, Carl Smith (tpt), George Hunt, Dan Minor (tb), Caughey Roberts (as), Herschel Evans, Lester Young (ts), Jack Washington (bar, as), Basie (p), Claude Williams (g), Walter Page (sb), Jo Jones (d)
New York 21 Jan 1937 **Honeysuckle Rose** (arr Fletcher Henderson)

add Jimmy Rushing (v) **Pennies from Heaven** (arr Don Redman)

omit (v)		**Swingin' at the Daisy Chain** (arr ?Buster Smith) **Roseland Shuffle** (arr Henderson)

Ed Lewis and Bobby Moore (tpt) replace Keyes and Smith, Freddie Green (g) replaces Williams; add Rushing (v)

	26 March 1937	**Exactly Like You** (arr ?Henderson) **Boo-Hoo** (arr ?Henderson) **The Glory of Love** (arr Henderson) **Boogie Woogie (I May Be Wrong)**

Earle Warren (as, bar) replaces Roberts; omit Rushing (v)

	7 July 1937	**Smarty** (arr Skippy Martin) **One O'Clock Jump** (arr Eddie Durham and Smith)
add Rushing (v)		**Listen My Children** (arr Redman)
omit (v)		**John's Idea** (arr Durham)

Clayton, Lewis, Moore (tpt), Durham, Hunt, Minor (tb), Warren (as), Evans, Young (ts), Washington (bar, as), Basie (p), Green (g), Page (sb), Jones (d), Rushing (v)

	9 Aug 1937	**Good Morning Blues** (take A) (arr Durham) **Good Morning Blues** (take B)
Warren (v) replaces Rushing		**Our love was meant to be** (arr Martin)
add Durham (elg); omit (v)		**Time Out** (arr Durham)
as ***Time Out****, but Durham (tb)*		**Topsy** (arr Durham)

Benny Morton (tb) replaces Hunt; add Rushing (v)

	13 Oct 1937	**I Keep Remembering** (arr Durham)
omit (v)		**Out the Window** (arr Durham)
add Rushing (v)		**Don't You Miss Your Baby?** (arr Durham)
Warren (v) replaces Rushing		**Let Me Dream** (arr Durham)

Karl George (tpt) replaces Moore; Rushing (v) replaces Warren

	3 Jan 1938	**Georgianna** (arr Durham) **Blues in the Dark** (arr Clayton)

Clayton, Harry 'Sweets' Edison, Lewis (tpt), Durham, Minor, Morton (tb), Warren (as), Evans, Young (ts), Washington (bar, as), Basie (p), Green (g), Page (sb), Jones (d), Rushing (v)

16 Feb 1938	**Sent for You Yesterday**
omit (v)	**Every Tub** (arr Durham)
add Rushing (v)	**Now Will You Be Good?** (arr ?Durham)
omit (v)	**Swingin' the Blues** (arr Durham)
add Rushing (v)	**Mama don't want no peas 'n' rice 'n' coconut oil** (arr Don Kirkpatrick)
*as **Every Tub**, but Young (ts, cl)*	**Blue and Sentimental** (arr Durham)
*as **Every Tub**, but Evans (ts, cl)*	**Doggin' Around** (arr ?Edgar Battle and ?Evans)

Clayton, Edison, Lewis (tpt), Minor, Morton, Dickie Wells (tb), Warren (as), Evans, Young (ts), Washington (bar, as), Basie (p), Green (g), Page (sb), Jones (d), Rushing and band (v)

22 Aug 1938	**Stop Beatin' Round the Mulberry Bush** (take A) (arr Redman)
	Stop Beatin' Round the Mulberry Bush (take B)
omit band (v)	**London Bridge is falling down** (arr Redman)
add Young (cl); omit Rushing (v)	**Texas Shuffle** (arr Evans)
Evans (cl) replaces Young (cl)	**Jumpin' at the Woodside**

Basie (p), Green (g), Page (sb), Jones (d)

9 Nov 1938	**How Long, How Long Blues**
	The Dirty Dozens
	Hey! Lawdy Mama
	The Fives
	Boogie Woogie

Clayton, Edison, Lewis (tpt), Minor, Morton, Wells (tb), Warren (as), Evans, Young (ts), Washington (bar, as), Basie (p), Green (g), Page (sb), Jones (d), Helen Humes (v)

16 Nov 1938	**Dark Rapture** (arr Redman or Jimmy Mundy)

omit (v)		**Shorty George** (arr Andy Gibson)
add Rushing (v)		**The Blues I Like to Hear** (arr Smith) **Do You Wanna Jump, Children?** (arr Gibson)
omit (v)		**Panassié Stomp**
add Shad Collins (tpt); Humes (v)	5 Jan 1939	**My Heart Belongs to Daddy** (arr Mundy) **Sing for Your Supper** (arr Mundy)
Basie (p), Green (g), Page (sb), Jones (d)	26 Jan 1939	**Oh! Red** **Fare Thee Honey, Fare Thee Well** (take A) **Fare Thee Honey, Fare Thee Well** (take B) **Dupree Blues** **When the Sun Goes Down** (take A) **When the Sun Goes Down** (take B) **Your Red Wagon**

Collins (tpt), Young (ts), Basie (p), Green (g), Page (sb), Jones (d), Rushing (v)
2 Feb 1939 **You Can Depend on Me**

Clayton, Collins, Edison, Lewis (tpt), Minor, Morton, Wells (tb), Warren (as), Chu Berry, Young (ts), Washington (bar, as), Basie (p), Green (g), Page (sb), Jones (d)
3 Feb 1939 **Cherokee** (arr Mundy)

add Humes (v) **Blame It on My Last Affair**

Clayton, Collins, Edison (tpt), Wells (tb), Young (ts), Washington (bar), Basie (p), Green (g), Page (sb), Jones (d)
4 Feb 1939 **Jive at Five** (arr Edison)

Clayton, Collins, Edison, Lewis (tpt), Minor, Morton, Wells (tb), Warren (as), Chu Berry, Young (ts), Washington (bar, as), Basie (p), Green (g), Page (sb), Jones (d), Humes (v)
Thursday (arr Clayton)

Rushing (v) replaces Humes **Evil Blues**

omit (v) **Lady Be Good**

CD

***April in Paris,* Verve 825.575-2 (USA)**

Wendell Cully, Reunald Jones, Thad Jones, Joe Newman (tpt), Henry Coker, Bill Hughes, Benny Powell (tb), Marshall Royal, Bill Graham (as), Frank Wess, Frank Foster (ts), Charlie Fowlkes (bs), Count Basie (p), Freddie Green (g), Eddie Jones (sb), Sonny Payne (d)

New York	26 July 1955	**April in Paris** (arr Wild Bill Davis)
		Corner Pocket (arr ?Greene)
		Did'n You? (arr Foster)
		Sweetie Cakes (arr Ernie Wilkins)

*as **April in Paris**, but Wess (as, ts)*

	4 Jan 1956	**Shiny Stockings** (arr Foster)
		What am I Here for? (arr Foster)
		Magic (arr ?Foster)

Newman (tpt), Wess (fl), Basie (p), Green (g), Jones (sb), Payne (d)

Midgets

*as **April in Paris**, but Green (g, per); add José Mangual, Ubaldo Nieto (per)*

	5 Jan 1956	**Mambo Inn** (arr Foster)

*as **April in Paris***

Dinner with Friends (arr Neal Hefti)

* * *

Chick Webb: *Spinnin' the Webb*

The central core of instrumental recordings by Chick Webb's big band is collected on the CD **Spinnin' the Webb**, issued in 1994 on the Decca Jazz label. Above all, the point of listening to these tracks is to hear Webb, one of the great swing drummers. Even with the best of mid-1930s technology, it can be hard to pick out of a big band's sound the individual drums, cymbals, blocks, bells and other accessories of the drum kit. Fortunately the fidelity of this new CD issue shows a vast improvement over the Webb LPs issued in 1967 on Decca and reissued on MCA.

Decca's anthology begins in 1929, when Webb's then three-year-old group recorded two titles as the Jungle Band, emulating Duke Ellington's orchestra (some 78 rpm labels issued the discs falsely under Ellington's name). *Dog Bottom* is a kaleidoscopic compendium of techniques of arranging for contemporary big bands, in which Elmer James's chunky two-beat tuba playing and John Trueheart's bright banjo strumming are never allowed to establish a foothold for any length of time. Highlights include the saxophone trio break, Webb's hot cymbal breaks, brass and reeds in overlapping pyramids of sound, Elmer Williams's tenor saxophone solo, and Ward Pinkett's wildly energetic scat singing. In the contrasting *Jungle Mama*, simple, traditional blues riffs serve as a theme and also as the background for a succession of solos, beginning with a trumpet muted and growling after the manner of Ellington's Bubber Miley. Webb is inaudible, except for a steady, soft bass-drum beat and a trace of snare drum at the very end.

In 1931 Webb led his first session under his own name. The best of the three titles recorded that day (two of which are included here) is Benny Carter's arrangement of *Heebie Jeebies*, a tune which Louis Armstrong had made popular. The performance has a lilting rhythm which is not at all hurt by James's having switched to string bass. In addition to excellent solos from tenor saxophonist Williams (whose playing here is unusually free rhythmically, floating away from the beat), pianist Don Kirkpatrick and trombonist Jimmy Harrison, *Heebie Jeebies* offers (following Kirkpatrick) an early example of one of Carter's characteristic devices, a twisting melody arranged for the saxophone section playing in chords.

Webb's band had played at New York's Savoy Ballroom occasionally since 1927, and late in 1931 it began regular long engagements there. But it was another two years before Webb recorded steadily. The Decca collection picks up the story yet another year later, in the autumn of 1934.

The central features of the band's mature instrumental style are Edgar Sampson's writing and Webb's drumming. In addition there are numerous strong soloists on these tracks, of whom the most creative are the two Williamses (tenor saxophonist Elmer and trombonist Sandy) and trumpeter Bobby Stark. The band plays tightly, and John Kirby (on bass) and Trueheart (now on guitar) help Webb drive the rhythm. Trueheart is most prominent on *Blue Minor* and *Blue Lou*.

Sampson had written *Stomping at the Savoy* (not on this collection) and *Don't Be That Way* in 1933 for Rex Stewart's band, and these later became anthems of the swing era in modified arrangements recorded by Benny Goodman. In the interim, Webb recorded both in performances faster and livelier than Goodman's. *Don't Be That Way* has the essence of the mainstream big-band style, presenting themes and accompanimental figures which straddle the boundary between repeated riffs and arranged melodies. *Blue Minor* shows Sampson writing in another vein. This is a two-part piece, setting Ellington-style jungle music with muted wa-wa brass playing in a minor key against a jauntier theme in a major key; one phrase of the minor theme returns to end the piece.

Finally, the star of these performances, Webb: he plays prominent drum fills in the last part of *Don't Be That Way*, ending with a neatly constructed series of breaks which slow from triplets to a duple division of the beat to a series of strokes on the beat, these last accented in such a way as to superimpose a fragment of waltz rhythm on the swing beat; in the context, this seemingly un-hip idea – playing on the beat, and in waltz time – provides the perfect climax to his solo. On *Go Harlem* (a riff tune arranged by Sampson), Webb is in the foreground from the start. He supplies another effective 'un-hip' idea, simply playing right on the beat for eight straight beats (drums and block, drums and cymbal) at the end of Teddy McRae's brief tenor saxophone solo. At the end he takes a series of solo breaks, exploring timbral contrasts as he moves constantly about the drum kit; rarely does he take more than two consecutive strokes at any one piece of it. The same may be said for the fast swing version of *Clap Hands! Here Comes Charley* (again arranged by Sampson), with drum breaks at the start and following the solos by Jordan and Sandy Williams. In contrast to these high-energy performances, in a sultry version of *Squeeze Me*, Webb appropriately plays relaxed, 'striptease' drum patterns and fills. *Harlem Congo* ends with a 24-bar drum solo on which the leader concentrates on dynamic snare-drum syncopations. In this collection, Webb's only bad moment occurs on *Spinnin' the Webb*. The *a* section of this *aaba* theme has the feel of rhythm and blues. Stark takes his best solo over it, spinning out a relaxed melody which contrasts a biting open tone with a growling one; but Webb's drum break breaks the groove, and the band members seem unsure where to place their punctuated notes. *Liza* (arranged by Benny Carter), however, has four solo segments featuring Webb at his energetic best.

The Decca collection also includes a track by one of the less important instances of a band within a band: the quintet Chick Webb and his Little Chicks. Their cute and dainty version of *I Got Rhythm* is notable only as proof that the pioneering jazz flautist Wayman Carver did not succeed in his effort to be the first to make that a convincing solo instrument in the swing style.

Unlike earlier Decca anthologies on LP, the CD **Spinnin' the Webb** is devoted to instrumental tracks (apart from Louis Bacon's rather insignificant vocal on *Blues in My Heart*) and hence omits Webb's other star, Ella Fitzgerald. She joined the band in 1935 and recorded with it from 1936 to 1942, having taken over the leadership after Webb's death in 1939. Her contributions are featured on the two-volume CD sets entitled **The Early Years**, Decca GRD-2-618 and GRD-2-623 (USA).

CD

***Spinnin' the Webb*, Decca GRD-635 (USA)**

(the Jungle Band:) Ward Pinkett (tpt, v), Edwin Swayze (tpt), Robert Horton (tb), Hilton Jefferson, Louis Jordan (as), Elmer Williams (ts), Don Kirkpatrick (p), John Trueheart (bj), Elmer James (bb), Chick Webb (d)

New York — 14 June 1929 — **Dog Bottom**

as **Dog Bottom**, *but Jefferson, Jordan, Williams (cl), Trueheart (g); omit (v)*

Jungle Mama

Shelton Hemphill, Louis Hunt, Louis Bacon (tpt), Jimmy Harrison (tb), Benny Carter, Hilton Jefferson (as), Williams (ts), Kirkpatrick (p, celeste), Trueheart (g), James (sb), Webb (d)

30 March 1931 — **Heebie Jeebies** (arr Carter)

omit (celeste); add Bacon (v) — **Blues in My Heart** (arr Carter)

Mario Bauza, Bobby Stark (tpt), Taft Jordan (tpt, v), Sandy Williams, Claude Jones (tb), Pete Clarke, Edgar Sampson (as), Elmer Williams, Wayman Carver (ts), Kirkpatrick (p), Trueheart (g), John Kirby (sb), Webb (d)

10 Sept 1934 — **Lona** (arr Sampson)
Blue Minor (arr Sampson)

19 Nov 1934 — **Don't Be That Way** (arr Sampson)
What a Shuffle (arr Sampson)
Blue Lou (arr Sampson)

Bauza, Stark, Jordan (tpt), Williams, Nat Story (tb), Clarke (cl, as), Louis Jordan (as), Teddy McRae, Carver (ts, bar), Tommy Fulford (p), Trueheart (g), Beverly Peer (sb), Webb (d)

24 March 1937 — **Clap Hands! Here Comes Charley**
That Naughty Waltz (arr Charlie Dixon)

Chauncey Haughton (cl), Carver (fl), Fulford (p), Peer (sb), Webb (d)

21 Sept 1937 — **I Got Rhythm**

as **Clap Hands! Here Comes Charley**, *but Haughton (cl, as) replaces Clarke, ?Carver (?bar or bass sax), Bobby Johnson (g) replaces Trueheart*

1 Nov 1937 — **Squeeze Me**
Harlem Congo (arr Dixon)

Bauza, Stark, Jordan (tpt), Williams, Story (tb), Garvin Bushell, Jordan (as), McRae, Carver (ts), Fulford (p), Johnson (g), Peer (sb), Webb (d)

17 Dec 1937 — **Midnite in a Madhouse (Midnite in Harlem)**

add George Matthews (tb)

3 May 1938 — **Spinnin' the Webb** (arr Benny Carter)
Liza (arr Carter)

Bauza, Stark, Jordan (tpt), Williams, Story, Matthews (tb), Bushell (as, cl), Hilton Jefferson (as), McRae (ts), Carver (fl, ts), Fulford (p), Johnson (g), Peer (sb), Webb (d)

18 Aug 1938	**Who ya Hunchin'?**
17 Feb 1939	**In the Groove at the Grove**

* * *

Jimmie Lunceford: *Stomp It Off*

Sweet and hot, old and modern, simple and complex, stiff and swinging, mannered and unrestrained, sentimental and bluesy, imitative and original, funny and serious, naive and hip, Jimmie Lunceford's orchestra presented all these qualities in ever changing combinations. Numerous great performances guarantee the group's inclusion in any discreet selection of big-band jazz, but often it is necessary to jump around quite a bit to find these. The first edition of this book favoured a reissue on Affinity that collects together several fine tracks within a representative sample of recordings made between 1934 and 1944. This LP, **Strictly Lunceford**, is now deleted, with no sign of a replacement on CD. Our current choice, **Stomp It Off**, offers a strong collection of tracks spanning only the years 1934–5. Listeners interested in the continuation of Lunceford's work and the band's most well-known tracks (Sy Oliver's *Organ Grinder's Swing*, recorded in 1936, and *For Dancer's Only*, 1937) will find chronological series on the Hep (UK) and Classics (France) labels, but be forewarned that slighter performances (featuring the exceptionally lightweight sort of singing heard on *Rain*) fill large portions of these multi-volume series. According to the pamphlet notes, **Stomp It Off** is the first disc in a parallel series on Decca Jazz in the USA. Hopefully the producers will avoid some of the fluff as the series continues into Lunceford's later recordings.

Lunceford founded the band in 1927, rehearsed and directed it until his death two decades later, and occasionally played alto sax, trombone, flute or guitar, and contributed compositions and arrangements. Among these tracks from 1934–5, he contributed the technically difficult and wonderfully strange piece *Stratosphere*, which sounds as if it could have served as a model for soundtracks on zany cartoons.

Sophisticated Lady and *Mood Indigo* are bold reworkings of Duke Ellington's ballads arranged by the orchestra's lead alto saxophonist and strongest soloist, Willie Smith (not to be confused with pianist Willie 'the Lion' Smith), who added complex, unusual lines to the original versions. On *Sophisticated Lady* he first plays the melody on clarinet, set against muted brass punctuations, and then, after a piano solo, pits the melody in the muted brass against a bizarre, old-fashioned passage of massed saxophones sharply articulating each note. Drummer Jimmy Crawford's few notes on the vibraphone announce an interlude, and there follows a well polished (if somewhat stilted) passage that no other big-band saxophone section of the mid-1930s could have pulled off so cleanly. *Mood Indigo* begins with a hurdy-gurdy sound, the combined saxophones and clarinets playing an eccentric, clipped line that dances around the theme, stated in the brass. Later in the piece, before the quiet ending, there is further eccentricity, as the saxophones provide first a co-ordinated, clipped, syncopated obbligato and then a series of swoops up and down, against swinging versions of the theme carried by Sy Oliver's solo trumpet and then by the massed brass. By contrast Oliver's arrangement of Bubber Miley and Ellington's *Black and Tan Fantasie* is far more conservative, amounting in essence to a cover version of the original, and on *Solitude* Henry Wells sings an unadorned and handsome interpretation of Ellington's melody.

The orchestra's rhythm section was known for its ability to generate a bouncing rhythmic feeling, as on *Stomp It Off*, the aptly named *Rhythm is our Business* and *Four or Five Times*. Generally speaking, Moses Allen would play a two-beat bass line (though the title track has a four-beat bass), while guitarist Al Norris and pianist Ed Wilcox contributed four-beat chords (perhaps emphasizing beats 2 and 4 more than 1 and 3) and drummer Crawford provided discreet swing patterns. But nothing was constant with this orchestra. Smith's Ellington arrangements provide examples of their rhythmic (and other sorts of) wackiness. So too does Wilcox's arrangement of Cole Porter's song about the lynching of a black woman, *Miss Otis Regrets*, taken here instrumentally in a fast-tempoed, energetic manner known in jazz as a 'flag-waver', but taken vocally by Oliver with a relaxed half-time feeling, in which he floats through the melody, laid far back against the beat. The track also features another of the band's strong soloists, Joe Thomas, one of the many tenor saxophonists who carried on Coleman Hawkins's high-charged style in American swing bands while Hawkins was in Europe.

CD

***Stomp It Off*, Decca Jazz GRD-608 (USA)**

Eddie Thompkins, Tommy Stevenson, Sy Oliver (tpt), Henry Wells, Russell Bowles (tb), Willie Smith (as, cl), Laforet Dent (as), Joe Thomas (ts, cl), Earl Carruthers (bar), Eddie Wilcox (p), Al Norris (g), Moses Allen (sb), Jimmy Crawford (d, vb)

New York	4 Sept 1934	**Sophisticated Lady** (arr Smith)
		Mood Indigo (take B) (arr Smith)

omit (vb)		**Rose Room** (arr Smith)
	5 Sept 1934	**Black and Tan Fantasie** (arr Oliver)
add Crawford (timpani)		**Stratosphere** (arr Lunceford)
omit timpani; add Oliver (v)		**Miss Otis Regrets** (arr Wilcox)
Wells (v) replaces Oliver (v)		**Star Dust** (take A) (arr Wilcox)
Oliver (v) replaces Wells (v)	29 Oct 1934	**Dream of You** (arr Oliver)
omit (v)		**Stomp It Off** (arr Oliver)
add Wells (v)	7 Nov 1934	**Solitude**
unidentified trio (v) replaces Well	18 Dec 1934	**Rain** (arr Oliver)
		Since My Best Girl Turned Me Down (arr Oliver)
Wells (v) replaces trio (cv)		**Jealous** (arr Wilcox)
Smith and chorus (v) replace Wells		**Rhythm is our Business** (take A) (arr Wilcox)
		Rhythm is our Business (take B) (arr Wilcox)
omit (v)		**Shake Your Head (from Side to Side)** (arr Oliver)

Thompkins, Paul Webster, Oliver (tpt), Bowles, Elmer Crumbley, Eddie Durham (tb), Smith (as, cl), Dent, Lunceford (as), Thomas (ts, cl), Carruthers (bar), Wilcox (p), Norris (g), Allen (sb), Crawford (d)

	29 May 1935	**Sleepy-time Gal** (arr Wilcox)

Dan Grissom (as) replaces Lunceford; add Durham (solo g)

		Bird of Paradise (arr Wilcox and Durham)
add Crawford (xylophone)		**Rhapsody Junior** (arr Wilcox and Durham)

omit (solo g), (xylophone); add unidentified vocal commentary

		Runnin' Wild (arr Smith)
add Oliver (v)		**Four or Five Times** (take B) (arr Oliver)

* * *

Benny Goodman: *Pure Gold* (by James Lincoln Collier)

Benny Goodman's orchestra started the swing craze, and it remains the best example of the genre. Although other groups, such as the Basie and Ellington bands, possessed more significant soloists, and Ellington certainly was writing arrangements that were musically superior to those of anyone else, the Goodman band more exactly typified what the swing style was all about. Goodman was a hard task-master and pushed his musicians to high musical levels; the arrangements on the anthology **Pure Gold** are worth listening to sheerly for the impeccable section work. The rhythm section, despite the sometime erratic drumming of Gene Krupa and the undistinguished bass playing of Goodman's brother Harry, had in pianist Jess Stacy and guitarist Allen Reuss two of the finest rhythm players of the period. The soloists were always competent, and in the case of Berigan and Goodman himself, of very high quality. And finally Goodman, through judicious selection and editing, possessed arrangements that were generally clean, bright and effective in their simplicity.

The formula was the one worked out in rudimentary form by the early dance bands of the 1920s and developed in considerable part by Fletcher Henderson's orchestra, of playing off brass and saxophone sections against each other. Two classic examples are *Stompin' at the Savoy* and *Don't Be That Way*, both composed and arranged by Edgar Sampson. The main theme of the former begins with two notes played by muted trumpets and answered by unison saxophones; in a contrasting phrase the saxophones lead, punctuated by the trumpets; the last eight measures repeat the opening. For the second chorus the saxophones play the brief motif, with the trumpets answering; Goodman takes a solo; and again the first measures are repeated. This relentless shifting back and forth between saxophones and brass is basic to the band's style.

It is not true, as is frequently said, that the early Goodman band was built around the arrangements of Fletcher Henderson: the major contributor in the early days was Spud Murphy, and others, such as Sampson, provided important pieces. But Henderson's arrangements were among Goodman's most successful works. They were, if anything, even simpler than Sampson's. *King Porter Stomp*, which Henderson recorded with his own band, opens with Bunny Berigan's muted trumpet playing the introductory theme. The main theme that follows is for harmonized saxophones, with no punctuation. Really, only at the end, do we have the call and answer system typical of the style.

The band had its biggest hit with *Sing, Sing, Sing*. The original kernel was taken from an arrangement by Jimmy Mundy, but over time the band added segments so that it eventually sprawled over two sides of a 12-inch 78 rpm record. The key portion comes on the second side, where Krupa, playing tom-tom, exchanges solos with Goodman and James, improvising on a static minor-key harmony. Krupa's drumming excited fans, and for a period Goodman used *Sing, Sing, Sing* for a closing number.

The Goodman Orchestra of course played the usual romantic ballads and light dance pieces all these bands were required to play, but it was the hard swingers that were critical to the band's success and that remain most closely associated with it. (**Pure Gold** also includes three small group tracks: *After You've Gone*, *Body and Soul* and *Avalon*. These are detailed in chapter 4.)

CD

***Pure Gold*, Bluebird 07863-50973-2 (USA) and ND 90684 (Europe)**

Bunny Berigan, Nate Kazebier, Ralph Muzzillo (tpt), Red Ballard, Jack Lacy (tb), Benny Goodman (cl), Toots Mondello, Hymie Schertzer (as), Art Rollini, Dick Clark (ts), Frank Froeba (p), George Van Eps (g), Harry Goodman (sb), Gene Krupa (d)

New York — 1 July 1935 — **King Porter** (arr Fletcher Henderson)

Joe Harris (tb) replaces Lacy; Bill DePew (as) replaces Mondello; Jess Stacy (p) replaces Froeba; Allen Reuss (g) replaces Van Eps

Hollywood — 27 Sept 1935 — **Goodbye** (arr Gordon Jenkins)

Harry Geller (tpt) replaces Berigan

Chicago — 24 Jan 1936 — **Stompin' at the Savoy** (arr Edgar Sampson)

Ziggy Elman, Chris Griffin, Zeke Zarchy (tpt), Ballard, Murray McEachern (tb), Benny Goodman (cl), Schertzer, DePew (as), Rollini, Vido Musso (ts), Stacy (p), Reuss (g), Goodman (sb), Krupa (d)

New York — 5 Nov 1936 — **Bugle Call Rag** (arr Jimmy Mundy)

add Ella Fitzgerald (v) — **Goodnight My Love**

omit Fitzgerald; Harry James (tpt) replaces Zarchy; George Koenig (as) replaces DePew

Hollywood — 6 July 1937 — **Sing, Sing, Sing** (arr Mundy)

add Benny Goodman (v), Martha Tilton (v)

New York — 12 Nov 1937 — **Loch Lomond** (arr Claude Thornhill)

Elman, Griffin, James (tpt), Ballard, Vernon Brown (tb), Goodman (cl), Schertzer, Koenig (as), Rollini, Babe Russin (ts), Stacy (p), Reuss (g), Goodman (sb), Krupa (d)

15 Feb 1938	**Don't Be That Way** (arr Sampson)
	One O'Clock Jump (arr Count Basie)

Elman, Griffin, Irving Goodman (tpt), Ballard, Vernon Brown (tb), Goodman (cl), Schertzer, Noni Bernardi (as), Rollini, Jerry Jerome (ts), Stacy (p), Ben Heller (g), Goodman (sb), Buddy Schutz (d), Tilton (v)

1 Feb 1939	**And the Angels Sing**

* * *

Artie Shaw: *Begin the Beguine*

From the perspective of jazz the recorded legacy of white swing orchestras is problematic in two significant ways. First, in their studio work during the heyday of swing-era sessions – from 1935 up to the recording ban set by the American Federation of Musicians in 1942 – none of the important white ensembles were anywhere near as orientated towards jazz as those of Henderson, Moten, Ellington, Webb, Earl Hines, Basie, and Jay McShann. Listening in depth to the orchestras of Charlie Barnet, Bunny Berigan, Bob Crosby Tommy Dorsey, Benny Goodman, early Woody Herman, Harry James, Gene Krupa, Glenn Miller, Artie Shaw, reveals a repertory dominated by popular singers, whose sounds – unlike those of Louis Armstrong, Cab Calloway, Ella Fitzgerald, Billie Holiday and Fats Waller – were often distantly removed from, if not diametrically opposed to, sounds derived from jazz traditions. (The distinction along racial lines is not a firm one: a similar balance between jazz and popular music may be heard in the recorded repertories of Lunceford's orchestra, as well as Andy Kirk's from mid-1937 onwards, and most of the vocals recorded under Lunceford sound less closely related to jazz than do those of the jazziest singers employed by white big bands.) Second, a sift through these sessions for jazz tracks, and for the jazzy portions of pop tracks, brings out entirely different obstacles. While there are plenty of fine soloists to hear, including Berigan (who also worked with Dorsey), Goodman, James (initially with Goodman) and Shaw, many of the rhythm sections are uninspiring and many of the arrangements depend on scores already recorded by the black big bands. These particular faults of dull rhythm and unoriginal scoring are especially true of the most jazz-orientated of the bunch, Goodman's orchestra.

Against this backdrop, Crosby's orchestra stands out for its successful union of swing and dixieland styles (discussed together with his small group, the Bob Cats, in chapter 5), and Artie Shaw's looks to be the most adventuresome and creative of the white big bands of the swing era. Selections of its successes and failures have been issued on several RCA anthologies, including **Begin the Beguine**, which gathers together tracks from several stops along Shaw's ever-changing and tumultuous career, during which he moved back and forth between a conventional big band and a bigger (not better) big band, while also maintaining a small group within the band, his Gramercy Five.

It would be a nice story if the collection showed the orchestra struggling its way towards success, but life was not so obliging. Shaw's first hit, *Begin the Beguine*, was his best one and, to undercut the drama further, the best note of the piece was the first one. There was nothing unusual about a brass punch co-ordinated with a snare-drum shot, but this device would usually be used by big-band arrangers as an answer to some gentler sound that had come before; here, in a brilliant stroke, arranger Jerry Gray begins the beguine with the punch and shot right on the downbeat of the first bar, the result being one of the most exhilarating starts in all of jazz. The hard accents continue, set against a catchy swinging riff, which in turn becomes the background for Shaw's entrance on the melody. The remainder of the piece not only continues to highlight Gray's skill, but more generally provides an extreme example of the importance of the big-band arranger: it is made entirely of statements and restatements of the theme, played variously by the leader, the full ensemble, the saxes, the trombones, and tenor saxophonist Tony Pastor. The whole thing is underpinned by a jaunty four-beat swing which drummer Cliff Leeman holds together. In addition to his rim shots, the special effect of his splash cymbal is worth noting – it is heard most clearly behind Pastor's solo. Leeman was one of a succession of first-rate drummers who worked for Shaw, helping set the band apart from the pack.

Following examples set by Barnet's big band and Goodman's combo, Shaw had brought into his orchestra a black musician, none other than Billie Holiday, who had used Shaw as a sideman on her own recordings earlier, and who here recorded his song *Any Old Time* at the same session as *Begin the Beguine*. The result is a demonstration of how far below Holiday's normal level of performance the band could be. Perhaps out of courtesy to the composer and leader, she stays closer to the shape of Shaw's melody than she might have done with her own and Teddy Wilson's groups, but she gives its rhythm her usual treatment, floating across and around the beat. In the process she shows up the band's plodding pulse, which not even Leeman could rescue. A detail worth noting in Gray's arrangement is that the interlude (just before Holiday enters) has the kernel of the theme of Glenn Miller's *A String of Pearls*, which Gray composed and arranged three years later.

Nightmare, again written by Shaw, was the orchestra's theme, and the sort of eccentricity it exemplified was another distinctive feature of the band. The composition, such as it is, consists of nothing but a slow, unrelenting, droning brood on a couple of bluesy minor chords, with Shaw's clarinet set against muted brass.

Holiday's roughly ten-month stay with Shaw ended in November 1938. By March, when *Deep Purple* was recorded, the unenviable task of filling her place had been given to Helen Forrest, who comes through admirably under the circumstances. Neither she nor anyone else could match Holiday's tone and improvisatory flair, but she had a reasonable sense of swing, which isn't hurt at all by having drummer Buddy Rich marking time behind her. More importantly, on this track at least, a cutting edge to her tone and an avoidance of a corny sentimental vibrato separated her approach from that heard on many white big-band vocal tracks, including some of her own work with Shaw, Goodman and James.

Rich is more prominent on other tracks, though, to my ear, less satisfying. On *Serenade to a Savage* he moves back and forth between an 'exotic' section (with a tom tom beat obviously meant to capitalize on Krupa's popular drumming on Goodman's *Sing, Sing, Sing*), and much more compelling swing segments, including a good muted wa-wa trumpet solo from Bernie Privin. On *Traffic Jam* Rich adopts a swing style which is so far on top of the beat that the beat accelerates: some listeners like this type of jazz drumming, feeling that the forward rush adds to the excitement of the performance, but it is not an approach that I find satisfying. Similarly, on the band's interpretation of *Oh! Lady be Good*, I think he pushes unnecessarily.

Two of the best solos that Shaw recorded may be heard on the aforementioned *Deep Purple* and on *Star Dust*, recorded in October 1940. On both he fashions deliberate, perfectly executed lines which bounce back and forth between a paraphrase of the melody and the invention of a new melody. Like his rival Benny Goodman, Shaw seems to have left in the rehearsal room whatever struggle he might have had, presenting for public view a finished, polished product of great originality. Far more than Goodman, he favoured a pure tone, without the vocalized effects of New Orleans clarinettists, and not coincidentally he was a much less convincing blues player. His tone in the lower register, best heard on *Frenesi*, could take on a gorgeous, woody, round quality, but this disappeared as he ascended through the instrument's range, and in the highest register his tone was positively shrill.

In the interim between the quasi-Caribbean exotica of *Carioca* and the quasi-Mexican exotica of *Frenesi*, Shaw had disbanded briefly and then re-formed the group on the strength of an unfortunate idea: he would add a string section, and sometimes orchestral winds as well, to the big band. This walk in the footsteps of Paul Whiteman's symphonic jazz resulted in some unbelievable juxtapositions of smarminess and swing. In addition to the sharp contrasts between the string lines and Shaw's playing on these tracks, there are great incongruities between the strings' rhythmic feel and drummer Nick Fatool's relaxed swing on *Moon Glow*. Also, the strings break up Billy Butterfield's glorious presentation of the melody of *Star Dust*; playing with his open but slightly burnished tone, he re-enters with a jolt by smacking a high note and holding on to it, as if to ask the strings to go away.

CD

***Begin the Beguine*, Bluebird 6274-2 RB (USA) and ND 86274 (Europe)**

Chuck Peterson, Johnny Best, Claude Bowen (tpt), George Arus, Harry Rogers, Ted Vesely (tb), Artie Shaw (cl), Les Robinson, Hank Freeman (as), Tony Pastor, Ronnie Perry (ts), Les Burness (p), Al Avola (g), Sid Weiss (sb), Cliff Leeman (d)

New York	24 July 1938	**Begin the Beguine** (arr Jerry Gray)
add Pastor and band (v)		**Indian Love Call**
omit (v)		**Back Bay Shuffle** (arr Teddy McRae)
add Billie Holiday (v)		**Any Old Time** (arr Gray)

Russell Brown (tb) and George Koenig (as) replace Vesely and Robinson; omit (v)

	27 Sept 1938	**Nightmare** (arr Shaw)
		What is This Thing Called Love?

Peterson, Best, Bernie Privin (tpt), Arus, Rogers, Les Jenkins (tb), Shaw (cl), Robinson, Freeman (as), Pastor, Georgie Auld (ts), Bob Kitsis (p), Avola (g), Weiss (sb), Buddy Rich (d), Helen Forrest (v)

	12 March 1939	**Deep Purple** (arr Gray)
Hollywood	12 June 1939	**Comes Love**
omit Forrest		**Traffic Jam** (arr McRae)
	22 June 1939	**Serenade to a Savage**

Harry Geller (tpt) replaces Best

New York	19 Aug 1939	**Carioca** (arr Gray)
	27 Aug 1939	**Oh! Lady be Good**

Dave Barbour (g) replaces Avola, add Forrest (v)

	11 Nov 1939	**Moon Ray**

Charlie Margulis, Manny Klein, George Thow (tpt), Randall Miller, Bill Rank, Babe Bowman (tb), Jack Cave (french horn), Shaw (cl), Blake Reynolds, Bud Carlton, Jack Stacey (as), Dick Clark (ts), Joe Krechter (bass cl), Morton Ruderman (fl), Phil Nemoli (oboe), Mark Levant, Harry Bluestone, Peter Eisenberg, Robert Barene, Sid Brokaw, Dave Cracov, Alex Law, Jerry Joyce (vln), David Sturkin, Stanley Spiegelman, Jack Gray (viola), Irving Lipschultz, Jules Tannenbaum (cello), Stan Wrightman (p), Bobby Sherwood (g), Jud DeNaut (sb), Carl Maus (d)

Hollywood	4 March 1940	**Frenesi** (arr William Grant Still)

Billy Butterfield (tpt), Shaw (cl), Johnny Guarnieri (harpsichord), Al Hendrickson (elg), DeNaut (sb), Nick Fatool (d)

	3 Sept 1940	**Special Delivery Stomp**
		Summit Ridge Drive

Butterfield, George Wendt, Jack Cathcart (tpt), Jack Jenney, Vernon Brown (tb), Shaw (cl), Bus Bassey, Neely Plumb (as), Les Robinson, Jerry Jerome (ts), E. Lamas, T. Klages, Bob Morrow, B. Bower, Al Beller (vln), A. Harshman, K. Collins (viola), F. Goerner (cello), Guarnieri (p), Hendrickson (elg), DeNaut (sb), Fatool (d)

	7 Sept 1940	**Temptation**
	7 Oct 1940	**Star Dust** (arr Lennie Hayton)
	4 Dec 1940	**Blues** (arr Still)
add Ray Conniff (tb)	23 Jan 1941	**Moon Glow**

* * *

Tommy Dorsey: *The Best of Tommy Dorsey*

The appropriately titled anthology **The Best of Tommy Dorsey** testifies to the trombonist's eclecticism during his decade of greatest popularity, from 1935 to 1944. It begins soon after he and his brother Jimmy went their separate ways, with the recording in October 1935 of what would become his theme song, *I'm Gettin' Sentimental Over You*. Dorsey was justly famous for the beauty and perfection of his trombone playing on this title, and by the following year he had acquired his lasting motto: 'the sentimental gentleman of swing'. He was, though, far more versatile than the motto implies, and indeed was dedicated to playing in as many contemporary popular and jazz styles as possible. Found among this variety are the dixieland-tinged swing of *Royal Garden Blues*, the straight-ahead (if somewhat stiff) big band swing of *Little White Lies* and *Boogie Woogie*, an unidentified adaptation of pianist Pinetop Smith's *Pinetop's Boogie Woogie*. At decade's end, arranger Sy Oliver joined from Jimmie Lunceford's big band and thereby enabled Dorsey to embrace a jazz style more firmly based in swing, for which the finest example, *Opus No. 1*, came later, in 1944. Finally, turning as far from jazz as toward it, Dorsey in the early 1940s began to feature dreamy, romantic performances by Frank Sinatra and the Pied Pipers, whose biggest hit was *I'll Never Smile Again*.

Often Dorsey's eclecticism operated on a moment-to-moment level. His greatest successes, *Marie* and *Song of India*, are stylistic conglomerates. *Marie* is the orchestra's rendering of an arrangement which by various accounts was either purchased from, traded for, or stolen from Doc Wheeler's Sunset Royal Serenaders. In any event, Dorsey supplied the spark that made it a hit. It begins with another example of his control of the trombone, in an unadorned rendering of the melody; then Jack Leonard sings that melody in the same straightforward, clear-toned, and pretty manner, while the bandsmen interject rhythmically syncopated and swinging comments on the lyrics; then trumpeter Bunny Berigan takes over, improvising one of his most acclaimed jazz solos. The tune was requested so often that, to avoid boredom, Dorsey commissioned a series of arrangements along the same lines, beginning with *Who?*. A different series of stylistic conglomerates, 'swinging the classics', stemmed from the popularity of an adaptation of Rimsky-Korsakov's *Song of India*, again featuring Dorsey's beautiful sound and Bergian's imaginative swing. No performances underscore better than these the difficulty – some might argue the folly – of trying to distinguish jazz from pop at the height of the swing era.

CD

***The Best of Tommy Dorsey*, Bluebird 07863-51087-2 (USA) and ND 90587 (Europe)**

Andy Ferretti, Sterling Bose, Bill Graham, Cliff Weston (tpt), Tommy Dorsey, Ben Pickering, Dave Jacobs (tb), Sid Stoneburn (cl, as), Noni Bernardi (as), Clyde Rounds (as, ts), Johnny Van Eps (ts), Paul Mitchell (p), Mac Cheikes (g), Gene Traxler (sb), Sam Rosen (d)

New York	18 Oct 1935	**I'm gettin' sentimental over you** (arr Bernardi)

Max Kaminsky, San Skolnick, Joe Bauer (tpt), Dorsey, Pickering, Walter Mercurio (tb), Joe Dixon (cl, as), Fred Stulce (as), Rounds (as, ts), Sid Block (ts), Dick Jones (p), William Schaffer (g), Traxler (sb), Dave Tough (d), Edythe Wright (v)

	25 March 1936	**You** (arr Paul Weston)
omit (v)	3 April 1936	**Royal Garden Blues** (arr Weston)

Bunny Berigan, Jim Welch, Bauer, Bob Cusumano (tpt), Dorsey, Les Jenkins, 'Red' Bone (tb), Dixon (cl, as), Stulce (as), Rounds (as, ts), Bud Freeman (ts), Jones (p), Carmen Mastren (g), Traxler (sb), Tough (d)

	29 Jan 1937	**Song of India** (arr Bone and Dorsey)

add Jack Leonard and band (v)

		Marie (arr Stulce)

Bauer (tpt, v), Pee Wee Erwin, Ferretti (tpt), Dorsey, Jenkins, Mercurio (tb), Johnny Mince (cl, as), Stulce, Skeets Herfurt (as), Freeman (ts), Howard Smith (p), Mastren (g), Traxler (sb), Tough (d), Edythe Wright, Leonard, Alex Stordahl (v)

	21 July 1937	**Once in a While** (arr Stordahl)

Lee Castle (tpt) replaces Bauer; Earle Hagen (tpt) replaces Mercurio; omit Wright, Stordahl; add band (v)

	14 Oct 1937	**Who?** (arr Weston)

Erwin, Castle, Ferretti, Dorsey, Jenkins, Frank D'Annolfo (tb), Mince, Stulce, Herfurt, Freeman, Smith, Mastren, Artie Shapiro (sb), Tough

	6 Dec 1937	**Little White Lies** (arr Stulce)

Charlie Spivak, Yank Lawson, Kaminsky (tpt), Dorsey, Jenkins, Buddy Morrow (tb), Mince (cl, as), Stulce, Hymie Schertzer (as), Herfurt, Deane Kincaide (ts), Smith (p), Mastren (g), Traxler (sb), Moe Purtill (d)

	16 Sept 1938	**Boogie Woogie** (arr Kincaide)

Ferretti, Lawson, Jimmy Blake (tpt), Dorsey, Ward Silloway, Dave Jacobs, Elmer Smithers (tb), Mince (cl, as), Bernardi (as), Herfurt, Babe Russin (ts), Smith (p), Mastren (g), Traxler (sb), Cliff Leeman (d), Leonard (v)

	27 Sept 1939	**Indian Summer** (arr Kincaide)

Berigan, Ray Linn, Blake, Leon Debrow (tpt), Dorsey, Jenkins, George Arus, Lowell Martin (tb), Mince (cl, as), Stulce, Schertzer (as), Don Lodice, Paul Mason (ts), Joe Bushkin (celeste), Clark Yocum (g), Sid Weiss (sb), Buddy Rich (d), Frank Sinatra, the Pied Pipers (incl. Jo Stafford) (v)

	23 May 1940	**I'll never smile again** (arr Stulce)

Ziggy Elman, Charley Peterson (tpt) replace Berigan, Blake, Debrow; Heinie Beau (ts) replaces Mason; Bushkin (p)

Hollywood	11 Nov 1940	**Star Dust** (arr Weston)

Elman, Peterson, Linn, Blake, Dorsey, Arus, Jenkins, Martin, Mince, Stulce, Beau (as), Lodice, Mason, Bushkin, Yocum, Weiss, Rich, Sinatra, Pied Pipers

New York	20 Jan 1941	**Dolores**

Stafford, Sy Oliver (v) replace Sinatra, Pied Pipers

	17 Feb 1941	**Yes, Indeed!** (arr Oliver)

George Seaberg, Mickey Mangano, Dale Pierce, Roger Ellick (tpt), Dorsey, Nelson Riddle, Tex Satterwhite, Red Benson (tb), Buddy DeFranco (cl, as), Al Klink, Gale Curtis (ts), Bruce Branson (bar), Milt Golden (p), Bob Bain (g), Sid Block (sb), Rich (d), Alex Beller, Leonard Atkins, Bernard Tinterow, Peter Dimitriades, Manny Fiddler, Ruth Goodman, Joseph Goodman (vln), Milt Thomas, David Uchitel (viola), Fred Camelia (cello), Reba Robinson (harp), Joseph Park (tuba)

Hollywood	14 Nov 1944	**Opus No. 1** (arr Oliver)

* * *

Jay McShann: *Blues From Kansas City*

At a concert given in 1974 at Foundation Hall in Kansas City during the making of the documentary *The Last of the Blue Devils*, the always self-effacing Count Basie deflected conversation away from himself to the pianist at his side: 'And I'll tell you it was a good thing that we left town when we did 'cause this man, Jay McShann, was about to run us out of town, anyhow!' (Mary Lee Hester: *Going to Kansas City*, Early Bird: Sherman, TX, 1980, pp. 40–1). **Blues from Kansas City** collects together McShann's big band and small group studio recordings from the years 1941–3. There is a strong emphasis on blues forms, especially on the small group sides, and *Confessin' the Blues*, featuring Walter Brown's singing, proved to be a hit song in the newly emerging rhythm-and-blues field. McShann himself is featured as a restrained boogie woogie (*Hootie's Ignorant Oil*) and blues pianist. But the big band was by no means one dimensional. Even within this small sampling from its repertory, there are performances of markedly different character: the Ellington-like blues flavour (but not blues form) of *Swingmatism*, with a growling solo from trumpeter Orville Minor and through-composed (rather than riff-like) reed and brass melodies; the pop swing tunes *Sepian Bounce* and *Say Forward, I'll March*; and Al Hibbler's sweet ballad singing on *Get Me on Your Mind*, recorded the year before he joined Ellington's orchestra.

For many the attraction of these sessions is the presence (on all but the last session) of Charlie Parker. The alto saxophonist improvises on *Swingmatism*, *Hootie Blues* (one of his simplest and most tunefully elegant solos), *The Jumpin' Blues* and *Sepian Bounce*. This is a young Parker, not yet creating consistently astounding improvisations and not yet fully identifiable. Indeed there is some dispute among experts as to the identity of the soloist on *Lonely Boy Blues* and *One Woman's Blues* (also known as *One Woman's Man*), whether Parker or the sweeter, more delicate altoist John Jackson, who is also featured on *Dexter Blues*.

The band as a whole, though, was fully mature. While Basie himself was favouring a more formal approach to arranging in the early 1940s, McShann was carrying forward the Basie orchestra's arranging style of riffs, rhythm, and solos, particularly on *The Jumpin' Blues*, an appropriate title if ever there was one. It features the leader's piano; a catchy, riff-like, swinging theme stated by the ensemble; Parker, with a riff in the background; Brown, with another riff in the background and a trumpet obbligato too; interlocking sectional riffs; and the theme again. This was the last great Kansas City big band.

CD

***Blues From Kansas City*, Decca GRD-617 (USA)**

Harold Bruce, Orville Minor, Bernard Anderson (tpt), 'Little Joe' Taswell Baird (tb), Charlie Parker, John Jackson (as), Bob Mabane, Harry Ferguson (ts), Jay McShann (p), Gene Ramey (sb), Gus Johnson (d)

Dallas 30 April 1941 **Swingmatism** (arr William J. Scott)

add Walter Brown (v) **Hootie Blues** (arr Parker)

omit (v) **Dexter Blues** (arr Scott)

McShann, Ramey, Johnson **Vine Street Boogie**

add Brown **Confessin' the Blues**

omit Brown **Hold 'Em Hootie**

Minor (tpt), Baird (tb), Jackson (as), McShann (p), Ramey (sb), Johnson (d), Brown (v)

Chicago 18 Nov 1941 **One Woman's Man**

McShann, Ramey, Johnson, Brown **'Fore Day Rider**

omit Brown **So You Won't Jump**

add Brown **New Confessin' the Blues**
Red River Blues
Baby Heart Blues
Cryin' won't make me stay
Hootie's Ignorant Oil

Bob Merrill, Minor, Anderson (tpt), Baird, Lawrence Anderson (tb), Parker, Jackson (as), Mabane, Fred Culliver (ts), McShann (p), Enois (g), Ramey (sb), Doc West (d), Brown (v)

New York 2 July 1942 **Lonely Boy Blues**

Al Hibbler (v) replaces Brown **Get Me on Your Mind** (arr Scott)

Brown (v) replaces Hibbler **The Jumpin' Blues**

omit (v) **Sepian Bounce** (arr Archie Hall)

Merrill, Dave Mitchell, Jesse Jones, Willie Cook (tpt), Alonzo Pettiford, Alfonso Fook, Rudy Morrison (tb), Jackson, Rudolph Dennis (as), Paul Quinichette, Bill Goodson (ts), Rae Brodely (bar), McShann (p), Ramey (sb), Dan Graves (d)

New York 1 Dec 1943 **Say Forward, I'll March**

add Merrill (v) **Wrong Neighborhood**

Brown (v) replaces Merrill **Hometown Blues**

* * *

Woody Herman: *The Thundering Herds 1945–1947*

Over the years a succession of reissues has presented the glorious work of Woody Herman's First and Second Herds for the Columbia label. With one exception, these big-band tracks require none of the equivocating appreciation with apologies given to Artie Shaw's orchestra. The compositions, arrangements, soloists and rhythm are consistently first-rate, and the only drag on the proceedings is Herman's unbearably bad singing. While countless white instrumentalists have rendered the blues convincingly, scarcely any white singers have grasped its language, tone and inflections. Jack Teagarden was one. Herman was not. The leader had the further handicap of an almost toneless voice, so that his ballad singing was even more dreadful than his blues. Enough said.

Before forming the First Herd (heard on all but two tracks on the CD) Herman led 'the band that plays the blues', and, as the First Herd was about to disband, in December 1946 it remade the earlier group's biggest hits, *Woodchopper's Ball* and *Blue Flame* (first recorded in 1939 and 1941 respectively). Although the Herds developed very much their own styles, not surprisingly these earlier compositions owe a debt to the fountainheads of big-band jazz, and they indicate in some sense the direction Herman followed – that of Count Basie – and the one he did not – that of Duke Ellington. *Woodchopper's Ball* is in Basie's mould, a blues built on the principle of riffs, swing rhythms and solos. The simple, toe-tapping ideas remind us what a short step it could be from swing, to rhythm and blues, to rock and roll, to rock. (Indeed, the rhythmically uncontrollable rock guitarist Alvin Lee made *Woodchopper's Ball* his theme song.) *Blue Flame*, Herman's theme song, is also a blues, but in the Ellingtonian 'jungle music' style, with a bass-register trombone du-wah and a deliberate tom-tom rhythm forming the background for a moody sax riff, Herman's bluesy clarinet, Bill Harris's trombone and Chuck Wayne's somewhat too cheery electric guitar.

The bulk of the recordings on this CD were new to the First Herd. They show a creative approach that provides to some extent a swing-era parallel to the relationship between the restrained New Orleans style and the no-holds-barred Chicago style. If Basie's work was a starting point for the First Herd, the group transformed that approach by injecting it with a high-powered intensity in the brass and rhythm. *Goosey Gander*, for example, has (after Harris's solo) wild three-part interlocking riffs which are repeated with trumpeter Pete Candoli screaming over the top. In the last chorus of *Panacea* a blaring Harris and a screaming Candoli play together over an ensemble riff, all supported by the rhythm of bassist Chubby Jackson and drummer Don Lamond, who enthusiastically takes the beat into double time for the first eight bars to kick the intensity up another notch. There are high-register brass riffs in *Wild Root,* a great performance marred by an annoyingly resonant droning pitch (perhaps emanating from the drums), and also in *Backtalk,* which in addition features brassy fanfares, Herman's clarinet riding above or alongside the brass and Don Lamond's forceful drumming. It is worth noting that the relationship came full circle a few years later, when one of the principal arrangers on these sessions, Neal Hefti, began writing for Basie; *The Good Earth* is a close cousin of his later scores for Basie, who adopted, together with Hefti's cute themes, a powerhouse brassy style in combination with Sonny Payne's extroverted drumming.

Adventuresome ideas went hand in hand with this energetic approach. The wildest ones include the ending to *Apple Honey,* as the band slithers upwards to an abrupt halt; the ending to *Goosey Gander,* where the saxophones' honks and slides in the 'Shortnin' Bread' theme are interrupted by overlapping downward glisses tossed around the brass; and the last chorus of *Your Father's Moustache,* where, eight bars after a wild brass break, Herman painstakingly bends a clarinet note against soft sax and muted brass riffs, and some combination of instruments (I cannot identify it) makes a low-pitched glowering sound. The First Herd also took conventional poses, as for example in the themes of *Northwest Passage* and *Backtalk,* reminiscent of Benny Goodman's combos in their velvety blend of vibraphone, electric guitar and reeds.

Three principal soloists return again and again throughout these tracks from 1945 and 1946: clarinettist Herman, tenor saxophonist Flip Phillips and trombonist Harris. Herman and Phillips, though never innovators on their instruments, none the less had the tone, time, taste and technique to justify their prominence. Harris was an outrageously innovative trombonist who married old-fashioned sounds – a heavy-handed vibrato and an overdriven, brash timbre – to highly original improvised melodies. Among other soloists, there is veteran swing vibraphonist Red Norvo, at his best on *Backtalk* (which he wrote in collaboration with Shorty Rogers). Candoli, as mentioned, filled the screaming trumpet solo chair until the band's last session, when it was handed over with poorer results to Al Porcino; the latter, on *Non-Alcoholic* at least, comes across as more a squealer than a screamer. Trumpeter Sonny Berman, though not a high-note specialist, takes his place alongside Candoli and Porcino in supplying a soloist's equivalent to the 'Chicago style' parallel drawn above: like Frank Teschemacher, Berman places enthusiasm over polish in his solo on *Your Father's Moustache;* having begun to hit clinkers in the second half of his improvisation, he stays with them, creating an original but completely 'out to lunch' melody. This band was not bashful.

Herman's intended retirement on Christmas Eve, 1946, did not last long. Soon he was back in the studios with a combo, a medium-sized band and a big band, and in September 1947 he formed his renowned Second Herd. It is represented on the CD by two tracks: *The Goof and I*, a carefully wrought, delightfully swinging piece composed and arranged by Al Cohn, and *Four Brothers*, Herman's greatest recording.

Four Brothers was written by Jimmy Giuffre, whose inspiration dated back to the previous year, when he was a member of a four-tenor-saxophone section in a rehearsal band that Gene Roland was leading in Los Angeles. Now, in December 1947, three of the same tenor players – Stan Getz, Zoot Sims and Herbie Steward – were sitting beside Herman's new favourite soloist, baritone saxophonist Serge Chaloff. Giuffre set their mellow sounds, modelled after Lester Young's style, against crisp brass and Lamond's sensational playing on drums. The theme has the four brothers gliding along in tightly packed harmony, with trebly brass punches and snappy drum accents articulating the smooth, cool sounds. Each man takes a solo – Sims, Chaloff, Steward and Getz – and the honours go to the first and last, who with this recording began to push Flip Phillips into the background in the larger history of outstanding tenor saxophonists in Herman's Herds. The contrast of hot brass and drums and cool saxes continues, moving through a powerful riff (to which lyricist and singer Jon Hendricks later conveniently set the words 'four brothers') and a series of loud, exhilarating, perfectly executed stop-time breaks for the saxes playing individually (Getz, Sims, Steward, Chaloff) but with a single conception, and then collectively in harmony.

One other extremely important recording, *Early Autumn*, with Getz's definitive cool ballad playing, is not in the collection for the simple reason that it was recorded for Capitol, to which label Herman switched at the conclusion of the second recording ban by the American Federation of Musicians in 1948. But it seems a shame that the compilers of the CD set chose the rightfully rejected, painful rendition of *A Jug of Wine* rather than the warm-up for *Early Autumn*, Ralph Burns's *Summer Sequence (part iv)*, which is on several of Columbia's LP anthologies of Herman's sessions. In addition to giving a good taste of Getz's future achievement, *Summer Sequence (part iv)* beautifully captures Herman's alto saxophone playing, modelled after Johnny Hodges's sensuous style. Also, the earliest tracks on this CD are not the master takes, which generally do appear on the LPs.

CD

***The Thundering Herds 1945–1947*, Columbia Jazz Masterpieces CK 44108 (USA) and CBS Jazz Masterpieces 460825-2 (Europe)**

Sonny Berman, Chuck Frankhouser, Ray Wetzel, Pete Candoli, Carl Warwick (tpt), Ralph Pfeffner, Bill Harris, Ed Kiefer (tb), Woody Herman (cl), Sam Marowitz, John LaPorta (as), Flip Phillips, Pete Mondello (ts), Skippy DeSair (bar), Marjorie Hyams (vb), Ralph Burns (p), Billy Bauer (elg), Chubby Jackson (sb), Dave Tough (d)

New York	19 Feb 1945	**Apple Honey** (take 3) (arr Burns)
	1 March 1945	**Goosey Gander** (take 2) (arr Burns)
		Northwest Passage (take 1) (arr Burns)

Berman, Conte Candoli, Pete Candoli, Irv Lewis, Neal Hefti (tpt), Pfeffner, Harris, Kiefer (tb), Herman (cl), Marowitz, LaPorta (as), Phillips, Mondello (ts), DeSair (bar), Tony Aless (p), Bauer (elg), Jackson (sb), Tough (d)

	10 Aug 1945	**The Good Earth** (take 2) (arr Hefti)
	20 Aug 1945	**Bijou** (arr Burns)

add Ray Linn (tpt), Red Norvo (vb), Herman and band (v); Buddy Rich (d) replaces Tough

	5 Sept 1945	**Your Father's Moustache** (arr Hefti and Harris)

Berman, Pete Candoli, Lewis, Hefti, Shorty Rogers (tpt), Pfeffner, Harris, Kiefer (tb), Herman (cl), Marowitz, LaPorta (as), Phillips, Mickey Folus (ts), Sam Rubinowich (bar), Aless (p), Bauer (elg), Jackson (sb), Don Lamond (d)

	16 Nov 1945	**Wild Root** (arr Hefti)

Berman, Candoli, Marky Markowitz, Conrad Gozzo, Rogers (tpt), Pfeffner, Harris, Kiefer (tb), Herman (cl, v), Marowitz, LaPorta (as), Phillips, Mickey Folus (ts), Sam Rubinowich (bar), Red Norvo (vb), Aless (p), Bauer (elg), Jackson (sb), Don Lamond (d)

	17 Feb 1946	**A Jug of Wine**
		Panacea (arr Burns)

add Neal Reid (tb); Cappy Lewis (tpt), Jimmie Rowles (p), Chuck Wayne (g), Joe Mondragon (sb) replace Markowitz, Aless, Bauer, Jackson; omit (v)

Los Angeles	20 Sept 1946	**Backtalk** (arr Rogers)

Al Porcino, Lewis, Gozzo, Chuck Peterson, Bob Peck (tpt), Pfeffner, Harris, Kiefer (tb), Herman (cl), Marowitz, LaPorta (as), Phillips, Mickey Folus (ts), Sam Rubinowich (bar), Rowles (p), Wayne (elg), Mondragon (sb), Don Lamond (d)

Chicago	10 Dec 1946	**Woodchopper's Ball** (take 1) (arr Hefti)
		Blue Flame (arr Jiggs Noble)
add Herman (v)		**The Blues are Brewin'**
omit (v)		**Non-Alcoholic** (arr LaPorta)

Ernie Royal, Bernie Glow, Stan Fishelson, Markowitz, Rogers (tpt), Earl Swope, Ollie Wilson, Bob Swift (tb), Herman (cl), Marowitz, Herbie Steward (as), Stan Getz, Zoot Sims (ts), Serge Chaloff (bar), Fred Otis (p), Gene Sargent (g), Walt Yoder (sb), Lamond (d)

Los Angeles	24 Dec 1947	**The Goof and I** (arr Al Cohn)

omit Marowitz; Steward (ts)

	27 Dec 1947	**Four Brothers**

Dizzy Gillespie: *'Shaw 'Nuff'; The Bebop Revolution*

Jazz history tells us that singer Billy Eckstine formed the first bop big band in 1944, and indeed its roster of sidemen reads like a who's who of the music: Dizzy Gillespie, Charlie Parker, Fats Navarro, Gene Ammons, Dexter Gordon, Sonny Stitt and Art Blakey, all in its first year. But with little exception the group's studio recordings focused on the leader's romantic ballads, light years away from the then new style. Path-breaking big-band bop recordings came not from Eckstine, but from Gillespie. The innovative trumpeter first led his own large ensemble in 1945, but it failed, and the start of his studio sessions had to wait until the following year, when he successfully re-established the orchestra and began recording for Musicraft. In 1947, with RCA Victor, he moved the group in a new and even more unusual direction, bringing swing, bop and Latin music together into a style that came to be known as Afro-Cuban jazz. The unifying factor among all these recordings is that the band was designed to feature Gillespie as its principal soloist, and for good reason: from start to finish his improvising is consistently nothing short of spectacular.

The fanciest modern equipment cannot do much for the Musicraft material, which was not well recorded. And, naturally, some of Gillespie's experiments did not come off. But these faults are outweighed by the music's greatness and its historical importance: excepting the Afro-Cuban idea, the Musicraft sessions lay out the directions Gillespie was to pursue for RCA and with subsequent big bands. One of the many innovations which came directly out of bop combos was Gillespie's dismissal of the guitar from the big band. He did not want that chugging chomp in his rhythm section. From the list of instruments, it may seem that Gillespie simply replaced the guitar with Milt Jackson's vibraphone. But the leader evidently required Jackson to leave aside his considerable ability as an accompanist and instead use the vibraphone strictly as a solo melody instrument.

Among these performances, *Things to Come* is technically the most difficult and conceptually the most simplistic, aiming to create bop big-band music by having everyone play as if they were in a giant bop combo, an assignment which the massed brass cannot possibly handle at a tempo resembling that of Bennie Moten's *Toby*. During his solo the leader's display of effortless originality at high speed underlines, by comparison, the unrelaxed, frenetic, sloppy ensemble work. Things hadn't come together yet. Of greatest interest, after Gillespie's trumpeting, are Jackson's bop vibraphone solo (partially drowned out by the brass) and a characteristic emphasis on weakly functional, suspended harmonies, culminating in the mysterious and unresolved final chords that lead to a glissando down and back up.

One Bass Hit no. 2 is a follow-up to a combo version that Gillespie made two months earlier. Both versions are meant to feature bassist Ray Brown, but the poor fidelity is especially hard on Brown's instrument, and in any event on both it is Gillespie who steals the show. Apart from in the solos, the bop style makes its presence felt in the rapid-fire licks that the trumpets trade around as an introduction to Gillespie's solo, in the complexity of the line arranged for saxophones, and generally – as with *Things to Come* and many pieces to follow – in the emphasis on strange, tense harmonies. The next year, RCA's far superior technology afforded Brown an opportunity to stand out on *Two Bass Hit*, particularly in the unaccompanied solo on blues harmonies that he takes at the end, but again he is upstaged by Gillespie's trumpeting as well as by the writing, credited to Gillespie and pianist John Lewis. Outstanding are the stuttering but catchy theme and the slithering chromatic dissonant lines accompanying Gillespie in his third blues chorus.

Our Delight, the first title recorded for Musicraft, marks the start of arranger Tadd Dameron's contributions to the band, which continued on RCA with *Good Bait*. The most swing-orientated of Gillespie's recordings, these have a tunefulness, a cheeriness, a wholesome brightness which immediately mark them as Dameron's, and which belie the circumstances of his turbulent life.

Good Dues Blues, devoted mainly to an absolutely dreary vocal by Alice Roberts, is rescued at the end by one of the most perfect blues improvisations that Gillespie ever recorded. Often he sacrificed polish for wildly creative ideas, but here he has both. The solo demonstrates how he combined traditional licks with his special sense of harmony, twisting familiar phrases in surprising directions. A few months later Roberts redeemed herself on *He Beeped when He Shoulda Bopped*, a joyful, tongue-in-cheek pop song about a musician who was 'draggin' them out of the groove' by beeping when he should have bopped. The tune confirms, and pokes fun at, the status of bop as an insider music, not for just anyone.

Despite the presence of Sonny Stitt and Leo Parker in the band, one weakness on its recordings was the lack of a saxophone soloist talented enough to stand up against the leader. The problem was relieved late in 1946, when Cecil Payne joined. Payne's was a straight bop style, modelled after Charlie Parker's, and his was no small achievement in transferring the nimble-fingered requirements of bop melody to the large and cumbersome fingering of the baritone saxophone. Gillespie wasted no time in featuring Payne, who appears on the first track for RCA, *Ow!*, both as a soloist and in the lead of the riff theme played by the sax section.

The Afro-Cuban element came into the band with the hiring of conga drummer Chano Pozo in 1947. Pozo was murdered in 1948, which happened to be the year of the second recording ban imposed by the musicians' union, and so his studio career was brief. It was none the less tremendously influential. On some tracks, his rhythmic contribution juxtaposes Latin-style even subdivisions of the beat against everyone else's swing-style uneven subdivisions, with the result that the rhythm seems to pulsate in and out of phase. This is most evident on Dameron's pieces *Cool Breeze* and *Good Bait*. Gillespie's composition *Woody 'n You* more convincingly incorporates Pozo's rhythmic conception, though the result is still a jazz-Latin hybrid, not a jazz-Latin fusion. It begins with stuttering syncopated saxophone lines, which are co-ordinated with the conga beat, and with bassist Al McKibbon playing a syncopated pattern rather than a walking line. But the *b* section of the *aaba* theme comes straight out of Duke Ellington's *Satin Doll* and cries out for a swing feel rather than the even-eighth treatment it gets. The band breaks into swing for the alto sax solo; Pozo leaps back to Latin rhythm for his solo break. The following ensemble passage swings; the restatement of the theme returns to the Latin beat.

The two-sided 78 rpm recording of George Russell's *Cubana Be* and *Cubana Bop* (also known as *Cubano Be* and *Cubano Bop*, because this is what the band members actually sing) is the famed art piece of Afro-Cuban jazz. While it convincingly presents the voodoo roots of Pozo's percussion playing, it does not hang together well at all, being composed of part lumbering elephantine ensemble hockets (i.e., a succession of sounds and silences resulting from the introduction of rests), part self-consciously 'different' and dissonant lines, part overly tame, old-fashioned sentimental melody.

Instead the really memorable recording, and the masterpiece of these collections, is *Manteca*, credited to Gillespie, Pozo and Fuller, who wrote the arrangement. The opening gradually builds up into an interlocking collection of repeated, two-bar Latin riffs, with the string bass on the one hand and baritone sax and trombone on the other playing rollicking lines, either of which alone would have been enough to carry the piece forward; together the effect is irresistibly propulsive. The theme emerges seamlessly out of the interlocking riff, but then there is a clear break into a swing-bop feel, with a walking bass line rather than the syncopated pattern. The cycle begins again as the introductory Latin riffs return, but this time the theme presents itself in the guise of swing, with the bass walking in support of Big Nick Nicholas's tenor sax solo; Nicholas even quotes from a swing standard, *Blue Moon*, to begin the second half of his solo. After Gillespie's solo the Latin rhythms return, and then the opening vamp moves in reverse, reducing down to bass and conga drum as Gillespie shouts out the title of this euphoric performance.

On reissues, Gillespie's essential big-band tracks appear in tandem with his bop combo recordings. Only the big-band tracks are listed below; the combo recordings are detailed in chapter 7. Additionally at the time of writing only a small selection of his RCA work is available on the general anthology **The Bebop Revolution**. Most significantly his delightful and comical style of scat singing is not represented here, apart from the combo performance of *Oop Bop Sh'bam* on the Musicraft CD.

CD

***'Shaw 'nuff'*, Musicraft MVSCD 53 (USA)**

Dizzy Gillespie, Dave Burns, Raymond Orr, Talib Daawud, John Lynch (tpt), Alton Moore, Charles Greelea (tb), John Brown, Howard Johnson (as), Ray Abrams, Warren Luckey (ts), Pee Wee Moore (bar), Jackson (p), Ray Brown (sb), Kenny Clarke (d)

New York	10 June 1946	**Our Delight**
add Alice Roberts (v)		**Good Dues Blues**

Gillespie, Burns, Daawud, Kenny Dorham, Lynch, Elmon Wright (tpt), Leon Comegeys, Gordon Thomas, Moore (tb), Johnson, Sonny Stitt (as), Abrams, Luckey (ts), Leo Parker (bar), John Lewis (p), Brown (sb), Clarke (d)

	9 July 1946	**One Bass Hit no. 2**
		Ray's Idea
add Jackson (vb)		**Things to Come**
add Roberts (v)		**He Beeped when He Shoulda Bopped**

Gillespie, Burns, Lynch, Wright, Matthew McKay (tpt), Thomas, Alton Moore, Taswell Baird (tb), John Brown, Scoops Carry (as), James Moody, Bill Frazier (ts), Pee Wee Moore (bar), John Lewis (p), Ray Brown (sb), Joe Harris (d), Kenny Hagood (v)

	12 Nov 1946	**I Waited for You**
add Jackson (vb)		**Emanon**

CD

***The Bebop Revolution*, Bluebird 2177-2 RB (USA) and ND 82177 (Europe)**

Gillespie, Burns, Wright, McKay, Raymond Orr (tpt), Baird, Bill Shepherd (tb), John Brown, Johnson (as), Moody, Joe Gayles (ts), Cecil Payne (bar), Lewis (p), Ray Brown (sb), Harris (d)

	22 Aug 1947	**Ow!**
		Two Bass Hit

Gillespie, Burns, Elmon Wright, Lammar Wright Jr, Benny Bailey (tpt), Ted Kelly, Shepherd (tb), John Brown, Johnson (as), Big Nick Nicholas, Joe Gayles (ts), Payne (bar), Lewis (p), Al McKibbon (sb), Clarke (d), Chano Pozo (conga drum)

	22 Dec 1947	**Woody 'n You**
add Pozo and band (v)		**Cubana Be**
		Cubana Bop

Gillespie (v) replaces Pozo and band

	30 Dec 1947	**Manteca**
omit (v)		**Good Bait**

Gillespie, Burns, Elmon Wright, Willie Cook (tpt), Andy Duryea, Sam Hurt, Jesse Tarrant (tb), Brown, Ernie Henry (as), Gayles, Budd Johnson (ts), Payne (bar), James Forman (p), McKibbon (sb), Teddy Stewart (d), Harris (conga drum), Sabu Martinez (bongo)

	29 Dec 1948	**Guarachi Guaro**

Gillespie, Little Benny Harris, Wright, Cook (tpt), Duryea, Hurt, Tarrant (tb), Brown, Henry (as), Gayles, Yusef Lateef (ts), Al Gibson (bar), Forman (p), McKibbon (sb), Stewart (d), Vince Guerro (conga drum)

Chicago	6 May 1949	**Dizzier and Dizzier**

Charles Greenlea, J. J. Johnson (tb) replace Hurt and Tarrant; omit Guerro

	6 July 1949	**Jumpin' with Symphony Sid**

CHAPTER 4
Swing-era Combos

Barry Kernfeld

As the 1930s rolled along, hot bands gave way to swing combos, not in the manner of the seemingly abrupt emergence of bop in the early 1940s, nor in that of the much more abrupt emergence in the late 1950s of free jazz, but rather in a seamless transition in which certain tendencies of early jazz received less prominence, while others came to the fore. There was less collective improvisation, though countless examples still remained, especially in the climactic last choruses of pieces (the 'ride out'). Instead, there were greater proportions of space given over to soloists; greater proportions of themes stated alone, or in unison, or in arranged block harmonies; greater proportions of simple repeated snippets of melody ('riffs') used as both themes and accompanimental figures. In the core repertory, multi-thematic pieces (rags, marches, multi-part blues) took a back seat to pop song forms, while the 12-bar blues remained as crucial as ever, and hand in hand with this simplification of the repertory came a greater complexity of its interpretation, in that for both accompanists and soloists the underpinning of fundamental three- and four-note harmonies became less transparent. The roles of instruments shifted somewhat. The saxophone began to push the trumpet out of its position as the foremost jazz instrument. In the completion of a years-long process that saw the rhythm grow smoother, guitar replaced banjo, string bass replaced tuba, and the drums more often simply kept time rather than participating actively as the main percussive element in collective improvisation. More generally, whole combos began to grasp 'swing', that rhythmic propulsion which such individuals as Jelly Roll Morton, Sidney Bechet and, above all, Louis Armstrong, already had under their control in recordings made in the previous decade.

Swing was so basic to the first 40 years of jazz recording that swing combos absorbed, or combined with, hot and bop combos in every imaginable way, with the result that sometimes their separate identity seems to depend as much on period and affiliation as on distinct sound. Thus it is that swing combos are the subject of four chapters in this book. This chapter and the one that follows begin with combos that flourished from the mid-1930s into the 1940s, the height of the swing era. Some were fairly stable groups, both dependent and independent. The former, as Benny Goodman's combo and Bob Crosby's Bob Cats, were affiliated with a big band, from which they partially, if not entirely, drew their personnel, and through such an affiliation they reached audiences far larger than the jazz community. The latter, such as the combo Sid Catlett led on 52nd Street in New York and the quintet Django Reinhardt and Stephane Grappelli led in Paris, generally did not reach out beyond jazz, and in this respect two groups, Fats Waller and his Rhythm and Nat 'King' Cole's trio, are atypical, since both entered segments of the popular market-place. Other types of swing combos made their way into the recording studios on an *ad hoc* basis, perhaps to accompany a soloist, as in the ever-changing all-star combos heard on Billie Holiday's sessions, or perhaps just to get away from big-band arrangements and let off some steam, as on the informal 'jam session' recorded by Roy Eldridge and Chu Berry.

The present chapter then leaps abruptly to a session recorded in the mid-1980s by tenor saxophonist Scott Hamilton, the most prominent representative of the permanent continuation of instrumental swing combos beyond the years of the swing era. Chapter 5, which surveys combos presenting a blend of swing and dixieland, moves into the 1950s to trace analogous continuations of that hybrid. Chapter 10 surveys a different hybrid, those combos blending swing and bop. Chapter 11, which focuses on singers, includes further selections exemplifying the continuation of the swing style in combos from the 1950s onwards.

* * *

Benny Goodman: *After You've Gone: the Original Trio & Quartet Sessions vol.1 (1935–1937)*; *Avalon: the Small Bands, vol.2 (1937–1939)*; Charlie Christian: *The Genius of the Electric Guitar*

While leading the ensemble which from 1935 was *the* most popular big band (giving way to Glenn Miller only as the decade ended), Benny Goodman also directed a swing combo. Anthologies recorded for the Victor and Columbia labels document his small group's growth from a trio of six, seven, and – for one recording session – eight pieces (all of the latter curiously called 'sextets'). These afford plenty of opportunity to hear Goodman's immaculate clarinet playing. Furthermore, the combo sessions, in comparison with the big-band ones, are far less heavily indebted to borrowings from other ensembles.

There is a sprinkling of significant performances by racially mixed groups to be found among early jazz recordings. Examples include Jelly Roll Morton with the New Orleans Rhythm Kings in 1923, Eddie Lang (masquerading as Blind Willie Dunn) with King Oliver and Lonnie Johnson in 1929, Billy Banks's Rhythmakers in 1932. But it was one thing to hold *ad hoc* sessions for a specialized buying public and quite another for America's most popular musician to follow up a jam session with pianist Teddy Wilson and drummer Gene Krupa by incorporating Wilson into his regular group, first in recording sessions and then in live performances, the mixed combo being presented as an adjunct to the white big band. Later other great black players joined, including vibraphonist Lionel Hampton (who in mid-1939 doubled as a drummer with the big band), guitarist Charlie Christian and trumpeter Cootie Williams (who also played with the big band); pianist Count Basie made several guest appearances.

These recordings testify to Goodman's sensitivity to instrumental sounds. There had only occasionally been jazz trios of clarinet, piano and drums (notably Morton again, with Barney Bigard and Zutty Singleton in 1929). The combination became still more unusual with the addition of vibraphone, with which Hampton produced a shimmering sound, setting the instrument's mechanically rotating discs to produce a vibrato at the fastest possible speed. The addition of string bass, tenor sax and trumpet moved the combo's overall sound towards the conventional, but at the same time along came Charlie Christian, playing electric guitar as if it were a wind instrument.

The first two anthologies date from Goodman's association with Victor. On the trio tracks, Krupa is far less heavy handed than he is with the big band. He keeps time on the snare drum, adding accents on other drums and cymbals as the more energetic pieces move along, and playing a solo on *Tiger Rag*. Wilson, while maintaining a striding left hand, improvises florid new melodies both in solos and in filling the spaces around Goodman's melodies. Wilson is a gentle player, and even when he is inventing a rhythmically charged solo, as in the second chorus of *Oh, Lady be Good!*, he does not hit the keyboard hard (as, say, Earl Hines would do). Goodman produces a beautiful sound, playing with a light, fast vibrato, yet he also distorts his sound when appropriate; in the same way, he moves freely between playing perfectly in tune and sliding around to produce blue notes. Within the context of these general approaches, the three men produce a varied sound, especially on *Tiger Rag*, which for contrast includes a chorus of Goodman's woody low-register playing and a series of stop-time solo choruses.

When Hampton joins to make the trio a quartet, he fully exploits the possibilities of his instrument. A second striking feature of these tracks, aside from the mere fact of the particular instruments played, is the multitude of ways in which the instruments combine. If the repertory and rhythms are weighted towards swing, other aspects of these performances are more closely related to Morton's goals for small-band jazz – to achieve a carefully rehearsed balance between composition and improvisation and to pull greatly varied textures out of a small number of players – than to the notion of a free-wheeling swing-era combo jam session. Examples include the dixieland ending to *Dinah*, in which clarinet, piano and vibes improvise as if there were a trumpeter anchoring the proceedings; in *Runnin' Wild*, the fast line played in harmony by clarinet and vibraphone at the beginning and ending and a vibes solo accompanied by a steady drum beat but a stop-time clarinet and piano riff; piano and vibraphone striking chords heavily against Goodman's sombre rendition of the melody of *The Man I Love*; and the riffing call and response between Goodman and Hampton that opens and ends *Smiles* (essentially big-band sectional playing translated to individual instruments). The most complex of these meticulous arrangements is *Opus ½*, a multi-thematic piece comprising an introduction, a first theme in a minor key, and a succession of blues choruses sandwiched between a second theme which returns at the end with its middle section omitted. *Opus ½* and a straightforward rendition of *Sweet Georgia Brown* were recorded in October 1938, by which time Krupa had left to form his own big band, thereby initiating a period of rapid personnel turnover in Goodman's group. Dave Tough replaces Krupa on these tracks.

By the time of the Columbia recordings featuring Charlie Christian (1939–41), Goodman's six- and seven-piece 'sextets' had moved completely into the mould of the free-wheeling swing-era combo jam session. The emphasis is on riffs and improvisation, with arrangement kept to a minimum. Among the principal soloists, Count Basie plays in the sparse style by then already well known from his work with his own big band. Cootie Williams keeps on his Duke Ellington mask, playing growling, muted 'jungle music' solos; the only exception is *Waitin' for Benny*, which he did not realize was being recorded. Tenor saxophonist Georgie Auld plays in a manner heavily indebted to Ben Webster. Goodman's playing complements what we have already heard on the Victor sessions, and he has an opportunity on *Wholly Cats, Gone with 'What' Wind* and *Breakfast Feud* to show what a fine blues soloist he is. But the main point of having this collection is to hear Christian.

Christian's period in the spotlight extended only a couple of months on either side of these recordings, from September 1939, when he joined Goodman, to June 1941, when tuberculosis caused him to be confined in a sanatorium permanently. In these two years he established an enormously influential approach to jazz electric guitar-playing. He was not the first jazz electric guitarist, but he was the first brilliant electric-guitar soloist. He preferred a clean, round tone, and this aspect of his playing had a stifling effect upon jazz; only 30 years later, after blues and rock musicians showed the way, did jazz electric guitarists stop imitating Christian's sound and begin exploring the sort of timbral variety that wind, brass and percussion players had been exploring all along. Christian balanced this single-minded approach to tone with his fertile imagination for melody. He effortlessly tossed out new swinging riffs and running lines, and in this respect he put his instrument on an equal footing with winds and brass. All of the commercial recordings have consistently creative guitar solos; possibly the best are on *Rose Room*, *Boy Meets Goy* (the offensive title was changed to *Grand Slam* early on), *Breakfast Feud* (on many issues as a composite of two takes to extend Christian's solo) and *I Found a New Baby*. To show off his ability in the freest possible jam session, the Columbia collections also include informal warm-ups: *Blues in B* and *Waitin' for Benny* were test recordings, subsequently released because of Christian's great playing. On *Blues in B* someone asks Charlie to play a blues in B. (Is this the recording engineer, who perhaps did not know the difference between B and B flat?) The horn players are flustered, this being a difficult key for them, and in the background you can hear 'what the hell ... in B!' as they noodle about, but for guitar this is one of the easiest keys, and Christian plunges right in. *Waitin' for Benny* begins as a one-chord jam without piano and bass, then segues into a fast version of *A Smoo-o-o-oth One* with pianist Johnny Guarnieri joining in. (The authorized version of *A Smoo-o-o-oth One*, recorded after Benny arrived, is much slower, more restrained, and more formal; it is included on a different set in the Columbia Jazz Masterpieces series: **The Benny Goodman Sextet 1939–41 Featuring Charlie Christian**).

Christian generally did not play with Goodman's big band, which kept its own rhythm guitarist. Among his occasional recordings with it, the best known is *Solo Flight*, which, except for a brief solo by Goodman, pits Christian's fluid lines against a busy succession of swing riffs and sustained chords, as arranged by Jimmy Mundy.

CD

***After You've Gone: the Original Trio & Quartet Sessions vol.1 (1935–1937),* Bluebird 5631-2 R (USA) and RCA ND 85631 (Europe)**

Benny Goodman (cl), Teddy Wilson (p), Gene Krupa (d)		
New York	13 July 1935	**After You've Gone**
		Body and Soul
		Who?
		Someday, Sweetheart
Chicago	24 April 1936	**China Boy**
		More Than You Know
add Helen Ward (v)		**All My Life**
omit Ward	27 April 1936	**Oh! Lady Be Good**
		Nobody's Sweetheart
add Ward		**Too Good To Be True**
omit Ward; add Lionel Hampton (vb)		
Hollywood	21 Aug 1936	**Moonglow**
	26 Aug 1936	**Dinah**
*as **Dinah**, but Hampton (v)*		**Exactly Like You**
add Hampton (vb)		**Vibraphone Blues**
omit Hampton		
New York	18 Nov 1936	**Sweet Sue – Just You**
add Hampton (vb)		**My Melancholy Baby**
omit Hampton	2 Dec 1936	**Tiger Rag**
add Hampton		**Stompin' at the Savoy**
		Whispering
	3 Feb 1937	**Ida, Sweet as Apple Cider**
		Tea for Two
		Runnin' Wild

CD

***Avalon: the Small Bands, vol.2 (1937–1939)*, Bluebird 2273-2 RB (USA) and ND 82273 (Europe)**

Goodman, Wilson, Krupa, Hampton		
Hollywood	30 July 1937	**Avalon**
		Handful of Keys
		The Man I Love
	2 Aug 1937	**Smiles**
		Liza
omit Hampton		
New York	29 Oct 1937	**Where or When**

add Hampton
2 Dec 1937 — **Vieni Vieni**
I'm a Ding Dong Daddy

omit Hampton; Dave Tough (d) replaces Krupa
25 March 1938 — **Sweet Lorraine**

add Hampton (vb) — **The Blues in Your Flat**

add Hampton (v) — **The Blues in My Flat**

omit (v) — **Dizzy Spells**
Chicago 12 Oct 1938 — **Opus 1/2**

Hampton (d) replaces Tough — **I Must Have that Man**

Goodman, Wilson, Hampton (vb), Tough — **Sweet Georgia Brown**
'S Wonderful

Goodman, Wilson, John Kirby (sb), Hampton (d)
29 Dec 1938 — **I Know That You Know**

Goodman, Wilson, Kirby, Buddy Schutz (d), Hampton (vb)
Pick-A-Rib
I Cried for You

Goodman, Jess Stacy (p), Schutz, Hampton
6 April 1939 — **Opus 3/4**

CD

Charlie Christian: *The Genius of the Electric Guitar*, Columbia Jazz Masterpieces CK 40846 (USA) and CBS Jazz Masterpieces 460612-2 (Europe)

Goodman (cl), Fletcher Henderson (p), Christian (elg), Artie Bernstein (sb), Nick Fatool (d), Hampton (vb)
New York 2 Oct 1939 — **Rose Room**
22 Nov 1939 — **Seven Come Eleven**

Count Basie replaces Henderson
7 Feb 1940 — **Till Tom Special**
Gone with 'What' Wind

Johnny Guarnieri replaces Basie
16 April 1940 — **Boy Meets Goy (Grand Slam)**

Dudley Brooks replaces Guarnieri
Los Angeles 20 June 1940 — **Six Appeal**

Cootie Williams (tpt), Goodman (cl), Georgie Auld (ts), Basie (p), Christian (elg), Bernstein (sb), Harry Jaeger (d)
New York 7 Nov 1940 — **Wholly Cats**
Royal Garden Blues

As Long as I Live
Benny's Bugle

Jo Jones replaces Jaeger
15 Jan 1941 — **Breakfast Feud**
I Found a New Baby

Goodman (cl, dir), Alec Fila, Jimmy Maxwell, Williams, Irving Goodman (tpt), Lou McGarity, Cutty Cutshall (tb), Skippy Martin, Gus Bivona (as), Auld, Pete Mondello (ts), Bob Snyder (bar), Johnny Guarnieri (p), Christian (elg), Bernstein (sb), Tough (d), Jimmy Mundy (arr)
4 March 1941 — **Solo Flight**

Williams, Auld, Guarnieri, Christian, Bernstein, Tough
13 March 1941 — **Blues in B**

omit Bernstein — **Waitin' for Benny**

add Goodman and Bernstein — **Good Enough to Keep (Air Mail Special)**

* * *

Fats Waller: *Jazz Classics in Digital Stereo: Fats Waller and His Rhythm, 1934–1936*

The sextet Fats Waller and his Rhythm was formed in 1934 and recorded steadily for the Victor label and its subsidiary Bluebird until the recording ban of 1942, shortly before Waller's death. Of various chronological slices of this large body of work, the best are found on reissues from the earlier period, including this volume from the series **Jazz Classics in Digital Stereo**.

Strictly as an instrumental swing combo, the Rhythm does not deserve a place in this book. Most of the horn solos are just average. Al Casey's guitar solos are pedestrian, consisting unvaryingly of syncopated chordal strumming. Waller himself coasts through stride piano paraphrases of the themes with a greater frequency here than on the unaccompanied recordings discussed in chapter 2 (of course, as mentioned there, Waller 'coasts' at a level most players never reach).

Yet some of the instrumentals reward careful attention. The rhythm section positively cooks on the dixieland-style collectively improvised final choruses of (*Oh Susannah*) *Dust off that Old Pianna* and *Swingin' them Jingle Bells*; on the former, drummer Harry Dial produces a compelling but curiously thumping beat (as if he were hitting a suitcase) by striking excessively hard with brushes, not sticks. They achieve a brisk, crisp swing on many performances, including Waller's hit songs *Honeysuckle Rose* and *It's a Sin to Tell a Lie*.

For the session of November 1934 trumpeter Herman Autrey was replaced by one of the better swing trumpet soloists, Bill Coleman. Eugene Sedric also rises above the norm in his solo on *Christopher Columbus*, playing tenor sax in the mould of Coleman Hawkins, though with a muffled tone. Waller is by far the best soloist, when he makes the effort. *Have a Little Dream on Me* begins with a delightful solo, while *(Oh Susannah) Dust off that Old Pianna* and *Swingin' them Jingle Bells* are representative of the bent-for-hell attitude in numerous fast, syncopated stride piano choruses.

What elevates this music to greatness is Waller's singing, a wholly original blend of jazz improvising, pop singing and comedy. Considered strictly as raw material, Waller seems an unlikely candidate for high praise. His raspy voice lacks fullness. But like Louis Armstrong, who had an even more unlikely voice and yet turned out to be jazz's best singer, Waller has a fabulous sense of rhythmic placement and swing; listen to his remaking of the melody of *Someboy Stole My Gal* and to the way he disconnects his voice from his hands on *What's the Reason?*, maintaining an emphatic stride piano solo while floating around the beat in a spoken reply to a woman's (unspoken) reason why he's 'not pleasin'' her. Also like Armstrong, the gruffness of his voice lent a biting attack to every syllable he uttered, imparting a special energy to his performances and thus sharply differentiating his school of jazz singing from the milky smoothness of male crooners and female songbirds in so many contemporary big bands. Unlike Armstrong, Waller does not regularly use scat singing, and he has a tendency to drift into ugly shouting, as for example in the last portion of *Swingin' them Jingle Bells*. (This piece incidentally serves as our book's representative of a perhaps excessively large seasonal subgenre, Christmas jazz, which each year begins to flood the jazz radio airwaves about two weeks before the event.)

With Waller's quick wit, there was little reason for him to sing the nonsense syllables of scat. The straightforward delivery of lyrics, improvised alterations to lyrics, commentaries on lyrics, commentaries on and instructions to instrumentalists, irreverent and irrelevant asides, all are his strengths. On *Bye Bye, Baby* he sounds quite jolly about the prospect of leaving. He gives a sincere and sweet reading of *Have a Little Dream on Me*, but then, taking up a related lyric, he throws acid in the face of *Dream Man* by turning this love song into a song about ducking out on the rent ('Woman get away from here ... I'm dreamin' ... I ain't got no money for you this morning.... Please go away and let me sleep. Landlady let me sleep some more.') He inserts words ('...I love you; yes, but if you break my heart, I'll break your jaw and then I'll die'), and at the end of his chorus he repeats the tune's title and introduces clarinettist Gene Sedric with the line: 'It's a sin to tell a lie; now get on out there and tell your lie.' He calls for Sherlock Holmes in *Somebody Stole My Gal,* sings the lyrics in a mock crying voice and at the end instructs Holmes to 'bring her back on roller skates.' On *The Curse of an Aching Heart* he tells his woman what she did to him: 'I look like something the cats had in the alley last night.' He then sings the lyrics with bizarre alterations of vocal tone and vibrato incorporating a mock-operatic sound and in the spoken ending says, 'Bump, bump, bump. That's the curse back at you.' His most off-the-wall comment comes during Autrey's solo on *Whose Honey are You?*: 'my, they're throwing the babies out the balcony, mercy!'

Some of the material is intentionally comic, not sentimental, providing suitable vehicles for his good-time jazz. *Christopher Columbus,* recorded just two weeks and one week respectively after Benny Goodman and Fletcher Henderson made their hit instrumental versions, has Waller at his zaniest: silly voices (falsetto, moving down into the baritone range), silly rhymes ('world is roundo ... safe and soundo ... goal is foundo ... rhythm boundo') and silly puns ('Since the crew was makin' merry, Mary got up and went home'). The excessively silly *Big Chief De Sota* (rhyming 'De Sota ... Minnesota ... Dakota ... bought a boata ... only mota ... cannot floata') has an unusually casual band arrangement and, as it aimlessly winds down, Waller cuts off the recording in the middle of a phrase and says 'cease, cease, De Sota has went'.

CD

***Jazz Classics in Digital Stereo: Fats Waller and His Rhythm, 1934–1936*, BBC CD 684 (UK)**

Herman Autrey (tpt), Gene Sedric (ts), Fats Waller (p, v), Albert Casey (g), Billy Taylor (sb), Harry Dial (d)

New York	17 Aug 1934	**Have a Little Dream on Me**

Bill Coleman (tpt) replaces Autrey; Sedric (cl)

	7 Nov 1934	**Honeysuckle Rose**
		Dream Man
add Dial (vb)		**I'm growing fonder of you**
add Sedric (ts); omit (vb)		**If It Isn't Love**

Autrey (tpt), Rudy Powell (cl), Waller (p, v), Casey (g), Charlie Turner (sb), Dial (d)

	6 March 1935	**Whose Honey are You?**
		What's the Reason?
add Waller (celeste)		**(Oh Susannah) Dust off that Old Pianna**

omit (celeste) 8 May 1935 **Lulu's Back in Town**

Autrey (tpt), Powell (cl, as), Waller (p, v), James Smith (g), Turner (sb), Arnold Boling (d)
Camden, NJ 24 June 1935 **Take it Easy**

omit (as) **There's going to be the devil to pay**
Somebody Stole My Gal

Autrey, Sedric (ts), Waller, Casey, Turner, Boling
New York 8 April 1936 **Christopher Columbus**

Autrey, Sedric (cl), Waller, Casey, Turner, Yank Porter (d)
5 June 1936 **It's a Sin to Tell a Lie**

(ts) replaces (cl) **Big Chief De Sota**

Autrey, Sedric (ts, cl), Waller, Casey, Turner, Slick Jones (d)
1 Aug 1936 **The Curse of an Aching Heart**

omit (cl) **Bye Bye, Baby**

add (cl) 29 Nov 1936 **Swingin' them Jingle Bells**

* * *

Quintette du Hot Club de France: *Souvenirs*

Despite the 'hot' in its name, and associations of that word with early jazz styles, the Quintette du Hot Club de France played swing tempered by gypsy string-band music. The combo grew gradually out of jam sessions among members of the band led by Parisian string bass player Louis Vola. It took its name in 1934 as a quintet led by guitarist Django Reinhardt and violinist Stephane Grappelli (spelled 'Grappelly' at the time), with two more guitarists and Vola fleshing out the rhythm section. An anthology of recordings made in London for Decca presents the quintet a few years down the road, now in its full maturity, just before World War II; and again later, when Grappelli, having settled in England during the war, was reunited with Reinhardt for a session with a British rhythm section in 1946.

The monumental playing on this collection is by Reinhardt. Fittingly, a Belgian-born Hungarian gypsy French guitarist was the first great non-American jazz musician, and the only European player to have significantly influenced the development of Afro-American music. In my opinion he is yet to be overtaken, even when considered against the international explosion of jazz which has taken place since the 1950s.

The reason is not his stinging, metallic tone, which I admire for offering an alternative to the limpid tone prevalent among jazz guitar soloists, an alternative which drew only a narrow following in swing and bop (though a wide one in blues). Nor is it his prodigious technique (notwithstanding the uselessness of two fingers on his left hand, damaged in a fire), evident in innumerable fleet lines; in passages played in octaves (foreshadowing Wes Montgomery's favourite device) at the end of his solo on *Sweet Georgia Brown* and at the start of his solo on *My Sweet*; and in his control of harmonics, played together with Grappelli momentarily at the beginning and steadily at the end of *H. C. Q. Strut*. Nor is it his imaginative use of harmony, including some wildly dissonant lower-register tremolos to begin the second half of the first chorus of the same solo on *Sweet Georgia Brown*. Nor is it his skill as a rhythm guitarist, cranking the energy and swing up several notches with his fast triplet strumming on the last chorus of *Sweet Georgia Brown*, and with his double-time strumming to wind up *My Sweet*. Great as all these things are, they do not account for his special stature. What overwhelms me about Reinhardt's playing is the way in which he spins out long, breathless improvised single-note melodies. His conception stands in opposition to that of wind players or singers, the fountainheads of jazz phrasing. He uses silence liberally, but the silences do not provide a place to breathe; rather, his phrases span silence, the end of one segment of melody being picked up and continued logically into the next. Sometimes he achieves this through simple motivic processes, repeating an idea sequentially at different levels of pitch, but usually the process is more complex: an idea breaks off without resolving, Reinhardt lets us wait for a dramatic moment until he picks it up – not to finish it off, but to carry it in a new direction and then again in yet another new direction. Ultimately this concept reaches back to baroque music, especially that of Johann Sebastian Bach, but this is heady improvised jazz, not some lightweight jazz–classical fusion. All of the solos in this collection well exemplify Reinhardt's approach, except *Daphne*. (*Daphne*, which Reinhardt and Grappelli had recorded the previous year under the leadership of violinist Eddie South, is based on the *a* section of the *aaba* theme of the jazz warhorse *I Got Rhythm*. But in place of the *b* section the piece repeats theme *a* one half step higher. In the quintet's version the soloists get tangled up, lunging gracelessly and hitting clinkers as they move back and forth between two unrelated keys.)

Grappelli, the other featured soloist, is always a happy player. An inveterate improviser, like Reinhardt he cannot wait to get rid of the themes and start making his own melodies. His style ranges more widely than Reinhardt's, embracing madcap swinging in the aforementioned strummed choruses; a lilting effect in *Honeysuckle Rose*; and romantic opening choruses to the popular song *Night and Day*, Reinhardt's 'gypsy blues' composition *Nuages* and his *Love's Melody*. Grappelli makes this last title into syrupy continental supper-club music, until Reinhardt enters to jolt the piece back into jazz with his solo.

One oddity is that both men use blue notes completely out of context, perhaps through a misunderstanding of this American idiom. Bending pitches on, for example, *Night and Day*, seems inappropriate, the resulting effect being a whine, not a lament.

Apart from Reinhardt's contributions, the rhythm sections are purely functional, laying down an adequate base and bass for swinging. Vola, who has no ability to sustain plucked notes, disastrously tries to make up for this with bowed held notes in the dreary two-beat bass line to *Souvenirs*; much more successful is his walking slap bass solo on *My Sweet*. His counterpart, expatriate Jamaican bassist Coleridge Goode, suffers more than anyone from the poorly recorded, cloudy postwar session; Goode's one brief solo on *Liza* typically is in imitation of Slam Stewart's humming while bowing, a style which Stewart had pretty well worn out by this time.

CD

***Souvenirs*, London 820.591-2 (UK)**

Stephane Grappelli (vln), Django Reinhardt, Roger Chaput, Eugène Vées (g), Louis Vola (sb)

London	31 Jan 1938	**Honeysuckle Rose**
		Sweet Georgia Brown
		Night and Day
		My Sweet
		Souvenirs
		Daphne
		Stompin' at Decca

Grappelli (vl, p), Reinhardt (g)

	1 Feb 1938	**Nocturne**

Grappelli (p), Reinhardt (g)

		I've Got my Love to Keep me Warm
	1 Sept 1938	**Please be Kind**
	10 Sept 1938	**Louise**

Reinhardt (g)		**Improvisation no.2**

as **Honeysuckle Rose**, *but Roger Grasset (sb) replaces Vola*

	30 Aug 1938	**Lambeth Walk**

Grappelli (vln), Django Reinhardt, Joseph Reinhardt, Vées (g), Emmanuel Soudieux (sb), Beryl Davis (v)

	25 Aug 1939	**Undecided**

omit (v)	**H. C. Q. Strut**
add Davis (v)	**Don't Worry 'bout Me**
omit (v)	**The Man I Love**

Grappelli (vln), Django Reinhardt, Jack Llewellyn, Alan Hodgkiss (g), Coleridge Goode (sb)

London	1 Feb 1946	**Love's Melody**
		Nuages
		Liza

* * *

Billie Holiday: *The Quintessential Billie Holiday, vol.5, 1937–1938; The Quintessential Billie Holiday, vol.9, 1940–1942*

Temperamentally, singer Billie Holiday was not stable enough to keep a single group together for long, or to work happily under another leader. Musically, she was the greatest jazz singer after Louis Armstrong. The result was that, in her steady studio work form 1935 onwards, she became a freelance star around whom *ad hoc* swing combos revolved. Favouring a more mainstream style than the string-band music of the Hot Club quintet, or than the novelty and comedy songs of Waller, Holiday attracted all but a few of the most important horn and rhythm players of the era to record with her. Two clumps of sessions stand out among the extraordinary riches of her recorded legacy, though not by much; apart from the occasional failure resulting from an inability to overcome a diabolically bad song, every bit of Holiday's swing combo work is worth hearing.

The first, from the years 1937 and 1938, comprises her collaborations with five sidemen from Count Basie's orchestra: soloists Buck Clayton (trumpet) and Lester Young (tenor saxophone), and rhythm section members Freddie Green (guitar), Walter Page (string bass) and Jo Jones (drums). They were joined by several pianists, most often and most importantly Teddy Wilson, who organized many of Holiday's recording dates. They were also joined by either a distinguished clarinettist – Benny Goodman, Edmond Hall, Buster Bailey – or a trombonist drawn from Basie's ranks – Benny Morton, Dicky Wells. Volume 5 of the chronologically ordered CBS Jazz Masterpieces series provides a good sampling of their achievements.

These were neither cameo appearances by big names, playing anonymous roles subsidiary to the singer, nor the sort of all-star mish-mash heard from jazz magazine poll-winner bands, but completely integrated performances which encapsulate the very best of swing. Indeed it was normal for Holiday to sing the first chorus and then give the rest over to the instrumentalists, perhaps returning at the end to sing a half chorus, perhaps not. Perfectly matched to Holiday's approach, the instrumental work is characterized by relaxation and understatement in many respects: in the embroideries woven around Holiday's singing, in the solos, in the accompanimental riffs which occasionally appear in the background (for example, Clayton and Young at the start of *When You're Smiling*, Clayton and Morton later in the tune), and most strikingly at the end of pieces, in the mellow collectively improvised passages – the musicians' interpretation of this remnant of New Orleans jazz is the very antithesis of the wild Chicago style, with each contribution soft, cool, unintrusive.

Musically, there was an especially empathetic understanding between Holiday and tenor saxophonist Young. Always a melodic player, Young developed his ideas even more slowly and caressingly during these sessions than in his remarkable work with Basie. The very best of his playing on the Jazz Masterpieces collection is his solo on the third take of *When You're Smiling*, which for this and many other reasons, if it weren't such a dreadfully corny piece of fluff to start with, could be a candidate for Holiday's greatest recording.

Well before these sessions, Holiday had formulated her unique singing style, some elements of which proved widely influential, though no one else has come close to reproducing the whole package. What strikes first, like a hammer, is the emotional depth of her singing. Here in 1937–8, and increasingly so later, tragedy is at the centre of her experiences. She could turn around the meaning of songs, reconstructing phrases through her use of blues inflections and the lamenting timbre of her voice, to bring out the tragic side. On *He's Funny That Way*, it seems less likely that 'I got that man crazy about me', more likely that 'he'd be better off if I went away'. On *If Dreams Come True*, her droning, sad melody tells us they won't. On *When You're Smiling*, she cries out the words 'smiling' and 'smiles' over and over and over again, sending the message that these vaudeville-style smiles are the tears of a clown. She also worked with songs which were inherently tragic: *Trav'lin' all Alone*, with its grim lyrics covered by numerous minor chords, and *When a Woman Loves a Man*, with its punch line 'tell her she's a fool – she'll say "yes, but I love him so"', give a taste of what would later come in larger doses. Holiday brought utter conviction to a lyric. Who cannot believe her, when she sings that she's 'hoping he'll think it over, be satisfied with a simple sort of person on the sentimental side'? (Never mind that Holiday was scarcely a simple sort of person.) In marked contrast to her contemporary Ella Fitzgerald, she was never buoyantly cheerful, and one of the few unsuccessful tracks in this collection is the Fitzgerald-style ditty *Now They Call it Swing*. Looking forward with a vulnerable, guarded optimism towards a possible future love, as on *My First Impression of You* and *Back in your own Back Yard*, was about as far as she wanted to go.

The other half of the package is her musicality. The measure of a jazz singer who is not a scat singer (that is, who is not directly imitating a jazz instrument) is the ability to overhaul a given melody, and in this Holiday was superb. Usually hers was devastatingly better than the original. Though gifted with a hauntingly beautiful vocal tone and a trumpet-like articulation of notes, she had a narrow range, especially evident on *He's Funny That Way*, which is set at what is, for her, a high pitch. And so she worked on nuances of pitch and rhythm, rebuilding the contours of a song (generally flattening it out), swooping and sliding into notes in all sorts of ways, and generating a powerful sense of swing, largely by the seemingly paradoxical method of retreating further and further behind the beat. The clearest of the abundant examples is *When You're Smiling*, because, uncharacteristically for a jazz musician, trombonist Benny Morton first plays the theme absolutely straight as an arrow, thus affording a structure against which Holiday's subsequent demolition and reconstruction job may be viewed. Also especially revealing from this point of view is *My Man*, recorded during this period, but with a different group of all stars joining Clayton, Wilson and Page: pianist Wilson plays the melody while Holiday is singing, effectively wrapping her inventiveness in a rhythmic-melodic straightjacket, and dissipating the energy of the performance.

The balance had shifted by the time of Holiday's sessions of 1940–2 (all under her own name, not Wilson's). The accompaniments are still peppered with famous names – Young, Wilson, Roy Eldridge, Kenny Clarke, Eddie Heywood, Emmett Berry, Shad Collins, Jimmy Hamilton, Al Casey, J. C. Heard, Benny Carter – but there are plenty of lesser-known players as well, because the emphasis is no longer on something approaching a jam session among peers, but rather on Holiday, with her singing supported by set arrangements involving choirs of horns in sustained chords and moving lines. There is still a good deal of room for soloists, most often Heywood's restrained swinging on piano and most importantly Young's gripping double-time break on the last chorus of *All of Me*, but now the stars, Young and Eldridge, come out for briefer periods. One does not need a Lester Young for all of the horn playing here; less gifted players will do.

After several years' absence from Holiday's recording sessions Young returned for that of March 1941, which proved to be one of Holiday's greatest and, for her, one of her cheeriest. Of the many recordings of Hoagy Carmichael's hit song *Georgia on my Mind*, I think that only Ray

Charles's emotive soul and country version can stand up against Holiday's interpretation, which, taking a different tack from Charles, subtly lays out a spellbinding mood of wistful reminiscence. *All of Me* has a justifiably famous moment of rewriting by Holiday. She gives the song a deeper and sexier meaning by changing the words the second time around, from 'you took the part that once was my heart', to 'you took the best, so why not take the rest?'.

The next three sessions present some of the darkest moments in all of jazz. In the last, Holiday's tragic bent goes over the edge. *Mandy is Two* is an absolutely bizarre performance: a tearful lament on the occasion of a little girl's second birthday; on *It's a Sin to Tell a Lie,* I cannot help recalling Fats Waller's wonderful 'punch' line, already mentioned ('if you break my heart I'll break your jaw'), while she is singing, entirely seriously, 'if you break my heart I'll die'. But the tracks from the previous two, from May and August 1941, are profoundly beautiful, even if depressing. The outstanding performances are her own song *God Bless the Child,* a streetwise anthem to those who take care of themselves; *I Cover the Waterfront* (note, by contrast to the earlier recordings, that Holiday sings the whole way through this); and *Gloomy Sunday,* a dream about suicide.

In detailing the last two sessions, neither standard nor specialist discographies have noted the extent to which the reed players use clarinets, not saxes. It is not easy to pick out the details exactly, but I believe that in the August session the musicians used clarinets, picking up their saxes only momentarily for the break on *Jim,* though there is a tenor solo, probably by Russin, on *Love Me or Leave Me.* The clarinets return, with Russin again doubling for the tenor solos, on tracks 1 and 3 from February 1942. The mere fact of reed players doubling is nothing unusual, and indeed there are plenty of places in this book where we would not presume to untangle the uncertain details of who plays which wind instrument at which moment. But here I think the clarinets have a special significance, worth hearing: the arranger has used them mainly in their low register, their dark sound adding to Holiday's dark mood.

CD

***The Quintessential Billie Holiday, vol.5, 1937–1938,* Columbia Jazz Masterpieces CK 44423 (USA) and CBS Jazz Masterpieces 465190-2 (Europe)**

Buck Clayton (tpt), Edmond Hall (cl), Lester Young (ts), James Sherman (p), Freddie Green (g), Walter Page (sb), Jo Jones (d), Billie Holiday (v)

New York	15 June 1937	**Born to Love**
		Without your Love (take 1)

Buster Bailey (cl) replaces Hall, Claude Thornhill (p) replaces Sherman

13 Sept 1937 — **Getting Some Fun out of Life**
Who Wants Love?
Trav'lin' all Alone
He's Funny That Way

(Teddy Wilson:) Clayton (tpt), Prince Robinson (cl), Vido Musso (ts), Wilson (p), Allan Reuss (g), Page (sb), Cozy Cole (d), Holiday (v)

1 Nov 1937 — **Nice Work if You Can Get it**
Things are Looking up
My Man
Can't Help Lovin' dat Man

(Wilson:) Clayton (tpt), Benny Morton (tb), Young (ts), Wilson (p), Green (g), Page (sb), Jones (d), Holiday (v)

6 Jan 1938 — **My First Impression of You** (take 4)
When You're Smiling (take 3)
I Can't Believe that You're in Love with Me (take 4)
If Dreams Come True

*(Holiday:) as **My First Impression of You***

12 Jan 1938 — **Now They Call it Swing** (take 2)
On the Sentimental Side (take 2)
Back in your own Back Yard (take 1)
When a Woman Loves a Man

CD

***The Quintessential Billie Holiday, vol.9, 1940–1942*, Columbia Jazz Masterpieces CK 47031 (USA) and CBS Jazz Masterpieces 469049-2 (Europe)**

Bill Coleman (t), Morton (tb), Benny Carter (cl, as), Georgie Auld (ts), Sonny White (p), Ulysses Livingston (g), Wilson Myers (sb), Yank Porter (d), Holiday (v)

New York 15 Oct 1940 — **St Louis Blues** (take 1)
Loveless Love

Shad Collins (t), Leslie Johnakins, Eddie Barefield (as), Young (ts), Eddie Heywood (p), John Collins (g), Ted Sturgis (sb), Kenny Clarke (d), Holiday (v)

21 March 1941 — **Let's do it**
Georgia on my Mind
Romance in the Dark
All of Me

Roy Eldridge (tpt), Lester Boone, Jimmy Powell (as), Ernie Powell (ts), Heywood (p), Paul Chapman (g), Grachan Moncur (sb), Herbert Cowens (d), Holiday (v)

9 May 1941 — **I'm in a Low Down Groove**
God Bless the Child

Am I Blue?
Solitude

Emmett Berry (tpt), Jimmy Hamilton (cl), Hymie Schertzer (cl, as), Babe Russin (cl, ts), Teddy Wilson (p), Al Casey (g), John Williams (sb), J. C. Heard (d), Holiday (v)

7 Aug 1941 **Jim**
I Cover the Waterfront
Love Me or Leave Me
Gloomy Sunday

Gene Fields (g) replaces Casey

10 Feb 1942 **Wherever You Are**
Mandy is Two
It's a Sin to Tell a Lie
Until the Real Thing Comes Along

* * *

Coleman Hawkins: *Body and Soul; Classic Tenors: Coleman Hawkins and Lester Young*

During his decade with Fletcher Henderson's big band, Coleman Hawkins more than anyone else established the tenor saxophone as a solo instrument in jazz, but it was only after leaving Henderson in 1934 that he began to develop the fully mature style heard on sessions made in Paris in 1937, as well as on *Body and Soul* (1939) and *The Man I Love* (1943). The Parisian sessions are discussed in chapter 10 in the context of Benny Carter's album **Further Definitions**. These recordings are a mixed bag. Multi-instrumentalist Carter and guitarist Django Reinhardt are among Hawkins's sidemen on the Parisian session, and the excellent trumpeter Arthur Briggs solos alongside Hawkins on a session made there under Michel Warlop's direction two years earlier, but on these and other tracks from Hawkins's expatriate years the majority of his fellow players range from competent to barely adequate – Europe at the time not yet having developed a large enough pool of world-class players. How far they had yet to go may be heard on various anthologies including these sides, especially ones that also have the track *Blue Light Blues*; made in 1938 under Carter's leadership, with Alix Combelle taking Hawkins's role, it is – excepting Carter's masterful trumpet playing – filled with wrong notes and shows no sense of swing, and even Reinhardt struggles with the blues.

The masterpiece of Hawkins's career, *Body and Soul,* was made for Victor shortly after he returned to the USA from his five-year stay in Europe. The CD reissue on RCA's Bluebird label includes swing combo tracks from 1939–40, a mixed swing-bop session from 1947, plus additional tracks from 1956, when RCA recorded Hawkins in orchestral contexts irrelevant to the present chapter. In the pamphlet notes Dan Morgenstern surveys Hawkins's career and all these diverse tracks, and hence there is no need to cover the same ground here. Listeners should not be confused by Morgenstern's reference to a session from 1946 and a few titles from 1956. The additional tracks appear on a double LP for which he wrote these notes, but not on the CD reissue.

As the 1930s ended, Lester Young was offering a fully developed alternative to Hawkins's conception of tenor sax playing, but the generation he influenced had not yet hit the professional ranks. Hawkins, despite his absence from New York, remained the model for jazz tenor saxophone playing, and on *Body and Soul* he showed that he was still a force to be reckoned with. Some idea of its unique and revered position within the jazz community may be gained from the status of Hawkins's improvisation as the only notated solo to have been published three times in *Down Beat* magazine, so that players and listeners might study it in detail. If any performance ever demonstrated that jazz need not be integrated into a single unified whole, that an individual part can be greater than the sum of the rest, this is it. Hawkins's rhythm section is dull and the section of brass and reed instruments is abysmal, playing lethargic chords hopelessly out of tune. But Hawkins's effort is so profound, the rest doesn't matter a whit.

Hallmarks of the solo are his manipulation of timbre, volume, harmony and range. Over a slowly paced 64 bars (two choruses of the theme) his playing snowballs towards a tremendous climax. He begins softly, with a breathy sound and a small and controlled vibrato, in a moderately low register, and in at least the first sweep of the solo the opening phrase of the melody of *Body and Soul* is easily recognized. Quickly it disappears, giving way to faster-moving new lines embroidered around the song's chord progression. Hawkins gradually alters his sound, getting louder, adding an edge to his tone, growling through the instrument, widening and loosening his vibrato and aiming towards a climax which falls on a pitch just above the 'normal' range of the instrument. (After decades of screaming tenor saxes in rhythm and blues, soul music and free jazz, any young player worth his salt can hit this note cleanly; at the time Hawkins's control was authoritative.) A brief cadenza ties up the solo by spinning sequentially through a chromatic descent, in the process summarizing Hawkins's preference for creating abstract melodies by playing out chords rather than playing tunes.

The LP (and now CD) **Classic Tenors: Coleman Hawkins and Lester Young** collects together low fidelity sessions made for the little label Signature before the musicians' union had finished settling its strike against the major companies. All but one of the tracks by Hawkins or Young are of minor importance to the careers of those great tenor saxophonists, but the one exception, *The Man I Love,* is so significant that this anthology has been reissued time and time again.

By the end of 1943 Charlie Parker, playing alto sax in the style which came to be known as bop, was beginning to turn around saxophonists' notions of how jazz might be played, and Hawkins himself would soon follow in that direction, as would the bassist and drummer in the quartet that recorded *The Man I Love*, Oscar Pettiford and Shelly Manne. In fact, at that very moment Pettiford was co-leading a combo with Dizzy Gillespie. But *The Man I Love* gives no inkling that a change was in the air. It is a classic of swing combo playing. By contrast with *Body and Soul,* here the accompanists are superb, and furthermore Hawkins has adjusted the nature of the accompaniment to the florid style of his solo playing. Both tunes are meant to be slow ballads, but *The Man I Love* is in double time, with the tempo twice as fast but the harmonies moving along at their normal deliberate rate (so that the 32-bar song becomes a 64-bar song).

Even though he is using brushes, not sticks, Manne establishes a vigorous swing rhythm on the snare and bass drums. With Pettiford playing walking lines and Hawkins holding notes softly in the background, pianist Eddie Heywood, obviously inspired by the opportunity to accompany Hawkins, launches into a deep, original solo. In a few spots he refers to fragments of the melody, but he concentrates on an approach which provides a refreshing compromise between repeating riffs and spinning out ever-new melodies: his crisply articulated right-hand phrases are more complicated than typical swing riffs, yet he is not reluctant to repeat a phrase, perhaps with a change in ornamentation, or at a higher or lower pitch.

The recording balance changes at the end of Heywood's choruses to capture Pettiford's solo. There was plenty of precedent by this time for a string bassist to put aside the bass line for a chorus and create a melody instead. Such players as Israel Crosby (with Gene Krupa), Milt Hinton (with Cab Calloway) and Jimmy Blanton (with Duke Ellington) had recorded solos. But, for the first time in Pettiford's agile solo (just as for the first time in Blanton's ensemble playing), everything is in place: intonation, tone quality, swing, mature ideas and melodic phrasing (the last marked by his gasping for breath, as if he were blowing a horn). Appropriately it is Pettiford, not Heywood or Hawkins, who pays close attention to the song's melody, paraphrasing a portion of it to begin the second half of his solo.

Hawkins finishes up the piece. His solo emphasizes another side of his musical personality: forthright, hard swinging, driving on top of the beat. Since Heywood and Pettiford have already started things churning there is no need to begin gently, and thus Hawkins starts at a higher intensity than on *Body and Soul*. All the other essentials of that most famous solo remain central to his aesthetic: weaving arabesques around the chord progression, widening his vibrato, and adding edge to his tone, with a special harshness reserved for climactic high notes.

CD

***Body and Soul*, Bluebird 5717-2 RB (USA) and ND 85717 (Europe)**

Tommy Lindsay, Joe Guy (tpt), Earl Hardy (tb), Jackie Fields, Eustis Moore (as), Coleman Hawkins (ts), Gene Rodgers (p), Oscar Smith (sb), Art Herbert (d)

New York	11 Oct 1939	**Meet Doctor Foo**
		Fine Dinner
add Thelma Carpenter (v)		**She's Funny that Way**
omit Carpenter		**Body and Soul**

Benny Carter (tpt), J. C. Higginbotham (tb), Danny Polo (cl), Hawkins (ts), Rodgers (p), Lawrence Lucie (g), Johnny Williams (sb), Walter Johnson (d)

	3 Jan 1940	**When Day is Done**
		The Sheik of Araby
		My Blue Heaven
		Bouncing with Bean

Fats Navarro (tpt), J. J. Johnson (tb), Budd Johnson (as), Marion DeVeta (bar), Hank Jones (p), Chuck Wayne (g), Jack Lesberg (sb), Max Roach (d), Tadd Dameron (arr)

	11 Dec 1947	**April in Paris**
		How Strange
		Half Step Down Please
		Angel Face
		Jumping for Jane
Hawkins, Jones, Wayne, Lesberg, Roach		**I Love You**

Jimmy Nottingham (tpt), Urbie Green, Tom Mitchell, Fred Ohms, Jack Satterfield (tb), Julius Baker, Sid Jekowsky (fl), Phil Bodner (oboe), Hawkins (ts), Paul Gershman, Leo Kruczek, Harry Lookofsky, Gene Orloff, Tosha Samaroff (vln), Izzy Zir (viola), Alan Schulman (cello), Hank Jones (p), Barry Galbraith (elg), Milt Hinton (sb), Osie Johnson (d), Marty Wilson (vb), Billy Byers (arr, conductor)

	17 Jan 1956	**There will never be another you**
		Little Girl Blue
		Dinner for one please, James

Bernie Glow, Lou Oles, Ernie Royal, Charlie Shavers, Nick Travis (tpt), Green, Ohms, Satterfield, Chauncey Welsh (tb), Hal McKusick, Sam Marowitz, Zoot Sims, Al Cohn, Sol Schlinger (reeds), Hawkins (ts), Jones (p), Galbraith (elg), Hinton (sb), Johnson (d), Wilson (vb), Byers (arr, conductor)

	18 Jan 1956	**His Very Own Blues**
		39″–25″–39″
		The Bean Stalks Again

Jimmy Buffington (french horn), Baker (fl), Bodner (oboe), Jekowsky (cl), Hawkins (ts), Orloff, Samaroff, Gershman, Dave Newman, Alvin Rudnitsky, Arnold Eidus, Max Hollander, Max Cahn, Cy Miroff, Stan Kraft, Dave Sarser (vln), Bert Fisch (viola), George Ricci, Bernie Greenhouse, Edgardo Sodero (cello), Jones (p), Lesberg (sb), Johnson (d), Wilson (vb)

	20 Jan 1956	**Have you met Miss Jones?**
		Body and Soul
		The Essence of You

CD

***Classic Tenors: Coleman Hawkins and Lester Young*, CBS Special Products AK 38446, Doctor Jazz WK 38446, and Signature AK 38446 (USA)**

Bill Coleman (t), Andy Fitzgerald (cl), Hawkins (ts), Ellis Larkins (p), Al Casey (g), Oscar Pettiford (sb), Shelly Manne (d)

New York	8 Dec 1943	**Voodte**
		How Deep is the Ocean
		Hawkins' Barrel House
		Stumpy

(Dickie Wells:) Coleman (tpt), Wells (tb), Lester Young (ts), Larkins (p), Freddie Green (g), Al Hall (sb), Jo Jones (d)

	21 Dec 1943	**I got rhythm**
		I'm fer it too
		Hello Babe
		Linger Awhile

Hawkins (ts), Eddie Heywood (p), Pettiford (sb), Manne (d)

	23 Dec 1943	**Crazy Rhythm**
		Get Happy
		The Man I Love
		Sweet Lorraine

* * *

Chu Berry: *A Giant of the Tenor Sax*; Ben Webster and Don Byas: *Giants of the Tenor Sax*

Soon after Victor and Columbia began the widespread dissemination of jazz by recording the Original Dixieland Jazz Band in 1917, there emerged a succession of small companies recording jazz. In ever-changing combinations the independents remained a part of the jazz landscape until the depression, when they either went bankrupt or were absorbed into the majors. Their permanent return was marked by the establishment at the beginning of 1938 of the Commodore label, an outgrowth of Milt Gabler's activities as owner of the Commodore Music Shop in New York. Owing to Gabler's devotion to improvised small combo jazz and his perceptive, tasteful selection of musicians, it became one of the most important jazz labels of its era.

Among many outstanding tracks on Commodore are two sessions led by Chu Berry while he worked as the featured tenor saxophonist in Cab Calloway's big band. Although these two sessions took place in the studio, they epitomize the spirit of the swing jam sessions that were then flourishing. In the first, later in 1938, Berry teamed up with his good friend trumpeter Roy Eldridge, formerly a colleague in the big bands of Teddy Hill and Fletcher Henderson. In the second, two months before Berry's death in an automobile accident in 1941, his partner was Hot Lips Page, who had just joined Artie Shaw's big band.

This collection invites a consideration of the question of invention and repetition, since there are two versions of six of the eight tracks. I must confess that, unlike many devoted listeners, I am not automatically enamoured of alternate takes; even for someone as spectacularly inventive as Charlie Parker, I find the reward of listening to his ever-new solos on five takes of *Billie's Bounce* somewhat dampened by the drudgery of hearing the theme played again and again and again. Happily, this is not a problem on Berry's sessions. These are free-wheeling performances and most of the alternate takes are drastically altered.

Following a time-honoured tradition of musicians angling for extra money from royalties, Gabler and Page claim credit as composers for *Sittin' In* (based on the 'hold that tiger' strain of *Tiger Rag*), *Forty-six West Fifty-two* (based on *Sweet Georgia Brown*), *Blowing up a Breeze* (based on *I Got Rhythm*) and *Monday at Minton's* (a blues). The claim is not outrageous, since all that is borrowed each time is a chord progression. The players avoid familiar melodies, as they plunge right into improvising at the start, and the only remotely thematic elements are some riffs traded between Berry and Page at the end of *Blowing up a Breeze* and *Monday at Minton's*. With one exception this philosophy carries over into the other performances, in which the notion of a fixed theme never advances further than a preset piano or guitar introduction or the extremely loose paraphrase of the melodies of *Star Dust* and *Body and Soul*. The exception is Page's prearranged solo and singing on the first half of both versions of *Gee Baby Ain't I Good to You*.

Berry was strongly influenced by Coleman Hawkins. He used a less pronounced vibrato than Hawkins, though it becomes heavy in his renditions of ballads. He was somewhat less overtly passionate, and this difference is heightened in the first session. Set against Eldridge, who is a firecracker, Berry sounds positively cool. This sense of restraint comes across in another way on *Monday at Minton's*, with Page, in which Berry's playing points towards the emerging rhythm and blues tenor saxophone style, but without crossing over into raucousness. And these recordings suggest that Berry could not handle fast tempos as well as

Hawkins. His rhythmic drive is impressive throughout, but as the tempo increases the shape of his melodies grows simpler, so that on two versions of *Sittin' In* he gets stuck repeating two-, three- or four-note figures when continuously moving lines might have provided more interest. By contrast, his melodic invention on slow tunes is creative and sophisticated. *Body and Soul,* recorded before Hawkins's famous version, begins strongly, Berry improvising at his best. Upon entering, Eldridge kicks up the tempo about two and a half times (rather than strictly double timing), with the result that Berry is hurried when he returns at half of this new tempo. There are no such glitches in *On the Sunny Side of the Street,* and the two sentimental versions afford a chance to hear Berry at his most inventive; except for a few fragments (for example, the beginning and ending of his second solo on each track, and the descent from a dramatic high point), the alternate take is entirely new and just as beautifully played.

The great tragedy of Eldridge's career was the well-publicized mid-1940s battle between the adherents of bop and the New Orleans revival, which had the side effect of forcing swing combo musicians into one camp or the other. Eldridge reluctantly abandoned swing tunes for a more traditional repertory. These earlier Commodore recordings testify how well he thrived on swing, and at the time – that is, in 1938 – he was the leading trumpet soloist in that style. On these tracks he is an exciting improviser, not at all daunted by fast tempos; indeed, on *Body and Soul,* where he throws Berry a curve, and also on *Sittin' In,* where he ignores the tempo of the introduction, he seems to be saying 'no, let's take this one faster'. Regardless of speed, he is consistently inventive, negotiating difficult leaps and fast lines which he sets against rhythmically charged repeated notes and dramatic high climaxes. He uses a mute for the opening solo on *Forty-six West Fifty-two* (in which, incidentally, about half of his solo recurs on the alternate take), but otherwise he plays with a bright, open tone, sometimes adding a burred edge to intensify his sound further.

Page is a simpler, more traditional player than Eldridge, and his improvising draws heavily from swing and blues riffs, recalling his more significant work as a soloist with the Bennie Moten and Count Basie big bands. In both sessions pianist Clyde Hart takes solos. In the main these present a functional style which provides a textural contrast to the horns' leading role; the best are on the ballad versions of *On the Sunny Side of the Street,* especially take 2. All these are fully in the swing style, with no indication as yet of Hart's involvement with bop. There are also brief drum and bass solos, but in the main the rhythm sections keep to an accompanimental role, laying down a solid, steady foundation.

The fidelity of these tracks is, for prewar technology, excellent. Throughout jazz recording, turntables have rotated at non-standard speeds, and some listeners may note that gremlins were at work on at least one track here: take 2 of *Forty-six West Fifty-two* is not merely slower than take 1, but at a lower pitch, thus indicating that something slipped in the long chain of mechanical steps between the making of the 78 rpm master and its remastering in modern formats.

A second Commodore collection presents the results of three sessions, two of which were originally recorded in the studio for that label in 1944: drummer Sid Catlett's quartet featuring tenor saxophonist Ben Webster, and Hot Lips Page's septet featuring tenor saxophonist Don Byas. The third segment is an excerpt from and the best part of a concert given at Town Hall in New York the following year, and it also features Byas, in duets with bassist Slam Stewart, and in a trio with Teddy Wilson added.

The four titles on the Catlett–Webster sessions were recorded during a period when the two men were working together at the Onyx Club in New York. These follow the spirit and format of Chu Berry's Commodore sessions. The few dull moments are John Simmons's walking bass solos and Catlett's tune *Just a Riff*, based largely on a plodding riff which forces the players into a long series of disconnected phrases, until Webster finally manages to build a solo in phrases which cut across the riff. The remainder of the session is magnificent, if possible surpassing Berry's. Again the emphasis is on improvised swing, with alternate and substantially new takes of the other three titles.

Catlett, who also accompanied Berry and Eldridge six years earlier, is the leader here and thus has a greater opportunity to show off his command of the swing style, particularly through his intricate snare drumming on several solos. The pianist is Marlowe Morris, whose playing here, and also with Catlett, Simmons, Lester Young and others in the film *Jammin' the Blues* this same year, marks his greatest contribution to recorded jazz. By setting fleet melodies against sparse chords in his solos, Morris suggests the growing influence of bop pianists on other New York musicians in 1944, but he displays none of the rhythmic trickiness of bop. Morris worked alone often. In this capacity he is one of the local players who might be mentioned in the same breath as Art Tatum, and here he occasionally quotes from Tatum's work (as for example in the droning figure in the second half of his solo on the first take of *Sleep*).

The star of the session is Webster. A comparison of alternate takes finds him inventing complex and convincing new melodies throughout these performances, and, unlike Berry, he is equally comfortable with the fast-tempoed *Sleep*, the medium-tempoed *Linger Awhile* and the ballad *Memories of You*. His sound is full of contrasts. These contrasts might build progressively, as on the two versions of *Sleep*. His opening statements of the melody and the solos that follow are delivered with a gentle tone and a pronounced, but not heavy, vibrato; when he returns, following Catlett's solos, he adds a growl to his tone, and this leads to ferocious climaxes on a repeated high note (which occurs earlier in take 1 than in take 2). Or the change may be sudden, as in the leap from hard-edged solo playing to a tender melodic phrase at the end of *Linger Awhile* and the explosive rip upwards inserted into the midst of the first take of his otherwise caressing version of *Memories of You*.

The remaining tracks include Page's bright, joyful blues singing and solos on *You Need Coachin'*, as well as alto saxophonist Earl Bostic's incongruous fast-running, unswinging, non-bluesy solo on that same title. But the focus is on Don Byas: his relaxed solo on *You Need Coachin'*, his soft sumptuous ballad playing on *These Foolish Things* and *Candy*, and his fleet variations on *Indiana* and *I Got Rhythm*. These last two titles, the duets with Stewart, follow an identical format. Stewart sets out a bass line, and, indeed, here the resemblance is more literal than intended: *Indiana* begins with the first 16 bars of the bass line of *I Got Rhythm*! Byas then launches into the melody of *Indiana* and Stewart follows along in a blink. On both titles Byas plays the theme clearly before improvising in a nearly perpetual motion manner that points towards the technical facility and some of the harmonic imagination of bop saxophonists, but again, as with Morris, lacks the surprising accentuation that would be peppered throughout a characteristic bop solo. While Byas plays, Stewart keeps up a strong bass line, sometimes using a slap bass technique to add a percussive effect in the absence of drums. Sandwiched between Byas's improvisation is Stewart's melodic solo, bowed and hummed simultaneously in the humorous style which is ever present in his work. If the two ballads are far less exciting than these two duets, their melodic content is certainly far more substantial. In his gentle, breathy sound and his florid imagination, Byas here invites comparison with any of his rivals on the instrument.

These Commodore sessions keep appearing and reappearing in anthologies of swing tenor saxophonists: Berry alone; Berry and Webster; Berry and Lucky Thompson; Webster and Byas. Byas's tracks have also been reissued within the context of the concert at Town Hall in New York, where he recorded the duos with Stewart. Some discs include alternate takes, and others offer master takes only. The two most closely related CD reissues are listed after the discographies of the main selections.

CD

A Giant of the Tenor Sax, Commodore 8.24293 (Germany)

Roy Eldridge (tpt), Chu Berry (ts), Clyde Hart (p), Danny Barker (g), Artie Shapiro (sb), Sid Catlett (d)

New York	11 Nov 1941	**Sittin' In**
		Sittin' In no.2
		Star Dust
		Body and Soul
		Forty-six West Fifty-two
		Forty-six West Fifty-two no.2

Hot Lips Page (tpt), Berry (ts), Hart (p), Albert Casey (g), Al Morgan (sb), Harry Jaeger (d)

New York	Sept 1941	**Blowing up a Breeze**
		Blowing up a Breeze no.2
omit Page		**On the Sunny Side of the Street**
		On the Sunny Side of the Street no.2
add Page		**Monday at Minton's**
		Monday at Minton's no.2
*as **Monday at Minton's**, but Page (tpt, v)*		**Gee Baby, Ain't I Good to You**
		Gee Baby, Ain't I Good to You no.2

CD

Ben Webster and Don Byas: *Giants of the Tenor Sax*, Commodore CCD 7005 (USA)

Ben Webster (ts), Marlowe Morris (p), John Simmons (sb), Sid Catlett (d)

New York	18 March 1944	**Sleep**
		Sleep no.2
		Linger Awhile
		Memories of You
		Just a Riff

Hot Lips Page (tpt), Don Byas (ts), Earl Bostic, B. G. Hammond (as), Clyde Hart (p), Al Lucas (sb), Jack Parker (d)

New York	29 Sept 1944	**Six, Seven, Eight or Nine**
		You Need Coachin'
omit Page, Bostic, Hammond		**These Foolish Things**

Byas (ts), Slam Stewart (sb)

New York	9 June 1945	**Indiana**
		I Got Rhythm
add Teddy Wilson (p)		**Candy**

Other CDs

incl. Berry's and Webster's tracks, master takes only:
(Webster and Berry:) *Classics in Swing: Ben Webster – Chu Berry*
Commodore 9031-72726-2 (Germany)
incl. Berry's tracks, master takes only, but both takes of **On the Sunny Side of the Street:**
(Berry and Lucky Thompson:) *Giants of the Tenor Sax*, Commodore CCD 7004 (USA)

* * *

Nat 'King' Cole: *Jumpin' at Capitol: The Best of the King Cole Trio*

Nat 'King' Cole had two careers. In 1937 he founded a swing trio in which he played piano alongside guitarist Oscar Moore and string bassist Wesley Prince; all three men also sang. In 1951, after only a few changes of bassists, and up to that point still with Moore, Cole abandoned the trio to devote himself fully to an activity he had taken up a few years earlier, singing romantic popular music to the accompaniment of studio orchestras. An anthology on the Rhino label focuses on his first, lesser-known career.

Bassist Johnny Miller replaced Prince on Cole's first hit, *Straighten up and Fly Right*. His own composition, it was a pioneering performance on the rhythm-and-blues edge of swing, though the term 'rhythm and blues' was not yet in currency when he recorded the song towards the end of 1943, just as the American Federation of Musicians was beginning to settle their strike against recording companies. Ostensibly about a buzzard and a monkey, *Straighten up and Fly Right* has a harmless pop quality about it and could easily be taken for a cute animal song. But it takes no great stretch of the imagination to hear the lyric as a metaphor for race relations in the USA, and Cole pops out the climactic break with a cool, streetwise air: 'your story's so touching, but it sounds just like a lie'.

Two weeks later, he was in the studio again, blending smoothly into the mainstream of American popular music with relaxed swing versions of *Sweet Lorraine* and *It's Only a Paper Moon* and a sensuous reading of the ballad *Embraceable You*, on all of which he sticks closely to the familiar melodies in carefully enunciated performances that focus on the mellow beauty of his voice. These, together with another slow ballad recorded in 1946, *For Sentimental Reasons*, show that the equipment for his second career was already fully in place.

As instrumentalists, the members of the trio achieved a marvellous sense of swing, setting feet tapping without the aid of a drummer. Only in those passages where Cole and Moore repeatedly pound out a riff does there seem to be a need for the contrasting rhythmic patterns that a swing drummer could supply. Moore's basic approach relied heavily on the standards of tone and single-note technique set by Charlie Christian, but he also provided strong support as a strumming rhythm guitarist (which Christian did not), and harmonically he was further down the line towards bop. Cole's approach was centred around the transitional swing-to-bop manner of a fast running right-hand line accompanied by sparsely placed fragments of chords in the left. He was one of the greatest pianists of his era.

A portion of the Rhino anthology – *Jumpin' at Capitol, I'm a Shy Guy, Come to Baby, do, The Frim Fram Sauce* – perpetuates a longstanding problem, whereby Cole's performances were imperfectly mastered, so that tempo, pitch and tone quality are respectively too fast, too high, too thin. These four tracks were repaired in the exhaustive collection on the Mosaic label, listed below. Happily the best tracks on the Rhino disc do not suffer from this problem.

CD

***Jumpin' at Capitol: The Best of the Nat King Cole Trio*, Rhino R2 71009 (USA)**

Nat 'King' Cole (p, v), Oscar Moore (elg), Red Callender (sb)		
Los Angeles	11 Oct 1942	**All for You**
Cole (p, v), Moore (elg, v), Johnny Miller (sb, v)		
	30 Nov 1943	**Straighten up and Fly Right**
Cole (p, v), Moore (elg), Miller (sb)		**Gee Baby, Ain't I Good to You**
omit (v)		**Jumpin' at Capitol**
add Cole (v)		**If You Can't Smile and Say Yes**
	15 Dec 1943	**Sweet Lorraine**
		Embraceable You
		It's Only a Paper Moon
omit (v)	17 Jan 1944	**What is This Thing Called Love?**
Cole (p, v), Moore (elg), Miller (sb)		
	13 April 1945	**I'm a Shy Guy**
New York	11 Oct 1945	**Come to Baby, do**
		The Frim Fram Sauce

Cole (p, v), Moore (elg, v), Miller (sb, v)

Los Angeles	15 March 1946	**Route 66!**

Cole (p, v), Moore (elg), Miller (sb)

New York	22 Aug 1946	**For Sentimental Reasons**
Los Angeles	6 Aug 1947	**When I Take My Sugar to Tea**

Ernie Royal (tpt), Charlie Barnet (ts), Cole (p, v), Irving Ashby (elg), Joe Comfort (sb), Earl Hyde (d), Nellie Lutcher (v)

	5 Jan 1950	**For You, My Love**

Other CDs

plus additional tracks:

The Complete Capitol Recordings of the Nat King Cole Trio, Mosaic MD 18-138 (USA)

* * *

Scott Hamilton, Jake Hanna and Dave McKenna: *Major League*

The span of the present chapter suddenly leaps four decades beyond the swing era, from the 1930s and 1940s into the 1980s, while remaining firmly tied stylistically to the sound of that era, as represented by a trio headed by tenor saxophonist Scott Hamilton. Since 1977, Hamilton has been making consistently fine albums for the Concord label, among which **Major League** provides an excellent place to start listening. Hamilton shares the billing equally with Jake Hanna, whose crisp drumming is perfectly recorded on this disc, and Dave McKenna, but clearly the spotlight is mostly on the saxophonist.

Somehow Hamilton received an intuitive insight into the style, enabling him to extract and recombine the most attractive features of the playing of the four or five best tenor saxophonists of the swing era. On this CD, the strongest influences are evidently Ben Webster and Lester Young. Hamilton recalls Webster most clearly in the breathy and unabashed romanticism of his ballad playing on *I'm through with love* and *This is all I ask,* and in his growling and emotional sound at the end of *Linger Awhile.* From Young come specific little gestures scattered about his improvisations (for example, during *Cocktails for Two,* an abrupt repeated note, beginning firmly on the downbeat of the measure), and more importantly, the absolutely perfect sense of melodic swing that he displays on *Cocktails for Two, Linger Awhile,* and *September in the Rain*. A whole school of saxophonists of the mid-1940s onwards had started from Young's conception but then mixed in elements of bop soloing – among them Brew Moore (closest to Young), Al Cohn, Zoot Sims, and Stan Getz (most independent and able to remake Young's approach into his own personal style). Hamilton, by contrast, has penetrated directly to the original, remarkably almost as if bop had never happened.

CD

***Major League*, Concord CCD-4305 (USA)**

Scott Hamilton (ts), Dave McKenna (p), Jake Hanna (d)

Boston	May 1986	**Swinging at the Copper Rail**
		A pretty girl is like a melody
		Cocktails for Two
		I'm through with love
		Linger awhile
		September in the Rain
		This is all I ask
		It all depends on you
		April in Paris

CHAPTER 5

We Called it Music: Dixieland and Swing

Digby Fairweather

We Called it Music was the self-effacing title chosen by guitarist Eddie Condon for his autobiography and a subsequent companion LP collection. Knowing the quality of jazz that Condon and the musicians who surrounded him always played, it's inconceivable now that anyone in our music's history could ever have called it anything else. Condon-style was a well-shaken cocktail of classic jazz freedoms stiffened with the sophistication of swing, and the swing era represents the great coming-out party for jazz – the 1930s years when she grew, instrumentally and conceptually, from rough-edged tomboyism to fully matured womanhood. Technical skills advanced, knowledge grew, and a whole bright generation from Benny Goodman to Harry James and their groundbreaking confrères established new state-of-the-art standards in some cases never to be surpassed. The sort of musicians who turn up in this chapter were – or are – contemporaries or sons of the swing era – young masters who grew up and shaped up in the generation closely following on after such true innovators as Armstrong, Noone, Hines, Teagarden and a few others. And consequently their music was technically equipped to express all the joyful new creative thoughts flooding their imagination. Bob Haggart, one of the great creators of the genre under discussion here, summed up the end-results blossoming in the music: 'What is there *not* to like?' he asked once. At that point Haggart was talking about *his* kind of 'dixieland', and the term is a controversial one, with at least two definitions, which was disliked and disowned by several of the jazz giants who turn up in these essays, notably Bobby Hackett! So, a definition: 'dixieland', for the purposes of this chapter, is neither classic New Orleans jazz nor the Euro-American tradition of revivalism. At the arranged end, it is the musical reinventions of Bob Crosby, Matty Matlock and their followers, and, at the free end, the free-for-all creativity born of sophistication applied to classic jazz principles for which Eddie Condon was the figurehead. It is the music of 'Jamboree Jones', of Muggsy's 'Great Sixteen', of Chicago and New York and of the grand jazz masters as well as their followers, from Charlie Lavere to Dick Cathcart, Billy Maxted and Rosy McHargue. They called it music – and jazz was never richer than when they did.

* * *

Bob Crosby: *Jazz Classics in Digital Stereo: Bob Crosby, 1937 to 1938*

For lovers of what is popularly (but sometimes confusingly) called 'dixieland', Bob Crosby's orchestra and small group, the Bobcats, are held in especially affectionate regard. This is logical, because Crosby's two ensembles were based on classic jazz designs and formed a dixieland oasis in the big-band years, well away from the blander trappings of swing written into the act by Tommy Dorsey, Benny Goodman or even Artie Shaw. Indeed, Crosby's band could lay some legitimate claim to having founded the American jazz revival. Much of its repertoire drew largely from classic jazz sources and several of its cornermen – Eddie Miller, Nappy Lamare, Ray Bauduc and Irving Fazola – came from New Orleans. And even though these players – as well as others such as Yank Lawson and Bob Haggart – grew up in the swing era, their formative influences had been the classic jazz of Armstrong, Oliver, Jimmie Noone and others.

The things that set Crosby's joyful music apart from fully fledged revivalism, of course, were its technical sophistication (founder-members of his organization were ex-members of Ben Pollack's highly proficient band) and a collection of written arrangements. These served most of all to create a separate developmental heritage of dixieland, running down through Muggsy Spanier's Ragtimers, Bud Freeman's Summa Cum Laude Orchestra and the Lawson–Haggart Jazz Band, via the brilliant creations of Crosby staff arranger Matty Matlock and finally to the World's Greatest Jazz Band (again of Lawson and Haggart), which finally disbanded in 1978. This line inspired a whole coterie of international imitators (including British players Sid Phillips and Harry Gold) and created a genre for itself quite separate from the deliberate or natural archaism of Lu Watters or Bunk Johnson and George Lewis.

Perhaps the best illustration of this difference is *South Rampart Street Parade*, a brilliantly conceived sound-picture of a New Orleans street parade which sets the standard features of the genre – free clarinet, parade drums and tailgate trombone against trumpet lead – into a totally sophisticated paraphrase that achieves new effects of its own. And this unique mix of revivalism and swing sophistication, of course, carries on through producer Robert Parker's representative collection of Crosby titles. Numbers such as *Gin Mill Blues* and *Dogtown Blues,* with their catalogue of cunningly played New Orleans-isms, perfectly illustrate one of the many essential points in John Chilton's liner note: that 'the band's rule was to discard any part of a score that sounded ostentatious or superfluous – the result was tough honest music that abounded with feeling'. The coda of *Gin Mill Blues,* with its throwaway lyric diminuendo, is a fine example of the sort of minutia of dixieland composition which is now a completely lost art. *Honky Tonk Train Blues* remains the definitive big-band development of the Meade 'Lux' Lewis piano solo original, and *Squeeze Me,* with its delicate playing by Zurke and perfect performance by Eddie Miller, is a definition of big-band dixieland. Only *Swingin' at the Sugar Bowl* (featuring Nappy Lamare's likeable singing and more fine Miller tenor) reverts to standard swing formats.

Twelve of Parker's 18 tracks feature the Bobcats' state-of-the-art small-group dixieland – a sometimes indistinguishable mix of cunning scoring and flyaway ad lib, all played with unflagging intensity and conviction. A few classic highpoints among dozens are Lawson's climactic two-note lead towards the close of *Five Point Blues* (like a man too overcome with emotion to express thought); Zurke's *Big Foot Jump,* which recalls the delicate stride of Willie 'the Lion' Smith; and more perfect dixie scoring in *Slow Mood* (to which Johnny Mercer later added words as *Lazy Mood*) and *Can't We be Friends?*. The dozens of other written finesses – such as the short, potent scored passages at either end of *Who's Sorry Now?* – are Bob Crosby-style jazz at its definitively greatest.

CD

***Jazz Classics in Digital Stereo: Bob Crosby, 1937 to 1938*, BBC CD 688 (UK)**

Andy Ferretti, Yank Lawson (tpt), Ward Silloway, Mark Bennett (tb), Gil Rodin, Matty Matlock (cl, as), Noni Bernardi (as), Eddie Miller (cl, ts), Deane Kincaide (ts), Bob Zurke (p), Nappy Lamare (g), Bob Haggart (sb), Ray Bauduc (d)

New York	8 Feb 1937	**Gin Mill Blues**

Zeke Zarchy, Billy Butterfield, Lawson (tpt), Silloway, Warren Smith (tb), Matlock (cl, as), Joe Kearns (as), Miller (cl, ts), Rodin (ts), Zurke (p), Lamare (g), Haggart (sb), Bauduc (d)

Los Angeles	5 Nov 1937	**Squeeze Me** (arr Haggart)

(Bob Cats:) Lawson (tpt), Smith (tb), Matlock (cl), Miller (cl, ts), Zurke (p), Lamare (g), Haggart (sb), Bauduc (d)

	9 Nov 1937	**Stumbling**

as ***Stumbling****, but Miller (ts)*

Who's Sorry Now?
Coquette
Fidgety Feet
You're Driving Me Crazy
Can't We be Friends?

as ***Squeeze Me****, but Charlie Spivak (tpt) replaces Zarchy*

	16 Nov 1937	**South Rampart Street Parade** (arr Kincaide and Haggart)
		Dogtown Blues

(Bob Cats:) as ***Stumbling****, but Irving Fazola (cl) replaces Matlock, Haig Stephens (sb) replaces Haggart*

New York	14 March 1938	**March of the Bob Cats**
		Slow Mood
		Big Foot Jump
		The Big Crash from China
		Five Point Blues

Haggart (sb, whistling), Bauduc (d)

Chicago	14 Oct 1938	**The Big Noise from Winnetka**

Zarchy, Sterling Bose, Butterfield (tpt), Silloway, Smith (tb), Fazola (cl), Kearns (as), Miller (cl, ts), Rodin (ts), Zurke (p), Lamare (g, v), Haggart (sb), Bauduc (d)

	19 Oct 1938	**Swingin' at the Sugar Bowl**

omit (v)

Honky Tonk Train Blues (arr Matlock)

* * *

Muggsy Spanier: *At the Jazz Band Ball: Chicago/New York Dixieland*

The 16 titles recorded by Muggsy Spanier's Ragtime Band for RCA Victor in July, November and December 1939 are hallowed classic jazz. After their issue, critics called Spanier's band 'the greatest since King Oliver's', and time has done nothing to diminish the 'Great Sixteen'; they remain for many listeners the finest dixieland on record – a pinnacle of stylistic expression which helped refocus attention on traditional jazz values amid the swing era and which led on, within a year, to the American jazz revival. Four of Spanier's 16 titles were recorded in Chicago on 7 July 1939 while the Ragtimers were resident at the

Sherman Hotel's Old Town Room, the remainder in New York after the band had moved on to Nick's club for a short residency. And every one is a cornucopia of dixieland perfection, full of dedicated musical intensity as much as of the choreographed detail which comes from nightly performance: a tightly knit ensemble, scored sustained tones behind solos (especially Spanier's), dynamic observation, and sudden texture changes in mid-performance creating the effect of electric light turned on to illuminate the dark area of a room. Spanier played the perfect lead cornet; his spare punchy phrasing, underpinned by a perfect sense of time and note-placement, was delivered in a broad, attractively sour-edged tone, and around this faithful lead his sidemen hung their ensemble lines in relaxed decorative compliment.

Just how perfectly this worked can be heard on *At Sundown*, in which it is difficult after repeated hearings to decide which parts of the ensemble opening statements were formalized and which not. *At Sundown* indeed represents one peak of the 'Great Sixteen'. It is a crafted performance which moves from fast-trot introduction to galloping ensemble; there are scored riffs behind Nick Caiazza (on tenor) and in contrary motion behind Cless (clarinet) before a bridge and key change to Bushkin's all-American piano solo, which echoes Basie for 16 bars before gambolling off into joyful dixieland expression. The great biting entry of Spanier's cornet leads to a controlled ensemble diminuendo, at which point Cless's clarinet takes over the lead for just three bars before reverting to harmony for an operatically voiced false ending. This leads the piece in near-ecstasy to a reprise capped with a mock-modest 'that's all' coda.

Were this the only side Muggsy Spanier's Ragtimers had ever recorded their reputation would be assured, but spread among the 15 others there are dozens of similarly unforgettable moments. One of them is *Relaxin' at the Touro* (named after the Touro Infirmary, New Orleans, where Spanier (just) weathered an illness in 1938), in which Joe Bushkin's solemn piano introduction ranks alongside John Lewis's opening to *Parker's Mood* as one of jazz's great scene-setters. Spanier's bitingly caustic and muted solo figures move unobtrusively into ensemble at bar 11 of the first chorus, and after Bushkin's piano solo (contemporary for its time, with its chromatic minor sevenths at bars 9 to 10) Georg Brunis's entry, voiced with the ensemble again, is a solemn funeral dirge. More of the same atmosphere turns up on *Lonesome Road*, in which Spanier's cornet, against hymn-like chords from the ensemble, creates a mock-gothic ambience. When Bushkin's piano enters after Caiazza's tenor, with ticking drum-rims in support, the effect is of a welcome *leitmotif* amid the stark blues landscape; then the humble, hushed trombone of Brunis, like a prayerful mourner, precedes 16 more bars of definitive Spanier, playing, plunger-muted, a substitute paraphrase of *Moanin' Low* in place of the original theme. Such creative thought is rare in dixieland music 50 years on, and illuminates every other track, from *Dinah* (with its dynamic introduction, irresistible out-of-tempo verse and hep Brunis vocal) to *Eccentric* (*a tour de force* for Cless) and *Black and Blue*, with Spanier's cutting solos and more definitive playing from Bushkin. The coda of this last track found its way into dixieland lore and beyond (to Count Basie's *Every Day I Have the Blues*, for one hit-making example), and there are dozens of other passages throughout the 'Great Sixteen' which – like the greatest of Armstrong, Beiderbecke or Parker – are now *de rigueur* in re-creative performance. Two examples are the upward cornet climb towards the final joyful ensemble of *Big Butter and Egg Man* and the alternation of long-noted ensemble passages and solo drum breaks towards the end of *That Da Da Strain* – dixieland tablets of hot stone!

At the time of writing, the newly available Bluebird issue of Spanier's 16 tracks also includes unrelated material: two tracks by Eddie Condon from 8 February 1929, cited in chapter 1; and four by Bud Freeman from his Summa Cum Laude orchestra's session of 19 July 1939. Track 2 is an alternate take, not the original 78 rpm master, though in this and other instances of alternate takes noted below, the versions are not very different from one another.

CD

***At the Jazz Band Ball: Chicago/New York Dixieland*, Bluebird 6752-2 RB (USA) and Bluebird ND 86762 (Europe)**

Muggsy Spanier (c), Georg Brunis (ts, v), Rod Cless (cl), Ray McKinstry (ts), George Zack (p), Bob Casey (g), Pat Pattison (sb), Marty Greenberg (d)

Chicago	7 July 1939	**Big Butter and Egg Man** (take 1)
omit (v)		**Someday, Sweetheart** (take 1)
		Eccentric (take 1)
		That Da Da Strain (take 2)

Spanier (c), Brunis (tb), Cless (cl), Bernie Billings (ts), Joe Bushkin (p), Casey (sb), Don Carter (d)

New York	10 Nov 1939	**At the Jazz Band Ball** (take 2)
add Brunis (v)		**I Wish I Could Shimmy like my Sister Kate** (take 1)
omit (v)		**Dipper Mouth Blues** (take 1)
		Livery Stable Blues (Barnyard Blues) (take 2)

Nick Caiazza (ts) replaces Billings
22 Nov 1939
Riverboat Shuffle (take 2)
Relaxin' at the Touro (take 1)
At Sundown (take 1)
Bluin' the Blues (take 1)

Al Sidell (d) replaces Carter
12 Dec 1939
Lonesome Road (take 2)
add Brunis (v)
Dinah (take 1)
omit (v)
(What Did I Do to Be so) Black and Blue (take 1)
Mandy, Make up your Mind (take 2)

* * *

Bobby Hackett: *Coast Concert/Jazz Ultimate*

Most jazz commentators avoid critical absolutes, but a number of years ago trombonist Bill Russo advanced one that is now widely accepted: 'Jack Teagarden', he proposed, 'is *the* greatest jazz trombonist'. Place Teagarden alongside Bobby Hackett, often cited (in my view, rightly) as the most profound and musical jazz cornettist of his or perhaps any generation, and you set a level for this deeply regarded album often called (to quote Hackett on another topic) 'the best in its field'. Leaving aside the shimmering quality of the recording (Hackett and Teagarden, like their confrères here, had raw-diamond tones ready to be polished into perfection by any engineer with ears), its content is worthy of scholarly transcription – not only for the solo *chefs-d'oeuvre,* but for the relaxed perfection of what Hackett would certainly have preferred *not* to call its dixieland ensembles.

Such perfection is heralded here with his simple five-note lead-in to *Big Butter and Egg Man,* which (like a lot of other Hackett inventions) has turned into a much-quoted adage, and carries on through gold-standard solos to an out chorus which is copybook ensemble; Hackett's flattened fifth in bar 3 is echoed with a musical friendly nod by Matty Matlock, and the root note from Abe Lincoln which follows both of them lingers like a man caught suddenly by an unexpected but beautiful view. And beneath all this genuine wit, the tuba-driven rhythm section skips along as if every member were playing jump-rope to a final 'skimmerlink' drum coda. All the glories of Hackett – sunshot tone, relaxed technical command and sophisticated guitarist's harmonic ear (he worked regularly with Glenn Miller as a rhythm guitarist) –

shine out on *New Orleans*, where his bright-toned lines light up Teagarden's dark and sonorous solemnities, and on *That's a Plenty* (a favourite Hackett vehicle) you hear him swing out to the top register with feathery lip-trills like a miniaturized Armstrong. The chase chorus between Teagarden and Lincoln which follows is such skilled pecking that you can hardly tell the musicians apart bar by bar, but Lincoln is the one with the challenges, and when he turns on the heat Teagarden's gentle answers deflect the wrath like a man refusing to take part in a shouting-match. Alongside such *délices*, Matlock – the most pure-toned Goodman follower of his generation – decorates ensembles and enhances with solos, playing the perfect artistic compliment to his fellows. And such stamps of quality are the hallmark of every other up-tempo tune on the recording, including *Muskrat Ramble*, whose jokey introduction and coda have passed into dixieland jazz-lore; *Royal Garden Blues*, where Teagarden's entry reaffirms him conclusively as 'King of the Blues Trombone' while Matlock's solo recalls the suspensions of the theme of *Sobbin' Blues*; and *Fidgety Feet*, where Hackett unexpectedly but perfectly quotes from *I Could Write a Book*.

Perhaps most attention, though, should be paid to the two remaining slow tunes of the session, for both are masterpieces. First, *Basin Street Blues*, a Jack Teagarden set-piece which, like many of Louis Armstrong's, was a monument; after his ever-disarming vocal refrain Matlock's clarinet is expectant against Fatool's brush *frissons*, and then Hackett comes in. His opening motif – pivoting on suspended fourths and ninths resolving to major sevenths and sixths – is often requoted, and, as his long rambling lines unfold, each new one picked up like an afterthought, you hear all of the harmonic-melodic Hackett 'ingredients' that Louis Armstrong revered and which made the cornetist uncopiable. The other great revelation of the session is *I Guess I'll Have to Change my Plans*. After its introduction, in which Hackett improvises gently over sustained chords (a frequent trademark), Teagarden's statement of the theme over a lilting $\frac{2}{4}$ rhythm is – like the song – rueful, wistful, somehow unfulfilled. When Hackett enters with a key change his solo is all embellishment, touching, then passing between the primary tones of Arthur Schwartz's melody like a butterfly between blooms, until the listener realizes that, by some divine process of artistic unity, the song provides the perfect structural base for the perfect Hackett solo. Throughout its 20 bars Hackett plays each and every one of Schwartz's melody tones, and the melody, thus gracefully embellished, responds to Hackett's touches like a lover in willing embrace. Teagarden's reprise of the theme is the perfect tactful capper. After his reference to *These Foolish Things* at the coda there was, on the original LP pressing, a longer-than-usual pause, as if in respect, before *Royal Garden Blues* began. It should still be there.

CD

***Coast Concert/Jazz Ultimate*, Dormouse DM1 CD X02 (UK)**

Bobby Hackett (c), Jack Teagarden, Abe Lincoln (tb), Matty Matlock (cl), Don Owens (p), Nappy Lamare (g, bj), Phil Stevens (sb, bb), Nick Fatool (d)

Los Angeles	18–19 Oct 1955	**Struttin' with some Barbecue**
		Muskrat Ramble
		New Orleans
add Teagarden (v)		**Basin Street Blues**
omit (v)		**That's a Plenty**
		Big Butter and Egg Man
		Fidgety Feet
		Royal Garden Blues
		I Guess I'll Have to Change my Plans

Hackett (tpt), Teagarden (tb), Peanuts Hucko (cl, ts), Ernie Caceres (bar, cl), Gene Schroeder (p), Billy Bauer (elg), Jack Lesberg (sb), Buzzy Drootin (d)

	16 Sept 1957	**Indiana**
		It's Wonderful
		'Way Down Yonder in New Orleans
		's Wonderful
		Baby Won't You Please Come Home
		I Found a New Baby
		Mama's Gone Goodbye
	17 Sept 1957	**Oh Baby**
		Sunday
		Everybody Loves My Baby
		55th and Broadway

* * *

Eddie Condon: *Dixieland Jam*

The 1950s saw the issue of a series of LPs by Eddie Condon which were to become a recorded definition of late Chicago-style jazz. 'Chicago-style' was a genre of which Condon firmly denied the existence, but in the 1950s, as before, Condon-style jazz existed, and at this period it was made up of several elements. First, a 'modern-style' flexibility from the rhythm section. Second, a stable of Condon regulars – cornetist Wild Bill Davison, trombonist Cutty Cutshall, pianist Gene Schroeder and drummer George Wettling – who, along with visiting magicians such as Bobby Hackett, Billy Butterfield, Dick Cary, Bud

Freeman and others, defined a highly individual house approach and therefore style. Third, a likeable informality on record – including Condon talking over and after the music on issued takes – which, when it was first heard, caused a sensation and matched the irreverent, often alcoholic ambience which surrounded Condon from the publication of his autobiography *We Called it Music: a Generation of Jazz* (with Thomas Sugrue) in 1947.

1950s recordings such as **Jamming at Condon's, Bixieland** and **The Roaring 20s** all highlighted these qualities. **Dixieland Jam** reissues eight newly mastered stereo takes from this third album (recorded in 1957) and adds six unreleased as well as one alternate take as a collectors' bonus. All three elements cited earlier are in plenteous supply, including the magnificent frank-vibratoed cornet statements of Wild Bill Davison, which made him, in Condon's view, the greatest lead in the business; placed alongside Vic Dickenson's equally motivic, deeply humorous counterpoints and young Bob Wilber's (then) underrated clarinet lines, the result is an archetypal Condon front line, as good as ever played for him.

St James Infirmary – a tune originally left unissued, perhaps because it was over-familiar then – turns into an effortless masterpiece; Davison's physico-musical flare bear-hugs the melody at its turnaround point (bars 16–17), and there are relaxed two-bar exchanges and a wonderful moment at which Condon's guitar pushes the music off into a new chorus like the swailing tail of a whale flipping away into deep water. His comments too – at track's end this time – say a lot about the true spirit in which recorded jazz is often made. On *That's a Plenty* there are more marvels; Vic Dickenson proves that – with Dicky Wells, Bill Harris and George Chisholm – he was and remains now one of the most humorous improvisers of trombone jazz; Wild Bill high-jumps two octaves and two tones from chorus 1 to chorus 2 of his solo and Wilber reminds us that reassessment of his early work is overdue. The timpani booms from Wettling after the ensemble are a further salutory reminder that Condon's men were goodtime jazzmen as well as musical curators of a style. *The Song is Ended* gives us Davison at his most sensitive, speaking through his cornet with broad Irish sentiment like all good Chicago gangsters, and a sit-down finish which sounds like a naturally completed sentence. On *Wrap your Troubles in Dreams* Billy Butterfield is heard at full power, and *When a Woman Loves a Man* (another good example of the kind of underplayed song that Condon's bands often came up with) is a perfect miniature of Condon formulae; split-led melody, tiny touches of arrangement which make all the music sound perfectly rehearsed and mid-performance key changes (to the trombone solo and final eight bars of the ensemble). Such small but vital points of finesse reveal the artistry which lay under the Condon crew's collectively bucolic exterior. They turn up again on *The Minor Drag* (a title from Condon's early recording session with Fats Waller) and elsewhere. *Why Was I Born?* – another lesser-known popular song of great value – has more archetypal Butterfield; his first three quarter notes are pure Armstrong, but the little unassuming lip-slur up a sixth at bar 10 is just as much pure Billy, and the tinkling piano of Schroeder complementing him is a historic microcosm of high jazz art. This, and other delights – Butterfield again striking out at the end of *Put 'em Down Blues*, the cheerful toddle-tempo of *Davenport Blues* and sheer dixieland exuberance of *What's the Use?* – make you realize that such music is now as rare, as precious, and as much a lost art as a late Beethoven string quartet.

CD

***Dixieland Jam*, Columbia Jazz Masterpieces CK 45145 (USA) and CBS Jazz Masterpieces 465680-2 (Europe)**

Wild Bill Davison (tpt), Vic Dickenson (tb), Bob Wilber (cl), Gene Schroeder (p), Eddie Condon (g), Leonard Gaskin (sb), George Wettling (d)

New York	19 Aug 1957	**Wolverine Blues**
		China Boy (take 2)
		China Boy (take 3)
		St James Infirmary
		That's a Plenty
		The Song is Ended
		Hindustan

Billy Butterfield (tpt) and Cutty Cutshall (tb) replace Davison and Dickenson

	24–5 Sept 1957	**Wrap your Troubles in Dreams**
		When a Woman Loves a Man
		The Minor Drag
		Why Was I Born?
		Put 'em Down Blues
		Davenport Blues
		Apex Blues
		What's the Use?

* * *

Vic Dickenson: *The Essential Vic Dickenson*

There are three reasons to include these classic recordings in this chapter. First, they are the perfect embodiment of 'mainstream' – the classification invented by Stanley Dance to define a style encompassing the rhythmic flexibility of (then) modern jazz, the techno-melodic sophistication of swing and the repertoire of the pre-bebop era. Second, they celebrate the best points of extended performance first made possible by 'long-play' recording in the 1950s. And third, by consequence, they set out in unhurried exposition the talents of trombonist Dickenson and – perhaps most dramatically (on five of the tracks) – those of his young partner, cornetist Ruby Braff, alongside clarinettist Ed Hall and a Basie-based rhythm section led by pianist Sir Charles Thompson.

For Dickenson these sessions from 1953–4 provided, at last, an opportunity to parade at leisure all of his magnificently original stylistic trademarks – trademarks which had sometimes been compacted too tightly on 78s in the past. These included a repertoire of wholly motivic ideas delivered with the lazy tension of a sleepy lion, a great soft-leather sound, and a vibrato which widened regularly into something like a good-humoured turkey-gobble. Behind these basics followed on a whole catalogue of improvisational originalities: runs of tricky triple-tongued triplets like a baby bounced on the knee, sudden half-veiled windy emissions, and great shouting blues phrases erupting from rumbling asides like a man goaded from submission into a sudden shout of anger. On tracks such as *When You and I Were Young, Maggie*, *Old Fashioned Love*, *Jeepers Creepers* and the classic *Suspension Blues*, all these qualities and more show up in glorious extended exposition – sustenance enough for any jazz-hungry listener.

Yet, surprisingly at the time, they were easily matched by Ruby Braff, then aged 26, whose performance, track by track, effortlessly demonstrated new levels of facility, tonal luxury and creative synthesis which were to win the hearts of trumpeters, cornetists, their followers and most of the jazz world from then on. At every turn Braff can be heard parading his peacock gifts. In a barrelling tone, bucket-deep, he heads the ensemble with open-throated, free-breathing lead, and once in solo swaggers up and down melodic lines and chord tones, often setting whirligig-spinning flurries of centred sound against sensuous, slowed phrases (like a woman stretching in the sun), and regularly placing pure-music lyric statements against huge castigating blues phrases which wrap melodic situations in a suffocating bear-hug as if to say, 'That's enough beauty! Let's get physical!'.

This was the era of the young, hard-blowing Braff, and set against the huge sounds and conceptions of both him and Dickenson it might have been a long search to find a clarinettist of equal power, flexibility and tonal perfection. Ed Hall supplied the perfect third voice. As melodically creative and harmonically aware as his partners, Hall had a sound that was comparably mellow and meaty, and his delivery had the crackling attack of Sidney Bechet without any of the (then) more controversial aspects of Bechet's dominant style. In short Hall was a supportive sophisticate, and his contributions did much to remind a new fashionable generation of West and East Coasters that the clarinet was still hip; hear him, say, on *Nice Work if You Can Get it*, and it's plain that Hall's was a voice of classic proportions. Against the Thompson-led rhythm section (sporting rhythm guitarist Steve Jordan) the wonders of these two sessions unfold: among them the jaunty *When You and I Were Young, Maggie*, which, like much of the set, sounds like a cosy homefire chat, *Keeping out of Mischief Now*, with its majestic solos and (now standard) counter-riff, and the architectural *I Cover the Waterfront*. Only one voice is less than definitive: trumpeter Shad Collins who, on that day in the studio, sounded dry-toned and short in breath – almost as if the magnificence of the company left him shy. For the best of Collins listen elsewhere; for the best of mainstream listen here.

CD

***The Essential Vic Dickenson*, Vanguard 99/100-2 (USA)**

Ruby Braff (c), Vic Dickenson (tb), Edmond Hall (cl), Sir Charles Thompson (p), Steve Jordan (g), Walter Page (sb), Les Erskine (d)

New York	29 Dec 1953	**Russian Lullaby**
		Keeping out of Mischief Now
		Sir Charles at Home
		Jeepers Creepers
		I Cover the Waterfront

Shad Collins (tpt), Dickenson (tb), Edmond Hall (cl), Thompson (p), Jordan (g), Page (sb), Jo Jones (d)

	29 Nov 1954	**Runnin' Wild**
		When You and I Were Young, Maggie
		Nice Work if You Can Get it
		Old Fashioned Love
		Everybody Loves my Baby
		Suspension Blues
		You Brought a New Kind of Love to Me

* * *

Buck Clayton: *Jam Sessions from the Vault*

'One day', Buck Clayton recalls in his autobiography, 'towards the end of 1953, ... I got a call from John Hammond. He wanted to know if I could make a recording session that he had planned with George Avakian for Columbia. ... As I entered the studio I found a lot of guys there that I didn't know. I knew about half of them personally, but the others I had to be introduced to. ... What John wanted was to record a real jam session in a studio. This is rather hard to do ... [but] before you knew it we were all playing like we had known each other for years. ... A few days later I was told that I had been named leader of that group and the albums are known as the *Buck Clayton Jam Sessions*. I think I must credit John Hammond for this.'

Extended jazz recording in all styles was a natural follow-on from the invention of the LP record, and the 'Buck Clayton Jam Sessions' made history as examples of a Kansas City genre which so far had been unrecordable. They received widespread critical accolade after their release – as well as discussion because of the (then) controversial use of tape editing and splicing by co-producer Avakian, who on one occasion combined sections of music recorded six months apart! In all, six sessions were recorded between 14 December 1953 and 5 March 1956, and the most famous of them – *The Hucklebuck* backed with *Robbins' Nest* on two sides of one LP – comes from 16 December 1953. **All the Cats Join In**, however, combines one track from 1953 (*Lean Baby*, recorded at the *Hucklebuck* session, but unissued as the tune was still a best-seller) with two from 1955 (featuring two definitive pairings: Buck Clayton with Ruby Braff, and Coleman Hawkins with Buddy Tate) and two more from the last Jam Session of all. This featured trumpeter Billy Butterfield teamed alongside Clayton and Braff, and untypically a singer – Jimmy Rushing – added for one title. On one album, therefore, this historic Hammond–Clayton–Avakian project is spanned from first to last, and there are other incidental virtues; tracks are not over-long (the longest, *Blue Lou*, lasts ten minutes four seconds), and occasional touches of Clayton arrangement (notably on *All the Cats Join In* and *Lean Baby*) make the soloists shine brighter in contrast. However, the prime aim of these great Columbia recordings always was to illustrate to the eager listener how jazz musicians sounded once allowed to 'stretch out' in extended solos, and, despite the problems of contending with clinical studio atmosphere, this was quickly achieved: 'we got into the best mood we could', recalls Clayton, 'and soon had a genuine session going'.

A perfect illustration is the appropriately named *All the Cats Join In* (surprisingly written by Alec Wilder and Eddie Sauter for the Walt

Disney feature *Make Mine Music*), where there are perfectly in-context solos from Coleman Hawkins (supremely at home in these gently competitive surroundings), J. C. Higginbotham in fine form, Ruby Braff at his most youthfully hard-blowing, the well-matched pair of Butterfield and Clayton, Tyree Glenn commuting between vibraphone and plunger-muted trombone, Julian Dash (who had been present at the very first of the sessions) and the under-rated pianist Kenny Kersey. *Out of Nowhere* has Clayton's definitive harmon-muted lead, architectural Braff, exploratory trombone from the little-known Dickie Harris (who later worked in Broadway pit bands) set against the easy mobility of Bennie Green, and a full chorus from Hawkins (unusually) followed by a capper from the titular head. *Don't You Miss your Baby* introduces a bonus, Jimmy Rushing, and before his now highly moving sign-off ('Anyone ask you who was it sang this song / tell 'em 'lil' Jimmy Rushing, he's been here and gone!') there is a definitive solo swing segue from Braff, Higginbotham, Clayton and then Hawkins, topped in turn by a three-trumpet chase (Braff, Clayton and Butterfield) which captures all three brass voices working to one style yet parading individualities as strong as three signatures. The *Lean Baby* which follows features a few soloists (Dash, Lem Davis and Charlie Fowlkes) of less import than the stars booked for the later sessions, but also outstanding contributions from trumpeter Joe Newman, trombonist Urbie Green and Clayton; all is highly acceptable. *Blue Lou*, which concludes the album, turns the heat back up to boiling point. The whole equals indispensable mainstream history.

CD

***Jam Sessions from the Vault*, Columbia Jazz Masterpieces CK 44291 (USA) and CBS Jazz Masterpieces 463336-2 (Europe)**

Buck Clayton, Joe Newman (tpt), Urbie Green, Henderson Chambers (tb), Lem Davis (as), Julian Dash (ts), Charlie Fowlkes (bar), Sir Charles Thompson (p), Freddie Green (g), Walter Page (sb), Jo Jones (d)

New York	16 Dec 1953	**Lean Baby**

Clayton (tpt), Ruby Braff (c), Bennie Green, Dickie Harris (tb), Coleman Hawkins, Buddy Tate (ts), Al Waslohn (p), Steve Jordan (g), Milt Hinton (sb), Jones (d)

	15 March 1955	**Out of Nowhere**
		Blue Lou

Clayton, Billy Butterfield (tpt), Braff (c), J. C. Higginbotham (tb), Tyree Glenn (tb, vb), Hawkins, Julian Dash (ts), Kenny Kersey (p), Jordan (g), Page (sb), Bobby Donaldson (d)

	5 March 1956	**All the Cats Join In**

omit (vb) **After Hours**

Jimmy Rushing (v) replaces Glenn (tb) **Don't You Miss your Baby?**

Other CDs

Plus additional tracks:
The Complete CBS Buck Clayton Jam Sessions, Mosaic MD6-144 (USA)

* * *

Henry 'Red' Allen and Coleman Hawkins: *Standards & Warhorses*

There are not many jazz recordings which catch a player in the midst of musical renaissance, but **Standards & Warhorses**, featuring trumpeter Henry 'Red' Allen, is one. By the late 1950s the overriding European image of Allen was of an energetic New Orleans trumpeter-entertainer whose music, at dixieland bars such as New York's Metropole, was flashy, rabble-rousing and shallow – geared to critically unacceptable ways of pleasing a clubful of customers drinking to the dawn of rock and roll. Around 1958, however, when tapes of Allen recorded with Earle Warren, Coleman Hawkins and a rhythm section began to circulate among collectors, the first seeds were sown for the great Red Allen reassessment of the 1960s, a reassessment based later on two great quartet recordings, one of them a live club session titled **Feeling Good!** which bannered Don Ellis's widely quoted view of the time that 'Red Allen is the most avant-garde trumpeter in New York'. On the titles which were to become **Standards & Warhorses**, however, Allen could be heard gloriously unveiling new creative profundities for the first time. It was as if his style had suddenly refocused from a blurred image into sharp relief, revealing brilliant new hues in his kaleidoscope of stylistic devices and – above all, perhaps – a calmly unhurried authority at ballad tempo, like a master philosopher whose last block to direct speech has been miraculously removed. Quite suddenly – or so it seemed – a great comedian was playing Hamlet, and magnificently, and reconsideration of his artistic status became urgent.

All of the necessary evidence for this turns up on the 1958 tapes, on which there are four grade-one jazz professionals (Earle Warren, Marty

Napoleon, Chubby Jackson and George Wettling) and one usually unconquerable genius, Coleman Hawkins. But with every track the listener finds himself waiting at seat's edge for Allen's tablet-of-stone statements which, with their calm, almost stilled directness, make Hawkins sound like a lesser speaker hectoring for attention and much else of the session seem merely very good. At this point in his career Allen was cocky-lipped, cream-toned and technically equipped for every one of his revelations. And they were unique. Where, by contrast, Ruby Braff's musical statements were positive acclamation. Allen's were often more like fascinating theories half-developed, then left; sudden self-revisions or just asides – sometimes neurotic, sometimes peremptory, but always to the point. Transcribe an Allen solo of the period and you find dramatic changes in note density, bar by bar; flurries of sound are followed by pausing tones like a thoughtful speaker demurring, 'Well, yes – but on the other hand...!' His re-entry on *Sleepytime Gal* is a perfect example of physical technique commanding a musical response, and from then on every note of his solo, even in the fastest phrase, is perfectly sure-centred. Plainly, at this time, Allen was enjoying every idea that sprang from his trumpet bell, and in the music the listener senses urgency, discovery and delighted surprise. This leads to top-of-the-heap musical liberties such as his entry, two bars early, on *Summertime* for a solo full of physical delights; growls, glissandi, and high, cloudy, half-valved notes in the top register. The effect is mesmeric; Allen is caught in the midst of a great redefinition, and against such jubilant affirmations Hawkins sounds for once like a man blustering his way to small conclusions.

After the coming-to-flower glories of this session, the tracks recorded a year earlier sound temporarily like a return to older, more barren lands; the arrival of J. C. Higginbotham's bucolic trombone amid a team of Metropole regulars, including clarinettist Sol Yaged, restores a dixieland format, and the band is plainly working to a different level. *Battle Hymn of the Republic*, with its hokum, features Higginbotham, all yawps and sighs, Allen playing to grandiose effect and Hawkins galloping after him like an avenging angel. This, the tension-building 'business' of *When the Saints* and the raunchy resentful-tempoed *South* embody the kind of performance that would have had Metropole habituées shouting for more drinks; Allen grandstands dutifully, but amid the industrious entertaining his emergent subtleties are easier to miss – an artfully sidestepping near-lead on *Bill Bailey* and just one veiled note on *The Blues*, at the crossover from piano to trombone solo, which sounds like a perceptive onlooker slipping in a sly word unnoticed. On the original LP *Stormy Weather* was tactfully placed at the end of this dixieland parade. The effect was like a second coming – as if to prove that it wasn't all a dream.

CD

***Standards & Warhorses*, Jass CD-2 (USA)**

Henry 'Red' Allen (tpt), J. C. Higginbotham (tb), Sol Yaged (cl), Coleman Hawkins (ts), Lou Stein (p), Milt Hinton (sb), Cozy Cole (d), Dewey Bregman (arr)

New York	16 Dec 1957	**Battle Hymn of the Republic**
		Frankie and Johnny
		When the Saints Go Marchin' In
		South
		Won't You Come Home, Bill Bailey?
		The Blues
		Maryland, My Maryland

Allen (tpt), Earle Warren (cl), Hawkins (ts), Marty Napoleon (p), Chubby Jackson (sb), George Wettling (d), Larry Clinton (arr)

	7 Aug 1958	**Stormy Weather**
		Mean to Me
		The Lonesome Road
		Sleepy Time Gal
		Summertime
		All of Me
		Tea for Two

CHAPTER 6

The New Orleans Revival

Mike Hazeldine

The New Orleans revival began in the mid 1930s, when white middle-class Americans began to collect jazz records made by blacks. These 'race records' had been made during the previous decade and were to be found in junk shops and by canvassing black people's homes. Virtually all of these old recordings were long deleted and the difficulty in acquiring them only added to the enthusiasm of the collectors. Recordings by King Oliver, Louis Armstrong, Johnny Dodds and Jelly Roll Morton were catalogued and studied. As the personnel were rarely printed on the labels, identification of musicians became a subject of discussion – a subject which still occupies the energies of collectors today. In 1935 collectors Bill Russell and Steve Smith formed the Hot Record Exchange and began to trade the vintage records by mail. In Britain, collectors met to form Rhythm Clubs, and in France the first discography was published by Charles Delaunay. Vintage jazz records began to be reissued on small collectors' labels. The Jazzman Record Shop opened in Los Angeles and the Commodore Record Shop opened in New York. Magazines devoted to New Orleans jazz, such as *Jazz Information* and *Record Changer*, began to appear.

The popular music scene had also given a nod to the New Orleans interest. Bandleader Bob Crosby had a number of notable New Orleans musicians in his orchestra and often organized them into a dixieland small group. New recordings by Johnny Dodds and Jimmie Noone were followed by the rediscovery and recording of Tommy Ladnier. Benny Goodman had a hit with Jelly Roll Morton's *King Porter Stomp*, and the composer took part in a historic series of interviews and piano solo recordings for the Library of Congress. Morton was to make several more new piano and band recordings during the next two years, but he died before he could exert any influence on the direction which the revival was to take.

Interest in the origins and originators of jazz was growing, and in

1939 Frederick Ramsey and Charles Edward Smith edited the first book to document a history of jazz – *Jazzmen*. The importance of this book cannot be overestimated. Through his research, one of its main contributors, Bill Russell, discovered Bunk Johnson, who was to become one of the major figures of the movement. It also included a chapter on New Orleans musicians currently working in the city. The musicians discussed were to form the basis of the first revival recording in New Orleans by Kid Rena in 1940.

In San Francisco, trumpeter Lu Watters formed a band to re-create the sounds and the spirit of King Oliver. The band proved to be very popular and its records sold well. Soon scores of amateur bands began to spring up throughout the USA. Some were inspired by King Oliver, others by Jelly Roll Morton; some got no further than imitating Lu Watters!

Finally, in 1940, two major record companies responded to the growing interest in New Orleans jazz. In February, Victor began a series of New Orleans-style sessions under Sidney Bechet's name. A few months later Decca issued an album entitled **New Orleans Jazz**, with new recordings by Louis Armstrong, Sidney Bechet, Johnny Dodds, Jimmie Noone and other New Orleans musicians. The American Federation of Musicians' recording ban then prevented further new recordings, and it was left to amateur enthusiasts such as Bill Russell to continue the work.

* * *

Bunk Johnson: *Bunk Johnson and his Superior Jazz Band*

Willie 'Bunk' Johnson's first recording was an important event, not only for the revival movement, but for Johnson himself. After achieving some early fame in New Orleans, he had left the city around 1914 to work with travelling shows. Had he then resided in Chicago or New York, he might well have made his recording debut during the 1920s. As for so many of his New Orleans contemporaries, the 1930s was an era of neglect for Bunk and, with no teeth and no trumpet, he retired from music. When the book *Jazzmen* was being compiled in the late 1930s, Louis Armstrong, Clarence Williams, Sidney Bechet and other prominent New Orleans musicians all singled out Bunk Johnson as the man to talk to about the early days of jazz. (Some of these musicians were later to disown him when he became famous.) His legendary reputation attracted the authors and he was found in New Iberia, a small town west of New Orleans. The veteran lost no time in impressing upon them that he still had 'what it takes to stomp trumpet yet'. Money was raised for a set of new teeth and a trumpet, and Bunk began to practise once more. He declined an invitation to record in 1940, and when he accepted in 1942 Bill Russell, Gene Williams and Dave Stuart of Jazzman Records hardly knew what to expect. The veterans Russell had interviewed for the *Jazzmen* book had either died (Jelly Roll Morton and Johnny Dodds) or were in poor health (Kid Rena and Big Eye Louis Nelson). As Bunk was not in the musicians' union, the choice of available musicians was limited. When a band was eventually assembled the members gathered at the house of pianist Walter Decou for a rehearsal. When Bunk hit the opening notes of an old spiritual, *Yes, Lord, I'm Crippled,* Russell, Williams and Stuart couldn't believe their ears. Here was no old-timer who was living on past glory, but a musician with tone and melodic ideas superior to any player then working in New Orleans.

After trying unsuccessfully to hire a studio for the recording, the organizers finally settled for the third floor of a piano storeroom, a borrowed portable disc-cutting machine and a box of acetates. From a recording point of view, the results were primitive. *Yes, Lord, I'm Crippled* was the first number recorded; the sound is still unbalanced and makes listening difficult at times, but moving some of the musicians around for the subsequent numbers improved the results slightly. Despite the lack of fidelity the recording still conveys all the zest and passion of New Orleans jazz at its best. None of the frictions that were later to beset the band are apparent. Bunk was an intelligent, highly articulate musician who could read, compose and arrange music. Although he had selected George Lewis and Jim Robinson to play at this session, he later found their musical shortcomings restrictive. However, here their hard-swinging style and mutual enthusiasm show complete empathy with the leader's own ideas. All the hallmarks of his unique style are in evidence. One is the unhurried phrasing which seems to fall so far behind the beat that one feels he will never catch up, yet, by running certain phrases together or with a few carefully placed notes either side of the beat, he is back. Lewis and Robinson also placed notes around the beat, but had a more conventionally melodic sense of time. This effect of a free-ranging lead against a busy clarinet and a driving trombone is one of the most exciting sounds in New Orleans jazz.

In *Panama,* Robinson quickly picks up the trumpeter's love of the riff. This device had become widely used in many swing-band arrangements, yet it had been a feature of New Orleans bands since the turn of the century. The long, blue, off-scale, bent notes in the final chorus between Bunk and Robinson make this (along with the wonderful 1930 Luis Russell version) the best rendition of this much recorded tune.

With the USA getting involved in the war, the spiritual *Ain't Gonna Study War No More* was released as *Down by the Riverside*, and has retained this title ever since. It later became Bunk's signature tune.

There are few solos on these recordings. Often Johnson will drop out for a chorus and then return to play a series of variations around his own imagined lead – similar to a second trumpet part. Much the same approach is employed when he does occasionally take a solo (*Bunk's Blues*). It is not a result of improvisation, but a carefully worked-out variation of the melody which he would retain every time he performed that number. Other New Orleans musicians, such as King Oliver, Kid Ory and even Louis Armstrong, had the same approach.

Weary Blues and *Moose March* match *Panama* for excitement. The band seems happiest with these tempos, and Robinson in particular is most effective. On the other hand, the trombonist seems unsure of *Ballin' the Jack*, and this is the least successful of the nine items released. The final track is made up from the three 78 rpm records of Bunk Johnson talking about his early life. In the past it has been fashionable to dismiss most of what he said as fiction, yet recent research has shown he was far nearer the truth than most of his detractors gave him credit for.

Bunk Johnson was to become even stronger during the next few years, and his playing on the 1944–5 American Music recordings is even more assured and confident. Many will argue that these are his better recordings, yet none captured the drive and the excitement of the tracks from this first session. If the revival was looking for a hero, it certainly found one in Bunk Johnson.

CD

***Bunk Johnson and his Superior Jazz Band,* Good Time Jazz GTJCD-12048-2 (USA)**

Bunk Johnson (tpt), Jim Robinson (tb), George Lewis (cl), Walter Decou (p), Lawrence Marrero (bj), Austin Young (sb), Ernest Rogers (d)

New Orleans 11 June 1942

Yes, Lord, I'm Crippled
Down by the Riverside
Storyville Blues
Weary Blues
Bunk's Blues
Moose March
Make me a Pallet on the Floor
Ballin' the Jack
Panama

Johnson (speech) **Bunk Johnson Talking Records**

* * *

George Lewis: *George Lewis and his New Orleans Stompers, vol.1; George Lewis and his New Orleans Stompers, vol.2*

Following Bunk Johnson's initial two sessions in 1942 (for *Jazzman* and *Jazz Information*, the latter being issued by Commodore), Bill Russell planned to visit New Orleans to record a further session with Johnson and George Lewis. In April 1943 he wrote to Johnson in New Iberia to tell him of his plans, but just as he was about to leave for New Orleans he received a telegram from San Francisco informing him that Bunk was there and playing at weekends with the Yerba Buena Jazz Band. Russell immediately wrote to George Lewis, saying that he would now like to record a band under the latter's leadership, and suggested various trumpet players to replace Johnson. On arrival in New Orleans he considered the possibility of using Kid Shots Madison or Herb Morand when Lewis recommended Kid Howard. Russell expressed doubts about Howard, having already heard him play, but Lewis assured him: 'You won't be disappointed, Mr Russell'.

Before the session, a rehearsal was organized at the home of drummer Edgar Mosley. Kid Howard and Chester Zardis were unable to attend, so the rehearsal went ahead without them. Bassist Jim Little (Sidney Brown) dropped by the house and sat in on tuba with the group. It was a tradition for many New Orleans bands to open with *Climax Rag*, and they do so here, both on the rehearsal and the next day at the actual session, which yielded a more exuberant take. Jim Little's tuba is well featured on the sombre *Two Jim Blues*.

The following day, when the band assembled at the Gypsy Tea Room to record, some union officials were in the hall. Pianist Walter Decou had been booked and was the only band member actually in the union; seeing the officials, he declined to enter, fearing expulsion. When the session was over Russell offered the best numbers to Alfred Lion of Blue Note. The American Federation of Musicians' recording ban was still in force, so Lion issued the tracks on the specially created Climax label to avoid union objections. The Climax 78s and the later Blue Note LP kept the best takes of the session in the catalogue for almost 40 years, and these records were amongst the most influential of all New Orleans revival recordings.

After the musicians had set up and the microphone was in position, the band exploded into *Climax Rag*. Listening to it after his doubts about Howard, Russell must have felt completely reassured. The trumpeter romps through the number with tremendous spirit, and there are few recordings in all jazz that better demonstrate the sheer joy of making music. The whole band bubbles with enthusiasm, and I have met few people impervious to the excitement generated here. In the second take, Howard omits his much-imitated downward run that has become an essential part of any revival trumpet player attempting this number. The second take is less exuberant, yet in chorus after chorus, it portends an imminent eruption that is skilfully held in check. After the familiar first take, this only adds to the excitement.

Since the days of Buddy Bolden, New Orleans bands would often combine two or three themes of other tunes into a new number. *Dauphine Street Blues* is an example of this. These sessions of 15–16 May marked the first ever recording of *Just a Closer Walk with Thee*. The number has been recorded hundreds of times since by numerous revivalist groups, yet none has come close to the haunting beauty of the first take of 16 May, which was the version originally issued. Lewis was a little sharp throughout the proceedings, yet his delicate placement of notes and phrases around the beat make this track one of the masterpieces of New Orleans music. Jim Robinson rarely played better, and his manner of making the ensemble swing is well illustrated on *Just a Closer Walk with Thee*. Apart from the solo choruses by George Lewis, most numbers feature the ensemble collectively, in the grand New Orleans jazz tradition, and where brief solos are taken they seem to grow out of the ensemble rather than to be separate from it. Generally the first takes are the better ones, although *Milneberg Joys* and *Don't Go 'way Nobody* are better on the second takes. Unlike many reissues of complete sessions, new takes are often at different tempos, and every new take has something fresh to say.

Chris Kelly was reputed to be the best blues trumpeter in New Orleans, though sadly his playing went unrecorded. Howard was his pupil, and something of Kelly's emotive style can be heard on *Careless Love* and *Deep Bayou Blues*. *Don't Go 'way Nobody, (Let's stay and have a good time)* was a number that Buddy Bolden used to feature after midnight, when respectable patrons had left, and its theme had also appeared in Sam Morgan's recording of *Everybody's Talking about Sammy*. It is a vehicle for a series of infectious breaks with everyone participating. Finally, the easy paced *Whenever You're Lonesome* completes one of the most satisfying CD sets in any New Orleans collection.

George Lewis took part in almost 90 recording sessions, yet these tracks remain his finest achievement. Along with the group that recorded Kid Ory's Crescent session, this band led by George Lewis set a standard for New Orleans ensemble playing of the 1940s that was never to be achieved again. Today, at Preservation Hall in New Orleans, and in hundreds of revivalist bands around the world, ensemble playing of this quality seems to be a lost art. George Lewis's Climax sessions should be required listening for any young band wanting to play New Orleans jazz.

CD

***George Lewis and his New Orleans Stompers, vol.1*, American Music AMCD-100; *George Lewis and his New Orleans Stompers, vol.2*, American Music AMCD-101 (USA)**

Jim Robinson (tb), George Lewis (cl), Lawrence Marrero (bj), Sidney 'Little Jim' Brown (bb), Edgar Mosley (d)

New Orleans	15 May 1943	**Climax Rag**
		New Orleans Hula
		Don't Go 'way Nobody
		Two Jim Blues
		Just a Closer Walk with Thee

add Kid Howard (tpt); Chester Zardis (sb) replaces Brown (bb)

	16 May 1943	**Climax Rag**
		Climax Rag
		Just a Closer Walk with Thee
		Just a Closer Walk with Thee
		Ain't Gonna Give Nobody None of this Jelly Roll
		Ain't Gonna Give Nobody None of this Jelly Roll
		Careless Love
		Careless Love
		Dauphine St Blues
		Just a Little While to Stay Here
		Just a Little While to Stay Here
		Just a Closer Walk with Thee
		Milneberg Joys
		Milneberg Joys
		Fidgety Feet
		Fidgety Feet
		Don't Go 'way Nobody
		Don't Go 'way Nobody
		Deep Bayou Blues
		Whenever You're Lonesome, Telephone Me

Other CDs

plus additional tracks:

The Complete Blue Note Recordings of George Lewis, Mosaic MD3 132 (USA)

* * *

Kid Ory: *Kid Ory's Creole Jazz Band 1944/45*

With their high standard of musicianship and wide choice of tempos, Kid Ory's recordings are the most approachable of all those made by the latter-day genuine New Orleans bands. The trombonist had been a successful bandleader since the earliest days of jazz, and in 1921 his group (which included two musicians listed here, Mutt Carey and Ed Garland) had been the first black jazz band to record. In the 1920s his uncanny ensemble sense contributed much to the success of the classic Armstrong, Morton and New Orleans Wanderers/Bootblacks sides. But his robust tailgate style found little favour with the swing bands and he retired from music in 1933. Had he never played another note, his reputation (like that of King Oliver, who died in 1938) would have been assured. His comeback in the 1940s produced a series of brilliant recordings, all of which illustrated the leader's principles of disciplined, yet relaxed New Orleans ensemble playing.

The best of Ory's 1940s recordings were those from his four Crescent sessions, made between August 1944 and November 1945. The nucleus of the band consisted of New Orleans exiles who, like Ory, were based in Los Angeles and had been associated with him for many years. Mutt Carey and Kid Ory were from the pioneer school of New Orleans brass players. Their occasional solos were often a straightforward statement of the main theme, but their ensemble playing, though appearing deceptively simple, always added great variety to the music, while leaving ample space for the other instruments. Although Carey was occasionally inclined to pitch sharp, his rattling lead was a perfect foil for Ory's unfailing ability to fill out the ensemble with a steady stream of perfectly placed notes and slurs. Together they formed the most exciting New Orleans brass team since King Oliver and Louis Armstrong. For the first two sessions, Ory added the New Orleans clarinettist Omer Simeon, then playing alto saxophone with Jimmie Lunceford's orchestra. As is the case with the 1926 Morton recordings, Simeon's fluent playing is ideal for this New Orleans ensemble playing. Another Ory trademark was his excellent rhythm sections. He preferred the lighter sound of Bud Scott's guitar to the banjo, and Ed Garland's light slapped bass left ample room for pianist Buster Wilson's telling support. When Minor Hall joined the band after the first session, the rhythm section became even better.

The first session produced the classic version of *Blues for Jimmie* – a tribute to the late Jimmie Noone, who had been appearing with the band when he died the year before. There are memorable solos by

Simeon and Garland, plus an intense solo by Carey playing into a bucket mute. *South* is completely ensemble and, with its well spaced breaks, shows the band's real strength. It demonstrates how the best New Orleans groups could introduce subtle variations into an ensemble without losing the melody, tempo and character of a number. Ory sings in creole on his own *Creole Song*, but the track is remembered mainly for Simeon's beautifully constructed clarinet solo. *Get Out of Here* is based on the first strain of *Tiger Rag* and is claimed to be an earlier variation of the tune.

The second session was recorded just over a year later, and if it didn't quite live up to the others it still produced some memorable moments. *Panama*, a favourite of countless New Orleans revival groups, is disappointing by the band's own high standards. Simeon's solos are excellent, but Carey's uncertain square phrasing causes some uneasiness in the ensemble. *Careless Love* is taken at a brisk pace, and one feels that a slightly slower tempo would have produced a greater swing. Bud Scott's vocal on *Under the Bamboo Tree* has just the right inflections for this old vaudeville number. He is slightly under-recorded, but the whole band (particularly Minor Hall) plays with tremendous swing. *Do What Ory Say* features the leader's craggy vocal over a superb rhythm section. Simeon's solo is the best of many fine solos from these early sessions, and it is a pity that he never recorded with the band again.

Simeon was replaced for the remaining two sessions by the Chicago clarinettist Darnell Howard, who plays quite beautifully at times. The ensemble on the three rags, *1919 Rag*, *Down Home Rag* and *Maple Leaf Rag*, is magnificent. The inventive ensemble with its beautiful balance and texture compares favourably with the best of Oliver's and Morton's classic bands. This version of *Maryland, my Maryland* is probably the best jazz march ever recorded and is only a shade better than their *Oh! Didn't He Ramble*, which is also excellent. *Weary Blues* also contains some brilliant ensemble playing, with fine solos by Howard and Ory. Only *Ory's Creole Trombone* and *Original Dixieland One Step*, though good by other bands' achievements, fail to match the high standard of the other tracks. Visually, their hokum strains would have been undoubted crowd pleasers, but set among so much brilliant music they often sound corny. *Ory's Creole Trombone* has some good moments, but a comparison with the Armstrong Hot Five version is inevitable.

Many who heard Ory's group live insist that it was the finest New Orleans band of the revival period. It is a pity (though understandable) that it was confined by the recording company to a dixieland repertoire, for it was also capable of playing a wide variety of popular tunes without losing its instinctive New Orleans approach.

CD

Kid Ory's Creole Jazz Band 1944/45, Good Time Jazz GTJCD-12022-2 (USA)

Mutt Carey (tpt), Kid Ory (tb), Omer Simeon (cl), Buster Wilson (p), Bud Scott (g), Ed Garland (sb), Alton Redd (d)

Hollywood	3 Aug 1944	**Get Out of Here**
		South
		Blues for Jimmie Noone (take 2)
add Ory (v)		**Creole Song**
omit (v); Minor Hall (d) replaces Redd		
	5 Aug 1945	**Panama**
		Careless Love
add Ory (v)		**Do What Ory Say**
Scott (v) replaces Ory (v)		**Under the Bamboo Tree**
omit (v); Darnell Howard (cl) replaces Simeon		
	8 Sept 1945	**1919 Rag**
		Maryland, my Maryland
		Down Home Rag
		Oh! Didn't He Ramble
	3 Nov 1945	**Original Dixieland One Step**
		Maple Leaf Rag
		Weary Blues
		Ory's Creole Trombone

* * *

Wooden Joe Nicholas: *Wooden Joe Nicholas*

In a city where so much music was played outdoors, powerful cornet players quickly gained attention and were often 'crowned' 'King' by their supporters and fellow musicians. Charles 'Buddy' Bolden (1877–1933) was the first musician to achieve this status, before he was committed to the East Louisiana State Hospital in 1907. Freddie Keppard (1889–1933) and then Joe 'King' Oliver (1885–1938) later held the crown. Both men were past their peak when they recorded in the 1920s, yet something of Keppard's power can be heard on the final choruses of *Here Comes the Hot Tamale Man*, made with Doc Cook's orchestra in 1926. Oliver's legendary power is almost totally absent on his 1923 classic recordings, although his intense solo on *Dippermouth Blues* gives an indication of what his hot style must have been like.

When the city's music began to be documented in the 1940s, there was no trumpet player more powerful than Wooden Joe Nicholas. He was older than Keppard and Oliver, but not in their class, nor was he ever crowned 'King'. But even though he was at that time over 60, he must have been close (or equal) to their power during their peak years. The strength of his lip and his endurance during 14-hour parades earned him the nickname 'Wooden' Joe. Bill Russell first heard Nicholas in 1943 and his power 'almost blew me right out on to the sidewalk'. When Russell recorded him in 1945, the acoustics of the Artesan Hall were far from ideal, yet we can get a clear indication of his powerful playing. Russell was concerned about the echo in the hall, and a few days later re-recorded Nicholas playing some of the same numbers at George Lewis's house. The small room was even less helpful in capturing his power, but Lewis's wife was concerned for the structure of the house when Nicholas began playing!

Wooden Joe Nicholas was originally a clarinettist and worked with Joe Oliver's band at the Big 25 in 1915. When Oliver began taking extended breaks to go to the pool hall, Nicholas began playing the leader's cornet to get the music started again. He took up cornet regularly in 1918. He was not a schooled musician and was limited in the keys in which he could play, yet his technique is adequate for his economical style. His musical approach was very different from that of the younger musicians such as Punch Miller, Lee Collins or Herb Morand. Possessing none of their fingering skills, he concentrated more on rhythmic drive, and notes and phrases are scattered around the beat. He displayed a greater freedom in his endless variations around the main theme, and his attack and phrasing continually change throughout a number. His single note values alter during a phrase and the phrases themselves vary in length. He constantly alters his vibrato to great effect and, with his variation of power, his playing has a considerable swing and momentum throughout this recording. On *Shake it and Break it* (not to be confused with the number that Sidney Bechet recorded in 1940, but the name often given by some New Orleans musicians to *Weary Blues*), his stabbing notes and fiery phrasing produce one of the most exciting tracks ever to be recorded in New Orleans.

The clarinettist Albert Burbank is also worthy of attention. His busy, extrovert playing is a perfect foil to Nicholas's economic style. On *Eh, La Bas* and *Up Jumped the Devil* he plays lead most of the time, allowing Nicholas even more rhythmic freedom. Trombonist Jim Robinson arrived late for the Artesan Hall date and his playing on *I Ain't Got Nobody* at the end of the session has a nice balance and provides another highlight. Baby Dodds was booked as the drummer, but he failed to appear – although he did record with the band later that week. Josiah 'Cié' Frazier was brought in as a replacement. In the 1960s Cié became the most sought-after drummer in the city, but in 1945 he was working with a navy big band. His drumming is not always in the best of taste and this band would have been better without him.

Even though Wooden Joe had lost much of his power when he recorded five more tracks in 1949, his playing still retained the same rugged swing. *Any Rags* recalled a song that the 'bottlemen' (rag and bone vendors) used on their rounds in earlier years. The two *Clarinet Blues* feature Nicholas's clarinet playing, and his solo, following that of Burbank, may seem crude by comparison. It owes nothing to the high standards of clarinet playing established by the Tio family (teachers of so many of the city's leading clarinettists), but it predates the rougher uptown style of John Casimir and Steve Angram.

Bill Russell had wanted to record Ann Cook since 1943, but her request of a high fee prevented it. By 1949 she had lowered her demands and she recorded two numbers with Nicholas's band. Since recording with Louis Dumaine in 1929 she had become very religious, yet *The Lord Will Make a Way* still had much of the old blues-shouter quality in evidence.

It would be a mistake to suggest that Wooden Joe Nicholas sounded like the legendary Buddy Bolden, yet his archaic and powerful playing must have had some links with the sound that poured out from the noisy uptown dance halls at the turn of the century.

CD

***Wooden Joe Nicholas*, American Music AMCD-5 (USA)**

Wooden Joe Nicholas (tpt), Albert Burbank (cl), Lawrence Marrero (bj), Austin Young (sb)

New Orleans	10 May 1945	**Shake it and Break it** (actually **Weary Blues**)
add Jim Robinson (tb)		**Lead Me On**
		Careless Love
add Cié Frazier (d)		**Artesan Hall Blues**
		Tiger Rag
		All the Whores Like the Way I Ride
		Eh, La Bas
		Up Jumped the Devil
		Don't Go Way Nobody
		I Ain't Got Nobody

Nicholas (tpt), Robinson (tb), Burbank (cl), Marrero (bj), Alcide 'Slow Drag' Pavageau (sb), Baby Dodds (d)

	15 May 1945	**Up Jumped the Devil** **Eh, La Bas**
Joe Petit (tb) replaces Robinson		**St Louis Blues**

Nicholas (tpt), Louis Nelson (tb), Burbank (cl), Johnny St Cyr (g), Austin Young (sb), Albert Jiles (d)

	20 July 1949	**Any Rags**
add Nicholas (cl)		**Clarinet Blues** **Clarinet Blues #2**
*as **Any Rags***	21 July 1949	**Seems Like Old Times**
add Ann Cook (v)		**The Lord Will Make a Way, Somehow**

* * *

Mutt Carey: *Jazz New Orleans, vol.1; Jazz New Orleans, vol.2*

Thomas 'Papa Mutt' Carey was undoubtedly the most underrated of all the major New Orleans musicians. After playing in his home town with Kid Ory, in 1917 he became one of the first New Orleans pioneers in work in Chicago. Not liking the Chicago winter, he returned home the following year. Had he remained in Chicago and recorded with a variety of musicians, posterity might now place him in the same class as King Oliver and Freddie Keppard. In 1919 he left for California, where he was to remain for the rest of his career. He immediately rejoined Kid Ory and recorded with him in 1921. The session was good, but gave Carey little opportunity to shine. When Ory left for greater fame in Chicago in 1925, Mutt Carey took over leadership of the band.

According to his pupil Buck Clayton, Carey was playing some of the most interesting trumpet to be heard in the 1930s. Early musicians never saw themselves as historical figures and paid little attention to recordings, but, sadly, musicians of his generation are today judged mainly on their recorded output from the 1920s and 1930s, and very few jazz recordings were made in California during this period. When Carey was once more reunited with Ory in the 1940s, the former was initially the leader. But by the time the band recorded commercially in 1944 he had become overshadowed by the stronger personality of Ory. His excellent recordings with Ory are discussed elsewhere, yet they do not demonstrate the quality in his playing to which all who heard him live testify.

As a master of the authentic New Orleans trumpet lead he had few equals. Yet the very nature of the role in controlled ensemble playing (particularly in the short time available on a 78 rpm record) demanded an unselfish approach. He always played his part brilliantly, but his subtle contributions are often misunderstood or overlooked. His light swinging style was often capable of power (as on *Ostrich Walk*), yet according to historian Bill Russell: 'He could play so softly when the band got rocking that the shuffling beat of the dancers' feet all but drowned out the band'. Recently, some previously undiscovered 1947 live recordings of the Ory band have come to light and, when issued, these should help to rectify Carey's reputation as one of the very best lead trumpet players in New Orleans jazz. Apart from those with the Ory band, his only other recordings were a 1946 duet session with blues singer and pianist Hociel Thomas and these 1947 tracks for the Century label with his own band.

Carey left the Ory band in the summer of 1947 over a disagreement about money. He travelled to New York and formed this group using local musicians. Baby Dodds and Pops Foster had been working with Art Hodes's small band and along with Danny Barker were regulars on Rudi Blesh's weekly 'This is Jazz' broadcasts. Individually the three musicians had been part of some of the most distinctive rhythm sections on record: Baby Dodds with Bunk Johnson's 1944 band, Pops Foster with Luis Russell's 1929 group and Danny Barker with one of the best big-band rhythm sections of all – that of Cab Calloway's 1940–2 orchestra, with Milt Hinton and Cozy Cole. With the combination of Dodds' infectious drumming, Foster's slapping bass and Barker's solid, swinging guitar playing, Carey's team had already become recognized as one of the best of all small-group rhythm sections. In the broadcasts, the pianists such as James P. Johnson or Joe Sullivan did not always fit perfectly with the rhythm trio. Under Carey's astute leadership, pianists Hank Duncan or Cliff Jackson completed one of the finest small-band rhythm sections ever to have recorded.

Albert Nicholas, Edmond Hall and Jimmy Archey were also taking part in the 'This is Jazz' broadcasts. Since early 1946 Albert Nicholas had returned to small-band playing, first with Hodes, then with Kid Ory, and was at this time working at Jimmy Ryan's. He shared the broadcasts with Edmond Hall, who had been working with outstanding success in small groups since 1939. Jimmy Archey had replaced Georg Brunis in the series and, like the rhythm trio, was a fixture in the broadcasts. Unlike most of this band, Archey was not from New Orleans. Although he had worked in the big bands of King Oliver and Louis Armstrong, his small-group experience was limited. Yet he was developing a unique ensemble style that fitted well with New Orleans musicians.

The first session included a long version of *Slow Drivin'*, issued on two sides of a 78. The sides have been spliced together into one of the most satisfying blues to have been recorded during the 1940s. Nicholas's solo is superb, as is his playing throughout the session. On the second chorus of *Cake Walking Babies*, Carey and Dodds prompt him into some electrifying ensemble and solo work. Archey also has a good solo on *Slow Drivin'*. On faster numbers such as *Fidgety Feet* and *Indiana* his tone has a persuasive swing, and these recordings established his small-band reputation. Carey's understated lead pushes (rather than drives) the band and leaves plenty of room for the other voices. He reacts quickly to ideas and his choppy ragtime lead on *Shim-me-sha-wabble, Cake Walking Babies* and *Fidgety Feet* produces some fiery playing from the other musicians.

A few days before the second session, New Orleans clarinettist Tony Parenti recorded an album of ragtime pieces with a seven-piece band that included Archey, Barker and Dodds. The results are interesting, but were too far removed from the authentic written scores that Carey was to use. A month later Bunk Johnson was also to record many ragtime numbers using the same 'Red Back' books that Carey read from, but these latter recordings lack the swing and the joy of Carey's versions. *Joplin's Sensation* and *The Entertainer* are taken at a faster speed than versions by many of today's revival bands, but have a better swing. Like that of King Oliver, Carey's ratty tone did not record well and his lead on *Chrysanthemum* sounds clumsy. Edmond Hall performs strongly on the rags and generally solos well, but his looser ensemble style on *Fidgety Feet* and *Indiana* does not always balance the band as well as Nicholas's playing had.

Following months of inactivity during 1948, Papa Mutt re-formed his band, but he died suddenly on the eve of a season of engagements in Los Angeles and San Francisco; he was only 55. After these recordings were issued they quickly became some of the most influential of the New Orleans revival. Carey's material takes up only one side of each of the Savoy albums detailed below; the remaining tracks are by groups led by Punch Miller. Although these important recordings have not yet been issued on CD, it can only be a matter of time before they appear.

LP

(Mutt Carey and Punch Miller:) ***Jazz New Orleans, vol.2*****, Savoy MG 12050 (USA)**

Mutt Carey (tpt), James Archey (tb), Albert Nicholas (cl), Hank Duncan (p), Danny Barker (g), Pops Foster (sb), Baby Dodds (d)

New York	18 Nov 1947	**Shim-me-sha-wabble**
		Slow Drivin'
		Ostrich Walk
		Cake Walking Babies

LP

(Carey and Miller:) ***Jazz New Orleans, vol.1,*** **Savoy Jazz Classics SJC 415 (originally MG 12038) (USA)**

Edmond Hall (cl) and Cliff Jackson (p) replace Nicholas and Duncan

27 Nov 1947

Joplin's Sensation
Chrysanthemum
The Entertainer
Fidgety Feet
Indiana

* * *

Eureka Brass Band: *Eureka Brass Band: New Orleans Funeral and Parade*

Brass bands had been an integral part of New Orleans musical culture before the earliest jazz bands made an appearance. The black Excelsior Brass Band was formed around 1880 and the white Reliance Brass Band about 1890. Most of the early brass bands were reading bands, and they provided a solid musical foundation for musicians who also performed in 'sit-down' bands for dancing.

During the 1940s an attempt had been made to capture the brass band sound in the recordings of Bunk's Brass Band and the Original Zenith Brass Band, using musicians who had been members of various brass bands in the past. With no rehearsal and limited to the playing time of a 78 rpm record, these pick-up bands featuring one trombone and two trumpets, often sounded like an enlarged jazz band rather than a true marching band.

The Eureka Brass Band had been formed in 1920 and remained active until the late 1960s. Besides playing for carnivals, church dedications and lodge parades, they were frequently engaged for funerals, where their repertoire of dirges dated back over half a century. When this recording was made in 1951, the Eureka had replaced the alto and baritone horns that had been a feature of earlier brass bands, with saxophones. Even so, with its steady personnel, disciplined approach and high musical standards, the band was the last link in the great tradition of New Orleans brass bands.

Since the turn of the century, most jazz musicians had also been members of brass bands, although, interestingly, some players performed only in brass bands. These were reading musicians who often lacked the ability to improvise. This was also the case with certain members of the Eureka. Its leader, Percy Humphrey, had grown up in the brass band tradition and was dedicated to maintaining the band's heritage. He was the grandson of Jim Humphrey, who had organized the Eclipse Brass Band of the Magnolia Plantation in 1900. Sunny Henry had played with the Eclipse, and Red Clark had studied with Dave Perkins of the Reliance Brass Band. For funeral dirges, Willie Pajeaud was the best solo trumpeter since Manuel Perez. Eddie Richardson, Albert Warner, Robert Lewis and Arthur Ogle were veterans of earlier brass bands. Emanuel Paul's massive sound on tenor saxophone was exactly right for taking over the role of the baritone horn on funeral dirges, and with Ruben Roddy the saxophones added a greater swing to the band. George Lewis had figured prominently in the jazzy brass band recordings of the mid-1940s, and by the early 1950s he was the best known musician in the New Orleans revival. Although he had played with the Eureka during the 1920s, he was no longer a regular member of the band. However, he was included in order to make the session more saleable; his clarinet playing also adds an exciting cutting edge to the band.

Even though there were a number of well-organized brass bands regularly playing in New Orleans in the early 1950s, the Eureka was still regarded as something special. Its manager, sousaphone player Clark, had collected and catalogued every old brass band score he could find. He encouraged the musicians to rehearse these and to incorporate them into the band's repertoire. Thus, while other bands played *Panama* and *Bye and Bye*, the Eureka could offer *Our Director* and *Eternity*. Frequent rehearsal was one of the secrets of the band's success; others were the impassioned playing of Humphrey and Paul, and the unity of the trombone team of Henry and Warner.

This was the first recording of an authentic brass band, and although the band was to record later for other labels, this session best demonstrates the range, power and cohesion of a true New Orleans brass band. The session was recorded by two students, Alden Ashforth and David Wyckoff, who had limited finances. Although union regulations stipulated that only four numbers could be recorded, they did manage to record the warm-up number, *You Tell Me Your Dream*. *Just a Closer Walk with Thee* is not really an extra number, but a coda to *West Lawn Dirge*. As the written dirges had been too long for previous 78 rpm recordings, the use of a tape recorder enabled Ashforth and Wyckoff to capture the full majesty of a music that was unique to New Orleans. *Garland of Flowers* and *West Lawn Dirge*, with their unconventional tuning and rigid sections, may prove difficult for the newcomer to accept at first hearing. Yet closer listening reveals a committed and passionate playing and passages of haunting beauty. At times the intensity is so powerful that it is awe inspiring, a great juggernaut of sound.

In the faster numbers, *Sing On* and *Lady Be Good*, the band exhibits a pulsating swing that vibrates between the bass drum and the trombones and rocks the entire band. The trombones play with a strutting syncopation that is a perfect foil for the surging saxophones and fiery trumpets. Although the musicians are using head arrangements for these numbers, there is a unity and collective discipline that is missing from today's more jazz-oriented brass bands. As one by one the older musicians died – Henry, Clark and Pajeaud – the unique qualities that they brought to the band died with them. This music is now gone for ever.

(In the following list, the instruments are ordered in a manner that indicates how the musicians lineup when marching, rather than in the conventional discographical sequence of brass, reeds and rhythm.)

CD

***Eureka Brass Band: New Orleans Funeral and Parade,* American Music AMCD-70 (USA)**

Percy Humphrey, Eddie Richardson, Willie Pajeaud (tpt), Arthur Ogle (snare drum), Robert 'Son' Lewis (bass drum), Emanuel Paul (ts), Ruben Roddy (as), George Lewis (E-flat cl), Charles 'Sunny' Henry, Albert Warner (tb), Joseph 'Red' Clark (bb)

New Orleans 25 Aug 1951

Garland of Flowers
Sing On
Sing On (alternate take)
West Lawn Dirge / Just a Closer Walk with Thee
West Lawn Dirge / Just a Closer Walk with Thee (alternate take)
Lady Be Good
Lady Be Good (alternate take)
You Tell Me Your Dream

* * *

Emile Barnes and Peter Bocage: *Barnes–Bocage Big Five*

One of the unfortunate results of the New Orleans revival was that most of its well-meaning enthusiasts (particularly in Europe) have tended to restrict the music to a so-called traditional instrumentation and confine the repertoire to the blues, rags, stomps and marches issued on the 1940s recordings. This 'purist' outlook was never present among the musicians. One of the strengths of real New Orleans music is its adaptability and its acceptance of new ideas, and early New Orleans bands of between two and eight or nine musicians reveal a wide variety of instrumentation. Every instrument was regarded as a rhythm instrument: often violins or clarinets took the straight melody, and cornets, piccolos and valve trombones played their own variations. With such diverse instrumentation, and before individual roles became fixed, this must have been a highly creative period. However, the piano and the saxophone (often the most important instruments in later forms of jazz) were never included in these early bands, and the banjo (often a symbol of the New Orleans revival) was rarely used. Today, owing to the same economic conditions to which the city's musicians have always been required to adapt, there are many three-, four- or five-piece bands (the terms trio, quartet and quintet are never used in New Orleans music).

This New Orleans adaptability is nowhere better demonstrated than in the 1954 session of the Barnes–Bocage Big Five. The band (with a different drummer) had been working at Mama Lou's, an old dance hall perched precariously on the end of a wooden pier at Lake Ponchartrain, but this recording was made at the San Jacinto Hall, where the best of the Bunk Johnson American Music recordings had been made ten years earlier.

The five musicians originate from a wide variety of different musical backgrounds, yet they respond to each other's ideas without losing their own identity. Emile Barnes had grown up with Sidney Bechet and, while he possessed none of the latter's majestic ideas and technique, as a gutsy blues player he had few equals among the older clarinettists. His archaic manner stems from the earliest of New Orleans styles. Playing close to the melody, he often ends a phrase with an upward run and holds the last note before sliding into the next phrase. A similar approach can be heard in the playing of the ODJB clarinettist Larry Shields as well as of such black players as Achille Baquet and Big Eye Louis Nelson. Like Bechet, Barnes was self taught and possessed a very distinctive sound. He could not have been more different from Peter Bocage, a schooled musician whose light tone and excellent taste had been influential in many of the city's best reading bands for almost 50 years. Bocage also played the violin, xylophone, banjo and trombone and was a skilled composer and arranger. Eddie Dawson had been a member of various string bands before 1906 and had adapted to every style of music since. Homer Eugene was a younger trombonist but here plays the amplified guitar, an instrument that had not even been invented when Barnes, Bocage and Dawson had reached the veteran stage of their careers. From a strict jazz point of view, Homer Eugene is the most interesting soloist on the recording. Bocage had been used to working with steady drummers such as Louis Cottrell Sr and, latterly, Alfred Williams, and the exuberant Albert Jiles, complete with cowbells, tom-toms and chimes, was hardly to his taste. On *The Sheik of Araby* he over-punctuates the melody and his time-keeping is often erratic, yet his sheer enthusiasm produces some highly spirited playing from the band.

Neither Barnes nor Bocage had been working regularly when these recordings were made, and there is often some uncertainty in Barnes's approach. Bocage plays in a relaxed manner, mainly in the middle register and slightly behind the beat. Barnes responds by toning down some of the rougher aspects of his performance and works in a quieter, more wistful style. He often plays the first chorus straight, just behind the trumpet, before embarking on a series of simple variations and riffs. His solos are simply a more intense version of one of his variations, often presented with an increased vibrato. It was hardly a style to win a *Down Beat* award, but it was a recognized way of playing for the old New Orleans dance-hall crowd rather than pleasing the jazz record buyer.

As the band had been playing for dances, most of the tracks are taken at a fairly gentle pace. It is even possible to dance to the faster pieces such as *Toot', Toot', Tootsie, Goodbye* and *Down in Honky Tonk Town*. Some of the slower blues numbers such as *Holler Blues* are a composite of other blues themes loosely strung together. *Mama Inez*, with its Spanish tinge, is played as a rumba and was a favourite in many New Orleans dance halls. Towards the end of the session, children and adults were let into the hall to enjoy the music and to dance, and their happy screams can be heard on the final tracks. As they were so uncommercial, these tracks remained unissued for many years. Eventually, Folkways issued two of the best numbers as a sampler (FA 2465) and the less interesting takes of *When my Sugar* and *Honky Tonk Town* are included here.

This recording will be the most difficult for the newcomer to New Orleans jazz to accept. It has many shortcomings. This recording will also be virtually impossible to find. None the less, having put it into the first edition of this book, we leave it in this new edition, in the hope that it will eventually reappear on CD. As the best documentary example of the uncompromising sound of a New Orleans dance hall its study is the key to understanding the nuances and richness of New Orleans music.

LP

***Barnes–Bocage Big Five*, Nola LP 9 (UK)**

Peter Bocage (tpt), Emile Barnes (cl), Homer Eugene (g), Eddie Dawson (sb), Albert Jiles (d)

New Orleans	9 Sept 1954	**When I Grow Too Old to Dream**

Rat's Blues
When my Sugar Walks Down the Street
The Sheik of Araby
Haltin' the Blues
Toot', Toot', Tootsie, Goodbye
I'm Gonna Sit Right Down and Write Myself a Letter
Holler Blues
My Blue Heaven
Down in Honky Tonk Town
Mama Inez

* * *

Louis Armstrong: *Louis Armstrong: the New and Revised Musical Autobiography*

Louis Armstrong's move back to leading a six-piece band was only partly owing to the revival of interest in New Orleans jazz; it was also an economic decision. In response to public taste, Armstrong had led a successful big band since the 1920s. By the mid-1940s, however, the public's interest in big bands began to wane, though Armstrong continued to front his orchestra until the spring of 1947. In 1944 he recorded with Jack Teagarden in a small group for V-Disc. This was a recording partnership that had brought the best out of both musicians back in 1929 and now, 15 years later, was equally successful. The following year he recorded with another small group, organized by Leonard Feather – the Esquire All-American Award Winners. By 1946 the interest in small-group New Orleans jazz was gaining momentum and Hollywood offered Armstrong a leading role in the film *New Orleans*. The film was a fictional account of how New Orleans jazz became accepted throughout the world after the closing of Storyville, and it reunited Armstrong with his former sidemen Kid Ory, Bud Scott and Zutty Singleton. Also engaged was Barney Bigard, who, like Scott, was a member of Ory's band. Under Armstrong's leadership the group recorded a dozen New Orleans numbers for the film soundtrack, then, with Ory's drummer Minor Hall replacing Singleton, re-recorded some of the pieces for Victor. When the film was released it was suggested that Armstrong should tour with the band as his regular unit. Ory declined the offer, although Bigard (who was about to leave Ory) expressed an interest. There were further small-band appearances with Edmond Hall, and Armstrong participated as a guest in a 'This is Jazz' broadcast, leading to the famous Town Hall concert in February 1947.

The occasion once again reunited Armstrong with Jack Teagarden, and the partnership scaled new heights with brilliant performances such as *Rockin' Chair* and *Save it Pretty Mama*. It was only natural that Teagarden and Bigard should be the basis of the first All-Stars, a group which made its recording debut in October 1947.

The original All-Stars made many excellent recordings, though few lived up to the promise of the Town Hall concert. In the 1950s the group underwent various personnel changes, with Teagarden and Bigard being replaced by Trummy Young and Edmond Hall. While the decade saw the production of many fine albums, such as the tributes to W. C. Handy and Fats Waller, none matches the achievement of the 1956–7 boxed set entitled **Satchmo: a Musical Autobiography of Louis Armstrong**. It was unfortunate that Decca also included some of the tracks from previous All-Star recordings, as these were often of lesser recording quality and the performances are generally less interesting.

Milt Gabler had been supervising many of Armstrong's Decca sessions. These usually featured the trumpeter fronting larger bands and singing popular tunes. However, Gabler was also a knowledgeable jazz enthusiast who was familiar with Armstrong's past achievements, and his suggestion to re-record the many jazz masterpieces made between 1923 and 1931 was eagerly accepted by Armstrong. It was a brave decision by both participant and recording company, for it could have had disastrous results. Unlike many musicians, Armstrong was neither ashamed of his early recordings, nor always fully aware of the extent to which jazz collectors lavished 'classic' status upon them.

The **Autobiography** was recorded over several sessions between December 1956 and January 1957. Armstrong was still a great trumpet player, but he no longer had the fertile imagination, lip agility and phenomenal strength of his earlier years. Bob Haggart was employed to update many of the old small-band arrangements, and he wisely lowered the keys on many numbers. But his 'modern' arrangements were often too fussy and sound today more dated than the originals. The other arranger, Sy Oliver, was more successful in scoring some of Armstrong's old big-band numbers for the smaller groups. Armstrong links each track with a spoken commentary written for him by Leonard Feather. He doesn't bother to correct some of the mistakes in the script, and is at his best when sounding more spontaneous with some of his own stories.

Milt Gabler persuaded Armstrong's manager Joe Glaser not to book the band elsewhere on the recording days, and the musicians thus arrived at the studios fresh and with an appetite for the night's work. Most of the big-band re-creations were recorded first, during three days in mid-December, and show that Armstrong was clearly enjoying the experience. The first session produced a magnificent *I Can't Believe that*

You're in Love with Me and *Lazy River*, and the third a wonderful *Memories of You*, but there are many excellent moments from all three. Five weeks later Armstrong returned to the studio for four further sessions which often produced performances of even more breath-taking quality. His lead on *High Society* and *Everybody Loves my Baby* displayed all the old skills, and every note he played had that New Orleans sense of timing. *Cornet Chop Suey* and *Potato Head Blues* didn't quite match the earlier masterpieces, though new versions of *Gully Low Blues* and *Two Deuces* came remarkably close. The original *Wild Man Blues* was also impossible to follow, yet the new version had its own poignant melancholy.

Away from the live club and concert routine, Armstrong's playing was more thoughtful, and a new urgency and intensity was present. The third of the 1957 sessions produced the unexpected: *King of the Zulus* had not been considered one of the classic recordings from Armstrong's Hot Five period, but it was better than many, and certainly in a different league from the vast majority of recordings made in 1926. This new version rolled back the years. It had the same zany humour as the original, but Armstrong's intense, imaginative and passionate playing surpasses that of the 1926 hit.

The most difficult tracks on the **Autobiography** to re-create were those from the classic blues sessions. The All-Stars' resident vocalist Velma Middleton hardly possessed the right voice for the blues of Ma Rainey, Bessie Smith, Clara Smith and Bertha 'Chippie' Hill. Her version of Ma Rainey's *See See Rider* is poor, yet she manages to project a little more composure on the other three numbers. Armstrong is magnificent. Using a straight mute to simulate his original cornet responses, he phrases with such uncanny timing that it transforms these tracks into minor classics.

The sessions were a tremendous achievement, both for Armstrong and for Milt Gabler. The performances were the last major statement by the music's greatest figure. When Louis visited Britain in 1956, many considered that he was well past his best. Few of us could have predicted that he was still to record some of his most memorable work.

CD

***Louis Armstrong: the New and Revised Musical Autobiography*, Jazz Unlimited JUCD 2003, JUCD 2004, JUCD 2005 (Denmark)**

Louis Armstrong (tpt), Jack Teagarden (tb), Barney Bigard (cl), Dick Cary (p), Arvell Shaw (sb), Sid Catlett (d)

Boston	30 Nov 1947	**Muskrat Ramble**

Earl Hines (p) and Cozy Cole (d) replace Cary and Catlett

New York	26 April 1950	**New Orleans Function: Flee as a Bird**
		Oh, Didn't He Ramble

add Armstrong (v)

Pasadena, CA	30 Jan 1951	**My Monday Date**

Armstrong (tpt), Trummy Young (tb), Bigard (cl), Billy Kyle (p), Shaw (sb), Kenny John (d)

New York	19 March 1954	**Struttin' with Some Barbecue**

add Freeman (ts), Armstrong (v) — **Basin Street Blues**

omit Freeman; Barrett Deems (d) replaces John

	21 Jan 1955	**When it's Sleepy Time Down South**

Armstrong (tpt, v), Young (tb), Edmond Hall (cl), George Dorsey (as), Lucky Thompson (ts), Dave McRae (bar), Billy Kyle (p), Everett Barksdale (g), Squire Gersh (sb), Deems (d)

New York	11 Dec 1956	**If I Could Be with You**
		Lazy River
		I Can't Give You Anything but Love
		Body and Soul
		I Can't Believe that You're in Love with me
		On the Sunny Side of the Street

omit (v); add Hilton Jefferson (as)

	12 Dec 1956	**Mahogany Hall Stomp**

add Armstrong (v)

When You're Smiling
Some of these Days
I Surrender Dear
Georgia on my Mind
Exactly like You

Armstrong (tpt), Young (tb), Hall (cl), Kyle (p), Gersh (sb), Deems (d)

High Society

as ***When You're Smiling****, but add Dorsey (fl), McRae (bass cl)*

	13 Dec 1956	**Song of the Islands**

as ***When You're Smiling*** — **That's my Home**

omit Hall — **Memories of You**

omit (v); add Hall — **Them There Eyes**

Armstrong (tpt, v), Young (tb), Hall (cl), Kyle (p), George Barnes (g), Gersh (sb), Deems (d)

23 Jan 1957 — **Hotter than That**

add Young (v) — **Gut Bucket Blues**

omit (v) — **Weary Blues**
Potato Head Blues
Cornet Chop Suey
All the Wrongs You've Done to Me

24 Jan 1957 — **Two Deuces**
Mandy Make up your Mind
Wild Man Blues

add Armstrong (v) — **Gully Low Blues**
Everybody Loves my Baby

add Young (v) — **Heebie Jeebies**

omit (v); add Armstrong, Young, Hall (speech)
25 Jan 1957 — **King of the Zulus**

omit (speech) — **Frog-i-more**

add Armstrong, Velma Middleton (v) — **Georgia Grind**

add Yank Lawson (tpt); omit (v) — **Snag it**

add Hall (shout) — **Dipper Mouth Blues**

omit Hall (shout) — **Canal Street Blues**

Armstrong (tpt, v), Young (tb), Hall (cl), Jefferson, Dorsey (as), Seldon Powell (ts), McRae (bar), Kyle (p), Barksdale (g), Gersh (sb), Deems (d)

28 Jan 1957 — **You Rascal You**
Hobo You Can't Ride this Train

omit (v) — **Knockin' a Jug**

Armstrong (tpt), Kyle (p) — **Dear Old Southland**

Armstrong (tpt), Young (tb), Hall (cl), Kyle (p), Barksdale (g), Gersh (sb), Deems (d), Middleton (v)

See See Rider
Reckless Blues
Trouble in Mind
Courthouse Blues

* * *

Kid Thomas Valentine: *Kid Thomas Valentine's Creole Jazz Band*

After the many recordings made during the 1940s by black New Orleans bands the 1950s were a lean time for a number of New Orleans collectors. Louis Armstrong, Sidney Bechet, Kid Ory and George Lewis continued to record, but most of their output was geared towards the touring circuit of younger white audiences. The Southland label in New Orleans issued numerous LPs that featured mainly white dixieland musicians and a few black musicians playing for the tourists on Bourbon Street, but produced few recordings of any distinction. However, the 1960s brought forth a new interest in black New Orleans jazz which, in sheer volume, was to more than treble the number of recordings ever made in the city. If Bunk Johnson and George Lewis were seen as the champions of the 1940s revival, then Kid Thomas and Capt. John Handy were the new heroes of the 1960s.

Kid Thomas Valentine made his recording debut for American Music in 1951, but, issued on a label that also offered Bunk Johnson, George Lewis, Kid Shots Madison and Jim Robinson, the album received little attention and did not stay in the catalogue very long. It featured Thomas with a pick-up band. His regular band was featured on several private recordings made at dance halls and parties during the 1950s, and these eventually appeared on small independent labels. Kid Thomas lived across the river in Algiers and the band was popular amongst the local population. In neighbourhood halls like Speck's Moulin Rouge, the Tip Top Ballroom and the Westwego Fireman's Hall, he produced a loose rhythmic brand of music that the locals liked to dance to.

The CD under discussion was the first official recording of Valentine's regular band. After previous informal recordings made in less than ideal conditions, Thomas might have expected that this session would be different. But recording studios were still closed to black musicians, and this session was held in the reception area of a local television studio, where the music had to be interrupted every 15 minutes for news, weather reports and commercials. Yet for a band that could keep playing even during fights and the occasional shooting, the adverse conditions did not affect the performance, except during the second take of *Maryland*, hurriedly finished as the second hand of the studio clock swept towards a prearranged time for a station break.

Recorded in 1959, the majority of the band had been working together since the 1940s. Valentine was a canny leader and possessed a powerful ringing tone that could be heard several blocks away, but his main asset was the nucleus of musicians he had gathered together. In trombonist Louis Nelson and tenor saxophonist Emanuel Paul he had soloists who were considerably more musically literate than he was himself. This not only extended the repertoire, but added a wide range of colour to the ensemble. The constantly shifting blend of the three instruments created a sound that was distinctive and exciting. Nelson once complained that Paul's busy tenor saxophone lines often crossed into the trombone parts. This was true, but it forced the trombonist into adopting a looser and less conventional role and gave the band greater variety. The band plays a mixture of popular dance numbers that would have been a typical evening's entertainment at the Moulin Rouge. Numbers usually associated with Xavier Cugat, such as *Mama Inez* and *Siboney*, are played with the same enthusiasm as pop tunes like *When My Dreamboat Comes Home* and *What am I Living for* or jazz standards like *St Louis Blues* and *Panama*. There was almost no tune that the Thomas band would not attempt. Like most New Orleans bands, if the customers requested it, they would play it.

The music is relaxed and reflects the ease and confidence that these musicians have for each other after many years of working together. The New Orleans philosophy that every instrument is really a rhythm instrument is nowhere better demonstrated than here. The texture of the music is loose and the lead frequently alternates between several instruments. Sammy Penn's busy drumming, banjoist 'Creole' George Guesnon's rolling beat, pianist Joe James's simple chordal style and bassist Alcide 'Slow Drag' Pavageau's rocking swing, together produce a flexible, shifting foundation for the three horns. Here, ideas are passed back and forth, the lead exchanged, and each horn moves between rhythmic and melodic duties with casual ease. Spaces are left that allow tremendous freedom to each musician. This accommodates perfectly Valentine's explosive style, the hallmark of his playing. After outlining the melody, he often roars into a broader variation with a series of rhythmic clusters of jabbing notes delivered in clipped phrases, with a wide vibrato and a searing tone. Scattered around the beat, his unpredictable, high voltage, unfinished, strangulated phrases give the band its drive. During some ensemble passages Nelson also introduces a series of single note blasts like a man with an uncontrollable hiccup. The notes appear to be placed at random, yet each one is perfectly positioned within the ensemble. Nelson also is given room to quote themes from other compositions during his solos (*Tin Roof Blues* during *A Closer Walk with Thee*, and *Stars and Stripes Forever* during *St Louis Blues*). Emanuel Paul's large tone and muscular playing derive from Coleman Hawkins's tenor saxophone style of the 1930s.

During the 1950s Kid Thomas Valentine's band was unusual, because it still identified itself with the noisy dance halls in which it originated. Inevitably as the band became more popular during the 1960s and began playing regularly for tourists in the French Quarter, its character changed. Happily, this CD captures something of the carefree atmosphere of a New Orleans band doing what it does best, entertaining the people in an unpretentious way with music that mirrored their lives.

CD

***Kid Thomas Valentine's Creole Jazz Band*, American Music AMCD-49 (USA)**

Kid Thomas Valentine (tpt), Louis Nelson (tb), Emanuel Paul (ts), Joe James (p), 'Creole' George Guesnon (bj, v), Alcide 'Slow Drag' Pavaveau (sb), Sammy Penn (d)

New Orleans	24 May 1959	**On a Coconut Island**
James (v) replaces Guesnon		**Stingaree Blues**
omit (v)		**Mama Inez**
add Guesnon (v)		**Eh, La Bas**
omit (v)		**Maryland, My Maryland** (alternate take)
		Maryland, My Maryland
		Siboney
		Panama
		When My Dreamboat Comes Home
		Just a Closer Walk with Thee
		St Louis Blues
add Penn (v)		**I Believe I Can Make It By Myself**
Guesnon (v) replaces Penn		**Confessin'**
omit (v)		**When the Saints Go Marching In**

* * *

Percy Humphrey: *Percy Humphrey's Crescent City Joy Makers*

In 1961 Herb Friedwald, a student at Tulane University, persuaded Bill Grauer of Riverside Records to let him make a series of recordings in New Orleans. Although many of the stalwarts who had recorded for Bill Russell in the 1940s had died – Bunk Johnson, Kid Shots Madison,

Wooden Joe Nicholas and Big Eye Louis Nelson – and George Lewis was under contract to Verve, there were still a number of musicians playing well enough to maintain the standards of earlier recordings.

Like Russell, Friedwald preferred to ignore the saxophone and amplified guitar featured in many bands playing in New Orleans at that time. Thus Kid Thomas Valentine's band was recorded without its regular tenor saxophonist Emanuel Paul, and the debut recording of the exciting alto saxophonist Capt. John Handy had to wait a little longer. In addition to Valentine, Friedwald recorded regular bands led by Peter Bocage and Sweet Emma Barrett (with slight changes in personnel) and other bands assembled under various nominal leaders. However, the jazz scene was changing drastically in New Orleans. Regulars at the dance halls had gradually become too old to dance, and younger blacks were more interested in rhythm-and-blues and rock-and-roll. Bands that had found steady work playing for dances were now looking for jobs.

Percy Humphrey was among those who witnessed the success that George Lewis had achieved on the college circuit, playing a mixture of traditional rags, stomps and blues for a white middle-class audience that had become familiar with this repertoire via local revival bands and phonograph records. Humphrey was the strongest and most original trumpeter in the city. He viewed the chance to record for a major company as simply an opportunity to obtain regular work on Bourbon Street. To achieve this, he was prepared to include a trombone and a banjo in his 'joy maker' band, to satisfy Friedwald's preconceptions about instrumentation. (In New Orleans, a joy maker band is a band specially assembled for an occasion.) Trombonist Louis Nelson and banjoist Emanuel Sayles were added, therefore, to Humphrey's group from the pool of musicians that Friedwald had selected for other recordings in this series.

Most of the bands that Friedwald recorded appeared content to perpetuate their usual manner of playing, while others strove to re-create an earlier musical tradition. Not Humphrey. He seemed aware that a simplified formula for performance might reach the potential new audience, and the session, for all its faults, is in this sense forward-looking.

The formula is partly based on the success that groups led by Papa Celestin, Paul Barbarin and, to some extent, Lewis had been enjoying on Bourbon Street. Confining themselves mainly to 'traditional' numbers, Humphrey's men opened with a brief statement by the whole ensemble. Then, to the accompaniment of the rhythm section, most of the musicians played a solo, usually two choruses in length, the first chorus sticking closely to the melody and the second offering simple variations. A lively, shouting, collectively played statement would finish the piece. This approach may have lacked the excitement of performances offering a greater amount of collective improvisation, but it was easier for the musicians and, more importantly, the customers preferred it and, feeling obliged to applaud after each solo, tipped generously.

The absence of a piano on this Joy Maker session produces a lighter sound in the rhythm section and somehow seems to give the band more forward thrust. The rhythms are lively, indeed too lively for older dancers. In any event the new audiences would come not to dance but to sit and listen. If the full ensemble sound sometimes lacks subtlety and light and shade, at least it offers strength. If Albert Burbank's clarinet solos sometimes lack ideas and logic, then at least he has a strong New Orleans tone. If most of the solos are taken in the same order – well, at least one could be sure that the banjo solo would be included! The fans loved it, and *Down Beat* magazine awarded this Riverside LP four stars. This band, perhaps above all others, anticipated the opening of Preservation Hall, and the musical policy that made that venue such a worldwide success. Naturally its opening was an enormous benefit to musicians and fans alike. But the resultant situation, bringing veteran musicians wanting to pace themselves, together with an uncritical audience, often lulled the musicians into set routines, fossilizing the style.

During the 1960s labels like Icon, Center, Pearl, Mono and San Jacinto, as well as Preservation Hall's own label, made excellent recordings that were superior to this one in many respects. But most of these have not been reissued on CD, and they do not represent the optimism and hunger for success that this portrays. For sheer drive and commitment the Joy Makers are hard to beat. Humphrey leads the front line with passion and a no-nonsense approach. Nelson is a thoughtful soloist and the rhythm section is first class. There is some variation in the solo routines on these tracks, and Sayles's acoustic guitar, heard on two tracks in place of the banjo, is an asset.

Percy Humphrey led several Preservation Hall bands that toured America and Europe over the next 30 years. The joy and vitality of New Orleans jazz was still often evident, and his bands brought happiness to millions of people. It was jazz with a smile on its face, but these countless subsequent performances rarely achieved the spontaneity and freshness that his Joy Makers brought to this record.

CD

***Percy Humphrey's Crescent City Joy Makers*, Original Jazz Classics OJCCD-1834-2 (USA)**

Percy Humphrey (tpt), Louis Nelson (tb), Albert Burbank (cl), Emanuel Sayles (bj), Louis James (sb), Josiah Frazier (d)

New Orleans	24 Jan 1961	**Milenberg Joys**
		Over in Gloryland
*as **Milenberg Joys**, but Sayles (g)*		**Lonesome Road**
*as **Milenberg Joys***		**We Shall Walk Through the Streets of the City**
		Weary Blues
*as **Milenberg Joys**, but Sayles (g)*		**Bucket's Got a Hole in It**
*as **Milenberg Joys***		**All the Girls Like the Way I Ride**
		Rip 'em up Joe
		Climax Rag

CHAPTER 7

The First Bop Bands

Mark Gardner

Bop crystallized and was perfected in New York. To be sure, many of the creators and leading exponents of this jazz form were from the American provinces. Alto saxophonist Charlie Parker, an acknowledged genius and virtuoso, came from Kansas City. Trumpeter Dizzy Gillespie, a brilliant instrumentalist, important teacher and leader of the first fully-fledged modern big band, was a son of South Carolina. Miles Davis, destined to be the most talented protégé of Parker and Gillespie, arrived in Manhattan from St Louis. His fellow trumpeter, the brilliant Fats Navarro, was an emigré from Key West, Florida. Drummers Kenny Clarke and Art Blakey were born in Pittsburgh, also the home of bass player Ray Brown. Guitarist Charlie Christian, from Texas, and bass player Jimmy Blanton, from Tennessee, died before bop flowered yet made significant contributions. The key arranger for the new sounds and one of its most melodic composers was Tadd Dameron, from Ohio.

All these men gravitated to New York in the early 1940s and found each other. They also discovered many kindred spirits who were native New Yorkers. Pianists Bud Powell, Thelonious Monk and Duke Jordan were residents, as were Walter Bishop Jr and Kenny Drew. Other New Yorkers who made substantial contributions to the style included drummer Max Roach, baritone saxophonist Cecil Payne, tenor saxophonist Sonny Rollins and alto saxophonist Jackie McLean. The bulk of the originators had worked under the disciplines of big bands from which they escaped with glee to the cramped cabarets of 52nd Street, which for half a dozen years was a unique centre of excellence.

Essentially a small-group idiom, this new music was an advance in harmonic and rhythmic complexity on the traditional and swing styles that preceded it. It became harder for two chordal instruments to agree, so more groups used a piano and dispensed with a guitar. The pianist set the chords in an understated, abstract way. Later the guitar was reintroduced, and when two closely attuned musicians such as pianist

Al Haig and guitarist Jimmy Raney, or pianist Lennie Tristano and guitarist Billy Bauer, worked together in a rhythm section, they were able to avoid clashes in accompaniment. The bass player emerged as the main time-keeper, providing a steady walking line to suit the harmonies and dovetail with the piano chords. Cymbals, especially the ride cymbal, also carried the rhythm, but otherwise the drummer was allowed a freer role which enabled him to punctuate solos with an apt commentary of his own. A key change was the elimination of the bass drum as a time-keeper, and its participation in punctuating solos came to be known as 'dropping bombs'.

Bop demanded greater facility from all instrumentalists, a feature of which was fast tempo playing to an extent not heard before. Many of the melodies, both improvised and composed, were terse and tense and had complex patterns of accentuation, this being a vital element in the rhythmic sophistication of the music. Often the composed themes were cryptic 'original' tunes written on the same chord progressions as popular songs. To confuse listeners further, groups occasionally would not even play the melody but would swiftly sail into apparently themeless improvisation, the result being more disorienting in this style than in the swing performances which had done the same thing. And it was a trademark of the boppers to end a piece on a note that sounded unresolved in conventional terms.

The rules of the game were soon assimilated and, after a period of controversy and turbulence, bop became an accepted style absorbed into the mainstream, to the considerable enrichment of the music. Originally known as bebop and also rebop, it was the basis for related styles that appeared rapidly: Afro-Cuban jazz, cool jazz, West Coast jazz, hard bop, soul jazz and bossa nova.

Bop is still heard, admired and played, although many of its finest interpreters have long departed. The present generation is learning to love this cerebral, intense and beautiful style which called for the highest musical ability. The recorded legacy is large and comprehensive.

* * *

Dizzy Gillespie: *'Shaw 'Nuff'*; (various artists:) *The Bebop Revolution*

Although their names will be linked forever, Charlie Parker and Dizzy Gillespie, the twin architects of bop, worked together for only 18 months or so. They recorded in tandem on just nine occasions and on four of those they were mere sidemen. Significantly, eight of their studio sorties were compressed into 12 months in 1945–6. Our knowledge of their partnership has been expanded greatly by the release of various broadcasts, transcriptions and private tapes, but in the 1940s much of their extensive influence on other musicians was distilled from their recordings of 1945 for the Guild and Musicraft labels. These seven performances were like commandments to the faithful, tracts to be studied and analysed, copied and recycled by the most gifted of a generation of both black and white jazz players.

The music stemming from the dates under Gillespie's name included pieces which the trumpeter and his alto saxophonist had shaped up during their engagement at the Three Deuces club on 52nd Street the previous autumn. There are strong suspicions that Parker should have been part of the proceedings at the session on 9 February 1945 when *Groovin' High*, in a version initially rejected but issued many years later, and the blues *Blue 'n Boogie* were recorded by Gillespie's sextet. In the event, Gillespie and tenor saxophonist Dexter Gordon carry the solo load, with assistance from pianist Frank Paparelli and guitarist Chuck Wayne. On the blues Gillespie's bravura trumpet passage is a particularly fine example of his ability to create at speed with complete confidence.

A few weeks later, Parker was present in an entirely different sextet. Inexplicably, the two men did not use the rhythm section which had accompanied them the previous year. The line-up, essentially a compromise personnel, consists of pianist Clyde Hart, guitarist Remo Palmieri, bassist Slam Stewart and drummer Cozy Cole. Hart is a sensitive accompanist whose piano chords are cast in the modern idiom, but his solos betray his preference for swing, and this is also true of Stewart, a little of whose vocal accompaniment in unison with his improvisations goes a long way. Cole did not favour the crisp, unexpected accents employed by Roach or Clarke, and for the most part merely keeps time with brushes or, on *Dizzy Atmosphere* only, sticks. Palmieri, thoroughly a modern soloist steeped in Charlie Christian's style, is called upon to play rhythm guitar on Gillespie's compositions *Dizzy Atmosphere* and *Groovin' High*, giving the rhythm section a curious chugging quality, well distanced from the clean, fleet support that Parker certainly preferred.

Yet with all these apparent debits, the three performances are of immense musical and historical value for the sweeping, unfettered trumpet and saxophone solos and the vivid unison lines in which the two sound like a single voice. Their tones may have appeared thin and their ideas strange and uncomfortable to lay listeners in 1945 still unfamiliar with the surprising rhythms, fast tempos and original combinations of notes, but time has proved the unerring logic and beauty of these inspired creations.

Groovin' High, based on the chord progression of *Whispering*, has a call-and-response pattern established from the onset, when a unison phrase by the horns is answered by the bass and continues over into the main theme with the piano responding to the catchy phrases of alto and trumpet. The figure that they repeatedly play translates into the spoken word as 'bebop.' Parker's improvisation strikes a wonderful balance between tension and relaxation, and, following a bizarre interlude by Stewart, Gillespie punches out a muted trumpet solo of great precision and power. After the guitar solo Gillespie, removing the mute, plays his specially composed solo ending, later adapted by Tadd Dameron to fit into his melody *If You Could See me Now*.

All the Things You Are, with its classic introduction, which was subsequently grafted on to virtually all modern jazz interpretations of the song, is a relatively straight reading. Gillespie hews fairly closely to the written melody, but Parker in his eight-bar passages improvises freely in a relaxed manner. Parker later adapted this standard as *Bird of Paradise*.

The gem of the session is the spirited *Dizzy Atmosphere* with its scene-setting opening from the trumpet, the crazy, heady dash by the horns, and the brilliance of their solos. In Parker's lissom chorus the notes seem to unravel from the saxophone with the swing and snap of an uncoiling spring. His placement of accents is continually startling yet eminently right. The same acute sense of timing, and a matching grace and guile, are present in the trumpet solo, after which Stewart's facile chorus of bowed bass and vocal comes almost as a relief. When the trumpet and saxophone return in unison it is on a smooth melodic variation of the original theme which resolves into the opening strain.

For his next assignment with Guild, Gillespie was able to present four-fifths of the Three Deuces band, including pianist Al Haig and string bass player Curly Russell. Drummer Max Roach was on the road with Benny Carter, so Gillespie chose Big Sid Catlett. The admirable Catlett had been a huge influence on Roach, Clarke, Blakey and most of the other early bop drummers. He was sympathetic to the new style and adapted to it more readily than Cole. This time there was no guitar to complicate the rhythm section.

The session was more tightly organized than its predecessor. As if to underline the atmosphere of confidence that prevailed, the musicians launch themselves immediately on a composition by Gillespie and Clarke first recorded by tenor saxophonist Georgie Auld the previous year, *Salt Peanuts*. This brusque, angular, stop-start theme was soon to become a testing ground for aspiring boppers. Jagged and dissonant, it was not intended to be pretty, and the trumpeter's vocal mugging is another strange element in this abrasive performance. Once the jarring theme, such as it is, has been despatched, the way is clear for free-wheeling solos by Haig, Parker and Gillespie, and then a meticulous drum solo by Catlett which shows in detail the influence he had on Blakey.

Catlett's drumming is also a potent ingredient of *'Shaw 'nuff'*, another up-tempo performance with intricate, highly charged lines. As was usually the case in fast pieces, the leader would yield to the saxophonist in the order of solos. Haig's solo benefits from its controlled understatement in the whirlwind of music that surrounded him.

By contrast, *Lover Man*, the other undisguised song among these recordings, is an impeccable ballad read by ultra-cool singer Sarah Vaughan, who had worked with Gillespie and Parker in the Earl Hines and Billy Eckstine orchestras. Haig and the horns constantly support and embroider Vaughan's true and pure voice. Gillespie's solo subtly embellishes the melody.

Hot House, created by Tadd Dameron, is based on the chord progression of *What is this Thing Called Love?*. A bustling burst from the drums announces this medium-tempo swinger, in which Gillespie emphasizes his rapport with Parker by picking up one of the last phrases of his companion's solo to launch his own. Aside from an eight-bar intervention by Haig towards the end, this warm, relaxed, unadulterated bop performance features Parker and Gillespie, singly or together, from start to finish. Their solos became model structures for most young jazz instrumentalists.

Upon returning to New York from an uncomfortable engagement in Hollywood, Gillespie began an extended stay at the Spotlite club. Vibraphonist Milt Jackson, pianist Haig and bassist Ray Brown were still in the group, but Parker and his permanent 'deputy' Lucky Thompson had both opted to remain in Los Angeles, and drummer Stan Levey quit. Within days Gillespie was in front of the microphone for a session under the aegis of Victor, the company which would sign the trumpeter to a contract the following year. Victor had been persuaded to record Gillespie after a certain amount of arm-twisting from critic Leonard Feather, who produced the session and also, under the pseudonym Floyd Wilson, arranged one title, *Ol' Man Rebop* (based on *Old Man River*). The company required that some of the *Esquire* magazine award winners participate. Gillespie brought in tenor saxophonist Don Byas, about to sail to Europe (whence he never returned), who had worked with Gillespie on 52nd Street in 1944; although he was a swing musician in tone and feeling, he was harmonically sophisticated and an excellent technician. Drummer J. C. Heard, another *Esquire* winner, was equally at home with mainstream jump bands as with a bop combo. For this date, the leader again called in a guitarist, the remarkably facile Bill DeArango, who had recorded alongside Gillespie at a session under Vaughan in 1945. DeArango was undoubtedly the most fluent and accomplished guitarist active at that time, but he made few recordings and none better than these tracks.

Master takes of the four titles, together with four sides by Coleman Hawkins, were rapidly issued in a 78 rpm album called **New 52nd Street Jazz**, which finished as the best-selling jazz album of 1946. In this respect, quite apart from its musical virtues, it was the most significant release in helping to attract a wide audience to the new style. Two decades later a Gillespie retrospective LP revealed alternate takes to all of the titles except Feather's contribution.

After years of contributing compositions and arrangements to various bands and collecting pieces from fellow modernists, Gillespie was virtually a walking archive of new music awaiting wider dissemination. Heard on record for the first time – pre-dating versions by Kenny Clarke, its composer Thelonious Monk and Bud Powell – was *52nd Street Theme*, built on a cunning bop riff pattern, part of which Monk borrowed from the novelty hit *Woody Woodpecker's Song*. This unwhistleable melody gained the immediate status of an anthem, invariably played at a frenetic tempo and thereby seen as a trial ground for any young bop musician. Parker adopted it as his set closer, usually launching into the turbulent contours with undisguised ferocity. Gillespie's arrangement calls for both horns along with guitar and vibes to play the main section of the melody in unison – no mean feat at a bristling tempo – but only Byas and Gillespie play the bridge. Although Jackson solos confidently, the engineering does not catch the nuances of his instrument. Byas is brusque and forthright, while DeArango executes a passage of stunning virtuosity. However, Gillespie caps them all with his invention. One senses his dissatisfaction with his own performance on the first take, which includes an uncharacteristic stumble, but no such blemish occurs in his meticulous upper-register work and cohesive integration of ideas at the second attempt. Brown also performs a bowed solo on both takes.

Gillespie wrote *A Night in Tunisia*, the first of his many 'exotic' pieces, around 1941 when he was working with saxophonist Benny Carter at Kelly's Stable. This piece had been recorded in a vocal version by Sarah Vaughan under the title *Interlude* in 1944. Here, though, was its first, brilliant instrumental reading in an arrangement which became standard and outstripped *52nd Street Theme* in popularity. It opens with a then unusual recurring bass figure, syncopated, not walking. Gillespie's muted trumpet, assisted harmonically by the tenor sax, carries the melody, which evolved from a happy accident when Gillespie was playing thirteenth chords. The piece includes an interlude which launches Gillespie into an immaculately executed solo of enormous excitement, energy and buoyancy. He rapidly removes the mute while Byas takes a few bars. Much of Gillespie's improvisation is concentrated in the upper register, and while the tone is thinner than, say, that of Louis Armstrong or Roy Eldridge, every note is crisp and clear.

Trumpet playing of such complexity and accuracy was a new element in jazz. Byas's solo and that of Jackson are inevitably anti-climactic after this precision piece of musicianship, replete with daring double-time passages and rhythmic twists.

Completing this momentous session was a pair of elaborations of Gillespie's composition *Anthropology*, a variation on *I Got Rhythm*. Again he uses a mute for the theme and open trumpet for his solos. More surprisingly, he chooses to unveil the tricky melody in unison with Jackson's vibraphone. Byas does not play, possibly because he was unfamiliar with the angular line. The quicker master take is far superior to the other attempt, illustrating that a speedy tempo was a necessary adjunct to certain aspects of bop. In many respects this piece is as complicated as the arrangements Lennie Tristano recorded for Capitol in 1949.

Three months later, with Jackson, Haig and Brown, Gillespie recorded four titles for the Musicraft company. Sonny Stitt, the undeniably fluent and gifted replacement alto saxophonist, had patterned his playing closely on Parker's style, and his allegiance to Parker is glaringly obvious in his solos on these recordings. Equally apparent are the differences. While Parker invariably delights with his rhythmic and melodic inventiveness, Stitt sounds rather predictable, even mechanical, by comparison. That he was able to absorb so many of Parker's lessons shows his aptitude as one of the latter's earliest disciples. Stitt was able to prevent himself being enveloped by Parker's style by switching to tenor saxophone later on.

Vibraphonist Milt Jackson, pianist Haig and bassist Ray Brown were all part of Gillespie's Hollywood line-up. Drummer Clarke was an old friend and fervent supporter of the trumpeter. On this session Gillespie shuns the mute, except for the blues track, and plays glorious open trumpet, which would be his strong suit in front of the big band he led for the following four years. By this stage he had worked hard to broaden and ripen his tone, with some success, as this date attests. Perhaps, too, he felt that his open sound blended better with Stitt's tone, which was altogether less pliant than Parker's.

As the title suggests, *One Bass Hit* features among its solos Brown's nimble and big-toned bass lines, but it is the flashing double-time passages by the trumpet that distinguish the performance. Arranger Gil Fuller was present in the studio and joined Gillespie for the vocal portion of the surreal conversation between voices and instruments on *Oop Bop Sh'bam*. *That's Earl, Brother* is a composition with more substance than many of the skeletal bop themes. Overall this date lacks the spark of the Parker–Gillespie collaborations, but it is an admirable showcase for the leader's verve and virtuosity, not to mention his skill at bandleading.

On reissues, Gillespie's essential combo tracks appear in tamdem with his big-band recordings. Only the combo tracks are listed below; the big-band recordings are detailed in chapter 3. Additionally at the time of writing only an incomplete selection of his RCA work is available on the general anthology **The Bebop Revolution**.

CD

***'Shaw 'nuff'*, Musicraft MVSCD 53 (USA)**

Dizzy Gillespie (tpt), Dexter Gordon (ts), Frank Paparelli (p), Chuck Wayne (elg), Murray Shipinski (sb), Irv Kluger (d)
New York 9 Feb 1945 **Blue 'n Boogie**

Gillespie (tpt), Charlie Parker (as), Clyde Hart (p), Remo Palmieri (elg), Slam Stewart (sb), Cozy Cole (d)
28 Feb 1945 **Groovin' High**
All the Things you Are
Dizzy Atmosphere

Gillespie (tpt, v), Parker (as), Al Haig (p), Curly Russell (sb), Sid Catlett (d)
11 May 1945 **Salt Peanuts**

omit (v) **'Shaw 'nuff'**

add Sarah Vaughan (v) **Lover Man**

omit (v) **Hot House**

Gillespie (tpt), Sonny Stitt (as), Milt Jackson (vb), Haig (p), Ray Brown (sb), Kenny Clarke (d)
15 May 1946 **One Bass Hit no.1**

add Gillespie, Gil Fuller (v) **Oop Bop Sh'bam**
That's Earl, Brother

CD

(various artists:) *The Bebop Revolution*, Bluebird 2177-2 RB (USA) and ND 82177 (Europe)

Gillespie (tpt), Don Byas (ts), Jackson (vb), Haig (p), Bill DeArango (elg), Brown (b), J. C. Heard (d)
New York 22 Feb 1946 **52nd Street Theme** (take 1)
52nd Street Theme (take 2)
A Night in Tunisia
omit Byas **Anthropology** (take 1)

* * *

Charlie Parker: *The Charlie Parker Story; Charlie Parker on Dial: the Complete Sessions*

Charlie Parker's inaugural recording session as a leader had its share of problems. His pianist, Bud Powell, had gone house-hunting in Philadelphia. Parker booked Dizzy Gillespie as a substitute, knowing that his trumpeter friend was a competent piano accompanist. He also asked pianist Argonne Thornton (Sadik Hakim) to come along. Barely had the proceedings for the Savoy company got under way when Parker realized that his saxophone had a defect which was causing squeaks. Later trumpeter Miles Davis disappeared and then a union official challenged Thornton, who had no union card. Given these unsettling circumstances, it is a wonder that any music of value resulted, yet such was Parker's concentration and inspiration that 26 November 1945 is perhaps the key date in postwar jazz. For the first time, all the musicians involved were of the same stylistic persuasion. The makeshift nature of the piano accompaniment affected Parker not one jot, and he seemingly took the other distractions in his stride.

His selection of Davis, whose instrumental proficiency at this stage was far from complete, indicated Parker's perception in spotting a talent of rare promise, and the inclusion of the exemplary percussionist Max Roach foreshadowed the composition of the regular quintet he would form in 1947 with Davis and Roach as key members. Bass player Curly Russell would also be a consistent companion for recording dates, including two more with the Savoy label.

By the end of 1945, Parker's artistry was well known and widely appreciated in the jazz community, although many listeners, including some musicians, were bewildered by the speed and execution of his ideas, the rhythmic complexity of his solos and compositions and his harmonic conception. His tart tone did not find favour with those reared on the sweeter sound of Johnny Hodges or the smoother delivery of Benny Carter. It had an abrasive cutting edge which could sound shrill when Parker was not himself. Even his detractors, though, had to acknowledge that the man was a powerful blues player who, more than Gillespie, refurbished and advanced the 12-bar form.

It was in blues territory that this session began as the musicians got to grips with *Billie's Bounce*, a melodically complex theme which Parker contrived on the morning of the session. The first three takes find him struggling with the deficient saxophone, although his first solo is a good one. By take 3, when Davis has settled down, the saxophone problem is glaringly obvious, and Parker decided to give the horn a thorough test. Musicians often tackle different material after unsatisfactory takes, returning refreshed to the original later. Parker's diversion was an up-tempo improvisation on the chord sequence of the popular tune *Cherokee*. Most of this unscheduled performance, released as *Warming up a Riff*, was recorded and it indicates no obvious mechanical difficulties. With Thornton at the piano, Parker soars through an improvisation of splendid invention, relishing the stimulating chord changes and quoting from such disparate sources as *High Society* (the old New Orleans favourite), *Tea for Two*, *Irish Washerwoman* and *Cocktails for Two*. Immediately after this brilliant interlude the group returned to *Billie's Bounce*, and at the fifth attempt a successful take was accomplished. Actually, the leader's best solo is on the fourth (incomplete) take, despite some reed squeaks.

The next task was the other blues Parker had concocted at the eleventh hour, *Now's the Time* (later lifted as the basis for the pop hit *The Hucklebuck*), with a piano introduction by Gillespie that has echoes of Thelonious Monk's style. On this slower, more classical blues, Davis sounds much more confident and poised. The richness of Parker's imagination, his projection of emotion and his links with jazz tradition are all apparent in the two completed takes, which contain quite different solos, replete with double-time passages. His solo on the master take inspired Eddie Jefferson to write a fitting lyric, neatly demonstrating that the improvisation was a melody in its own right.

The most challenging business was left to the end – *Thriving on a Riff* and *Koko*. The first title was rooted in the chord changes of *I Got Rhythm*. Parker would later retitle this clever piece *Anthropology*, and it was first recorded under that name by Gillespie the following year. Three surviving takes find Parker in startling form. His solo on the opening attempt is near perfect, but slight blemishes in the restatement of the theme probably led to its original rejection. The entire opening theme is dropped for the other completed take, which is a series of improvisations by Parker, Davis and Thornton, who sounds distinctly tense after the fine solos by the two horns.

With Gillespie on piano, the quartet (minus Davis) detailed a loving interpretation of one of Parker's favourite ballads, *Embraceable You*, eventually issued under the title of *Meandering*. His playing here is gentle, tender and romantic without being either rhapsodic or sentimental. Right at the end of this unscheduled warm-up, which was never intended for release, Parker reminds himself with a quotation from *You'd Better Go Now* that the saxophone had to be fixed before he could again assay the contours of *Cherokee* (this time under the title *Ko-ko*) at the blinding tempo he reserved for this speciality (on which he had been featured in the Jay McShann orchestra). At this juncture he left with producer Teddy Reig to get the recalcitrant saxophone sorted out. On their return, Davis was missing, so Gillespie was charged with doubling on trumpet and piano, with Thornton filling in at the keyboard on the theme of the first take and at the beginning of Parker's solo on the master take.

The initial try is soon whistled to a halt because Parker and Gillespie start playing the original melody of Ray Noble's *Cherokee*, which would have cost Savoy royalties. The second take is suitably themeless. Both, however, include the new intricate introduction, in unison, then with solo breaks by muted trumpet and saxophone, and again in unison. The only accompaniment for the horns on this swirling theme is the flashing brushes on Roach's snare drum. The routine serves as a propulsive launching pad for Parker's scintillating two choruses of unbroken inspiration at a crippling tempo. Its cohesive shape, fluidity and development of rapid but logical ideas mark this as one of the master works of his substantial discography. The only other soloist is Roach, whose drum passage was a landmark in technique and the controlled building of excitement.

Koko, the definitive summation of all Parker had absorbed and created by the end of his 25th year, heralded his most creative and productive period. During the years 1946–8 he completed seven sessions for the Dial label and five more for Savoy. His output thereafter for Norman Granz's various labels tended to be unsatisfactory owing to the unhelpful nature of some of the contexts in which Granz placed him.

The Dials constitute his most consistent and satisfying work. Despite being treated for drug addiction and mental stress for six of the 15 months he spent in California, he functions at a highly inventive level on all but one date. Among the ensuing albums, the first volume of the Dial sides in chronological order encapsulates his highs and lows.

The opening performance, *Diggin' Diz* (based on the chord progression of *Lover*), is the only fragment to survive from a chaotic session nominally led by Gillespie. It is by a septet including tenor saxophonist Lucky Thompson and guitarist Arvin Garrison, both of whom Parker kept on when he mustered his own septet for Dial. More importantly, however, he was reunited with Davis, lately arrived in Hollywood with Benny Carter's orchestra. The brilliant, classically trained pianist Dodo Marmarosa led the rhythm section. Bass duties were assigned to Victor McMillan (his one and only studio appearance of any import), while behind the drums was the advanced and adventurous Roy Porter.

Every surviving scrap of music – ten complete performances and one edited item – detail five hours of concentrated creativity. With Parker at the peak of his form, Davis was suitably inspired to improvise with hitherto unsuspected daring. Thompson's smooth, rounded sound with its well-shaded vibrato supplied an engaging contrast to Parker's vocal tone with its keen, cutting edge. The responsive rhythm section – Garrison was exclusively a soloist, not an accompanist – maintains an insistent and unflagging pulse, with Marmarosa's percussive chording a constant source of helpful prompting to the soloists. The arrangements are precisely worked out (not always the case in Parker's sessions) and the ensembles tightly rehearsed. The understanding of producer Ross Russell, who believed in letting the musicians go about their work without interference, and the quality of the engineering also contributed to the birth of these classic sides.

To some extent preparations were as usual for Parker, who came up with the melody of *Moose the Mooche* in a taxicab on the way to the session. On the first take Davis plays open trumpet, but on the next, taken slightly faster, he inserts a mute which he used for the remainder of the date, producing a distinctive, plaintive tone closer to that of Howard McGhee than Gillespie. Parker's best flourish is on the third take, but an uncertain wobbling led to the selection of the second take for original release. The arrangement benefits from a conversational ending to which Parker, Thompson and Marmarosa each contributes two bars. Garrison lays out on these takes.

Parker had composed the melody of *Yardbird Suite*, an airy, dancing line, several years earlier. Take 1 follows a conventional pattern, with Parker playing a whole chorus, Davis, Thompson and Marmarosa halves, and Garrison a quarter. By the fourth take the routine had been altered, the net result being a performance half a chorus longer, more relaxed and of greater interest on account of the double juxtaposition of Davis and Thompson. The revised set-up runs like this: Marmarosa (8-bar introduction), unison (16 bars), Parker (8), unison (8), Parker (32), Davis (16), Thompson (8), Davis (8), Thompson (16), Garrison (16), Marmarosa (8), ensemble (8). Parker's chorus on this extended master take is a miracle of structure, unusually economical and rhythmically attuned closely to the intricacies of the design of his melody. Demonstrating his ability to conjure up a memorable phrase, the altoist, in the first eight bars of his solo, inserts the main theme of what would be recorded as *Cool Blues* almost a year later. Thus many Parker themes grew within actual improvisations – a neat reversal of standard jazz practice.

Parker had also long before composed the scintillating and serpentine melody of *Ornithology* (written down by trumpeter Benny Harris), based on the chord pattern of *How High the Moon*. The first take was clearly a run through, because Parker does not solo. The relay ending of the theme was tricky, calling for trumpet, alto, tenor, guitar and piano each to contribute one bar apiece. On take 3 they have this together at the end of the opening and closing themes. The fourth take, the master, opens with an explosive four-bar drum break from Porter and is notably quicker than its predecessors. It is the crispest cut of all.

To this trio of themes by Parker, all destined to become quintessential parts of the bop repertory, was added Gillespie's *Night in Tunisia*. Three of five takes survive, but one is a mere fragment comprising a snatch of ensemble, Parker's glorious cadenza and solo and part of Davis's solo. This was the opening sally, and Parker felt he would be unable to reproduce the soaring spontaneity in subsequent efforts, so Russell issued this 47-second miniature as *The Famous Alto Break*. Actually, Parker's forays on the two surviving complete takes are by no means anti-climactic, although on the fragment the cadenza itself is marginally more virtuosic in its ascent. The arrangement is unusual because the piano and guitar combine in unison to play the hypnotic droning line above which trumpet (in the *a* section) and alto (in the *b*) soar. Porter's strategic 'bombs' on the bass drum are most effective.

The next four tracks, recorded just four months later, come as a deep shock. On the day of the session Parker was disintegrating, in the depths of traumatic drug withdrawal. He was not fit to play (having consumed a quart of whisky) and that he managed any coherence at all was a tribute to his innate musicianship. On one of the few occasions of his career the saxophonist flounders on fast pieces, *Max is Making Wax* and *Bebop*. His struggle is emphasized by the accurate, crackling trumpet work of Howard McGhee. *Loverman*, the first of two ballads, is sluggish and halting yet strangely moving as Parker unnaturally wrestles with an instrument of which he was a master. The same slow, deliberate manner is apparent on *The Gypsy*, which he never played again, so much did he dislike the song and its associations. Parker's fury at the release of these four sides is understandable.

The Spotlite label's compact disc edition of Parker's Dial recordings includes, in chronological order, every single surviving performance the saxophonist made for that company. As such it is an essential aid in appreciating the scope of Parker's invention from take to take. This brilliant body of work is indispensable.

CD

***The Charlie Parker Story*, Savoy Jazz SV–0105 (Japan)**

Miles Davis (tpt), Charlie Parker (as), Dizzy Gillespie (p), Curly Russell (sb), Max Roach (d)

New York	26 Nov 1945	**Billie's Bounce** (take 1)

	Billie's Bounce (take 2)
	Billie's Bounce (take 3)
omit Davis	**Warming up a Riff**
add Davis	**Billie's Bounce** (take 4)
	Billie's Bounce (take 5)
	Now's the Time (take 1)
	Now's the Time (take 2)
	Now's the Time (take 3)
	Now's the Time (take 4)

Argonne Thornton (p) replaces Gillespie

	Thriving on a Riff (take 1)
	Thriving on a Riff (take 2)
	Thriving on a Riff (take 3)
*as **Warming up a Riff***	**Meandering**

Gillespie (tpt) replaces Davis; both Gillespie and Thornton (p)

	Koko (take 1)
	Koko (take 2)

Other CDs

plus additional tracks:

The Complete Savoy Studio Sessions, Savoy ZDS 5500 (USA)

CD

***Charlie Parker on Dial: the Complete Sessions*, Spotlite SPJ-CD4-101 (UK)**

(Gillespie): Gillespie (tpt), Parker (as), Lucky Thompson (ts), George Handy (p), Arvin Garrison (elg), Ray Brown (sb), Stan Levey (d)

Glendale, CA	5 Feb 1946	**Diggin' Diz**

Davis (tpt), Parker (as), Thompson (ts), Dodo Marmarosa (p), Victor McMillan (sb), Roy Porter (d)

Hollywood	28 March 1946	**Moose the Mooche** (take 1)
		Moose the Mooche (take 2)
		Moose the Mooche (take 3)
add Garrison (elg)		**Yardbird Suite** (take 1)
		Yardbird Suite (take 4)
		Ornithology (take 1)
		Ornithology (Bird Lore) (take 3)
		Ornithology (take 4)
		The Famous Alto Break (Night in Tunisia)

Night in Tunisia (take 4)
Night in Tunisia (take 5)

Howard McGhee (tpt), Parker (as), Jimmy Bunn (p), Bob Kesterson (sb), Porter (d)

26 July 1946 — **Max is Making Wax**
Loverman
The Gypsy
Bebop

(Chuck Kopely Jam Session): McGhee, Shorty Rogers, Melvyn Broiles (tpt), Parker (as), Russ Freeman (p), Arnold Fishkin (sb), Jimmy Pratt (d)

Los Angeles — 1 Feb 1947 — **Yardbird Suite**
Blues on the Sofa
Kopely Plaza Blues

omit (tpt) — **Lullaby in Rhythm** (part 1)
Lullaby in Rhythm (part 2)
Home Cooking (part 1)
Home Cooking (part 2)
Home Cooking (part 3)

Parker (as), Erroll Garner (p), Red Callender (sb), Doc West (d), Earl Coleman (v)

Hollywood — 19 Feb 1947 — **This is Always** (take C)
This is Always (take D)
Dark Shadows (take A)
Dark Shadows (take B)
Dark Shadows (take C)
Dark Shadows (take D)

omit (v) — **Bird's Nest** (take A)
Bird's Nest (take B)
Bird's Nest (take C)
Hot Blues
Blowtop Blues
Cool Blues (take C)
Cool Blues (take D)

McGhee (tpt), Parker (as), Wardell Gray (ts), Dodo Mamarosa (p), Barney Kessel (elg), Callender (sb), Don Lamond (d)

26 Feb 1947 — **Relaxin' at Camarillo** (take A)
Relaxin' at Camarillo (take C)
Relaxin' at Camarillo (take D)
Relaxin' at Camarillo (take E)
Cheers (take A)
Cheers (take B)
Cheers (take C)
Cheers (take D)
Carvin' the Bird (take A)
Carvin' the Bird (take B)
Stupendous (take A)
Stupendous (take B)

Miles Davis (tpt), Parker (as), Duke Jordan (p), Tommy Potter (sb), Roach (d)

New York	26 Oct 1947	**Dexterity** (take A)
		Dexterity (take B)
		Bongo Bop (take A)
		Bongo Bop (take B)
		Prezology
		Dewey Square (take B)
		Dewey Square (take C)
		The Hymn
		Superman
		Bird of Paradise (All the Things You Are) (take A)
		Bird of Paradise (take B)
		Bird of Paradise (take C)
		Embraceable You (take A)
		Embraceable You (take B)
	4 Nov 1947	**Bird Feathers**
		Klact-oveeseds-tene (take A)
		Klact-oveeseds-tene (take B)
		Scrapple from the Apple (take B)
		Little Be-bop (Scrapple from the Apple) (take C)
		My Old Flame
		Out of Nowhere (take A)
		Out of Nowhere (take B)
		Out of Nowhere (take C)
		Don't Blame Me
add J. J. Johnson (tb)	17 Dec 1947	**Giant Swing (Drifting on a Reed)** (take B)
		Drifting on a Reed (take D)
		Air Conditioning (Drifting on a Reed) (take E)
		Quasimado (take A)
		Quasimado (take B)
		Charlie's Wig (take B)
		Charlie's Wig (take D)
		Charlie's Wig (take E)
		Bongo Beep (Bird Feathers) (take B)
		Bongo Beep (Bird Feathers) (take C)
		Crazeology (excerpt) (take A)
		Crazeology (excerpt) (take B)
		Crazeology (take C)
		Crazeology (take D)
		How Deep is the Ocean? (take A)
		How Deep is the Ocean? (take B)

Other CDs

same contents:
The Complete Dial Sessions, Stash CD-567 / 68 / 69 / 70(USA)
master takes plus some alternate takes:
The Legendary Dial Masters, vol.1, Stash ST-CD-23, and *The Legendary Dial Masters, vol.2*, ST-CD-25 (USA)

* * *

Thelonious Monk: *Genius of Modern Music, vol.1*; Milt Jackson: *Milt Jackson*; Monk: *Brilliant Corners*

Of all the major contributors to shaping a course for modern jazz, Thelonious Monk was considered the most eccentric. The pianist and composer was quickly recognized by his contemporaries for his unusual and distinctive writing abilities. His individual perception of harmony was undoubtedly influential within the bop workshop sessions of the early 1940s, and his themes were highly valued by Dizzy Gillespie, Charlie Parker and others. But his instrumental work was a subject for scorn in the 1940s and his idiosyncratic melodies were not properly explored until he indicated through his own recordings how they should be interpreted.

His highly personal piano style evolved in a mysterious manner. His earliest recordings, made in 1941, reveal that he was strongly under the influence of Teddy Wilson at this stage of his career. It was also apparent that he had listened to such stride pianists as James P. Johnson, Willie 'the Lion' Smith and Fats Waller, but three years later, on sides with swing tenor saxophonist Coleman Hawkins, his own keyboard concept is fully defined in typically uncompromising fashion.

While certain critics felt that Monk's playing displayed a lack of technique, the evidence suggests he deliberately chose a brusque, percussive stance, and consciously rejected the Wilsonian smooth sophistication which he had earlier favoured. Monk's improvisations bristled with angular dissonance, surprising intervals and craggy runs. His wit, never far away in any performance, often took an ironic turn; at times he was capable of tongue-in-cheek self-parody. He would frequently insert a few bars of stride piano into an otherwise obtuse statement. He disapproved of glib, fast 'blowing' on his melodic structures and sought to involve his fellow musicians in deeper exploration of what were invariably intriguing, surprising themes. Some, notably *'Round Midnight*, were so expertly cast that even highly imaginative players found them difficult melodies on which to improvise. The tunes therefore added a further challenge to Monk's own unconventional accompaniment.

Since Monk was not given to talking about his work, he left listeners to unravel his puzzles and draw their own conclusions. Initially the majority of musicians were certainly baffled. Even though Hawkins employed him for nearly two years, Monk was not a popular pianist with many of the boppers. Some simply could not play with him. So while such of his pieces as *Epistrophy*, *'Round Midnight*, *52nd Street Theme* and *Well You Needn't* gained increasing currency, their composer found work scarce and little call for his keyboard style. In 1946 he was fired from Dizzy Gillespie's orchestra for persistent lateness, and he had scant reason for any optimism about the future until Blue Note Records began recording him in the autumn of 1947. His five sessions for that label, made between 1947 and 1952, are invaluable documents, showing Monk at the helm of assorted quintets and sextets and, for one date, a trio.

The performances from 1947 include 25 of his compositions. Never a prolific writer, he would recycle many of these early works throughout his career. They would be heard in solo, group and even orchestral contexts and would continue to offer provocative challenges to their creator and his numerous sidemen.

The way he played and his style of writing were closely related. Unlike Duke Ellington, he did not compose with other soloists in mind; he wrote primarily to suit his own pianistic approach. After the songs emerged from his keyboard investigations, he would cast about for suitable colleagues to lend his ideas substance. Sometimes the recruits were simply not up to the task. On his first Blue Note session, saxophonists Danny Quebec West and Billy Smith were less than satisfactory associates, whereas trumpeter Idrees Sulieman displayed sympathy and understanding. Monk's most compatible sideman was drummer Art Blakey, who perfectly understood the aims of the pianist and over many years provided the rhythmic stimulation he sought. It is no accident that Blakey is on four of the five Blue Note dates directed by Monk, who appreciated the strong rhythmic undertow and flourishing accents that he supplied. Blakey seldom played loudly in Monk's company, his accompaniment on *Humph*, a jagged up-tempo discursion on the harmonies of *I Got Rhythm*, being somewhat of an exception in this respect. The drummer on the fifth date, Shadow Wilson, was another favourite who subsequently worked alongside Monk in 1957 in the quartet which included John Coltrane.

Evonce and *Suburban Eyes*, the latter based on the chord sequence of *All God's Children Got Rhythm*, are both untypical themes, since they were written not by Monk, but by Ike Quebec and Sulieman respectively. The real gem of Monk's inaugural date was his own *Thelonious*, a telling, repetitive theme built largely around just two notes. Monk enlarges this trifle with inspired skill. The only soloist, he includes a lengthy passage of pure stride piano in his second chorus and affectionately quotes from *Salt Peanuts* in his third.

Nine days after this respectable debut, Monk returned to the same studio with the same rhythm section – veteran bass player Gene Ramey and Blakey – to perform three of his most durable compositions, *Ruby, my Dear*, *Well You Needn't* and *Off Minor*. Some nine years later, a fourth original, *Introspection*, was unearthed.

In a trio context Monk becomes noticeably more expansive and communicative, completely secure in his own structures, with no other soloists to worry about. *Ruby, my Dear* is a beautifully poignant 32-bar ballad destined to become a standard in the jazz repertory. Monk's interpretation is seminal in its economy and feeling, with Blakey's crisp brush punctuations an asset throughout. The sinewy *Well You Needn't*, another much played piece, has a most satisfying hypnotic line with a dancing contrasting melody that rises and falls through a pattern of alternating steps and leaps drawn from the opening. Monk swings hard, occasionally letting a bar or two roll by without striking a note and humming along with his improvisations; he closes with a traditional phrase from Scottish folk music. *Off Minor* also has a memorable theme, and a disconcerting second melody. *Introspection*, opening with an out-of-tempo introduction, has a more complex melody with a call-and-response pattern. In this instance, Monk only lightly embroiders his own creation. Clearly, a piece of this subtlety would have been too much for the front-line sidemen on the previous session, and even the trio required four takes before striking the mood that Monk wanted.

Possibly to show Monk at work in a context more familiar to lay listeners, he played, with unconcealed gusto and considerable distinction, the standard song *April in Paris*. Here his chord combinations and melodic embellishments are more easily comprehended, along with his personal rhythmic preferences. That Monk was part of a tradition, albeit an expander of it, is fully apparent. There is nothing weird or strange about what he plays here, but in 1947 Monk had to contend with ears and minds which were not attuned to the sounds that were the natural expression of his originality.

At his third session, again including Blakey, Monk opted for a quintet with alto saxophonist Sahib Shihab, who unlike trumpeter George Tait was an understanding interpreter of Monk's music. Monk's composition *In Walked Bud*, dedicated to his fellow pianist and protégé Bud Powell, is a clever elaboration of the chord progression of *Blue Skies* and contains a suitably optimistic piano solo. *'Round Midnight*, a dignified

32-bar ballad of classic quality, had already been recorded by the contrasting orchestras of Cootie Williams and Dizzy Gillespie before Monk delivered this masterpiece. The composer handles the melody, with a subdued commentary supplied by the horns, and he elects to improvise during the *b* section of the *aaba* melody. The piece has a late-night mood that is highly evocative of the subject.

With a completely new cast highlighting the vibraphone solos of Milt Jackson, Monk's quartet refurbished his admired *Epistrophy* and *I Mean You*, and detailed a fine new piece, *Misterioso*, at a date in 1948. Wilson replaced Blakey, and the sturdy bass playing of John Simmons was heard alongside Monk for the only time in a recording studio.

Misterioso, sounding like a pianistic exercise but played in harmony by Monk and Jackson, reverts to a lazy beat for the solos, following the urgent theme. The vibes and piano work splendidly together, Jackson clearly enjoying Monk's sparse accompaniment. The pianist's solo is deliberate and ruminative, full of cunning phrases and wicked little runs. The jabbing punctuations he deploys when Jackson returns to the theme are gems of timing.

Epistrophy, written in collaboration with drummer Kenny Clarke, was also recorded by Williams, and it subsequently served as a closing theme for many bop groups. Through its dissonant line the *a* section of the melody builds tension which finds a vivid release in the *b* segment. Jackson's flowing manner of improvisation is by no means at odds with Monk's more rough-hewn lines.

I Mean You, earlier recorded by Hawkins, has a basic quality and a shape that appealed to the saxophonist. Again one is struck by the superior interplay of vibes and piano, a partnership that was to be revived in a famous session in 1954 at which a testy Miles Davis instructed Monk not to play during his solos. Had Davis properly listened to the way Jackson adapted to Monk's accompaniment, he might have had second thoughts. Here, as on *Epistrophy*, the solos are restricted to half choruses, but they are miniatures filled with interest and more than 40 years later still make an impact.

Monk was handicapped by his reputation as an eccentric pianist, an image he did nothing to alter by his bizarre behaviour, and his direct influence on keyboard styles was marginal. Randy Weston and Stan Tracey are two pianists who clearly are disciples, and possibly Monk's percussive touch influenced the young Horace Silver. Many others absorbed aspects of Monk's playing only via his friend Powell. Yet Monk is now seen, with hindsight, as a vital contributor to the jazz mainstream. His compositions have kept entire groups in employment, and these pieces still merit investigation by today's musicians. Monk was certainly ten years ahead of his time. Fortunately, players and listeners eventually caught up, and from the late 1950s he reaped the benefits that were his due. These Blue Notes were the brave beginnings that should not be missed.

The current reissue of the quartet session of 2 July 1948, available under Jackson's name, includes nine tracks from 1952 that do not involve Monk. These tracks are not detailed below.

Following his sporadic recorded ventures for Blue Note in the early 1950s and an unsatisfactory period with Prestige, Monk produced some of his most durable and adventurous work for Riverside in the late 1950s. **Brilliant Corners** is arguably the finest of the many sets he taped for that label. Not only does it contain four excellent compositions by Monk, but the quality of work by the composer–pianist's companions ensures that these selections receive the performances they deserve.

The leader's playing is bold and confident, not in the slightest introverted as was the case on some of his earlier sessions. His sense of irony is well matched by both tenor saxophonist Sonny Rollins and alto saxophonist Ernie Henry, and on one track by trumpeter Clark Terry, who replaces Henry. Rollins seems to understand Monk's aims perfectly and his tone and phrasing are even better suited to the contours of Monk's compositions than were those of John Coltrane.

The tunes presented here are typically unorthodox Monk structures, filled with harmonic interest and, to the unfamiliar ear, unexpected resolutions. The title track, *Brilliant Corners,* is notable for its juddering, stuttering passages and its shifts in tempo. Double-time (in which the pace of the melody or the accompaniment doubles) is a common device in improvised melodies and in transitions from an introduction to the body of a piece, but here on *Brilliant Corners,* unusually, Monk organizes a succession of alternations back and forth between time and double-time, and the melody itself recurs at twice its original speed. Monk adds the surprisingly apt colouration of a celeste for his stately ballad *Pannonica,* employing the bell-like tones for ensemble and solo passages to lend this piece a special piquancy. The twin saxes blend beautifully. Switches in instrumentation also inform the rolling blues *Bemsha Swing,* on which Max Roach plays both the conventional drum set and timpani, the latter supplying a menacing boom to his percussive commentary. Clark Terry has no difficulty moving from Ellington's ensemble to fruitful small group labours with an equally personal leader in the shape of Monk. The other blues, *Ba-lue Bolivar Ba-lues-are,* is slower and sinewy and provokes Henry into one of his finest recorded solos.

The bon-bon of the set is Monk's unaccompanied treatment of *I Surrender, Dear,* on which the pianist systematically strips away the melody's layered sentimentality, replacing it with a measured poignancy all of his own. It is a striking example of re-composition and mood change.

CD

***Genius of Modern Music, vol.1*, Blue Note CDP 7-81510-2 (USA)**

Idrees Sulieman (tpt), Danny Quebec West (as), Billy Smith (ts), Thelonious Monk (p), Gene Ramey (sb), Art Blakey (d)

New York 15 Oct 1947

Humph
Evonce (take 1)
Evonce (take 4)
Suburban Eyes (take 1)
Suburban Eyes (take 2)
Thelonious

Monk (p), Ramey (sb), Blakey (d)

24 Oct 1947

Nice Work if You Can Get it (take 0)
Nice Work if You Can Get it (take 1)
Ruby, my Dear (take 0)
Ruby, my Dear (take 1)
Well You Needn't (take 0)
Well You Needn't (take 1)
April in Paris (take 0)
April in Paris (take 1)
Off Minor
Introspection

George Tait (tpt), Sahib Shihab (as), Monk (p), Bob Paige (sb), Blakey (d)

21 Nov 1947

In Walked Bud
Monk's Mood
Who Knows (take 0)
'Round Midnight
Who Knows (take 7)

Other CDs

same contents:
Blue Note B21Y 81510-2 (USA)
plus additional tracks:
The Complete Blue Note Recordings, Blue Note CDP 7243 8 30363 2 5 (USA)

CD

***Milt Jackson*, Blue Note CDP 7-81509-2 (USA)**

Milt Jackson (vb), Monk (p), John Simmons (sb), Shadow Wilson (d), Kenny Hagood (v)

2 July 1948

All the Things You Are
I Should Care (take 1)
I Should Care (take 2)

omit (v)		**Evidence** **Misterioso** (take 0) **Misterioso** (take 1) **Epistrophy** **I Mean You**

CD

***Brilliant Corners*, Original Jazz Classics OJCCD-026-2 (USA)**

Clark Terry (tpt), Sonny Rollins (ts), Thelonious Monk (p), Paul Chambers (sb), Max Roach (d, timpani)

New York	17 Dec 1956	**Bemsha Swing**

Ernie Henry (as), Rollins (ts), Monk (p, celeste), Oscar Pettiford (sb), Roach (d)

	23 Dec 1956	**Pannonica**
omit (celeste)		**Brilliant Corners** **Ba-lue Bolivar Ba-lues-are**
Monk (p)		**I Surrender, Dear**

* * *

Bud Powell: *The Amazing Bud Powell, vol.1; The Amazing Bud Powell, vol.2*

Once the innovations of Charlie Parker and Dizzy Gillespie were out in the open during the early 1940s, jazz players of all other instruments strove to incorporate the lessons. The piano found its most advanced and accomplished modernist in Bud Powell, a young New Yorker who had hung out with Parker, Gillespie and Monk and understood and absorbed the new style completely.

By the age of 21, Powell had forged a technique of formidable proportions which enabled him to produce with his adroit right hand the incredibly fast and complex lines that Parker had achieved on the alto saxophone. Powell's left hand punched out complementary chords to suit each line. He was gifted in all areas of expression. His melodic sense was fine, his rhythmic perception acute and his harmonic knowledge, gained from close study of Art Tatum, highly advanced. Thus he became the idol of his fellow pianists. All the other early bop keyboard players, including Al Haig, Duke Jordan, Hank Jones, Dodo Marmarosa and George Wallington, adopted his procedures and borrowed from his vocabulary.

Intense is the word that best describes Powell's style. When attacking a rhythmic exercise such as *Un Poco Loco* or tearing into a bop anthem such as *52nd Street Theme* he would build almost unbearable, highly charged tension, even to a greater pitch than Parker on occasion. Powell was a man completely driven by a search for musical perfection. So involved was he in this obsession that at times his bass player George Duvivier would shine a flashlight to bring him out of a long, involved solo.

His greatest achievements emerged from the late 1940s and early 1950s when mind and hands were perfectly co-ordinated, when the pianist's responses allowed him to play precisely what he heard. In this highly creative period, Powell frequently recorded for the Blue Note label, for which he produced sessions of rare quality in the company of some of his peers. Just as Art Blakey was the perfect drummer for Thelonious Monk, Max Roach proved to be the ideal percussionist for Powell. Roach's presence on three of these titles is crucial. Such is the strength and flexibility of his support on *Un Poco Loco* and *A Night in Tunisia* that the presence of bass player Curly Russell is almost superfluous.

The three takes of *Un Poco Loco* (A Little Crazy) enable us to hear the evolution of a masterpiece. The first and briefest version of this hypnotic Latin jazz exercise builds broodingly, but Powell becomes increasingly dissatisfied with his own level of performance and a slight sag in tension makes him call a halt before Roach can launch into his solo. Take 2 traces the gathering improvement in the performance. A repetitive left-hand figure from Powell runs through the piece like the print through a stick of rock candy and is reflected in Roach's own figure on the cowbell. The original master take is indisputably the finest of the three. Powell probes deeper and his invention never flags as the right hand unfolds cunning thoughts.

It is beyond belief that Powell, an extremely competitive musician in certain respects, was unaware of the acclaim that had greeted Charlie Parker's 'famous alto break' on *A Night in Tunisia*, for the pianist obviously took special care to make his break of sustained interest. Again we are afforded the luxury of two takes, and the break on the shorter, alternative version is particularly memorable. Powell's fingers fly and he keeps the listener suspended with a teetering, poised pause. As for the solos, both are beautifully conceived and executed. On the longer, master take, he inserts a descending Monk-like run towards the end of the performance.

A further jewel from this important date is a charming interpretation of Powell's own *Parisian Thoroughfare*, an evocative piece that became a jazz standard. The pianist wrote it years before he ever visited Paris, yet it accurately suggests in sound the busy boulevards of that city.

The four quintet tracks, recorded nearly two years earlier, show Powell in another guise, as the leader of an unusually compatible group. Beside the dash and drive of trumpeter Fats Navarro – like Powell, a perfectionist – there are early glimpses of the fine playing of tenor saxophonist Sonny Rollins as the unit assays two of Powell's finest compositions, *Dance of the Infidels* and *Bouncing with Bud*. Powell's certainty on these performances is reflected in his compact and concise solos and firm supportive accompaniment. His solo on *Wail* is also outstanding, but his digital dexterity is at its most commanding in the swirling rapids of *52nd Street Theme*, at a testing tempo. Small wonder that enigmatic, complicated lines such as these bewildered musicians of earlier styles!

From the same session stems a relaxed trio rendition of Parker's *Ornithology*, on which drummer Roy Haynes's tidy brushwork and bass player Tommy Potter's springy lines help Powell create an improvisation of memorable design. Powell is closest to his mentor, Tatum, in the unaccompanied solo elucidation of *It Could Happen to You*, in which his regard for the older man is fully apparent as he moves with supple ease in and out of tempo. Here, surely, is a respectful tribute from one piano master to another.

CD

***The Amazing Bud Powell, vol.1*, Blue Note B21K 81503 (USA)**

Fats Navarro (tpt), Sonny Rollins (ts), Bud Powell (p), Tommy Potter (sb), Roy Haynes (d)

New York	9 Aug 1949	**Bouncing with Bud** (take 0)
		Bouncing with Bud (take 1)
		Bouncing with Bud (take 2)
		Wail (take 0)
		Wail (take 3)
		Dance of the Infidels (take 0)
		Dance of the Infidels (take 1)
		52nd Street Theme
omit Navarro and Rollins		**You Go to my Head**
		Ornithology (take 0)
		Ornithology (take 1)

Powell (p), Curly Russell (sb), Max Roach (d)

	1 May 1951	**Un Poco Loco** (take 1)
		Un Poco Loco (take 2)
		Un Poco Loco (take 4)
Powell (p)		**Over the Rainbow**

Other CDs

same contents:
Blue Note CDP 7-81503-2; B21Y 81503 (USA)

CD

***The Amazing Bud Powell, vol.2*, Blue Note B21K 81504 (USA)**

Powell (p), Russell (sb), Roach (d)

New York	1 May 1951	**A Night in Tunisia** (take 0)
		A Night in Tunisia (take 1)
Powell (p)		**It Could Happen to You** (take 0)
		It Could Happen to You (take 1)
Powell, Russell, Roach		**Parisian Thoroughfare**

Powell (p), George Duvivier (sb), Art Taylor (d)

	14 Aug 1953	**Autumn in New York**
		Reets and I (take 1)
		Reets and I (take 2)
		Sure Thing
		Collard Greens and Black-eyed Peas (take 0)
		Collard Greens and Black-eyed Peas (take 2)
		Polka Dots and Moonbeams
		I Want to be Happy
		Audrey
		The Glass Enclosure

Other CDs

same contents:
Blue Note CDP 7-81504-2; B21Y 81504 (USA)
plus additional tracks:
The Complete Blue Note and Roost Recordings, Blue Note CDP 7243 8 30083 2 2 (USA)

* * *

Fats Navarro and Tadd Dameron: *The Fabulous Fats Navarro, vol.1; The Fabulous Fats Navarro, vol.2*

Two musicians of the 1940s who were inextricably linked, trumpeter Fats Navarro and composer, arranger and pianist Tadd Dameron, forged a memorable partnership. Navarro's brilliant trumpet sound provided Dameron's small groups with star quality, while the leader's melodic compositions were the ideal basis for the perfectly formed improvisations of the great brass soloist.

Navarro, who died from tuberculosis at the age of 26, was among the most accomplished of the bop instrumentalists and, unlike many of the trumpeters who worked in the style, he had a big, brassy sound, in the tradition of his relative Charlie Shavers. Such was his facility that he could compete in the fastest company, and that included Charlie Parker and Bud Powell. Dameron had proved his value as a composer and arranger with a series of commissions for big bands including those of Harlan Leonard, Georgie Auld, Count Basie and, most significantly, Dizzy Gillespie. He also contributed important pieces to the library of Billy Eckstine's bop big band. His charts incorporated both melodic appeal and harmonic challenge; sidemen enjoyed performing them because the written parts in themselves were beautiful.

The teaming of Navarro and Dameron was heard on half a dozen recording sessions for Blue Note, Savoy and Capitol as well as on numerous broadcasts from a lengthy residency at the Royal Roost club in New York. The supporting cast was apt to change but usually included Ernie Henry, Allen Eager or Charlie Rouse on saxophone, while the first choice for drummer was Kenny Clarke.

In a group that varied between quintet and septet size, Dameron was stimulated to write some of his finest lines, including *The Squirrel, Lady Bird, Jahbero* (a reworking of *All the Things You Are*) and *Symphonette.* Subtle arranging skills enabled him to make a sextet sound like a much larger ensemble. He invariably selected brass and reed players with big tones and would fully utilize them in ensembles. With a front line of only one trumpet and two saxophones at his disposal, he would assign varied roles to each in the ensemble passages. These were not confined to thematic statements alone, for Dameron also scored entirely new passages between or after solos. This technique, unusual in most bop combos (which typically proceded rigidly through a pattern of theme–solos–theme), is most strikingly employed in *Our Delight*, where the scored penultimate chorus is like a new melody, richer and more complex than the original.

Dameron's experience grafting and crafting arrangements for the big swing bands was also evident in his skilful isolation of one instrument to set up a conversation with others within a theme. He pulls off this risky process with quiet authority on *The Squirrel*, wherein he poses solo questions from the keyboard to draw responses from his front line. In miniature here is what he did with a large orchestra when contrasting his trumpet and saxophone sections, for example. He also enjoyed writing variations on his own themes and saving them up for the end of a performance, so that the listener, anticipating a restatement of the main melody, is pleasantly surprised by a fresh theme. Sometimes, as in *Dameronia*, it might be simply an eight-bar segment, but it showed the composer did not wish stolidly to retread the same ground. On the other hand, he was just as likely to pop a written sequence between solos, as on *Lady Bird*, where the two contributions from the tenor saxes are separated by eight bars of ensemble and eight of piano chords.

No soloist himself, Dameron was more than contented to have quality improvisers such as Navarro, Eager and saxophonist Wardell Gray expounding on his compositions. At the piano, Dameron restricted himself to the occasional break or brief chorded solo, but his broad, emphatic chordal accompaniment was an undervalued asset to his groups which lent them a highly distinctive sound. The riffy pattern of *The Chase* even prompts a couple of breaks by the reserved Dameron. However, it cannot be counted among his most satisfactory compositions, which are usually stronger than the average, skeletal bop original.

The items from the Blue Note sessions of 1947 and 1948 have been collected in several different packages, all issued under Navarro's name. They present Dameron's originals with alternate takes in every case, enabling the listener to make immediate comparisons between the solos. Close study reveals that the orderly, mathematical mind of Navarro invariably had his solo contours well shaped on the first cut and made only minor adjustments thereafter. This has led to his being categorized as a calculating improviser when compared with, say, Clifford Brown, whose variations would be enormous in rapid, successive takes. The truth is that Navarro's perfectionism and clarity meant he could fully deliver before his colleagues had properly got their act together. In this special ability to get things right on the first take, he was rather like Lester Young and Art Tatum.

The sides from 1947 benefit from the presence of Ernie Henry, who employed the sort of wide vibrato that Dameron loved to hear in his ensembles, and the contrasting tenor sax of Charlie Rouse, not at this point the mature soloist of Thelonious Monk's quartet, but still a worthy individual performer. However, it is Navarro's commanding lead work that sets the pace for the sextet. There are some typically complex and daring passages in his solo on *Our Delight* which Navarro executes with ridiculous ease and fluency, but these are only small effects in the meticulous construction. Navarro favours long lines and a careful attention to detail; his climaxes are always in just the right place. Henry also contributes fine solos, modern yet not too deeply cut in Parker's mould. Rouse strains slightly, no doubt finding it hard to follow the other two. He is considerably more relaxed on *The Squirrel,* but Navarro's controlled intensity and superbly cohesive contributions are in a class of their own on this chirpy blues. By the time the players reached *Dameronia,* Rouse was taking all the first solos so that Navarro did not give him an inferiority complex, and the tactic worked well. How could anyone have topped the trumpeter's scintillating entrances on either take? Indeed, Dameron discovered this was one of the problems of having Navarro in his bands – other musicians were inhibited by his brilliance.

The septet tracks are a notch or two above the sextet items because of the presence of two exceptional tenor saxophonists in Wardell Gray and Allen Eager, each of whom had the resilience and self-belief to follow Navarro. Both are in excellent fettle on *Lady Bird* (Eager is the first sax soloist) despite shimmering trumpet lessons from Navarro. *Jahbero,* with Afro-Cuban drumming supplied in tandem by Kenny Clarke and bongo player Chino Pozo, is rightly celebrated for the staggering invention of Navarro's solos and begins with one of the most electrifying entrances in the recorded annals of jazz. The trumpeter surges in with a climbing phrase of astonishing beauty. Nobody could touch Navarro in this mood.

Finally, there is the perky *Symphonette,* a somewhat neglected Dameron theme which has a more boppish opening line than many of his pieces, but a gently flowing contrasting section. Wardell Gray is most comfortable in this climate, but once again the trumpet interludes are dazzling examples of Navarro's majestic power. Eager copes with the awkward third solo spot with far more élan than anyone had a right to expect.

These sessions combine the elegance of an unusually gifted trumpeter with the perception of a marvellous melodic composer, both at their creative peak. Together they showed an intriguing route that could have been more fully explored in bop, but in the event was really never revisited, save briefly in Dameron's band in 1953.

(All issues cited include tracks from other sessions.)

CDs

***The Fabulous Fats Navarro*, vols.1–2, Blue Note B21K 81531 and B21K 81532 (USA)**

(Tadd Dameron:) Fats Navarro (tpt), Ernie Henry (as), Charlie Rouse (ts), Dameron (p, arr), Nelson Boyd (sb), Shadow Wilson (d)

New York	26 Sept 1947	**The Chase** (take 0)
		The Chase (take 2)
		The Squirrel (take 0)
		The Squirrel (take 1)
		Our Delight (take 0)
		Our Delight (take 5)
		Dameronia (take 0)
		Dameronia (take 2)

(Dameron:) Navarro (tpt), Allen Eager, Wardell Gray (ts), Dameron (p), Curly Russell (sb), Kenny Clarke (d), Chino Pozo (bongos)

	13 Sept 1948	**Jahbero** (take 0)
		Jahbero (take 1)
		Lady Bird (take 0)
		Lady Bird (take 1)
		Symphonette (take 1)
		Symphonette (take 2)

Other CDs

same contents:

Blue Note CDP 7-81531-2 and CDP 7-81532-2; Blue Note B21Y 81531-2 and B21Y 81532-2 (USA)

* * *

J. J. Johnson: *J. J. Johnson's Jazz Quintets*

Bop presented special difficulties for jazz trombonists, almost all of whom played the slide trombone, more awkward to manipulate than valve trombone, and far more awkward than the saxophone with its keys. Adapting the trombone required a complete reappraisal of technique, so that it could negotiate the blistering tempos that were so much a part of the new style. Charlie Parker and Dizzy Gillespie caused many a trombonist to retreat to the rehearsal room to grapple with the problem. Trummy Young, a fine swing trombonist, effected a half-way style. He incorporated bop phrasing, but struggled on fast numbers. It was left to the prodigiously gifted J. J. Johnson to find the complete solutions and point the way for practically all the trombonists of his generation and those that followed.

Influenced by Vic Dickenson, Fred Beckett and Dicky Wells, Johnson also admired Jack Teagarden and John 'Streamline' Ewing, but while he was working in Snookum Russell's orchestra an even bigger influence was trumpeter Fats Navarro, whose technical facility was tremendous. While he was honing his technique in the trombone sections of the Benny Carter and Count Basie big bands, Johnson's goals were set by the solos by Parker and Gillespie he heard on records. He overcame the innate awkwardness of the instrument by developing a lightning wrist action co-ordinated with amazingly accurate articulation. His smooth, round, open tone was perfect in a bop context, and he also employed a variety of conventional mutes (and a bop beret) to alter that tone effectively. His legato phrasing displayed a deep admiration for Lester Young, and he invariably sounded unhurried and unflurried. Johnson's mastery of the instrument was so complete that many critics, and even fellow musicians, hearing his early recordings, believed he was 'cheating' by using a valve trombone! He never played that version of the instrument.

By 1946, when Johnson was only 22, his style was already fully formed and would show no radical departure thereafter, although his mature work of the 1950s revealed a heightened emotional involvement and depth. However, the sides from his three key sessions for the Savoy label in the 1940s possess a verve and enthusiasm that bespeak the youthful artist in the first flush of unbounded creativity, setting new boundaries for what Johnson himself once described as 'a beastly, horrid instrument' (Leonard Feather, liner notes for the Savoy double album **Mad Be Bop**, which included alternate takes of five of the titles listed below).

For his debut as a leader, Johnson could not have wished for better companions than pianist Bud Powell and drummer Max Roach, the leading exponents of the new style on their respective instruments. Cecil Payne, soon to become a formidable baritone saxophonist but heard here on alto, played a satisfying amalgam of the approaches of Parker and Benny Carter. Bass player Leonard Gaskin was fleet of finger and sure of tone.

Johnson wrote three of the four pieces that exercised this quintet. The opening *Jay Bird* (also known as *Jaybird* and *Fly Jay*) departs from rigid conventions, following the pattern *abca* rather than the usual *aaba* bop formula and thus providing three melodic strands to make the solos more interesting. Even the title is portentous, combining the nicknames of Johnson and Parker, as if to underline the fact that the trombonist was playing in the manner of the genius of the alto saxophone. Powell's introduction is a gem; so impressed with it was Tadd Dameron that he scored the eight-bar passage for trumpet and tenor sax and used it to introduce Navarro's recording of *Nostalgia*. The three versions (preserved on the LP **Mad Be Bop**, but not on the CD) differ in the order of solos. Johnson and Powell are commanding at each attempt, but Payne is not fully together until the master take, on which he sounds more boppish, infusing his solo with tension.

Max Roach composed *Coppin' the Bop*, notable for its use of suspended time and for the contrast between on-the-beat notes and typical bop phrases. Roach's drum punctuations are also a vital element, and he takes a crisp eight-bar solo during the out chorus. Payne and Johnson, who quotes from *High Society*, are both relaxed and confident, while Powell is commanding.

Johnson's helter-skelter *Jay Jay* is our old friend *I Got Rhythm* in new guise. Johnson really shows his mettle here with clarion clear lines and beautifully separated notes. It wasn't often that soloists could top Bud Powell, especially when he was in the consistent form evident throughout this session, but Johnson caps every one with his lithe improvisation on the master take.

Like Thelonious Monk's *Evidence* and Coleman Hawkins's *Spotlite*, Johnson's *Mad Be Bop* is based on the chord progression of *Just You, Just Me*, which is beefed up rhythmically by Gaskin and Roach. Johnson's admirable mobility and logical development of ideas are both apparent in his forthright solo on a piece that marked the conclusion of a most impressive debut.

Eighteen months later Johnson was at the helm of an entirely different quintet, drawn largely from the ranks of the band of the brothers Illinois and Russell Jacquet, with whom the trombonist was also working at the time. The roaring baritone saxophone of Leo Parker formed an effective partnership with Johnson, while the able rhythm section contained pianist Hank Jones, bass player Al Lucas and drummer Shadow Wilson.

On the ballad *Yesterdays* Johnson is heard throughout, save for eight bars of piano. Respectful of the melody, he restricts himself to a minimum of elaboration, yet it is a moving and meaningful interpretation, unmistakably the work of a jazz player of considerable sensitivity.

Johnson composed the balance of the pieces. *Boneology* has a lazy, legato quality, and in the *aaba* theme Johnson allocates the fourth bar of the *a* section to Jones, who plays a trilling bop phrase in response to the horns in unison. Always a shrewd deployer of quotations, Johnson inserts one from *'s Wonderful* in his solo, full of dash and pep, yet smoothly flowing. *Down Vernon's Alley* contrasts Parker wailing at full throttle in his most abrasive manner and Johnson, poised, urbane and perfect in an elegant solo. *Riffette* is exactly what the title implies, a repetitious riffy blues on which Johnson gets quite heated. Jones is also thoroughly involved, while Parker revels in this kind of stomping ground, inventing a few riffs of his own in a blistering example of fire-eating. This evidence suggests that Johnson and company spent a fruitful Christmas Eve in 1947, just a week before the second recording ban by the American Federation of Musicians came into effect.

The third session, held some 15 months later, was significant for several reasons. The leader's own style had been refined in the interim and by 1949 he was the complete trombonist. He chose as his front-line partner the young tenor saxophonist Sonny Rollins, who had impressed Johnson on a recording they made with singer Babs Gonzales a few weeks earlier. The choice was astute, for Rollins's rugged and jagged lines served as fitting foils to Johnson's smoothly rounded improvisations. Rollins further enhanced Johnson's selection by bringing in two original themes.

The saxophonist's *Audobahn* (also incorrectly known as *Audubon* and *Auduban*) has been released in two versions. On both Johnson placed a felt (probably his bop beret) over the bell of his trombone so that he could achieve the required blend with his saxophonist. *Don't Blame Me* is as good a ballad performance by Johnson as the earlier *Yesterdays*. Rollins's *Goof Square* is a neat bop blues which seems to suit Johnson perfectly at the medium-bounce tempo employed on all three issued takes. It is the sort of line that Charlie Parker tossed off to finish a session, and Rollins was certainly strongly under Parker's influence (instrumental and otherwise) at the time. His solos are occasionally rough in spots but consistently lively.

The trombonist had also come to know pianist John Lewis through their work with Miles Davis's cool jazz nonet and employed him on several sessions during 1949. Lewis's solo on *Goof Square* is, as ever, tidy and precise. Another blues, *Bee Jay*, this time by Johnson and much faster than *Goof Square*, concludes a sparkling date. Rollins musters his best solo on the master take, which is also enlivened by an improvisation of spry movement, wit and studied understatement by the urbane Johnson. Here was a man who knocked the abrasive corners off the instrument and substituted an undreamt-of polish and flow.

CD

***J. J. Johnson's Jazz Quintets*, Savoy Jazz SV-0151 (Japan)**

J. J. Johnson (tb), Cecil Payne (bar), Bud Powell (p), Leonard Gaskin (sb), Max Roach (d)

New York	26 June 1946	**Jay Bird** (take 11)
		Coppin' the Bop
		Jay Jay (take 2)
		Mad Be Bop

Johnson (tb), Leo Parker (bar), Hank Jones (p), Al Lucas (sb), Shadow Wilson (d)

	24 Dec 1947	**Boneology**
		Down Vernon's Alley
		Yesterdays
		Riffette

Johnson (tb), Sonny Rollins (ts), John Lewis (p), Gene Ramey (sb), Wilson (d)

11 May 1949

Audobahn (take 3)
Don't Blame Me
Goof Square (take 8)
Bee Jay (take 5)

Other CDs

plus additional tracks: *Mad Bop*
Savoy 881919; Savoy 650119 (Europe)

* * *

Wardell Gray: *One for Prez*

The life of tenor saxophonist Wardell Gray closely paralleled that of Charlie Parker. Born just six months later in another midwestern city (Oklahoma City), Gray survived for less than 11 weeks following Parker's death. Both men were originally inspired by Lester Young, and both worked with the big bands of Billy Eckstine and Earl Hines. Later, Gray, who recorded with Bird on two occasions, showed traces of Parker's influence in his style. Sadly, each was a victim of narcotics addiction and of racial and musical intolerance.

Few musicians had so rapidly and comprehensively digested the tonal and rhythmic lessons of Lester Young or the harmonic extensions wrought by Dizzy Gillespie and Parker as Wardell Gray, who by 1946 was probably the most modern and personal tenor saxophonist in jazz. His tone recognizably sprang from Young's sound, but Gray's was more open and he employed a subtle and unique vibrato. He had a terrific knack of creating melodic phrases, and his solos could be whistled or sung (as they were later by Annie Ross). His gift was for simplifying the complex. Like his frequent companion in tenor battles, Dexter Gordon, Gray had an engaging capacity for weaving quotations from other songs into his improvised solos. These familiar reference points were never self-consciously introduced, but formed an important part of the improvised fabric.

That Gray was technically adept and remarkably imaginative had been apparent in his early solos with Earl Hines's orchestra and was subsequently confirmed on his recordings in 1947 with Parker and Gordon. But the jazz audience at large did not fully realize just how advanced Gray was in 1946 until the systematic release of the superlative tracks from this session more than 40 years later. Supervised by

Eddie Laguna after Gray had left Hines to work as a freelance in Los Angeles, the material, inexplicably, never appeared in the USA. Five of the performances were issued on small European labels and four additional tracks came out on an LP in the 1970s, but it was not until 1988 that the full wealth of 16 items from this productive date was arranged for release on CD.

For the first time it was possible to hear Gray eloquently appraising *Dell's Bells,* his lovely line based on *What is This Thing Called Love?,* in five different versions. A similar number of takes is also accorded to his tribute to Lester Young, *One for Prez,* a clever new melody based on the chord sequence of *How High the Moon.* A plethora of alternative takes can become exceedingly tedious, especially when the participants are predictable and merely polishing pet phrases until they shine to their satisfaction. But Gray was different – a thrilling off-the-top player who would create an entirely new improvisation at each attempt. This was an ability he shared with Parker and trumpeter Clifford Brown. His aptitude for instant composition is also convincingly heard in the three versions of *The Man I Love,* in none of which is Gershwin's original melody ever stated!

Laconic, erudite and composed, Gray's work carried a sense of deep inner conviction. He could suggest a wide spread of emotions. On a ballad such as *The Man I Love,* he displayed a touching tenderness and humanity, and the introduction has an Ellingtonian flavour that suggests Gray was prepared to listen beyond his immediate stylistic preoccupations. At medium tempos he conveyed a jaunty optimism with an occasional ironic touch. Even at a comparatively speedy pace, preferred for *One for Prez,* he never sounds rushed. The quality of relaxation which makes his extemporizations so satisfying remains a constant.

While Gray had reason to feel bitter and angry about his lack of acclaim, neither self-pity nor frustration clouded his musical vision. Rather we turn to him for a joyous lift, a well-adjusted, happy perspective. The essence of what Wardell Gray was about is to be found on the two versions of his aptly named *Easy Swing,* which Parker recorded a couple of years later under the title of *Steeplechase.* The sequence of these chords is borrowed from *Perdido,* which Gray artfully paraphrases on each take. Possibly because this was delivered at his favourite moderate tempo, he felt the need for only two takes, each of which is a gem of pithy understatement. Unhurried and unflappable, Gray is the epitome of relaxation as he phrases fractionally behind the beat in the manner of Lester Young. Both these solos have an engaging continuity and inevitability as Gray matches long and short phrases with effective pauses in truly conversational style. The piece has a surprising, abrupt ending because he elects not to retrace the theme – a slice of boppish humour.

Gray was singularly fortunate to have the services of pianist Dodo Marmarosa for this programme. He was another brilliant individualist whose erratic lifestyle denied him the recognition his distinctive playing would have otherwise surely achieved. Marmarosa's lightning fingering in unison with Gray on the blistering theme of *One for Prez* foreshadows the complex melodic structures that Lennie Tristano would contrive for his sextet. A conservatory-trained musician, Marmarosa employed much fuller chords than were generally favoured by many of his contemporaries, and lent Gray dashing, percussive accompaniment on this occasion. His own solos reflect not only an interest in bop but an appreciation of earlier stylists, especially Art Tatum, Teddy Wilson and Earl Hines. He and Gray were wholly compatible in their approach, as they would prove on location and in other studio performances from the period.

The uncluttered drumming of Doc West and the assured bass playing of Red Callender blend cohesively, as well they might since both men regularly worked together in Erroll Garner's trio. Chuck Thompson replaces West for an impromptu version of *The Great Lie*, based on the standard *Fine and Dandy*. Once again fine playing results in what was for those times an extended recording.

CD

***One for Prez*, Black Lion BLCD 760 106 (UK)**

Wardell Gray (ts), Dodo Marmarosa (p), Red Callender (sb), Doc West (d)

Hollywood	23 Nov 1946	**Dell's Bells** (take 5)
		Dell's Bells (take 4)
		Dell's Bells (take 1)
		Dell's Bells (take 2)
		Dell's Bells (take 3)
		One for Prez (take 5)
		One for Prez (take 4)
		One for Prez (take 1)
		One for Prez (take 2)
		One for Prez (take 3)
		The Man I Love (take 3)
		The Man I Love (take 2)
		The Man I Love (take 1)
		Easy Swing (take 2)
		Easy Swing (take 1)
Chuck Thompson (d) replaces West		**The Great Lie**

* * *

Gene Ammons: *Gene Ammons All Star Sessions*

Saxophone partnerships in modern jazz enjoyed unprecedented popularity during the 1950s, when a pair of free-booting tenor players with sufficiently contrasting styles to maintain consistent interest and excitement could pack clubs and dances and make recordings for a rash of new independent labels that were springing up. The origins of these saxophone duels were the big bands. In Count Basie's orchestra, Lester Young and Herschel Evans had shown the way in the late 1930s. Norman Granz, who knew a good thing when he heard it, had encouraged saxophone battles at his earliest concerts, and the jousts between such frenetic saxophonists as Flip Phillips and Illinois Jacquet became a frenzied focus for his Jazz at the Philharmonic presentations. The two-tenor groups that cut a swinging swathe across the 1950s included Dexter Gordon and Wardell Gray, Al Cohn and Zoot Sims and above all Gene Ammons and Sonny Stitt. Companions in the saxophone section of Billy Eckstine's orchestra in 1946, Ammons and Stitt were sufficiently different stylistically to ensure listeners' attention never lapsed.

Stitt had started out on alto saxophone, but concentrated on the tenor from 1949. His fleet muscularity sat well alongside the thicker-toned Ammons, who favoured a simpler, more economical approach. The band these two formed in January 1950 was a septet of like-minded players. To balance the two reeds were the trumpet of Bill Massey and the warm, flowing trombone of Bennie Green (or the equally facile Eph Greenlea). Pianist Duke Jordan and bass player Tommy Potter had served both Charlie Parker and Stan Getz, but now found themselves in a much more basic climate.

The Ammons–Stitt band purveyed a no-frills brand of straight-ahead jazz with a repertory that was comprised of blues, the occasional standard, riffy melodies, bizarre band vocals and novelty numbers. The group was equally popular with jazz and rhythm-and-blues audiences. Dancers enjoyed the beat laid down by either swing veteran Jo Jones or the hard-bopping Art Blakey. The leaders were clearly at home with either percussionist's style. Indeed, the unit was all things to all listeners, and even after the direst vocal there was always a good saxophone solo to enjoy.

One of the band's earliest sessions for the newly launched Prestige label was held in the spring of 1950. An archetypical tenor battle is Ammons's *Blues Up and Down*, heard here in three takes. The first shot starts well enough with Ammons opening the chases after the utilitarian theme, but Stitt has reed trouble in his first chorus and an uncertain moment in the third, and the performance ceases abruptly with Ammons still blowing. The second take is much more assured. Both men sound confident and inventive as they trade virile choruses back and forth and then indulge in some brisk four-bar breaks. Again there is a breakdown, this time in the restatement of the theme when the players were clearly signalled to halt. The third (master) take snaps along. Ammons and Stitt maintain the fluency and flow of ideas that had marked the previous attempt, and at one point both give nods in the direction of Lester Young by using a little honking phrase that was one of Young's trademarks. There are no fluffs on this occasion. The performance is a classic of the 'tough tenor' genre, characterized by hard-driving swing, a no-frills, uninhibited approach to improvisation and, in this partnership, a necessary competitive edge.

Another side of the group's character is disclosed on the two takes of *You Can Depend on Me*, each briskly delivered as a tenor conversation. Ammons, with the broader tone and more pronounced vibrato, is again the first soloist; Stitt has a tighter tone and greater mobility. The two tones blend perfectly in the unison passages. Both saxophonists are in scintillating form as they speak in leaping, jaunty phrases without becoming repetitious or tired. Potter's great beat and the sure drumming of Jones drive the pair on splendidly. The second take is just a mite faster, but if anything Ammons and Stitt are even more inspired.

CD

***Gene Ammons All Star Sessions*, Original Jazz Classics OJCCD 014-2 (USA)**

(Gene Ammons and Sonny Stitt:) Bill Massey (tpt), Eph Greenlea (tb), Ammons, Stitt (ts), Duke Jordan (p), Tommy Potter (sb), Jo Jones (d)

New York	5 March 1950	**Bye Bye**
omit Massey and Greenlea		**Blues Up and Down** (take 1)
		Blues Up and Down (take 2)
		Blues Up and Down (take 3)
		You Can Depend on Me (take 1)
		You Can Depend on Me (take 2)

(Ammons and Stitt:) Ammons, Stitt (ts), Junior Mance (p), Gene Wright (sb), Wesley Landers (d)

	28 Oct 1950	**Stringin' the Jug**
omit Stitt		**When I Dream of You**
		A Lover is Blue

Massey (tpt), Al Outcalt (tb), Stitt (ts), Ammons (bar), Charles Bateman (p), Wright (sb), Art Blakey (d)

	31 Jan 1951	**New Blues Up and Down**

Art Farmer (tpt), Lou Donaldson (as), Ammons (ts), Freddie Redd (p), Addison Farmer (sb), Kenny Clarke (d)

16 June 1955 **Juggernaut**
Woofin' and Tweetin'

* * *

Stan Getz: *Stan Getz at Storyville*

Categorizing jazz soloists can be a futile and inexact pursuit, especially when the labelling is applied to a musician as versatile and adaptable as Stan Getz. After his solo on *Early Autumn* with Woody Herman, Getz was pegged as the iceman – the coolest tenor saxophonist in existence, a chilly, precise balladeer with a frosty tone. This analysis overlooked Getz's choice of Dexter Gordon as an early role model, and ignored a good deal of recorded evidence to the contrary. Getz subsequently made a nonsense of the 'deep freeze' tag by displaying his mettle in Jazz at the Philharmonic packages and jam sessions, where he took the measure of such 'hot' players as Roy Eldridge and Sonny Stitt. Getz's superficially gentle style contained a steely centre that made him a formidable adversary in a competitive blowing session. Like Lester Young, he would score by his invention and understatement.

While not strictly regarded as a bop figure, Getz used the vocabularly of Parker and Gillespie, and even shared with Parker the same rhythm section for a year or two in the early 1950s. The quintet Getz fronted briefly in the autumn of 1951 was cast in the bop mould and performed with a fire and feeling well distanced from the cool school. It remains to this day, some four decades later, the most homogeneous band Getz led in his consistently interesting career.

With pianist Al Haig and guitarist Jimmy Raney, Getz rapidly achieved a telepathic understanding that enhanced their unity of purpose. In Tiny Kahn he found a drummer of unusual perception whose grasp of polyrhythms and ability to complement the soloist's line made him an asset in any context but especially this one. Bass player Teddy Kotick chose his notes with care and maintained impeccable time. His tone was resilient. In this responsive company Getz thrived and threw caution to the wind. The speed of his delivery evoked Parker while in his phrasing he betrayed a deep admiration for Lester Young, particularly in performances such as *Jumpin' with Symphony Sid* and *Thou Swell*.

The accommodation of the soft-toned electric guitar of Raney was achieved with the minimum of fuss. As an accompanist, Raney does not play rhythm guitar, but usually offers counterpoint to Getz's saxophone on the theme or drops into a unison role. He never gets in the way of the measured piano feeds by Haig. The addition of Raney gave the group three distinctive yet empathetic solo voices, ensuring a uniformly excellent level of improvisation. The three shared a lyrical approach to making music, so their solos were invariably melodic, yet harmonically sophisticated and rhythmically adventurous.

Recorded in front of an appreciative audience at Boston's Storyville Club, the tracks capture an electric atmosphere of creativity in which relaxation is the key. Few rhythm sections in jazz have worked together with such fluent ease as the Haig–Kotick–Kahn combination. At any tempo, they seem just naturally to fall into the groove that will be most beneficial to Getz and Raney and, of course, the splendid Haig, who shared with the tenor saxophonist a gift for understatement.

On a brisk version of *The Song is You,* Raney contrives neat contrapuntal lines to Getz's revelations on the theme. Kahn starts out with brushes but soon switches to sticks and drives along Getz's soaring work. Kahn's sticks also prod Raney, but he reverts to brushes to shade Haig's balletic mood. Saxophonist Gigi Gryce's composition *Mosquito Knees* has a boppish line, played in accurate unison by Getz and Raney, and it hurls Getz into some unexpected corners, out of which he nimbly skips. In a typically witty Haig solo there is a mellow reference to *Honeysuckle Rose.* The four-bar conversation pieces between Getz and Kahn find the saxophonist evoking Lester Young and the drummer suggesting Art Blakey.

On *Pennies from Heaven,* taken at a brisk bounce, Getz juxtaposes clipped, staccato phrases against more integrated passages, and uses Lester Young-style honks for effect. Along the way he quotes randomly from such tunes as *Fascinating Rhythm* and *How Are Things in Glocca Morra?* Apart from an eight-bar introduction by Haig, the performance is Getz's all the way, and the warmth of his solo ending is right in keeping with his amplifications of the melody that precede it.

The saxophonist's sense of order and ability to build and relate his choruses at a fast tempo is underlined by his fleet work on drummer Denzil Best's composition *Move,* on which he sails through the rapid chord changes. Raney and Kahn show similar objectivity, with Getz and Kahn again perking brightly in their exchanges. Kahn executes his drum solo beautifully, reinforcing the impression that he was rarely better captured on tape than on these sides.

Parker 51, Raney's cunning derivation from the melody of *Cherokee,* is also given express delivery, and is notable for the delightful counterpoint struck by guitar and tenor on the theme. One feels that Haig was more effective and comfortable at a gentler pace than this furious gallop. The descending contours of Getz's *Hershey Bar,* derived from *Tea for Two*, are more to Haig's liking, as he unfolds one of his neat and precise solos. The abrupt ending in the middle of the last chorus may have been the result of a tape unexpectedly running out.

On Raney's *Rubberneck*, a theme in a minor key, the tenor, guitar and piano solos are amazingly unified in style and feeling, serving as a further indicator of the close empathy between the musicians. *Signal* is also Raney's, and not surprisingly he makes the most telling contribution. Charlie Parker had lately revived the ballad *Everything Happens to Me*, performed here with restraint and sensitivity. The band plays *Yesterdays* in sturdy fashion and not at the sort of drag tempo which is apt to choke rhythmic movement. This is a feature for Getz, who carries the performance with unfailing charm, wit and vision. *Budo*, composed jointly by Bud Powell and Miles Davis, ends this invaluable set on a high, with its intricate unisons by Getz and Raney and sterling solos, including Kahn's explosive drumming.

The plum of the collection, though, is Lester Young's memorable blues *Jumpin' with Symphony Sid*, to which Getz appends an opening and closing variation also drawn from Young's phrasebook. Getz is not normally thought of as a blues player, but his eight superb choruses in this instance evince a splendid conviction and an absence of clichés. His use of double-time in the sixth chorus and the Young-like honks in the eighth are climaxes placed exactly to achieve the optimum effect. After Raney and Haig take solos, Kotick in his three choruses shows a wry sense of humour by inserting a quotation, which had earlier been used by Haig, from *An English Country Garden*. These are among the most enticing and sublime seven minutes in postwar jazz.

CD

***Stan Getz at Storyville*, vols.1–2, Cap. C2-7-94507-2 (USA)**

Stan Getz (ts), Jimmy Raney (elg), Al Haig (p), Teddy Kotick (sb), Tiny Kahn (d)

Boston	Oct 1951	**Thou Swell**
		The Song is You
		Mosquito Knees
		Pennies from Heaven
		Move
		Parker 51
		Hershey Bar
		Rubberneck
		Signal
		Everything Happens to Me
		Jumpin' with Symphony Sid
		Yesterdays
		Budo

Other CDs

same contents:

Roulette CDP 7945072 (UK)
Vogue VG 651-600093 (France)

plus additional tracks:

The Complete Recordings of the Stan Getz Quintet with Jimmy Raney, Mosaic MD3 131 (USA)

CHAPTER 8

The First Cool Jazz and West Coast Jazz Bands

Mark Gardner

Cool jazz, the first style to fragment from bop, formed as a coherent style well before the end of the 1940s. The term 'cool' was appropriate, particularly in describing personal sounds employed by many of this sub-idiom's stylists. Brass and reed players favoured gentle tones, used scarcely any vibrato and tended to play more quietly than the leading solo performers of bop, although their musical language had been learned from the first modernists and their phrasing remained rooted in the twists and turns of Parker and Gillespie's improvisations.

The cool style, a sober reaction against the sometimes frenetic, headlong rush of bop, was more calculating and brought the arranger back into play. Proponents of this music paid far greater attention to ensemble playing. By comparison with the staccato and sketchy bop unisons, often for only a couple of wind instruments, the cool formation, expanded to as many as five or six melodic instruments, was able to engender greater subtlety and variety, requiring properly scored arrangements. To bring out the richness of ensemble playing, slower tempos were employed, and the use of arranged and improvised counterpoint was encouraged, especially in the intimate cool trios and quartets. In all these contexts the studied tones of musicians like Miles Davis and Lee Konitz were most effective.

West Coast Jazz grew directly from the cool innovations, but here the mixture was apt to be on the tepid side, since a dilution took place, and over-writing became far too common. The arrangers really ran the show in many of the Hollywood-based groups, and the importance of soloists diminished.

Some musicians associated with the cool movement were tailor-made for the bossa nova, a decade later. This stylistic tributary is discussed in chapter 12, on Latin jazz.

* * *

Miles Davis: *Birth of the Cool*

The advent of the cool style in jazz was the outcome of a friendship and discussions between trumpeter Miles Davis and arranger Gil Evans as early as 1947. Davis, whose temperament and instrumental ability were not entirely suited to the torrid tempos and minimal arrangements favoured by his then employer, Charlie Parker, was thinking of a more restrained and polished setting for his low-key, economical style. He had enjoyed the unusual ensemble patterns and instrumental combinations created by Evans for Claude Thornhill's orchestra of the early and mid-1940s, and the pair worked out that, with just four brass players, two reeds and a rhythm section, they could reproduce the essential sound elements of Thornhill's band.

Davis's nonet began as a rehearsal band and quickly attracted musicians and composers who were thinking along similar lines. Gerry Mulligan had also written for Thornhill, while alto saxophonist Lee Konitz had been a soloist with the orchestra. John Lewis, another talented composer and an able pianist, also joined this exclusive workshop unit with some alacrity, as did trumpeter Johnny Carisi, though not in an instrumental role but as a composer and an arranger.

What lent the nonet its distinctive sound was the presence of a french horn and tuba in addition to the conventional brass and reed instruments; the tuba was in addition to, not in place of, string bass, and it functioned as a member of the brass section. None of the front line was called upon to play in a loud, strident manner. Soft unison and contrapuntal work was required to achieve the cloudy, restrained blend that Evans and Davis had in mind. The emphasis in this group was on a subtle melding of tones and a good deal of precisely scored passages for the ensemble, an area that had been somewhat neglected in the stampede of bop virtuosity.

Although Davis and Evans were the overall guiding hands, the chief writers were Mulligan, who arranged his own pieces *Jeru*, *Venus de Milo* and *Rocker* as well as *Godchild* (written by pianist George Wallington) and the ballad standard *Darn that Dream*, and Lewis, who arranged his own piece *Rouge* and also provided charts for *Move* (composed by drummer Denzil Best) and *Budo* (by Davis and pianist Bud Powell). A writer of an earlier era, Chummy MacGregor, was represented in *Moon Dreams*, arranged by Evans. Evans also supplied the framework for *Boplicity*; the piece is attributed to Cleo Henry (the name of Davis's mother), but it was co-composed by the trumpeter and Evans. Carisi wrote and scored *Israel*, and it is believed that Davis arranged his own *Deception*.

Considering that the 12 Capitol recordings involved so many writers, the oneness of feeling they achieved is a tribute to their unity of purpose and commitment to Davis's concept. The trumpeter was undoubtedly the catalyst for the band and the cool movement as a whole for, as we shall see, the leading individuals from the nonet went on to examine in other contexts the possibilities that had been opened – Davis in his own groups and through the later orchestral collaborations with Evans (discussed in chapter 3), Lewis through the Modern Jazz Quartet, Mulligan in his quartet, tentet and Concert Jazz Band, Konitz within a series of combos and elaborations with Lennie Tristano. The influence was also spread via the orchestral compositions of J. J. Johnson and Gunther Schuller, two of the ensemble players who passed through the nonet's changing ranks. (Two decades later, the process would recur, with Davis's sidemen spreading out into the leading fusion bands.)

The band was actually a commercial disaster. Its public appearances were restricted to a couple of brief engagements at the Royal Roost and the Clique Club, and five months elapsed before Davis, through Pete Rugolo (who supervised the dates), was able to persuade Capitol to record them. But for the fact that Capitol at the time were signing up every jazz name of consequence, this music would not exist. Even when he had a contract, Davis was forced to spread the sessions over a 15-month period, which accounts for the shifts in personnel. The key constant factor, enabling the ensemble to maintain a consistency of sound, was the ever-present contingent of Davis, Konitz, Mulligan and tuba player Bill Barber.

While other musicians quickly perceived the subtle beauty of the music and set about emulating the distinctive ensemble sound and writing procedures, thereby reviving an interest in orchestration, the public was slow to catch on, although **Birth of the Cool** became a big seller when 11 of the tracks were collected on LP in 1957. Irritatingly, in repeated reissue packages, Capitol consistently omitted *Darn that Dream*, featuring a sensitive vocal by Kenny Hagood, a supple arrangement and a gem of a solo by Davis. Not until the early 1970s were all 12 pieces released together in an essential compilation by Dutch Capitol; the compact discs also include all 12.

What is immediately obvious from the improvisations of Davis, who naturally enough is the leading soloist, is the calm assurance and meticulous execution that he displays. With Parker, it seemed that the trumpeter was always fighting to keep up, struggling to compete with a soloist of unprecedented ability. This was most certainly invaluable experience, but by 1949 Davis was a considerably more confident and adept improviser. His solos brim with a new authority and his leadership is apparent within ensemble segments. He has no difficulty negotiating the tricky contours of *Move* in company with Konitz, and his solo on this item is bold and forthright. A decade later Davis would make frequent use of mutes, but with the nonet he played open horn all the way, varying the dynamics and tone by his own instrumental skill. The trumpet is the focal point of most of the writing, and Davis's solos of consistent quality illuminate every track save one. He is especially engaging in *Budo* and *Venus de Milo*.

Konitz's sound was ideally cast in this context, his thin tone blending perfectly with Davis in the unisons, and his imagination is voluminous, as can be heard in a lilting solo on *Rouge*. Mulligan, on the other hand, has a sound which is far from cool. However, he modifies his normal approach in order to knit with his colleagues, playing in gently restrained fashion. Similarly, the occasional piano solos by Lewis and the trombone interventions of Kai Winding and Johnson are in complete accord with the context. Johnson is particularly good on *Deception*.

Two of the most interesting pieces are *Israel*, a very clever treatment of the blues in a minor key, and the elegant *Moon Dreams*, a flowing, slow score by Evans, whose use of harmonies and textures indicates his originality of thought. A trifling song takes on a completely new dimension under his skilful control. Davis contents himself with an ensemble role here; Konitz and Mulligan solo briefly.

Ironically, **Birth of the Cool** even had its effect on bop's hottest soloist, Charlie Parker, who, a few months after Davis's recording was released, commissioned Mulligan to arrange *Rocker* for a string ensemble that the alto saxophonist was fronting. *Rocker* became a fixture in Parker's book with the stiff string section, and he would even play the composition with his quintet. Mulligan also recycled the tune for his 1953 tentet.

What Davis and company demonstrated, particularly in their treatments of bop originals such as *Move* and *Godchild*, was the existence of new avenues and possibilities for modern jazz. It didn't have to be fast and frantic or phrased in the astringent musical shorthand of Parker and Gillespie. Many fell in to follow Davis, but found it tough to keep up because he was already moving on.

CD

***Birth of the Cool*, Capitol C21K 92862 (USA) and Capitol CDP 792862-2 (Europe)**

Miles Davis (tpt), Kai Winding (tb), Junior Collins (french horn), Bill Barber (tuba), Lee Konitz (as), Gerry Mulligan (bar), Al Haig (p), Joe Schulman (sb), Max Roach (d)

New York	21 Jan 1949	**Move** (arr John Lewis)
		Jeru (arr Mulligan)
		Godchild (arr Mulligan)
		Budo (arr Lewis)

Davis (tpt), J. J. Johnson (tb), Sandy Siegelstein (french horn), Barber (tuba), Konitz (as), Mulligan (bar), Lewis (p), Nelson Boyd (sb), Kenny Clarke (d)

22 April 1949 — **Venus de Milo** (arr Mulligan)
Rouge (arr Lewis)
Boplicity (arr Gil Evans)
Israel (arr Johnny Carisi)

Davis (tpt), Johnson (tb), Gunther Schuller (french horn), Barber (tuba), Konitz (as), Mulligan (bar), Lewis (p), Al McKibbon (sb), Roach (d)

9 March 1950 — **Deception** (arr ?Davis)
Rocker (arr Mulligan)
Moon Dreams (arr Evans)

add Kenny Hagood (v) — **Darn that Dream** (arr Mulligan)

* * *

Lennie Tristano: *Crosscurrents*

Few musicians in the history of jazz have prompted so much strong debate as pianist, composer and teacher Lennie Tristano. Even today, more than 40 years after these recordings were made and a decade on from Tristano's death, the arguments about his contribution to the music continue to rage. In assessing Tristano there appears to have been no middle ground of appreciation. On one side he was depicted as a man who could do no wrong, whose disciplines should have been adopted and embraced by the entire jazz community. On the other, he was portrayed as a bloodless technician, a demanding martinet whose music was over-formalized and devoid of warmth and feeling. The truth was a considerable distance from either viewpoint.

Tristano certainly preached the importance of a disciplined approach, insisting on precise ensemble playing at all times, but he also espoused the importance of pure improvisation and spontaneity within a logical framework. He did not believe in emotions ruling the head and deplored the arbitrary use of excitement and superficiality in jazz performances. He had certain idols, including Roy Eldridge (the tasteful early Eldridge, not the Eldridge who sometimes violated these very principles), Lester Young and Charlie Parker, and in getting his students and colleagues to understand the import of such soloists he would instruct them to sing the instrumental solos of Eldridge and company.

Blindness probably made Tristano more of a perfectionist when it came to music, and he was indeed a hard taskmaster. He gathered around him some extremely gifted acolytes who shared both his musical and philosophical beliefs. His two leading spokesmen were saxophonists Lee Konitz and Warne Marsh, whose light tones on alto and tenor respectively were identified with the new cool order. Indeed, Konitz, as we have already seen, was also immersed at this time in Davis's nonet and was making a copious input as a soloist to both bands.

In the first half of 1949, Tristano organized seven performances for Capitol Records which accurately encapsulated his highly personal approach to jazz. The music was difficult, spiky, introverted. It held out no easy route of understanding for the listener, who was expected to do his or her homework by concentrated listening. Here were not to be found the tonal variations, the spark, the recognizable blues phrases that were integral parts of Parker's style. Tristano's music conveyed austerity despite its complexity. Konitz and Marsh deliberately effected flat tones; it was their ideas that audiences were expected to appreciate, and these two with Tristano fashioned an abundance of intriguing melodic lines. Harmonies were also important, but rhythm in this music had a less vital role.

Tristano never yearned for inventive, dramatic percussionists such as Art Blakey or Max Roach; he merely required steady time-keepers who would not clutter up the lines with what he heard as distracting or ephemeral accents. As a proponent of 'pure improvisation', Tristano had a natural admiration for the intricate lines of Bach, which also served as rehearsal exercises, and some of the contrapuntal forays of Konitz and Marsh have their roots in the theories of Bach rather than accepted jazz procedures. At its best, Tristano's method produced an intellectually satisfying musical outpouring. At its worst the results could sound coldly cerebral, devoid of human warmth and passion.

The Capitol sides are actually among the most fully realized of his ensemble recordings and were clearly preceded by typically thorough preparation and rehearsal. This is evident in the flawlessly synchronized playing of the themes by the two saxophonists and guitarist Bill Bauer, all three perfectly together in the twisting lines of *Wow*, *Crosscurrent* and *Marionette*. Tristano was something of a martinet about ensembles, but the drilling of his men produced the super-cool sound he was aiming for. This was by no means the first time a guitar had been placed into the front line, but never before had it blended so seamlessly. Only on *Sax of a Kind*, which as the title suggests focuses on the saxophones, does the guitar drop back into a subsidiary accompanying role.

The two pieces that were both controversial and futuristic are *Intuition* and *Digression*, since they were the first 'free' improvisations to be recorded. Without a fixed chord progression, metre or tempo, these performances were off-the-top examples of total spontaneity, but, possibly because the relationships between the participants were so close, the music is neither aimless nor chaotic. They follow each others' patterns in a controlled manner so that a definite unity of purpose prevails.

Capitol failed to perceive any value in these pioneering efforts by Tristano and company, and they were released only after considerable hectoring by enthusiasts.

In a more conventional vein are the well-integrated band performances that make up the bulk of the output from these sessions. *Wow* has intense solos from all four men, while the bass and drums are as unobtrusive as they could possibly be. *Crosscurrent* is another finely tuned, intricate line in which the unified approach becomes apparent as each solo sounds like a logical continuation of the last; there is more than a hint of atonality in the running chromatic lines within all the contributions. Bauer's *Marionette* is a more relaxed, uncrowded piece which allows the composer to inspect its contours in calm fashion. Tristano is coolly detached and of the saxophones Marsh has the expressive edge here.

The Tristanoites were not averse to adopting the bop tenet of writing new melodic themes upon the chord changes of standard songs, and this is exactly what Konitz and Marsh do with *Sax of a Kind*, their joint exercise borrowed from *Fine and Dandy*. The seventh track is a quartet performance (minus the saxophones), ostensibly of Jerome Kern's *Yesterdays*, although the original melody is never stated as Tristano invents his own luminous and impressionistic variations, with some invaluable assistance from Bauer. As the piece progresses the piano and guitar lines intertwine in an extraordinary singularity of purpose, and the performance ends enigmatically without any attempt to retrace the opening atmosphere.

Here, on these recordings, is delineated a singular individualist's uncompromising attitudes to music. According to Lee Konitz, *this* was the real birth of the cool.

(The seven sides are not in themselves long enough to make an album, and reissues have been filled out with various unrelated material, not detailed below. According to Tristano's daughter, there was, as of October 1994, still no prospect of these Capitol recordings being issued on CD.)

LP

(with Tadd Dameron and others:) *Crosscurrents*, Affinity AFF 149 (UK)

Lee Konitz (as), Warne Marsh (ts), Lennie Tristano (p), Billy Bauer (g), Arnold Fishkin (sb), Harold Granowsky (d)

New York	4 March 1949	**Wow**
		Crosscurrent
omit Konitz and Marsh		**Yesterdays**

as ***Wow****, but Denzil Best (d) replaces Granowsky*

	23 April 1949	**Marionette**
		Sax of a Kind
		Intuition
		Digression

Other LPs

incl. tracks 1–7: (with Buddy DeFranco and others:) *Crosscurrents*
Capitol M 11060 (USA)
Capitol 5C052-80853 (Netherlands)

* * *

Red Norvo: *Move!*

Showing a commendable open-mindedness, Red Norvo, a star soloist since the 1930s on xylophone and then vibraphone, selected two young modernists as partners in a forward-looking trio that he formed in the spring of 1950. On guitar he chose Tal Farlow, a 29-year-old virtuoso from North Carolina, who had already worked with another vibraphonist, Margie Hyams, in a small group. For string bass, Norvo recruited a refugee from Lionel Hampton's orchestra, Charles Mingus, temporarily out of music and working for the US Post Office.

Norvo's style, rooted in the swing era, altered little in the context of his trio, but it sounded more modern on account of the accompaniment of Farlow and Mingus. Norvo was sophisticated harmonically, and he had found no difficulty playing with Charlie Parker and Dizzy Gillespie as early as 1945. In the trio's performances, his prodigious technique enabled him to manage comfortably tricky bop charts such as Denzil Best's *Move* and George Wallington's *Godchild*. It was only when Norvo improvised that his allegiance to older jazz tenets became obvious. His form of musical embroidery, with its skittering phrases and slight rhythmic stiffness, had its counterpart in Teddy Wilson's keyboard style. However, when accompanying Farlow's improvisations, he was invariably sensitive and unobtrusively supportive.

The sound of the trio was an interesting amalgamation of instrumental elements which had already been heard in two highly popular groups of the 1940s, the Nat Cole Trio (piano, guitar and bass) and the George Shearing Quintet (vibraphone, piano, guitar, bass and drums). With a resourceful bass in Mingus and chordal assistance from Farlow, Norvo reasoned that he did not need a drummer to disrupt a calm, orderly environment. The group turned out to be a pioneer of the 'chamber jazz' concept, and in some respects foreshadowed the establishment of the Modern Jazz Quartet a year or two later. The instrumentation undoubtedly gave Norvo's unit a cool sound. The vibraphone frequently conveys an air of detachment, even in the passionate hands of a Lionel Hampton or a Milt Jackson. The amplified guitar is not necessarily a cool instrument, but definitely so in the timbre achieved by Farlow, whose smooth round tone was in distinctive contrast to the raw tone of, say, T-Bone Walker, and certainly more mellifluous than the sound of Django Reinhardt. Together, this particular combination of vibes and guitar reinforced the suspicion that studied effect was the name of the game. The sometimes overly precise, even pedantic, arrangements used by Norvo heightened that impression.

Godchild, although recorded in an exultant version by a studio band under Chubby Jackson's leadership, was perceived as one of the ultra-cool anthems; after all, it had been one of the dozen 'scriptures' handed down by Miles Davis's Capitol band. Norvo's trio made at least three takes which afforded each man ample solo space, with Mingus making the most telling contribution in a nimble solo on the master version.

Swedish Pastry, a theme by guitarist Barney Kessel which Norvo had recorded with the composer and Swedish clarinettist Stan Hasselgård in 1947, also had a cool, smooth melodic shape which the trio delineated deftly. With its clipped contours enunciated in unison by Norvo and Farlow against Mingus's walking bass, the piece is ably developed by Norvo, Farlow and Mingus in turn. For all his reservations about the musical aims of the group, Mingus enjoyed a prominence accorded to no other bass player in modern jazz up to that time. He was truly a third solo voice rather than an occasional contributor.

The express delivery of the angular *Move* and its overt modernity are far removed from the rather old-fashioned amble through *I Can't Believe that You're in Love with Me*. Some of the arrangements, for example *I'll Remember April* and *September Song*, veer towards the writing of George Shearing at his blandest and verge on the somnolent, but then, in an unpretentious up-tempo offering such as *Zing! Went the Strings of my Heart*, everyone forgets to be cool and the music ignites. In this instance Norvo shows an aptitude for blending bop and swing phrasing, and the effect is most curious.

One case of an arrangement enhancing a performance is the dressing provided for Cole Porter's *I Get a Kick out of You*, in which fairly static unison passages by vibes and guitar are offset by running bass lines from Mingus. Norvo's slow burn approach and the intimate quality of the trio's music made the group popular not only with jazz musicians but in the smart supper clubs, where couples had no problems dancing to the friendlier tempos. *If I Had You*, taken at a real businessman's bounce, was part of that other repertory. They could even manage nifty turns to the excellent *Godchild* at a quickstep tempo! A winsome aspect of this side is Farlow's attractive rhythm-guitar stroking during the course of Mingus's solo.

Farlow's instrumental command is never in doubt. He was at that time among the most technically gifted guitarists alive, with a boundless capacity for inventing a plethora of ideas at any tempo. He would toss off the most complicated written parts with unfailing accuracy. He might have benefited, however, by some occasional percussive support other than the vibraphone. One senses his need for drums most obviously on *Swedish Pastry* when after his own solo, which cries out for a tasty backbeat, he does exactly that for Mingus, alternately plucking a held string and patting the body of his guitar, a process which helps the movement of the bass passage.

Norvo's trio was heard at its freshest in the year that Mingus was a member. After his departure it was never quite the same, although his replacement, Red Mitchell, was no mean bass player. The later Decca and Fantasy sides do not measure up to the unification that marked the material undertaken for the Discovery label. Norvo and Farlow also ultimately tired of the format, but by then their place in the development of 'chamber jazz' was assured, if sometimes perversely overlooked by many of the music's historians.

CD

***Move!*, Savoy Jazz SJ-0168 (Japan)**

Red Norvo (vb), Tal Farlow (elg), Charles Mingus (sb)

Los Angeles	3 May 1950	**Swedish Pastry** (take 2)
		Cheek to Cheek (alternate take)
Chicago	31 Oct 1950	**September Song**
		Move
		I've Got You under my Skin
		I'll Remember April
		I Get a Kick out of You
		I Can't Believe that You're in Love with Me (alternate take)
		Zing! Went the Strings of my Heart
Los Angeles	13 April 1951	**If I Had You** (alternate take)
		This Can't Be Love (take 3)
		Godchild (take 3)
		I'm Yours (alternate take)

* * *

Modern Jazz Quartet: *Django; Concorde*

The Modern Jazz Quartet is the longest-running small group in the history of the music. It existed from 1952 to 1974, was re-formed in 1981 and is still going strong in the 1990s. The origins of the foursome stretch back to the 1940s when Milt Jackson (vibraphone), John Lewis (piano) and Kenny Clarke (drums) were members of Dizzy Gillespie's big band. Frequently, at after-hours sessions, they would be joined by Gillespie's bass player Ray Brown. This unit recorded under Milt Jackson's name for the Dee Gee label in 1951, but it was not yet the MJQ. The music was loose and informal, reflecting Jackson's personality.

With Ray Brown on the road with Jazz at the Philharmonic, Percy Heath, who had worked with Lewis and Clarke in Paris in 1948, was recruited for bass duties, and Lewis became musical director of the small cooperative. The MJQ signed to record under that name for Prestige in 1952, and the disciplined, shaping hand of Lewis was immediately evident in its debut recordings. Although the band had only four instruments, Lewis created detailed and precise arrangements for optimum effect, with frequent use of unison lines by vibes and piano. He even wrote bass parts for Heath and had definite instructions for his vastly experienced drummer. Lewis, who had been a contributing arranger and pianist for Miles Davis's nonet, liked the cool sounds and the MJQ was certainly a cool little band, a feeling enhanced by the detached sound of the vibes and his own sparse piano style. Little was left to chance in Lewis's careful approach, and perhaps for this reason the quartet's music did sometimes sound a trifle too calculated for comfort.

The pianist's knowledge of and interest in European classical music was also reflected in his compositions for the quartet, most especially in such early pieces as *The Queen's Fancy* and *Milano*. Bach-like phrases, contrapuntal playing and echoes of Tudor melodies were apt to crop up in Lewis's tunes. Sometimes they were incongruous, often engaging. Just when listeners might feel the atmosphere was verging towards the twee, Jackson, and occasionally Lewis, would cut loose with improvisations that proclaimed their musical origins. Lewis also wrote some splendid original melodies, not least the eminently attractive *Django*, which became a jazz standard, and the rather neglected *Delaunay's Dilemma*, a graceful and charming line which the group accorded a lightly swinging and entirely appropriate treatment.

The quartet's music was primarily cerebral. Jackson was the only passionate soloist and the tight arrangements provided him with too few chances to be his extrovert self, at least in the early life of the band when recording procedures dictated performances of limited duration. This was chamber jazz, put together with patience, precision and some dedication. By endeavouring to forge links between contemporary American jazz and European art music, Lewis and cohorts were treading new ground and anticipating by many years the later dabblings with so-called Third Stream. The neat, well-tailored nature of these sounds carried considerable appeal to a much wider audience than hard-core jazz listeners. The music was understandable and logical, with none of the raucous, spontaneous edge that is apt to frighten off middle-of-the-road concertgoers. Lewis and his companions seemingly felt more at home in concert or recital halls than in the informal atmosphere of jazz clubs. Larger, more attentive audiences provided fewer distractions than the usual patrons drinking at the bar in nightclubs.

La Ronde Suite, actually four variations on an old composition by Lewis entitled *Two Bass Hit,* was ideally cast for a concert context since it presented each member of the group in turn showing off his instrumental prowess. The tune had actually been recorded a couple of years earlier at the MJQ's inaugural session in a much less self-conscious version. *The Suite,* by contrast, places the emphasis on organization and arrangement. Lewis, for all his obsession with the classical element, did not feel hidebound by convention, particularly when he was recasting standard tunes. His frameworks for *Autumn in New York* and *But Not for Me* afford us new perspectives on these familiar songs by Vernon Duke and George Gershwin. The group gives *Autumn in New York* a slow, meditative exposition, and there is an effective striking clock sequence before the paraphrase of the theme. *But Not for Me* carries an out-of-tempo introduction but quickly moves into time, with Clarke pushing the beat forward with his immaculate brush strokes on the snare drum.

Actually Clarke, the father of modern drumming, is one of the reasons why the first edition of the quartet was so satisfying. His successor, Connie Kay, could never match Clarke's smooth, easy swing. Clarke disliked the tiny cymbals, triangles and other percussive paraphernalia which Kay readily deployed, leading some observers to suggest his drumming had too many effects and too little substance. It was no real surprise that Clarke grew tired of the MJQ's constrictions and sought more red-blooded jazz activity.

However, the MJQ undoubtedly attracted many listeners to jazz, and the members were great ambassadors for the music, earning respect and forcing listeners to take the group seriously. This was part of the trouble, for under Lewis's influence they were a shade too serious in demeanor and about their art.

CD

***Django*, Original Jazz Classics OJCCD 057-2 (USA)**

Milt Jackson (vb), John Lewis (p), Percy Heath (sb), Kenny Clarke (d)

New York	25 June 1953	**The Queen's Fancy**
		Delaunay's Dilemma
		Autumn in New York
		But Not for Me
	23 Dec 1954	**Django**
		One Bass Hit
		Milano
	9 Jan 1955	**La Ronde Suite**

CD

***Concorde*, Original Jazz Classics OJCCD 002-2 (USA)**

Jackson (vb), Lewis (p), Heath (sb), Connie Kay (d)

	2 July 1955	**Ralph's New Blues**
		All of You
		I'll Remember April
		Gershwin ballad medley:
		Soon
		Love Walked in
		Our Love is Here to Stay
		For You, for Me, For Evermore
		Concorde
		Softly as in a Morning Sunrise

* * *

Shorty Rogers: *Short Stops*

Several years after the release of the **Birth of the Cool** recordings, the instrumentation employed in Miles Davis's nonet began to appear in groups on the West Coast of the United States. In the case of the Gerry Mulligan tentet, which added a second trumpet to the front line, there was no real surprise, since Mulligan had been closely involved with Davis's group and simply wished to continue writing for such an ensemble. Mulligan even made a fresh recording of *Rocker*, which had figured in the nonet's repertory.

By a strange coincidence, in the same month of 1953 which saw the recording debut of Mulligan's new band, trumpeter Shorty Rogers, who had written for Woody Herman and Stan Kenton among others, took his nine-piece unit into the Los Angeles studios of Victor for two sessions which were to be influential in the evolution of West Coast Jazz. Like many of his contemporaries, Rogers had been completely won over by the Miles Davis sides and wished to emulate their sound. Shorty Rogers and his Giants carried an instrumentation that differed in only one respect from the Davis blueprint: tenor saxophone was substituted for baritone. The leader's arrangements, however, were quite another matter, being slick, tidy and rather conventional. There was none of the challenge or originality to be found in the charts by Gil Evans, John Lewis and Mulligan that had made the sound of Davis's band so memorable. One or two of the compositions were attractive, but they fell short of the collective inspiration that had shaped Davis's library of tunes.

Rogers's adaptation of the cool had already been heard on six numbers recorded by Capitol in the autumn of 1951, when his octet had been lacking a trombonist. The trumpeter's tidy but slightly twee arranging methods became one of the hallmarks of the West Coast style. There was a bland, cloying quality about a Rogers ensemble that was to be repeated in so many Hollywood bands, including those of such leaders as Marty Paich and Dave Pell. The same sound would also infuse Howard Rumsey's Lighthouse All Stars and Bob Cooper's groups. A curiously flat, dead sound, the fact that it was so repetitious and ubiquitous was explained by the presence of so many of the same faces in all these bands. French horn player John Graas, for example, seemed to crop up in most Hollywood groups, along with alto saxophonist Art Pepper. Jimmy Giuffre was another who would turn up with predictable frequency. There was a definite clique of highly proficient white musicians who cornered much of the jazz market (and most of the studio assignments) in Los Angeles.

To be fair to Rogers, he equipped himself with an array of impressive soloists in the Giants, notably Pepper, later replaced by Bud Shank, and pianist Hampton Hawes, associated with a much gutsier form of jazz but adaptable to this context, although he was, on his own admission, a poor reader. Hawes, Sonny Clark and Buddy Collette were three black musicians who were occasionally used on Hollywood dates, but their musical preferences lay elsewhere. Rogers made no attempt to emulate Davis in his trumpet solos, for, while he was certainly proficient, there was no hint of Davis's beauty or clarity of thought in his efforts.

In the rather stiff version of *The Pesky Serpent* space is found for no fewer than five soloists, of whom trombonist Milt Bernhart and Pepper are the most impressive. Hawes is guilty of some misfingering and Rogers sounds bland. Giuffre is just warming to his task when he has to stop. *Diablo's Dance* is a fast-moving showcase for Hawes, who enunciates the staccato, ascending theme which the horns then repeat. The real joy, though, is Hawes's fluent improvisation, filled with the blues phrases that were such an integral part of his style. His brisk, single-note lines sound somewhat at odds with the lumbering ensemble.

Easily the most attractive of Rogers's lines is the winsome *Pirouette,* in which he uses the ensemble textures in a way reminiscent of Mulligan's writing. The melody is a good one, and the variation is cleverly related to it. Rogers interweaves ensemble passages behind segments of the solos by Pepper, the leader and Giuffre. Taking a leaf out of Tadd Dameron's book, he also presages the piano solo with an eight-bar ensemble passage. A feature of the theme's contrasting melody is one bar when the time is deliberately suspended, producing a curiously attractive effect within an otherwise smooth, even performance. Drummer Shelly Manne's meticulous brushwork and accents that are faithfully attuned to the ensemble lines are excellent examples of his thoughtful craftsmanship.

Indian Club, with a nice rising tempo set by Manne, lacks any pretence of subtlety and is a far cry from, say, *Move* by Davis's nonet. Rogers contributes an energetic opening solo, and, although Giuffre is also heard, it is the vibrant Pepper who steals the show. *Morpo* sounds contrived and is again too stiffly performed to allow for relaxed solos. Pepper gives it his best shot and Hawes is listenable, but the contributions from Giuffre and Rogers are as staid as the rhythm. The leader endeavours to make greater use of the tonal colours available on the slow *Bunny,* which is a most effective arrangement. Pepper springs a surprise by doubling the tempo and the device is not misplaced. The only intrusive element is the use of a triangle, which contributes nothing other than an unwelcome distraction.

Pleasantly inoffensive but hardly stirring stuff is *Powder Puff,* which finds Bernhart and Hawes making nonsense of the twiddly arrangement and pointed title by delivering powerfully macho solos. Pepper's unforced elegance makes one believe he would have held his own in Davis's group and his sound would have blended as well with Davis as Konitz's did. *Mambo del Crow* is an authentic mambo complete with excellent rhythmic percussion by Manne, an amusing crow call, Latin style piano by Hawes and assorted chants from the bandsmen. Manne takes a superb solo, making effective use of timbales, and Bernhart weighs in with a virile trombone statement. But on this track there is no justification for the chosen instrumentation.

All too often the Giants sound mechanical, yet we know that this was not the natural stance of most of these musicians, so some of the fault must lie in that direction. The music has not worn nearly so well as the **Birth of the Cool** material, and that is usually the fate of blurred copies of originals. Rogers merely adopted an instrumentation with a sound that appealed to him, but was unable to use its pastel textures in a strikingly original way. Where the West Coasters went wrong was their perception of cool as a fixed style rather than as a successful experiment by some of the sharpest musical minds who regarded the episode as a brief phase in their development.

CD

***Short Stops*, Bluebird 5917-2 (USA) and RCA CD 90209 (Europe)**

Shorty Rogers (tpt), Milt Bernhart (tb), John Graas (french horn), Gene Englund (tuba), Art Pepper (as), Jimmy Giuffre (ts), Hampton Hawes (p), Joe Mondragon (sb), Shelly Manne (d)

Los Angeles	12 Jan 1953	**Powder Puff**
		The Pesky Serpent
		Bunny
		Pirouette
	15 Jan 1953	**Morpo**
		Diablo's Dance
		Mambo del Crow
		Indian Club

Rogers, Conrad Gozzo, Maynard Ferguson, Tom Reeves, John Howell (tpt), Bernhart, John Halliburton, Harry Betts (tb), Graas (french horn), Englund (tuba), Pepper, Bud Shank (as), Giuffre (ts, cl), Bob Cooper (bar), Marty Paich (p), Curtis Counce (sb), Manne (d)

	26 March 1953	**Coup de Graas**
		Infinity Promenade
		Short Stop
		Boar-Jibu
	2 April 1953	**Contours**
		Tale of an African Lobster
		Chiquito Loco
		Sweetheart of Sigmund Freud

Rogers, Gozzo, Ferguson, Reeves, Ray Linn (tpt), Bob Enevoldsen, Jimmy Knepper, Betts (tb), Graas (french horn), Paul Sarmento (tuba), Herb Geller, Shank (as), Bill Holman, Bill Perkins (ts), Giuffre, Cooper (bar), Russ Freeman (p), Joe Mondragon (sb), Manne (d)

	14 July 1953	**Blues for Brando**
		Chino
		The Wild One
		Windswept

Rogers, Gozzo, Ferguson, Harry 'Sweets' Edison, Clyde Reasinger (tpt), Bernhart, Betts, Enevoldsen (tb), Graas (french horn), Sarmento (tuba), Geller (as), Shank (as, ts, bar), Zoot Sims, Cooper (ts), Giuffre (cl, ts, bar), Paich (p), Counce (sb), Manne (d)

	2 Feb 1954	**Topsy**
		Basie Eyes
		It's Sand Man
		Doggin' Around

Pete Candoli (tpt) replaces Reasinger; Holman (ts) replaces Sims; Bob Gordon (bar) replaces Cooper

9 Feb 1954 — **Jump for Me**
Over and Out
Down for Double
Swingin' the Blues

Sims (ts) replaces Holman; Cooper (ts, bar) replaces Gordon

3 March 1954 — **H & J**
Tickletoe
Taps Miller
Walk, Don't Run

* * *

Gerry Mulligan: *The Best of the Gerry Mulligan Quartet with Chet Baker*

Formed six months before the MJQ and 3,000 miles away was a quartet of a very different stripe which bestrode the West Coast and cool-jazz categories. The Gerry Mulligan Quartet was one of those happy accidents that litter the history of jazz. Mulligan, as already discussed above, had made significant contributions to Miles Davis's **Birth of the Cool**, both as an arranger and the nonet's baritone saxophonist. On arrival in Hollywood in the summer of 1952, Mulligan was keen to do more instrumental work and cast about for some suitable sidemen in the Los Angeles area.

Trumpeter Chet Baker, a 22-year-old who had already worked with Charlie Parker and was lately discharged from the army, auditioned for the assignment and was given the job. Meanwhile the leader called pianist George Wallington in New York and asked him to come out to join his new quintet. Wallington declined and, because Mulligan could not find a suitable replacement, the famous piano-less quartet was born. Bob Whitlock was his initial choice for bass duties, and he hired Chico Hamilton as the drummer, although bassist Carson Smith and drummer Larry Bunker were the group's rhythm section later on.

This intimate environment enabled Mulligan to get through more playing than opportunities had allowed for several years. His bluff, cheery baritone formed a nicely contrasting sound to the lyrical, cool tones of Baker's trumpet. An instinctive player with a penchant for graceful, melodic lines, Baker flourished among the popular songs and catchy originals worked up by Mulligan. Neither musician was hampered by the absence of keyboard feeds, although each would often provide helpful riffs when the other was improvising. A natural outcome of this procedure was that an abundance of contrapuntal interweaving between saxophone and trumpet became one of the distinctive features of the group's recordings. The musical understanding within this partnership was remarkably close, each man seemingly able to anticipate the next thought of the other. Their personal relationship was less harmonious, yet these discords were buried when it was time to play. Mulligan has stated on more than one occasion that working with Baker provided some of the most inspired and satisfying musical experiences of his career.

The quartet existed as a working unit for just about a year, but before personal problems split it asunder an impressive collection of recordings was made for the newly formed Pacific Jazz label. Such well-shaped and neat Mulligan compositions as *Walkin' Shoes* produced cool, reflective performances from the principals, both of whom excelled in the unhurried climate of an even medium tempo. However, neither was averse to accelerating a few notches and Baker's staccato piece *Freeway* finds them bowling confidently along. The slower the beat, the cooler Mulligan and Baker became, and in pieces such as *My Funny Valentine* and *The Nearness of You* they are completely unruffled, achieving a sonorous instrumental blend that sounds like a scaled-down **Birth of the Cool**.

In contrast to these somewhat detached ballad inspections, their assessments of intrinsically hearty pieces such as *I'm Beginning to See the Light* and *Makin' Whoopee* are brimming with bounce and bonhomie. In *Love Me or Leave Me* perky, whimsical moods are struck. For such an intimate ensemble the range of textures and moods achieved was surprisingly broad.

Although a basically intuitive musician, Baker was not the poor technician depicted by some commentators. Certainly, he generally opted to play in the middle range of his instrument, but his vivid improvisation of the presto *Freeway* shows an ample technique at work and intelligent use of the trumpet's full scope.

There is good reason to suppose that Baker and Mulligan in this intimate milieu, without a piano, did not welcome undue distraction, for attentive listening was one of the prerequisites for their passages of simultaneous improvisation. Perhaps this factor led them to insist that the drummer, whether Hamilton or Bunker, accompany with brushes, laying down a crispy, springy swish rather than a penetrating cymbal sizzle. No group before or since has relied so heavily on brushes, which undoubtedly contributed to the already unusual sound. Hamilton, in particular, was a master of this percussive art, and his snare-drum accents and bass-drum punctuations were always pertinent to the moment.

If Mulligan's deep-throated playing occasionally veered towards the lugubrious, it was more often robustly expressive. His rhythmic perception was different from that of many modernists; sometimes he would slip into a two-beat, dixieland feel which gave his solos a dancing quality. His liking for improvised ensemble playing also harks back to earlier jazz styles. Hear the ending of *I'm Beginning to See the Light*; it is pure dixieland.

Mulligan's compositions were usually new tunes in their own right, but he was not unwilling to follow the bop procedure of basing a piece on a popular song. Thus his *Swing House* is cut from the chord progression of *Sweet Georgia Brown*. The one direct link between the quartet and the **Birth of the Cool**, apart from Mulligan himself, was his seminal composition *Jeru*, which served to inspire Chet Baker as it did Miles Davis before him. This piece, perhaps more than any other from his early career, demonstrates Mulligan's considerable originality as a composer.

CD

***The Best of the Gerry Mulligan Quartet with Chet Baker*, Pacific Jazz CDP 7 95481 2 and B21Y 95481 (USA)**

Chet Baker (tpt), Gerry Mulligan (bar), Bob Whitlock (sb), Chico Hamilton (d)

Los Angeles	16 Aug 1952	**Bernie's Tune**

Whitlock (sb) replaces Smith

Los Angeles	15–16 Oct 1952	**Nights at the Turntable**
		Walkin' Shoes
		Freeway
		Soft Shoe

Carson Smith (sb) replaces Whitlock; Larry Bunker (d) replaces Hamilton

	24 Feb 1953	**Carson City Stage**
		Makin' Whoopee
	27 March 1953	**My Old Flame**
	27 April 1953	**Love Me or Leave Me**
		Jeru
		Swing House
	29–30 April 1953	**I'm Beginning to See the Light** (master take)
		Darn that Dream (master take)
	20 May 1953	**My Funny Valentine**

Baker (tpt), Mulligan (bar), Henry Grimes (sb), Dave Bailey (d)

New York	Dec 1957	**Festive Minor**

Other CDs

plus additional tracks and takes:

The Complete Pacific Jazz and Capitol Recordings of the Original Gerry Mulligan Quartet and Tentette with Chet Baker, Mosaic MD 3-102 (USA)

Paul Desmond: *Take Ten*

For the greater part of his career, alto saxophonist Paul Desmond was ensconced as a permanent and invariably pleasing fixture in pianist Dave Brubeck's quartet. After a 16-year run with this group, Desmond finally broke from that rather arid musical climate, and for the last decade of his life worked as a freelance and was heard in more creative contexts alongside the Modern Jazz Quartet, Gerry Mulligan and Jim Hall.

This collection – one of a handful of felicitous collaborations with guitarist Hall – dates from a period when Desmond was seeking fresh musical stimulation in the recording studios, where he could hand pick kindred spirits for sessions under his own leadership. A most sensitive musician with a light, dry tone and a polished, lyrical turn of phrase, Desmond shared certain points of style with both Lee Konitz and Art Pepper. He was fond of using the upper register of his instrument, and his solos were invariably studded with witty quotations. He was a supremely relaxed performer who swung with the ease and unhurried eloquence that are associated with such saxophonists as Lester Young, Zoot Sims and Wardell Gray. His playing, although superficially cool and on early acquaintance even detached, was infused with a charm and gentleness rarely found in jazz. Desmond eschewed raw emotion, preferring a calm, cerebral climate.

His partnership with Hall was especially rewarding. These players were closely attuned and receptive to each other's ideas. On the CD **Take Ten**, Hall's sophisticated and supporting accompaniment gives Desmond a perfect frame, and the inventiveness of Hall's solos matches the leader's. Drummer Connie Kay plays with meticulous time, never distracting or disturbing the partnership of saxophone and guitar. Both bass players are dedicated to the beat and the group cause.

Like many jazz musicians, Desmond became interested in bossa nova melodies and rhythms during a period of over-exposure for this delicate Brazilian samba style. The pieces on **Take Ten** are divided between bossa nova performances and popular songs, with a couple of original melodies by Desmond included for good measure. These originals include the title track, written in the spirit of his commercially successful piece for Brubeck, *Take Five*, with the unusual metre of that earlier piece, $\frac{5}{4}$, now reprised in a melodic line that has a quasi-Eastern flavour. Desmond is assured in this metre, and his deft craftsmanship in turning the bossa nova to good account is exemplified on that Brazilian anthem, *Samba de Orpheu* (from the movie *Black Orpheus*).

However, the saxophonist's propensity for straight swinging is not neglected when he bears down on *Alone Together*, and his winsome way with a ballad is underlined by a moving interpretation of *Nancy*. All the music is instantly accessible and appealing to the lay listener and simultaneously satisfying to connoisseurs of improvisational technique.

CD

***Take Ten*, Bluebird 07863 66146 2 (USA)**

Paul Desmond (as), Jim Hall (elg), Gene Cherico (sb), Connie Kay (d)

New York	5 June 1963	**The One I Love (Belongs to Somebody Else)**
	10 June 1963	**The Theme from Black Orpheus**
		Samba de Orpheus
	12 June 1963	**Alone Together**
	14 June 1963	**El Prince**
		Embarcadero
		Nancy

Gene Wright (sb) replaces Cherico

	25 June 1963	**Take Ten**

Other CDs

plus additional tracks:

The Complete Recordings of the Paul Desmond Quartet with Jim Hall, Mosaic MD4-120 (USA)

CHAPTER 9

The First Hard Bop Bands

Mark Gardner

For a decade from 1954, the most popular style to enjoy currency among jazz musicians was hard bop. Stemming from bop, it sought to simplify the complexities of the earlier pioneers, placing a heavier emphasis on the rhythmic element while introducing material that was easier for the average listener to assimilate.

Like cool jazz, hard bop put a greater reliance on composition. Tunes were not so angular as bop pieces and frequently offered more substance to the soloist. Improvisation remained paramount, and the style was refreshed by drawing on blues and gospel sources for inspiration. Many compositions by the likes of Horace Silver, Hank Mobley and Ray Bryant, along with Benny Golson and Bobby Timmons, had a churchy, sanctified feel about them that gave hard bop a spirited impetus. This 'downhome' feeling was somewhat overdone at times by such groups as Art Blakey's Jazz Messengers and Cannonball Adderley's quintet, and ultimately became predictable and tired. In some circles, words such as 'funky' and 'soulful' developed into terms of critical abuse. Yet throughout that decade of pre-eminence, hard bop proved a pliable medium for many highly distinctive and original soloists. Their best work has continued to inspire and is the basis for much of the music being played as the millenium approaches. Hard bop undoubtedly brought the heat and heart back into the music, stressing not only passion and muscularity but also the value of well-conceived themes.

* * *

Clifford Brown and Max Roach: *Clifford Brown and Max Roach*

Hard bop became a cause and a positive movement in 1954 with the formation of two quintets in which the motivating forces were pioneer bop drummers Max Roach and Art Blakey. It was appropriate that these potent percussionists should be up front in their respective bands, because the drums took on an even more definitive role as the catalyst in hard bop.

It was particularly ironic that Roach decided to form a new band in California, where for several seasons the super-cool West Coast sounds had reigned supreme. In the spring of 1954 he invited the brilliant young trumpeter Clifford Brown to join him from New York to co-lead a combo which would provide positive alternatives to the Los Angeles style. Brown had modelled his style on that of the virtuoso Fats Navarro, but, unlike the first modernists, he did not emerge from the big bands. His workshop milieu had been rhythm-and-blues groups which offered greater freedom to soloists, but as the name implied emphasized both the beat and the 12-bar form. Later, these characteristics were carried over into hard bop by a flock of other soloists from the genre – Blue Mitchell, Junior Cook, Tommy and Stanley Turrentine, Johnny Griffin and many more. Brown did work briefly with Lionel Hampton's orchestra, which synthesized big-band swing and rhythm and blues during the early 1950s. However, the trumpeter had little stomach for grinding section work and escaped from Hampton's ranks at the earliest opportunity following a controversial European tour in 1953. Thus he promptly answered Roach's request on the understanding that both men would select the rest of the personnel from the pick of the Hollywood musicians.

The Clifford Brown–Max Roach group existed for around two and a half years and left behind a body of music that encapsulated all the best virtues of hard bop. After some experiments with personnel – tenor saxophonist Teddy Edwards, pianist Carl Perkins and bassist George Bledsoe were charter members – a settled line-up emerged with tenor player Harold Land, pianist Richie Powell (brother of Bud Powell) and bassist George Morrow. Land, from Texas, had a muscular tone and a down-to-earth, unflashy style that served to complement the daring and dash of Brown's manner. Powell and the steadfast Morrow were ideal anchormen. The five points of the group were in perfect accord, which resulted in an unusually close unity of purpose. When Land eventually departed, his replacement, Sonny Rollins, although a much more inventive and original player, failed to fit in as harmoniously as his predecessor.

The numerous felicities of this tightly knit working band were seldom better displayed than in these dynamic performances. The group successfully continued a tradition of playing that had been established by Charlie Parker's quintet of 1947. There were differences, mainly to do with greater rhythmic drive, in no small measure owing to the fact that Roach was an even better drummer in 1955 than he had been eight years earlier. Brown, like Parker before him, discovered that Roach was a repository of rhythmic subtlety, a source of consistent inspiration and urgency in the act of improvisation. An almost telepathic understanding existed between them. The co-leaders projected a controlled heat, a co-ordinated discipline that never denied expressiveness but stopped short of an emotional deluge.

Such was the perspicacity of this wholly integrated band that they could even invest an old and creaking warhorse such as *What am I Here For?* with an agreeably surprising zest, zipping through the unpromising chord sequence at a fast clip and discovering unimagined beauty along the way. Brown made significant contributions to the repertory in the nicely turned *Daahoud*, the headlong charge that is *The Blues Walk* and, best of all, the piquant melody of *Joy Spring*, so evocative of its subject matter. Both Bud Powell's atmospheric *Parisian Thoroughfare*, on which Brown and Land skilfully simulate traffic sounds, and Duke Jordan's minor masterpiece *Jordu* had been in the group's book since its inception, while the exotic mood of *Delilah* was cleverly exploited in a very pretty arrangement on which Land plays a vamping counter-melody to Brown's muted theme statement. In Brown's sweeping solo, the commentary supplied by Roach is worthy of special study, as he seemingly anticipates every nuance of his co-leader's line. Their compatibility is further enunciated in the four-bar exchanges that flow between trumpeter and drummer. Anyone doubting the musicality of the finest jazz drummers would do well to hear Roach in this collection. His use of sticks and brushes is exemplary, his accents and fills are integral parts of each performance and his beat never falters, no matter the complexity of the cross-rhythms he compounds. His playing, ever crisp and tasteful, bespeaks an intellect of logic and clarity.

By all accounts Brown was a warm, outgoing, unaffected and humble man. His essentially optimistic outlook was reflected in an adventurous style, which was vibrant and cheerful, far removed from the moody melancholia of Miles Davis. Brown's good-natured wit was infectious and coloured the band's music. Thus, Powell humorously interjects wry quotations from *Can Can* and *The Marseillaise* into an apt arrangement of *Parisian Thoroughfare* to epitomize the happy, carefree spirit that prevailed.

Brown was a prototype hard bopper. He, together with his main influence, Navarro, combined three often unrelated streams in bop trumpet playing: beautiful timbre, super technique, creative improvisation. His playing was to affect deeply almost all the young brassmen that followed, most prominently Lee Morgan, Freddie Hubbard and Woody Shaw. Others would synthesize aspects of Brown's style with borrowings from Davis's.

The pivotal position of Brown is shown by the fact that early in 1954 he had briefly served in a short-lived edition of the Jazz Messengers (then billed as the Art Blakey Quintet) which recorded at Birdland. He could so easily have been a permanent star in that other vital unit but for Roach's offer.

CD

***Clifford Brown and Max Roach*, EmArcy 814645-2 (USA)**

Clifford Brown (tpt), Harold Land (ts), Richie Powell (p), George Morrow (sb), Max Roach (d)

Los Angeles	2 Aug 1954	**Delilah**
		Parisian Thoroughfare
	3 Aug 1954	**Jordu**
	6 Aug 1954	**Joy Spring**
		Daahoud (take 1)
New York	24 Feb 1955	**The Blues Walk**
	25 Feb 1955	**What am I Here For?**

Other CDs

Brownie: The Complete EmArcy Recordings of Clifford Brown, EmArcy 838306-2 (Japan)

* * *

Horace Silver: *Horace Silver and the Jazz Messengers*; Art Blakey: *Art Blakey and the Jazz Messengers at the Jazz Corner of the World*

A lengthy parade of superior soloists passed through the ranks of Art Blakey's Jazz Messengers in the 1950s – trumpeters Kenny Dorham, Donald Byrd, Bill Hardman and Lee Morgan, saxophonists Hank Mobley, Jackie McLean, Johnny Griffin, Benny Golson and Wayne Shorter, pianists Horace Silver, Sam Dockery, Junior Mance, Walter

Bishop Jr and Bobby Timmons. Those who weren't good enough didn't last long; Blakey blew them away.

Blakey, who with Max Roach defined the rhythmic surge and intensity of hard bop, was a leader who sought out brilliant young players with fire in their bellies and an unquenchable thirst for driving swing. In Blakey's opinion, if listeners' feet were not tapping and fingers not snapping, the Jazz Messengers were not getting their message through.

Almost any of the Jazz Messengers' recordings from this period would be representative because of Blakey's huge inspirational presence and pulse. However, the quintet's first album, under Silver's leadership, shows the pianist's permanent contributions to the group's spirit and the direction it would take, while the live recordings of the 1950s have a special atmosphere of uninhibited excitement, for here was a band which ignited in the presence of a warmly responsive audience.

Silver was in the vanguard of the hard-bop movement from the outset and proved to be one of its most influential and charismatic figures. Hired by the cool and bop tenor saxophonist Stan Getz and brought to New York in 1950, he was soon recording with Miles Davis, J. J. Johnson and other leading lights. After making some spirited trio sessions for Blue Note he was asked to assemble a quintet for a further album; thus the Jazz Messengers were reborn in the autumn of 1954.

Blakey had used this group name for a Blue Note date with an octet as early as 1947, and he was the man to stir the rhythm for Silver. On bass, young Doug Watkins, a recent arrival from Detroit, was recruited. Bop veteran Dorham, a late developer whose personal sound and articulate melodic ideas had suddenly come into perfect focus, was an excellent choice to partner tenor saxophonist Mobley, still relatively unknown despite a recent stint in Dizzy Gillespie's combo. Dorham, incidentally, was a member of the original 1947 Messengers. In the group's reincarnation, Silver was clearly the motivating force in the four-sided role of composer, arranger, pianist and musical director. Then just turned 26, he possessed refreshing originality. His infectious piano style owed a debt to Bud Powell, but Silver had a bubbling, optimistic perspective, a bright, cheerful quality expressed in a percussive touch and a penchant for outrageous quotations and soulful, gospel phrases. His busy, choppy accompaniment kept soloists on their toes.

The blues had been somewhat neglected by cool and West Coast musicians, and Silver's music was a positive reaffirmation of the durability of a constant form in jazz. Similarly his use of gospel music showed how the old could inform and refresh the new. Silver wrote relatively simple melodies, often with the feel of the swing style, but juxtaposed these lines cleverly against a modern rhythm section. This effective hybrid style rapidly became the norm and was reflected in hundreds of hard-bop albums disgorged by the Blue Note, Prestige and

Riverside labels. This apparent simplification made the music much more accessible than bop, which had never sought to court its audience. Silver's tunes – many of them catchy and attractive – could be whistled and danced to. Their appeal, which was neither fake nor contrived, opened the way for a much wider appreciation of jazz.

Silver and his colleagues also restored red-blooded emotion, excitement and the importance of the individual soloist to jazz after a period of arch, over-arranged confections. All members of the group were gifted, resourceful soloists, and in Silver's compositions there was a vigour that infused their playing. In his seven pieces and one by Mobley (*Hankerin'*) the level of invention is high.

Hankerin' is notable for the particularly nimble solos by Mobley and Dorham as they lightly ride a rhythmic switchback supplied by Blakey. *Room 608*, taken at a fast bop tempo, illustrates Silver's concern for detail as he inserts neatly arranged riffs between the solos. His own pair of vibrant choruses are matched by a molten drum break by the dynamic Blakey. *Creepin' in* explores a more sinuous, slow mood. The theme is in a minor key, a feature by no means new to jazz, but one which with hard bop for the first time became a regular element of the music. Dorham indicates how well suited he was to this setting. Silver's emphatic touch and deliberate use of repetitious, bluesy phrases makes his a potent solo, wholly in keeping with the spirit of the piece.

To Whom it May Concern, with a staccato melodic line and an attractive Latin contrasting theme, finds Silver developing clear, well-resolved phrases in his first solo, but he cannot resist an amusing reference to *The Donkey Serenade* along the way. The composer's ready wit is also displayed on *Hippy*, which sounds as if it will have a conventional *aaba* structure, but has a tag to extend the composition in *ccdc* fashion, giving the impression of two tunes in one. It is a delightful piece of writing. In keeping with the happy atmosphere, Silver launches his solo with a hilarious borrowing from *Bye Bye Blackbird*.

The piece from this session which became an instant jazz standard is *The Preacher*, subsequently in the repertory of all manner of bands, large and small. It inspired Eddie Jefferson to write an eminently suitable lyric. An adhesive 16-bar theme, it is littered with blues and gospel phrases but stands as a memorable melody. The solos are in keeping with the atmosphere, and again Silver has the two horns play unison passages where another solo might be expected. The blues *Doodlin'* is as attractive in its way as *Creepin' in* and *The Preacher*. The soul phrasing that Silver employs in his solo became overdone and exaggerated by some of his lesser imitators, but in his hands it sounds unpretentious and unforced.

The pattern of Horace Silver's future development and substantial recorded output was firmly established on this exceptional album, brimming with zest, vitality and music that has withstood the test of time quite superbly. In little over a year he was following this course with his own quintet, after having left the cooperative Jazz Messengers in Blakey's firm hands.

The selection from Blakey's live recordings features a transitional personnel which briefly brought back charter Messenger Mobley, in a positively electrifying partnership with trumpeter Lee Morgan. Mobley, a consistently inventive soloist, tended to be overshadowed during his most creative years by such contemporary saxophonists as Sonny Rollins, John Coltrane and Johnny Griffin. His even, unflashy tone made his work superficially less distinctive than that of those three, but his great rhythmic perspicacity and improvised lines of unfailing logic and clarity were revealed on closer acquaintance. Undoubtedly a 'musician's musician', Mobley, rather like Wardell Gray before him, remained largely unappreciated by a wider audience throughout a career notable for a consistency of craftsmanship.

The unsuppressed vivacity of trumpeter Morgan provided a most satisfying counterbalance to Mobley's dark and sinuous lines. Blakey's barrage provoked Morgan to fashion his most durable improvisations when in the drummer's company; his crackling delivery was never quite so crisp when other drummers were feeding the beat. The same would be true, to a slightly lesser extent, of Morgan's successor, Freddie Hubbard, who also thrived on the pulsations of this extraordinary drummer.

At this stage of their existence the Messengers had no current musical director – a role first taken by Silver and later ably filled by Benny Golson and Wayne Shorter – so Blakey commissioned compositions by writers outside the band's ranks. Pianist Ray Bryant came up with the delightfully catchy *Chicken an' Dumplins*, a chuckling theme eminently suited to the potent ensemble. Pianist Gildo Mahones supplied the minor-keyed *Art's Revelation*, and from pianist Randy Weston Blakey borrowed the attractively melodic original *Hi-Fly*. Mobley, not renowned for composition, contributed the sturdy *M and M* (standing for Mobley and Morgan), a good blowing line with an arrangement that showed the saxophonist had learned a lesson or two from Silver's methods. As for *The Theme*, this bop riff pattern had been claimed by many composers, but was most probably written by Wardell Gray, although authentication is now virtually impossible and the matter will surely remain an unsolved jazz mystery. On this album the piece is uncredited.

The live atmosphere of these recordings made at Birdland in New York is apparent in not only the applause, but the shrill huckstering of pint-sized MC Pee Wee Marquette and the occasional verbal exhortations of Blakey himself. Fortunately a fine recording balance was achieved and the only slight drawback is the rather casually tuned piano with which Bobby Timmons had to deal.

Chicken an' Dumplins, wherein Blakey lays down a powerful backbeat, sets the proceedings aflame with its comical, stuttering line, which proves to be a launching pad for earthy solos by Mobley and Morgan. Timmons feeds a steady supply of broad chords for the strutting soloists, and then immerses himself in an infectious gospel groove. Blakey takes a typically potent and pithy break before the quiet, stalking ending. After this leisurely stroll, the band hurls itself into a frightening charge tempo on *M and M*. Mobley, despite having trouble with an unresponsive reed, keeps his cool and builds a solo of admirable cohesion. Morgan deploys a host of vocal effects and displays his ultra-fast technique in a scintillating solo. Timmons has a tough row to hoe in following such virtuosity but struggles to keep up, while Blakey appends a series of eight- and four-bar explosions in a rushing, climactic conversation with the horns. Allowing the temperature to cool somewhat following this fervid flourish, the Messengers play *Hi-Fly*, and in his solo Timmons indicates his admiration for Bud Powell. The piece was neatly arranged by trombonist Melba Liston, whose pleasant scored interlude allows Blakey time for tension-building accents on his snare and even four bars by bass player Jymie Merritt before the thematic reprise.

A rapid burst of *The Theme* is merely an appetizer for a much more detailed and lengthier exploration of the piece, this time at a medium tempo. Mobley shows his harmonic understanding in some unexpected twists. Horn riffs assist the penultimate chorus of Timmons's cogent solo, and Morgan's little growling phrases provide a delicious touch in the closing statement of the theme. *Art's Revolution* employs another scorching tempo which once again finds Morgan and Mobley highly inventive and Timmons striving, but the joy of this track is Blakey's richly detailed and enormously stimulating solo, his only extended workout of the set.

Blakey's own volcanic playing and the style and general approach of his groups in the three decades after this album was recorded did not really change one jot. While others were diverted to new stylistic areas, Blakey hewed closely to the hard-bop sound with which he was so closely identified. In the process he succoured many young talents who went on to make important contributions to jazz, including trumpeters Woody Shaw, Chuck Mangione and Wynton Marsalis, saxophonists Branford Marsalis and Gary Bartz, pianists Keith Jarrett and JoAnne Brackeen, and many others. All found that a spell with the Messengers was helpful and educational. Blakey's commitment to fostering good, young players certainly enriched the music. Without his dedication it is unlikely that hard bop would have become such a potent force.

CD

***Horace Silver and the Jazz Messengers,* Blue Note B21K 46140 (USA)**

Kenny Dorham (tpt), Hank Mobley (ts), Horace Silver (p), Doug Watkins (sb), Art Blakey (d)

Hackensack, NJ	13 Nov 1954	**Room 608**
		Creepin' in
		Doodlin'
		Stop Time
	6 Feb 1955	**Hippy**
		To Whom it May Concern
		Hankerin'
		The Preacher

Other CDs

same contents:

Blue Note CDP 7046140-2; Blue Note B21Y 46140 (USA)
Blue Note 746140.2 (Germany)

CD

***Art Blakey and the Jazz Messengers at the Jazz Corner of the World,* Blue Note CDP 7243 8 28888 2 6 (USA)**

Lee Morgan (tpt), Hank Mobley (ts), Bobby Timmons (p), Jymie Merritt (sb), Blakey (d, speech)

New York	15 April 1959	**Just Coolin'**
*as **Just Coolin'**, but Pee Wee Marquette (speech)*		**The Theme** (short version)
Blakey (speech) replaces Marquette		**Close Your Eyes**
omit (speech)		**M and M**
add Marquette (speech)		**Hipsippy Blues**
Blakey (speech) replaces Marquette		**Chicken an' Dumplins**
omit (speech)		**Hi-Fly**
		Art's Revelation
		Justice
add Marquette (speech)		**The Theme** (long version)

* * *

Miles Davis: *'Round about Midnight*

Despite the artistic success and considerable influence of his **Birth of the Cool** recordings, Miles Davis had some lean times in the early 1950s. Without a group of his own and struggling with personal problems, he was forced to take jobs as a guest soloist, and but for recordings on the independent Blue Note and Prestige labels we would know little of his progress during that period of temporary public eclipse. Fortunately, those sessions provide a faithful account of his development and interest in the burgeoning hard-bop style which was being embraced by all the rising young talents in New York and Detroit, a centre for a seemingly inexhaustible supply of gifted jazz players. Davis was the first to give alto saxophonist Jackie McLean a chance to record, and subsequently employed such hard boppers as Horace Silver, Art Blakey, Sonny Rollins and drummer Philly Joe Jones on his dates.

After Davis's career was buoyed by a standing ovation at the 1955 Newport Jazz Festival, he cast about for personnel to fit a quintet he was forming. Pianist Red Garland and Philly Joe Jones had impressed Davis on a quartet recording and were both engaged for the new group. The trumpeter then recruited 20-year-old Paul Chambers, one of the most promising young bass players. As a front-line partner he selected tenor saxophonist John Coltrane, who had worked with Dizzy Gillespie, Earl Bostic and Johnny Hodges without making much of an impression.

Thus one of the most important small groups of the decade was born. Typically, Davis adapted hard bop to his own ends. The rhythm section was certainly in the hard-swinging mould associated with the style, but neither Davis nor Coltrane favoured the overtly declarative manner of the horn players operating in the genre. Neither did Davis embrace the catchy original themes or soulful, gospel influence introduced by Horace Silver, Hampton Hawes and others. Davis's book consisted largely of older popular standards, bop originals, compositions by Thelonious Monk and the occasional line from the leader's own pen. In this unit, possessing the same instrumentation as the classic bop group, Davis skilfully merged his cool perception with the heat of hard bop in a unique blend.

The cool overlay stemmed largely from Davis's own trumpet style, which increasingly was projected through a Harmon mute. His leisurely readings of ballads with long, held notes in the middle register occasionally suggested a frosty detachment in his solos. Coltrane's rough and jagged improvisations with a steely centre were a surprisingly apt contrast to the leader's work. Another positive factor was Garland's unobtrusive piano, with solos that balanced single-note lines with personally framed passages of block chording. However, the source of much of the band's momentum was drawn from the explosive yet meticulous drumming of Jones, whose high-octane performances Davis rightly regarded as crucial. Neither should the perceptive and lean bass lines of Chambers be undervalued in this context. He was considerably more mobile than the bop bass players. Whether 'walking' or 'running', Chambers had an infectious time feel, and his choice of notes was not as predictable as that of the majority of bass players. Davis's regard for him is indicated by the fact that the trumpeter employed him for well over seven years, longer than any of his other sidemen, excepting drummer Al Foster.

While still working out his contract with Prestige, Davis unveiled this quintet for the first time at a session for Columbia Records, with which he would be affiliated for the next three decades. It was fitting that the debut title should have been *Ah-leu-cha,* an intricate theme by Charlie Parker which Davis had recorded with his erstwhile employer some eight years earlier. In a clever arrangement, its repeated eight-bar theme on which the horns play contrapuntal lines is divided by punching breaks by Jones. Davis's open horn solo is flowing and outgoing, and a bold spirit also infuses Coltrane's effort. Garland sounds spry and there isn't a block chord to be heard. Jones's dynamic drumming lifts everyone. Davis also eschews the mute for a rapid inspection of Tadd Dameron's *Tadd's Delight* (also known as *Sid's Delight*), which has the melodic appeal and harmonic interest that one associates with this composer's works. The brisk nature of the performance has as much to do with Jones's percussive urgency as the involvement of the soloists.

Elsewhere, though, on this thoughtful and ingeniously conceived album, Davis opts for the mute as a device to help express his calm, order and sparse ideas. Never a man aimlessly to fill up every bar with the maximum number of notes, Davis would often let several measures ride before continuing his improvisation. By contrast, Coltrane's solos were positively verbose and at this juncture lacked the incisive execution of which Davis was now possessed.

Davis's rhythmic certainty was such that his clipped treatments of hoary old standards such as *Bye Bye Blackbird* and *All of You* became the accepted manner of dealing with the compositions, which rapidly found their way into the repertory of many other bands of the day. Both pieces, incidentally, remained as regularly inspected components of the trumpeter's repertory for five or six years, suggesting that he found their melodic contours and chord progressions consistently stimulating.

Among the most moving tracks on this inaugural set by the quintet is Davis's emotive exploration of Thelonious Monk's distinctive composition *'Round Midnight,* as perfect a reading of the tune as you could hope to find. The trumpeter's melody statement is spare and pristine in quality. Coltrane elects to double the tempo for his solo, into which he is launched by a tension-building insert where Davis removes the mute for eight biting notes. Such felicitious touches in the arrangements were a carryover from his discoveries with the earlier nonet.

Saxophonist Stan Getz had introduced a jazz version of a Swedish folk melody, *Dear Old Stockholm*, several years earlier, and Davis redefined the brooding theme with the aid of an excellent arrangement. Chambers is prominent in both the theme and the solo roster. Surprisingly, he is the opening soloist and this platform provides an ideal view of his nimble elasticity. Undoubtedly this was one of the most satisfying bass solos put on record up to that time, and his contemporaries studied it with the sort of attention that the previous generation had reserved for Jimmy Blanton's improvisations. Listening to this and the other sides, it is not difficult to understand why, once again, many would follow where Davis led.

CD

***'Round about Midnight*, Columbia Jazz Masterpieces CK 40610 (USA)**

Miles Davis (tpt), John Coltrane (ts), Red Garland (p), Paul Chambers (sb), Philly Joe Jones (d)

New York	27 Oct 1955	**Ah-leu-cha**
	5 June 1956	**Dear Old Stockholm**
		Bye Bye Blackbird
		Tadd's Delight
	10 Sept 1956	**All of You**
		'Round Midnight

Other CDs

same contents:

CBS CD 62323; CBS Jazz Masterpieces 460605-2 (Europe)

* * *

Phil Woods: *Woodlore*

Of the second wave of alto saxophonists who took Charlie Parker as their starting point, Phil Woods and Jackie McLean were perhaps the two most creative and influential. Although they developed along contrasting lines, each has stayed the course and remains a model for younger musicians. Both were employed by pianist George Wallington in editions of his mid-1950s quintet, and they were affiliated to the Prestige label for several years. Whereas McLean effected an even more biting tone than Parker's and infused his playing with a searing 'cry', Woods revealed a love for the bubbling exuberance which was another aspect of Parker's multi-layered musical personality. Cannonball Adderley was another of the 'second wave' who took an optimistic stance, though he lacked Woods's resilience.

Woods had, and still has, the ability to elate with his fierce attack, devotion to the beat and love of medium-fast sorties through standard tunes and compositions of his own creation. The boldness and vibrancy of his leaping improvisations carry the listener along. He revels in swinging lithely, never holding back, ever becoming emotionally involved.

First works are not invariably prescient in informing listeners of the course of a jazz musician's career, but Woods's first album for Prestige proved to be a reliable and extremely impressive pointer to his artistic progress. Made in 1955 on his 24th birthday, the quartet album entitled **Woodlore** showed Woods to be an inventive soloist of considerable ability and sure technical accomplishment. Excitement is endemic to his music, but even at this early juncture he showed himself well capable of projecting all kinds of emotional moods. *Falling in Love All Over Again* is an infinitely tender and perceptive study in the ballad form. Yet on *Be my Love*, previously associated with the theatrical voice of Mario Lanza, Woods strips away the song's sentimentality and substitutes a bustling, extrovert sense of optimism. Woods's winsome way with show tunes is also apparent on his fast inspection of *Get Happy*, but the gem of this rewarding set is his jaunty and uninhibited canter through the chords of the unlikely *On a Slow Boat to China*, a pop melody that Charlie Parker also used on occasion. Tearing into the piece with unconcealed pleasure, Woods unleashes four choruses of perfectly symmetrical improvisation, his dry tone and spry, limber phrasing combining to memorable effect above the choppy chord pattern laid down by pianist John Williams. Who, after hearing this track alone, could doubt the allegiance of Woods to hard bop? His mercurial solo on *Get Happy* reinforces the conclusion, as at a flying tempo he inserts some positively shouting 'vocal' effects and gets increasingly heated as the choruses flash by. His instrumental command on this track is quite remarkable, and shows how far jazz had travelled in terms of technique by 1955.

Strollin' with Pam is an impressive example of Woods's blues playing. When a pianist was advised to 'stroll' it meant he didn't play, and Woods's first three choruses are to an accompaniment of bass and drums – hence the title. Woods laces his neatly developed statement with the smearing blues phrases which had been heard in this idiom many years earlier, but they come out sounding newly minted, and the saxophonist builds tension by an economical use of double-time passages in his fifth chorus. Much of his playing in this instance is what used to be termed 'funky' – earthy and basic – and it is all delivered with a deceptive ease.

His other original composition from this date, *Woodlore,* is of considerably more substance, and its interestingly structured chord changes enable Woods to deploy his harmonic knowledge, but his undoubted skill in this area and his rhythmic flexibility do not disguise that he is also a melodic player of considerable sensitivity.

While primarily a style associated with young black musicians, hard bop was not exclusively their domain. Woods and his colleagues here play four square in that manner. They clearly regarded it as the natural style to adopt, the contemporary music of their time. Pianist Williams had unashamedly listened to Horace Silver and adapted the idea of laying down a jumpy, highly percussive accompaniment which particularly suited Woods's stream of long-lined phrases in *On a Slow Boat to China* and elsewhere. Drummer Nick Stabulas and bass player Teddy Kotick had worked with Woods in Wallington's band and were closely attuned to his rhythmic needs. Their presence helps explain Woods's supremely confident air throughout this satisfying recital. Stabulas sounds as assured as Arthur Taylor, and like that drummer tends slightly to accelerate during a performance, but this tendency in no way detracts from the performance; it actually enhances it. Kotick, having worked extensively with Charlie Parker, would later slot into Silver's quintet. On *Get Happy* he contributes an excellent running solo and dancing support lines. He was also a fine walking-bass player, as he is able to show on *Strollin' with Pam.*

Phil Woods went on to create music of richer texture and greater variety in the years that followed, but the freshness, involvement and devil-may-care mood of this set retain an appeal that transcends time and style.

CD

***Woodlore,* Original Jazz Classics OJCCD 052-2 (USA)**

Phil Woods (as), John Williams (p), Teddy Kotick (sb), Nick Stabulas (d)

New York	25 Nov 1955	**Be my Love**
		Woodlore
		Falling in Love All Over Again
		Get Happy
		Strollin' with Pam
		On a Slow Boat to China

* * *

Sonny Rollins: *Saxophone Colossus*

If ever there was a career turning-point in the life of tenor saxophonist Sonny Rollins it was this remarkable recording. To be sure, Rollins already had a growing reputation and at the age of 26 was certainly no novice, having salted away invaluable learning experience with such seminal modernists as Charlie Parker, Miles Davis, Thelonious Monk, J. J. Johnson and Max Roach, but the quality of his pre-1956 recordings had been decidedly uneven and inconsistent. Rollins was a comparatively late developer, despite his taking part in sessions with Bud Powell and Johnson when he was only 19.

His raw, rumbustious talent received its final polish during the first half of 1956 when he was the front-line partner of trumpeter Clifford Brown in the Brown–Roach quintet. Aside from the challenge of measuring up to Brown's exhilarating solos, Rollins discovered anew in this unit the inspirational drumming of Roach, the most disciplined, musical and commanding percussionist of that time. Roach knew how to fire and control a soloist of Rollins's potential; his polyrhythms extracted consistently adventurous playing from the tenorman. To place the album in its historical context, it was recorded just four days before the horrific road accident which claimed the lives of Brown and the band's pianist Richie Powell and effectively ended one of the most important hard-bop combinations.

Although by this juncture Sonny Rollins had outgrown his obsession with the style of Coleman Hawkins, his approach and gruff, even brusque, tone owed more to Hawkins than to Lester Young. In his reappraisal of Hawkins's innovations, Rollins offered new alternatives to his contemporaries. Hawkins had been unjustifiably neglected during the 1950s; Rollins's enthusiasm for him would revive interest in the work of the older man.

The close collaboration between Rollins and Roach is apparent throughout this programme, and the drummer is a potent solo voice in the proceedings, but it should also be noted how skilfully pianist Tommy Flanagan and bass player Doug Watkins slot into the quartet with the two New Yorkers. Flanagan and Watkins were two of the able exports from a flourishing bop scene in Detroit, and both rapidly established their credentials on the East Coast. Flanagan's neat, melodic and understated manner was suitable to all manner of contexts, and his thoughtful accompanying chords allowed soloists a multiplicity of options. Rollins disliked being confined by over-emphatic leads from the keyboard, and it would be no surprise when, in later years, he frequently shunned pianistic support, preferring to operate with strong drummers and resilient bass players. However, he suffered no constriction from the thoughtful and sympathetic presence of Flanagan. Yet, in *Strode Rode*, for example, one senses a soaring surge from Rollins in the choruses on which Flanagan lays out.

A number of elements that were to become associated with Rollins are displayed here. His own *St Thomas* vividly demonstrates his love for the intoxicating rhythms and cheerful melodies of calypso. The music of the West Indies is part of his heritage, and in later years he would consistently evaluate these roots in such pieces as *Don't Stop the Carnival, Hold 'em Joe, Mangoes* and *The Everywhere Calypso*. Both Parker and Dizzy Gillespie had found Caribbean rhythms fertile fields for improvisation, but for Rollins harnessing that droning beat to the demands and disciplines of jazz proved especially stimulating.

A penchant for unlikely, at times bizarre, popular melodies was another of his trademarks. In this case the man who had already energetically sifted the contours of *No Business like Show Business, Love is a Many-Splendoured Thing, Sonny Boy* and *Count your Blessings*, casts an ironic eye over *Moritat* (*Mack the Knife*). Granted this piece had provided a pop-chart hit for Louis Armstrong, it was hardly the stuff of the modernists' repertory until Rollins indicated the possibilities with a loosely swinging exploration. After his close inspection, though, the song was quickly embraced by many of his contemporaries.

Rollins also took the opportunity to exhibit his strong allegiance to the blues form in the deceptively casual *Blue Seven*, which affords him the space to structure two solos of irresistible fluency. There is nothing condescending or superficial about his probings of this traditional structure. Like the majority of the great creative improvisers, he seeks to enlarge that tradition, regarding the blues framework as a challenge to his powers of invention. Between Rollins's solos, Roach gives one of the finest demonstrations of how a drum solo may be musical rather than technical. Keying the various rhythms and timbres of his drums and cymbals to the 12-bar blues structure, he plays percussion phrases which build up into a succession of 12-bar patterns. The walking bass of Doug Watkins opens this minor blues and is a constant hypnotic thread that runs through the fabric of Rollins's studied extemporizations. Watkins, a back seat musician of rare quality, had few peers at this particular game. Only Leroy Vinnegar and Paul Chambers had the necessary patience for such an unselfish yet vital role. Fittingly he is the final soloist.

On the two briefer selections from this delightfully informal but quintessential session, *You Don't Know What Love Is* and *Strode Rode*, Rollins invests the former with a stern masculinity, deploying a broad sweep of tonal inflections with frequent double-time passages to spice what in other hands can lapse into a dreary dirge. Rollins blows away the self-pitying atmosphere of the song, substituting a hard-edged realism. The Rollins–Roach blend is at its best on *Strode Rode*, where tenor sax and drumsticks punch out in a staccato duet an electrifying insert within the theme and later indulge in a two-way dramatic conversation. Rollins has a genuine swagger in his rhythmic step here – a self-belief engendered by his ability and the assurance of his companions. His vocal and mobile approach was certainly an attractive alternative to the mesmeric messages of his contemporary and fellow saxophonist John Coltrane.

CD

***Saxophone Colossus*, Original Jazz Classics OJCCD 291-2 (USA)**

Sonny Rollins (ts), Tommy Flanagan (p), Doug Watkins (sb), Max Roach (d)

New York	22 June 1956	**You Don't Know What Love Is**
		St Thomas
		Strode Rode
		Blue Seven
		Moritat

* * *

John Coltrane: *Blue Train*

John Coltrane, a standard-bearer for change in the 1960s, had a contradictory relationship with hard bop. He could perform fluently in this branch of the idiom; but whether he was wholly comfortable in this climate is open to question. Sometimes he seemingly ignored his accompanists to unravel long, steely, multi-noted solos that were stretching for a different context.

Between 1955 and 1959 the tenor saxophonist participated in scores of recording sessions, most frequently for Prestige, with Miles Davis, with all-star ensembles, or with quartets and quintets of his own choosing. He made only four appearances on the rival Blue Note mark, two of which were jam sessions and another a favour for his bass player friend from Davis's group, Paul Chambers. **Blue Train** was to be his solitary Blue Note date as a leader, and the cohesive and satisfying nature of the music it produced makes it a matter for regret that there were no successors.

The sombre, intense, almost puritanical voice that Coltrane favoured in the late 1950s needed companions of a sunnier disposition to offset a single-minded abrasiveness that could be overwhelming. In this respect, bright and bubbly trumpeter Lee Morgan and underrated trombonist Curtis Fuller, whose round tone and cliché-free solos were always plus factors, served to frame Coltrane's saxophone in a genial setting.

Members of the rhythm section – pianist Kenny Drew, bassist Chambers, drummer Philly Joe Jones – were anything but strangers to the saxophonist. Chambers and Jones had been colleagues with him in the Miles Davis Quintet and would be again in the later sextet. With Drew at the keyboard, Chambers and Jones had also backed the tenorman at a notable quartet session in Los Angeles the previous year. Drew's nimble and witty contributions provided another welcome dimension to the roster of soloists, a light leavening absent from so many of Coltrane's offerings from the period.

In the autumn of 1957 Coltrane was still engaged in a stimulating spell of employment with Thelonious Monk. It was a challenging and instructive assignment for the saxophonist as he grappled with the gripping but nourishing material of the master composer and wayward pianist. On **Blue Train** one senses a new awareness of form in Coltrane's improvisations and perhaps a feeling of release from the particular disciplines imposed by Monk. On the title track, for example, there is a brilliant buoyancy about his double-time runs, and the blues unison riffs of Morgan and Fuller spur him forward. If humour is largely absent from Coltrane's perception, there is no shortage of spirit or resilience. His austere tone has an edge that demands attention, and he executes ideas, no matter how complex, with a technical perfection that bespeaks a serious musician.

A driving passion infuses Coltrane's monumental solo on *Moment's Notice*, which shows his harmonic sophistication and his sheer patience in building the interlocking flurries of notes that would be accurately dubbed 'sheets of sound'. Coltrane does not make listeners smile, but in this mood he creates an air of exultation. Conversely, Morgan's daring and limber statement is warmingly agreeable; his dashing cut and thrust is the epitome of youthful expression, as affecting and effective in its way as the messianic mood struck by the leader. Both men are well served by the energizing current that flows from Philly Joe Jones's drum kit. It is too bad that Morgan and Coltrane recorded together on only one other occasion, because each seemed to play with unusual fire.

In the up-tempo blues *Locomotion*, both men construct dashing solos, but the palm here really goes to Fuller, who defies the physical limitations of his instrument in an immaculately designed improvisation. Coltrane evinced his most satisfying projection of emotion on slow ballad performances, and his reading of *I'm Old Fashioned* has a sublime poignancy and tenderness that are not to be found in the saxophonist's presto exercises. He would explore this side of his musical character many times, most notably in an entire programme of songs with singer Johnny Hartman some years later.

Lazy Bird is the composition by Coltrane from this set which made the greatest impact on his fellow musicians, and in short order it became a jazz standard, much relished by other saxophonists. Its attractive chord changes certainly suited the leader's colleagues in this instance. Morgan sets the temperature soaring with a contribution of great ferocity. Fuller, by contrast, opts for a cool interlude before Coltrane holds sway with a logical compilation of precisely chiselled notes. In this mood, Coltrane's control over his material was positively awesome.

It is possible to hear, within this sophisticated expression of hard bop, the move by Coltrane to the harmonic testing grounds of his 1959 recording of *Giant Steps* and even the course his work would take beyond that milestone. He was a man restless for change and thirsty for fulfilment. He felt he had absorbed all that he could of his predecessors and contemporaries, and after the years with Dizzy Gillespie, Johnny Hodges, Davis and Monk he was ready to strike out in pursuit of a wholly personal objective. So while belonging to the hard-bop movement for several years, his long-term commitment lay elsewhere.

Coltrane's purposeful, even calculating, approach was actually the antithesis of that adopted by Dexter Gordon, one of his early idols. Perhaps the most notable omission from Coltrane's perception was a sense of humour. His progress towards far horizons allowed no time for the jocularity of Gillespie or the hip amusement of Charlie Parker. And in truth Coltrane's time afforded scant reason for mirth. However, in a hard bop setting he never made a better recording than **Blue Train**, which proved to be among the highlights of his extensive output in the East Coast studios.

CD

***Blue Train*, Blue Note B21K 46095 (USA)**

Lee Morgan (tpt), Curtis Fuller (tb), John Coltrane (ts), Kenny Drew (p), Paul Chambers (sb), Philly Joe Jones (d)

Hackensack, NJ 15 Sept 1957

Lazy Bird
Moment's Notice
Blue Train
Locomotion
I'm Old Fashioned

Other CDs

same contents:

Blue Note CDP 7-46095-2; Blue Note B21Y 46095 (USA)

* * *

Lee Morgan: *Leeway*

Carrying the identical instrumentation to that of Charlie Parker's classic quintet of a decade earlier, this homogeneous Lee Morgan unit exemplified the changes wrought in the jazz mainstream during the immediate post-Parker period. Gone are the astringent bop themes. The new compositions are rounder and more melodic. The music is more relaxed. And the rhythms these men danced to were set to emphasize the beat – especially when Morgan's then employer, Art Blakey, was providing the propulsion.

That bop was already one step removed was apparent from the playing of trumpeter Morgan, who had absorbed the influences of Dizzy Gillespie and Fats Navarro via the work of Clifford Brown, even though he had become a trumpet soloist in Gillespie's big band in the 1950s; in the blazing context of that crew, Morgan's solos showed him to be much closer in conception to Brown than to his employer.

Pianist Bobby Timmons had drawn considerably on the inspiration of Bud Powell, but with half an ear cocked to Horace Silver's keyboard delineations. Utilizing blues and gospel motifs, Timmons, a much maligned musician, wrote some catchy tunes that helped instigate the brief fad for 'soul jazz'. This aspect of his work certainly helped the record sales of his current group, again the Jazz Messengers, as well as Cannonball Adderley's combo, in which Timmons served from 1959 to 1960.

The easier sense of swing induced by groups like this one was also due in part to the improving ability of the new young bass players, of whom Paul Chambers was one of the finest. Only in the playing of alto saxophonist Jackie McLean are to be found the astringency and concentrated tension that were omnipresent ingredients in the first phase of modern jazz. Six years older than Morgan and already a youthful veteran of service with Miles Davis, the Jazz Messengers and George Wallington, McLean brought his experience and challenging attack to these proceedings. His harsh, acidic tone and biting, jagged lines made for difficult initial listening. But familiarity with his sound and methods invariably provided rewards to listeners. A strongly emotional player, McLean uses a searing 'cry' without affectation.

The material from this date includes a pair of compositions by the trumpeter and brilliant writer Calvin Massey, from Philadelphia. The first, *These Are Soulful Days*, is a minor key, 24-bar *aaba* pattern of some charm, and it contains one typical soul phrase that appears right at the end of the melody, taken at a purposeful march tempo. Reversing the expected order, Chambers has the first solo. Blakey is particularly restrained behind Chambers and Timmons, but articulates appropriate rim shots and press rolls in the course of the statements by McLean and Morgan.

Morgan, albeit the composer and arranger of *The Lion and the Wolff* (named after the owners of the Blue Note label), was not an especially assertive leader, and on this sinewy blues he again yields the first solo spot, this time to McLean. In his own solo Morgan occasionally creates riffs for himself to answer in following phrases. Chambers has an especially effective solo, and Blakey's artfully constructed exercise, building in intensity, is a model of its kind. The fashionable fade out to end the piece is, for once, wholly justified: the closing Latin phrase is only partially resolved, but its repetition by the horns induces a satisfying hypnotic effect as engineer Rudy Van Gelder reduces the volume to a distant echo.

McLean's functional 12-bar *Midtown Blues* provides more scope for Morgan to conduct his own inner conversation with musical queries and equally personal responses. By this time McLean had moved well clear of Charlie Parker's shadow, and only the occasional characteristic trill betrays his profound admiration for Parker. Blakey bears down heavily on this track, but in tandem with Chambers spreads the firmest of bases for McLean's long, impassioned solo. Timmons's keyboard passage includes a portion played in the two-handed, block chord style popularized by Milt Buckner, George Shearing and Red Garland, with the chords spelled out in Garland's manner.

The plum of the session is unquestionably Massey's *Nakatini Suite*, not in fact a suite at all but a striking *aaba* composition of 66 measures, with the *b* section 18 bars long, rather than the usual 16. Massey had written this a decade earlier, and it was certainly an advanced work for 1948. The tune seems to lie perfectly for Morgan, probably because it was created by a fellow trumpeter, and it inspires him to unleash his finest solo of the set, a leaping, lithe improvisation that shows his resilience and control. A splendid achievement this, for a man only just turned 20. *Nakatini Suite* is a tantalizing fragment from a genuine composer whose output, slender though it was, suggested he was a melodic writer in Tadd Dameron's mould. Massey's works were also admired and recorded by John Coltrane and others, but unfortunately he made only a single album of his own pieces with a somewhat ill-assorted personnel. The two tracks here are more fitting reminders of his ability, brought to life by the quicksilver trumpet of Morgan and a band that existed for just this one revealing recording.

CD

***Leeway*, Blue Note B21Z-32089-2 (USA)**

Lee Morgan (tpt), Jackie McLean (as), Bobby Timmons (p), Paul Chambers (sb), Art Blakey (d)

Englewood Cliffs, NJ	28 April 1960	**Nakatini Suite** **These Are Soulful Days** **The Lion and the Wolff** **Midtown Blues**

* * *

Freddie Redd: *The Music from 'The Connection'*

A watershed year for hard bop was 1960, when so many exponents of the style seemed to hit a creative peak. One thinks especially of the work of Donald Byrd, Kenny Dorham, Hank Mobley, Tina Brooks, Kenny Drew, Sonny Clark, the entire Jazz Messengers and the two principals on this album, pianist Freddie Redd and Jackie McLean, who never sounded better than in their 1960 collaborations.

McLean, of the biting, searing sound and highly personal stance in the music, and Redd, a restless wanderer and one of the hardest swinging pianists of his generation, were perfectly matched associates who each eschewed compromise and imbued their music with an urgent excitement. The pair were able to work together for many months in the Off-Broadway production of Jack Gelber's hard-hitting play *The Connection*, about junkies and their preoccupations. Redd and McLean not only played this music on stage as an integrated part of the action, they also took acting roles in the drama. They later transferred with the company to the West End of London, where the play had a brief and controversial season. For British audiences, though, *The Connection* was important chiefly because it enabled them to hear these dynamic players for the first time.

Redd had made a number of recordings before 1960, but none did him real justice until this Blue Note session of his vibrant score for *The Connection* which, incidentally, was also made into a movie featuring Redd and company. McLean took to the pianist's richly melodic compositions with glee, and his tone and attack became inextricably identified with these songs. When Redd made another version of exactly the same material with a different personnel, without McLean, much of the magic was missing. Both soloists were immensely helped by the surging power of two relatively little-known musicians, bassist Michael Mattos and drummer Larry Ritchie, who with Redd formed a rhythm section of unflagging energy and sure swiftness.

McLean completely immersed himself in Redd's clever chord changes, churning rhythms and satisfyingly resolved melodic lines, which he found a constant challenge and source of renewal. The results are positively explosive, as an emotional torrent of notes poured from the bell of his saxophone. Similarly inspired was Redd himself. Influenced by Bud Powell and Horace Silver, he favoured a firm touch and chordal clusters which put a solid underfelt beneath the soloist. Redd was never the most technically accurate of pianists, but his playing was notable for its bustling impatience and sheer verve. He was daring and uninhibited, and a joyous, casual air infused his unpredictable solos. His willingness to take chances in a disarming and invariably vigorous manner made his improvisations infinitely more exciting than those of pianists gifted with far greater technical expertise. Glib boredom has no place in Redd's jazz.

His seven pieces for *The Connection* hang together as clearly the stylistic work of one composer, yet each serves to clarify a different mood, and just how well can be fully appreciated only by seeing the movie. However, without any visual aids this fine music exists in its own right. Redd was one of the most direct and felicitous of the hard-bop composers, and such is the sincerity and strength of his themes that many listeners will have regretted that writing has been only a sporadic pursuit for him over the past 35 years. He never found a more fitting interpreter for his music than McLean.

The fast action of this recital is set by *Who Killed Cock Robin?*, a rollicking, fluid melody that features cohesive, expressive work by McLean, who barely pauses for breath in the onrush of improvisation. Redd plays in a warmly relaxed manner with his fulsome chords counteracted by some lively interjections from his mobile right hand. *Wigglin'*, a soulful blues shuffle, is lit by emphatic yet appropriate contributions in a succinct statement by McLean and Redd, both of them excellent interpreters of the blues, and Mattos, who sticks to basics and reveals the wonderful tone of his instrument.

Redd's joyous spirit is most effectively expressed in the heated climate of *Music Forever*, another fast exercise coupled with a winsome melodic line. McLean boosts the tension by enunciating the theme in half time while his accompanists lay down a mercurial four beat. Redd has fun with the beat at several points in his intense solo, riding on and behind the feverish rhythm by turn. It is an exhilarating experience. This piece seems to capture the very essence of Redd's musical persona.

Time to Smile is much more relaxed, and, as he punches out the melody, the pianist brings Erroll Garner to mind. McLean compiles a solo of stunning design in which the tone, dynamics and vocal effects are all melded into an unwavering line that conveys a bittersweet feeling. Redd's touch here is particularly percussive and his broken accompaniment is truly enhancing. *Theme for Sister Salvation* introduces a gospel march tempo that is redolent of its Salvation Army subject, but the piece is cleverly cast in two moods, because the meat of the composition is an entirely different slow melody. This allows McLean and Redd to fashion tender ballad solos before the brisk march is reinstated and played to a fade ending.

Jim Dunn's Dilemma has an edgy, neurotic line, encapsulating a glorious contrasting theme. There is concentrated ad-libbing by an inspired McLean who loves moving through minor keys at such insinuating tempos. Redd floats with the time, his forward momentum being generously assisted by the whirling percussive patterns worked by Ritchie. *O.D.* is a fittingly declamatory statement, opening with a menacing tribal 'cry' which leads into the sinewy melody. McLean's playing, passionate and intense, is closer than usual to Charlie Parker here, but the keening tone remains wholly distinctive. The emotion is so strong it almost overwhelms. Redd follows this with equal fervour but no flamboyance. His playing is occasionally reminiscent of Sir Charles Thompson; the two share a penchant for pungent chords.

None of this music is for the timid; it has a compelling, turbulent atmosphere, but it informs and rewards in generous measure. Here is undiluted honesty, raw, uplifting and occasionally disturbing.

CD

***The Music from 'The Connection'*, Blue Note B2-89392 (USA)**

Jackie McLean (as), Freddie Redd (p), Michael Mattos (sb), Larry Ritchie (d)

Englewood Cliffs, NJ	15 Feb 1960	**Time to Smile**
		Jim Dunn's dilemma
		Wigglin'
		Music Forever
		Theme for Sister Salvation
		Who Killed Cock Robin?
		O.D.

Other CDs

plus additional tracks:

The Complete Blue Note Recordings of Freddie Redd, Mosaic MD2-124 (USA)

* * *

Harold Land: *The Fox*

West Coast jazz coexisted on the West Coast with other jazz styles. Alongside the white musicians playing neat and precise arrangements by the likes of Shorty Rogers and Marty Paich in the 1950s was the continuing revival of traditional jazz as played by white musicians and centred in the San Francisco Bay Area, and, somewhat less prominently, a few white musicians (including Art Pepper) and a large contingent of gifted black players who were closely attuned to the hard-bop camp in the East.

Among these last were tenor saxophonist Harold Land, pianist Elmo Hope and drummer Frank Butler, all of whom were more advanced than many of their better-known brothers in New York. Land at least had a fairly wide reputation, via his years with the Clifford Brown–Max Roach group. Hope, however, despite a boyhood association with Bud Powell and several excellent albums, was unfamiliar to most listeners. Butler, once hailed by Jo Jones as 'the greatest drummer in the world', was also an obscure figure. Yet the three were all long on ability, and their work together in the group led by bassist Curtis Counce gave them at least some sort of platform to show their mettle. When Land was invited to make this album for the short-lived Hifijazz label, he pulled in Hope and Butler, and added the obscure trumpeter Dupree Bolton and an 18-year-old bass player, Herbie Lewis.

If this sounds an unpromising cast, the music they made exhibited a quality and originality that defied those who would pass hasty judgements. Hope, a quirky, unpredictable player who enjoyed manufacturing themes of off-beat complexity, was one of the main reasons for the electrifying atmosphere that exists on this date. Four of the six provocative pieces are his, and one suspects he also had a hand in arranging the two originals by Land. All the writing is distinctive and unhackneyed. It seems to say: 'Hard bop is understood, but here's another way of phrasing it.'

In the centre of this jazz maelstrom is the solid professionalism of Harold Land, a man who could play anything that was put in front of him. His darkhued tenor sound blended with Bolton's tart trumpet tone to create memorable textures, and swirling behind them were the tempestuous but precise rhythms of Butler and the curious and questioning chords of Hope. For young Lewis this intense and idiosyncratic music must have seemed a daunting assignment, but he shows both insight and feeling and copes with the tricky twists and turns of charts that call for high technical accomplishment.

The challenging nature of the material is set by *The Fox,* taken at a blinding, blurring tempo that never flags for an instant. Among the soloists, Hope finds unsuspected combinations of notes in a minimalist approach. Hope's *Mirror-Mind Rose* is performed in the deliberate manner of Thelonious Monk. On *One Second, Please*, probably Hope's most conventional piece in this collection, Butler's astute placement of crisp accents helps the soloists to take wings. *Sims-a-Plenty* has by contrast the jagged edges and chordal shifts that formed so many of Hope's musical minefields. Besides being tough to execute, Hope's tunes make for hard listening. They are not pieces the layman would whistle readily, and their order and logic are revealed only on repeated auditions. That they served to refresh the imaginations of Land and Bolton is obvious from the verve that illuminates their solos. Hope was undoubtedly the best interpreter of his own originals, but he never again mustered men who understood his music so deeply.

Land's *Little Chris* contains echoes of *Broadway* and the soul-jazz fad in its whimsical melody. The suspended time breaks build-up and then releases tension, making the soloists' task more absorbing. The performance elicits from Bolton a statement of acute melodic sensibility. What a shame that we subsequently heard so little from him and nothing to rival the quality of his accomplished work on this programme.

One Down is a satisfying exploration of a flowing structure by Hope. As Land once observed of his esteemed colleague, Hope's compositions expressed a sure sense of form while his playing was loose and free. Hope shared with Land a background of apprenticeship in rhythm-and-blues bands, which presupposed an ability to swing that neither man ever lost or sacrificed in the cause of complexity.

Thus this album has great intellectual appeal but at once provokes body movement. Coming right at the end of the decade, it shakes a fist at the pallid fare peddled by the makers of musical mediocrity in the Los Angeles of the 1950s.

CD

The Fox, Original Jazz Classics OJCCD 343-2 (USA)

Dupree Bolton (tpt), Harold Land (ts), Elmo Hope (p), Herbie Lewis (sb), Frank Butler (d)

Los Angeles	Aug 1959	**The Fox**
		Mirror-Mind Rose
		One Second, Please
		Sims-a-Plenty
		Little Chris
		One Down

* * *

Art Pepper: *Intensity*

Alto saxophonist Art Pepper lived dangerously in music and in life. All improvising jazz musicians take risks every time they perform in front of an audience or a microphone. By exposing so honestly the emotions they feel, they make themselves vulnerable. But the act of instantaneous composition also produces a stimulus to excitement. Pepper seemed to thrive on high risk, and often created some of his finest music under the most severe strain, when, to compound the contradiction, his playing would be supremely relaxed.

This album, for example, was made while he was on bail awaiting what he knew would be a lengthy term of imprisonment, yet Pepper performs with total composure, icy professionalism and sustained artistry in the most taxing of circumstances. In this respect at least, he was able to show remarkable resolve and strength of character by shutting out the most intrusive aspects of a chaotic lifestyle when music-making was on the agenda.

Pepper, a graduate of the orchestras of Benny Carter and Stan Kenton, had won admiration for his deft and driving solos with Kenton. In the 1950s he emerged as a potent small-group leader and a busy guest soloist in the Hollywood studios. Through his work with Shorty Rogers, Marty Paich, Chet Baker, Dave Pell and Shelly Manne, he became closely identified with the West Coast jazz movement. He was by far the most distinguished improviser to emerge from that amorphous grouping. Pepper favoured a cool tone, drawn from Lester Young and his early mentor Carter, and his style owed nothing to Charlie Parker, although he certainly drew in some measure from the latter's vocabulary. His sound was deceptive. At first hearing apparently lightweight and thin, it revealed on closer acquaintance a hard edge. When buried in larger ensembles with heavily arranged orchestrations, Pepper's flame burned only intermittently. While no listener could dispute the precision and clarity of his work in such settings, he was properly ignited only by an intimate context with a mobile rhythm section and one or two brass or reed players of similar persuasion.

Pepper shared with Young an instinct for recasting tunes to extract the optimum melodic appeal. Superficially sophisticated and definitely accomplished in the area of harmonic knowledge, he was actually an intensely emotional player, capable of expressing and communicating deep feeling. He could play the blues with genuine conviction, his ability to swing was unquestionable and his well-shaded and powerfully personal solos were invariably beautifully resolved. Pepper had previously shown a liking for assertive accompanists and had made two stunning albums with Miles Davis's rhythm sections, along with a recording in the company of the individualistic and quirky pianist Carl Perkins. However, while the supporting cast for **Intensity** may be lesser known, its members formed a unit of considerable flexibility and ability.

Pianist Dolo Coker, possibly because he elected to live and work in California, had a small reputation, yet he was a musician of manifest sensitivity and stylistic awareness whose solos and accompaniment here are a revelation. Only many years later, in the last chapter of his life, did he enjoy deserved recognition. Similarly, Jimmy Bond, a close companion of Coker's, was a bass player of accomplishment and drive. As for drummer Frank Butler, he gave Pepper the same resourcefulness and supportive swing that he had brought to Harold Land's **The Fox**.

Because of the hurried nature of the session, standard songs that would be familiar to all four participants were chosen. That they sound so satisfyingly integrated is testimony to the superb professionalism of these men who thrived in each other's company and the impromptu atmosphere that was established.

Bond's fleet bass line introduces *I Can't Believe that You're in Love with Me*, and Bond and Pepper handle the entire melody, save for the bridge when Butler joins in, so when Coker does enter the performance there is a pleasant surprise. Pepper's use of blues phrases imbues the piece with qualities not implicit in the tune. Coker's compact chorus is in accord with the mood, and the stimulating four-bar trades between saxophone and drums are punchy and pertinent.

Pepper was fond of Latin rhythms, and the arrangement of the theme of *I Love You* is in this vein, but the treatment for the ad-libbing is at a heady swing tempo. Butler is alive to every twist of Pepper's subtle improvisation, and his reflexes are such that at one point he repeats in the following instant the shape of a rhythmic phrase played by the leader. Coker's carefully controlled solo benefits from an interlude when Butler pauses for part of a chorus to leave the pianist to run with the bass.

A master of the slow ballad performance, Pepper made *Come Rain or Come Shine* into one of the masterpieces in the genre. Tender, deeply affecting yet unsentimental, it enshrines Pepper's awesome integrity. As with all the great players, even when performing the melody, Pepper recomposes it by tone, inflection and note placement.

Long Ago and Far Away delineates the fierce, concentrated exhilaration of which Pepper was capable at fast tempos. His command of instrument, material and ideas is complete in this agile exercise. By virtue of his technique, he makes it all sound easy and relaxed. Coker nibbles at the keys in a cryptic solo which somehow fits after the elegance of the alto.

The group adopts a medium-tempo shuffle rhythm for a cool account of *Gone with the Wind*, in which Pepper deploys his personal vibrato and singing sound to brilliant effect, sparingly using double-time runs and snatches of blues phrasing in his deft design. Showing how the band was thinking on its feet, instead of following the solos with the conventional exchanges between sax and drums, Pepper this time begins by trading ideas with the bass. Another variation in treatment is the statement of the first segment of *I Wished on the Moon* by drums and saxophone. Pepper's solo is heated and he repeats a riff-like motif to raise the tension, clearly enjoying Butler's off-beat contributions at every stage.

Even in an unpromising tune such as *Too Close for Comfort* Pepper finds unsuspected quality, as he unfolds an improvisation brimming with crisp, cutting ideas that transform the trite melody. Using the whole range of his instrument, he creates a solo of unerring logic and unwavering interest – Pepper personified.

CD

***Intensity*, Original Jazz Classics OJC CD 387-2 (USA)**

Art Pepper (as), Dolo Coker (p), Jimmy Bond (sb), Frank Butler (d)

Los Angeles	23 and 25 Nov 1960	**I Can't Believe that You're in Love with Me**
		I Love You
		Come Rain or Come Shine
		Long Ago and Far Away
		Gone with the Wind
		I Wished on the Moon
		Too Close for Comfort
		Five Points

* * *

Jimmy Smith: *Crazy! Baby*

Organist Jimmy Smith's debut as a Blue Note recording artist early in 1956 was ideally timed for him to add to the growing momentum which hard bop was gathering as it became the dominant international jazz style of the late 1950s. A native of Pennsylvania, Smith had studied both piano and bass, which made him well qualified to exploit the duality of the electric Hammond organ, supplying his own bass lines on the foot pedals while giving full expression to his copious ideas on the keyboard. Smith transferred the conventions of bop piano playing to the organ with a horn-like use of his right hand, fashioning fast, single-note lines while his left hand punched out appropriate chords. He favoured a bright, sharp sound and avoided the instrument's muddier reaches.

His preference was for either the organ–guitar–drums trio, to which he would frequently add a tenor saxophone, or loose blowing sessions featuring a queue of good soloists. The trio was his perfect vehicle, for of the organ he was able to make an entire orchestra of his own. Smith's energy was inexhaustible. He could improvise daringly and satisfyingly for chorus after chorus. As an interpreter of blues he was earthy, authentic and hugely adventurous. Indeed, blues phrases are a recurring motif in all his work. He also had a prodigious sense of swing and built excitement through his use of sustained and repeated riff patterns at strategic points in his driving solos.

Crazy! Baby, his first album of the 1960s, contains several selections that certainly must be counted among his outstanding recorded performances. He is to be found at the peak of his musical potency on *When Johnny Comes Marching Home* in the archetypal trio format. This surging, uninhibited exercise gives Smith an opportunity to display his fecund preaching while always showing his rhythmic flexibility and astuteness. In many respects guitarist Quentin Warren and drummer Donald Bailey were the most appropriate of sidemen. Each works hand in glove with the organist and helps to maintain the intensity of this dramatic performance, which opens with a clever combination of bagpipe drone and Middle Eastern commentary by Smith – bizarre, but effective! Bailey's lithe ad-libbing sets things up considerably for the leader's torrid outpouring, which stops just the right side of frenzy. His astute and snappy rim shots, his tom-tom raps and his shimmering cymbal patterns are the spurs for Smith's inspiration. After the excitement has passed, the organist allows the atmosphere to calm, gently and naturally.

Smith's playing assumes a muted quality for a perky passage through *Makin' Whoopee*, a hoary standard that he infuses with a spry, bluesy air. In this attractively trilling performance, he occupies the entire solo space and justifies the decision with some bubbling, staccato lines.

Tackling a bop express exercise like *A Night in Tunisia* holds no terrors for Smith, who unzips a sparkling and original introduction before warming to the task of enlarging Dizzy Gillespie's composition in a highly personal manner. The neat and sparse solo by Warren shows the poise of this under-valued performer.

Smith brings equal fervour to Sonny Rollins's blues *Sonnymoon for Two*, allowing his guitarist to fire the opening shots before homing in himself with a solo rich in pungent organ effects and rhythmic variety. Towards the close of a vividly exciting, blues-drenched improvisation, he builds the tension to fever pitch by holding a sustained note for four entire choruses!

Mack the Knife takes on a new life as Smith tosses it around playfully but with just a touch of dark humour, deploying his monstrous technical facility to excellent purpose in a running improvisation of considerable guile. It was tracks of this quality that persuaded all the organists that followed to use Smith's style as the blueprint.

The pent-up physical energy that seems to permeate most of Smith's performances is held in check for a good-natured assessment of *What's New,* but even here Smith is not content to recline and opt for a smoochy slow ballad offering. Instead he brings into play crashing chords and shrill piping effects which are certainly lively, if a trifle over-emphatic. Any sentimentality that may have been lurking in the song is well and truly wrung out.

Smith's only original composition of this set, *Alfredo,* is an attractive minor-key melody which prompts Warren to yield up his most refreshing solo of the date. As if in appreciation of his sideman, Smith takes up Warren's last phrase to launch himself into a steely-fingered contribution of compelling swing and sureness.

Smith's style has altered very little since those first mind-blowing, ear-tweaking debut albums caused a justifiable sensation. The validity of that style and its architect's strength are never in doubt for one instant in this definitive example of his work. Thanks to Smith and the Blue Note label, the organ trio became a fixture in jazz for which only the most snobbish purist can find no room.

CD

***Crazy! Baby,* Blue Note B21K 84030 (USA)**

Jimmy Smith (org), Quentin Warren (elg), Donald Bailey (d)

Englewood Cliffs, NJ	4 Jan 1960	**Alfredo**
		Mack the Knife
		Makin' Whoopee
		What's New
		Sonnymoon for Two
		When Johnny Comes Marching Home
		A Night in Tunisia
		If I Should Lose You
		When Lights Are Low

Other CDs

same contents:

Blue Note CDP 7-84030-2; Blue Note B21Y 84030 (USA)

* * *

Dexter Gordon: *Doin' Allright*

Dexter Gordon, a forceful influence from the early years of pure bop, found little difficulty in adjusting to the somewhat differing demands of the hard-bop idiom. It is regrettable, therefore, that for much of the 1950s the tenor saxophonist was musically inactive, making only a handful of recordings during the decade. When he eventually resumed his career in 1960 he made an arguably greater impact than during his first emergence 15 years earlier. An initial album, recorded in Los Angeles, indicated that his ebullience and rhythmic certainty were undiminished. His harmonic knowledge had deepened and his lengthy solos continued to evince a bountiful stock of melodic touches. These hints of a well-developed and wholly personal style were fully displayed in the first recording session he completed under a productive association for the Blue Note label. The music flowed from him with an ease and purpose which eclipsed the long years of denial. Gordon, fairly bursting with ideas and inventiveness, strongly signalled that he intended to make up for lost time. His solos have a breadth and shape which confirm a satisfying inner logic, yet they are at once packed with emotion and coloured by a personable wit. A musical vocabulary which had always been rich showed a positive expansion. In a sojourn remote from the epicentre of jazz, Gordon had kept abreast of innovations, and his work on **Doin' Allright** shows an awareness of the styles of both John Coltrane and Sonny Rollins. Not that he was overly swayed from either quarter, for an intense conviction in his own ability was an enduring characteristic.

The supporting cast for a dynamic debut on Blue Note was of the high calibre calculated to bring out the best from the saxophonist. The bright brashness of Freddie Hubbard's trumpet provided the ideal foil to Gordon's powerful voice. Each man draws inspiration from the other. It was a memorable first meeting of minds from two generations. The addition of a supple, loose-jointed, working rhythm section was probably the critical factor that ensured the success and durability of the date. Pianist Horace Parlan, bass player George Tucker and drummer Al Harewood had functioned as a regular unit for several seasons. With saxophonist Booker Ervin they were integral components of the Playhouse Four, and they had recorded as a trio and with horns. A funky sense of swing was their special forte and they possessed a mutual understanding which enabled them to conjure up an irresistible groove immediately. This they achieved in most telling fashion on Gershwin's standard *I Was Doing All Right*, where the course of the performance is determined by the jogging, relaxed medium tempo set by Parlan, Tucker and Harewood. On this track the responsive and flexible underfelt they supply is trodden with gleeful confidence by Gordon in his assertive opening statement. Hubbard's crisp contribution takes its cue from Gordon's relaxed delivery. Hubbard does not feel obliged, as on some outings elsewhere from this period, to crowd notes into every available space, but instead uses rests to enhance the cascading runs and occasional held notes. Parlan is the epitome of laid-back assurance, as he begins sparsely and then switches to rolling block chords for the closing measures of a lucid solo. While fadeout endings could be a feeble way of not knowing how to finish, the suspended final phrases and fade in this instance are the perfect exit for the mood of *I Was Doing All Right*.

In the terrain of the jazz ballad Gordon has few peers, and his majestic exploration of *You've Changed* carries an authority seldom achieved in this type of slow performance. Gordon's deployment of a wide range of tonal effects, including a pronounced vibrato on low notes, enhances his unsentimental but romantic statement, while his harmonic astuteness is consistently in evidence. With Harewood using brushes, Tucker's sonorous and unfussy bass lines assume some significance here. Gordon's confidence is underlined by his unaccompanied passage at the close.

The thematic variety to be found in hard bop certainly appealed to Gordon, and his ability to write in the idiom was amply illustrated by his compositions *For Regulars Only* and *Society Red*. The stuttering phrasing of the opening of *For Regulars Only*, counterbalanced by its joyous contrasting theme, make for an intriguing composition. Gordon's penchant for humour in the shape of an apt quotation is never more apparent than in his solo here. He also uses such devices as the honk and the shake to spice up his improvisation, but these shots from his locker are fired with judicious placement – never overdone. The alternate take of this piece, eventually made available some 27 years later, proffers an entirely different solo by Gordon with only a couple of similar reference points, showing he was definitely an off-the-top player with awesome inventive power.

The vigorous *Society Red*, the longest performance from the session, is an almost archetypal hard-bop composition with more than a few touches of Horace Silver's soul style gleaming in the melody. In this instance Gordon redistributes the solo routine, giving Hubbard first bite, and his arrangement includes catchy breaks for the two horns between solos. The leader is decidedly earthy in his swaggering passages on this item, and his dramatic flair is apparent in a series of beautifully sustained choruses which are never repetitive.

Mounting the popular warhorse *It's You or No One*, Gordon imbues it with a distinctive flavour in a neat arrangement. At a brisk tempo, the ideas tumble in a deluge from Gordon's horn in a cohesive display that marks him as a virtuoso. The occasional bagpipe drone set by Parlan at strategic points is a refreshing means of heightening the tension.

Another composition by Gordon, unknown until its appearance on the CD compilation in 1988, is *I Want More*, an attractive melody on which the leader's work is as spirited and buoyant as on the remainder of the material. It completes the picture of a highly original musician, at the peak of his powers, who had drawn on the language of Lester Young and Charlie Parker without for one moment submerging or sacrificing his individuality.

CD

***Doin' Allright*, Blue Note B21S 84077 (USA)**

Freddie Hubbard (tpt), Dexter Gordon (ts), Horace Parlan (p), George Tucker (sb), Al Harewood (d)

Englewood Cliffs, NJ	6 May 1961	**I Was Doing All Right**
		You've Changed
		For Regulars Only (take 1)
		For Regulars Only (take 2)
		Society Red
		It's You or No One
		I Want More

Other CDs

same contents:

Blue Note CDP 7-84077-2; Blue Note B21Y 84077 (USA)

* * *

Sonny Clark: *Leapin' and Lopin'*

Pianist Sonny Clark was perhaps the classic case of a musician to whom genuine recognition came many years after his death. Of course there are others, including his fellow pianists Carl Perkins and Herbie Nichols, but those two perhaps lacked the lyricism and ability to communicate that are characteristic of Clark's entire discography. His early career was spent on the West Coast, where his employers included Buddy DeFranco, Oscar Pettiford, Wardell Gray and Howard Rumsey. Although he was hampered by a chaotic lifestyle, in 1957 he moved to New York, and in the last six years of his short life he recorded for the

Blue Note label around 30 sessions yielding a remarkably consistent and fine level of performance.

Leapin' and Lopin' dates from his final flush of creativity, and it was the last date he undertook as a leader. Clark, bass player Butch Warren and drummer Billy Higgins formed the last great Blue Note house rhythm section in the early 1960s, and their intelligent support was lent to such diverse soloists as Jackie McLean, Dexter Gordon, Kenny Dorham and Grant Green. They were a supremely relaxed and responsive team with a loosely swinging unity which afforded soloists a wide choice of options. In this congenial company, Tommy Turrentine, a small-toned but expressive trumpeter, and tenor saxophonist Charlie Rouse, already embarked on a lengthy stay with the group of Thelonious Monk, were moved to deliver some of the most luminescent playing of their respective careers.

Clark is the fulcrum of their inspiration, not only through his attentive and considerate accompaniment and beautifully resolved solos, but also in the crafting and texture of his melodic compositions, *Somethin' Special*, *Melody for C* and *Voodoo*. Warren's piece *Eric Walks* is in perfect accord with his leader's writing, and rehearsal time was clearly fruitful in perfecting the neat arrangements. *Midnight Mambo*, by Turrentine, is arguably the weakest of the originals, but the standard of improvisation compensates for the rather corny line. In its incarnation on compact disc a further gem by Clark, *Zellmar's Delight*, was revealed. Only the time limits of the LP format can have led to its original exclusion.

Clark's chief influence was Bud Powell, but his playing also displayed an awareness of Horace Silver and Hampton Hawes, a close friend, in its earthy quality. In solo recordings he invariably paid homage to Art Tatum, the pianist revered by all the modernists for his harmonic depth and rhythmic richness, and on slow ballads he would occasionally adopt the deliberate, emphatic approach of Powell. He had a strong right hand which fashioned lightning, single-note lines, and his left hand provided soft and sparing chordal commentary. He possessed a firm, distinctive keyboard touch, and even if his fingering was not always precise it did not seem to matter, such was the spirit of adventure in his improvisations, which were mercurial and inevitably betrayed his gift for the creation of melodic phrases. His liking for minor-key excursions is evident in the dark-hued blues *Somethin' Special*, and his improvisational powers are displayed in two strikingly different solos on the takes of *Melody for C* which have been released.

On record, at least, Sonny Clark seldom enjoyed the opportunity to work alongside musicians from an earlier era, so his relatively few sessions with tenor saxophonist Ike Quebec, a devotee of the Coleman Hawkins–Ben Webster school of influence, are especially valuable and clearly afforded the pianist much pleasure. For the opulent, romantic ballad *Deep in a Dream*, Clark sidelined Turrentine and Rouse, bringing in Quebec as a special guest. This was a masterstroke of planning, for Quebec's sensuous and breathy style suits the song's beauty. Clark limns a pretty introduction and then quietly unfolds the touching melody. Just when it seems this is to be a gently restrained trio performance, Quebec makes his moving entrance. His blend of sophistication and emotion recalls Webster, but the saxophonist had a singularly personal voice and in this solo conveys a vulnerability which is implicit in the song itself. Aside from any other considerations, this tender treatise emphasizes the unimportance of stylistic divisions and indicates how effectively men of different generations could work together. (By one of those strange strokes of fate, both Clark and Quebec died within three days of each other in January 1963.) The common ground existing between the best swing players and post-bop musicians was far greater than many commentators appreciated. Here is a pertinent example of how varied elements could comfortably meld in the jazz mainstream.

There may be more brilliant samples of Clark's piano playing available, not least his illustrious trio sessions for the Blue Note and Time labels, but none that provides a better picture of the leader, composer, arranger, accompanist *and* improviser than **Leapin' and Lopin'**.

CD

***Leapin' and Lopin'*, Blue Note BCT 84091 (USA)**

Tommy Turrentine (tpt), Charlie Rouse (ts), Sonny Clark (p), Butch Warren (sb), Billy Higgins (d)

Englewood Cliffs, NJ	15 Jan 1961	**Voodoo**
		Somethin' Special
		Midnight Mambo
		Melody for C
		Eric Walks
		Melody for C (alternate take)
		Zellmar's Delight
omit Turrentine and Rouse; add Ike Quebec (ts)		**Deep in a Dream**

Other CDs

same contents:

Blue Note CDP 7-84091-2 (USA)

* * *

Donald Byrd: *At the Half Note Café, vol.1*

Shortly before the accidental death of Clifford Brown, another talented trumpeter arrived in New York and immediately caused a stir. Donald Byrd, from Detroit, had more in common with Kenny Dorham than Brown or Miles Davis. Byrd's ability to blow long, inventive and imaginative melodic lines was aided by a bright and pure sound.

During his early years as a professional, Byrd was somewhat overused for recordings and, as a consequence, judged harshly for some indifferent performances. He was also hampered by lip problems that resulted in an uneven quality of performance. At his best, during 1958–64, the trumpeter performed at a highly creative level, maintaining an enviable excellence in recordings with Thelonious Monk, John Coltrane, Jackie McLean, Hank Mobley and others.

Of his own small groups, the one featured here with baritone saxophonist Pepper Adams and pianist Duke Pearson is unusually stimulating. Byrd's clarion-clear tone and lithe improvisations contrast superbly with Adam's gritty gruffness and relentless attack. The gifted Pearson provides a lyrical balance and three attractive compositions. The one that really catches fire is *My Girl Shirl*, a 32-bar minor mode piece that finds Byrd articulating every note with crispness and feeling, employing half-valve effects to produce a muffled tone in contrast to his normal clarity, and exhibiting his magnificent lung power in some incredibly long phrases. Adams's apparent bluffness conceals a sharp mind that seemingly squeezes every last drop from the piece in an atmosphere of sustained excitement. Pearson's fleet contribution ensures no loss of momentum. In the eight-bar exchange with the drummer, Byrd and Adams show the wit and skill that are needed for such instantaneous repartee.

Almost as good as *My Girl Shirl* is the performance of another of Pearson's delightful compositions, *Child's Play*, a tune of considerable charm, assessed here at a chirpy tempo. Byrd's embroidery enhances the pretty nature of the song. This is trumpet playing of a very high order, beautifully lit by Pearson's typically thoughtful arrangement, featuring his clock-tick chords behind a static unison from the horns and leading in turn to a surging contrasting section of the piece. Byrd thrives in this climate.

CD

***At the Half Note Café, vol.1*, Blue Note CDP-7-46539-2 (USA)**

Donald Byrd (tpt), Pepper Adams (bar), Duke Pearson (p), Laymon Jackson (sb), Lex Humphries (d)

New York	11 Nov 1960	**My Girl Shirl**
		Soulful Kiddy
omit Adams		**A Portrait of Jennie**
add Adams (bar)		**Chant**
		Cecile
		Child's Play

* * *

Art Farmer and Benny Golson Jazztet: *Blues on Down*

Trumpeter Art Farmer and tenor saxophonist Benny Golson shared more than a musical philosophy; they were temperamentally compatible and after years of working for others as important contributing sidemen it seemed natural they should pool their considerable artistic resources at the end of the 1950s to form the co-operative sextet named the Jazztet. Farmer, still mainly on trumpet at this juncture before his permanent switch to the flugelhorn, was a concise and precise improviser who played with a burnished tone and neat turns of phrase. If his solos occasionally sounded too pat, they were invariably orderly and well resolved. Golson's saxophone style was rooted in Don Byas and Lucky Thompson, and tonally he was a throwback to the breathy Hawkins school. An expert arranger for ensembles of any shape or size, Golson was strongly influenced by Tadd Dameron and showed similar concern for attractive ensemble harmonies and melodic purity.

In the Jazztet these main protagonists appeared for several years with a variety of rhythm sections and different trombonists, of whom Tom McIntosh (also an able composer and orchestrator) was the most frequent. Given Golson's admiration for Dameron, it is not surprising that the Jazztet reflected the tenets of that composer and was a performing reaffirmation of his 1940s small group values. Arranged passages and subtle voicings for the front line reveal Golson's imagination and care. Unlike Dameron's quintets and sextets of the 1940s, the Jazztet was not constrained by the three-minute time limit when recording, yet generally their recordings are not overblown, five or six minutes being the norm. A notable exception is a beautifully detailed perusal of *'Round Midnight*, replete with passionate solos from the co-leaders who evaluate Monk's classic without recourse to imitation of more famous interpretations of the song. Farmer chooses to use flugelhorn here and the sound is most appropriate to the brooding quality of the piece.

The selections, culled from a pair of LPs, were chosen for CD reissue by Golson himself and define most satisfactorily an articulate and cohesive unit that was not overly concerned by contemporary preoccupations, drawing instead from swing, bop, hard bop and cool sources to achieve an enviable mainstream amalgam.

CD

***Blues on Down*, Chess GRP 18022 (USA)**

Art Farmer (tpt), Tom McIntosh (tb), Benny Golson (ts), Cedar Walton (p), Tommy Williams (sb), Albert 'Tootie' Heath (d)

New York	16 and 19 Sept 1960	**Hi-Fly**
		Blues on Down
		Five Spot after Dark
		My Funny Valentine
		Wonder Why
		Con Alma
		Bean Bag
Chicago	15 May 1961	**Junction**
		Farmer's Market
*as **Hi-Fly**, but Farmer (flugelhorn)*		**'Round Midnight**
*as **Hi-Fly***		**A November Afternoon**

* * *

Roland Kirk: *Rip, Rig & Panic/Now Please Don't You Cry, Beautiful Edith*

Jazz is truly the art of the impossible, as its more adventurous practitioners have proved consistently – none more so than the late lamented extrovert virtuoso Roland Kirk. Like Art Tatum, Kirk was blinded from an early age but overcame this handicap and developed into one of the most individualistic, vital forces in music during the 1960s. Not content with being arguably the leading flute stylist in jazz, Kirk was also a resilient tenor saxophonist. But his most amazing feat involved a technique which enabled him to play three saxophones simultaneously. At the age of 16 he dreamed that this was possible and promptly acquired a pair of antique saxophones, the stritch (a straight sax but a rough equivalent of the alto) and the manzello (a hooked instrument that sounded like the soprano). These curious reeds were added to his tenor sax, and, having worked out a clever pattern of false-fingering that enabled him to produce a blend of three-part harmony, Kirk astonished listeners and fellow musicians with his unique invention.

Some sceptics, choosing to overlook Kirk's impelling work on single instruments, dismissed his discovery as a gimmick. Sour words failed to deflect him from continued research into multi-instrumental technique, and by the mid-1960s he was including the oboe in his triple deliveries. In *Mystical Dreams* on this set, he deploys the oboe alongside stritch and tenor sax, a combination that posed unprecedented problems since the embouchure for the two single-reed saxophones is scarcely compatible with that required for the oboe's double reed. Inevitably, with his inquisitive mind and ready facility operating in tandem, Kirk was able to resolve the difficulty and manage a most convincing three-part ensemble.

It was frequently stated when Kirk was alive that he combined the energy and enthusiasm of the untutored street musician with the knowledge and skill of the modern jazz player. This unusual amalgam meant that he was always open to a wide range of influences and, with his broadminded outlook, was capable of fitting in with all manner of bands and styles. His appreciation of jazz encompassed such early individualists as Sidney Bechet, Duke Ellington, Fats Waller and Barney Bigard, yet his admiration also extended through Lester Young and Don Byas to Thelonious Monk, Clifford Brown and John Coltrane. His own work reflected no single, overwhelming influence, since Kirk was one of a kind and matched any strand he may have adopted with something of his own.

This hugely entertaining and enjoyable recording affords an invaluable introduction to Kirk in some of his numerous guises – as superb flute soloist, warm tenor saxophonist, multi-instrumentalist, experimenter with electronic sound (years before synthesizers came into use), composer, and master of those obscure reeds manzello and stritch. Sharing in his delights are three players who also took risks to innovate. Pianist Jaki Byard, another man of many instruments, found fun in music, as did Kirk. The fierce originality of drummer Elvin Jones, architect of many a percussive barrage behind Coltrane, and the technically adroit bass playing of Richard Davis were pooled to serve Kirk's expansive imagination.

Two pieces in the set utilize pre-recorded backing tracks devised by Kirk himself and made up of all manner of sounds, including chimes, his own voice amplified, his baby screaming. Some of the sounds were slowed down before being played together. On *Rip, Rig and Panic,* another element is Kirk's 'live' tenor sax which he makes creak and vibrate with shuddering intensity. He ends the electronic introduction by smashing a glass on the studio floor. In the closing segment the human cries can be heard. In between these experimental episodes there lies an oblique theme and a driving tenor sax solo of wild and uninhibited scope.

Slippery, Hippery, Flippery also mixes a manifest of effects to which Byard contributes by plucking the piano's strings. Kirk used a cycle of notes from a computer to make the line. His darting stritch solo is followed by a startling keyboard excursion from Byard, who between fast, intricate lines actually bangs the keys at several points to obtain an explosive effect.

Kirk delivers his flowing waltz *Black Diamond* on the sonorous manzello, which has a slightly more colourful tone than the soprano. Performances like this show his melodic sensibility and superior instrumental command. The same might also be said of his exceptionally passionate interpretation of *Once in a While,* inspired by trumpeter Clifford Brown. Kirk uses his three saxophones as textural devices but feelingly delivers the body of his improvisation on tenor, where more than a hint of his early idol, Byas, may be detected. At the close he hits top notes that few people realized were within the tenor's range.

From Bechet, Byas and Fats is a tribute on which Kirk plays both manzello and tenor while Byard recalls Waller's style, both in his stride piano accompaniment behind Kirk and in his solo, which astutely quotes from Waller's piece *Jitterbug Waltz.* Jones enriches the serpentine theme through his use of chimes, and Kirk tosses off his multi-noted and complex tenor passage with incredible élan.

Many listeners regretted that Kirk's preoccupation with the saxophone did not allow him more time to devote to the flute, because his control of this instrument, often in the wrong hands too thin and watery for jazz, was exceptional. Jazz flute enjoyed considerable popularity in the 1950s following recordings by Frank Wess with Count Basie's orchestra, but only a handful of musicians were able to give it sufficient body and expertise to sustain serious examination. James Moody, Yusef Lateef and Sam Most all achieved individual styles, but none of them quite managed the true, strong sound that Kirk seemed to obtain with an effortless ease. There is an excellent example of his flute playing on *Mystical Dreams,* a fast piece which draws a solo of wit, beauty and free-wheeling momentum from Kirk. His tone is firm and clear and the vibrato expertly controlled. Occasionally, Kirk would use a buzzy throat growl to accompany the flute line, but he shuns that procedure in this instance.

Sirens and whistles, castanets and numerous other devices for making unusual sounds – all had a place in the turbulent, creative world of Roland Kirk, a musician who was fascinated by everything he heard and often recycled effects from the most unlikely sources in his solos and compositions. To Kirk the seemingly impossible was always within his grasp, yet he was essentially a modern traditionalist with a keen appreciation of both the music's history and its contemporary strivings. His catholicity of taste and eclecticism were the signs of an ever open mind.

CD

***Rip, Rig & Panic/Now Please Don't You Cry, Beautiful Edith*, EmArcy 832 164-2 (USA)**

Roland Kirk (ts, manzello, stritch, oboe, castanets, siren, v), Jaki Byard (p), Richard Davis (sb), Elvin Jones (d)

Englewood Cliffs, NJ	13 Jan 1965	**No Tonic Pres**
		Once in a While
		From Bechet, Byas and Fats
		Mystical Dreams
		Rip, Rig and Panic
		Black Diamond
		Slippery, Hippery, Flippery

Kirk (ts, manzello, stritch, flute, whistle, tambourine), Lonnie Smith (p), Ronnie Boykins (sb), Grady Tate (d)

Englewood Cliffs, NJ	April 1964	**Stompin' Grounds**
		Fallout
		Blue Rol
		Why Don't They Know?
		Alfie
		It's a Grand Night for Swingin'
		Silverlization
		Now Please Don't You Cry, Beautiful Edith

Other CDs

plus additional tracks:

Rahsaan: the Complete Mercury Recordings of Roland Kirk, Mercury 846630-2 (USA, Germany)

* * *

Wes Montgomery: *The Incredible Jazz Guitar of Wes Montgomery; Wes Montgomery Live in Paris, 1965*

Wes Montgomery was a self-taught virtuoso who pushed the guitar to limits which the instrument had not experienced since the experiments of Charlie Christian some 20 years earlier. By unravelling the mysteries of the instrument by himself, Montgomery stumbled on techniques that came easily to his nimble, responsive fingers. He learned to play simultaneously in octaves to perfection, a procedure first engineered by Django Reinhardt. He also reintroduced four-note chording, used by earlier guitarists, to lend texture to his work. Unlike most jazz guitarists he did not pick the strings with the fingers or a plectrum but employed an unusually mobile right thumb.

Although he was a member of Lionel Hampton's orchestra from 1948 to 1950, few listeners had any idea of his exceptional facility until his emergence a decade later in a group which included his brothers, electric bass guitarist Monk and vibraphonist Buddy. A contract with Riverside Records enabled him to reveal his mature talent on a series of sparkling albums, of which *Incredible Jazz Guitar* is, in many respects, the most satisfying. Accompanied by a cohesive rhythm section, including in Tommy Flanagan a pianist who knows when to stay out of the way, Montgomery prospered.

The guitarist's famous trademarks are all in evidence. His use of octaves is readily apparent in his original tune *Four on Six*, where the technique recalls the locked-hands style of pianists like Phineas Newborn and Red Garland. His single-note improvisations share common ground with Grant Green, but tonally he is softer and closer to the Jimmy Raney school.

Montgomery had a flair for originality of treatment. *West Coast Blues* is that comparative rarity, a blues in waltz time that works wonderfully well. *Polka Dots and Moonbeams* illustrates his capacity for restraint in creating a subdued atmosphere, while Sonny Rollins's tune *Airegin* demonstrates the guitarist's technical expertise in negotiating a very fast tempo in crisp and logical fashion.

If some of these performances, especially *D-natural Blues* and *Mr Walker*, have not worn well, being dated by the drum patterns and arrangements, Montgomery's inspection of *Gone with the Wind* continues to pass muster as an exemplary sample of his unwavering invention. Even the dead studio sound so characteristic of Riverside productions is forgotten as he weaves his spells.

Montgomery's career at the top encompassed only the last ten years of his life, which was ended by a heart attack in 1968. European audiences enjoyed the benefit of only one tour, in the spring of 1965, and this admirable recording on location at the Théâtre des Champs-Elysées, Paris, stems from that all-too-brief visit.

For this concert, the guitarist was faithfully served by his regular rhythm section of pianist Harold Mabern Jr, bassist Arthur Harper and drummer Jimmy Lovelace. And somebody had the creative idea of adding tenor saxophonist Johnny Griffin, with whom Montgomery had worked in the USA. The presence of Griffin on two tracks is a further delight and allows listeners to savour two virtuosos for the price of one. These vivid recordings, far superior in most respects to Montgomery's studio output, which suffered from dead sound quality, were scarcely known beyond a small group of French cognoscenti until the late 1980s, when they were finally cleared for release, greatly enhancing the available knowledge of the guitarist. Possibly inspired by the appreciative audience and fired by the rare chance to combine with Griffin, Montgomery was moved to muster some of his most plangent playing on four extended performances comprising 50 minutes of pure, concentrated inspiration.

Never one to linger over lachrymose ballads, here Montgomery's concerns are his own compositions and a blues by Dizzy Gillespie. The atmosphere is hard swinging and tensile, as guitarist and saxophonist improvise in uninhibited style with useful solo support from pianist Mabern. Montgomery's *Full House*, a bright and bubbly waltz, sidesteps the polite mood this time is apt to engender. Indeed, the guitarist gives the piece a $\frac{6}{8}$ feel while sounding perfectly at ease swinging in either metre. He drops into octaves for his second chorus and stays there for the remainder of a dramatic solo. Griffin, revelling in the rhythmic impetus, opens in fragmented manner, gradually pulling together his ideas and reaching an electrifying, double-time climax in his penultimate chorus. The muted out chorus in which everyone paraphrases the melody is attractively executed, as is the subdued suspended ending. No wonder the audience roared its approval.

Jingles, also by Montgomery, features a stop-time procedure on the main melody, with a fast contrasting section. It is taken at a presto tempo which the guitarist uses to deploy some of his fleetest single-note lines in the first part of his solo. The expected octaves come as a pleasant contrast, stalked by Mabern's urgent piano chords. Montgomery also inserts a passage of running rhythm guitar which is both agreeable and adventurous at this kind of pace. Mabern takes a solo in McCoy Tyner's manner, with dense, off-centre chords punctuating his busily modal right hand. His emphatic verbosity becomes a shade too heavy in his final chorus. There are some crisp eight-bar exchanges between guitar and drums which segue into a percussive barrage by Lovelace before the nifty theme resumes.

Griffin sits out *Jingles* and also the perky *Twisted Blues*, the third of the guitarist's functional compositions. This one has a soul phrase inserted in the melody line. Montgomery improvises his first chorus against the support of bass and drums. Then Mabern joins the fun as Montgomery's earthy extemporization unravels. It is noticeable in this performance that he plays squarely on top of the beat and uses riff patterns to squeeze the tension. Like Horace Silver, Montgomery enjoyed tossing quotations from gospel music into his mixture. It must be admitted that the temperature drops considerably when Mabern shifts to the fore and gets hung up on some corny keyboard runs. However, a solid solo by Harper helps to repair this flaw in the treatment.

Although first recorded at the onset of the bop era, Gillespie's *Blue 'n Boogie* was very popular among musicians of the 1950s, especially after its revival by Miles Davis in 1954. It is meat and drink to Montgomery and Griffin, who each assay the riffy blues with unconcealed delight. Montgomery even quotes extensively from the counter-melody often used in arrangements of the piece. His is a busy, precariously balanced solo. Griffin finds the insistent pulse to his taste and elects to navigate without the aid of either piano or guitar for much of his adroit exercise in forward motion. Actually his flow is slightly disrupted when Mabern eventually enters the picture. He picks it up again, though, in a remarkable unaccompanied passage that brings the house down at the close of a tremendously stimulating set which ends with a smidgeon of *West Coast Blues* and the crowd stamping for more. This is the best possible way to remember the glowing gift of Wes Montgomery.

CD

***The Incredible Jazz Guitar of Wes Montgomery*, Original Jazz Classics OJCCD-036-2 (USA)**

Tommy Flanagan (p), Wes Montgomery (elg), Percy Heath (sb), Albert 'Tootie' Heath (d)

New York	26 and 28 Jan 1960	**Airegin**
		D-natural Blues
		Polka Dots and Moonbeams
		Four on Six
		West Coast Blues
		In Your Own Sweet Way
		Mr Walker
		Gone with the Wind

***Wes Montgomery Live in Paris, 1965*, France's Concert FCD 108 (France)**

Johnny Griffin (ts), Harold Mabern (p), Wes Montgomery (elg), Arthur Harper (sb), Jimmy Lovelace (d)

Paris	27 March 1965	**Full House**
		Blue 'n Boogie
omit Griffin		**Jingles**
		Twisted Blues
		West Coast Blues

CHAPTER 10

Swing–Bop Combos

Barry Kernfeld

Swing and bop combos have their own identities. In archetypal performances, there can be no mistaking, say, Roy Eldridge and Chu Berry with Sid Catlett for Dizzy Gillespie and Charlie Parker with Max Roach. Earlier chapters have surveyed characteristics of each, but it may be useful to add one grand overview: in crossing over, the greatest challenge for swing musicians was the rhythmic complexity of bop; for bop musicians, it was the tunefulness of swing. Those uninterested in meeting, or unable to meet, either challenge or have kept their separate traditions through what has now become generations of players. But the two styles have much in common – a basic instrumentation, walking bass lines, swinging cymbal rhythms, a common foundation of pop songs and blues, a devotion to solo improvisation – and many musicians have wanted to bring them together.

Having followed this thread through big bands in chapter 3, and having introduced Don Byas's special blend of bop speed and swing accentuation, Nat 'King' Cole's unsatisfying bop pieces within an eclectic and otherwise highly successful body of recordings, Jo Jones's drumming with Gene Ammons and Sonny Stitt, Red Norvo's swing-style solos within the framework of his cool jazz trio, the book now introduces performers who achieved a deeper fusion in their work with small groups. For Erroll Garner, whose music falls mainly on the swing side of the equation, it was a matter of his having grasped, in his improvisations, the rhythmic jaggedness which lies at the heart of bop. For Benny Carter, a veteran swing musician, it meant not only absorbing elements of bop into his personal improvisatory style, but also working with musicians who had grown up with the new music. Eddie 'Lockjaw' Davis and Shirley Scott took a common path, bringing bop's complexity to the rhythm-and-blues edge of swing. And for Oscar Peterson and Clark Terry, it was a matter of being completely comfortable in either style, and consequently jumping fluently between them, piece by piece, chorus by chorus, phrase by phrase.

It must be said that chronology, a crucial consideration for other selections, is not terribly important in the union of swing and bop combo styles, except of course that bop needs to have been around long enough for the musicians to have comprehended it. The recordings here represent, I think, the leaders' (and organist Scott's) very best work, and though they happen to span the years 1955 to 1964, that particular span does not carry special significance.

* * *

Erroll Garner: *Concert by the Sea*

In 1955, in the midst of a long and successful career touring as the leader of a trio, Erroll Garner recorded his deservedly best-known album, **Concert by the Sea**. At the time of this performance, in a building situated on the northern California coast, his assistants were bass player Eddie Calhoun and drummer Denzil Best, who has already figured prominently in this book as a member of Lennie Tristano's group, as well as, in a different way, for having composed the bop and cool jazz theme *Move*.

In an idiom which attracts players clumped around a popular technique – the busy stride of Johnson and Waller, a Basie-like sparseness, the relentless boogie-woogie bass lines of Albert Ammons and Meade 'Lux' Lewis, the fast-running single-note lines of Powell – Garner, like Thelonious Monk, was off in a room of his own. Most original was his use of the left hand, which on this and other trio sessions (he also recorded unaccompanied) is carefully integrated with the roles of his sidemen. With the touch of a cat pawing at a pillow, Garner plays soft, gentle, steady, swinging chords on each beat, producing an effect which frequently has been described as a pianistic equivalent to a swing guitarist's four-beat strum. Rhythmically intertwined with this strumming, but sharply differentiated in loudness and energetic attack, are unpredictably placed notes played with the same hand (sometimes it seems as if he must have an extra hand!), producing a pianistic equivalent to a drummer 'dropping bombs' on the bass drum. In using his left hand this way for so much of the concert, Garner depends on Calhoun to provide the bass line; at the same time, Best stays well out of Garner's way, playing swing and swirling patterns with brushes on the snare drum and cymbals, and (except in arranged passages) leaving to the pianist the job of providing random rhythmic punctuations.

One aspect of his right-hand technique also stands out, in those passages where he duplicates the melody an octave lower, or harmonizes it. This technique is not unusual in itself, but Garner's mastery of it is noteworthy: he nimbly articulates long, fast stretches of two- or three-part lines, his right hand more or less locked into position.

By combining these devices with more conventional ones – single-note lines, two-handed block chords and (infrequently on this album) flowery arpeggios – Garner creates several distinct textures, invariably linked to changes in volume and characterized by a tremendous sense of swing. The first track, *I'll Remember April*, is representative of the procedures he follows (not necessarily in this order) on much of the album. It begins with pounding chords and a dissonant, twisted version of the opening melody. (Garner's propensity for inventing long, fanciful introductions, a general element of his style, is only hinted at during the issued portions of this recorded concert.) The theme comes in softly, harmonized in the right hand, as the strumming left hand keeps time together with the bass and drums. To delineate the structure of the tune, left-hand bombs intensify at the end of a phrase, then fall away suddenly as a new phrase quietly emerges. When he has finished presented the theme and begins to improvise, Garner changes the texture, his right hand keeping now mainly to a fast-running, single-note line. The third time through the *aba* tune, the trio's arrangement makes differentiations within and between the sections: the first half of each *a* section draws them together, hammering out a syncopated rhythm, two notes to every three beats; the second half is at a moderate level of volume, akin to that during Garner's improvisation; and the *b* section is soft, in a breath-taking manner that elicits applause. Unusually among jazz musicians, Garner uses softness for emphasis.

On one piece, *Autumn Leaves*, these sorts of contrasts go too far. Garner plays a fine solo in the middle of the piece, but the unaccompanied introduction is mawkish and the ending leaps back and forth between bombastic chords and soft tremolos. By contrast, in the blues *Red Top* he shows impeccable taste. Here too, at the end, the theme returns in the guise of chords and tremolos, but these Garner plays at a moderate volume, which in the context proves to be a delightful surprise.

Garner's improvising is an amalgam of swing and bop techniques, a reflection of experiences and associations from his formative work in the mid-1940s, when he deputized for Art Tatum and then later recorded with Charlie Parker. His continuously changing single-note lines approach the bop style in their jaggedness and irregular accentuations, but he also commonly repeats ideas, either swing riffs or motifs of a more abstract nature. He is fond of inserting quotations. Fittingly, he places the most swing-like of Parker's blues themes, *Now's the Time*, into his version of *Red Top* and refers to *The Last Time I Saw Paris* at the end of *April in Paris*.

Prospective buyers should be forewarned that the fidelity, without being anywhere near as bad as that of King Oliver's Gennett recordings from 1923, is not anywhere near the standards of a good 1955 studio recording. The sound is murky, the concert having been given in an echoic building that had formerly been a church. Also, Garner, like many of the great jazz pianists, moans and grunts while he plays, and the microphone has managed to pick up these sounds better than some of the instrumental ones. But the murkiness and vocalizing are easily ignored, the music is so good.

CD

***Concert by the Sea*, Columbia Jazz Masterpieces CK 40589 (USA) and CBS Jazz Masterpieces 451042-2 (Europe)**

Erroll Garner (p), Eddie Calhoun (sb), Denzil Best (d)

Carmel, CA	19 Sept 1955	**I'll Remember April**
		Teach Me Tonight
		Mambo Carmel
		Autumn Leaves
		It's All Right with Me
		Red Top
		April in Paris
		They Can't Take That Away from Me
		How Could You Do a Thing like That to Me?
		Where or When
		Erroll's Theme

* * *

Eddie 'Lockjaw' Davis: *The Eddie 'Lockjaw' Davis Cookbook, vol.1; The Eddie 'Lockjaw' Davis Cookbook, vol.2*

The rhythm-and-blues edge of jazz carries with it connotations of particular and deep connections to black-American religion, the toughness of inner-city life and macho swaggering. But music and humanity are quirky, always reminding us to beware of stereotypes. Thus it is that on the albums originally issued individually as volumes of **The Eddie**

'Lockjaw' Davis Cookbook, the tough tenor saxophonist Davis, who is in excellent form, is upstaged by the incredibly great playing of Hammond organist Shirley Scott, who comes across as one of the 'baddest', most 'virile' players in jazz. Her gospel roots run deep, but her gentle personality belies the toughness of her playing, and clearly it's not safe to presume that you need to be male to translate virility into sound.

This album also brings to the fore an entirely different issue. Jazz need not be consistent. As with Coleman Hawkins's *Body and Soul*, the success of the whole is often unimportant, especially in improvised jazz. On these performances, the intensity and interest plummet when Davis and Scott stop playing: the other soloists are either competent or downright poor, and the compositions and their arrangements are commonplace – conventional renditions (theme, solos, theme) of blues, ballads and unremarkable bop melodies. When Davis and Scott re-enter, the level shoots right back up to where it was, and this is so high that the rest does not matter much. It is nice to imagine a perfect album without the unexciting segments, but even with its faults **The Cookbook** should fall onto any short-list of the very best jazz.

The drummer is Arthur Edghill (not Edgehill, by the way), whose experiences in swing, hard-bop, and rhythm-and-blues groups made him the ideal accompanist on an album which brings together these three styles. Bassist George Duvivier was an even more wide-ranging accompanist, comfortable with players as different as Benny Carter and Eric Dolphy. His solos on these tracks do not indicate what a marvellous melodic improviser he could be, and it is strictly as a time-keeper that he makes his critical contribution to the group's success. The weak link is Jerome Richardson, who later went on to hold a respected position as the lead alto saxophonist in the Thad Jones–Mel Lewis Orchestra. He is a good jazz musician, but being matched up against someone as strong as Davis was a mistake. Richardson's flute sounds absurdly delicate in the context of this gutbucket music, and when he tries to add body to the sound by flutter-tonguing the result is not the gruff tone that flautist Roland Kirk was able to make, but an annoying buzz. To compound these problems, his disconnected improvisations cannot stand up against the competition. This is most painfully obvious when Richardson takes up his tenor saxophone for the hard bop tune *Three Deuces*, ostensibly a duel following in the tradition of improvised tenor sax battles between Dexter Gordon and Gene Ammons, Gordon and Wardell Gray, Ammons and Sonny Stitt. The contest is over after Davis's first shot. Following the theme, Davis's solo opens the piece. Richardson enters after the organ solo, and a minute later Davis jumps in after him, initiating a series of quick exchanges. As a soloist with Count Basie's big band in 1952–3 and again in 1957, Davis had been well prepared for such battles, and it was not until 1960, when he formed a quintet with Johnny Griffin, that he found a suitable tough tenor to serve as his partner.

On most parts of **The Cookbook**, Davis charges ahead, playing bop lines or swing and rhythm-and-blues riffs with a hard, vibratoless tone that moves frequently into grittiness; this is especially effective on repeated high notes, as for example during his solos on *Have Horn, Will Blow* and *In the Kitchen*, where his intentional distortion of the tone lends character to what otherwise would be a thin squeal. He shows his versatility on such ballads as *But Beautiful*, playing pretty melodies with a warm, breathy, sensuous tone and a pronounced but soft vibrato.

Scott, having taken up the organ in 1955, shortly after Hammond organist Jimmy Smith made a dramatic impact upon Philadelphia jazz musicians, was in the midst of a five-year association with Davis at the time of this recording. By comparison with Smith, there is an old-fashioned quavering quality to her sound, as she keeps the mechanical vibrato of the organ's Leslie speaker horn literally whirling on its fastest setting. Like Smith, she prefers a deep tone, but places this against biting, trebly percussive attacks. She lacks Smith's ability to keep a convincing bass line going on the foot pedals, but when string bassist Duvivier is a member of your group this is not an issue.

Block chords are central to Scott's accompanying and improvising. She may present them in fundamental rhythm-and-blues chord progressions (for example, at the conclusion of her solo on the slow blues *In the Kitchen*, leading into Davis's entrance) or coloured by the harmonic complexities of bop.

Scott has a complete command of blues formulas. Owing to her keen sense of how to build a melody, she uses these in a traditional way which is neither trite nor boring, no matter how familiar the material may be. On the contrary, her blues improvising is exhilarating, and Davis, who disposes of Richardson quickly, more than meets his match on these tracks.

CD

***The Eddie 'Lockjaw' Davis Cookbook, vol.1*, Original Jazz Classics OJCCD 652 (USA)**

Eddie 'Lockjaw' Davis (ts), Jerome Richardson (fl, ts), Shirley Scott (org), George Duvivier (sb), Arthur Edghill (d)

New York	20 June 1958	**The Chef**
		Have Horn, Will Blow
		In the Kitchen
		But Beautiful
		Three Deuces

CD

***The Eddie 'Lockjaw' Davis Cookbook, vol.2*, Original Jazz Classics OJCCD 653 (USA)**

Davis, Richardson, Scott, Duvivier, Edghill

New York	5 Dec 1958	**The Broilers**
		Star Dust
		Skillet
		I Surrender Dear
		The Rev

* * *

Coleman Hawkins: *The Hawk in Europe, 1934–1937*; Benny Carter: *Further Definitions*

What is being defined further on Benny Carter's album **Further Definitions** are two of his arrangements recorded by an octet under Coleman Hawkins's leadership in Paris in 1937, *Honeysuckle Rose* and *Crazy Rhythm*. Here, in 1961, are eight of Carter's arrangements for an octet of the same instrumentation – two alto saxes, two tenor saxes and rhythm section – including new versions of *Honeysuckle Rose* and *Crazy Rhythm* which draw upon aspects of the original ones. Martin Williams's liner notes to this album are tremendously informative, outlining the circumstances of the session, identifying the sources of borrowed material, describing each player's style and Carter's arranging, and detailing the order in which the soloists appear on each track. It seems most sensible, then, to leave these central topics to Williams and address the album from other angles.

The Parisian and New York sessions have quite different strengths. Hawkins's solos on the 1937 recordings are landmarks in his career. On *Honeysuckle Rose* – substantially slower than Carter's remake – Hawkins locks into the groove and concentrates more on swinging variations of a small number of simple figures than on the continuous and harmonically oriented spinning-out of ever-changing lines for which he is best known; interestingly, to accompany Hawkins's second chorus, Carter arranged a sax riff which would become, a week short of 16 months later, the main idea of Count Basie's *Jumpin' at the Woodside*. The most renowned of Hawkins's solos from this date is that on *Crazy Rhythm*. The tempo is fast – substantially faster than the remake, in fact – and Alix Combelle, the first tenor saxophonist to take a solo, seems frantic and scattered trying to keep up; after Carter's alto sax solo intervenes, Hawkins shows how it is done, driving through the song with such energy that guitarist Django Reinhardt urges him on to an unplanned second chorus. The other two titles from this acclaimed swing-era session have a different instrumentation, with multi-instrumentalist Carter switching from alto sax to trumpet. Hawkins plays just as well. After the muted trumpet states the melody of *Out of Nowhere*, Carter's arrangement features the tenor sax all the way, and he begins with a relaxed solo, not nearly as busy as the previous ones, before moving into his usual double-time feel. On *Sweet Georgia Brown* Hawkins plays florid and swinging choruses, entering for his second solo with a spectacular upward swoop which must have had a lot of tenor players scratching their head, wondering how to keep up with this man's originality. As well as Hawkins was still playing in 1961, this early work couldn't possibly be improved upon.

The rhythm section is driven by Reinhardt, whose sparkling chordal work at the beginning of *Crazy Rhythm* is sorely missed in the remake. But John Collins is a respectable rhythm guitarist, and in the rest of the rhythm section the decision goes hands down to the modern players: pianist Dick Katz rather than Stephane Grappelli (Grappelli is a great violinist, but as a piano accompanist he provides little better than a clumping beat); bassist Jimmy Garrison rather than Eugene d'Hellemmes; drummer Jo Jones rather than the expatriate American Tommy Benford. It is worth noting as a curiosity that at this time Garrison was a member of John Coltrane's group and less than two weeks earlier had made Coltrane's radical series of recordings released under the rubric **Live at the Village Vanguard**. With Carter the bassist shows his versatility by suppressing all his impulses towards modal and free-jazz bass playing and instead provides rock-steady walking lines, as if he were, say, John Simmons or Leroy Vinnegar.

A trademark of Carter's arranging is his scoring for saxophone sections playing melodies harmonized in block chords, and again the advantage goes to the tighter American version, where Carter and Hawkins are joined by alto saxophonist Phil Woods and tenor saxophonist Charlie Rouse, rather than André Ekyan and Combelle. They work in this fashion on the opening theme and closing riffs of *Honeysuckle Rose*, the theme and ensemble chorus of *Cottontail* (borrowed from Duke Ellington's recording of 1940), the opening of *Body and Soul* (a four-part harmonization of the first phrases of Hawkins's famous improvisation on this piece, from the recording of 1939 discussed in Chapter 4), and the section work on *Blue Star*, newly written for this performance. Especially characteristic of Carter's practice is the sort of intricate section work that gives the impression of a solo improvisation harmonized for a group of saxes, though his melody lines were usually written anew, rather than borrowed as on these recordings. A further excellent example occurs on Carter's arrangement of *Happy as the Day is*

Long (1934) from among the recordings of Fletcher Henderson's big band cited in chapter 3.

Yet another advantage of the 1961 tracks is Carter's solo playing, which is drastically different in style – in the interim he had moved significantly in the direction of bop – and, I would argue, much better. At the risk of being the Grinch who stole Christmas, I must confess that I do not at all like the early alto sax solos by the man who, at the time of writing, has been feted widely as the dean of surviving swing musicians. His improvisation on the Parisian version of *Crazy Rhythm* is oddly mannered and unswinging, with untuneful lines incorporating a weird selection of pitches, with too many notes placed squarely on the beat and with no sense of phrasing, each note being detached from the next. His improvising on this and all other tracks of **Further Definitions** is not so idiosyncratic, yet just as individually creative, and more elegant.

CD

***The Hawk in Europe, 1934–1937*, ASV Living Era CD-AJA 5054 (UK)**

Coleman Hawkins (ts), Stanley Black (p), Albert Harris (g), Tiny Winters (sb)

London	18 Nov 1934	**Lullaby**
		Lady Be Good

Hawkins, Black — **Lost in a Fog**

Michel Warlop (director), Arthur Briggs, Noël Chiboust, Pierre Allier (tpt), Guy Paquinet (tb), André Ekyan, Charles Lisee (as), Hawkins, Alix Combelle (ts), Stephane Grappelli (p), Django Reinhardt (g), Eugène d'Hellemmes (sb), Maurice Chaillous (d)

Paris	2 March 1935	**Avalon**
		What a Difference a Day Made

Hawkins, Grappelli, Reinhardt — **Star Dust**

(accompanied by The Ramblers:) Jack Butlerman, George van Helvoirt (tpt), Marcel Thielemans (tb), Wim Poppink (cl, as, bar), André van den Ouderas (cl, ts, vln), Hawkins (ts), Nico de Rooy (p), Jack Pet (g), Toon Diepenbroek (sb), Kees Kranenburg (d)

Laren, Netherlands	26 Aug 1935	**Meditation**
		Netcha's Dream

(accompanied by The Ramblers:) Butlerman, van Helvoirt (tpt), Thielemans (tb), Poppink, van den Ouderas (as, cl), Hawkins (ts), de Rooy (p), Pet (sb), Kranenburg (d)

	26 April 1937	**A Strange Fact**

Benny Carter (as, arr), Ekyan (as), Combelle, Hawkins (ts), Grappelli (p), Reinhardt (g), d'Hellemmes (sb), Tommy Benford (d)

Paris	28 April 1937	**Honeysuckle Rose**
		Crazy Rhythm

*as **Honeysuckle Rose**, but Carter (tpt, arr), Combelle (cl)*

		Out of Nowhere
		Sweet Georgia Brown

(Carter:) Carter (tpt, as, arr), George Chisholm (tb), Jimmy Williams (cl, as), Hawkins (ts), Freddy Johnson (p), Ray Webb (g), Len Harrison (sb), Robert Montmarche (d)

The Hague	18 Aug 1937	**Somebody Loves Me**
		Mighty Like the Blues
		Pardon Me Pretty Baby
		My Buddy

Hawkins, Johnson

Laren, Netherlands		**Well All Right Then**

CD

***Further Definitions*, MCA Impulse! MCAD 5651 (USA)**

Benny Carter (as, arr), Phil Woods (as), Coleman Hawkins, Charlie Rouse (ts), Dick Katz (p), John Collins (g), Jimmy Garrison (sb), Jo Jones (d)

New York	13 Nov 1961	**Honeysuckle Rose**
		The Midnight Sun Will Never Set
		Cherry
		Crazy Rhythm
	15 Nov 1961	**Doozy**
		Blue Star
		Cottontail
		Body and Soul

* * *

Oscar Peterson: *The Oscar Peterson Trio + One: Clark Terry*

This joyous album, made in August 1964, brings together men who were already jazz veterans, though still young. Trumpeter and flugelhorn player Clark Terry had sandwiched stints with Count Basie and Quincy Jones around an eight-year stand as the featured soloist with Duke Ellington's big band. Now he was concentrating on studio work, while he and trombonist Bob Brookmeyer also led a combo which aimed for the same seamless blend of swing and bop styles heard on this album. Pianist Oscar Peterson, bassist Ray Brown and drummer Ed

Thigpen were into their sixth year as a trio, Peterson having previously worked for years with Brown and a guitarist. Too often I find myself disappointed by this sort of all star session, because reputation (hence guaranteed record sales) often takes precedence over compatibility in bringing together the principals. On this occasion the outcome was nothing short of magnificent.

Peterson is regularly mentioned and not infrequently damned as a follower of Art Tatum. Among all the pianists who have come along after Tatum, he is best equipped to match the latter's prodigious technical command of the keyboard. But the consequent assumption, that having this ability he would use it, turns out not to be true. In a music filled with close relationships between innovators and imitators (followers of Louis Armstrong, of Charlie Parker, of John Coltrane, etc.), Tatum and Peterson are distantly removed from one another. This observation is no novel idea on my part. Listeners who have thought about what Peterson plays have noted that his greatest strengths – group playing and hard-driving swing – are not Tatum's. But the notion of the connection remains so pervasive that it seems worth while to challenge it once again. Indeed, Peterson himself encourages the idea in his own liner notes to the original issue, which mention his debt to Tatum with regard to the younger man's unaccompanied introduction to the ballad *They Didn't Believe Me*, an introduction which then proves to have none of the swooping arpeggiated interruptions which Tatum certainly would have supplied.

Peterson's concentration on swinging takes several forms. He improvises abstract, lightning-quick bop lines (*Squeaky's Blues*), but also plays more tuneful melodies. For example, his solos on *Brotherhood of Man* and *Roundalay*, laced with flashy lines, include soul jazz licks and, on the latter, passages in block chords. On *Jim* his touch and tone are sumptuous as he plays standard bluesy phrases in two-part harmony, using tremolos to hold out the ends of phrases, as if he were singing his ideas. At some points, as for example in portions of Peterson's solo on the jump tune *Blues for Smedley*, the microphone picks up the pianist grunting out melodies in unison with his fingers, like some of the earthier jazzmen with whom he might not be immediately associated.

Like his first inspiration, Oscar Pettiford, Ray Brown has all of the equipment to be a major soloist – perfect time and intonation, clean articulation, mature melodic ideas – but Brown is more content than Pettiford was to remain an accompanist. In fact, his greatest moment on this album is not the three-chorus solo on *Blues for Smedley*, but his accompaniment to Terry in the sections of *Mack the Knife* where Peterson lays out. He deftly varies the style of his bass line, playing a rocking two beat, walking deliberately from beat to beat, dancing about in broken triplet rhythms, all the time keeping the trumpeter's harmonic support crystal clear. And in the more usual segments of the album, when Peterson is playing, the pianist uses his left hand sparingly and in the middle register of the keyboard, thus staying respectfully out of Brown's domain.

All these actions in the interest of discretion and taste, tunefulness and swing apply equally to Terry, who has the technique to hit high notes (*Blues for Smedley*) and to articulate with speed (*Mack the Knife*, *Squeaky's Blues*) and the good sense not to overdo either. One of his main concerns is tone colour. He plays flugelhorn and trumpet, uses several types of mutes and sings (well, mumbles) in different 'voices'. On *Jim*, his burnished, open flugelhorn, played in its low-to-middle register, contrasts with his tightly muted trumpet, played in its middle-to-high register, in a series of four-, two- and one-bar internal dialogues, culminating in downward glisses for which he moves between the two horns note by note to the end of the piece. He also uses flugelhorn (again unmuted) in a bop-oriented solo on *Roundalay* and an uncluttered reading of the pretty melody of *They Didn't Believe Me*, played with a warm tone and a pronounced vibrato which recalls jazz brass from an earlier era.

Playing trumpet, he either keeps the mute on or plays wa-wa melodies by moving between open and muted sounds. This does not mean, though, that the two instruments are always easy to distinguish. Forays into the high register and a slight lack of ease in the low register are the only clues to reveal that he is playing trumpet on the ballad *I Want a Little Girl*, which otherwise pours out with such a gorgeous, full-bodied, mellow sound that the instrument could easily be mistaken for a flugelhorn.

Mumbles (which became Terry's nickname) and *Incoherent Blues* mark the start of Terry's recording career as a hilarious singer who simultaneously celebrates and pokes fun at down-home blues. As the titles suggest, he intentionally sings in a poorly enunciated manner which confuses the nonsense syllables of scat singing with the characteristic love-life lyrics and the black-American dialect of blues songs. *Mumbles* leans towards the scat singing side of the line, while *Incoherent Blues* is a surrealistic conversation between an impressionable woman (portrayed in a mousy falsetto voice) and a self-assured man, whose boasting descends at the very end into a gravelly leer.

CD

***The Oscar Peterson Trio + One: Clark Terry*, EmArcy 818840-2 (USA)**

Clark Terry (tpt, flugelhorn), Oscar Peterson (p), Ray Brown (sb), Ed Thigpen (d)

New York	17 Aug 1964	**Brotherhood of Man**
		Jim

	Blues for Smedley
	Roundalay
*as **Brotherhood of Man**, but Terry (v)*	**Mumbles**
*as **Brotherhood of Man***	**Mack the Knife**
	They Didn't Believe Me
	Squeaky's Blues
	I Want a Little Girl
*as **Brotherhood of Man**, but Terry (v)*	**Incoherent Blues**

CHAPTER 11

Singers Since the 1950s

Barry Kernfeld

This chapter might well be titled 'Swing and Bop Singers since 1950s', but the extra words of qualification seem unnecessary, because singers have made scarcely any steps outside the mainstream to contribute significantly to the stylistic upheavals that swept through jazz from the late 1950s onwards. Notable among the few exceptions are Polish singer Urszula Dudziak, whose most wildly innovative free jazz album **Newborn Light** is unfortunately unavailable at the time of writing, and Cassandra Wilson (discussed in chapter 19). By the mid-1950s, boundaries for jazz singing had been set by Louis Armstrong, Billie Holiday, Ella Fitzgerald and Sarah Vaughan, together with a host of blues singers extending from Bessie Smith to Dinah Washington and also together with comedians Fats Waller and Dizzy Gillespie. Their approaches have held steady. If consequently the singers surveyed in the present chapter have not gotten caught up in jazz's fascination for ever-new stylistic innovation (Abbey Lincoln excepted), they none the less have refined their art considerably over the years. Time and again in this chapter we encounter the best modern jazz singers making their greatest jazz recordings in mid-career.

* * *

Sarah Vaughan: *Sarah Vaughan With Clifford Brown*

Like many singers, Sarah Vaughan maintained a dual career in popular music and jazz. This duality was formalized contractually during the 1950s when she began recording with popular ensembles (typically a studio orchestra, including strings) for the Mercury label and with jazz groups for the Mercury company's subsidiary label EmArcy. **Sarah Vaughan With Clifford Brown** is probably the finest of these latter sessions, offering her characteristic style plus the brilliant trumpeting of Brown, especially on *Jim* and *It's Crazy*. The rest of the group is strong too, with the exception of flutist Herbie Mann, who is completely overmatched. His presence on this session is a puzzle.

Following Roy Haynes's drum solo on *Lullaby of Birdland* (both takes), Vaughan delves into scat singing during improvised exchanges with Mann, tenor saxophonist Paul Quinichette and Brown. She also contributes gentle instrumental sounds to the arranged passage that begins and ends this track, and again at the end of *Jim*. Her scat singing syllables and melodies owe a substantial debt to Ella Fitzgerald's style. Otherwise this is an album of popular songs with the lyrics kept reasonably intact. As was the case throughout her career, Vaughan presents a mixture of moderate swing tunes and slow ballads, the latter predominating. Her approach is to enunciate these songs clearly, singing in a rich alto voice, perfectly in tune, with a pronounced classical vibrato at the end of her multitude of gorgeous held tones.

In spite of Vaughan's devotion to articulating lyrics with luxurious clarity, it would be difficult to identify a vocalist who cared less about their meaning (apart from those jazz musicians who are strictly scat singers and whose lyrics consequently have no explicit meaning). Indeed sometimes she stretches out a song so deliberately and so reconfigures its melody, that the lyrics lose sense, linguistic phrasing having been replaced by musical phrasing. Listen, for example, to how completely she remakes Kurt Weill's melody when she re-enters after Brown's solo on *September Song*. It is perhaps this pure devotion to the exploration of sound that has made her such a favourite of jazz listeners.

CD

***Sarah Vaughan With Clifford Brown*, EmArcy 814 641-2 (USA)**

Clifford Brown (tpt), Herbie Mann (fl), Paul Quinichette (ts), Jimmy Jones (p), Joe Benjamin (sb), Roy Haynes (d), Sarah Vaughan (v), Ernie Wilkins (arr, conductor)

New York	16 Dec 1954	**September Song**
		Lullaby of Birdland (alternate take)
		Lullaby of Birdland (master take)
		I'm glad there is you
		You're Not the Kind
	18 Dec 1954	**Jim**
		He's My Guy

April in Paris
It's Crazy

Jones, Benjamin, Haynes, Vaughan

Embraceable You

* * *

Dinah Washington: *For Those in Love*

Dinah Washington initially made her mark in the mid-1940s as a blues singer, but a decade later she was recording mainly with jazz groups and studio orchestras, activities differentiated (although less strictly than in Vaughan's case) by her association with the Mercury and EmArcy labels. Probably the best of her EmArcy jazz sessions is **For Those in Love**, on which Washington sings with an all-star group of swing and bop musicians, playing arrangements by Quincy Jones. Reissued with a hazy, miniature facsimile of the original LP cover, the CD now includes two additional tracks from the same session of March 1955. Those of us who have excellent vision (or a good magnifying glass) will find some useful biographical information and musical description in the original and uncredited LP liner notes.

For the sake of variety, EmArcy could not have offered a greater contrast to Vaughan's style. The basic tone quality of Washington's voice was razor-sharp rather than full-bodied. On held notes she routinely added a fast vibrato, an effect that attenuated the cutting tone. Alternatively the unrestrained blues singer might come popping out, as for example near the end of the opening track, when she nearly shouts out the lyrics, 'Say I get a kick. You give me a boot. Say I get a kick out of you'. Washington was comfortable grafting familiar lyrics on to newly improvised melodies, but she was mainly devoted to investing lyrics with deep meaning, rather than exploring the voice as a musical instrument, as Vaughan did. When Washington sings *You Don't Know What Love Is,* a song of love leading to agony, she convinces us that she knows this fully, from direct experience. Then in a nice touch of programming, the next track, *This Can't Be Love,* celebrates the opposite experience in an equally convincing fashion, with her account of love leading to joy. Less systematically, the whole album is constructed in this manner, juxtaposing slow ballads and relaxed swing tunes, with the emotional mood changing accordingly. Her renditions of *Easy Living* and *I Could Write a Book* are delightful.

Jones's arrangements focus on small group sounds in a style derived from swing and cool jazz. There is no clue of the then-emerging hard bop style, in which some of Washington's accompanists would soon figure prominently. Barry Galbraith's electric guitar is integrated into smooth harmonized lines, in co-ordination with the brass and reeds, and even the baritonist saxophonist Cecil Payne (who was fully capable of cutting through Dizzy Gillespie's big band) plays with a gentle tone both in ensemble passages and in his solo on *This Can't Be Love*. Clearly the arranger Jones understood that the fire in Washington's voice could be heard to advantage in an understated instrumental setting.

This is Washington's showcase of course, but the playing of trombonist Jimmy Cleveland should not be overlooked. Improvising pretty melodies and hybrid swing-bop lines, he is the outstanding instrumental soloist, heard on the majority of tracks from this session. The disc also features Clark Terry, then with Duke Ellington's orchestra. On *Easy Living* Terry might be playing flugelhorn, though he was fully capable of producing on trumpet the mellow, low-pitched sound that leads directly into Cleveland's solo.

CD

***For Those in Love*, EmArcy 314 514 073-2 (USA)**

Clark Terry (tpt), Jimmy Cleveland (tb), Paul Quinichette (ts), Cecil Payne (bar), Wynton Kelly (bar), Barry Galbraith (elg), Keeter Betts (sb), Jimmy Cobb (d), Dinah Washington (v), Quincy Jones (arr)

New York 15–17 March 1955

I Get a Kick Out of You
Blue Gardenia
Easy Living
You Don't Know What Love Is
This Can't Be Love
My Old Flame
I Could Write a Book
Make the Man Love Me
Ask a Woman Who Knows
If I Had You

* * *

Ella Fitzgerald: *The Cole Porter Songbook, volume one; The Cole Porter Songbook, volume two; Ella at Juan-les-Pins*

In a book of essays on great recordings I cannot resist beginning Ella Fitzgerald's segment by saying that neither her **Cole Porter Songbook** nor *Ella at Juan-les-Pins* is her best disc. That honour goes to **The George and Ira Gershwin Songbook** (1959), a collection of faithful renditions of American popular songs on which the singer is accompanied by a studio orchestra under the direction of Nelson Riddle. There are few things in the world more beautiful than her version of *Embraceable You*.

But for Fitzgerald in all her diversity as a jazz singer, the definitive collection is the album recorded in France at the fifth Festival Mondial du Jazz Antibes-Juan-les-Pins in 1964. Strangely this LP has at the time of writing not yet been reissued on compact disc. Hence what follows, carried over from our first edition, is the text and listing for a completely unavailable LP, on the theory that it is so fine that it *must* appear eventually (unless some contractual dispute prevents its reissue). To avoid the perversity of selecting only a Fitzgerald collection that no-one can find, this essay is now supplemented by a discussion of the **Cole Porter Songbook**, which has been readily available on CD.

Beginning in 1956 with the two-volume **Cole Porter Songbook**, Fitzgerald made a series of definitive albums of the music of great composers of American popular song. This first set is not quite as fine as the subsequent companion for the Gershwins, but it serves better to represent Fitzgerald's relationship to jazz. The **Cole Porter Songbook** places Fitzgerald in diverse settings. Evidently the Verve company files are unreliable: details of instrumentation are both missing and mangled in Michel Ruppli's usually reliable book *The Clef/Verve Labels: a Discography* (New York: Greenwood, 1986). A more accurate outline appears below. Fitzgerald sings with Bunny Bregman's amalgamated orchestra and big band, that is to say, the sort of ensemble that would normally present Porter's songs in musical theatre (*It's Delovely*). She is accompanied by an orchestra of strings, oboe, flute and harp (*Ev'rytime We Say Goodbye*). She is heard in a Latin pop orientation, in which bongos, clavés and a plucked string bass (playing a syncopated Latin dance rhythm) are added to that orchestra (*I am in love*). Elsewhere she is joined by orchestral strings functioning as a section of a big band, a combination that Harry James, Artie Shaw and Tommy Dorsey had pioneered during the war years (*Begin the Beguine*). And producer Norman Granz places her with a conventional jazz big band (*Ridin' High*) and quartet (*Easy to Love*). Indeed here in Fitzgerald's Porter, and far more broadly speaking, throughout the popular music of the twentieth century, the nature of the accompaniment rather than the individual style of the vocalist often distinguishes jazz from other genres: *Just One of Those Things* is jazz; *I Love Paris* is not.

Never the sort of singer to interpret lyrics with profound depth, as Billie Holiday and Dinah Washington did and Abbey Lincoln does,

Fitzgerald in her devotion to sound sometimes loses all sense of meaning, as on *Miss Otis regrets (she's unable to lunch today)*, where the cynical bite of Porter's song about the lynching of a black woman is lost in an interpretation of vocalized beauty that borders on the absurd. Her personality seems far better suited to songs like *Always True to You in My Fashion* and *Let's do it (Let's fall in love)*, with their lighthearted and mildly risqué humour. In any event one usually listens to Fitzgerald not for the interpretation of Porter's brilliant poetry, but for the sound of her fabulous voice singing his brilliant melodies. Across the variety of these songs and settings Fitzgerald presents her personal style of consistently pristine enunciation (the songbook is not a forum for her scat-singing), melodic perfection, a sumptuous tone with just the occasional hint of grittiness (the end of *Ace in the Hole*) and where appropriate (*Too Darn Hot*), a perfect sense of swing.

Ella at Juan-les-Pins has trumpeter Roy Eldridge at the head of a quartet that included two longstanding members of Fitzgerald's regular trio: Gus Johnson, formerly one of the best of Count Basie's drummers, and Tommy Flanagan, whose extensive credentials as a bop pianist in Detroit and New York should not deceive anyone about his appropriateness for this mainstream swing album.

As always, popular songs are at the heart of Fitzgerald's repertory. (The exception is *The Cricket Song*, a throwaway made on the spot in response to the insects which were disrupting the second evening of her performance.) What is astonishing about this album is her versatility, the breadth of interpretation which she brings to these standards. Closest to the spirit of the studio song books are the tunes without Eldridge. *Summertime* shows off the beauty of her voice on what is, for her, a fairly high-pitched melody; using a languid tone which matches the lyrics, she stays close to the original tune, modifying it with bluesy inflections and gospel melismas. By contrast, *Somewhere in the Night*, a duet with piano until the very end, affords in its opening verse an opportunity for Fitzgerald to revel in the deep, creamy end of her range. Eldridge also lays out on the ballad-style introduction to *I've Got You Under my Skin*, which turns into a not entirely successful hybrid of swing and bossa nova, and he is absent on all but the last note of *How High the Moon*. Again in these songs Fitzgerald stays fairly close to the given melodies. The latter is taken as a slow ballad, no doubt as an antidote to the countless up-tempo versions she had given after the success of her bop-influenced scat singing on a recording of *How High the Moon* in 1947. For one phrase of its second chorus she takes up the trumpeter's role, giving the melody over to pianist Flanagan while she weaves around it an improvised obbligato, which in a moment of reverse tone-painting dips down into her lowest range at the words 'somewhere there's heaven'.

Just as with Chu Berry's combo nearly three decades earlier, Eldridge is a firecracker here. With his support, another side of Fitzgerald's artistry opens up, revealing a hard driving, swinging, adventuresome improviser whose gritty sound is in the tradition of Kansas City blues shouters, even if her repertory is not. For the most part she avoids scat singing, preferring instead to keep to the given lyrics; but these she divorces from their melodies, supplying instead her own pitches and rhythms, while also modifying her tone with crackles and growls for emphasis. In the middle of *Day in, Day out,* she inserts *Come Rain or Come Shine* and then sings to the words 'there it is, there it is' the melody of *Mean to Me,* with Eldridge jumping right in together with her. *Just a Sittin' and a Rockin'* begins with a laid-back delivery of the opening verse, but builds through Eldridge's heated, bluesy, muted trumpet solo into Fitzgerald's most intense shout singing, as she strains at the top of her range. On the opening verse of *The Lady is a Tramp* she borrows a characteristic female vocal style from Broadway musicals, and for a few phrases sounds every bit like a New York teenager. But she moves out of this style, into her full alto voice and then into more shout singing, this time demonstrating that the intense approach can be wedded to precisely controlled, virtuoso improvisation; for example, after the phrase ending 'my shape is my own', she effortlessly negotiates the leaps on 'tha-hat's why-hy the la-hady is a tramp'. (This, incidentally, exemplifies the semi-scat singing which is a trademark of Fitzgerald's style, stretching out words into sounds, like 'tha-ha-ha-ha-hat' and 'suh-huh-huh-huh-humwhere'.)

St Louis Blues, the second half of which offers the only 12-bar blues progression on the album, carries the leader's fervour over the boundary into crassness, with especially distorted shouting on the word 'feelin''. At the end she reveals that her heart wasn't in it: 'the only reason we sang this song, it was a request from our record'. Much more successful in this vein, though it is another popular song with a theme in the form *aaba* rather than a blues, is *They Can't Take That Away from Me,* performed at an unusually sultry pace and heavily coloured by blues phrases in Fitzgerald's recasting of the melody of the *b* section.

You'd be so Nice to Come Home to offers the most straightforward testimony to Fitzgerald's abilities as an improviser: going through the words three times, she changes the melody drastically at each repetition. But this lesson in jazz creativity is topped by *Honeysuckle Rose.* From the first note she remodels Fats Waller's familiar tune. Scarcely referring to the original, she makes new melodies on the given chord changes, while also inventing riffs in exchanges with Eldridge and scat singing. The performance is a *tour de force* in improvised swing.

CD

***The Cole Porter Songbook, volume one; The Cole Porter Songbook, volume two,* Verve 821-989-2 and 821-090-2 (USA)**

Buddy Bregman orchestra (including fl, oboe, strings, harp; details unknown), Ella Fitzgerald (v)

Los Angeles	7 Feb 1956	**Why can't you behave**
		I love Paris
		Do I love you
		Ev'rytime We Say Goodbye
add (Latin per)		**I am in Love**
Bregman big band; Fitzgerald		**Ridin' High**
		It's all right with me
		From this Moment on
		Just One of Those Things
		Too Darn Hot
Paul Smith (p), Fitzgerald		**Miss Otis regrets (she's unable to lunch today)**

Smith (p), Barney Kessel (elg), Joe Mondragon (sb), Alvin Stoller (d), Fitzgerald

		Get Out of Town
		Easy to Love

Bregman orchestra (including Latin per), Fitzgerald

	8 Feb 1956	**So in Love**
Bregman big band, Fitzgerald		**You do something to me**

Bregman orchestra (including jazz brass section, Latin per), Fitzgerald

		In the Still of the Night
Bregman big band plus strings, harp, Fitzgerald		**Begin the Beguine**
Bregman orchestra and big band		**All Through the Night**
		Always True to You in My Fashion
		It's Delovely
		Ace in the Hole
		Love for Sale
		Anything Goes
Smith, Kessel, Mondragon, Stoller, Fitzgerald		**Let's do it (Let's fall in love)**
	9 Feb 1956	**I get a kick out of you**
Bregman big band, Fitzgerald		**I've got you under my skin**
		What is this thing called love
		All of You
		Don't fence me in

Bregman big band plus strings, Fitzgerald	27 March 1956	**Night and Day** **You're the Top**
Bregman orchestra, Fitzgerald		**I concentrate on you**

LP

***Ella at Juan-les-Pins*, Verve 4065 and 64065 (USA)**

Roy Eldridge (tpt), Tommy Flanagan (p), Bill Yancey (sb), Gus Johnson (d), Ella Fitzgerald (v)

Antibes, France	July 1964	**Day in, Day out** **Just a Sittin' and a Rockin'** **The Lady is a Tramp** **Summertime** **St Louis Blues** **Honeysuckle Rose** **They Can't Take That Away from Me** **You'd be so Nice to Come Home to** **Somewhere in the Night** **I've Got You Under my Skin** **The Cricket Song** **How High the Moon**

* * *

Nancy Wilson and Cannonball Adderley: *Nancy Wilson and Cannonball Adderley*

Nancy Wilson's career has been mainly in popular music, but in 1961 she made a delightful excursion into the realm of jazz in association with her friend Cannonball Adderley, alto saxophonist and co-leader of a quintet with his brother, cornetist Nat Adderley. In a chapter as selective as this one, aiming to offer samples of the very finest of jazz singers, some readers may well wonder 'Why include Nancy Wilson?' when others more centrally active in jazz have been disregarded, and why this album, with five tracks given over to instrumentals by the hard bop quintet. The answer is simple. It is difficult to imagine a better summary of the art of jazz singing than Wilson offers in the first two tracks, representing bluesy ballads (*Save your love for me*) and buoyant swing tunes (*Never Will I Marry*). Wilson sings these with a poignant and arrow-tipped concentration of tone quality and articulation that has an uncanny resemblance to the sound of Dinah Washington's voice, and it might be argued that here, momentarily, the emulator has outdone the originator. In mood Wilson differs substantially from Washington's blues-tinged outlook, instead sharing with the Adderleys a fundamentally cheery nature. She is, however, fully capable of unleashing soulful cries, heard, for example, at the end of *The masquerade is over*.

Coming to prominence just after Charlie Parker's death, Cannonball Adderley was one of the leading hard bop soloists. He had a reputation for going overboard, cramming too many notes into too small a space, but on this session he was relaxed and in top form, both in support of Wilson and as the featured soloist himself, the latter including an alternately passionate and abstract interpretation of the ballad *I can't get started*. The disc also affords an opportunity to hear Joe Zawinul in his early manifestation as a subdued hard bop pianist, before he became co-leader of the fusion group Weather Report (see chapter 18).

CD

***Nancy Wilson and Cannonball Adderley*, Capitol Jazz CDP 0777 7 81204 2 1 (USA)**

Nat Adderley (c), Cannonball Adderley (as), Joe Zawinul (p), Sam Jones (sb), Louis Hayes (d), Nancy Wilson (v)

New York	27 and 29 June 1961	**Save your love for me** **Never Will I Marry** **The Old Country** **Happy Talk**
omit Adderleys		**The masquerade is over**
add Adderleys		**A Sleepin' Bee** **Little Unhappy Boy**
omit (v)	23–24 Aug 1961	**Teaneck**
omit Nat Adderley		**I can't get started**
add Nat Adderley (c)		**One Man's Dream** **Never Say Yes** **Unit 7**

* * *

Joe Williams: *A Swingin' Night at Birdland*

One need not repeat details of the definitive CD pamphlet notes written for this reissue by Count Basie's biographer, Chris Sheridan, who sets the atmosphere at the nightclub Birdland in New York and explains the circumstances of Joe Williams's appearance there. A professional singer in the Chicago area since the mid-1930s, Williams had toured with Basie's big band from 1954 to 1961. Some tension had arisen from his desire to focus on American popular song and not to be typecast exclusively as a blues singer. Now in 1962 he was embarking on a solo career with Basie's blessing, the entrepreneural support of Basie's management, and the musical support of Basie's former trumpeter Harry 'Sweets' Edison. **A Swingin' Night at Birdland** was one of the happy results in this redefinition of his career.

High points in Williams's presentation of popular songs include *September in the Rain,* which also features Edison's improvising; the great swing of *By the River St Marie,* with an arrangement for trumpet and tenor sax pushing the singer along; a tantalizing and too brief *Have you met Miss Jones?*, with a little explosion of Edison's trumpeting and Williams's scat singing; and *Falling in Love with Love,* which can only have been omitted from the original issue because of an engineering flaw that causes Williams's voice to distort just before the end of the track, not because of the quality of the performance. Williams also sings five blues: *Come Back Baby, 5 O'Clock in the Morning, Well alright ok you win, Roll 'em Pete,* and *Goin' to Chicago Blues.* On the whole these involve urbane and occasionally elaborate lyrics delivered with clear enunciation and conveying a restrained emotion, and on the fast blues *Roll 'em Pete* he shows his talent for bop scat singing as he trades four-bar phrases with drummer Clarence Johnson. Only rarely does he unleash the downhome side of his musical personality, imitating the blues shouting style of Basie's most famous singer Jimmy Rushing for the 'Goin' to Chicago' chorus in the middle of *Goin' to Chicago Blues,* and breaking into a banshee wail 'oooooooooooo' at the end of *Come Back Baby* and again as he finishes his scat singing on *Roll 'em Pete.*

CD

***A Swingin' Night at Birdland,* (Blue Note) Roulette Jazz CDP 7 95335 2 (USA)**

Harry 'Sweets' Edison (tpt), Jimmy Forrest (ts), Hugh Lawson (p), Ike Isaacs (sb), Clarence Johnson (d), Joe Williams (v)

New York	June 1962	**September in the Rain**
		Come Back Baby

5 O'Clock in the Morning
By the River St Marie
This can't be love
Teach Me Tonight
Well alright ok you win
I was telling her about you
Have you met Miss Jones?
Roll 'em Pete
You're everything but mine
Falling in Love with Love
Goin' to Chicago Blues
The Very Thought of You

* * *

Betty Carter: *The Audience with Betty Carter*

Betty Carter's tenure as a singer with Lionel Hampton's big band from 1948 to 1951 was her only important affiliation with a leading ensemble, disregarding her later period with Ray Charles's orchestra (1960–3), in which obviously it was not Carter whose singing was featured. For nearly four decades she struggled to be accepted on her own terms, and in the course of this struggle she formed her own record label, Bet-Car, in 1972, so as not to be obliged to accommodate her idiosyncratic jazz style to the tastes of producers for major record labels. Finally, as the 1980s ended, she achieved that sought-after success on her own terms, winning a Grammy award and signing with the Verve label, which subsequently reissued the Bet-Car albums on CD. The best of these is **The Audience with Betty Carter**, recorded live at the Great American Music Hall in San Francisco in 1979.

Within the intertwining realms of jazz, blues and pop, an essential element that distinguishes jazz performance is its tendency to be preoccupied first and foremost with sound rather than lyrics. But singers of necessity deal with lyrics anyhow (scat singers excepted) and thus tend automatically to raise the question whether jazz singing has its own identity, separate from blues and pop. For Betty Carter, the answer is yes, certainly it does. The opening track on this collection confirms her central interest by its very title, *Sounds*, a 25-minute *tour de force* in which she explores the voice as a jazz instrument, while the text consists of inconsequential phrases – 'we're movin' on' – or the nonsense of scat singing. This preoccupation is nearly as obvious on *The Trolley Song*, as she luxuriates in trolley sounds ('bump bump bump bump bump bump went the brakes'); she also builds musical tone painting into the arrangement, with a fast-paced introduction and ending evoking the movement of the trolley, and particularly with pianist John Hicks playing a final descending sequence as she sings, 'we held hands to the end of the line'.

Indeed, like Vaughan, Carter is often so interested in sound that she warps the meaning of lyrics; hence for example, on her own composition *Tight*, she drops out the words 'let him go' towards the end of the song, for musical effect, but with the result that the phrase reverses its meaning: 'don't let him go; hold on to him tight' becomes instead 'don't ... hold on to him tight'. Also like Vaughan, while delivering familiar popular song lyrics Carter remakes popular song melodies with an individuality sometimes bordering on the bizarre, as in the latter parts of *Everything I Have is Yours* and *I Could Write a Book*. This individuality is heightened by a musical mannerism completely at odds with Vaughan's singing: Carter swoops through melodies, obscuring pitch, as if a free jazz conception of non-western intonation had been transferred into a mainstream repertoire; examples need not be cited, for this mannerism permeates her performances. The tone and range of her voice may reach down into a full-bodied low alto range (though with none of Vaughan or Fitzgerald's timbral beauty); alternately she may sound like a cute little girl. Also unlike Vaughan and Fitzgerald, Carter is a great scat singer, controlling a wide array of appropriately idiomatic syllables and comfortably scatting her way through any style, whether fast modal jazz (portions of *Sounds* and *My Favorite Things*), slow blues (toward the last part of *Sounds*), Latin jazz (the opening and ending of *Caribbean Sun*, including a final saxophone-like unaccompanied cadenza) or relaxed swing (the first half of *I Could Write a Book*).

CD

***The Audience with Betty Carter*, Verve 835 684-2 (USA)**

John Hicks (p), Curtis Lundy (sb), Kenny Washington (d), Betty Carter (v)

San Francisco 6–8 Dec 1979

Sounds (Movin' On)
I Think I Got It Now
Caribbean Sun
The Trolley Song
Everything I Have is Yours
I'll Buy You a Star
I Could Write a Book [medley:]
  Can't We Talk It Over
  Either It's Love or It Isn't
Deep Night
Spring Can Really Hang You Up the Most
Tight
Fake

So....
My Favorite Things
Open the Door (Theme Song)

* * *

Mel Tormé and George Shearing: *An Evening at Charlie's*

London-born pianist George Shearing established himself during the war years as the leading British jazz pianist. Like his contemporary Marian McPartland (Marian Turner at the time), he showed an ability to assimilate styles ranging from stride and swing to the newly emerging bop. Emigrating to America in 1947, he was immortalized in Jack Kerouac's novel *On the Road;* Kerouac, an ardent jazz fan, called Shearing 'God'. During the 1950s he then found popular success, at least for a jazz musician, with a quintet featuring the co-ordinated sound of vibraphone, electric guitar, and Shearing's own two-handed 'block' chords. Singer Mel Tormé is six years younger, but made his mark (and presumably a lifelong income) around the same time, after having written a huge hit, *The Christmas Song,* in 1946. It is not typical in the youth-orientated jazz and pop life for two musicians to recognize their compatibility after four decades in the business, but such was the experience of Shearing and Tormé, whose collaboration flowered with a series of outstanding albums for the Concord label. The first two, recorded in 1982–3, won Grammy awards; this third, **An Evening at Charlie's**, is perhaps even better.

Tormé is a magnificent singer. He has Billie Holiday's sense of time, the ability to float along pulling this way and that against the rhythm section's strict beat, as for example on *Just One of Those Things* and *Love is just around the corner.* He relies heavily on Ella Fitzgerald's mannerisms, particularly her scat singing formulas, as well as a gesture in which a syllable repeats at various pitches, thereby temporarily submerging sense beneath sound. Like Holiday (not as well, but who could match her!) and far better than Fitzgerald, he conveys the depth and meaning of lyrics. As Shearing points out in a tongue-in-cheek introduction, Tormé is the perfect man to deliver Bob Dorough and Dave Frishberg's song *I'm Hip,* skewering phony, fashion-conscious jazz fans. As well as he understands hipness, Tormé is anything but the detached hipster. Indeed his versatility extends to sincere, unabashed romanticism, notably on a beautiful rendition of *Then I'll be Tired of You* ('If my throbbing heart should ever start repeating that it is tired of beating, then I'll be tired of you'). **An Evening at Charlie's** offers assorted nods toward bop, including Charlie Parker's theme *Moose the Mooche*, which oddly ends the set, and Shearing and bassist Don Thompson's hurried romp through Horace Silver's hard bop tune *Nica's Dream*, but it is Tormé's swing that wins the day.

CD

***An Evening at Charlie's*, Concord CCD-4248 (USA)**

George Shearing (p), Don Thompson (sb), Donny Osborne (d), Mel Tormé (v)

Washington, DC	Oct 1983	**Medley:** **Just One of Those Things** **On Green Dolphin Street**
Shearing		**Dream Dancing**
Shearing, Thompson, Osborne, Tormé		**Dream Dancing** **I'm Hip** **Then I'll be Tired of You**
Shearing, Tormé		**Medley:** **Caught in the Middle of My Years** **Welcome to the Club**
Shearing, Thompson		**Nica's Dream**
Shearing, Thompson, Osborne, Tormé		**Chase Me Charlie** **Love is just around the corner**

* * *

Dee Dee Bridgewater: *Live in Paris*

In New York during the mid-1970s Dee Dee Bridgewater rose to prominence as a gospel-influenced singer with the Thad Jones–Mel Lewis Orchestra and a Tony-award winning actress in the musical *The Wiz*. Over the next decade, during which time she settled in France, her career was the familiar jazz story of youthful promise unfulfilled. Then in 1987 the story took a happy twist with the issue of this spectacularly fine album **Live in Paris**. It rightfully returned Bridgewater to the attention of an American jazz audience, and by year's end she had embarked on an international tour with the all-star Phillip Morris Superband.

The trio heard on these tracks are not all-stars. Drummer André Ceccarelli is the best known of the three, for his playing in European bop and swing groups. Yet they prove to be talented soloists (pianist Hervé Sellin shows off his bop licks on *Cherokee*) and perfectly accomplished, sensitive accompanists for Bridgewater. This in itself says something about the consistently high level that jazz performance had reached internationally by the 1980s.

Bridgewater is the star of the set. She is as versatile as a jazz singer can be. She can sing a pretty ballad like *Here's that Rainy Day* with gentle beauty or deliver the *Medley Blues* with the force of a Kansas City shouter: listen to her sing 'nobody loves me, nobody seems to care'. Even more impressive is her ability as an improviser. For singers the main threads of jazz improvisation involve sticking close to the original melody while focusing on the manipulation of tone quality and the placement of notes; retaining familiar lyrics while remaking the melody (the most difficult approach); or discarding the given melody and lyrics for instrumentally inspired scat singing. Very few jazz singers excel at all three approaches. For example, Billie Holiday did not attempt to be a scat singer. Ella Fitzgerald and Sarah Vaughan did, but with unsatisfying results (owing largely to their selection of unidiomatic syllables, offering 'la' and 'doe' when they needed 'zwa' and 'oop'). Those who have excelled at scat singing, like Dizzy Gillespie and Jon Hendricks, are not the sort of singers whom we would want to hear caressing a ballad melody. But Bridgewater (like Louis Armstrong before her) has the whole package. There is not a weak track on this album, but best of all are *Misty*, *There Is No Greater Love* and an especially ecstatic rendition of *On a Clear Day*, each displaying her irrepressible sense of invention and swing.

CD

***Live in Paris*, Impulse! MCAD-6331 (USA)**

Hervé Sellin (p), Antoine (Tony) Bonfils (elb), André (Dédé) Ceccarelli (d), Dee Dee Bridgewater (v)

Paris	24–25 Nov 1986	**All Blues**
		Misty
		On a Clear Day
		Dr Feelgood
		There Is No Greater Love
		Here's That Rainy Day

Medley Blues:
Every Day I Have the Blues
Stormy Monday
Cherokee

* * *

Carmen McRae: *Carmen Sings Monk*

Carmen McRae performed with the orchestras of Benny Carter and Count Basie in the mid-1940s, but it was another decade before she began making recordings that established her as one of the leading jazz singers. McRae is versatile, comfortable with lyrics or scat singing, capable of fluently delivering romantic songs or the blues, offering a correspondingly wide sonic palette that ranges from rounded shimmering tones to a tart dryness and equipped technically to swoop through blue notes (as Betty Carter does, but in a less exaggerated manner) or to cleanly pop out a fast and difficult line. She has a considerable devotion to the bop style. This interest found its fullest expression in 1988 with the performance in San Francisco (where two tracks were also recorded) and the subsequent recording in New York of **Carmen Sings Monk**, a collection of Thelonious Monk's tunes set to lyrics.

Lyrics for the first half of McRae's version of Monk's *'Round Midnight* were written by Bernie Hanighen in the early 1940s (although this tune is routinely performed without a vocalist). Otherwise, all of the lyrics, including Jon Hendricks's contribution to the second half of McRae's *'Round Midnight*, have been supplied by Hendricks, Mike Ferro, Sally Swisher and Abbey Lincoln, and accordingly all of the other tracks have been retitled (to clarify publishing royalties). The original titles appear in the CD pamphlet notes and also below, in brackets. Of course Monk sometimes utilized the standard practice of reworking existing chord progressions into new jazz themes. Hence the result may be twice removed from the original, for example, the lyrics of *Suddenly*, fitted to the melody of Monk's *In Walked Bud*, based on the chord progression of Irving Berlin's *Blue Skies*. What seems especially interesting – and this is characteristic of Monk's work, whether partially borrowed or wholly new – is that his quirky new melodies are completely memorable and distinctive, so that, in this case, Berlin's contribution sounds almost irrelevant. **Carmen Sings Monk** confirms that originality, fortifying our sense of Monk as a composer.

Outstanding among the new settings are Ferro's cutting celebration of the end of a love affair, *It's Over Now* ('You're takin' off weight, well you needn't. You're lookin' great, well you needn't. You're settin' the bait, well you needn't. It's over now'.); Hendricks's hipster-era poetry on *Suddenly*; his lament on a lost chance for love, *How I Wish*... ('You asked me could I care. My attention was elsewhere. How I wish you'd ask me now'.); and above all Swisher's *Dear Ruby*, which McRae's singing makes as touchingly beautiful as Monk's versions for unaccompanied piano.

Among the instrumentalists, the consistently finest soloist is string bassist George Mraz, heard on *It's Over Now*, *Monkery's the Blues*, *Little Butterfly* and two versions each of *Get it Straight* and *Suddenly*, these last tracks having been recorded live with Monk's own tenor saxophonist Charlie Rouse and then again in the studio as CD bonus tracks, with Clifford Jordan replacing Rouse. Also worth noting is the utterly appropriate drumming of Al Foster, the consummate professional. Here with McRae is the man who had driven the most ponderous of Miles Davis's bands, instead inventing carefully structured solos and accompanying with complete sensitivity, as when he plays a delicate brushed swing rhythm (known in the trade as the 'businessman's bounce') beneath tenor saxophonist Jordan's relaxed double-time solo on *Dear Ruby*.

CD

***Carmen Sings Monk*, Novus 3086-2 N (USA)**

Charlie Rouse (ts), Larry Willis (p), George Mraz (sb), Al Foster (d), Carmen McRae (v)

San Francisco	30 Jan or 1 Feb 1988	**Get it Straight [Straight, No Chaser]**
		Suddenly [In Walked Bud]

Clifford Jordan (ts), Eric Gunnison (p), Mraz, Foster, McRae

New York	April 1988	**Dear Ruby [Ruby, My Dear]**
		It's Over Now [Well You Needn't]
		Monkery's the Blues [Blue Monk]
		You Know Who [I Mean You]
		Little Butterfly [Pannonica]
		Listen to Monk [Rhythm-a-ning]
		How I Wish ... [Ask Me Now]
		Man, That Was a Dream [Monk's Dream]

omit Jordan		**'Round Midnight**
		Still We Dream [Ugly Beauty]

add Jordan (ss)	**Looking Back [Reflections]**
(ts) replaces (ss)	**Suddenly [In Walked Bud]** **Get it Straight [Straight No Chaser]**

* * *

Shirley Horn: *You Won't Forget Me*

Around 1962 Miles Davis was intrigued by an album recorded by pianist Shirley Horn, and he invited her to alternate with his group in performances at the Village Vanguard in New York. This fortuitous contact led to further recordings, and it quickly became apparent that Horn not only was a first-rate jazz pianist, but also had a gorgeous voice. She was featured as a singer with Quincy Jones's orchestra on LP and on the soundtrack to the movie *For Love of Ivy*. Thus to her dismay, she was sometimes required to sing with other pianists, rather than supplying her own accompaniment, which she is fully capable of doing in a manner synchronized with and complementing her voice, and yet at the same time astonishingly independent of that voice.

Horn never disappeared from the scene, but from the mid-1960s to early 1980s she worked in the Baltimore and Washington area, while raising her daughter. Gradually from 1978 onwards her career blossomed again, this time far better than before. First came recordings in New York for the Danish label SteepleChase and a festival appearance in the Netherlands and then came America's discovery that here is a major jazz artist. The CD **You Won't Forget Me**, from 1990, is perhaps the best of the recordings that she has made on the Verve label from 1987 into the 1990s, but all these are consistently fine. If **You Won't Forget Me** becomes unavailable, listeners should not be disappointed by an alternative choice.

You Won't Forget Me is an album of love songs spanning the emotional compass from celebration to resignation. There is not a weak track on the disc. Along the way the CD offers two rock-solid rhythm sections – pianist Horn with bassist Buster Williams and drummer Billy Hart (both of whom had been on her first SteepleChase album in 1978), and the pianist with bassist Charles Ables and drummer Steve Williams. It also features cameo appearances by distinguished guests, notably Toots Thielemans and Miles Davis. Thielemans, who has no rival as a virtuoso jazz harmonica player, also performs on his second instrument, guitar, in a 'trio' with Horn on *Beautiful Love* (actually a duo with harmonica overdubbed). Davis makes an extremely rare appearance as a sideman, playing the stemless harmon-muted trumpet in his characteristically haunting and off-the-wall manner on the title track, *You Won't Forget Me*. Interestingly drummer Williams superimposes a quiet, metronomic jazz fusion beat on top of this slow ballad, no doubt to accommodate Davis's having stepped out of his fusion band as a favour to Horn. Of course the centre of attention is Horn. Like Sarah Vaughan, she has a deep, warm, full voice, but she avoids Vaughan's warbling vibrato, and the resulting sound is altogether different (and I think, more appropriate to jazz). She hits notes squarely in tune and swings in a delicate way, and she conveys the emotion and meaning of the lyrics. There are a few joyous tracks (*Come Dance with Me; I just found out about love*) and one bluesy, biting song (*Don't let the sun catch you crying*), but in the main these are gentle romantic performances, allowing us to luxuriate in the sound of her intertwining voice and piano.

CD

***You Won't Forget Me*, Verve Digital 847 482-2 (USA)**

Shirley Horn (p, v), Charles Ables (sb), Steve Williams (d)		
New York 12, 14 June 1990		(sequence of tracks unknown)
11–13 Aug 1990		**The Music that Makes Me Dance**
		Come Dance with Me
add Wynton Marsalis (tpt)		**Don't let the sun catch you cryin'**
Toots Thielemans (harmonica, g), Horn (v)		**Beautiful Love**
Horn (p, v), Buster Williams (sb), Billy Hart (d)		**Come Back to Me**
Horn, Ables, Steve Williams		**Too Late Now**
		I just found out about love
add Branford Marsalis (ts)		**It Had to be You**
Thielemans (harmonica) replaces Marsalis		**Soothe Me**
Horn, Buck Hill (ts), Buster Williams, Hart		**Foolin' Myself**
Horn, Ables, Steve Williams		**If You Go**
Horn, Ables (g), Buster Williams, Hart		**You Stepped out of a Dream**

Horn, Miles Davis (tpt), Ables, Steve Williams	**You Won't Forget Me**
omit Davis	**All My Tomorrows**

* * *

Abbey Lincoln: *You Gotta Pay the Band*

Although jazz is a music in which its participants routinely find themselves at a young age, it occasionally offers up examples of extensively prolonged and ultimately rewarding searches for a personal musical identity. Abbey Lincoln's musical life is one such story, perhaps the most uplifting of all. In the mid-1950s she found considerable success as a romantic jazz singer. In 1960 she staked out a claim in jazz's contribution to the civil rights movement with her unforgettable primal screams on *Triptych: Prayer, Protest and Peace* on the album **We Insist! (Freedom Now Suite)** by Max Roach (then her husband) and Oscar Brown Jr. She became an actress, starring in *For Love of Ivy* and other movies. In the 1970s she began writing original songs and writing lyrics to existing tunes. Through this path, she found her individuality. Her repertory percolated and grew for over a decade, but Lincoln struggled for steady work until, in 1988, she resumed her recording career, now in association with producer Jean-Philippe Allard. Among the consistently stunning results is the disc **You Gotta Pay the Band**. Recorded in 1991, this CD subsequently topped the jazz charts in a happy example of agreement between popularity and good taste.

You Gotta Pay the Band features pianist Hank Jones and tenor saxophonist Stan Getz, whose veiled, shadowy tone, and cool, slippery, swinging melodies are perfectly matched to Lincoln's own wry and understated manner. In jazz, unlike blues or rock or folk or gospel, the message is usually in sound rather than in the words. One can enjoy this album simply for its wonderful sounds, without paying any attention to the lyrics.

Alternatively, considerable rewards come from paying close attention to Lincoln's interpretations of musical poetry. In her re-emergence as a singer and her new birth as a songwriter, Lincoln continues to be a master of love songs (as is obvious from several titles on the disc), but she also addresses other types of substantive issues – loneliness (*Bird Alone*), responsibility (*You gotta pay the band*), poverty (*Brother, can you spare a dime?*), a failure to 'fit in' (*You made me funny*), and death (*When I'm Called Home*). Indeed Lincoln is perhaps unparalleled in her ability to deliver weighty lyrics without undermining the sound of jazz (as happens when, for example, Joni Mitchell or Nina Simone attempt to operate within this realm).

CD

***You Gotta Pay the Band*, Verve 314 511 110-2 (USA)**

Stan Getz (ts), Hank Jones (p), Maxine Roach (viola), Charlie Haden (sb), Marc Johnson (d), Abbey Lincoln (v)

New York	25–26 Feb 1991	**Bird Alone**
omit Roach		**I'm in love**
		You gotta pay the band
		Brother, can you spare a dime?
Johnson (d), Lincoln (v)		**You made me funny**
Getz, Jones, Haden, Johnson, Lincoln		**And how I hoped for your love**
		When I'm Called Home
		Summer Wishes, Winter Dreams
		Up Jumped Spring
add Roach (viola)		**A Time for Love**

CHAPTER 12

Latin Jazz

Barry Kernfeld

Syncopated Latin rhythm was probably a part of jazz from its beginning (whenever that was). Certainly it could be heard in ragtime pieces that probably pre-date jazz, in the second strain of W. C. Handy's *St Louis Blues* (1914), and on *New Orleans Joys* and *Mamamita*, two unaccompanied piano pieces recorded in 1923–4 by Jelly Roll Morton, who called that rhythmic quality the 'Spanish tinge'. But a couple of decades passed before Latin rhythm was used in something that had a sufficient identity to be called a Latin jazz style. First, beginning in the mid- to late-1940s, came Afro-Cuban jazz, involving the orchestras of Dizzy Gillespie (discussed in chapter 3), who blended bop, swing, and Latin rhythms, structures, and instrumentation, and Machito, who shifted the balance of these same components more toward the Latin side of the equation. This approach became a permanent part of the musical landscape. Next, from the early 1960s onward, came bossa nova, a union of cool jazz and subdued Brazilian samba, with composer Antonio Carlos Jobim and saxophonist Stan Getz at its vanguard. A craze for bossa nova followed, temporarily vulgarizing and exhausting the style, but bossa nova proved to be resilient, and it too became a permanent part of the musical landscape. The late 1960s and 1970s brought a further development: many fine Brazilian musicians, above all percussionist Airto Moreira, began playing jazz in the United States, and Latin rhythm came to be incorporated into jazz–rock and other fusions, with which it shared duple divisions of the beat (as opposed to the triplet feeling of swing rhythm), and with which it therefore could conveniently be used as yet another component of these fusions, as heard in Chick Corea's group Return to Forever (blending bop, rock, and bossa) and later in Pat Metheny's group (discussed in chapter 18).

As with all other styles of jazz, the years since the mid-1970s have been for Latin jazz a time of consolidation and recombination, rather than new invention. Apart from an unusual Argentinian jazz–tango fusion involving Astor Piazzolla and Gary Burton, the later selections in this chapter focus on the continuation of the Afro-Cuban tradition. Over the years there have been any number of jazz-orientated recordings in which the Afro-Cuban rhythm is smoking, but the content of the improvisations is rather fluffy. For example, Mongo Santamaria's recorded output is characterized by such shortcomings; Tito Puente's Latin jazz is from this standpoint uneven – sometimes fluffy, sometimes meaty. (Unfortunately his best albums are unavailable at the time of writing.) And there have been numerous recordings by ensembles that come from the other side of the synthesis to offer a combination of heady improvisation and lame rhythm, because their percussionists lack a proper knowledge of the style (Stan Kenton's orchestra having recorded the most prominent examples). It would seem, then, that a successful Afro-Cuban jazz synthesis has been quite difficult to achieve. Yet since the late 1980s the situation seems to have changed, and sessions by Jerry Gonzalez, Gillespie, Luis Bonilla and Eddie Palmieri testify to a vigorous revival of the style. Perhaps after all these years musicians have finally figured out how to be consistent in uniting idiomatic Afro-Cuban rhythm with substantial soloing.

* * *

Machito and his Afro-Cuban Salseros: *Mucho Macho*

The leading exponents of Afro-Cuban jazz in the late 1940s were Gillespie (whose contributions from this era are discussed in chapter 3), Cuban-born singer and percussionist Machito, and a lesser-known link between them, trumpeter Mario Bauza, who had brought Gillespie into Cab Calloway's big band before joining Machito's group in 1941. (Kenton was also prominent in the flowering of the style, but anyone who learns to hear the essence of Afro-Cuban rhythm should recognize that Kenton never 'got it', however sincere and enthusiastic he might have been.) **Mucho Macho** is a fabulous collection of Machito's recordings from this period. It summarizes the multi-faceted relationships among swing, bop, and American and Cuban popular music.

Vaya Niña, composed by Chico O'Farrill, offers a characteristic example of the importance of repeated and interlocking syncopated patterns in Latin jazz, as heard on string bass, several percussion instruments, brass and reeds. Also typical is René Hernandez's piano solo, played in octaves and built in a relaxed but staggered fashion. This track illustrates the then-popular dance rhythm of the mambo, as do several others, including *Tumba el Quinto* and *Llora Timbero* (both sung by Machito) and of course also those tracks with the word Mambo in the title; *Hall of the Mambo King* is a latinized version of Grieg's *In the Hall of the Mountain King*. The group presents a slower, crisper dance, of the sort that would come to be known as cha-cha-cha, on *Un Poquito de tu Amor* and *Vive Como Yo*, both featuring Machito's sister, Graciela. Their singing on some of these tracks carries the stylistic concoction away from jazz and into the realm of salsa, but when Machito is improvising while members of the group chant in response, there seems little distance between African-American English and Afro-Cuban Spanish in tracing the roots of this device, so closely associated with jazz.

Not all such connections work smoothly. *U-bla-ba-du* is an effort to make an Hispanic version of Gillespie's *Oop-pop-a-da*, but where Gillespie's bop scat singing is magnificently funny, Graciela is merely silly. O'Farrill's *Gone City*, without any singing, proves to be a much more successful meld of bop and Cuban styles. The latinization of American popular songs also yields mixed results, but the uncredited arrangement of *The World is Waiting for the Sunrise* is outstanding. Also worth noting is the piano solo on *Tea for Two*, for in its development of a loping, staggered descending pattern, it presents an idea that has become ubiquitous in latin-flavoured performance since Stevie Wonder popularized it in the early 1970s. Amusingly, the collection also testifies to America's indiscriminate fondness for musical exotica. Suddenly on *Asia Minor* and *Cleopatra Rumba*, Cuba is transported to the Muslim world, as an unidentified oboist (presumably one of the saxophonists) plays the melodic clichés associated with Hollywood's conception of that world, within the context of sounds that otherwise represent the heart and soul of Latin jazz.

CD

***Mucho Macho*, Pablo PACD-2625-712-2 (USA)**

Mario Bauza, Frank Davila, Bobby Woodlen (tpt), Gene Johnson, Fred Skerritt (as), José Madera (ts), Leslie Johnakins (bar), unidentified (oboe), René Hernandez (p), Roberto Rodriguez (sb), José Mangual (bongos), Luis Miranda (conga), Ubaldo Nieto (timbales), Machito (maracas, clavés)

New York	1948–9	**Asia Minor**
omit (oboe); add Graciela (v)		**Un Poquito de tu Amor**
Machito and group (v) replace Graciela		**Tumba el Quinto**
omit (v)		**Jungle Drums**

add Machito (v)	**Llora Timbero**
Graciela and group (v)	**Vive Como Yo**
Machito (v) replaces Graciela	**Babarabatiri**
omit (v); add (oboe)	**Cleopatra Rumba (Desert Dance)**
add Graciela and group (v)	**U-bla-ba-du**
add Machito (v)	**El Sapon**
omit (v); add unidentified (tb)	**Gone City**
omit (tb); add Machito and group (v)	**Babalu**
omit (v)	**Vaya Niña** **Hall of the Mambo King** **Donkey Serenade**
add group (v)	**Mambo Jambo**
omit (v)	**At Sundown** **Why do I love you?**
add Machito and group (v)	**Mambo is here to stay**
omit (v)	**Rose Room** **Tea for Two**
add Graciela (v)	**Finaliza un Amor**
omit (v)	**The world is waiting for the sunrise** **St Louis Blues**

* * *

Stan Getz and Charlie Byrd: *Jazz Samba*

After having been dominated by the brassy, extroverted, piercing Afro-Cuban style during the 1940s and 1950s, the realm of Latin jazz embraced a new style that could not have presented a greater contrast: breathy, introverted, quiet Brazilian bossa nova, introduced into the USA in 1962 with the release of the album **Jazz Samba** by tenor saxophonist Stan Getz and acoustic guitarist Charlie Byrd. Their discovery was a curious side effect of the cold war. In brief: in reaction to the Soviet's cultural exchange programme with South American countries, the USA set up a similar programme. Byrd applied to participate and soon thereafter, when Dave Brubeck was forced to cancel his tour, Byrd's group was sent instead; in Brazil he encountered the full-blown bossa nova style and set about learning to play it; he brought home records and music, including songs by the superlative composer Antonio Carlos Jobim, and shared these with Getz. The rest, as they say, is history.

Jazz Samba is an uneven recording. Byrd had not yet identified the finest songs, and hence the album includes only two titles by Jobim, the now classic tune *Desafinado* and the comparatively lightweight *Samba de Uma Nota So* (*One Note Samba*). He had not yet developed an appropriate improvisatory style, and consequently his guitar solos have an inappropriately bluesy orientation, akin to Stephane Grappelli's misuse of blues phrases in non-blues contexts. And he was not yet sufficiently familiar with the particular songs that he chose, evidently getting lost in his solo on *Desafinado* and playing through half of Jobim's chord progression before settling into a two-chord ostinato and then ceasing to play altogether, so that bassist Keeter Betts and the percussionists are left alone to reiterate softly the tune's characteristically delicate, bouncing, syncopated background, until Getz re-enters to rescue them. (Perhaps all this is intentional, but it sure sounds like a mistake.) Today the bossa nova style has been so completely absorbed into the mainstream of jazz – to which it offers bop-like chord progressions, but with Latin rather than swing rhythm – that we can easily underestimate just how different and difficult it might have sounded in 1962.

Despite these apparent flaws, **Jazz Samba** is a magnificent recording, not because of its historical role in the internationalization and popularization of a Brazilian music (though this is certainly interesting), but because of Getz's extraordinary playing. Having received his lessons second-hand through Byrd, without having himself been to Brazil, Getz immediately grasped the style more deeply than anyone else had or would (with perhaps the exception of Jobim), and he made it his own. There is no sound more appropriate to the bossa nova style than his cool, understated, airy tenor saxophone, flowing gently through the melody.

CD

***Jazz Samba*, Verve 810 061-2 (USA)**

Stan Getz (ts), Charlie Byrd (g), Gene Byrd (g, sb), Keeter Betts (sb), Buddy Deppenschmidt (d), Bill Reichenbach (per)

Washington, DC 13 Feb 1962

Baia
Samba Triste
Desafinado
E Luxo So
O Pato
Samba dees Days
Samba de Uma Nota So

* * *

Chick Corea and Return to Forever: *Light as a Feather*

Listeners may raise their eyebrows at the selection of **Light as a Feather**, for it offers a good dose of fluff in Chick Corea and Stanley Clarke's lyrics and wordless vocalizings, as performed by their colleague Flora Purim. These features, which have not worn well over time, are overwhelmed by Chick Corea's fine compositions, involving meaty material delivered by his group, Return to Forever, with a crisp relaxation and seeming ease that downplays their virtuosity (that is, until you hear a different group try to play these pieces).

In all respects – composition, improvisation, ensemble playing – the outstanding track is *Spain*. Jazz has always (and rightly) avoided complex compositional structures, so as not to disrupt the business of improvising. This is one way in which the building blocks of jazz – and hence the aesthetic standards with which it operates – are diametrically opposed to those of classical music. Corea in this respect succeeds where many have failed, in stretching the sophistication of jazz composition to its limit, without undermining jazz itself. The theme of *Spain* is constructed seamlessly, ingeniously, and elegantly from a group of little subthemes that interconnect in more than one way. For those listeners who wish to trace its course, here is an outline of the opening theme, following the freely paced, flamenco-flavoured introduction.

It begins with three segments, consisting respectively of a rapid, staircase descent followed by repeated notes (six bars long; we may call it subtheme A), phrases that mainly ascend in quarter-note triplet rhythms (four plus eight bars; subtheme B), and a fast, virtuosic, twisting, syncopated alternation of unison notes and silences sounding above simple, steady handclapping on the beat (11 plus two bars; subtheme C). The whole segment repeats with the last two bars eliding into a fourth subtheme, a pretty melody with held notes flowing over the fast rhythmic underpinning (24 bars long; subtheme D). The ascending subtheme B returns (its last eight bars only), then the flashy syncopated subtheme C (11 bars), and subtheme D, which now cycles over and over for improvisations by flutist Joe Farrell, Fender Rhodes electric pianist Corea, and electric bass guitarist Clarke, all of whom place a bop-influenced melodic intricacy into the context of double time Latin rhythm. A recurrence of little subthemes B and C separates each solo. Finally the opening segment, with its staircase motive, signals the last portion of the piece, which ends with a final repetition of subthemes B and C.

Light as a Feather is not a showcase for Airto Moreira, who plays a perfectly appropriate role as timekeeper, but who is afforded no opportunity to showcase his extraordinary gifts as a Latin percussionist. But Farrell, Corea, and Clarke shine, presenting thoughtful and intricate ideas delivered with a well defined, cutting edge (by means of which Corea and Clarke extended the potential of their instruments in jazz). Together during each statement of that syncopated third theme (with handclapping), their playing really is light as a feather, and nothing short of astonishing.

CD

***Light as a Feather*, Polydor 827148-2 (USA)**

Joe Farrell (ts, fl), Chick Corea (elp), Stanley Clarke (elb), Airto Moreira (d, per), Flora Purim (v, per)

London	autumn 1972	**Light as a Feather**
omit (ts)		**You're My Everything** **Captain Marvel**
omit (fl); add (ts)		**500 Miles High**
omit Farrell, Purim		**Children's Song**
add Farrell (fl), Purim		**Spain**

* * *

Astor Piazzolla and Gary Burton: *The New Tango: Suite for Vibraphone and New Tango Quintet*

Argentinian composer, bandleader and button accordion (bandoneón) player Astor Piazzolla stands in a relationship to jazz similar to that of composer, bandleader and saxophonist John Zorn (discussed in chapter 19). Jazz sometimes informs each man's music, but only as a component of a highly personal musical catholicism that shatters attempts at categorization. Zorn's rebellious spirit has led to a sort of high-brow parallel to MTV's titillation, the majority of his pieces exploiting restless, ever-changing, radical juxtapositions of style. By contrast, Piazzolla's equally rebellious spirit has resulted in a much gentler and more accessible juxtaposition of stylistically diverse musical sources within the context of the Argentinian tango. It might be said that Zorn's patchworks offer us nightmares (*Spillane*) and Piazzolla's, dream music. The **Suite for Vibraphone and New Tango Quintet**, recorded in performance at the Montreux Jazz Festival in 1986, is representative, although with the virtuosic improvisations of vibraphonist Gary Burton having been added to the stylistic mix, Piazzolla's *Suite* achieves a somewhat greater orientation toward jazz than is the norm in his music. Hence its selection here.

In addition to its solo and collective improvisations (certainly inspired by jazz, insofar as Burton is concerned), Piazzolla's *Suite* incorporates traditional syncopated Argentinian tango dance ostinatos, including the *milonga*, heard on *Milonga is Coming*, and it utilizes a traditional tango-band instrumentation of violin, piano, bandoneón, guitar, and string bass. Piazzola's musical language offers sweetly romantic pop themes and improvisations, including pianist Pablo Ziegler's rhapsodic, unaccompanied jazz–pop introduction to *Little Italy 1930*, and on that same track, Fernando Suarez Paz's lyrical violin solos, much more closely linked to European Salon music than to jazz. It incorporates changes of pace and mood, as for example in the romantic pop song progression that alternates with the *milonga* ostinato on the opening track, and in the contrasts of tango, waltz and ballad on *Operation Tango*. Piazzola composes complicated unison lines, he presents tango in odd metres (considerable portion of *Laura's Dream* are in $\frac{5}{4}$ time), and he explores quietly subversive *avant-garde* sounds, such as the dissonant harmonies of *Nuevo Tango* and booms, squeaks and squeals of *Operation Tango*. Unlikely as it may seem when described on paper, the resulting sound is beautiful and delicately passionate. For those of us unfamiliar with the role of tango as a political and social force in Argentinian culture (not least in its manifestation as the *tango-canción*, with lyrics of protest), it is difficult to understand just how outrageous Piazzola's instrumental music was felt to be when he established his tango quintet, and how reviled he was in his own country. In the CD pamphlet, Fernando Gonzalez's historical notes and Piazzolla's triumphant comments give us some introduction to this battle.

CD

***The New Tango: Suite for Vibraphone and New Tango Quintet*, Atlantic Jazz 7 81823-2 (USA)**

Fernando Suarez Paz (vln), Pablo Ziegler (p), Astor Piazzolla (bandoneón), Gary Burton (vb), Haracio Malvicino (g), Hector Console (sb)

Montreux, Switzerland July 1986

Milonga is Coming
Vibraphonissimo
Little Italy 1930
Nuevo Tango
Laura's Dream
Operation Tango
La Muerta del Angel

* * *

Jerry Gonzalez: *Rumba para Monk*

Percussionist and trumpeter Jerry Gonzalez formed the Fort Apache Band in 1982 after extensive experience in many distinguished hard bop, free jazz, fusion and Afro-Cuban groups, including those of Kenny Dorham, Dizzy Gillespie, Eddie Palmieri, Tony Williams and Manny Oquendo. **Rumba para Monk**, recorded in the autumn of 1988 and winter of 1989, is but one in a succession of fine recordings that his Fort Apache Band has been making. For its title alone, it deserves mention in a chapter on Latin jazz. What better programmatic description could there be for the idea of latinizing Thelonious Monk's compositions? – a rumba for Monk. Happily the performance is as fine as the title.

Monk's Mood and *Ugly Beauty* are done as mainstream bop ballads, without the Latin flavour. Actually, the disc might have been called 'Rumba para Monk y Miles', because the sound of Davis's mid-1960s quintet echoes in Gonzalez's devotion to the stemless harmon mute (Davis's trademark sound on trumpet), heard on these two titles and others as well, and in the pliability of the rhythm section after the manner of Davis's then-sidemen Herbie Hancock, Ron Carter and Williams, heard here particularly toward the end of the trumpet and tenor sax solos on the opening track.

Gonzalez's Latin jazz may involve the superimposition of bop or hard bop on Afro-Cuban rhythm, as for example on *Bye-Ya*, where herky-jerky, interlocking patterns on bells, timbales, congas and rattle, accompany first Monk's melody and then boppish solos from trumpeter

Gonzalez, tenor saxophonist Carter Jefferson and pianist Larry Willis, before percussionists Gonzalez and Steve Berrios come to the fore. His Latin jazz also may involve a stark differentiation of the two styles. The rendition of *Nutty* juxtaposes the two within the course of Willis's excellent piano solo, beginning with a stereotypical Afro-Cuban ostinato (its rhythmic steadiness being the antithesis of Monk's personal style as a pianist, but none the less fitting in perfectly well with an interpretation of Monk the composer), moving into hard bop and then returning to Latin rhythms for the remainder of the piano solo. *Little Rootie Tootie* is done with a smoothly bouncing, $\frac{12}{8}$ Afro-Cuban rhythm that gives way to conventional hard bop for Jefferson's solo, and then returns, no longer so smoothly, for what proves to be the most rhythmically sophisticated passage on the disc, a lengthy improvisation that alternates between time and double-time (or operates simultaneously in those realms) while functioning as an accompaniment to Willis's solo and then on its own. The interweaving, polyrhythmic, percussion feature on *Jackie-ing* is nearly as great, although its strict 12-bar periodicity puts a cap on possibilities for improvisational development.

A few words on Afro-Cuban instrumentation should prove helpful: the batá is a double-headed hourglass drum, the chekeré, a rattle, and the güiro, a hollow gourd made into a scraper. Clavés are a pair of sticks, and timbales, a pair of single-headed cylindrical drums, often played in combination with a cymbal mounted alongside one of the drums. Russ Musto's detailed CD pamphlet notes also mention a home-made instrument, the guataca, a garden hoe made into a bell.

These sessions of 1988–9 also require a sombre footnote. Five years later, Carter Jefferson died of general circulatory failure while on a dreary winter tour with a pickup band in Poland. In his experiences we encounter a paradox that has become one of the most important features of contemporary jazz performance, as represented in the last four selections in this chapter and time and time again in portions of the remaining chapters of this book (although not with such dire consequences). Jazz styles have gradually become more historical than original during the last quarter of the twentieth century, and as one consequence of this transformation, instrumental virtuosity has become commonplace, because the historical models are now so well defined. Playing jazz has always been a competitive profession, but more than ever before there are any number of spectacularly talented players competing for its tiny financial resources. Hence from this perspective someone as seemingly exceptional as Jefferson may be considered unexceptional and find himself leading the life of a 'mere' journeyman jazz tenor saxophonist.

CD

***Rumba para Monk*, Sunnyside SSC 1036D (France)**

Jerry Gonzalez (tpt, flugelhorn, congas, chekeré, bells, guiro), Carter Jefferson (ts), Larry Willis (p), Andy Gonzalez (sb), Steve Berrios (d, batá, timbales, clavés, chekeré, bells)

New York	27–28 Oct 1988 and 16 Feb, 3 March 1989	(sequence of tracks unknown)
		Monk's Mood
		Bye-Ya
		Nutty
		Little Rootie Tootie
		Misterioso
omit Jefferson		**Ugly Beauty**
add Jefferson (ts)		**Reflections**
		Jackie-ing

* * *

Dizzy Gillespie: *Dizzy Gillespie and the United Nation Orchestra: Live at Royal Festival Hall*

From 1988 to 1992, at the end of his life, Dizzy Gillespie led the United Nation Orchestra, his finest big band since the late 1940s. On the strength of this concert recorded in 1989 at the Royal Festival Hall in London, the Latin Jazz Orchestra would have been a more precise name, for its personnel and stylistic orientation focus on this musical hybrid of the Western hemisphere, notwithstanding Gillespie's titular tributes to a North African city, *A Night in Tunisia*, and historical nation, *Kush*.

The first part of *Tin Tin Deo* is done as relaxed Latino soul, with brief interludes of big band swing, both styles serving as accompaniment to the leader's extended trumpet solo. At the time of recording Gillespie was 71 years old, at which point the task of blowing a trumpet is not a practical idea for most people. Yet here and throughout the rest of the performance, he improvises as in decades past, playing brilliantly original, quicksilver and unpredictable melodies in a typically sloppy manner. That technical sloppiness, which has characterized his playing ever since he tried to match the speed of Charlie Parker's saxophone melodies, seems especially inconsequential when the heady content of his inventions is compared to the technical virtuosity and shallow content of trumpeter Arturo Sandoval's contributions elsewhere at this concert. When Gillespie's segment ends and alto saxophonist Paquito D'Rivera enters, the rhythm of *Tin Tin Deo* moves gradually into

Afro-Cuban double-time. D'Rivera's energetic solo is one of the highlights of the disc.

Taking a step away from the concert's emphasis on Cuban and Brazilian jazz, *Seresta* represents the *vals criolla* (creole waltz), a sentimental, European-derived popular music of the middle class of Lima and the Peruvian coast. Mainly a gentle duo for clarinet and piano, played by D'Rivera and Danilo Perez, this arrangement of *Seresta* becomes ponderous at the end, when the full ensemble bashes through the theme. After a brief pause the track continues with D'Rivera's composition *Samba for Carmen*, featuring trombonist Slide Hampton, trumpeter Claudio Roditi, and D'Rivera, back on saxophone again, all improvising on a fast Brazilian dance pattern.

Tanga begins as another Brazilian samba, but that style gives way to fast bop during Flora Purim's scat singing solo. The finest moments come later, in the alternating and then collective bop improvisations of tenor saxophonists Mario Rivera and James Moody (Gillespie's sideman in combos of the 1960s) and alto saxophonist D'Rivera, and in unaccompanied solos by Ignacio Berroa on the standard drum set, Airto Moreira on an unconventional drum set and Gilvanni Hidalgo, on conga drums, during which time the samba rhythms return.

After Moody's pretty introduction on flute, Gillespie's *Kush* settles into Latin-flavoured funky jazz. A minor-key pattern in a brisk $\frac{6}{8}$ metre serves to accompany Gillespie, Moody, who gradually works toward his wildest personal style of alto saxophone playing, and guitarist Ed Cherry, whose relaxed solo draws from the techniques of Wes Montgomery and Bill Frisell. *Dizzy Shells* features Steve Turré's unique sea shell playing, first in a folk-like melodic improvisation, with occasional rhythmic accompaniment, and then in the context of an Afro-Cuban dance.

The best track is a long version of Gillespie's Afro-Cuban bop standard *A Night in Tunisia*, which, he tells us, 'has withstood the vicissitudes of the contingent world'. The arrangement has a new twist to it: the introduction and the first six bars of the theme's opening eight-bar phrase are done at half-speed and in $\frac{6}{8}$ metre, creating the same sort of hybrid Latin-jazz and funky-jazz style heard previously on *Kush*. The last two bars of each phrase, and the eight-bar bridge theme, are fast and in the bop style that obtains throughout the improvisations. These are by Moody on alto sax, trumpeters Gillespie, Claudio Roditi and Sandoval (the disc notes place Sandoval before Roditi, but the flashy high-note playing is Sandoval's) and electric bass guitarist John Lee, whose nimble melody perhaps outdoes the trumpeters. Gillespie returns to lead the half-speed theme and a series of unaccompanied cadenzas. His own moves into a passage of bluesy soul music. Moody's cadenza sustains a sense of thoughtfully unresolved harmonic tension through a mainly boppish but also bluesy and momentarily explosive solo. Roditi's includes a passage in which he makes the trumpet sound like a Brazilian friction drum. At the end, Sandoval (again the disc notes have Sandoval and Roditi in the wrong order) unfortunately kicks the legs out from underneath the table by playing inappropriate and in the context meaningless classical piccolo trumpet melodies.

CD

***Dizzy Gillespie and the United Nation Orchestra: Live at Royal Festival Hall,* Enja 6044-2 (Germany)**

Dizzy Gillespie, Claudio Roditi (tpt), Arturo Sandoval (tpt, flugelhorn), Slide Hampton (tb), Steve Turré (bass tb), Paquito D'Rivera (as), James Moody (as, ts), Mario Rivera (ts, ss, per), Danilo Perez (p), Ed Cherry (elg), John Lee (elb), Ignacio Berroa (d), Airto Moreira (per), Giovanni Hidalgo (congas, per)

London 10 June 1989 **Tin Tin Deo**

add D'Rivera (cl) **Seresta/Samba for Carmen**

omit (cl) **And Then She Stopped**

add Gillespie (speech), Flora Purim (v, speech) **Tanga**

add Moody (fl); omit Purim **Kush**

Turré (sea shells), Perez (p), Cherry (elg), Lee (elb), Berroa (d), Moreira (per), Hidalgo (congas, per) **Dizzy Shells**

as ***Tin Tin Deo****; add Sandoval (piccolo tpt); Gillespie (speech)* **A Night in Tunisia**

* * *

Luis Bonilla Latin Jazz All Stars: *Pasos Gigantes*

As our own contributor Mark Gardner explains in his pamphlet notes to **Pasos Gigantes**, Luis Bonilla's Latin Jazz All Stars comprised in 1991 a group of young instrumentalists who had grown up in environments where jazz, Latin music and popular American styles intermingled comfortably. Gardner's notes supply accounts of their individual activities.

The title track is tenor saxophonist Justo Almario's arrangement of

John Coltrane's *Giant Steps*. (Just in case it is not obvious: *Pasos Gigantes* is Spanish for *Giant Steps*.) After a brief percussive introduction, the band plays Coltrane's theme twice, substituting a fast Latin beat for fast swing rhythm. Almario and alto saxophonist Ken Goldberg play a blistering unison line reminiscent of Coltrane's improvisation from 1959. Brass and reeds present the theme again, with a chorale-like flavour. Tenor saxophonist Almario and pianist Otmaro Ruiz take bop-orientated solos. Then, without disrupting the tempo, the rhythmic feeling changes to half-time, an Afro-Cuban chordal ostinato replaces Coltrane's labyrinthine harmonies and a riff-like Latin theme begins. Over this new context, Bonilla solos on trombone and Goldberg on tenor sax. The Latin theme repeats. After another transitional passage for the ensemble, the track leaps back into bop for trumpeter Tony Lujan's solo and then just as quickly back to Latin, as drummer Alex Acuña and percussionist Mitchito Sanchez step into the spotlight. Coltrane's theme returns to end the piece. If on paper this description makes the performance seem like a disjunct stylistic pot-pourri, in actual sound the result is seamless and impressive. Almario succeeds in bringing together Coltrane's tortuously fast and harmonically obscure bop test piece, and the rhythmic grooves and harmonical stability of Afro-Cuban jazz.

The band versions of Wayne Shorter's *Deluge* and Tadd Dameron's *If You Could See Me Now* are less elaborate Latin transformations of the original, with the emphasis on soloing rather than arrangement (although there are some elaborate ensemble passages in the uncredited arrangement of Dameron's tune). On *Deluge* pianist Ruiz takes the outstanding solo on this disc. The band's remaining tribute to the standary repertory is *Caravan*, composed by trombonist Juan Tizol for Duke Ellington's orchestra in the 1930s, at a time when jazz musicians had not yet figured out how to work with Latin rhythm. Like *Pasos Gigantes*, the performance uses a stark stylistic contrast, with Bonilla soloing in a conventional bop context during the middle of the piece. Tizol would probably have loved to have heard what the rhythm section does during the Latin portions of this piece, and particularly, at the opening, Abraham Laboriel's rollicking electric bass line, studiously avoiding beats one and three as if he were playing while gracefully dancing on nails.

Goldberg's *Eva* is a beautiful jazz balled, slightly latinized by a syncopated bass line and the use of conga drums. The other original tunes – Goldberg's *Panama* (not to be confused with the dixieland tune of the same name), the leader's *Irazú*, and Almario's *Mambo Barbara* – offer strong examples of Afro-Cuban harmonic and rhythmic grooves. Additionally, Goldberg weaves a bossa nova chord progression into *Panama*, while Almario pays tribute to a mid-1960s, harmonically indeterminate bop style in the introduction to *Mambo Barbara*. Listening to this album, one realizes that any difficulties that earlier may have existed in bringing together Latin music and jazz, have now evaporated.

CD

***Pasos Gigantes*, Candid CCD 79507 (USA)**

Tony Lujan (tpt, flugelhorn), Luis Bonilla (tb, bass tb), Ken Goldberg (as, bar, fl), Justo Almario (ts, ss, fl), Otmaro Ruiz (p, syn), Abraham Laboriel (elb), Alex Acuña (d, timbales), Mitchito Sanchez (congas, per)

Los Angeles	26 Feb 1991	**Pasos Gigantes** (Giant Steps) (arr Almario) **Deluge** (arr Bonilla)
omit Goldberg		**Panama** **Caravan**
add Goldberg		**The Dolphin** **If You Could See Me Now**
omit Goldberg		**Irazú** **Eva**
add Goldberg		**Mambo Barbara**

* * *

Eddie Palmieri: *Palmas*

Pianist Eddie Palmieri, a native New Yorker, comes out of the tradition of American Afro-Cuban popular music. As he explains in his pamphlet notes to **Palmas**, he gradually became more interested in jazz and more skillful at it, although without ever losing his focus on Afro-Cuban rhythm (the core of the music). On this disc he modifies his usual approach, carrying the synthesis much further to the jazz side of the equation.

With one exception the entire disc offers a powerful Afro-Cuban rhythmic underpinning defined by four types of drum – bongos, congas, timbales, and the standard drum set – interlocking in syncopated patterns with bass and piano lines. At times the performances are positively seething with energy. (The exception is *Bolero Dos*, a moderately paced ballad oriented toward swing rhythm and utilizing the Latin percussion in a manner that is superfluous.) Upon this energetic base Palmieri uses simple, oscillating harmonic patterns and cutting, brassy horn riffs of the sort that traditionally typify the Afro-Cuban style. But for his compositions he also utilizes American structures that are more closely associated with jazz. The title track, *Palmas,* is built on a popular song form that underlies the piece throughout the individual solos, until the collective percussion solo settles into a two-chord Latin vamp. *Slowvisor* combines a deliberate Latin rhythm with a 24-bar blues form. *Bolero Dos* begins with a bit of free jazz from Palmieri and then, as his unaccompanied piano playing continues, it settles into a jazzy chord progression composed by the leader.

Palmieri also turns toward jazz in a much more significant way by eliminating the focus on Hispanic lyrics. In fact there is scarcely any vocalizing at all, apart from a brief passage of chanting on *Mare Nostrum* and the leader's occasional emotive grunting in co-ordination with his piano playing. Serving in place of a Machito or a Graciela are a succession of talented instrumentalists: trumpeter Brian Lynch, alto saxophonist Donald Harrison (both of whom are veterans of Art Blakey's Jazz Messengers), trombonist Conrad Herwig, Palmieri himself, and the percussionists. Their solos are consistently fine and need not be graded, except perhaps to point with particular joy to Harrison and the rhythm section's funky improvisation on *Mare Nostrum.*

CD

***Palmas*, Elektra Nonesuch American Explorer Series 9 61649-2 (USA)**

Brian Lynch, Barry Danielian (tpt), Conrad Herwig (tb), Donald Harrison (as), Eddie Palmieri (p), Johnny Torres (elb), Robbie Ameen (dr), Anthony Carrillo (bongos), Richie Flores (congas), José Claussell (timbales)

New York	April 1993	**Palmas**
omit Danielian		**Slowvisor**
add Johnny Benitez (elb), Palmieri, Eddie Palmieri II, Torres (v)		**Mare Nostrum**
omit Benitez and (v)		**You Dig**
		Doctor Duck
		Bolero Dos
add Danielian (tpt)		**Bouncer**

CHAPTER 13

Leaving Hard Bop

Barry Kernfeld

As quickly as hard bop became the dominant jazz style of the mid-1950s, so quickly did it fall away from the cutting edge of innovation. After all, the parent style, bop, had been well established a decade earlier, which is a long time in this ever-searching genre of music, and the rules governing hard bop, if considered from anything but the closest distance, seem not drastically different from those governing its parent. Thus it was that, even as hard bop was inspiring into the 1960s the many notable new albums cited in chapter 9, groups of musicians were searching for new styles, to avoid feeling that their playing was sounding conventional. The radical results of these searches – free jazz and fusion – broke away as no previous style had done and in the process eventually served by contrast to consolidate all earlier forms, from New Orleans to hard bop, into a broader than ever notion of the mainstream.

At the turn of the 1960s free jazz was already well established, but fusion would have to wait another decade while blues and rock musicians showed the way. Miles Davis, Charles Mingus, Yusef Lateef, John Coltrane and Herbie Hancock would later embrace one or other of these approaches. For the time being, they, together with Bill Evans (who never took the final stylistic step away from hard bop), Booker Little and Eric Dolphy (whose early deaths rendered moot the question of their relationship to subsequent stylistic developments), were extending rather than breaking away from the mainstream, retaining some aspects of hard bop while leaving others behind. In the process these leaders made albums which are landmarks in the history of jazz. Perhaps it was the very ambiguity of their situation, their desire to remain in touch with tradition and yet also to invent new sounds on an *ad hoc* basis, which pushed them to the limits of their creativity. And when players such as these are at the top of their game, the results are nothing short of astonishing.

* * *

Miles Davis: *Kind of Blue*

The album **Kind of Blue** is as accessible and beautiful as it is creative and important. By 1959, when his sextet recorded it, Davis was only beginning down the path that would lead a decade later to jazz-rock. But **Kind of Blue** offered a new approach which has come to be known as modal jazz, or modal playing. It is easy to get tied up in knots trying to figure out what 'modal' means, and a crucial mistake in Bill Evans's liner notes to the original LP issue (referring to 'a few modal changes') tightens the knots further (more on that below).

It seems best to use the word simply because everybody else does, but to ignore its meaning, vaguely tied to the modes of medieval church music, or the major-minor modes of classical music, or some scalar pattern used in the music of India, China, Bulgaria, West Africa, Spain, etc. The key element of modal jazz is a single and, for its time, profound idea: the slowing of 'harmonic rhythm'; that is, the slowing of the rate at which chords change. In hard bop and related styles, harmony moves along at a good clip, the chords usually changing at least once every one or two bars, and sometimes as fast as once every beat; to accord with the accompaniment, the typical soloist consequently plays a fast-moving and ever-changing line. Davis did not want to play early jazz or swing, both of these being predominantly tuneful styles, but he wanted to create an environment in which he could invent tuneful melodies. For much of the album, he simply slowed down the harmony. This is modal jazz.

The album was recorded at two sessions a month apart, with (according to Evans) little rehearsal, although to my ears Cannonball Adderley's vastly improved playing at the second session suggests that at least he had thought about this new musical situation for a while, and figured something out. Davis plays brilliantly throughout, and it didn't hurt a bit to have the equally brilliant John Coltrane among his sidemen. Paul Chambers, a rock-steady, conservative player, was the perfect man to maintain the inevitably restrictive bass lines which the new style required. Jimmy Cobb, far less fiery than Davis's former drummer Philly Joe Jones, was right for the relaxed rhythms on every track. The sessions begin chronologically (not in the order on the album) with Wynton Kelly playing piano on *Freddie Freeloader*. The most conventional track, this is a blues in a toe-tapping rhythmic groove, but still there is a considerable nod in the direction of modal playing, in that the blues progression is less complex than that of the usual hard-bop theme. The sighing motif played at the start by the trumpet and saxes underscores this simplicity.

Evans replaces Kelly for the remainder of the tracks. Like *Freddie Free-*

loader, *So What* has a relaxed groove, and its song form (a 32-bar *aaba* pattern) is equally as familiar as the blues. But, following a rhythmically free and harmonically wandering introduction, the harmony is static, the *a* section resting on one sound corresponding, essentially, to the white keys of the piano, the *b* section moving that sound one pitch upwards. After the theme's 'melody', such as it is, Davis plays a lyrical solo. Coltrane discovers Davis's method for himself: confronted with the challenge of playing without the supporting crutch of fast-moving harmonies, he repeats and varies a series of ideas, rather than just 'running the changes'. He came to like this approach so much that it became the backbone of his most famous work while leading a quartet throughout the early 1960s; his *Impressions*, from 1962, is based directly on *So What*. Adderley fails to meet the same challenge and never quite locks into the feeling of the piece. Evans's contribution before the return of the theme is unremarkable. He is mainly filling the spaces between the trumpet and sax riff.

Blue in Green, on which Adderley does not play, shares the subdued atmosphere of the album as a whole, but harmonically it is diametrically opposed to modal jazz. What I find remarkable are the pretty melodies which Davis (playing with his patented brooding sound, produced with a stemless Harmon mute) and Coltrane fashion from the tortuous theme. It moves through an obscure, complex chord progression at a slow ballad tempo when Davis and Coltrane take the lead, then doubles into a moderately swinging pace whenever Evans has it. The best way to learn this theme is to listen to the ending, where Evans repeats it above Chambers's bowed bass notes. This sort of tonally ambiguous writing probably influenced the compositional style of two of Davis's future sidemen in the mid-1960s, Herbie Hancock and Wayne Shorter.

Endless confusion arises from the disagreement between the original liner notes and record label as to the respective identities of *Flamenco Sketches* and *All Blues*. All subsequent recordings of *All Blues* (not to mention good old common sense) confirm that it is, indeed, a blues, but unfortunately this has the uncomfortable result that the label is right and Evans's notes are wrong. The confusion has been carried widely into the literature, including Benny Green's notes for the LP issue in the UK (CBS BPG 62066). *All Blues*, then, is a 12-bar blues in $\frac{6}{8}$ rhythm; repetition of the opening pattern stretches some of the choruses to 16 bars. Cobb plays bop waltz patterns with brushes during the theme and with sticks during the solos, and Chambers, foreshadowing jazz-rock, eschews walking bass lines in favour of a repeated figure closely synchronized with the drum accents. The harmony is even simpler than that of *Freddie Freeloader*, and, for those interested, Evans's cryptic comment that the form 'produces its mood through only a few modal changes' means that, in bars 1 to 8 and 11 to 12 of each chorus, the harmony sits on the pitches G–A–C–D–E–F, the only change being from the major mode (with B) to the minor mode (with B flat, in bars 5 to 6). By this session there is outstanding solo playing from all four men, including Adderley, who has picked up some ideas about this new method; instead of trying to insert bursts of hard-bop playing, he spends much of his bouncy solo developing motifs that move up and down three steps.

Flamenco Sketches is, Evans obliquely tells us, 'a series of five scales, each to be played as long as the soloist wishes until he has completed the series'. This isn't quite true: each segment is either four or eight bars long. But it is true that the number is not exactly fixed, and on more than one occasion Chambers is fooled by a soloist who does or does not move on to the next segment when Chambers expects him to. This open-ended approach was a first step towards Coltrane's modal albums and towards jazz-rock, with its extended improvisations on chordally static patterns. I think this ethereal performance is one of the most beautiful recordings in all of jazz, with the soloists at their very best. Davis, with an eye to his album **Sketches of Spain** (recorded soon afterwards), deliberates over the half-step oscillations characteristic of flamenco music. Coltrane plays with the tender warmth which he was increasingly bringing to performances at ballad tempos. Adderley contributes a complex solo, in part romantic and singing, in part dashing and complex. Evans presents his unique sense of chordal voicing, spreading out and clustering together the piano keys in combinations all his own. Although all the compositions are credited to Davis, at least the first segment of *Flamenco Sketches* comes directly from Evans, who had recorded it as *Peace Piece* in 1958.

CD

***Kind of Blue*, Columbia Jazz Masterpieces CK 40579, CBS CK 08163 (both USA) and CBS Jazz Masterworks 460603-2 (Europe)**

Miles Davis (tpt), Cannonball Adderley (as), John Coltrane (ts), Wynton Kelly (p), Paul Chambers (sb), Jimmy Cobb (d)

New York	2 March 1959	**Freddie Freeloader**
Bill Evans replaces Kelly		**So What**
omit Adderley		**Blue in Green**

Davis, Adderley, Coltrane, Evans, Chambers, Cobb

	22 April 1959	**Flamenco Sketches**
		All Blues

* * *

Charles Mingus: *Mingus Ah Um; Charles Mingus Presents Charles Mingus*

Among the giants of jazz, composer, bandleader and string bass player Charles Mingus ranged the furthest stylistically. While focusing on bop, especially hard bop, his performances explored all of the other main currents in jazz – the New Orleans style, swing, free jazz and fusion – and other genres as well – blues, rhythm and blues, boogie-woogie and gospel music. Two albums recorded a year and a half apart, **Mingus Ah Um** and **Charles Mingus Presents Charles Mingus**, exemplify all these interests excepting fusion, which occupied Mingus in the last three years of his life (he died at the beginning of 1979) and which, I think, yielded the least successful results from among the diverse areas he touched. **Mingus Ah Um** (a pun on Latin declension), recorded by a five- to seven-piece band in a Columbia studio in 1959, is a virtual catalogue of his great compositions. **Charles Mingus Presents Charles Mingus** shows off his talent for improvisation alongside that of the formidable alto saxophonist and bass clarinettist Eric Dolphy, the two men together as part of a quartet which simulated a nightclub performance for the Candid label in 1960.

Better Git it in your Soul is a revised version of a gospel-influenced soul-jazz piece which Mingus had recorded a few months earlier as *Wednesday Night Prayer Meeting*. The theme, shouted out in a medium-fast $\frac{6}{8}$ rhythm by the reed and brass congregation, is in song form (*aaba*), but the body of the piece consists of blues improvisations of changing character. During these a one-note riff intoned by the horns either alternates with or accompanies first a boppish sax solo; second, oscillating piano chords in a pattern not far removed from that of Miles Davis's *All Blues*; third, stop-time choruses in which Booker Ervin's preaching on the tenor sax is accompanied by rhythm only (hand-clapping, bass drum, hi-hat cymbal); finally, before the theme returns, Dannie Richmond's drum solo, which maintains the 12-bar blues pattern in a rhythmic and timbral analogy to it.

Bird Calls, a vehicle for hard-bop improvisation, is notable for the moments of free jazz in the introduction, where the saxes imitate bird calls over atonal piano and bass lines and random drum accents, and at the end, where Mingus adds his shrieking bowed bass to the soft, squeaking saxes. During the main theme, the saxophones are not quite together. This may be one of the examples of Mingus's reputation for rehearsing insufficiently, but I find the push and pull exciting and wonder if it isn't intentional.

Fables of Faubus exists here in two versions, the second one being 'Original', because, according to Nat Hentoff's liner notes for the

Candid LP, the biting and satirical lyrics protesting against racism in America were suppressed for the Columbia LP (Orval Faubus was the notoriously racist governor of Arkansas). The other side of the coin is that Columbia had the good sense to omit Mingus and Richmond's singing, which is horribly incompetent, however noble their intentions. The version from 1959 is well polished and exemplifies one of the ideals of the groups Mingus had been leading under the rubric Jazz Workshop: the interweaving saxophones and trombone move between playing composed material and improvising in a way that obscures boundaries between the two processes. Strictly, as a composition, *Fables of Faubus* is one of Mingus's great achievements, a rare success among attempts in jazz to create substantial structures without losing touch with what makes the music tick. The theme, a 71-bar structure, lasts for over two minutes and takes a complex approach to conventional song form, subdividing each part of the familiar *aaba* pattern into an *aabc* pattern. Separate phrases have a markedly different character, including an eerie chord which builds up in the last subsection of each *a*; a double-time bop passage in the second subsection of *b* and a taunting oscillating figure in the last subsection of *b*; a machine-gun-like attack by the combined bass and drums in the first part of *a* during the improvisations; and a breaking up of the theme's double-time passage into two separate segments during the improvisations.

Pussy Cat Dues and *Jelly Roll* pay homage to earlier styles. The former is a slow blues, and, except in the theme, clarinet replaces alto sax, both for solo work and to participate in the earthy, relaxed riffs accompanying other solos. The latter, recorded earlier the same year as *My Jelly Roll Soul*, has a charming old-fashioned theme. Mingus sets the saxes and piano, playing together in harmony, against trombonist Jimmy Knepper, who improvises and plays composed counter-melodies. There is unfortunately a crude parody of early jazz, with Mingus's slap bass accompanying a ricky-ticky alto sax. Once again the body of the piece is hard bop, which has been lurking just around the corner throughout the album. The final series of false endings and solo breaks again recalls early jazz.

Mingus was fond of Duke Ellington's orchestra and frequently performed pieces from its repertory. *Open Letter to Duke*, Mingus's own composition, has a more tangential relationship to Ellington. After a hard-bop tenor sax solo and a drum interlude which moves into a Latin-jazz rhythm, a theme emerges. It begins in the Latin mood, but slows to a ballad which suggests Ellington as seen through Mingus's curved mirror. Imitating Johnny Hodges, one of the alto saxophonists takes the lead, scooping up to notes in a sensuous manner. But the harmony intentionally goes haywire, with stark dissonances peppered throughout this section. The ballad segues back into the Latin-jazz rhythm and then to a calypso beat beneath a happy alto sax solo; this last part might well have been called 'Open Letter to Sonny Rollins'.

Other references to past styles occur in *Boogie Stop Shuffle* and *Goodbye Pork Pie Hat*. On the former, trombonist Willie Dennis uses a wa-wa mute in the theme and for a riff beneath the alto saxophone's bop blues solo. On the latter, dedicated to Lester Young and his preferred style of hat, the saxophonists recall Young's cool, pure, vibratoless timbre. The theme, one of Mingus's most singable tunes, is built on a completely original 12-bar pattern with a bluesy feeling, yet not strictly the blues.

The album **Charles Mingus Presents Charles Mingus**, as Hentoff's liner notes explain, was recorded just as trumpeter Ted Curson and reed player Dolphy were leaving the Jazz Workshop, after it had held a long residency at the Showplace in New York. This album captures the spirit of their performances, complete with Mingus's instructions to the audience (don't talk, don't rattle your glasses, don't applaud) and his arguments with band members. And it captures Mingus's unmatched skills as a bass player: his roaring, vocalized string tone; his driving time-keeping, on top of the beat; his ability to provide a solid, sophisticated harmonic foundation for the others, without the help of a chordal instrument; his inventiveness and quickness as a melodic improviser.

The form of *Folk Forms, No.1* is a standard 12-bar blues, which this performance carries far from its folk roots, but without losing touch with a blues feeling. Largely disregarding traditional divisions into soloist and accompanists, the four men improvise collectively and take turns in playing solos, duos and trios, textural contrast being a key element in the conception of the piece. The harmonic pattern of the blues moves along steadily, as does the beat. Intermittently Richmond maintains swinging hard-bop cymbal patterns and occasionally, especially during the climactic ending, Mingus maintains a walking-bass line, but for the most part the beat is implicit, the compelling rhythmic drive determined more by the interlocking lines of the four men than by any single time-keeper's contribution. Notable features are, on the one hand, the many variations on basic blues riffs and, on the other, a nearly free-jazz passage in which the alto saxophone and trumpet stab out points of sound (following the bass solo). As he had done on *Better Git it in your Soul* and *Boogie Stop Shuffle*, Richmond follows the 12-bar blues pattern in his solos here; the first one is an especially clear example which breaks into a series of percussive calls and responses.

Original Faubus Fables is much rawer than the Columbia version. The theme is by necessity reduced to a skeletal four-part arrangement, with voices supplying, in addition to the previously unheard lyrics, only a few of the extra lines evident on the fuller version from the previous year. There is one fine new accompanimental figure: during the trumpet (later alto saxophone) solo, Mingus sings in falsetto voice a haunting line which moves either along with or in contrary motion to the accompanying alto sax (later trumpet). The high point of this version is Dolphy's fantastically original improvisation, putting together wide leaps, smeared fast-running bop lines, squeals, simple little motifs repeated at different pitches, and a distorted quotation from *When Johnny Comes Marching Home Again*, all played with a quavering, cutting timbre and a non-Western conception of pitch.

All the Things You Could Be by Now if Sigmund Freud's Wife was your Mother and *What Love* are based loosely on the popular songs *All the Things You Are* and *What is This Thing Called Love?*, but Mingus claims credit as composer on both tunes. The claim is a reasonable one. Unlike many mainstream performances of pop songs, these are radical transformations of the originals.

A motif which had the same shape (not the same rhythm) as that heard in Sergei Rachmaninoff's *Prelude in C sharp minor* found its way into bop versions of *All the Things You Are*. Mingus had put the two together in his 1955 recording *All the Things You Are in C Sharp Minor*, with Rachmaninoff's motif pounded out in a dreary and too-cute trombone counterpoint to Jerome Kern's melody. By 1960 the piece had evolved in a different direction. On the subjunctive *All the Things You Could Be ...* Mingus completely recomposed the theme. Curson's bop-oriented solo generally follows the chord progression of Kern's original, but only listeners truly familiar with it will be able to keep their place, and I am not sure what the point of that would be. In *Folk Forms, No.1* the players make blues the focus of their esoteric performance, but here they mean to blow apart the underlying form. There are extreme changes of tempo, and Mingus regularly leaves the song altogether to invent counter-melodies to Curson's line. Dolphy's solo carries things further away. He was known for his ability to play 'outside', that is to improvise lines which are not in accord with the accompanying harmonies. Playing mainly fast-running lines, he demonstrates this approach, although the notion of 'outside' gradually loses its meaning, because the accompanists, excepting Richmond, get freer and freer. Ultimately, before Mingus's new theme returns, there is a dissonant passage in which Curson again and again repeats a grating three-note riff against Dolphy's wild melody.

What Love departs even further from the original song. There is little reason to classify this interpretation as anything but free jazz. Again Mingus has composed a new theme, which the four men play at a freely varied slow tempo. In the context Curson's solo is somewhat conservative, with the borrowed chord progression peeking out regularly, but portions of it move into free collective improvisation, and a flamenco-like drone recurs where the opening chords of the popular song might have been.

After the theme Curson begins to improvise while Dolphy switches from alto sax to bass clarinet. He single-handedly made this instrument into a viable jazz voice, his style of severe contrasts being well suited to the inherent sound of the bass clarinet, round and full-bodied in its lowest range, harshly edgy at the top. Dolphy begins by doodling in the background. There follows a bass solo, in which Mingus humorously quotes the song *Oh What a Beautiful Morning* and overtly plays the opening melody of *What is This Thing Called Love?*. Dolphy's entrance marks the beginning of a bizarre, hilarious free-jazz duet, in which the two men conduct an argument in an instrumental parallel to street talk, each insulting the other. At one point, just before Dolphy begins an incredible series of growling popping sounds, Mingus intones his playfully obscene speech patterns with the precision of *Pygmalion*'s Professor Higgins.

CD

***Mingus Ah Um*, Columbia Jazz Masterpieces CK 40648 (USA) and CBS Jazz Masterpieces 450436-2 (Europe)**

Jimmy Knepper (tb), John Handy (as), Shafi Hadi, Booker Ervin (ts), Horace Parlan (p), Charles Mingus (sb), Dannie Richmond (d)

New York	5 May 1959	**Better Git it in your Soul**
omit Knepper; Hadi (as)		**Bird Calls**
add Knepper; Hadi (as)		**Fables of Faubus**
*as **Better Git it in your Soul**, but Handy (cl)*		**Pussy Cat Dues**
*as **Better Git it in your Soul***		**Jelly Roll**

Willie Dennis (tb), Handy (as), Hadi, Ervin (ts), Parlan (p), Mingus (sb), Richmond (d)

	12 May 1959	**Open Letter to Duke** **Boogie Stop Shuffle** **Self Portrait in Three Colors** **Goodbye Pork Pie Hat**

CD

***Charles Mingus Presents Charles Mingus*, Candid CD 9005 and CCD 79005 (USA)**

Ted Curson (tpt), Eric Dolphy (as), Charles Mingus (sb), Dannie Richmond (d)

New York	20 Oct 1960	**Folk Forms, No.1**
add Mingus, Richmond (v)		**Original Faubus Fables**

*as **Folk Forms, No.1**, but Dolphy (bass cl)*	**What Love**
*as **Folk Forms, No.1***	**All the Things You Could Be by Now if Sigmund Freud's Wife was your Mother**

Other CDs

plus additional tracks:
The Complete Candid Recordings of Charles Mingus, Mosaic MD3-111 (USA)

* * *

Booker Little: *Out Front*

'A Talent Cut Down – A Promise Unfilled.' Thus read the headline of Booker Little's obituary in *Down Beat* (9 November 1961), when a month earlier the 23-year-old trumpeter suddenly died of uremia, after having suffered from arthritis-like symptoms that hampered his playing. And yet despite this tragedy, Little left a small legacy of recordings far richer than that of many prolific and long-lived colleagues. Among these albums is his aptly titled third effort as a leader, **Out Front**, for which producer and writer Nat Hentoff afforded Little the opportunity to stand out front individually – as the featured soloist and composer, and stylistically – as a participant in the transition from hard bop to free jazz.

Alongside Donald Byrd, Freddie Hubbard and Lee Morgan in the late 1950s, Little followed Clifford Brown in a select circle of trumpeters blessed with a pretty tone, formidable technique and (perhaps more so than Byrd or Hubbard) consistently mature ideas. **Out Front** finds Little playing with considerable restraint and beauty. The other soloists include Max Roach, who finds in Little's music an apt setting for an unusually successful incorporation of spongy and sliding timpani notes into the standard drum set, and Little's frequent companion Dolphy, who pursues his unique style of playing 'outside' (as described above, with Mingus in 1960).

Little's compositions are far less traditional than his trumpeting. Little may have been attempting to adapt to a small group the orchestral collaborations of Miles Davis and Gil Evans, particularly in *Moods in Free Time* and *Man of Words*, where he sets soulful ballad playing against harmonically quirky ostinatos. Another prominent characteristic of his personal writing style is the presentation of themes that are paradoxically tuneful but dissonant, as he combines his trumpet in densely packed block chords with Dolphy's alto saxophone and Julian Priester's trombone. Finally, the quality that carries his pieces furthest from the hard bop style is an interest in contrasting tempos, metres, and rhythmic styles. In his CD notes (taken from the original LP sleeve), Hentoff describes many details of these contrasts, to which a few further comments may be appended: in *Strength and Sanity*, Roach plays a fast Latin jazz rhythm that intrudes upon the slow theme and returns again during Little's solo; and *A New Day* provides yet another example of odd metre, in this instance presenting the hard bop style in $\frac{5}{4}$ time. If these attractive pieces have not moved into the standard repertory of jazz, it is probably because the difficulty of Little's brand of deviant hard bop has dissuaded any attempt at revivals.

CD

***Out Front*, Candid CD 9027 (USA)**

Booker Little (tpt), Julian Priester (tb), Eric Dolphy (as), Don Friedman (p), Art Davis (sb), Max Roach (dr, timpani)

New York	17 March 1961	**We Speak**
add Dolphy (bass cl)		**Quiet, Please**
omit (bass cl); add Dolphy (fl)		**A New Day**

Little (tpt), Priester (tb), Dolphy (as), Friedman (p), Ron Carter (sb), Roach (dr)

	4 April 1961	**Strength and Sanity**
add Roach (timpani)		**Moods in Free Time**
omit Roach; add Dolphy (bass cl)		**Man of Words**
omit (bass cl); add Dolphy (fl), Roach (dr, timpani)		**Hazy Hues**

* * *

Bill Evans: *Waltz for Debby; Sunday Evening at the Village Vanguard*

After leaving Miles Davis's sextet in 1959, pianist Bill Evans mainly led trios. The best of these, with bassist Scott LaFaro and drummer Paul Motian, recorded at the Village Vanguard in New York on 25 June 1961, just ten days before LaFaro died in an automobile accident. Five of the selections are closely associated with Davis: the bop theme *Solar*, the popular song *All of You*, the modal theme *Milestones*, and two excerpts from *Porgy and Bess, My Man's Gone Now* and *Porgy* (this last is an additional title not on either of the single albums). The remainder consists of four pop songs, the waltz *Alice in Wonderland* (taken from the Walt Disney production), Evans's own *Waltz for Debby* (the body of which is not in waltz time) and two themes written by LaFaro. One, *Gloria's Step*, well captures the esoteric side of the trio's playing, with its oblique chord progression and its unusual length of 20 bars (in phrases of five plus five plus ten, rather than the usual four plus four plus eight); the other, a lugubrious tune entitled *Jade Visions*, offers the only dull moment (no doubt the musicians were tired by this time after a day-long marathon of recording 23 pieces, including alternate takes). The trio perform all these extremely quietly at slow to moderate tempos, and they might collectively be described as playing the coolest of cool jazz, were it not for the intensity generated by the looseness and extraordinary creativity of Evans and LaFaro's improvising above Motian's light bop rhythms, as well as the lovingly romantic interpretations of the ballad themes of *My Foolish Heart, Some other Spring* and *Detour Ahead*.

Solar summarizes much of the trio's approach and achievements. After Davis recorded this piece in 1954, it became a jazz standard. In straightforward little segments it moves quickly and endlessly through four keys (D minor – G – F – E flat – D minor – G – F – E flat...) and thus it has the potential to be treated as an exercise, with mechanical melodies and bass lines resulting from a key-by-key run through sequential patterns. But Evans and LaFaro avoid this trap. In part this is on account of a general notion which was then coming into free jazz – conceiving of the string bass as a melodic instrument rather than as a keeper of time and harmony – but more directly it derives from their personal styles. After playing the theme twice Evans lets his left hand rest, and one of the distinctive textures of the trio emerges: two interweaving melody lines supported by the drums. LaFaro, who not coincidentally was also recording with Ornette Coleman at the time, restlessly moves throughout the range of his instrument, from a soft boom at the bottom to a plaintive quiver at the top. He plays perfectly in tune and with great dexterity in a manner which engages Evans in a dialogue more than supporting his solo playing. This dialogue is mostly improvised, although just after the start LaFaro plays the melody of *Solar* against Evans's new line. At times *Solar* seems to disappear altogether, with nothing but the bop cymbal patterns separating this performance from a highly accessible type of free jazz. Finally Evans brings the chords back in to accompany his own melody and the beginning of LaFaro's solo. Later, another convention is slightly altered: we might expect normally to hear the three players together, then bass with drums, then briefer segments with the three alternating with the drums alone; but here, when this improvised trading back and forth begins, the irrepressible LaFaro keeps right on playing through the drum 'solos'. Here and elsewhere this enthusiasm also comes through on endings, where he is the last to stop playing. On *Milestones* someone (Evans?) starts laughing at LaFaro's refusal to quit.

All the tracks from this session demonstrate Evans's original conception of harmony. His playing is at one and the same time cutting, in his use of two- or three-note clusters within chords; precise, in his careful working out of the logical movement of individual notes; and smooth, in his use of the pedal to build overlapping pyramids of sound, as well as reiterating notes (usually from within the clusters) to obscure the boundaries between one chord and the next. Examples include the chordal rendition of the theme of *Milestones* (compare Red Garland's playing with Davis on the album of the same name from 1958), the opening of *Some other Spring* (borrowed from Evans's previous recordings of *Peace Piece*, made under his own name, and *Flamenco Sketches*, on Davis's album **Kind of Blue**) and his reharmonization of the theme of *All of You*.

It may not be surprising, given Evans's tremendous concentration on an imaginative approach to harmony and voice leading, that he sometimes neglects one aspect of rhythm, the independence between his hands. There are sections of boppish playing, with jabbing left-hand chords irregularly accentuating, or filling spaces between, the right-hand melodies. But far more often the two hands attack simultaneously, not in the locked-hands style of such pianists as Milt Buckner, George Shearing and Erroll Garner, but in a disappointingly undifferentiated presentation of melodic and accompanimental rhythms.

Evans's trio was enormously influential. Most specifically, in all but one way (namely that there are no gentle rock rhythms here) these performances foreshadow and define what would become more than a decade later the house style of the recording company ECM. If this session had taken place, say, in Oslo in 1980, no doubt we would be reading in lots of reviews and interviews about the perfect musical manifestation of nordic winter!

CD

***Sunday Evening at the Village Vanguard*, Original Jazz Classics OJCCD 140-2; *Waltz for Debby*, Original Jazz Classics OJCCD 210-2 (USA)**

Bill Evans (p), Scott LaFaro (sb), Paul Motian (d)

New York	25 June 1961	**My Foolish Heart**
		My Romance (takes 1 and 2)
		Some other Spring
		Solar

Gloria's Step (takes 2 and 3)
My Man's Gone Now (take 2)
All of You (takes 2 and 3)
Alice in Wonderland (takes 1 and 2)
Porgy
Milestones
Detour Ahead (takes 1 and 2)
Waltz for Debby (takes 1 and 2)
Jade Visions (takes 1 and 2)

* * *

Yusef Lateef: *Live at Pep's*

The stylistic eclecticism rampant in jazz of the 1990s may be traced back at least three decades to a series of albums that multi-wind player Yusef Lateef made for many labels, including this exemplary collection, **Live at Pep's**, recorded for Impulse! in Philadelphia around the time that Lateef left Cannonball Adderley's sextet to focus on leading his own groups. The reissue on CD includes three bonus tracks and fortunately retains from the original album the informative notes written by Don Heckman, who identifies Lateef's instruments and establishes Lateef's position as a pioneer in the incorporation of elements of world music into jazz and as a contributor to the incorporation of elements of classical music. This present essay adds a few supplementary comments to Heckman's own.

Number 7 is a multi-part exploration of the blues. It begins with Lateef improvising a steaming hard bop solo on tenor sax, which he plays with a muffled tone, reminiscent of Hank Mobley's instrumental sound and altogether different from the hard edge that was beginning to dominate jazz tenor saxophone timbre as a consequence of John Coltrane's influence. The fast opening section blends into a slow blues, at the start of which Lateef invents a strikingly original melody, played 'outside' of the harmony. The blues in turn becomes a drone, and Lateef picks up his bamboo flute, played both with a pure tone and with an added vocalized rasp. Another slow blues begins, and New Zealand-born pianist Mike Nock shows his command of this idiom, in the process making a statement about how far the internationalization of jazz had advanced in the 1960s. A return to the drone and Lateef's bamboo flute ends this elaborate *Number 7*.

Gee Sam Gee, one of the bonus tracks, is a gentle but highly dissonant ballad. *The Weaver*, while mainly a hard bop blues, moves into free collective improvisation for the last minute or so, as do the opening and closing moments of *The Magnolia Triangle*. These three tracks thus find Lateef willing to touch the edges of the free-jazz style, but without making a full break from hard bop. *Slippin' & Slidin'* points elsewhere: it is a simple soul jazz tune underpinned by the sort of straight-eighth (not swing-eighth) drum rhythm that would be commonplace in jazz fusion a few years later. The last minute of this last track is an altogether different tune, not acknowledged on the disc or in the notes: *Delilah* (also known as *The Song of Delilah*), a Middle-Eastern flavoured theme that fits in well with Lateef's vision of jazz. Max Roach and Clifford Brown had recorded this tune in 1954 (see chapter 9).

CD

***Live at Pep's*, Impulse! GRD-134 (USA)**

Richard Williams (tpt), Yusef Lateef (shenai, tambourine), Mike Nock (p), Ernie Farrow (sb), James Black (d)

Philadelphia	29 June 1964	**Sister Mamie**
*as **Sister Mamie**, but Lateef (ts, bamboo fl)*		**Number 7**
omit (bamboo fl)		**Twelve Tone Blues** **Oscarlypso** **Gee Sam Gee** **Rogi**
*as **Sister Mamie**, but Lateef (oboe)*		**See See Rider**
*as **Sister Mamie**, but Lateef (argol, ts)*		**The Magnolia Triangle**
omit (argol)		**The Weaver**
*as **Sister Mamie**, but Lateef (fl)*		**Slippin' & Slidin'** unacknowledged title **[Delilah]**

* * *

John Coltrane: *A Love Supreme*

The 1960s witnessed repeated efforts to wed jazz with an explicitly religious programme: Lalo Schifrin's *Jazz Suite on the Mass Texts*, Mary Lou Williams's *Black Christ of the Andes*, Duke Ellington's first two sacred concerts, Michael Garrick's *Jazz Praises at Saint Paul's*, and, by far the most successful one, John Coltrane's *A Love Supreme*. The spiritual inspiration for the piece dates from 1957, when a strengthening of his religious convictions helped Coltrane overcome the debilitating effects of drug addiction and alcoholism. But the music dates from 1964, by which time he was nearly at the end of a decade-long search after creativity and perfection which led him from hard bop to free jazz. At this point he was playing with his quartet – pianist McCoy Tyner, bassist Jimmy Garrison, drummer Elvin Jones – in a manner which consolidated elements of both styles together with a droning approach to accompaniment derived from Miles Davis's modal jazz (described above).

A Love Supreme is a suite in four movements of widely differing character, the pairs on each side linked by bass solos. Coltrane's opening fanfare and solo in *Acknowledgement* summarizes the salient features of his mid-1960s style on his principal instrument, tenor saxophone (he also played soprano sax). There is his tone: hard, penetrating and metallic in the main range of the horn, it becomes edgy, harsh and sometimes distorted (breaking into two or more simultaneous pitches) in the highest register; he avoids vibrato. This has become a widely imitated sound, though many imitators have developed a facile ability to pop out the highest pitches, not realizing that Coltrane's harshness connects his sound to traditional gritty-voiced black-American timbres, and moreover his very struggle to reach these high notes yields some of the strongest emotional content in his music. There is also his manner of improvising melody by repeating and embellishing motifs. Several plain three- and four-note ideas form the basis for large segments of his playing. Garrison states one of these after the fanfare. Coltrane picks it up in the midst of his solo. The two men restate it together in various keys (without any intention of settling at the same time on the same key). Finally the group chants this motif in gruff voices, to the words 'a love supreme'. Throughout the body of the piece, Jones maintains a samba rhythm, not of the meek bossa nova variety, but rather an eruption of accents, as if a whole corps of Brazilian street drummers had been stuffed into his four limbs. Although Garrison and Tyner have some freedom, Garrison improvising counter-melodies to Coltrane's lines and Tyner following Coltrane into distant keys and higher levels of dissonance, both men return regularly to anchor the piece through drones and simple repeated patterns. Taken together, this combination of factors make the quartet's playing at once esoteric and accessible.

Garrison intermittently plays walking-bass lines on *Resolution* and *Pursuance*, but these two movements of the suite are driven by Jones, who plays hard-bop rhythms in an ever-changing manner which is, if possible, even more effusive than Art Blakey's. Both pieces include piano solos partially indebted to the hard-bop style, but both are based more on drones and slithering blocks of chords than on boppish harmonies, and *Pursuance* has freer elements. It begins with a drum solo emphasizing colour and speed, not the beat. The theme, based on the blues, uses one of the main motifs heard in *Acknowledgement*, and Tyner develops this motif during a good portion of his solo, thus helping to unify the whole. Coltrane's solo is highly charged and at its intense climax the bop rhythms break apart. The movement concludes with Jones and Garrison improvising simultaneously; Jones drops out, leaving Garrison to prepare the calm finale.

Coltrane always had a fondness for ballads. If on one track he was playing at a mile a minute, on the next he might be giving a caressing rendition of a song associated with Frank Sinatra and Tommy Dorsey. In 1963 he invented a new equivalent to the standard jazz ballad, accommodating the idea of a ballad to the aesthetics and emotion of his non-standard style: *Alabama* was a meditative piece dedicated to black schoolchildren killed in the state. *Psalm* follows in this new path and carries it one step further by supplying a text. As Coltrane himself explains in his liner notes, *Psalm* is literally that, a musical narration of the prayer 'A Love Supreme' printed there. (At one point I purchased a reissue which had no liner notes. Did complaints over this omission lead to the appearance of a sticker on later reissues, stating 'all original liner notes & photos appear on inner sleeve'?) *Psalm* proceeds at a free rhythm, as would be appropriate for the singing of a psalm by a church choir, and accordingly the accompaniment is colouristic, with Jones using soft mallets rather than sticks. At the very end an unidentified second saxophonist plays two notes (a musical 'amen') and Coltrane restates at a higher pitch level a bit of the opening fanfare of *Acknowledgement*, thus neatly tying things up.

CD

***A Love Supreme*, MCA Impulse! AS 77 and ASC 77 (USA)**

John Coltrane (ts, v), McCoy Tyner (p, v), Jimmy Garrison (sb, v), Elvin Jones (d, v)

New York	9 Dec 1964	**Acknowledgement**
omit all (v)		**Resolution**
		Pursuance
		Psalm

Other CDs

same contents:

MCA Impulse! MCAD 5660 (USA)
MCA Impulse! DMCL 1648 (UK)

* * *

Herbie Hancock: *Maiden Voyage*

In 1965, when the three men were finishing their second year as the rhythm section of Miles Davis's quintet, pianist Herbie Hancock brought bassist Ron Carter and drummer Tony Williams into the studio to record the album **Maiden Voyage**. Fleshing out his quintet were tenor saxophonist George Coleman, who had been their companion in Davis's group from 1963 to 1964, and trumpeter Freddie Hubbard. Over a decade later, this widely influential album provided the inspiration for Hancock's taking a break from jazz-rock and pop music to tour and record with his group VSOP (also known as '*the* quintet'), with Wayne Shorter taking Coleman's place.

The quintet recorded five of Hancock's compositions. Like Davis's *So What*, the theme of the title track *Maiden Voyage* has a conventional song form (32-bar *aaba*) but fills this out with slow-moving, lush chords (two in each section) which have no strong harmonic interrelationships. The piece is glued together by a reiterated rhythm which shows Hancock's talent for making something new out of a cliché. He takes the stereotypical bossa nova rhythm, accented as on the first line, but turns the accents around, as on the second:

ONE and two AND three and FOUR and / one and TWO and three AND four and ONE and TWO and three AND four and / one and two AND three and four and

The esoteric theme of *The Eye of the Hurricane*, while taking hard-bop rhythm as a point of departure, has changing metres and dense harmonies. The theme of *Little One* has an introspective line played slowly but loosely, accompanied in part by a droning bowed bass, and it recalls such pieces as Ornette Coleman's dirge *Lonely Woman*. But these pieces take no further steps towards free jazz. The body of *The Eye of the Hurricane* is a fast hard-bop blues. The body of *Little One* is a moderately paced hard-bop waltz, but with oblique harmonies.

Survival of the Fittest is a more complex composition without such inconsistencies between the theme and the improvisations. In the first part, a Latin-jazz rhythmic vamp and a fanfare led by Hubbard announce a short, colouristic, unmetred drum solo by Williams. This segues into a trumpet solo, which builds over fast hard-bop rhythms and droning harmony before moving into free collective improvisation among Hubbard, Hancock, Carter and Williams. The cycle begins again, without the opening Latin rhythm: fanfare, drum solo (exploring a different part of the drum kit) and now saxophone. George Coleman is a more conservative player than the others. His solo never moves closer to free jazz than the playing of a dissonant trill, and so Hancock returns to the more comfortable drone. The fanfare announces the second part, an improvised duet between Williams's impressionistic drumming and Hancock's ethereal, atonal piano playing. It is astounding that Hancock has the ability both to create chart-topping pop music videos and to play free jazz in this rarefied manner.

The final piece, *Dolphin Dance*, again shows off Hancock's ability to combine the accessible with the esoteric. A light-hearted melody (constructed largely from a few simple motifs) twists its way gracefully through a tortuous succession of harmonies, juxtaposing aspects of blues, bop chord progressions, sweet static pop chords and bitonal conglomerates of sound, supported by Carter's nimble, dancing bass line and Williams's crisp swinging ride cymbal.

George Coleman takes John Coltrane's tenor saxophone tone as his point of departure, but draws his ideas from the blues end of the hard-bop style. He builds a majestic solo on the open form of *Maiden Voyage*, charges through standard hard-bop lines on the blues section of *The Eye of the Hurricane*, and perhaps proceeds cautiously in negotiating the more difficult pieces. It may be unfair, however, to judge Coleman against the company he is keeping at this moment. I think this is the finest album that Hubbard ever made. As always, following in the footsteps of Fats Navarro and Clifford Brown, his tone is beautiful and his technique impressive. But he has a bad habit of letting technical displays get in the way of music-making. Here for once that does not happen, and Hubbard, for his tasteful inventions, earns the right to be viewed as Miles Davis's substitute in this quintet. His impressive solos on *Maiden Voyage* and *Dolphin Dance* are far more complex than the usual 'well-constructed' jazz solo (that is, start slow and low and soft, end fast and high and loud), and he subtly varies speed, tunefulness and volume throughout.

Then there is the exemplary playing of the Hancock–Carter–Williams rhythm section, renowned as the best of its era. It should be clear from the description of Hancock's compositions that no single style of harmony, no moment-by-moment transition between styles, is beyond his and Carter's abilities. The three men together are equally at ease with rhythm, dancing around the beat with great flexibility while maintaining a metronomically precise internal pulse. They listen intensely to one another and to the horns, and react instantly. Some examples of their fluid work on *Maiden Voyage* are as follows. After establishing the 'warped' bossa nova rhythm, Williams increasingly departs from and ornaments it, such that his playing (especially from Hubbard's solo onwards) is more of a drum solo than accompanimental time-keeping. As Hubbard varies the loudness of his playing the three men follow suit immediately, and when Hubbard (towards the end of his solo) develops a swirling motif, Hancock echoes it (and later repeats the idea in his own solo) while Williams swirls around the drums. Hancock, to start his solo, begins to emphasize groups of three eighth notes, and Carter and Williams join in, not in a simple juxtaposition of three against four, but in an elastic, broken manner which creates an ambiguity between the two rhythms. At the end, as the piece is about to fade out, Williams, having played with a beat that is no longer Latin jazz but not quite yet jazz-rock, introduces a touch of swing rhythm.

CD

***Maiden Voyage*, Blue Note B21K 46339 (USA)**

Freddie Hubbard (tpt), George Coleman (ts), Herbie Hancock (p), Ron Carter (sb), Tony Williams (d)

Englewood Cliffs, NJ	17 March 1965	**Maiden Voyage** **The Eye of the Hurricane** **Dolphin Dance** **Survival of the Fittest** **Little One**

Other CDs

same contents:

Blue Note CDP 7-46339-2; Blue Note B21Y 46339 (USA)

* * *

CHAPTER 14
Big Bands Since the Late 1950s

Barry Kernfeld

The development of jazz big bands from Fletcher Henderson in the 1920s through Duke Ellington in the 1950s was traced in chapter 3. Ensembles based on traditional notions of jazz big bands would never again be so popular, but none the less they retained a large enough audience to guarantee their continuation, even as new jazz styles were developing from the late 1950s onwards. This chapter begins, exceptionally, with an example of Gil Evans's orchestral collaborations with Miles Davis, the most original and successful departure from this tradition. Their collaborations had little consequence in the larger picture, for the simple reason that no-one (including Evans himself) could later match, yet alone develop further, the genius for orchestration that Evans exhibited in these recordings. The remainder of this chapter surveys the continuation of conventional big bands from the 1960s onwards. Gillespie's United Nation Superband, which also forms a part of this tradition, has already made its appearance in the book for its contributions to Latin jazz (chapter 12).

Unfortunately there is of necessity a gap in the survey, owing at the time of writing to the absence of CD reissues of the finest recordings made in 1967–8 by Buddy Rich's big band (particularly the album **Mercy, Mercy, Mercy**) and to the absence of individual CD reissues for Rich's still more distinguished contemporary in those same years, the Thad Jones – Mel Lewis orchestra. (The selection of Mosaic's comprehensive five-CD Jones–Lewis reissue would overstate, for the purposes of this book, that band's significance.) Presumably these keepers of the big band tradition can be covered in a future edition, as new CDs appear.

A very different type of big band, exploring free jazz, developed from the mid-1960s onwards under such leaders as John Coltrane, Don Cherry, Sun Ra, Alexander von Schlippenbach and Henry Threadgill. Their recordings are discussed in chapters 17 and 19.

* * *

Miles Davis: *Porgy and Bess*

In 1957, seven years after concluding their leading roles in the 'birth of the cool' (see chapter 8), arranger Gil Evans and trumpeter and flugelhorn player Miles Davis began to make a series of albums presenting by far the most successful new conception of how a jazz big band might sound. The second of these collaborations, recorded in 1958, is Evans's adaptation, without vocal parts, of selections from George Gershwin's opera *Porgy and Bess*.

From the first phrases of *The Buzzard Song*, with screaming trumpets blending directly into trilling flutes, Evans's originality shines through. In part the newness results automatically from the unusual instrumentation, which expands the orchestral palette developed in their earlier cool-jazz nonet: there is no piano in the rhythm section; french horns and a tuba join the conventional brass sections of trumpets and trombones; flutes join the saxophones. But mainly it comes from the imaginative, ever-changing colours that Evans draws from these instruments. In *The Buzzard Song* and again just before Davis enters with the melody to the title line of *Bess, You is my Woman Now*, the string bass of Paul Chambers and tuba of Bill Barber are paired together, but not as bass instruments; instead they play a jumpy low-pitched melody. On the same track Evans uses massed winds in constantly changing textures of chordal accompaniment to Davis's mellow flugelhorn, such that the overall texture is one of soft colours, but forceful trumpets or dissonant accompanimental lines fleetingly intrude and retreat. On *Gone*, powerful block chords, in unpredictable combinations with and without Davis, provide a framework for Philly Joe Jones's drum solo and a hard-bop trio improvisation (Davis, Chambers and Jones) on an obliquely stated 12-bar blues progression. This provides a strong contrast to *Gone, Gone, Gone*, where the same block chords return in a gentle guise, against which Davis provides a stabbing version of Gershwin's music. On *Summertime* Evans brings an unusual twist to notions of big-band riffs, by having french horns and then flutes lead the riff that accompanies Davis. On *Prayer*, again there are wondrous combinations of sound in the orchestra's 'congregational shouts' accompanying Davis's bluesy 'preaching'. And halfway through *I Loves You, Porgy*, which threatens to coagulate into a sugary gel through its too-heavy reliance on orchestral winds, Evans brings Davis's intense trumpet back in to set the mood to a slow burn.

A good deal of rhythmic ambiguity goes hand in hand with Evans's diverse colouristic effects. *Bess, You is my Woman Now* deviates from being exclusively a slow ballad through arranged changes of tempo and metre. The block chords of *Gone, Gone, Gone* proceed at a slow, free tempo. On the slow ballad *Bess, oh Where's my Bess?* an undercurrent of double-time in the brushwork of drummer Jimmy Cobb breaks through into true double-time in portions of the second half of the track. *Prayer* has no explicit beat at all, and near the end Cobb's cymbals are there to provide tone, not rhythm. *My Man's Gone Now* moves back and forth between a slow and double-time pace. Finally, at the start of both *It Ain't Necessarily So* and *I Loves You, Porgy,* Evans devises rhythmic swirls; on the former the bass and on the latter the flutes play triplet figures, obscuring what turns out to be the true metre of each piece.

Rivalling this *tour de force* in colouristic and rhythmic orchestration is the quality of Davis's improvisations. He plays in a restrained, spacious manner, swinging devilishly in the trio passages and always keeping closely in touch with the blues through his use of bent notes, through the toughness of his attack, and through the plaintive quality of his open and muted timbres. He is not afraid to repeat ideas, and in doing so he has few peers in his ability to restate phrases in a microscopically varied continuum of positions around the beat. On the whole he avoids light witticisms, though he does paraphrase a snippet of *It's All Right with Me* in the fourth blues chorus of the trio's segment of *Gone.* Don't miss the sarcastic kiss he throws into his horn at the last instant of *It Ain't Necessarily So,* as if to underscore the meaning of the title.

This special big band also took up a path usually associated only with Davis's sextet, though it was in fact a general concern of his at the time: segments of three pieces provide examples of what came to be known as 'modal jazz', in which improvisation takes place over static harmony rather than over fast-moving chord progressions. These are the main section of *The Buzzard Song* (beginning at the move from a waltz rhythm into a swinging four beat); the oscillating accompaniment in *Prayer* (resembling a slow version of the title track of Davis's album **Milestones**, recorded by his sextet four months earlier) and the main section of *It Ain't Necessarily So* (closely resembling *Milestones*).

CD

***Porgy and Bess*, Columbia Jazz Masterpieces CK 40647 (USA) and CBS Jazz Masterpieces 480985-2 (Europe)**

Miles Davis (tpt, flugelhorn), Louis Mucci, Ernie Royal, Johnny Coles, Bernie Glow (tpt), Jimmy Cleveland, Joseph Bennett, Dick Hixon, Frank Rehak (tb), Willie Ruff, Julius Watkins, Gunther Schuller (french horn), Bill Barber (tuba), Cannonball Adderley (as), Danny Banks (sax), Phil Bodner, Romeo Penque (fl), Paul Chambers (sb), Philly Joe Jones (d), Gil Evans (arr)

New York	22 July 1958	**My Man's Gone Now**
		Gone
		Gone, Gone, Gone

Jimmy Cobb (d) replaces Jones

29 July 1958	**Here Come de Honey Man** **Bess, You is my Woman Now** **It Ain't Necessarily So** **Fisherman, Strawberry and Devil Crab**

Jerome Richardson (fl) replaces Bodner

4 Aug 1958	**Prayer (Oh Doctor Jesus)** **Bess, oh Where's my Bess?** **The Buzzard Song**
18 Aug 1958	**Summertime** **There's a Boat that's Leaving Soon for New York** **I Loves You, Porgy**

* * *

Gerry Mulligan: *Gerry Mulligan Concert Jazz Band*

In 1960, when this album was recorded, Gerry Mulligan formed what was for its era a 'small' big band – 13 pieces – in which he carried the sound of his pianoless (and for that matter guitarless) cool jazz quartet into an orchestral setting. (*Let My People Be*, the least interesting title on the album, has Mulligan himself on piano.) The arrangements, by Mulligan, Bob Brookmeyer, and Al Cohn, are wonderfully drawn: lush, yet transparent and not at all overblown. This is due in part to the absence of a chordal instrument and hence of any of the incidental conflicts that normally occur in a big band when pianists or guitarists improvise harmonies while the reeds and brass play arranged harmonies. Here reeds and brass alone sound out the details of chords above the walking string bass lines of Buddy Clark or Bill Crow. The lush transparency is also due to the technical perfection of the instrumentalists, whose ensemble work rivals that of Basie's band of the 1950s, an achievement made all the more amazing when one considers that these tunes were recorded in 'live' performance rather than in the studio. Here, in marked contrast to the monolithic, powerhouse playing of that Basie band, is a band that sings gorgeously and swings hard in a delicate and varied way.

Mulligan features his own baritone saxophone playing, trombonist Brookmeyer, and trumpeter Clark Terry throughout these sessions. Four tracks date from performances in Milan and Berlin in November 1960, when tenor saxophonist Zoot Sims supplied yet another strong solo voice. The remaining seven tracks date from a performance at the Village Vanguard in New York the following month, when Sims was absent. The finest tracks are ballad performances of the standards *Body and Soul* and *Come Rain or Come Shine*, the latter with swinging double-time passages, and a frisky romp through *Blueport*, a blues equally interesting for Cohn's subtle arrangement, the drive of bassist Crow and drummer Mel Lewis, and the solos from Mulligan and Terry.

CD

***Gerry Mulligan Concert Jazz Band*, Verve 838 933-2 (USA)**

Conte Candoli, Don Ferrara, Nick Travis (tpt), Willie Dennis, Alan Ralph (tb), Bob Brookmeyer (valve tb), Gene Quill (as, cl), Bob Donovan (as), Jim Reider, Zoot Sims (ts), Gene Allen (bar, bass cl), Gerry Mulligan (bar), Buddy Clark (sb), Mel Lewis (d)

Milan, Italy	Nov 1960	**Go Home**
		Barbara's Theme
		Apple Core
Berlin		**Theme from *I Want to Live***

Clark Terry (tpt) replaces Candoli; omit Sims; Bill Crow (sb) replaces Clark

New York	Dec 1960	**Lady Chatterley's Mother** (arr Al Cohn)
		Body and Soul (arr Brookmeyer)

*as **Lady Chatterley's Mother**, but Mulligan (p)* — **Let My People Be**

*as **Lady Chatterley's Mother***

Come Rain or Come Shine (arr Mulligan)
Blueport (arr Cohn)
Black Nightgown

* * *

Toshiko Akiyoshi and Lew Tabackin: *The Toshiko Akiyoshi – Lew Tabackin Big Band*

Having already spent two decades as a bop musician in Japan and the USA, the Manchurian-born pianist Toshiko Akiyoshi first worked with tenor saxophonist and flutist Lew Tabackin in New York in 1967. Six years later and now married, they founded a big band in Los Angeles, with Tabackin as its featured soloist and Akiyoshi as its driving force, composing and arranging nearly all of the orchestra's repertory. A stylistically representative sweep through their ensuing recordings has been reissued on a self-titled CD, **The Toshiko Akiyoshi – Lew Tabackin Big Band**.

Studio J is situated in the mainstream of big band writing from this period: Akiyoshi opens with a sample of her bop improvising, trombonist Bill Reichenbach solos in the same context, and the ensemble delivers elaborate lines in a tightly rehearsed rhythmic unison. The remainder of the CD shows off the band's individuality, in Tabackin's solo style and in Akiyoshi's orchestral and compositional idiosyncracies.

At a time when the influence of John Coltrane was overwhelming and when it was not yet hip to be historical and eclectic, Tabackin favoured a swing and rhythm-and-blues tenor saxophone style modeled after that of Coleman Hawkins and Don Byas, via Paul Gonsalves. His playing in this manner is featured on *Since Perry/Yet Another Tear*, a patchwork piece comprising a drum solo, a ponderous chromatic ascent, a frenetic passage alternating between reeds and brass, the co-leader's solo (based mainly on the chord progression of *I Got Rhythm*), his unaccompanied cadenza (all these segments constituting *Since Perry*) and finally his ballad playing on *Yet Another Tear*.

One of Akiyoshi's distinctive interests is her use of varied combinations of wind instruments for colouristic effects. The 1960s and 1970s were a time when many jazz saxophonists were doubling on flute. That phase, which has faded away, is well represented on these selections, and Akiyoshi takes it several steps further, using piccolo and alto flute as well as the standard flute, and also bringing clarinet, alto clarinet and bass clarinet into the mix. Hence, for example, *Road Time Shuffle* is situated almost as firmly as *Studio J* in the big-band mainstream, but in the midst of this swing piece incorporating saxophones as expected, Akiyoshi inserts a passage for other winds, their extremes bounded registerally by piccolo and bass clarinet. Not coincidentally, Tabackin himself is one of the best jazz flute soloists, and on several titles the instrument is prominent in improvised passages.

By the mid-1970s, the idea of incorporating world music into jazz (a process surveyed in chapters 17 and 19) had become sufficiently common that it could even be introduced into as conservative an idiom as big band writing. Akiyoshi made her most original contribution by inventing ways to express her musical heritage in this idiom. *Children in the Temple Ground* begins with Tokuko Kaga singing unaccompanied, apart from some unidentified (and overdubbed?) vocal swoops that punctuate her melody. The flutes take up these downward swoops in the body of the piece. It proves to be a gently swinging riff-like ballad in $\frac{5}{4}$ time, featuring beautiful timbral combinations among flutes, saxophones, muted and unmuted trumpets, trombones and rhythm section (including bells). *Kogun* begins with Tabackin's flute, Japanese hourglass drums (the kotsuzumi and ōtsuzumi) and Japanese vocalizing. The introductory idea expands to include the whole ensemble, and it is interrupted by the co-leader's brief flute solo, again in a passage of $\frac{5}{4}$ time. A segment of modal jazz follows, reminiscent of McCoy Tyner's style but with a Japanese-tinged flavour remaining in Akiyoshi's writing for the ensemble. Tabackin returns to the original mood with a virtuosic unmetred and unaccompanied solo. Then the opening segment returns, varied in its order and orchestration and serving now as an ending.

A discographical postscript and disclaimer are needed here. **The Toshiko Akiyoshi – Lew Tabackin Big Band** is a retrospective collection drawn from four of the band's albums of the mid-1970s. The CD pamphlet gives the personnel for a version of *Kogun* recorded in 1974, but the actual version on the CD is from 1976, and accordingly the personnel and instrumentation are corrected in the list below. Also, and again despite the pamphlet notes, general discographies agree that the issued version of *Quadrille, Anyone?*, is from separate performances of 28 February and 4 March 1975 (as indicated below), these having been spliced together. It might be added that these same discographies present numerous disagreements of detail that are not resolved in the following list of musicians and instruments, and as is characteristic in the coverage of big bands, no attempt has been made to sort out the reed players' fluid movements among saxophones, flutes and clarinets.

CD

***The Toshiko Akiyoshi – Lew Tabackin Big Band,* Novus 3106-2 N (USA) and 83106 (Europe)**

John Madrid, Mike Price, Don Rader (tpt), Bobby Shew (tpt, flugelhorn), Charlie Loper, Jim Sawyer, Britt Woodman (tb), Phil Teele (bass tb), Dick Spencer (as, fl, cl), Gary Foster (as, fl, alto cl), Lew Tabackin (ts, fl), Tom Peterson (ts, ss, cl, fl), Bill Perkins (bar, ss, cl, fl), Toshiko Akiyoshi (p, arr), Gene Cherico (sb), Peter Donald (d)

Los Angeles	3 April 1974	**American Ballad**

Stu Blumberg, Price, Rader (tpt), Shew (flugelhorn), Loper, Bruce Paulson, Woodman (tb), Teele (bass tb), Spencer (as, fl, cl), Foster (as, ss, fl, cl), Tabackin (ts, piccolo), Peterson (ts, as, cl), Perkins (bar, as, fl, bass cl), Akiyoshi (p, arr), Cherico (sb), Donald (d)

	28 Feb 1975	**The First Night**

add Tabackin and Peterson (fl)	**Quadrille, Anyone?**

Lynn Nicholson (tpt) replaces Blumberg; ?Joe Roccisano (as) replaces Foster

	4 March 1975	**Quadrille, Anyone?**

?Blumberg or ?Nicholson, Price, Rader, Shew (tpt), Loper, Paulson, Woodman (tb), Teele (bass tb), Spencer (as, fl, cl), ?Foster (as, ss, fl, cl), Tabackin (ts, as, fl, cl), Peterson (ts, as, fl, cl), Perkins (bar, as, fl, bass cl), Akiyoshi (p), Cherico (sb), Donald (d), Tokuko Kaga (v), unidentified (bells)

		Children in the Temple Ground

Richard Cooper, Steve Huffstetter, Price, Shew (tpt), Jimmy Knepper, Bill Reichenbach, Sawyer (tb), Teele (bass tb), Spencer (as, fl, cl), Foster (as, ss, fl, cl), Tabackin (ts, fl, piccolo), Peterson (ts, fl, cl), Bill Byrne (bar, bass cl), Akiyoshi (p), Don Baldwin (sb), Donald (d)

Tokyo	30 Jan 1976	**Since Perry/Yet Another Tear**
		Road Time Shuffle

add Kisaku Katada (kotsuzumi, ?v) and Yataka Yazaki (ōtsuzumi, ?v)

Osaka, Japan	8 Feb 1976	**Kogun**

as ***Since Perry****, but add Jerry Hey (tpt); Loper and Woodman (tb) replace Knepper and Sawyer; Perkins (bar, as, fl, bass cl) replaces Byrne*

Los Angeles	22–4 June 1976	**Studio J**

* * *

McCoy Tyner: *Uptown/Downtown*

Pianist McCoy Tyner played hard bop in Art Farmer and Benny Golson's Jazztet before coming to prominence during the 1960s as a member of John Coltrane's modal jazz and free jazz groups (discussed in chapters 13 and 17). Having quit the group at the end of 1965, owing to his lack of interest in the radical edge of Coltrane's style, Tyner has subsequently maintained a long, steady and consistently successful career in his own right as a leader of small groups, and additionally since the 1980s, an unaccompanied soloist and the leader of an exuberant big band.

In his excellent pamphlet notes for **Uptown/Downtown**, Kevin Whitehead outlines the band's history, describes the tunes on this disc and identifies the featured soloists. Tyner's big band offers nice touches of instrumentation. Reflecting Gil Evans's contributions to big band jazz, the group incorporates orchestral winds and brass: flute, french horn and tuba. Tyner and his fellow arrangers place Howard Johnson's tuba into the role normally reserved for a baritone saxophone in big bands or use it to double the bass line. Listen to Johnson's dexterity as he plays together with bassist Avery Sharpe at the end of *Genesis*.

What might be added to Whitehead's essay is a comment on Tyner's method in its historical context. Even without the explicit tribute in the title of the final track, *Blues for Basie,* it could be argued that this big band of the 1980s and 1990s is a direct descendant of Count Basie's orchestra of the late 1930s. Like Basie, Tyner emphasizes riffs, solos and swing rhythm, rather than complicated arrangements, and the result is a big band that has the sound and feel of a small group, as did Basie's. Like Basie, Tyner draws upon blues for the structures upon which the riffs, solos and swing operate; this is the connection that *Blues for Basie* makes explicit. The main methodological difference – and indeed this may be Tyner's most significant contribution to the big band tradition – is that in place of the popular song forms that Basie also relied upon, Tyner (particularly on this disc) bases his band's performances on static chordal patterns of the sort that he developed while with Coltrane. The results are probably not everyone's cup of tea. Some listeners may find the backgrounds boring. I think the repetitiveness is far outweighed by the inspirational nature of Tyner's compositions, the band's joyful enthusiasm and the creativity of its best soloists, most notably Tyner himself throughout the session and the piercingly emotional tenor saxophonist Ricky Ford on *Love Surrounds Us.*

CD

***Uptown/Downtown,* Milestone MCD-9167-2 (USA)**

Kamau Adilifu, Earl Gardner, Virgil Jones (tpt), Steve Turré, Robin Eubanks (tb), John Clark (French horn), Howard Johnson (tuba), Joe Ford, Doug Harris (as, ss, fl), Ricky Ford, Junior Cook (ts), McCoy Tyner (p), Avery Sharpe (sb, elb), Louis Hayes (d), Steve Thornton (per)

New York	25–26 Nov 1988	**Love Surrounds Us** (arr Jerry Hey)
		Three Flowers (arr Dennis Denizio)
		Genesis (arr Eubanks)
		Uptown (arr Tyner)

add Turré (didjeridu [Australian aboriginal trumpet])

Lotus Flower (arr Turré)

omit (didjeridu) **Blues for Basie** (arr Tyner)

CHAPTER 15

Soul Jazz and Jazz–Soul Fusion

Barry Kernfeld
(and Mark Gilbert on David Sanborn)

In the mid-1950s jazz instrumentalists – above all Hammond organists and saxophonists – found their way toward an instrumental vocabulary which quite specifically expressed the sound of gospel music, particularly the mannerisms of black preachers. Their playing was felt to represent 'soul', after the church. It was also called 'funk', a vulgar term meaning vaginal odor and thus emphasizing the equally important influence of the blues on this area of jazz. Early exponents included pianist Horace Silver (see chapter 9, *The Preacher*), saxophonist Eddie 'Lockjaw' Davis with Hammond organist Shirley Scott (chapter 10, Davis's **Cookbook**), composer Charles Mingus (chapter 16, *Better Git It in your Soul*), and alto saxophonist Cannonball Adderley, in whose group soul jazz emerged as a distinct substyle of hard bop. The present chapter traces highlights in the continuation of that tradition. It ranges from tenor saxophonist Gene Ammons, whose swing and bop style – drenched in bluesy and soulful elements – was easily transformed into soul jazz, to alto saxophonist Maceo Parker, who stepped out of soul music proper (he was James Brown's featured and finest soloist) to make an outstanding jazz album. The chapter also surveys jazz–soul fusion on recordings that share with soul jazz a strong link to blues and the gospel church, but utilize the duple rhythmic patterns of popular soul music, rather than the triplet feeling of swing rhythm.

* * *

Gene Ammons: *Boss Tenor*

From 1960 to 1962, his years at liberty during what was otherwise a decade of incarceration for drug problems, tenor saxophonist Gene Ammons returned to the recording studio to make several excellent albums epitomizing the style that was coming to be known as soul jazz. Mingus and Adderley had explicitly used references to soul in the late 1950s, but Mingus's music was too eclectic to be pinned down to any one style and Adderley's approach with his new quintet (after he left Miles Davis's sextet) was too lightweight to match Ammons's production, as represented by **Boss Tenor**.

There are many connections between these tracks and those in swing and bop styles that Ammons had been making earlier in his career. The repertory itself bears this out, what with his delivering straightforward swing classics, including *Savoy*, as well as one of Charlie Parker's bop standards, *Confirmation*. (Incidentally, despite the credit in the CD pamphlet, the former tune is not Lucky Millinder's riff blues *Savoy* but Edgar Sampson's song *Stompin' at the Savoy*, written for Rex Stewart's big band and first recorded by Chick Webb before Benny Goodman popularized it.) Two elements – one technological, the other musical – separate this music from what Ammons had done before. In 1960, when **Boss Tenor** was recorded, stereophonic sound was just becoming firmly established as the standard in the industry, and the celebrated engineer Rudy Van Gelder took advantage of the device by having Ammons play directly into one channel while locating the second near the rhythm section and with an echo mixed in, with a resulting overall sound that is full and glossy. This type of recording fidelity relates to soul, because of its similarity to the slickness of contemporary popular recordings in that vein (and perhaps also by analogy with the resonant sound of churches). The second and more significant departure from his earlier work involves a greater orientation toward soulful simplicity in his delivery of melody. This is true throughout the disc, and it is particularly obvious in his playing on the slow blues *Blue Ammons*, the riff blues *Hittin' the Jug* (his nickname was Jug) and the ballad *My Romance*, which he plays with a sumptuous tone.

CD

***Boss Tenor*, Original Jazz Classics OJCCD-297-2 (USA)**

Gene Ammons (ts), Tommy Flanagan (p), Doug Watkins (sb), Art Taylor (d), Ray Barretto (conga)

New York	16 June 1960	**Close Your Eyes**

Savoy
Blue Ammons
Confirmation
Hittin' the Jug

omit Barretto **Canadian Sunset**
My Romance

* * *

Les McCann and Eddie Harris: *Swiss Movement*

As the disc notes explain, pianist and singer Les McCann's trio and tenor saxophonist Eddie Harris's quartet performed separately at the beginning of the Montreux Jazz Festival in June, 1969, and then, later that same week, quickly organized a joint concert utilizing bassist Leroy Vinnegar and drummer Donald Dean from McCann's trio, with expatriate trumpeter Benny Bailey sitting in as well. The result, collected on **Swiss Movement**, was five tracks of absolutely compelling, toe-tapping music, including one of the greatest jazz–soul fusion tracks ever recorded, *Compared to What*.

Normally, jazz–soul fusion separates itself from popular soul music by the absence of lyrics, with the focus instead on an individual instrumentalist whose playing fills a function analogous to that of the soul singer. But our subject being music rather than mathematics, there may always be an exceptional procedure offering an alternative way to cross over from one genre to the other. Hence *Compared to What*, which establishes its connection to jazz via harmonic complexities, improvisational style and rhythmic audaciousness, while delivering not merely lyrics *per se*, but politically charged lyrics of considerable poetic beauty. Written by Gene McDaniels (who earlier in the decade had sung the soul hit, *Hundred Pounds of Clay*), the song *Compared to What* is a sweeping indictment of perversions of values and behaviour in American life. Notwithstanding a few specific references to the Vietnam era (and at the beginning, McCann's piano quotation of *The Age of Aquarius*), it remains as relevant today as it was in 1969. McCann sings it with complete conviction, as a gruff-voiced jazz–soul minister preaching to the nation, even as he indicts that very experience: 'Church on Sunday, sleep and nod. Tryin' to duck the wrath of God. Preachers fillin' us with fright. They all tryin' to teach us what they think is right. They really got to be some kind of nut. I can't use it. Tryin' to make it real, compared to what?'.

There are equally fine musical moments, including strong solos from all three principals. Additionally, *Compared to What* has an extraordinary interlude, played just before McCann first begins to sing and then a second time, before the verse with the lyrics 'Uh where's that piano, where's that honey? Uh where's my God and where's my money? Unreal values, crass distortion. Unwed mothers need abortion'. As the harmonies of this interlude ascend chromatically, gradually at first, and then quickly, and after Harris enters, improvising in a swirling and somewhat avant-garde style (rather than in his forthright soulful manner), drummer Donald Dean introduces a rhythmic twist, by pounding the bass drum between each beat (rather than on each beat). The effect is wonderfully disorienting, being completely at odds with the straightforward jazz-rock beat that Dean plays in the main body of the piece. The release of tension at the end of these interludes, as the harmony resolves, the rhythms reorientate, and the improvisatory style settles down, numbers among those moments in jazz that reward listening time and time again.

CD

***Swiss Movement*, Atlantic 1537-2 (USA)**

Benny Bailey (tpt), Eddie Harris (ts), Les McCann (p, v), Leroy Vinnegar (sb), Donald Dean (d)

Montreux, Switzerland	21 June 1969	**Compared to What**
omit (v)		**Cold Duck Time**
omit Bailey		**Kathleen's Theme**
add Bailey (tpt)		**You Got it in Your Soulness** **The Generation Gap**

* * *

Stanley Turrentine: *Sugar*

Working in small combos with organists Jimmy Smith and Shirley Scott, tenor saxophonist Stanley Turrentine was a key figure in the emergence of soul jazz as a substyle of hard bop and subsequently as a style in its own right through the late 1950s and 1960s. In the 1970s he began to reach a wider audience with similar though more straightforward melodies placed into an orchestral and more formal setting. **Sugar**, recorded in 1970, bridges these stages of his career: it still features a small combo, but his blues-tinged melodies are on the whole accessible and quite far removed from the complexity that may be heard in hard bop improvisation.

This album carries modal jazz into the domain of soul jazz. Turrentine's melody for the title track *Sugar* is made from a five-note modal scale, with the accompaniment designed to allow a conventional (i.e. not modal) chord progression underneath. Improvisers are then free to deliberate on the mode or to pursue an harmonically more ornate path. *Impressions* has an even more direct link to the tradition, having been composed by John Coltrane as a paraphrase of Davis's *So What*. In Coltrane's fabulous version (recorded in 1961), the static modal accompaniment modestly influences Coltrane's improvisation, which in the main is free and chromatic. On this new *Impressions* saxophonist Turrentine is characteristically more concerned than saxophonist Coltrane with inventing melodies that accord with the accompaniment, and hence he provides one of the best representations of the idea of modal improvising.

This analytical excursion notwithstanding, the reason for selecting **Sugar** lies elsewhere and requires no analysis. This is wonderful, toe-tapping, funky soul jazz – Turrentine at his best. His companion trumpeter Freddie Hubbard is not at his best (compare Hubbard's work on Dexter Gordon's **Doin' Allright** and Herbie Hancock's **Maiden Voyage**), but there are fine solos from electric guitarist George Benson and the lesser-known Hammond organist Butch Cornell. The title track also has a tasteful Fender Rhodes electric piano accompaniment played by Lonnie Liston Smith, who shows a sophistication that was soon thereafter lost when he went off into the realm of relentlessly boring jazz–soul musical mantras. The other two tracks introduce, from conga drummer Richard Landrum, the soul jazz backbeat rhythmic pattern, a by-this-time conventional device that has a lot to do with why all those toes are tapping.

CD

***Sugar*, CTI/CBS Associated ZK-40811 (USA)**

Freddie Hubbard (tpt), Stanley Turrentine (ts), Lonnie Liston Smith (elp), George Benson (elg), Ron Carter (sb), Billy Kaye (d)

New York	Nov 1970	**Sugar**

Butch Cornell (org) replaces Smith; add Richard Landrum (conga drum)

		Sunshine Alley
		Impressions

* * *

Grover Washington Jr: *Winelight*

Soul jazz, and soul music as a component of jazz fusion, both conjure up first and foremost the idea of unbridalling musical emotion. Yet there is another approach to the incorporation of soul into jazz, in which restraint overrides passion. Saxophonist Grover Washington Jr's album **Winelight** is one such collection, dominated by an aesthetic of clean and careful control.

Washington, the featured soloist, has a complete command of the manner of 'preaching' an improvised saxophone melody, which by the 1980s was a well-established technique, but he keeps a tight cap on it. The sole exception is a let-it-loose passage in the midst of *Take Me There,* at the point where the sweet and slow theme, having moved into a double-time tempo, cranks up another notch, doubling the double-time. The saxophonist, however, stops somewhat short of taking himself there, and the piece relaxes back down to where it began. His guest Bill Withers has a singing style even better suited to this understated approach, and indeed his song *Just the Two of Us* is the best track on the album. And restraint is equally evident in the cautiously funky, deliberately interlocking rhythms laid out by the accompanists, among whom keyboardist Richard Tee, guitarist Eric Gale, electric bass guitarist Marcus Miller, drummer Steve Gadd, and percussionist Ralph MacDonald were all (and often together) ubiquitous in the studios during this era, making just these sorts of albums for diverse leaders (including, most surprisingly, Carla Bley's LP **Dinner Music**) or under their own names.

Before the decade was out, Washington had lost his position as the pre-eminent exponent of this approach, to saxophonist David Sanborn. Though no match for Washington as an improviser, Sanborn had an extraordinary vocalized tone, which added the sense of a soulful cry to whatever he played, however carefully controlled that might be. All in all, this branch of jazz suggests a drastically modified rediscovery of a musical ambience that dates back to Fred Astaire and Cole Porter in the 1920s. The musical sound is unrelated and the social setting comparatively inelegant (tuxedos and gowns giving way to disco glitter suits and dresses), but the same musical impression – characterized by the term 'dicty' (indicating an expensive, sophisticated shallowness) – still well applies. (For a discussion of Washington's work in the context of Withers's career, see 'Supper Club Soul' in *The Blackwell Guide to Soul Recordings*, edited by Robert Pruter, 1993.)

CD

Winelight, Electra 305-2 (USA)

Grover Washington Jr (as), Richard Tee (elp), Raymond Chew, Paul Griffin (clarinets), Eric Gale (g), Marcus Miller (elb), Steve Gadd (d), Ralph MacDonald (congas, per, syndrums)

	June–July 1980	**Winelight**
*as **Winelight**, but Washington (ss)*		**In the Name of Love**
Washington (as); Griffin (elp) replaces Tee; add Ed Walsh (syn)		**Let It Flow (For 'Dr. J.')**
*as **Let It Flow**, but Washington (ts)*		**Take Me There**
Tee (elp) replaces Griffin, Bill Eaton (syn) replaces Walsh; add Robert Greenidge (steel drums), Bill Withers, Hilda Harris, Yvonne Lewis, Ullanda McCullough (v)		**Just the Two of Us**
Washington (as); omit (syn, steel drums, v)		**Make Me a Memory (Sad Samba)**

* * *

David Sanborn: *Close-up* (by Mark Gilbert)

'What I do is very superficial and very obvious. What I do takes about five minutes to figure out': alto saxophonist David Sanborn (interviewed by the author). Few people are likely to argue with Sanborn's assessment of the technical content of his music, yet paradoxically the emotional depth of his playing has made him perhaps the most imitated alto saxophonist of his generation. There is no better example of that intensity than the tortured but defiant scream some two minutes into *Pyramid* on **Close-up**, an album that forms the most comprehensive and effective statement of Sanborn's style.

Soon after recording **Close-up**, Sanborn was heard to regret any contribution he had made to the blandness of pop-jazz. However – another paradox – it is chiefly in the hands of his imitators that the idiom has tended to hollowness. Even at times of greatest danger – here when reading the Stylistics' maudlin old hit *You Are Everything* – Sanborn is able to scrape through with creativity, conviction and perhaps a few redeeming touches of irony.

Sanborn himself is not without precedents. He cites the 'human cry' in the tone of alto saxophonist Hank Crawford as his chief inspiration. Yet as **Close-up** demonstrates, he has added enough to the idiom to become one of its most immediately recognizable voices. Like countless other performances, *Pyramid* well represents his manner of bringing bluesy vocalization of tone to a new level. Additionally, and thanks in large part to bassist and producer Marcus Miller's grasp of contemporary idiom and technology, Sanborn's album also expanded the form and content of soul-jazz, incorporating and refining techniques originating in mainstream soul and pop. Before **Close-up**, the intricately-arranged, metallic funk and crisp, compressed production of *Slam*, *Pyramid* and *Tough* were unknown in instrumental jazz. After this, as was the way in the early 1990s, Sanborn sought 'new' but ironically regressive directions in post-modern, low-tech reprises of 1960s rhythm-and-blues, thus leaving **Close-up** to stand as his finest and most original statement.

CD

***Close-up*, Reprise 7599-25715-2 (USA)**

David Sanborn (as, v), Hiram Bullock, Nile Rodgers (elg), Marcus Miller (elb, kbd, percussion syn, v), Steve Jordan (d, drum syn), Terry Bardani, Cliff Braithwaite, Adam Dorn, Ava Gardner, Bibi Green, Bill Jones, Wayman Tisdale (v)
*c.*1987 **Slam**

Sanborn (as), Ricky Peterson (elp), Jeff Mironov (g), Miller (elb, elg, kbd, percussion syn), Andy Newmark (d)
J. T.

Sanborn (as), Peterson (elp), Bullock (elg), Mironov (g), Miller (elb, kbd), Vinnie Colaiuta (d), Paulinha da Costa (per), Michael Ruff (v)
Leslie Ann

G. E. Smith (elg) replaces Bullock; omit Ruff **Goodbye**

Sanborn (as), Miller (p, kbd) **Same Girl**

Sanborn (as), Ricky Peterson (elp, kbd), Paul Jackson, Jr. (elg), Miller (elb, kbd, percussion syn), William Ju Ju House (d)
Pyramid

Sanborn (as), Peterson (kbd), Bullock, Jackson (elg), Miller (elb, kbd, percussion syn)
Tough

Sanborn (as), Peterson (elp), Jackson, Smith (elg), Miller (elb, kbd, elg), Coliauta (d), da Costa (congas, per)
So Far Away

Sanborn (as), Peterson (elp), Jackson (elg), Miller (elb, kbd), Coliauta (d), da Costa (per)
You Are Everything

omit Jackson; add Don Alias (per) **Camel Island**

* * *

Groove Holmes: *Blues All Day Long*

This type of album (of which there are many) and in particular the opening minutes of its title track, *Blues All Day Long*, exemplify the heart of soul jazz. In the rhythm section, Groove Holmes punches out a bop- and blues-based chord progression on Hammond organ, while simultaneously providing a walking bass line with deep, lush and velvet-smooth organ tones serving in place of a string bass; Jimmy Ponder deftly strums his electric guitar in co-ordination with the organ bass; and drummer Cecil Brooks starts out with a gentle swing rhythm on the cymbal, bringing in a heavy backbeat as the emotion of the performance intensifies. Above this soul jazz underpinning, and following a rifflike blues theme, tenor saxophonist Houston Person 'signifies' the blues, blending the passion of rhythm-and-blues tenor saxophone licks with the intellectuality of hard bop improvisation. Ponder follows with a tasty solo, and then Holmes displays his blues style, nipping out bop lines before building up to a level of volume and density that only the organ can supply.

More broadly speaking, **Blues All Day Long** exemplifies how soul jazz partakes of blues, gospel, soul, and hard bop, and by the fact of this diversity distinguishes itself from these styles. As expected, the CD includes soulful blues tracks: *Minor Inconvenience*, a boppish blues in a minor key; *Groove's Groove*, based on a traditional Charleston riff and shuffle rhythm; and *Slo Blooze* (yes, a slow blues). But on two tracks the style has been filtered through soul music of the 1970s: *Cheeka's Dance*, a soul-jazz bossa-nova hybrid with Ponder paying homage to Wes Montgomery's manner of soloing in octaves, but also with the rhythms of Latino soul, recalling El Chicano's *Viva Tirado*; and a version of Benny Golson's hard bop composition *Killer Joe*, now updated to resemble the O'Jays' *For the Love of Money*. The CD also features a timeless, pan-stylistic ballad, *These Foolish Things*, again featuring Person. Great musicians know that if one is going to play a ballad in a convincing manner, one had better know not just the melody, but the words too. In this simple and elegant demonstration, Person 'sings' the lyrics on his saxophone.

CD

***Blues All Day Long*, Muse MCD 5358 (USA)**

Cecil Bridgewater (tpt), Houston Person (ts), Groove Holmes (org), Jimmy Ponder (elg), Cecil Brooks III (drums)
Englewood Cliffs, NJ 24 Feb 1988 **Blues All Day Long**

omit Bridgewater	**These Foolish Things**
add Bridgewater	**Killer Joe** **Cheeka's Dance**
add Ralph Dorsey (conga)	**Minor Inconvenience**
omit Dorsey	**Groove's Groove**
omit Bridgewater	**Slo Blooze**

* * *

Dirty Dozen Brass Band: *The New Orleans Album*

New Orleans brass bands made crucial contributions to the development of jazz, and as such their work should have figured prominently in our chapter on the first hot bands. Unfortunately the leading bands – the Excelsior, Onward, Reliance, Tuxedo and Eureka – did not record during that era, probably because their semiprofessional status, their ever-changing personnel, and their intimate connection to the social life of New Orleans precluded their coming to the major studios centred around New York and Chicago. Later developments brought about a modest body of recordings, including a homemade recording of the Eureka in 1951 (discussed in chapter 6) and studio sessions by the Young Tuxedo Brass Band (1958) and the Eureka (1962), but only with the flowering of the Dirty Dozen Brass Band in the mid-1980s did brass band recording break out of its confines to reach a non-specialist audience.

Some basic awareness of this historical background should help not only to lend meaning to the group's name, but also to explain a few features of instrumentation and style. Although nowadays the Dirty Dozen are far more likely to be found in a nightclub or on a festival stage than on the streets of New Orleans, they are essentially a marching band, comprising brass (trumpets and trombone), reeds (in this instance saxophones, not clarinet), brass bass (the sousaphone, a wraparound tuba designed for marching), drums (the bass drum and snare drum chores handled separately, rather than by a single drummer sitting at a drum set) and miscellaneous hand-held percussion. The resultant sound most closely linking the Dirty Dozen to their predecessors, and most distinctively separating them from modern traditions, is a particular emphasis on continuous and often elaborate patterns played on the snare drum (perhaps supplemented by syncopated patterns struck on the cowbell), these functioning in place of continuous patterns played on a cymbal.

At the same time, it is equally important to understand that the Dirty Dozen draw heavily from bop, rhythm-and-blues, and jazz–funk fusion. Consequently they offer a radical transformation of the New Orleans brass band tradition (however that may have sounded originally). In a tribute to popular styles that have been equally as important as jazz in the cultural heritage of New Orleans, the band carry their stylistic syntheses further than usual on **The New Orleans Album**, with guest stars singing novelty and party songs and adding piano and guitar to the instrumental mix. The heart of the group's sound, though, is heard on such strictly instrumental brass band pieces as *Inside Straight*, *Hannibal* and *Snowball*. These offer simple (and often static) harmonies; crisp horn riffs; funky improvisations (with jazz elements entering via moments of dissonant or free playing, as well as via the instrumentalists' technical virtuosity); and parade rhythms, all anchored by Kirk Joseph's extraordinarily punchy sousaphone lines. His solo opening to *Snowball*, in which the sousaphone coos like a dove, is not to be missed.

CD

***The New Orleans Album*, Columbia CK 45414 (USA)**

Gregory Davis (tpt, per), Efrem Towns (tpt), Kevin Harris (ts, per), Roger Lewis (bar, per), Kirk Joseph (sousaphone), Jenell Marshall (snare drum, per), Lionel Batiste (bass drum, per)

New Orleans Aug–Dec 1989 **Inside Straight**

add Charles Joseph (tb), Lewis (ss), Eddie Bo (p, v)

When I'm walking (let me walk)

as Inside Straight **Hannibal**

add Bo (p), Danny Barker (g, v) **Don't you feel my leg**

omit Bo; Elvis Costello (v) replaces Barker (v) **That's how you got killed before**

add Bo (p); omit Barker, Costello **Song for Bobe**

omit Bo; add Dave Bartholomew (tpt, v) **The Monkey**

Davis (tpt, per), Towns (tpt), Harris (ts, per), Lewis (ss, bar, per), Joseph (sousaphone), Batiste (snare drum, per), Marshall (bass drum, per)

Snowball

add Davis (v), Charles Joseph (tb) **Me like it like that**

omit (v), (tb), (ss) **Kidd Jordan's Second Line**

* * *

Maceo Parker: *Roots Revisited*

As a star in James Brown's band for many years, alto saxophonist Maceo Parker is one of the most revered soloists in all of soul music. Here on **Roots Revisited** he takes a rare step away from the rigorous formality required of instrumentalists in that genre, to cross over instead into the somewhat looser domain of soul jazz and jazz–soul fusion. Hence alongside the qualities that make him so spectacular with Brown – a hefty, biting tone, and the ability to invent deft, skittering, syncopated melodies articulated with unbelievable clarity – in this new context we additionally get the bonus of hearing Parker present themes and then stretch out for extended improvisations.

The band's personnel and repertory also exemplify the jazz–soul synthesis. With the altoist are fellows from Brown's band, trombonist Fred Wesley and tenor saxophonist Pee Wee Ellis, neither of whom is a match for Parker in this arena. The three horn players are joined by jazz organist Don Pullen (who carries the bass lines playing the organ foot pedals), guitarist Rodney Jones, and drummer Bill Stewart. Pullen has an amazing ability to leap effortlessly between free jazz and the most downhome jazz style and displays a far more esoteric side elsewhere among our selections (see chapter 19). Bootsy Collins, another of Brown's colleagues, replaces Pullen to provide characteristically sparkling electric guitar chords and a strutting and popping electric bass guitar line for the disc's funkiest selection, *In Time*. Serving in the role of singer Ray Charles, Parker offers a joyful, bouncy reading of *Them that Got*. He delivers a tender but pointedly unsentimental reading of the classic ballad *Over the Rainbow*. On a funked up remake of Charlie Parker and Jay McShann's riff tune *The Jumpin' Blues*, here retitled *Jumpin' the Blues*, Pullen supplements the leader's contribution with a wonderfully imaginative solo contrasting snappy little melodies with grand sweeps up and down the keyboard. In a version of Charles Mingus's *Better Get Hit in Yo' Soul* quite faithful to the original, Parker (that is, Maceo, not Charlie!) delivers a soulful solo unmatched by any altoist who recorded the tune in Mingus's Jazz Workshop. Particularly striking is the way that he leads the band through one of Mingus's arranged passages, punching out isolated syncopated notes. This occurs shortly before the portion of his solo accompanied by drums and handclapping alone. Among the other tracks is Curtis Mayfield's soul hit *People Get Ready* and Parker's relaxed and lengthy improvisation on a chordal background borrowed from James Brown's hit *It's a Man's World*, here retitled *Children's World* and credited to Parker himself.

CD

***Roots Revisited*, Verve 843 751-2 (USA) and Minor Music 801015 (?)**

Fred Wesley (tb), Maceo Parker, Vince Henry (as), Pee Wee Ellis (ts), Don Pullen (org), Rodney Jones (elg), Bill Stewart (d)

New York	*c.*1990	**Them that Got**
omit Henry		**Children's World**
		Better Get Hit in Yo' Soul
		People Get Ready
		Up and Down East Street
		Over the Rainbow
		Jumpin' the Blues

Wesley, Parker (as, p, org), Ellis, Jones, Bootsy Collins (elg, elb), Stewart

Cincinnati	*c.*1990	**In Time**

* * *

Malachi Thompson: *The Jaz Life*

Trumpeter Malachi Thompson's disc **The Jaz Life** belongs to the bop revival for its general stylistic approach, and within bop's derivatives, to soul jazz, for the leader's blues *In Walked John*. This is a two-headed piece in which a rhythm-and-blues flavoured theme frames a second double-time hard bop theme, the latter serving as the basis for solos, of which the finest is tenor saxophonist Carter Jefferson's soulful improvisation. But the real reason for calling attention to **The Jaz Life**, and its relation to soul jazz, is a sensational re-creation of Ray Charles's song *Drown in My Own Tears*, on which trumpet and saxophones take the place of singers. Every jazz fan knows how central the repertory of American popular song is to jazz. What seems surprising is how little has been done to develop a parallel relationship for rhythm-and-blues songs and soul songs, bringing them into the standard repertory. Perhaps it is just too difficult, the transformation requiring not only the ability to improvise over a given theme, but also to capture instrumentally the flavour of those rhythm-and-blues and soul singers. Of those who have made the effort, trumpeter Lester Bowie has been a leading practitioner since 1981, when he remade the song *The Great Pretender* (on the album of the same name). But with Bowie, there is always a feeling of laughing at things instead of with them, and almost of contempt, as if he thought he were taking inferior music and uplifting it into jazz. With Thompson's *Drown in My Own Tears*, no such feeling arises. If the performance evokes laughs (or tears), these are joyful. The last minutes – with 'preacher' Joe Ford testifying on his alto sax as the trumpet and tenor sax 'congregation' joins in with its accompanying riffs – constitute another of those magical moments in jazz.

CD

***The Jaz Life*, Delmark DD–453 (USA)**

Malachi Thompson (tpt), Joe Ford (as), Carter Jefferson (ts), Kirk Brown (p), Harrison Bankhead (sb), Nasar Abadey (d)

Chicago	30 June 1991	**In Walked John**
omit Ford		**My Romance**
add Ford		**Drown in My Own Tears** **Mystic Trumpet Man**
Ford (ss); add Richard Lawrence (conga drums)		**Croquet Ballet**
omit Ford		**Lucky Seven**

CHAPTER 16

The Bop Revival

Barry Kernfeld
(and Mark Gardner on Johnny Griffin)

The golden years of rock were a dark age for bop in America. From the mid-1960s into the 1970s bop was too old to be fashionable and too young to be classic. Several leading players moved to Europe, including Dexter Gordon, Johnny Griffin, Kenny Drew and Albert 'Tootie' Heath (some of whom had left the USA for non-musical reasons), and there they discovered better opportunities to perform their preferred style. They also encountered prodigious homegrown talents, including Niels-Henning Ørsted Pedersen and Tete Montoliu. A few of their mid-1970s recordings for SteepleChase, a Danish label, serve to introduce, in effect, a prehistory of the bop revival.

The revival encompasses bop in the broadest sense of the term, stretching stylistically from Parker and Gillespie's bop through cool jazz, hard bop and soul jazz, to the transitional style modal jazz; it also embraces ballad playing and Latin jazz (both Afro-Cuban and Brazilian). Blossoming from the mid-1970s onwards, it gained impetus from many directions. Gordon and Griffin resumed performing in the USA and thereby sparked an interest in veteran players that continues to be strong. Other veterans (most notably Phil Woods, also an expatriate from 1968–72), having tried their hand at jazz-fusion, eventually realized that their talents were better suited to bop and that the musical climate now encouraged their return. Some *avant-garde* musicians, motivated by musical interests and also by the recognition that free jazz was not commercially viable, began to take up 'the tradition' (i.e., bop and its derivatives). And a new generation of players grew to musical maturity.

Given the revival's prehistory in Europe, it is perhaps not surprising that a young player like French pianist Michel Pettruciani (born in 1962) would have developed his extraordinary skills. But during the style's dark age, no-one could possibly have anticipated the extent of contributions that would be forthcoming from young African-Americans, who then were overwhelmingly interested in soul music and (within jazz) *avant-garde* or fusion styles, rather than bop. The defining moment of change came in 1980, when Art Blakey hired Wynton Marsalis. Marsalis subsequently has acquired substantial clout in the world of jazz (in so far as that is possible within this often powerless realm). He and his colleagues, veterans and young alike, have made the bop revival into one of music's two prevailing popular styles, alongside jazz fusion. As a consequence of their often self-conscious efforts (and also as a consequence of a different and more eclectic approach, discussed in chapter 19), the identity of jazz seems to be changing, as it increasingly becomes a music of historical performance.

* * *

Kenny Drew and Niels-Henning Ørsted Pedersen: *Duo*

In the spring of 1973 pianist Kenny Drew and string bassist Niels-Henning Ørsted Pedersen recorded an album simply entitled **Duo**. It helped launch the then fledgling label SteepleChase, and it remains today one of the loveliest documents of the preservation and continuation of the bop style in Europe during that period. As Ib Skovgaard explains in LP liner notes (reproduced in the reissue on CD) tracing their biographies up to the early 1970s, the two men had held many residencies at the Montmartre Jazzhus in Copenhagen since the mid-1960s. This work involved playing in a conventionally high-charged hard bop style, but it also allowed them to develop the sensitive, interactive musicality and unusual repertory displayed on **Duo**.

As far as possible, the musicians strive to create varied textures. They present their normal combination of piano and string bass, and perhaps not coincidentally their experience with this instrumentation contributes to the strength of the two takes of *I Skovens Dybe Stille Ro* (In the Forest's Deep Stillness) (take one having been added as a bonus track on the CD), Drew's balled *Serenity*, and his *Duo Trip* (this last title being incidentally the only performance on the disc even remotely related to the skittery, energized side of bop). In addition to the duos with conventional instrumentation, they offer one little bit of 'cheating' – the duo becomes a trio, guitarist Ole Molin having been added for a reading of the swing tune *Do you know what it means to miss New Orleans*; two unaccompanied tracks, Drew showing his romantic skill on his own composition *Come Summer* and Ørsted Pedersen presenting a brief

Lullaby; and a few tracks on which Drew doubles on Fender Rhodes piano (playing sometimes with one hand on that electric instrument and the other on the conventional piano). Ørsted Pedersen adds a fourth part on Antonio Carlos Jobim's tune *Wave*, by droning out a syncopated bossa nova rhythm while soloing melodically. This feat is just one manifestation of the bassist's astonishing technical skills. Throughout the album he functions every bit as Drew's equal in the presentation of themes and in improvisation. His bowed playing on *Kristine* displays somewhat questionable intonation, but elsewhere, plucking the instrument, he presents bass lines precisely with a remarkably full and roaring tone and then leaps into the instrument's unwieldy upper register, handling it as if he were playing cello.

One intriguing aspect of the album is the duo's selection of traditional Scandinavian tunes. *Det Var en Lørdag Aften* (It Was a Saturday Night) has the sort of cutie-pie fluffiness that might be expected in the union of Danish folk music with jazz, but *I Skovens Dybe Stille Ro* works perfectly well. The duo give hauntingly beautiful performances that now, with the bonus track added, are positioned fittingly to frame the disc. Their renditions anticipate electric guitarist Pat Metheny's later evocations of the midwestern cowboy song as a vehicle for jazz. This musical-cultural connection between Scandinavian melancholy and American cowboy loneliness is perhaps not surprising, but many of us might be surprised at how well these qualities may be integrated with the African-American gospel tradition, brought in via Drew's soulful playing.

CD

***Duo*, SteepleChase SCCD-31002 (Denmark)**

Kenny Drew (p), Niels-Henning Ørsted Pedersen (sb)

Copenhagen	2 April 1973	**I Skovens Dybe Stille Ro** (take 2)
Drew		**Come Summer**
Ørsted Pedersen		**Lullaby**
Drew, Ørsted Pedersen		**Kristine** **Serenity**
add Drew (elp)		**Det Var en Lørdag Aften**
omit (elp); add Ole Molin (g)		**Do you know what it means to miss New Orleans**

add (elp); omit Molin	**Wave**
omit (elp)	**Duo Trip**
add (elp)	**Hush-a-bye**
omit (elp)	**I Skovens Dybe Stille Ro** (take 1)

* * *

Johnny Griffin: *Blues for Harvey* (by Mark Gardner)

No other jazz tenor saxophonist sounds remotely like Johnny Griffin, whose breathy, vocal, bluesy and ultra-fast lines have a unique flavour, redolent of highly spiced but delicious cuisine. Griffin embarked from his native Chicago at the age of 17 with the frenetic Lionel Hampton Orchestra, which already had a tradition for saxophone hysteria. From there he jumped into Joe Morris's rhythm-and-blues combo, which boasted such sterling assets as pianist Elmo Hope and drummer Philly Joe Jones. Griffin's career really blossomed in the 1950s when he moved to New York and enjoyed two productive spells in the group of Thelonious Monk and a stint with the Jazz Messengers. He later co-led a quintet with fellow saxophonist Eddie 'Lockjaw' Davis before emigrating to Europe.

Griffin became renowned for his dexterity in up-tempo exercises, but in his case technique was used as a means to an end; his bubbling personality sought expression with the rhythmic accelerator pressed hard down. In excessive moments this can be positively exhausting to the listener, but at his best Griffin brings a splendid sense of exhilaration to his music, pouring out great smears of notes that form a logical pattern. His penchant for breakneck gallops and the pressure they put him under should not disguise the fact that Griffin is also a most capable interpreter of slow ballads and the most basic of blues, to which his edgy tone is best suited.

While many observers have cited John Coltrane's collaboration with Monk as being of particular significance, there can be little doubt that Griffin also brought a fine appreciation to the pianist's compositions. His rhythmic fluidity lent Monk's spiky, angular pieces a feeling not previously indicated, and Griffin's sly and ready wit matched that of his keyboard employer. The experience with Monk made a lasting impact on Griffin who, for many years thereafter, used Monk's melody

Rhythm-a-ning as an opening and closing theme in club performances. Indeed, on this album he appends a flashing fragment of Monk's tune at the very end.

The album stems from a relaxed and happy stage of Griffin's career and was recorded on location in one of his favourite haunts, the Jazzhus Montmartre in Copenhagen. He had been a European resident for a decade, and his frequent partner for engagements of this kind was fellow expatriate Kenny Drew, a seasoned and accomplished bop-inspired pianist. Griffin and Drew, having worked and recorded together extensively in New York years before, were intimately versed in each other's styles. Drummer Ed Thigpen, a former cohort of Oscar Peterson, was a more recent arrival in Europe, but was a welcome addition to Copenhagen's jazz community of the early 1970s. His alert, responsive drumming is a continual source of refreshment to both Griffin and Drew in the four extended performances that form the backbone of this energizing set, and he conceives an especially fecund solo on *Blues for Harvey* after trading a series of snappy eight-bar breaks with Griffin. Mads Vinding typifies the new breed of European bass player, highly competent as soloist or accompanist, and more than capable of holding his own in celebrated company.

Griffin's occasionally brash but always breezy outlook infuses the music, not only through his exhilarating playing but also via his own compositions. The tone is set by the righteous blues *That Party Upstairs,* in which Griffin paints a convincing picture of a good-time gathering with his shouting, keening and wobbly phrases. Long before the advent of the jazz new wave, Griffin had used shrieks, barks, waspish smears, squealing honks and shrill top notes as parts of his arsenal of diverse effects to colour a performance; these were the stock-in-trade of a good booting rhythm-and-blues saxophonist. This performance is laced with such devices, and his tonguing technique has rarely been heard to better advantage. A solo by Griffin is never a smooth ride, but invariably a provocative, surprising jaunt. The steadfast rhythm also proves to be to the taste of Drew, whose flowing solo juxtaposes earthy blues phrases with darting and complex single-note runs. Unrepressed joy is the order of the day in this derivative from an earlier blues, Gene Ammons's *Red Top*.

Alone Again explores a more subdued mood, but the stately tempo does not preclude Griffin from doubling up when he feels the need. The piece is gentle and tender without being maudlin, and the leader's commitment to honest emotion is never in doubt during the course of his delineation. The tune bears a passing resemblance to *The Nearness of You*.

Soft and Furry, a stealthy, slow piece, is one of Griffin's most memorable originals, with its expressive theme stated by bowed bass and tenor in unison with creeping assists from the piano. Opening in restrained fashion, Griffin imperceptibly raises the heat but remains fully controlled. Somehow, he is even more exciting when keeping some of his virtuoso power in reserve.

Blues for Harvey is a repetitious riffy opus that allows Griffin to unleash a torrent of extrovert ideas, operating initially without pianistic support and demonstrating the full gamut of his stimulating vocal style and rhythmic sophistication. This is the Griffin that, once heard, is never forgotten, the archetypal jazz improviser, bursting with enthusiasm and preaching with uninhibited zeal.

CD

***Blues for Harvey,* SteepleChase SCCD 31004 (Denmark)**

Johnny Griffin (ts), Kenny Drew (p), Mads Vinding (sb), Ed Thigpen (d)

Copenhagen	4–5 July 1973	**That Party Upstairs**
		Alone Again
		Soft and Furry
		Blues for Harvey
		Rhythm-a-ning

* * *

Tete Montoliu: *Tete!*

During bop's encampment on the continent Ørsted-Pedersen was in great demand, his skills within this style being far in advance of other European bassists (excepting Englishman Dave Holland, who had already come to America and turned his interests elsewhere, toward fusion and free jazz). Roughly one year after the delicate session with Drew, Ørsted-Pedersen found himself in an equally familiar but dramatically contrasting setting, recording with American drummer Albert 'Tootie' Heath (the younger brother of bassist Percy Heath and saxophonist Jimmy Heath) in the trio of Catalan pianist Tete Montoliu. As for the duo above, Ib Skovgaard's pamphlet notes give a brief summary of the musicians' association, which again dates back to the 1960s. Two albums resulted from this session in 1974, **Catalonian Fire** and our selection **Tete!**.

That a pianist as talented as Montoliu could have emerged from Spain, a country in which jazz had little significance, is a testimony to the internationalization of the music and to the possibility of a purely musical inspiration divorced from the standard socio-cultural context. Montoliu did have the opportunity to work in Barcelona with tenor saxophonist Don Byas, who no doubt provided instruction in the jazz life. It is also possible that Byas's perpetual motion hybrid swing-bop style (as manifested on *I Got Rhythm*, discussed in chapter 5) was of some influence, but well before these sessions, Montoliu had become devoted to a mid- to late-1950s bop style. Occasionally he allows his instrument to sing out a pretty tune, but mainly he hammers out lightning-fast lines articulated with a crystalline clarity that is matched by drummer Heath, who defines each individual boom, bip, snap, swish and click within his rhythmic kaleidoscope, and nearly so by bassist Ørsted Pedersen.

The trio's performances on this disc represent the hyperactive side of bop. John Coltrane's *Giant Steps* is one of the standard test pieces for bop musicians, most of whom strive just to get through it without falling apart, so difficult is the chord progression and so fast the tempo. Montoliu and his fellows are among the few to have really made something musical out of this labyrinth (indeed more so than did Coltrane himself). Further opportunities to work out in this manner are afforded by another fast étude, *Solar*, and by *Hot House* (Tadd Dameron's bop version of the song *What is This Thing Called Love*), on which, after stating the theme, Montoliu builds portions of his improvisation upon angular, dissonant ideas reminiscent of Thelonious Monk's playing, although handled in a manner much more verbose than Monk's. Ostensibly the remaining titles are ballads, but after spending a couple of minutes with the quiet beauties of *Theme for Ernie* and *I Remember Clifford*, and giving only the slightest nod to those of *Body and Soul*, Montoliu launches into double-time and double double-time. If **Duo** is fine wine, **Tete!** is six cups of coffee after dinner.

CD

***Tete!*, SteepleChase SCCD-31029 (Denmark)**

Tete Montoliu (p), Niels-Henning Ørsted Pedersen (sb), Albert 'Tootie' Heath (d)

Copenhagen	18 May 1974	**Giant Steps**
		Theme for Ernie
		Body and Soul
		Solar
		I Remember Clifford
		Hot House

* * *

Chico Freeman: *Spirit Sensitive*

Tenor saxophonist Chico Freeman's album **Spirit Sensitive** is a lovely document of the early years of the bop revival. The main spirit to be revived is John Coltrane, his gentler side as heard on albums of the late 1950s to mid-1960s. Particularly on *Lonnie's Lament* and *Wise One* (the latter being one of four CD bonus tracks not on the LP), the resemblance of Freeman's sound to Coltrane's is uncanny. Countless players have imitated Coltrane, but few have done it so well. Freeman is aided by sidemen who obviously have a great sympathy for this task: pianist John Hicks (who has embarked on similar projects with Coltrane's former sideman Pharoah Sanders), string bassist Cecil McBee, and drummer Billy Hart.

Apart from Coltrane's dominant presence, the album offers a pianoless trio interpretation of the swing-era standard *I don't get around much anymore*, with drummer Don Moye replacing Hart and playing in a swing and bop style that gives not a hint of his foremost job, as percussionist for the Art Ensemble of Chicago. Freeman and Hicks are featured in a straightforward rendering of the ballad *A Child Is Born* (written by Sir Roland Hanna, not Thad Jones, according to Hanna). Among the bonus tracks, Freeman delivers the pop song *You don't have to say you're sorry* in a sentimental version not far removed from its hotel lounge origins. Also worth noting throughout is the bass playing of Cecil McBee, whose burred, quavering tone quality is unsurpassed and who has the uncommon ability to play adventuresome bass lines and solo melodies on the instrument without going out of tune.

Pianist Paul Bley's liner notes on the album **Paul Bley with Gary Peacock** (ECM 1003), issued in 1970, offer some sense of what was at that time the prevailing attitude of the *avant-garde* toward the mainstream repertoire of jazz. These notes comprise three sentences in large, boldface type, reminiscent of a warning on a bottle of medicine: 'This current album contains some standards. Chord changes have never interfered with my own way of hearing melody. Whether playing standards with steady time and a given set of chord sequences or free rhythm and free harmony pieces where the only guide to the improviser is the vivid character of the given written composition, one's own personality should be apparent to the listener'.

In the mid- to late 1970s this attitude began to change. *Avant-garde* jazz was struggling to hold its audience, as was jazz in general, what with the competition from rock to disco. Within the profession there was considerable hand wringing over the possible death of jazz. This did not happen, and one reason was that *avant-garde* musicians made the practical decision to begin playing in a more accessible manner, to regain an audience. Reed player Anthony Braxton had heralded this trend with his two albums entitled **In the Tradition**, recorded for SteepleChase in 1974, although he gave the tradition a free jazz twist by playing bop on the unwieldly contrabass clarinet. Freeman was also a leader in the *avant-garde* during these years, but by contrast his upbringing had prepared him to make the full leap away: his father, Von Freeman, was then a prominent swing and bop tenor saxophonist in Chicago. (Indeed by the 1990s the father had become at least as famous internationally as the son.) Hence **Spirit Sensitive** became one of the most conservative documents of the bop revival from the perspective of previous expectations raised by its leader. As such it takes on a modest historical importance, apart from being just plain pretty music.

CD

***Spirit Sensitive*, India Navigation IN 1045 CD (USA)**

Chico Freeman (ts), John Hicks (p), Cecil McBee (sb), Billy Hart (d)

New York	Sept 1979	**Autumn in New York**
		Peace
		A Child is Born
		Lonnie's Lament
as ***Autumn in New York****, but Freeman (ss)*		**You don't have to say you're sorry**
as ***Autumn in New York***		**Wise One**
		It never entered my mind
		Close to You Alone
Freeman (ss); Don Moye (d) replaces Hart; add Jay Hoggard (vb)		**Carnival**
Freeman (ts), McBee, Moye; omit Hicks, Hoggard		**Don't Get Around Much Anymore**

* * *

Phil Woods: *Birds of a Feather*

By the time that the SteepleChase label was underway in 1973, one of the foremost expatriates had already returned to the USA. In October of that year, after having made one last excursion into the realm of electrified instruments, alto saxophonist Phil Woods established an 'acoustic' group that has remained at the core of the bop revival for over two decades. Woods, string bassist Steve Gilmore and drummer Bill Goodwin have been permanent members. Hal Galper had just replaced the group's first pianist Mike Melillo in 1981, when Woods recorded **Birds of a Feather**. The title evidently refers to his devotion to Bird (Charlie Parker) and to the stability of the group. Given this stability, it should come as no surprise that his recorded output has been consistently fine. Perhaps the outstanding disc is the quintet album **Integrity**, recorded in 1984 in the second year of trumpeter Tom Harrell's long tenure with Woods. This CD has been discontinued, but **Birds of a Feather** serves perfectly well as an alternative choice.

In advocating an 'acoustic' group, Woods did not abandon amplification altogether. A microphone amplified the piano, Gilmore used the conventional string bass amplifier, and during the mid-1970s electric guitarist Harry Leahey joined the group. None the less, in terms of volume and timbre their style contrasted drastically with the then-prevailing fusion style and with the still-prevailing tendency of in-house engineers to filter the whole sound (including each component of the drum set) through a public address system, no matter how traditional the group or how intimate the setting.

Woods's personal sound took the opposite approach. By comparison with his contributions to bop in the 1950s, the tone quality of his alto saxophone had become broader and coarser, approaching that of a tenor saxophone. He heightened the effect by introducing a growl into many passages.

Performances of the swing tune *Star Eyes*, associated with Parker, and Horace Silver's hybrid Latin-bop piece *Nica's Dream*, are 'burners', each taken much faster than the famous earlier versions of these titles. As such, they well represent a practical aspect of bop performance. Here is a working group presenting familiar tunes and maintaining their interest and a sense of challenge by setting tempos at a lightning pace. Driving the band, supporting the arranged passages and soloing in this context, Goodwin shows himself to be one of the best drummers in the bop revival.

Woods's composition *Goodbye Mr Evans* is dedicated to pianist Bill Evans, who died the previous year. For Woods himself, the tribute is in the title only. The alto saxophonist plays with unabashed romanticism and with that growling edge added to his tone. In the course of his solo an undercurrent of double-time rhythm gradually emerges into the foreground, with Goodwin eventually switching over from brushes to sticks, so as better to support the leader's fervent ballad style. All in all the effect is much more reminiscent of Woods's Grammy winning contribution to Billy Joel's *I love you just the way you are* than of Evans's introspective approach. After the alto sax solo, the tribute acquires a greater musical meaning, as Gilmore and Galper invent delicate solos over Goodwin's brushed drum accompaniment, this trio evoking the memory of Evans's early trio with Scott LaFaro and Paul Motian. The mood switches right back when Woods re-enters.

Similar contrasts obtain throughout the session, including the relaxed swing tune *Summer Night* and the other original composition that the leader contributed to the session, the bop waltz *Petite Chanson*. Galper and Gilmore take carefully articulated, restrained routes through these tunes, while Woods charges ahead, even throwing in a few unmetred flurries of notes in a brief nod toward the free jazz style of saxophone improvisation.

CD

***Birds of a Feather*, Antilles 422-846 165-2 (USA)**

Phil Woods (as), Hal Galper (p), Steve Gilmore (sb), Bill Goodwin (d)

Stroudsburg, PA	11–12 Aug 1981	**Star Eyes**
		Goodbye Mr Evans
		Petite Chanson
		Summer Night
		My Old Flame
		Nica's Dream

* * *

Michel Petrucciani: *Pianism*

Having already established himself as one of the young lions of the bop revival, particularly for his performance in saxophonist Charles Lloyd's group at the Montreux Jazz Festival in 1982, French pianist Michel Petrucciani recorded the splendid album **Pianism** with his own trio late in 1985, eight days before his twenty-third birthday. In extensive notes that fortunately have been retained for the issue on CD, Mort Goode discusses the trio's history, the circumstances of recording, the genesis of the titles on this recording (four compositions by Petrucciani and two standards), the pianist's upbringing and his instrumental and improvisational skills.

Pianism well shows off the two sides of Petrucciani's playing: a serene introspection after the manner of Bill Evans, as heard on *The Prayer*; and an energetic brilliance after the manner of Oscar Peterson, heard on all the other tracks, including the ballad *Here's that Rainy Day* (on which he selects the energetic rather than the serene route). This brilliance is intellectually and emotionally more substantial than Peterson's playing. It is also less closely tied to swing, focusing instead on bop and Latin-bop styles, including an outstanding version of *Night and Day*. The work of bassist Palle Danielsson and drummer Eliot Zigmund as accompanists and soloists also deserves mention, for their sensitivity to and interaction with Petrucciani. As Goode explains, the trio had recently completed a 32-concert tour, and they were able to bring that cohesive experience straight into the recording studio.

CD

***Pianism*, Blue Note CDP 7 46295 2 (USA)**

Michel Petrucciani (p), Palle Danielsson (sb), Eliot Zigmund (d)

New York	20 Dec 1985	**The Prayer**
		Our Tune
		Face's Face
		Night and Day
		Here's that Rainy Day
		Regina

* * *

Woody Shaw: *Solid*

In 1963, at the tender age of 18, trumpeter Woody Shaw became a musical partner of Eric Dolphy. Invited by Dolphy to Europe the following year, only to have the saxophonist die from a heart attack brought on by diabetes, Shaw decided to go abroad anyway and there figured in the maintenance of the bop style, before returning to the USA to join Horace Silver's quintet in 1965. In these early years of his career Shaw was often mistaken for Freddie Hubbard, so similar (and so beautiful) were their tones and their dexterity on the instrument. In 1971–2, during bop's darkest years, he stayed true to his stylistic preferences, joining Art Blakey's Jazz Messengers. With drummer Louis Hayes, Shaw co-led a quintet that Dexter Gordon used for his homecoming tour in 1976, thus participating in the event that marked the start of the bop revival in the USA. The consequent publicity led to his securing a Columbia recording contract in 1977 and thereafter leading his own groups. Unfortunately the pressures of leadership and an affiliation with a major label overwhelmed Shaw, and his personal life plunged from great promise to tragedy. At the time of recording this album

Solid in 1986, he was debilitated by narcotics addiction and only three years away from a horrid death.

Shaw's musical life none the less somehow stayed on an even keel. Although during his career in the studio Shaw never achieved the brilliant originality and conceptual perfection of Hubbard's finest work, he never stooped to Hubbard's strong penchant for crassly commercial jazz, badly done. This combination of caution and good taste is captured on the aptly named **Solid**, recorded with an *ad hoc* assemblage, rather than his working group (which often included Steve Turré, whose trombone and conch-shell playing figures elsewhere in the book). Apart from Shaw's adaptation of *The Woody Woodpecker Song*, there is not meant to be anything even mildly innovative here. Instead, **Solid** draws from the central repertory of the bop revival for performances done in a masterful way – joyful romps through *There Will Never Be Another You* and *You Stepped out of a Dream*, a relaxed bossa nova and swing version of *Speak Low* (the latter done in an altogether more restrained manner than Gary Bartz's version, discussed below), the riff blues *Solid* and Rodgers and Hammerstein's ballad *It Might as Well be Spring*. By this time Shaw had been deeply involved in jazz education, and no doubt had spent considerable time working with players who were trying to improvise on bop chestnuts such as these. Here, propelled by the rhythm section of bassist Neil Swainson and drummer Victor Jones, the leader and his featured soloists – the veteran pianist Kenny Barron (see below, **People Time**) and the then-emerging new star, alto saxophonist Kenny Garrett – show students how the professionals do it.

CD

***Solid*, Muse MCD 5329 (USA)**

Woody Shaw (tpt), Kenny Barron (p), Neil Swainson (sb), Victor Jones (d)

Englewood Cliffs, NJ	24 March 1986	**You Stepped out of a Dream** **It Might as Well Be Spring** **The Woody Woodpecker Song**
add Kenny Garrett (as)		**There Will Never Be Another You** **Speak Low**
add Peter Leitch (elg)		**Solid**

* * *

George Coleman: *At Yoshi's*

Youth has always been prominent in jazz, often rightfully so, because of the genre's many precociously brilliant musicians. What a shame, though, that since the 1980s so much corporate publicity has focused on teenage and twenty-something young lions of the bop revival, few of whom can touch the abilities of tenor saxophonist George Coleman and his boyhood friend from Memphis, pianist Harold Mabern, who at the time of recording **At Yoshi's** were respectively 52- and 51-year-old veteran lions. Coleman's fondness for John Coltrane manifests itself in his tone quality, his serious romanticism on ballads, his occasional use of squealing altissimo notes, his usual manner of inserting fast swirling passages into the context of hard bop melody, and his energy. Mabern is equally energetic: more than one title begins as a ballad, doubles in tempo, and then doubles again, and on *Soul Eyes* in particular the pianist seemingly can hardly bear to wait for this to happen. But Mabern is more firmly grounded in the hard bop style, and with the similarly minded bassist Ray Drummond and drummer Alvin Queen, he brings a perfect foundation for Coleman's ideas. *Laig Gobblin' Blues* is the least interesting track on the CD, but just in case listeners are curious about the reference to odd metres in the pamphlet notes, it might be worth mentioning that in this 12-bar blues, bars 1–8 and 11–12 are in $\frac{5}{4}$ time, and bars 9–10 in $\frac{7}{4}$; this sort of too-clever structure tends to put a straitjacket around the improviser. All of the remaining tracks are outstanding, and it is hard to decide what most deserves mention. Certainly no-one should miss the rhythmic pliability of *Everything Happens to Me*, including a passage of Latin jazz toward the end; and *Good Morning Heartache*, which from a gentle opening (with Coleman soon reaching into his low register to coax out a breathy tone) builds and builds in tension, Drummond walking his bass line, Queen pounding out a backbeat rhythm, Mabern supporting Queen with his own repeated riff, while Coleman pours his heart out in instrumental flurries and screams. If someone wants to know, 'What is jazz all about?' – this moment is it.

CD

***At Yoshi's*, Evidence ECD 22021-2 (USA)**

George Coleman (ts), Harold Mabern (p), Ray Drummond (sb), Alvin Queen (d)

Oakland and San Francisco	Aug 1987	**They Say It's Wonderful** **Good Morning Heartache** **Laig Gobblin' Blues**

Io
Up Jumped Spring
Father
Soul Eyes

Other CDs

same contents:
Theresa TRCD-126 (USA)

* * *

Branford Marsalis: *Trio Jeepy*

Since the 1970s Herbie Hancock and Chick Corea have juggled dual careers in pop and jazz. Among the musicians who have most successfully followed their lead is the eldest of the Marsalis brothers, saxophonist Branford. He is a popular entertainer – most notably he has been a sideman with singer and guitarist Sting and he leads the Tonight Show band on television – and he is a prominent figure in the bop revival. His transparent and beautifully recorded CD, **Trio Jeepy**, belongs to this latter half of his musical personality. This performance testifies to Marsalis's stature as one of the most technically accomplished tenor saxophonists of his generation (and a substantially more interesting soloist than his famous brother Wynton).

Originally issued as a double LP, including a bonus track (*Stardust*) that could not be fitted onto the CD, **Trio Jeepy** presents a standard repertory extending from swing-era ballads, with references to the hefty tone quality of tenor saxophonists like Chu Berry and Ben Webster, to the edge of mid-1960s free jazz, with references to John Coltrane's sheets of sound. The album was produced by the third of the Marsalis brothers, Delfeayo, who achieves a delightful informality by leaving in conversation, false starts, saxophone squeaks, and other bits and pieces of studio sound that usually would be edited away. Yet in spite of this intentional looseness in the production, Branford's playing has an overall feeling of tightness, precision and intellectual deliberation. As such he seems to declare his allegiance above all to Sonny Rollins's work of the mid-1950s. Certainly Marsalis's restrained improvising on the slow blues *Gutbucket Steepy* should not be mistaken for, say, Eddie 'Lockjaw' Davis's freewheeling, heart rending approach to this sort of tune; nor, at the other end of the neo-classical compass, would Coltrane have played a piece like *Random Abstract* with such caution.

In his notes for the LP liner and CD pamphlet, Delfeayo supplies a patchwork quilt of ignorance and insight. On record packaging one often encounters notes mangling fancy words and musical concepts, and grossly overestimating the significance of the disc (in this instance, Delfeayo's claims for the achievements of bop revivalists of the 1980s and particularly his big brothers). Usually one simply disregards such silliness, but in this case Delfeayo also provides intriguing descriptions of the music, and he identifies the contributions of Marsalis's sidemen: veteran bassist Milt Hinton, and Marsalis's contemporaries, bassist Delbert Felix and drummer Jeff Watts. Hence Delfeayo's outrageous notes are none the less worth reading with care (and selectivity).

CD

***Trio Jeepy*, Columbia CK 44199 (USA)**

Branford Marsalis (ts), Milt Hinton (sb), Jeff Watts (d)

?New York	3–4 Jan 1988	**Housed from Edward**
		The Nearness of You
		Three Little Words
		Makin' Whoopee
		UMMG
		Gutbucket Steepy
Delbert Felix (sb) replaces Hinton		**Doxy**
Hinton replaces Felix		**Makin' Whoopee (reprise)**
Felix replaces Hinton		**Peace**
		Random Abstract (Tain's Rampage)

* * *

Frank Morgan: *Yardbird Suite*

No disc represents the bop revival more exactly than alto saxophonist Frank Morgan's **Yardbird Suite**, which features traditional bop interpretations of six tunes closely associated with the genius of the style, Charlie Parker. (The ringer on the disc is the swing-era ballad *Skylark*, first popularized by Billy Eckstine in Earl Hines's big band; the connection is that Parker played for both of these men, and anyway he loved the tune.) As a teenager, Morgan became friends with Parker, who played at an after-hours jazz club that Morgan's father ran in Los

Angeles. Having acquired his hero's addiction, he shared heroin with Parker, although he discovered to his surprise that Parker was not pleased to have inspired such misguided appreciation from Morgan and other imitators.

Morgan became an accomplished improviser in Parker's mould and made his first album in 1955, the year Parker died, but then spent the next three decades in and out of prison for narcotics violations. In 1985, with considerable attention being focused on such bop-orientated young lions as Marsalis and Petrucciani, the time was ripe for Morgan's rediscovery. He recorded a new album, returned to prison to assure that his addiction was under control, and then initiated a career of international performance that now extends into the 1990s.

Morgan produces a huge, liquid tone, precise and cutting rather than sentimental, and as an improviser he seems to have grasped a fundamental idea that eluded some of the greatest of Parker's successors (most notably Cannonball Adderley): that in Parker's personal style, relaxation, space and a strong feeling for the blues are as crucial as continuous fleet melody. Interestingly, in the face of the formidable challenge of recording an album of Parker's favourites, he shows himself not to be a Parker clone, stringing together time-worn licks, but a soloist of considerable originality and substance.

CD

***Yardbird Suite*, Contemporary CCD-14045-2 (USA)**

Frank Morgan (as), Mulgrew Miller (p), Ron Carter (sb), Al Foster (d)

Berkeley, CA	10–11 Jan 1988	**Yardbird Suite**
		Night in Tunesia
		Billie's Bounce
		Star Eyes
		Scrapple from the Apple
		Skylark
		Cheryl

* * *

Gary Bartz: *West 42nd Street*

Alto saxophonist Gary Bartz's **West 42nd Street** offers another instance of a CD issued with nicely informative pamphlet notes (these by our own contributor, Mark Gardner). Hence there arises an opportunity to complement Gardner's effort, rather than duplicating it, by placing

Bartz's achievement in a somewhat broader stylistic context. But first a few instrumental details might be mentioned. Despite the listing of alto and soprano saxophones on the back cover, Bartz plays only his main instrument, the alto, on these tracks. If indeed Claudio Roditi is playing flugelhorn on Wilbur Harden's *West 42nd Street*, then it is not at all easy to distinguish that sound from the tone of his trumpeting, and my identifications may be mistaken in the listing below. And an instrumental effect not to be missed occurs near the end (beginning at 18:17 of *The night has a thousand eyes*), when Roditi momentarily casts aside his allegiance to bop and instead shows his roots in Brazilian samba, by making the trumpet sound like a talking drum, as noted previously in his work with Dizzy Gillespie (chapter 14).

The early 1970s were a disastrous time for bop. Many leading practitioners turned away from the style and toward jazz–soul fusion, with wildly varied results. For someone like Chick Corea or Herbie Hancock, the move was a financial and artistic success, leading in Hancock's case to an even greater success the following decade when his creations crossed over into MTV video. For someone like George Benson or Donald Byrd the results were mixed: along with undeniable commercial appeal came a feeling that these musicians were working well below their full creative potential. For someone like Freddie Hubbard or Gary Bartz, the attempt was a disaster in both respects, financial and musical. How satisfying it is, then, to hear such musicians returning in the late 1980s and 1990s to the bop style, where their talent is situated. And how fascinating it is to listen again to the then-hip jazz–soul syntheses of the 1970s, and to recognize that much of this music now seems old-fashioned, while bop has worn its years – now decades – quite well.

CD

***West 42nd Street*, Candid CCD 79049 (USA)**

Claudio Roditi (flugelhorn), Gary Bartz (as), John Hicks (p), Ray Drummond (sb), Al Foster (d)

New York	31 March 1990	**West 42nd Street**
as **West 42nd Street**, *but Roditi (tpt)*		**Speak Low**
omit Roditi		**It's easy to remember**
add Roditi (tpt)		**Cousins**
		The night has a thousand eyes

* * *

McCoy Tyner: *Soliloquy*

However strong and lasting the success of his independent career may be, McCoy Tyner will best be remembered as a sideman, together with Jimmy Garrison and Elvin Jones, in John Coltrane's extraordinary quartet of 1961–5. Tyner was always the most traditionally orientated of the four – often it was his repeated chording that anchored the group's explorations – and he was the first to quit, in December 1965, when he felt that Coltrane's style had gone too far away from modal jazz into free jazz. (Jones quit the following month.) Many of his subsequent efforts have accordingly been firmly in the stylistic mainstream, avoiding free jazz, and focusing instead on hard bop and modal jazz. Tyner most often works in small groups utilizing the conventional instrumentation (piano, bass and drums, often with saxophone and trumpet as well), but he has also found considerable success with his big band (chapter 14) and as an unaccompanied soloist, this last activity including a romantic and tuneful collection, **Soliloquy**.

Bop piano playing is to a considerable extent fundamentally incompatible with the orchestral approach of unaccompanied stride and swing pianists like Johnson, Waller, Tatum and Hines, because it requires the musician to avoid steadily-paced chords and any sort of steady bass line, so as not to get in the way of the other members of the group. Tyner replicates the characteristic resulting sound in the first part of *Bouncin' with Bud* (a quintessential bop theme written and recorded by Bud Powell), but he understands full well that such a spare approach cannot sustain interest over an hour of unaccompanied playing, and in its place he offers lush irregular chording, occasional snippets of a bass line, passages of rhapsodic rather than rhythmic playing, and frequent contrasts in register, texture, and volume, as a solution to the challenge of developing a solo style within the bop idiom. The outstanding tracks are Jerome Kern's song *All the Things You Are*, in which Tyner slices apart the song registerally and texturally without for a moment losing a sense of continuity and swing, almost as if he were transferring to the piano Jones's method of swirling about the drum set; and to open and close the collection, two versions of Coltrane's *Crescent*, utterly transformed and sweetened from the original of 1964.

CD

***Soliloquy*, Blue Note CDP 7 96429 2 (USA)**

McCoy Tyner (p)

New York	19–21 Feb 1991	**Crescent**
		Española

All the Things You Are
Twilight Mist
Willow Weep for Me
Lonnie's Lament
Tivoli
Tribute to Lady Day
I Should Care
Three Flowers
Bouncin' with Bud
After the Rain
Effendi
Crescent (alternate take)

* * *

Stan Getz and Kenny Barron: *People Time*

By this point in the book, Getz needs no further introduction. Terminally ill with cancer, he recorded this live performance with pianist Kenny Barron at the Café Montmartre in 1991, the tenor saxophonist playing as perfectly as ever. The detached, icy coolness that he had brought to Woody Herman's band in 1947 was now long gone, replaced by an occasional splatty honk and more significantly by repeated instrumental cries that shatter the overriding delicacy of his sound. His partner Barron had spent his career in steady but unspectacular continuations of the bop tradition, working with Dizzy Gillespie, Freddie Hubbard, Yusef Lateef, Ron Carter (though never during their finest years) and then co-leading the group Sphere, a quartet devoted to Thelonious Monk's compositions as well as their own pieces. On **People Time**, Barron seems to have been pushed to a higher level. No doubt he was stimulated by the maturity and depth of Getz's improvising, and perhaps also he felt liberated from the familiar accompaniment of string bass and drums. Here, when playing alone, he offers by comparison with Tyner's **Soliloquy** a more traditional but also a more varied approach to unaccompanied bop piano, at times even managing to work in an old-fashioned oom-pah stride-piano technique without subverting the smooth flow of bop-orientated rhythm. With Getz joining in, Barron functions as both accompanist and equal, and in the latter capacity there are splendid moments of improvisation when the two men's interlocking lines are dizzying.

The tracks are too consistently fine to require singling out the best ones, except perhaps to say that a few lesser-known pieces yield somewhat less exhilarating performances than the many bop standards, among which the fleet and hybrid Latin-swing rendition of Cole

Porter's *Night and Day* is unforgettable. Here, as is sometimes the case in the bop revival, familiarity with the repertory breeds brilliance rather than boredom, the artists being so comfortable with these pieces that they are able to carry them in new directions.

CD

***People Time*, Verve 314-510823-2 (USA) and EmArcy 510134-2 (Europe)**

Stan Getz (ts), Kenny Barron (p)

Copenhagen	3–6 March 1991	**East of the Sun, West of the Moon**
		Night and Day
		I'm Okay
		Like Someone in Love
		Stablemates
		I Remember Clifford
		Gone with the Wind
		First Song (for Ruth)
		There is No Greater Love
		The Surrey with the Fringe on Top
		People Time
		Softly as in a Morning Sunrise
		Hush-a-bye
		Soul Eyes

* * *

Joe Henderson: *Lush Life: the Music of Billy Strayhorn*

Tenor saxophonist Joe Henderson first made his mark working with Horace Silver (for whom he improvised a now classic solo on *Song for My Father*), Andrew Hill and Kenny Dorham in the 1960s. One element that particularly distinguished his improvising was the way in which it sometimes turned away from the complexities of bop in favour of a simpler, clipped, tuneful, funky style reminiscent of contemporary saxophonists playing soul music. Despite this potential connection, he had no interest whatsoever in participating in jazz fusion of any sort. Instead he waited patiently through the 1970s and early 1980s, working mainly in Europe and Japan, but maintaining his residence in San Francisco (rather than joining Gordon, Griffin and others as an expatriate). Finally, bop came back into fashion, and subsequently Henderson has become both a father figure within the bop revival and one of its finest exponents, directing, soloing in and composing and arranging for two big bands (in New York and San Francisco) and leading diverse small groups. In this latter capacity he recorded his most highly regarded discs in 1991–2, one devoted to Billy Strayhorn's compositions and the next to pieces associated with Miles Davis.

On **Lush Life: the Music of Billy Strayhorn**, Henderson selects ten compositions written by Duke Ellington's amenuensis Strayhorn and interprets them within the stylistic realm of the bop revival, with, for example, *Rain Check* (dating from 1941) becoming a hybrid bop/calypso piece after the manner of Sonny Rollins's *St Thomas* and *Johnny Come Lately* (from 1942) becoming a hard bop/modal jazz piece performed here by a quintet that includes trumpeter Wynton Marsalis. Henderson adds considerable variety to the disc by varying instrumental textures track by track. Rather than staying with the quintet throughout, he has a quartet performing Strayhorn's strange and difficult ballad *Blood Count*. *Rain Check* is delivered with a pianoless trio (in a further tribute to Rollins's manner). *Drawing Room Blues*, the other trio track, is a soft blues, and it swings so well that one scarcely realizes that the drums are missing. The three duos include a heady and abstract version of Strayhorn's best known swing tune, *Take the "A" Train*, by Henderson and drummer Gregory Hutchinson alone, and a fittingly esoteric reading of another of Strayhorn's elusive melodies, *Isfahan*, by Henderson and the exceptionally talented young string bassist Christian McBride. Finally, the saxophonist gives an unaccompanied reading of Strayhorn's loveliest ballad, *Lush Life*. Throughout these tracks, Henderson is wildly imaginative and bursting with seemingly endless ideas for improvisation, though in a controlled and quiet way. He roams effortlessly through Strayhorn's music, seemingly playing as well as he ever has.

CD

***Lush Life: the Music of Billy Strayhorn*, Verve 314-511-779-2 (USA)**

Joe Henderson (ts), Christian McBride (sb)

Englewood Cliffs, NJ	3, 6, 8 Sept 1991	**Isfahan** (arr Don Sickler)

Wynton Marsalis (tpt), Henderson, Stephen Scott (p), McBride, Gregory Hutchinson (d)

Johnny Come Lately

omit Marsalis — **Blood Count**

Henderson, McBride, Hutchinson — **Rain Check**

Henderson, Scott	**Lotus Blossom**
Marsalis, Henderson, Scott, McBride, Hutchinson	**A Flower is a Lovesome Thing** (arr Sickler)
Henderson, Hutchinson	**Take the "A" Train**
Henderson, Scott, McBride	**Drawing Room Blues** (arr Sickler)
Marsalis, Henderson, Scott, McBride, Hutchinson	**U.M.M.G. (Upper Manhattan Medical Group)**
Henderson	**Lush Life**

* * *

Joshua Redman: *Joshua Redman*

Potential means that you haven't done it yet. Thus it has been with large segments of the bop revival. Since Wynton Marsalis recorded his debut as a leader in 1981, recording companies, talent agents and sometimes the musicians themselves have been asking us to judge young neo-classicists not only for what they are – talented keepers of the flame, focused on re-creation and imitation – but also for what they might become. We are in effect supposed to give them a handicap for their youth and to support their careers (even while more talented veterans like George Coleman scuffle for steady work!) with an eye towards a time when the creative juices begin to flow and we may finally evaluate them by the same standards that we apply to the giants of jazz.

How wonderfully refreshing it is, finally to come upon a young man's debut, the self-titled CD **Joshua Redman**, containing tenor saxophone playing of such quality and depth that there is no need to talk about his future potential. If anything, his problem will be matching this first achievement, though that is a nice sort of problem to have.

Redman is the son of free jazz tenor saxophonist Dewey Redman, but Joshua's musical interests lie elsewhere. As is common in the bop revival, his repertory ranges from swing and bop standards of the 1930s and 1940s up through bossa nova, skittery aharmonic bop and hypnotic modal jazz of the 1960s, this last area represented by *Sublimation*, performed after the manner of Coltrane's quartet. He also throws in a cover version of soul singer James Brown's hit song *I got you*, which he delivers with far more restraint than the original and yet with an uncanny feeling for the nuances of Brown's vocalizing: don't miss the perfect little tenor saxophone scream – modeled exactly after Brown's own yelp – just before the end of the piece.

Among Redman's own compositions, the soul jazz tune *Blues on Sunday* deserves mention for its distinctive interrupted theme and for the virtuosity of Redman's improvising, particularly when he moves fluently back and forth between full-bodied notes in the normal register of the instrument and squeezed, raspy notes in its altissimo register. But the outstanding performances are on two standards, both exhibiting a musical and emotional maturity seemingly beyond Redman's years. He presents the ballad *Body & Soul* in breathtaking long phrases, sliding gracefully into notes in a caressing manner reminiscent of Johnny Hodges's playing (though less exaggerated than Hodges's manner) and weaving in and out of the familiar melody. He tops this performance with a rendition of *On the Sunny Side of the Street* in a duo with string bassist Christian McBride, who supplies percussion sounds by slapping the instrument. In title and spirit this performance recalls Sonny Rollins, and Redman and McBride explore the piece with a witty perfection worthy of Rollins's best efforts.

CD

***Joshua Redman*, Warner Bros 9 45242-2 (USA)**

Joshua Redman (ts), Mike LeDonne (p), Paul LaDuca (sb), Kenny Washington (d)

New York	27 May 1992	**Body & Soul**

Redman (ts), Christian McBride (sb), Clarence Penn (d)

	4 June 1992	**Trinkle Tinkle**
Redman, McBride	15 Sept 1992	**On the Sunny Side of the Street**

add Kevin Hays (p), Gregory Hutchinson (d)

Blues on Sunday
Wish
Echoes
I got you (I feel good)
Tribalism
Groove X (By Any Means Necessary)
Salt Peanuts
Sublimation

* * *

Wynton Marsalis: *In This House, On This Morning*

Like Joshua Redman's first disc, Wynton Marsalis's heavily promoted recording début as a leader was perfectly competent, but unlike Redman's, it was not particularly memorable, either for Marsalis's playing or his tune writing. Indeed through the 1980s none of Marsalis's albums seemed to fulfil his artistic potential. Despite possessing an unprecedented fluency in both jazz and classical performance, he struggled for over a decade to find an innovative niche within jazz's neo-classicist movement. How encouraging and satisfying it is, then, that he finally found that niche as an inspired innovator, with the première in 1993 of his composition *In This House, On This Morning*, a wonderfully creative and ambitious programmatic sacred piece.

In terms of architectural grandeur, *In This House, On this Morning* is unparalleled in jazz. Among the musical building blocks of jazz, structure is usually the most trivial and nuance the most important. Those composers who have forgotten this – in an effort to emulate complex structures in classical music – have floundered badly. Exceptionally, Marsalis succeeds in building a large-scale piece without sacrificing the attention to nuance that makes jazz work. Its principal structural glue is programmatic, notably the sequence of tune titles, ordered to conform to an African-American Christian church service; within this sequence, Marian Williams's lyrics of prayer; the periodic and stunning evocation of church bells ringing (on the piano); and Herlin Riley's use of tambourine (an instrument appropriate for this portion of the gospel church service) rather than his drum set (heard, for example, through most of the *Processional*). Other interconnections are more purely musical, of which perhaps the most obvious are recurrences of the fanfare that opens the piece; and Marsalis's melody to the lyric 'In the sweet embrace of life', played and sung by Reginald Veal in the *Father* portion of the *Sermon* (at the start of the second of the two CDs) and then taken up by alto saxophonist Wes Anderson four tracks later, on *Invitation* (not to be confused with the jazz standard of the same title).

Marsalis's interest in large-scale form, his restricted stylistic eclecticism (essentially the hard bop style, but expanded to incorporate sounds ranging from New Orleans jazz to modal jazz), his use of a horn section that is, for a bop combo, larger than usual (trumpet, trombone and two saxophones) and his creation of a music in which the compositions are consistently more striking than the associated improvisations, all recall some of the efforts of Charles Mingus in his Jazz Workshop groups of the late 1950s to mid-1960s. But whereas Mingus in his striving after ambitious composition was notorious for being disorganized and unable to finish what he started, Marsalis here has done it, and spectacularly well.

CD

***In This House, On This Morning,* Columbia C2K 53220 (USA)**

Part I

Wynton Marsalis (tpt), Wycliffe Gordon (tb), Wessell Anderson (as), Todd Williams (ts, ss), Eric Reed (p), Reginald Veal (sb), Herlin Riley (d, per)

New York	28–29 May 1992 and 20–21 March 1993	**Devotional**
		Call to Prayer
		Processional
		Representative Offerings
		The Lord's Prayer
Part II		**Hymn**
		Scripture
		Prayer
		Introduction to Prayer
add Marian Williams (v)		**In This House**
omit (v)		**Choral Response**
		Local Announcements
		Altar Call
		Altar Call (Introspection)
Part III: In the Sweet Embrace of Life		
add Veal (v)		**Sermon**
omit (v)		**Father**
		Son
		Holy Ghost
		Invitation
add group (handclapping, v)		**Recessional**
omit (handclapping, v)		**Benediction**
		Uptempo Postlude
		Pot Blessed Dinner

* * *

Eddie Harris: *For You, For Me, For Evermore*

As Mark Gardner explains in the pamphlet notes to **For You, For Me, For Evermore,** tenor saxophonist Eddie Harris was supposed to record a duo session in Copenhagen, but the pianist never showed up. Perhaps this disappointment had some influence on Harris's having selected the title Everything Happens to Me for the ensuing disc. In any event, ever the professional, he made himself into a duo by recording nine tracks of competent chordal piano accompaniments (with melodies as well at the openings of *The End of the Day* and the title track) and then recording nine tracks of tenor sax overdubbed and a tenth, *If I Should Lose You*, for the sax unaccompanied. The result is a magnificent display of saxophone playing that stretches stylistically from Hawkins to Coltrane, these borrowings sounding against the considerable originality of his own personal style.

One quality of Harris's individuality is an earthy tunefulness. On its own, funky playing has brought him considerable commercial success (notably his song *Listen Here*), and has perhaps caused him to be underappreciated in jazz criticism. Here on this disc, the soul licks operate within a comparatively more cerebral approach to swing and bop tunes.

A more specific quality of Harris's individuality is his sensitivity to registral timbre and contrast. From the days of Illinois Jacquet in Lionel Hampton's band, through Coltrane and Albert Ayler, to countless players nowadays, the altissimo register of the tenor saxophone has offered an area for various types of hefty squalling, including the sort that Harris plays briefly at the end of his Coltrane-influenced version of *Night and Day*. But his usual procedure is quite different. Rather than generating screams or cries, he tweaks out precise little notes and uses these to create an independent area of melody. An extreme example occurs toward the end of *Everything Happens to Me*, when he tweaks out an entire passage of the melody, but his use of this device is even more effective on the opening track, a funky bossa nova version of Johnny Mercer's song *I Remember You*, where these startling notes act as if they were commentaries interjected into the principal stream of melodic thought. On his Hawkins-influenced rendition of George Gershwin's ballad *For You, For Me, For Evermore*, Harris explores other areas of the horn, concentrating the melody in the instrument's lower range during the opening sax chorus (following the piano solo) and then, for the next chorus, moving up roughly an octave and softening his tone, to create the effect of another saxophonist having just joined the session. These various possibilities are integrated in astonishing improvisations in the middle of *Everything Happens to Me* and throughout trumpeter Donald Byrd's tune *Fly Little Bird, Fly*, as Harris dances about the horn, leaving two or more lines dangling momentarily while he picks up another. This ability to play as if he were three saxophonists is one reason that this potentially too thin, bass- and drumless overdubbed duo session works so well.

CD

***For You, For Me, For Evermore*, SteepleChase SCCD 31322 (Denmark)**

Eddie Harris (ts, p)		
Copenhagen	Oct 1992	**I Remember You**
		The End of the Day
		For You, For Me, For Evermore
omit (p)		**If I Should Lose You**
add (p)		**You Stole My Heart**
		Night and Day
		Everything Happens to Me
		Salute to Bags
		All Alone
		Fly Little Bird, Fly

CHAPTER 17
Free Jazz

Ekkehard Jost

At the end of the 1950s Ornette Coleman made a startling statement: 'Let's play the music and not the background' (in Martin Williams: *The Jazz Tradition*, New York, 1970, p. 207). With this sentence, Coleman, who was then one of the pioneers of a new form of music that was soon to be called free jazz (after one of his recordings), proclaimed an aesthetic programme that paved the way for one of the most radical moves in the stylistic evolution of jazz, which until then had flowed comparatively smoothly. By 'background' Coleman obviously meant the traditional framework of jazz improvisation which had been established in the music's early years and which had never before been questioned seriously. This background consisted of a couple of rules and agreements that more or less controlled the individual means of expression of improvising musicians and that regulated musical interaction within a group: the elementary formal framework of a jazz piece (theme – improvisation – theme), its harmonic and metric structure (derived from the theme) and the normative character of a constant fundamental beat. Whereas most of the preceding stylistic developments manifested themselves in gradual changes of technical and expressive means of creation, and sometimes also in the growing complexity of the structure of the background, in the years around 1960 the background itself started to disintegrate. The break from a traditional system of rules led to a precarious situation full of contradictions and insecurity, for with the liberation *from* old norms the question arose what this liberation should be *for*.

The musicians who set out to find their ways through the stylistic mazes of the new music developed a large repertory of expressive means and principles of creation which, in its broadness, proved to be unique in jazz. The repertory not only concentrated on the new and unheard, but also encompassed blues, many traditional forms of jazz, musics of the Third World, and the European *avant-garde*. To free oneself from the norms of strict formal patterns, a common harmonic and rhythmic language and a fundamental beat did not mean that all this was now and forever forbidden, but that it was not automatically required.

Free jazz as a stylistic term is therefore only valuable when the freedom promised by the little word 'free' is understood as a freedom of choice among an infinite number of alternatives and not merely as a rebellion against tradition. And this of course means that free jazz cannot be understood as a compact style of jazz with definite characteristics and sharply drawn borders, but rather as a stylistic conglomerate, the most essential feature of which is its potential diversity. A few central points among the vast variety of musical changes and innovations that came along with free jazz are as follows:

The questioning (not the abolition) of any kinds of rules.

The growing importance of spontaneous interaction among players and, connected with this, the partial nullification of traditional divisions between soloists and accompanists, and a growing tendency toward collective instead of solo improvisation.

The emancipation of sound colour, which becomes an independent means of creation and consequently opens the possibility of improvising amelodically.

The importance of energy and intensity as communicative elements and sources for collective ecstasy.

A turn towards musical cultures of the Third World and thereby the integration of diverse 'exotic' elements into jazz.

A growing consciousness of social, political and economic problems among musicians and the consequent development of a new form of self-understanding.

All these points mark tendencies and are, taken together, not to be related to one single musician or group. Their individual relevance during the evolution of free jazz should become apparent in the following essays.

* * *

Ornette Coleman: *The Shape of Jazz to Come; Free Jazz*

Ornette Coleman grew up – musically speaking – near the roots of jazz. Born in the black ghetto of Forth Worth, Texas, he spent his years of apprenticeship in the rough atmosphere of tent shows, where musicians played the blues in a rude and original way that was untouched by the polish of jazz. When, around 1955, Coleman left rhythm and blues and turned to jazz, he adapted his playing to the established principles, but only partly and not for long.

The first recordings that Coleman, after years of hunger and frustration, recorded with his partner, trumpeter Don Cherry, in Los Angeles in 1958–9 show a hesitating revolutionary, hampered by an inadequate rhythm section and by the image of a record label, Contemporary, attached to the then contemporary West Coast jazz style. Coleman's aesthetic programme, the abolition of the 'background', was not to be solved in these surroundings.

The turning-point came in 1959 with a six-month engagement at the Five Spot in New York and with recording a couple of albums for Atlantic Records. In the meantime Coleman had settled upon some appropriate partners who, together with Cherry, not only followed his concept of playing freely but also made their own decisive contributions: bassist Charlie Haden and drummer Billy Higgins, both of whom had earlier played with Coleman in Los Angeles.

Coleman's musical innovations, and their shock effect on jazz listeners at the time, proceeded mainly from the negation of a quasi-axiomatic prerequisite of late 1950s jazz: the use of a predetermined harmonic framework as a formal element and as a basis for improvisation. This negative definition alone does not, of course, capture the character of Coleman's music, but it is important to realize that it was mainly the *lack* of these features that collided with the listening habits of jazz audiences. What Coleman had to offer in place of the rules which he threw overboard was less apparent and became evident only with intensive listening. His compositions, the themes or 'heads' of his pieces, are no longer functioning just to supply a set of chord changes to the improvisers, but in fact in most of his pieces there is a much deeper unity of theme and improvisation. The nature of that unity is more emotional than formal in so far as the expressive character of his themes often determines the emotional content of his improvisations, as is apparent from the lamenting character of *Lonely Woman* and the boppish *Chronology*. A most interesting relationship between composition and improvisation is represented by *Congeniality*, which would become a model for many other of Coleman's themes. The expressive content of this rather complex thematic structure is happy, sad and hectic, all three together, and it is up to the improviser to choose from the reservoir of emotional content. *Congeniality*, therefore, is a free jazz theme in the truest sense.

Both Coleman's themes and his improvisations reveal a peculiar mixture of complexity and simplicity. Both reflect a definite blues character, which by means of an extremely angular phrasing often becomes distorted without ever losing its identity. And, as in archaic blues singing, Coleman ignores not only the border lines of established formal frameworks but also the norms of intonation, especially those following the laws of equal temperament. Nevertheless, his improvisations are by no means so 'disorderly' as they appeared to audiences at the time. On the contrary, independent from the limiting structures of chord changes, his solos reveal a fascinating inner logic: one musical thought develops from another, becomes transformed, distorted, and leads into another one – a process of motivic improvisation in which the details very often show a rather simple, folksong-like character and yet the total structure gives the impression of high complexity. One is reminded of Bix Beiderbecke's notion of the 'correlated chorus', but with the 'chorus' left out!

In his notes to **Change of the Century** (recorded in October 1959), Coleman wrote: 'Perhaps the most important new element in our music is our conception of free group improvisation'. Considering the time it was written, this should be appraised as a plan whose realization still had to wait some time. To be sure, by that time Coleman's music was already free from norms previously held to be inviolable. But he had not given up the dominating role of the *soloist* and the resultant auxiliary role of the *accompanists*. The bassist had been liberated from playing chord progressions, but he and the drummer still had to mark the beat. The universally common sequence of composed ensembles and improvised solos was only rarely broken by faint-hearted free collective improvisation.

This all radically changed in December 1960 with *Free Jazz*, a performance that named a whole musical era. To record it, two quartets gathered in the Atlantic studio: with Coleman were Cherry, Haden, and drummers Higgins and Ed Blackwell (all members of his groups), plus bass clarinettist Eric Dolphy, trumpeter Freddie Hubbard, and string bass player Scott LeFaro. These eight musicians carried Coleman's conception of 'free group improvisation' to a degree of completeness such as had never been heard before in jazz. In terms of freedom, as it was understood in 1960, the outer framework of this 36-minute piece is infinitesimal. Transitional ensemble passages link single complexes, each led by a different 'soloist'. Some of the ensembles are written out and have the character of Coleman's typical lines. Others are partially improvised structures which he misleadingly calls 'harmonic unisons'; here he provides the players with tonal material, the timing of which is not fixed. This procedure was to be highly important as a compositional technique in later developments of free jazz.

The players have obviously agreed on a tonal centre and the tempo, to which they adhere from start to finish. Coleman also allotted roles: Haden and Blackwell are responsible for the fundamental rhythm, which LaFaro and Higgins constantly challenge and consciously 'endanger'. The music played on the basis of these agreements depends for coherence almost exclusively on the players' readiness to interact. Within a traditional framework, an uninspired collective improvisation with no interactions among the players might be hard to take, but would not end in a musical catastrophe. The same unrelated simultaneity within the boundlessness of free jazz could only end in chaos. Coleman and his musicians must have been aware of this danger. They avoided it by a method that had already given shape to Coleman's solo improvisations: motivic chain associations. In *Free Jazz* these are evolved by the group as a whole, not just by a single improviser. Ideas introduced by the 'soloist' of a given section are spontaneously paraphrased by the other players, developed further, and handed back to the originator in altered form. Despite an abundance of motivic interaction, the overall character of *Free Jazz* must be called static rather than dynamic. Only rarely do emotional climaxes occur, and there is hardly any differentiation of expression. The wealth of musical ideas and the continuous exchange of thoughts takes place on an unvarying expressive level. Now and then there are passages in which folksong-like phrases by Coleman suggest a kind of bucolic peacefulness; and Dolphy's rumbling, vocalized bass clarinet sound adds an occasional humorous touch. But these passages are both short and relatively incidental.

Thirty years later, one can only speculate about the causes of this emotional – not musical – sameness. Perhaps Coleman and his musicians were too occupied articulating a newly acquired vocabulary and conquering a musical terra incognita to devise a palette of moods and temperaments in the process. It may also be that Coleman set out to create a static, homogeneous whole, his main point being the integration of individual ideas to form an interlocking collective. His later music would seem to support the latter theory.

CD

***The Shape of Jazz to Come*, Atlantic 1317-2 (USA)**

Don Cherry (pocket c), Ornette Coleman (as), Charlie Haden (sb), Billy Higgins (d)

Hollywood	22 May 1959	**Focus on Sanity**
		Chronology
		Peace
		Congeniality
		Lonely Woman

Other CDs

same contents:
Atlantic 19238-2 (USA)
Atlantic 781339-2 (Europe)

CD

***Free Jazz*, Atlantic 1364-2 (USA)**

Cherry (pocket c), Freddie Hubbard (t), Coleman (as), Eric Dolphy (bass cl), Haden, Scott LaFaro (sb), Ed Blackwell, Higgins (d)
New York 21 Dec 1960 **Free Jazz**

* * *

Cecil Taylor: *Unit Structures*

'Call Ornette the shepherd and Cecil the seer.' In these words tenor saxophonist and poet Archie Shepp characterized the two musicians who are at once the true initiators of free jazz and its musical and psychological antipodes ('A View from the Inside', *Down Beat Music '66*, Chicago, 1966, pp. 39–44). One side of the coin is the 'shepherd' Coleman, with a new and almost folkloristic simplicity of expression whose roots – for all Coleman's abrogation of traditional norms – go back to the blues, the bedrock of jazz. The other side is the 'seer' Cecil Taylor, whose music is marked by unremitting tension between emotionality and a structural complexity that is due in part to assimilating tendencies of contemporary European and American new music into the language of free jazz.

Born in New York and raised in a middle-class milieu, Taylor attended the New England Conservatory in Boston, where he became familiar with the music of Bartók, Stravinsky and Schoenberg. Clearly it was there that he developed the idea of trying 'to consciously utilize the energies and techniques of European composers, and to blend them with the traditional music of the American Negro, and in this way create a new energy' (Shepp, op. cit.).

Two aspects are essential to an understanding of Taylor's music: his rhythmic approach and his attitude towards musical form. His music generally has no fixed tempo and therefore most of the time lacks the elementary quality of mainstream styles, swing. Nevertheless, his music generates an immense drive, a phenomenon that is sometimes called by contemporary theorists 'rhythmic energy'. 'Energy', of course, is a metaphor whose terminological virtues are problematic. In any event, energy is not to be misunderstood as loudness, measured in decibels, but it is – in the sense of kinetic energy – a variable of time. It creates motion or results from motion, in a process by which the level of loudness is just one variable and by no means a constant. Taylor's concept of rhythmic energy was very influential on younger free-jazz musicians, especially in Europe.

Similarly, Taylor creates *ad hoc*, open forms which none the less follow certain creative principles. He organizes many pieces in three parts, and he may repeat the second or third, each time with a different content. He calls these formal units *Anacrusis*, *Plain* and *Area*. The title of the first part is taken from antique prosody and means 'upbeat'. Its purpose, then, is to lay down a general 'programme' rather than to provide material for improvisatory elaboration. That happens in the section called *Plain*. There the actual thematic (or motivic) material evolves. In the process of improvisation the players state, juxtapose and reshape predetermined structures. New melodic and rhythmic patterns grow out of given patterns. As Taylor obscurely explains in his own liner notes, 'content, quality and change growth in addition to direction found [*sic*]'. In the third part, *Area*, 'intuition and given material mix group interaction'. An 'unknown totality, made whole through self analysis (improvisation), the conscious manipulation of known material'. The realization of this method of spontaneous formal construction in his compositions proves to be extremely flexible. What happens is not that traditional formal schemes are replaced by others whose novelty lay only in an unorthodox terminology; the formal disposition of *Anacrusis*, *Plain* and *Area* does not create boundaries, but directions, not predictable structures, but progressive developments.

Taylor's principles may be deduced very well from his composition-improvisation *Unit Structures*, a piece which draws its title from the large repertory of structural units which build its substantial material. The *Anacrusis* here is a brief (one minute long) episode in which the production of sound colour plays the dominant role. *Plain 1* follows, in which collective improvising presents and develops the different structural units. The two reedmen, Ken McIntyre and Jimmy Lyons, dominate *Area 1*, which is freely improvised. In the rather brief *Plain 2* again some structural units are established and transformed. *Area 2* follows, in which trumpeter Eddie Gale Stevens Jr and finally Taylor himself step into the foreground. The whole ensemble then joins in, improvising into the finale.

What Taylor does in *Unit Structures* illustrates several things that are of great importance to free jazz as a whole. Beneath the emotional impact of his music, which is what the listener primarily responds to, is an intricate network of formal relationships. These inner formative aspects – created by composition and agreement, as well as by spontaneous interaction on the part of the players – are utterly independent of traditional schematic demarcations and thus have only a low degree of predictability for the listener. The German jazz critic Manfred Miller correctly states that a first unprepared encounter with Taylor's music usually causes complete confusion ('Cecil Taylor: Schlüsselfigur der Avantgarde', *Neue Musikzeitung*, xix/1, Feb/March 1970, 10). And, especially at live performances by his group, again and again one meets listeners who are willing but irritated. Overwhelmed by the energy and intensity of the music, they are rarely able immediately to grasp the inner structures. But it is precisely the formative details – which become apparent only after several listenings – that set Taylor's music apart from that of his many cluster-clumping emulators. By demonstrating that spontaneity and structure need not be mutually exclusive, Taylor shows that the freedom of free jazz does not mean complete abstention from every kind of organization. Freedom lies, first and foremost, in the opportunity to make a conscious choice from boundless material. Further, the idea is to shape this material in such a way that the end result is not only a psychogram of the musicians involved, but a musical structure, balancing in equal measure emotion and intellect, energy and form.

CD

***Unit Structures*, Blue Note CDP 7-84237-2 (USA)**

Jimmy Lyons (as), Ken McIntyre (as), Cecil Taylor (p), Henry Grimes, Alan Silva (sb), Andrew Cyrille (d)

Englewood Cliffs, NJ	19 May 1966	**Steps**

Eddie Gale Stevens Jr (tpt), McIntyre (oboe), Taylor (p and bells), Grimes, Silva (sb), Cyrille (d)

Enter Evening (Soft Line Structure)

Stevens (tpt), Lyons (as), McIntyre (bass cl), Taylor (p), Grimes, Silva (sb), Cyrille (d)

Unit Structures (As of a Now; Section)

Taylor, Grimes, Silva, Cyrille — **Tales (8 Whips)**

Other CDs

same contents:
Blue Note BCT 84237; Blue Note B21Y 84237 (USA)
Blue Note BNZ 217 (UK)

* * *

John Coltrane: *The Major Works of John Coltrane*

In 1965 the evolution of free jazz received a new central figure and thus a new stylistic focus. John Coltrane, who had worked his way from the rhythm-and-blues sounds of Earl Bostic's group, through hard bop. Miles Davis's modal concept and his own harmonic adventures (*Giant Steps*), now joined the young generation of free players. This step not only had far-reaching musical consequences but also a strong symbolic value: Coltrane, the established artist, demonstrated his solidarity with a group of socially underprivileged young musicians of the New York scene.

The first and, at the same time, most famous musical document of this coalition is an approximately three-quarter-hour piece, *Ascension*, recorded on 25 June 1965 in the Impulse! studios in New York, in two takes of uncertain order. (Confusingly, both takes were released at one time or another under the original catalogue number, Impulse! 95; they were distinguished by the order of solos, listed below, and by the words 'Edition I' or 'Edition II', stamped on the vinyl near the LP label.) Taking part were trumpeters Dewey Johnson and Freddie Hubbard, alto saxophonists Marion Brown and John Tchicai, tenor players Coltrane, Pharoah Sanders and Archie Shepp, pianist McCoy Tyner, string bassists Art Davis and Jimmy Garrison, and drummer Elvin Jones.

From the list of players alone, it is clear that this session meant a great deal more than just another free-jazz recording. But what is really special about *Ascension* goes beyond the personnel of the group and the length of the piece. 'This is possibly the most powerful human sound ever recorded', began the review of *Ascension* by jazz theorist and critic Bill Mathieu in *Down Beat* (5 May 1966, p. 25). His words are just as valid today as they were in the mid-1960s, a significant reflection of the emotional impact *Ascension* had on listeners at the time.

Even while *Ascension* was being made, that is, during the recording session, the musicians must have been aware that they were involved in an experience of total communication and that the product could never match that experience completely. Marion Brown said later: 'We did two takes, and they both had that kind of thing in them that makes people scream. The people who were in the studio *were screaming*' (liner notes to **Ascension**, HMV CSD 3543, by A. B. Spellman). Here we arrive at a problem that looms even larger as free jazz develops: being in on the act of creation, the 'now', becomes at least as significant as the musical end-product, the 'after'. Whether or not the acoustical result, the recording, transcends the event of total communication is, likely as not, of secondary interest to the musicians themselves. Nevertheless, one of the most apparent features for the listener is the extraordinary emotion of *Ascension*. This very intensity may obscure the fact that the piece has thoroughly traditional elements, and, where one might assume that each man is playing exactly what he pleases, there is actually a definite musical organization.

As many listeners have pointed out, the construction of *Ascension* has parallels to that of Ornette Coleman's double quartet recording from 1960, *Free Jazz*. In both, the formal framework is an alternation of collective improvisations and solos, and there is a minimum of preset material and a maximum of spontaneous, free creation. But although the two show a similar radical stance in their renunciation of convention (and thus similarly triggered the development of jazz in ensuing years), their internal structure and their emotional content represent fundamentally different dialects of the same language.

In *Ascension*, the formal disposition into collective improvisations and solos has a second framework superimposed on it, which is a source of structural differentiation, especially during ensemble passages. It consists of systematic changes of modal levels, and occurs with only slight deviations in all eight collective improvisations. Such an organization – however elementary it may be – naturally needs a certain amount of steering, especially when, as in *Ascension*, organization occurs spontaneously, being subject to no schematic breakdown with a fixed timing. Usually the steersman is Coltrane. He gives signals for changing modes by holding tones related to the modal level towards which the music is moving. In the collective improvisations, changes thus initiated are then usually defined by complete scales or scale fragments – played as a rule by Hubbard – and stabilized by chordal patterns from Tyner.

The melodic nucleus of *Ascension*, a short motif played by Coltrane to open the first collective improvisation, doubtless has a symbolic character; its similarity to the main theme of his suite *A Love Supreme* cannot be missed. But this motif has only a secondary function in the piece. The principal model used to steer the group improvisations consists of descending lines which both define the mode and create a distinct body of sound. These lines, often scalar fragments or broken chords drawn from the modal framework, are obviously prearranged only as to the general course they take, not as to their melodic shape or exactly where they occur.

Thus a large number of rhythmically independent lines are set against one another by seven wind instruments, with resultant overlapping. This superimposition produces rapidly moving sound-fields whose rhythmic differentiation is provided as a rule by the rhythm section, rather than coming from within. When seven independent lines coincide, the relationships among them lose clarity, fusing into a field of sound enlivened by irregular accentuations. On the other hand, there are passages in *Ascension* in which individual musicians, by incessantly repeating short rhythmic motifs, create a driving, drilling rhythm whose impulses, when taken up by the other improvisers, awaken associations with the energetic rhythms of Cecil Taylor's groups.

In spite of the variety and density of sound and the occasionally dissonant cutting edge of these group improvisations, it is evident that their elements, namely what the various musicians play, are less 'revolutionary' melodically than the sum of those parts. Whereas in the group improvisations of Coleman's *Free Jazz* every melody has a clearly drawn intervallic structure (the result of motivic give and take between the musicians), the horn lines in *Ascension*, taken singly, are relatively simple in shape.

Here we can lay hold of one of the essential differences between these two recordings, whose consequences are probably the most important and far reaching in the evolution of free jazz. In the collective improvisations of *Free Jazz* the contributions of each and every improviser have a certain melodic life of their own; motivic connections and dove-tailing of the various parts create a polyphonic web of interactions. In *Ascension*, on the other hand, the parts contribute above all to the formation of changing sound-structures, in which the individual usually has only a secondary importance. Quite plainly, the central idea is not to produce a network of interwoven independent lines, but dense sound complexes.

The musical significance of *Ascension* for the further course of jazz history lies in part in its chronological position. Coming five years after Coleman's piece, it signals a second phase of free collective improvisation: the chamber-music dialogue between musicians, which was Coleman's principal aim, is succeeded by orchestral sound structures. No longer does the whole take its meaning from the constituent elements. Just the reverse: the elements now cannot be understood except by reference to the whole.

CD

***The Major Works of John Coltrane*, Impulse! GRD-2-113 (USA)**

Freddie Hubbard, Dewey Johnson (tpt), Marion Brown, John Tchicai (as), John Coltrane, Pharoah Sanders, Archie Shepp (ts), McCoy Tyner (p), Art Davis, Jimmy Garrison (sb), Elvin Jones (d)

Englewood Cliffs, NJ	28 June 1965	**Ascension** (Edition I) **Ascension** (Edition II)

Coltrane (ts), Sanders (ts, per), Donald Garrett (bass cl, per), Joe Brazil (fl, per), Tyner (p), Garrison (sb), Jones (d)

Lynwood, WA	1 Oct 1965	**Om**

Coltrane, Sanders (ts), Garrett (bass cl, sb), Tyner (p), Garrison (sb), Jones (d), Frank Butler (d, per), Juno Lewis (per, v)

Los Angeles	14 Oct 1965	**Kulu Se Mama**
omit (v)		**Selflessness**

Other CDs

Ascension (Edition I):
Impulse! 254745-2 (Europe)

Ascension (Edition II):
MCA Impulse! AS 95 (USA); Impulse! 254618-2 (Europe)

* * *

Archie Shepp: *Fire Music*

Tenor saxophonist, composer, publicist, poet, actor, dramatist, high school teacher, and eventually, professor of African-American music – when Archie Shepp appeared on the New York jazz scene in 1959, he soon became known as *the* angry young man of free jazz, not so much because of his musical work but more so because he was so vociferous about defects in American society, racial discrimination and the absurdities of the music business and its journalistic appendices. After working with Cecil Taylor for a while, Shepp, together with trumpeter Don Cherry and alto saxophonist John Tchicai, formed the New York Contemporary Five, a group that produced some of the most cohesive music in the early years of free jazz. In 1964, with the support of his mentor John Coltrane, Shepp managed to get a contract with the Impulse! label and consequently began leading groups.

Fire Music, recorded in 1965, is the second album that Shepp made for Impulse! It features him in four of his most important roles: as an improvising artist with a highly personal style, as a composer and arranger of intricate pieces, as a poet and as a reciter. At the same time **Fire Music** shows Archie Shepp at the first height of his creative potential. The initial upheavals of the free jazz revolution were over, and the time had come to formulate the new musical language in a clear and relaxed manner.

Fire Music consists of five pieces, each distinctive in structural design and emotional content. *Hambone*, referring to a character in a children's television show, is a complex, multi-thematic and also multi-stylistic composition, with changes in tempo, metre, melodic density and rhythmic configurations. References to rhythm-and-blues gestures play an important role, but also some very sensitive rubato melodies and elements of bop are brought into play. *Los Olvidados* (the forgotten ones), a poly-thematic structure as well, shows Charles Mingus's influence, in the considerable variety of its themes and musical climates, as well as in its use of continuous accelerations and retardations. *Malcolm, Malcolm – Semper Malcolm* of course deals with the late Malcolm X, a central figure of the black Muslim movement. The piece features Shepp as poet and reciter, and also as a sensitive creator of musical sounds that blend in a fascinating way with the bowed playing of string bassist David Izenson. *Prelude to a Kiss*, a ballad composed by the great Duke Ellington, shows Shepp in one of his most typical roles, as a custodian of the tradition of African-American music and also of the school of big-toned tenor saxophonists playing in the manner of Coleman Hawkins and Ben Webster. The final track is, in light of the then-current mid-1960s craze for commercialized versions of the bossa nova style, obviously meant to be an ironic gesture toward pop culture: *The Girl from Ipanema*, which had been recorded by Stan Getz and singer Astrud Gilberto the previous year, is here treated by Shepp in a highly satirical way. Leaving intact only two bars of this world-famous anthem of the style, he deforms the rest, especially the bridge. This girl has her roots not in Brazilian Ipanema but in the heart of black America.

CD

***Fire Music*, MCA Impulse! MCAD 39121 (USA)**

Ted Curson (tpt), Joseph Orange (tb), Marion Brown (as), Archie Shepp (ts), Reggie Johnson (sb), Joe Chambers (d)

New York	16 Feb 1965	**The Girl from Ipanema** **Prelude to a Kiss** **Hambone** **Los Olvidados**
Shepp (ts, v), David Izenzon (sb), J. C. Moses (d)		**Malcolm, Malcolm – Semper Malcolm**

* * *

Albert Ayler: *Spiritual Unity*

'Never try to figure out what happens, because you would never get the true message.' By saying this, tenor saxophonist Albert Ayler did not want to imply that his music does not have any rational foundations, but that its essence lies in its content and expressive character (the message), rather than its structural design. Maybe this is one of the reasons why Ayler's music has rarely been the object of musicological research, more often serving instead as the subject of polemics and philosophical controversies. Yet it is quite possible to decipher the essence of Ayler's music in structural terms, if only one gets to its basic principle, which lies in the dualism of simplicity versus complexity, as manifested in the tension between Ayler's compositions and his improvisations.

The most prominent feature of the thematic material composed by Ayler is its simplicity. But unlike the music of Ornette Coleman, for example, this is not the simplicity of the blues, but of an imaginary genre of folk songs, or folk dances, whose character seems more Euro-American than African-American. And whereas Coleman, however simply he may write, always gives his 'folk song' pieces some surprising edges and twists, the folk character of Ayler's themes is never impaired. Ayler said of these pieces: 'I'd like to play something – like the beginning of *Ghosts* – that people can hum. And I want to play songs like I used to sing when I was real small. Folk melodies that all the people would understand' (Nat Hentoff, 'The Truth is Marching In', *Down Beat*, 33 (17 November 1966): 18). Hence for thematic material he chose the most elementary melodic, harmonic and rhythmic structures. In general, Ayler's melodies are strictly diatonic and frequently move in arpeggiated chords, and their harmonies utilize correspondingly rudimentary cadential patterns. Their rhythm is simple and more or less confirms (or helps to establish) the metre.

The most characteristic piece is *Ghosts*, an imaginary children's song of striking simplicity and tunefulness. Ayler not only recorded at least five different versions of *Ghosts* (two of them on this album **Spiritual Unity**), but also used its melody as a *leitmotif* in his improvisations in many other pieces. Another type of composition is represented by themes like *The Wizard*, which consists primarily of riff-like motives of high kinetic density.

The complex side of Ayler's music is to be found in his improvisations. It is a form of complexity that is reached not by constructive means, but by distortion or melodic deformation and by dynamics. In fact, most of the time Ayler replaces melody in the traditional sense with amelodic contours of overblown sound having no definite pitch.

Often these waves develop into motivic structures that follow – in a highly distorted way – the periodicity of a given folk-like theme, making clear that in the seemingly complete irregularity of Ayler's improvisations, there does exist an inner connection with his simple thematic materials. At the same time, Ayler's improvisations reveal an extremely high degree of dynamic differentiation, hardly to be found anywhere else in jazz (a genre in which possibilities for contrasts in volume are vastly underexplored). He begins phrases (or sound waves) loudly and then lets them subside gradually to a quiet level, or until they end in whispered tones that are barely audible.

Albert Ayler's musical career was all too short. His life ended under mysterious circumstances in 1970, when he was only 34. **Spiritual Unity**, recorded in 1964, no doubt belongs with his most inspired and inspiring recordings.

CD

***Spiritual Unity*, ESP 1002-2 (USA)**

Albert Ayler (ts), Gary Peacock (sb), Sunny Murray (d)

New York	10 July 1964	**Ghosts** (1st variation)
		The Wizard
		Spirits
		Ghosts (2nd variation)

* * *

Don Cherry: *Eternal Rhythm*

Don Cherry first became known on the jazz scene as the trumpeter of the original Ornette Coleman quartet. (Actually he did not play trumpet but a pocket cornet.) After he left Coleman's group in the early 1960s Cherry played with Sonny Rollins, Archie Shepp and Albert Ayler, among others. In 1965 he moved to Europe, where he formed his own groups and started developing a new concept for the integration of composition and improvisation into large suites, exemplified on his albums **Complete Communion** (1965) and **Symphony for Improvisers** (1966). At the same time, Cherry became involved in non-Western musics, especially those of India, Turkey and North Africa. From these sources he not only adapted different stylistic means (rhythmic patterns, circular melodies) but also expanded his own instrumental scope by learning to play wooden flutes, conch horns, berimbau, and a large array of percussion instruments.

The first recorded document of this evolution is an LP Cherry made in Berlin in 1968, **Eternal Rhythm**. It was made in the wake of a concert during the Berlin Jazztage, for which he was given the chance to assemble an orchestra in line with his own ideas. At the concert, between the big bands of Maynard Ferguson and Count Basie, Cherry's orchestra ultimately demolished everything the Berlin audience was accustomed to thinking about big bands as an institution. Cherry accomplished this by employing his ten musicians not as members of sections, not as players who either lead or accompany, but as the individualists they were.

The musicians he brought together in the studio to record the suite *Eternal Rhythm* on 11 and 12 November 1968 were among the best available on the European free-jazz scene at that time: trombonists Albert Mangelsdorff and Eje Thelin, saxophonist Bernt Rosengren, pianist Joachim Kühn, bassist Arild Andersen and drummer Jacques Thollot; Karl Berger, a former member of Cherry's groups then working in New York, played various metallophones. The American guitarist Sonny Sharrock also came over to work with this ensemble.

A necessary point in understanding *Eternal Rhythm* is that, despite its *ad hoc* assembly, put together for Berlin, the piece is by no means all a product of spontaneous ideas organized and laid down in a few rehearsals, but rather an extract of Cherry's previous work with his European groups. The group conception of *Eternal Rhythm* consists of a composed or agreed-upon system of references, within which the musicians have a maximum amount of individual freedom and where Cherry acts as the catalyst: 'Don is a natural conductor of music through his playing', said Berger in the programme notes for the festival ('Das Don-Cherry-Märchen', *Berliner Jazztage 1968*, p. 12).

Themes occur at strategic points of the piece. They create structural differentiation and formal articulation, but they hardly figure as motivic material in the improvisations. All in all, the work seems to be designed from the outset for evolving sounds and rhythms rather than for developing motivic and melodic interconnections. Part of this shift of emphasis is the fact that the solos are relatively few and short; collective improvisation predominates. When solo instruments do emerge, they are almost always surrounded by a dense web of sounds, partly diffuse and partly accentuated, which provide a constantly changing background. Occasionally, as in Kühn's piano solo, the background gradually heightens in dynamics, intensity and density until it becomes the foreground and submerges the solo.

A new element in Cherry's music underscores the dominance of tone colour and rhythm: third-world music. The most obvious indications of its influence are the many instruments which are in addition to each man's main horn. Cherry, for instance, plays a whole assortment of differently tuned flutes and recorders of Eastern origin. Rosengren plays a normal Western oboe, but he uses it more like an Indian sanāī. The percussion section makes the chief contribution to the oriental coloration of the orchestra. Its arsenal includes gongs, chimes and the Balinese gamelan instruments gender and saron; the latter are metal idiophones resembling the xylophone in form and owe their special sound to the tuned bamboo resonators fixed below the metal bars.

Don Cherry's *Eternal Rhythm*, with its own particular emphasis on Near and Far Eastern musical elements, by no means stands alone in the history of free jazz. It must be viewed together with similar ventures undertaken by musicians such as John Coltrane, Pharoah Sanders, Archie Shepp, Sunny Murray, Sun Ra, etc., as the consequence of a growing sympathy for the musical cultures of Africa and Asia. Within this stylistic metamorphosis, *Eternal Rhythm* has the status of an individual variant. On no account should it be placed in the same category as the **Jazz Meets the World** recordings made about the same time in Germany, which signalled (sometimes in a very self-conscious way) that the Third World was in vogue, just as bossa nova or Baroque jazz before it, and jazz-rock later. For Cherry, as opposed to most of the European musicians riding the oriental wave, occupation with African and Asian music signified more than just a short-lived fad. *Eternal Rhythm* should be considered as one long stride in a march which gradually increased the distance between Cherry and the rules of the game of the free-jazz mainstream.

LP

***Eternal Rhythm*, Saba MPS 15204 (Germany)**

Don Cherry (c, bamboo fl, bengali fl, metal fl, plastic fl, gender, saron, northern bells, Haitian gourd, v), Albert Mangelsdorff, Eje Thelin (tb), Bernt Rosengren (cl, ts, fl, oboe), Joachim Kühn (p), Sonny Sharrock (g), Arild Andersen (sb), Jacques Thollot (d, saron, bells, gong, v), Karl Berger (vb, p, gender)

Berlin	11–12 Nov 1968	**Baby's Breath** **Sonny Sharrock** **Turkish Prayer** **Crystal Clear** (exposition) **Endless Beginnings**
Cherry unaccompanied		**Baby's Breath**
full orchestra		**Autumn Melody** **Lanoo** **Crystal Clear** (development) **Screaming** **Always Beginnings**

Other LPs

same contents:
BASF 21 20680–7; MPS 15007; Saba MPS 68225 (Germany)

* * *

Art Ensemble of Chicago: *A Jackson in your House*

There is hardly any other group of individuals in free jazz as tightly enclosed by a classification as those Chicago musicians who banded together in the mid-1960s under the heading of the Association for the Advancement of Creative Musicians (AACM) and who later, in several formations, spread throughout the world the tidings of a new kind of Chicago jazz.

The specific nature of Chicago free jazz can be explained partly by geographical location and the nature of the jazz community in the city, where the music arose relatively unaffected by what was happening musically in New York. In New York, constantly increasing competition led jazzmen to do their own thing, that is, to strive for uniqueness and individuality. Chicago was different. There was a unifying bond from the outset, in that the musicians were members of a larger organization and renounced all claims to individual fame. This ultimately had an effect on the stylistic evolution of their music. When we speak of Chicago free jazz, then, we have to describe not only a certain group of musicians and a certain kind of music, but also an interdependence of social and musical factors to which that music owes its individual status within the stylistic conglomerate of free jazz.

The first musical core of Chicago free jazz became the Experimental Band, led by pianist Muhal Richard Abrams. Practically every AACM member played in this ever-changing orchestra, which thus became a kind of school for upcoming Chicago avant-gardists. During the second half of the 1960s a number of bands within the band emerged from Abrams's workshop. Proceeding from a common musical basis but employing different means, these smaller groups consolidated knowledge gained in the experimental workshop of the big band into the specific Chicago style of free jazz. The most prominent group within this context became the Art Ensemble of Chicago, consisting of Lester Bowie, Joseph Jarman, Roscoe Mitchell and Malachi Favors. Building on a distinct jazz foundation, this quartet expanded and consolidated into an unmistakable musical language the experience gained in the various AACM groups. Their music represents the maturity of Chicago free jazz.

One of the most important stylistic factors in AACM music from the very beginning was an exploration of tone colour, which led to the use of an unusual quantity of diverse instruments and also had a direct effect on creative principles, such as the development of static sound-fields. When the quartet went to Europe in 1969 it took along more than 500 musical instruments. A first impression of what that array included can be gained by summarizing the instruments listed on recordings made by the group in France:

Lester Bowie: trumpet, flugelhorn, cowhorn, bass drum.

Roscoe Mitchell: soprano, alto and bass saxophone, clarinet, flute, cymbals, gongs, conga drums, logs, steel drum, gongs, bells, siren, whistles.

Joseph Jarman: soprano, alto and tenor saxophone, clarinet, oboe, bassoon, flutes, marimba, vibraphone, guitar, conga drums, bells, gongs, whistles, sirens.

Malachi Favors: double bass, Fender bass, banjo, zither, log drums, other percussion.

Some recordings also have piano and accordion. (Later, in 1970, while still in Paris, Don Moye, playing drums and a wide variety of percussion, joined the group, making it a quintet.)

Considering the quantity of equipment and the availability of a wide range of sounds and colours, there is an astounding economy in their use. One of the decisive achievements of the Art Ensemble lies precisely in turning away from every kind of musical muscle-flexing. What creates the impression of intensity and enhancement is not decibels, but density and drive. Moreover, the music gains greatly in transparency by dispensing with a drummer. Actually, what is dispensed with is jazz percussion of the traditional kind, for each of the musicians plays several percussion instruments. However, by spreading the instruments over the quartet, by a division of labour into bass drum, cymbals, melodic percussion (marimba and vibraphone) and other struck devices, they employ percussion selectively and to a considerable degree as a means of structural differentiation. It is not constantly present as a matter of course.

Isolating the various elements of conventional jazz percussion goes hand in hand with a partial rejection of customary ways of playing other instruments. The piano, for example, which the Art Ensemble paradoxically puts in the 'little instrument' category, generally provides just a background of sound. The accordion does not play melodies – its traditional function – but produces long, sustained, static tones. Favors does not pluck the strings of the zither, but strikes them with a stick to produce either sharply accentuated clusters of indeterminate pitch or a rhythmic continuum. These and other examples of denatured sound rarely appear for their own sake and should not be understood as isolated occurrences sufficient unto themselves. In general, each stands in a dialectical relationship to the music around it, complementing some other musical element. For example, the interpolation of denatured sounds and noises sometimes deliberately disrupts standard themes, such as Dexter Gordon's *Dexterity*. Similar things happen during some lyrical trumpet solos by Bowie, whose beauty of melody and tone contrasts with the rattle and click of little instruments. This confrontation of various levels of expression and style, in which the expressive power of one level relativizes the other, is an important part of the Art Ensemble's basic conception, even though the passages in question may not be preplanned in detail but result from spontaneous interactions among the musicians.

Compared with the music of other AACM groups up to 1968, there is a considerable expansion in the Art Ensemble's thematic material. The group shows a partiality for traditional elements from all conceivable musical and cultural areas. The CD **A Jackson in your House** provides excellent examples of this. The title piece, a suite, begins with a pompous overture whose baroque grace is considerably impaired by percussive interjections and laughter. There follows a dixieland piece with slapped bass and a clarinet whose syncopated phrasing is insistently corny. Finally, an episode imitates the swing style. *Get in Line* goes at an unmilitary headlong pace until it ends in the total pandemonium of a collective cymbal-crashing session. The Viennese charm of *The Waltz* is rather adversely affected by the bass's hacking accentuations.

Without a doubt, this is music about music, for the 'historical' material appears unfiltered only in the rarest instances. Otherwise, the Art Ensemble shapes it to match the group's specific stylistic features. Clichés remain recognizable by allusion and occasionally by ironic overstatement, but they are never brought directly into play. Many of these pieces are funny (to use a word that is taboo in jazz criticism) and are doubtless meant to be. Others, such as the album **Message to our Folks**, are obviously tied up with the socio-critical message of the Art Ensemble, which takes a much more direct and aggressive line than was the case in earlier AACM productions; ideology, no longer disguised as poetry, appears as a sermon (*Old Time Religion*). On the album **Certain Blacks**, from 1970, open agitation replaces metaphorical trappings on the title track *Certain Blacks Do What They Wanna! – Join Them!*. Getting these messages across in a medium as non-political as music necessarily means going back to models whose meaning the listener can decipher. But reversion does not unavoidably have to end in triviality. The Art Ensemble's 'traditional' themes demonstrate this conclusively. To measure them exclusively by an aesthetic yardstick, however, would be just as senseless as to interpret the group's improvisations in sound as protest.

CD

***A Jackson in your House*, Charly CDCHARLY 78 (UK)**

Lester Bowie (tpt, flugelhorn, bass drums, horns, v), Roscoe Mitchell (as, ss, bass s, cl, fl, cymbals, gongs, conga drums, logs, bells, siren, whistle, steel drums, v), Joseph Jarman (as, ss, cl, oboe, fl, marimba, vb, conga drums, bells, whistles, gongs, siren, v), Malachi Favors (sb, elb, bj, log drums, zither, perc, v)

Paris	23 June 1969	**A Jackson in your House**
		Get in Line
		The Waltz
		Ericka
		Song for Charles

* * *

Sun Ra: *The Heliocentric Worlds of Sun Ra, vol.I: 'Other Worlds'; The Heliocentric Worlds of Sun Ra, vol.II: 'The Sun Myth'*

One of the most controversial personalities within the history of free jazz is pianist, composer and bandleader Sun Ra. Scolded as a charlatan by one faction of the jazz community, he is celebrated as a charismatic figure and genial innovator by another. Reasons for this discrepancy are more easily found in his intergalactic philosophy than in the musical output of his orchestra (which he calls 'Arkestra'), which was very convincing from the outset.

Like the AACM groups, Sun Ra developed his musical language in Chicago during the early 1960s. But before the mid-1960s his music could not be called free jazz. The first step in this stylistic direction is represented by two CDs recorded in 1965, **The Heliocentric Worlds of Sun Ra**, volumes 1 and 2. It is difficult to subject the albums to objective musical analysis. When one hears them today, they suggest comparisons with things that originated at the same time, or just before or after, in adjacent stylistic areas of free jazz. One is reminded of the monumental collective improvisation in Coltrane's *Ascension* (recorded the same year), of the unorthodox tone colours and the courageous use of silence in the AACM's music, of the collective composing in Cecil

Taylor's groups. But beyond all musical and technical parallels – and having nothing to do with the extent to which tradition is overcome – there is a component in Sun Ra's music, at the time of **Heliocentric Worlds**, that distinguishes it from every other kind of free jazz: creative principles of composition and improvisation interweave with programmed emotional qualities.

On **Heliocentric Worlds**, one can hardly speak of composition in the customary sense. Not one of the ten pieces has fixed thematic material; there are no written-out horn arrangements; there is not even a tiny unison melodic line. Abstaining in this way from everything that can be prefabricated in the form of notes does not, however, lead to disorganization. On the contrary, the music of these two CDs has extraordinary clarity of structure and a broad range of emotional levels. This circumstance can presumably be traced to three different factors: the use of programmes to establish musical processes; a specific kind of communication between Sun Ra and his sidemen; and the high standard of these musicians.

There are clear indications in **Heliocentric Worlds** that Sun Ra's real 'thematic material' is found in the titles of his pieces, that the 'themes' are thus formulated verbally and not musically. Numerous interviews with Sun Ra and his musicians testify that he has always been concerned with translating ideas into music, illustrating emotional states or sketching pictures. The titles of his pieces function in that process as captions or mottos. During the 1950s translation of a verbal programme was more or less accomplished in the composition (that is, the arrangement, instrumentation, etc.), while improvisation by the soloists – who were still playing hard bop – was for the most part untouched by the programmatic aspects of the thematic material. Now, in 1965, the transformation of figurative or emotional ideas no longer occurs by writing out a composition. Instead, the motto expressed in the title of a piece directly intervenes in the process of improvisatory creation.

(With a good conscience, one may call this programme music, but one should not overlook the fact that in highly emotional music like jazz the expression of something, be it happiness, sadness, anger, sex, loneliness, peace, or whatever, has always been one of the triggers of musical creation. Renouncing emotion does not necessarily result in bad music, but it often does result in dull jazz.)

So that these theoretical considerations do not remain as mysterious and cryptic as Sun Ra's own explanations of his music generally are, I shall illustrate the translation of programmatic ideas into musical form in three pieces from the first volume of **Heliocentric Worlds**.

Outer Nothingness: the group translates the 'emptiness' of space into a musical context by coupling two expressive ideas: a strong emphasis on low instrumental registers, and tonal and rhythmic indeterminacy. Timpani, bongos and bass marimba (the last played by Sun Ra) provide a rhythmic background that is lively but diffusely accentuated. Against it, trombone, bass trombone, bass clarinet and baritone saxophone play long, sustained, dissonant, loud sounds in their lowest registers. The entrances do not all occur at once; sounds overlap, creating an impression of turgid, narrow clusters. The combination of bass register, atonality, rhythmic diffuseness and aggressive dynamics sets off that magical and threatening atmosphere which is present as an emotional basis in the ensemble passages. The collective improvisations in this piece, then, are as it were verbally pre-programmed, and some of the solos also realize the motto. A good example of the latter is John Gilmore's tenor saxophone solo, in which he suggests 'nothingness' in a significant way: he dispenses with melodic evolution. There are fragmentary phrases in half-steps, irregular single accents, and a great deal of 'space' (rests). He takes the solo at a free tempo and plays against a rhythmically unorganized, diffuse backdrop of drums, cymbals and bass marimba. He ends with overblown multiphonics (producing several pitches simultaneously in the highest register).

Dancing in the Sun: rhythm translates the title into music. This is the only piece on **Heliocentric Worlds** that has a continuous beat, and the improvisations swing in a traditional manner.

Nebulae: this is a solo improvisation by Sun Ra on celeste, an instrument whose timbre is relatively thin and yet diffuse. The sound itself is enough to awaken associations with something 'nebulous' and indeterminate, and therefore Sun Ra frequently uses the instrument in ensemble passages to create a quasi 'spheric' background of sound. The way Sun Ra improvises augments the non-transparency of the celeste's timbre: atonal lines in free tempo criss-cross, becoming interwoven into a dense melodic web, while irregularly interjected dissonant chords or clusters contribute to rhythmic insecurity.

The relationships between verbal theme and musical structure in **Heliocentric Worlds** are not all as easy to pin down as in these three examples. In particular the longer compositions – *Sun Myth, House of Beauty* and *Cosmic Chaos* – contain a profusion of forms and a diversity of emotional levels which can hardly be reduced to a single programmatic theme. The tendency to translate ideas or emotional states into music is nevertheless noticeable almost throughout. And that translation of thoughts or feelings proves to be what really governs the progress of Sun Ra's music. 'My rule is that every note written or played must be a living note. In order to achieve this, I use notes like words in a sentence, making each series of sounds a separate thought' (Barry McRae: 'Sun Ra', *Jazz Journal*, xix, August 1966, 15–16).

CD

The *Heliocentric Worlds of Sun Ra, Vol.I: 'Other Worlds'*, ESP 1014–2 (USA)

Chris Capers (tpt), Teddy Nance (tb), Bernard Pettaway (bass tb), Danny Davis (as, fl), Marshall Allen (as, fl, piccolo, per), John Gilmore (ts, timpani), Robert Cummings (bass cl, woodblocks), Pat Patrick (bar, per), Sun Ra (p, electric celeste, bass marimba, per, arr), Ronnie Boykins (sb)

New York 20 April 1965 **Heliocentric**

as ***Heliocentric****, but Gilmore (ts), Sun Ra (timpani)*

Outer Nothingness

as ***Heliocentric****, but Gilmore (ts), and add Jimhmi Johnson (per)*

Other Worlds

as ***Heliocentric****, but Allen (spiral cymbal), Gilmore (ts), Johnson (per, timpani)*

The Cosmos

as ***Heliocentric*** **Of Heavenly Things**

Sun Ra unaccompanied (p, electric celeste) **Nebulae**

as ***Heliocentric****, but Gilmore (ts)* **Dancing in the Sun**

Other CDs

same contents:

Cosmic Equation, Magic Music 30011–CD (Italy)

CD

The *Heliocentric Worlds of Sun Ra, Vol.II: 'The Sun Myth'*, ESP 1017–2 (USA)

Walter Miller (tpt), Allen (as, fl, piccolo, per), Gilmore (ts), Patrick (bar, per), Cummings (bass, cl, per), Sun Ra (p, clavoline, per, tuned bongo), Boykins (sb), Roger Blank (per)

New York 16 Nov 1965 **The Sun Myth**

A House of Beauty

Cosmic Chaos

* * *

Charlie Haden: *Liberation Music Orchestra*

Charlie Haden's 'liberation music' can be understood as the musical expression of a growing tendency towards political consciousness among jazz musicians during the 1960s and early 1970s, a tendency that of course had its roots in the general social and political upheavals and the mental climate of that time. Political ideas infiltrated the work of such musicians and groups as Charles Mingus, Sonny Rollins, Max Roach, Archie Shepp and the Art Ensemble of Chicago. Haden, in explaining his motives for the production of this liberation music, wrote in the liner notes: 'The music in this album is dedicated to creating a better world; a world without war and killing, without racism, without poverty and exploitation; a world where men of all governments realize the vital importance of life and strive to protect rather than to destroy it. We hope to see a new society of enlightenment and wisdom where creative thought becomes the most dominant force in all people's lives.'

The problem with any kind of political music is how to get the message across by means of such an abstract art. The most common and not always very convincing solution seems to lie in adding titles or texts to the music. Haden, with the help of pianist, arranger and composer Carla Bley, took another path. He avoided the direct meaning of texts and instead used a musical material with political connotations that, at least potentially, communicate indirectly by memory and historical experience. The nucleus of the liberation music consists of socialist songs from the Spanish Civil War (1936–9). In addition, Haden uses the *Song of the United Front*, written by Hanns Eisler; the unofficial hymn of the American civil rights movement, *We Shall Overcome*; Ornette Coleman's *War Orphans*; and his own graceful *Song for Ché* (as well as a functional introduction, mid-point ending and interlude composed by Bley). Thus the political meaning establishes itself through the use of the music within a certain political context, and listeners who do not know anything about this context will hardly be able to decipher Haden's political concerns. And so once again, despite the path Haden has taken, one has to have recourse to titles, commentaries and explanation.

The general aesthetic problems of political music notwithstanding, Haden's **Liberation Music Orchestra** is a most important document for the specific mental climate of jazz in the 1960s. It is also a very convincing example of the integration of historical musical material into the context of free jazz. Arranging for an ensemble drawn from the ranks of the Jazz Composer's Orchestra, which she had headed with trumpeter Mike Mantler since 1966, Bley tackled the challenge of finding a balance between scored big-band passages and free improvisation, the result being a combination of rowdy ensemble work and fiery solos, with recurring and essentially unaltered references to the borrowed songs.

CD

***Liberation Music Orchestra*, MCA Impulse! AS 9183 (USA)**

Mike Mantler (tpt), Roswell Rudd (tb), Bob Northern (french horn, bells, crow call, whistle, woodblocks), Howard Johnson (tuba), Gato Barbieri (ts, cl), Dewey Redman (ts, as), Perry Robinson (cl), Carla Bley (org, p, tambourine, v), Sam Brown (g, Tanganyikan guitar, thumb piano), Charlie Haden (sb), Paul Motian (d, per)

New York	27–29 April 1969	**The Introduction**
omit Brown		**Song of the United Front**

add Don Cherry (c, flugelhorn, Indian bamboo fl, Indian wood fl) and Brown

	El Quinto Regimiento (The Fifth Regiment)
	Los Cuatro Generales (The Four Generals)
	Viva la Quince Brigada (Long Live the Fifteenth Brigade)
omit Cherry	**The Ending to the First Side**
add Cherry	**Song for Ché**
omit Cherry	**War Orphans**
	The Interlude (Drinking Music)
omit Brown and Cherry; add Andrew Cyrille (per)	**Circus '68, '69**
omit Cyrille	**We Shall Overcome**

Other CDs

same contents:
Impulse! MCAD 39125 (USA)
Impulse! 254633–2 (Europe)

* * *

Anthony Braxton: *Five Pieces 1975*

Like the Art Ensemble of Chicago, multi-instrumentalist reedplayer and composer Anthony Braxton came out of the ranks of the AACM, Chicago's musicians' co-operative. But whereas the Art Ensemble took its main impulses from traditional Afro-American music as well as from musical cultures of the Third World, Braxton drew much of his inspiration from studying the works and concepts of the Second Viennese School, and of John Cage and Karl-Heinz Stockhausen. These different points of reference in fact mark what might be called different schools of the Chicago jazz *avant-garde*: one down to earth, colourful and extroverted, the other intellectual, austere and introspective (which does not mean that Braxton's music cannot be highly emotional at times).

For the development of contemporary jazz Braxton's role as a composer and conceptualist is of equally high importance as his role as an instrumentalist. In his compositions, which show a great variety of constructive principles, he often draws from mathematical concepts and graphic schemes, most of the time leaving large parts for the improvising musicians to fill out with their ideas. As an instrumentalist, using the whole consorts of saxophones, clarinets and flutes, he is a true virtuoso, with a distinctive style.

The LP **Five Pieces 1975** features Braxton as a composer and improviser with one of his most coherent groups of the 1970s, consisting of Canadian trumpeter Kenny Wheeler, who in England became at home in many contemporary jazz idioms; bassist Dave Holland, who came out of the English free-music scene, turned towards jazz-rock upon being 'discovered' by Miles Davis, and developed into one of the most inspiring free-jazz players; and American drummer Barry Altschul, an extremely sound-conscious percussionist and a master of playing 'free time'.

The **Five Pieces** each show a distinct character demonstrating a different principle of collective creation. *You Stepped out of a Dream* of course is not by Braxton, but an old standard. Braxton performs it in a duet with Holland, the latter playing the changes conventionally, whereas Braxton constantly moves in and out of the harmonic framework, thus accepting the traditional formal structure of the tune but at the same time filling it with new content.

The second piece starts out with an extended multi-part thematic structure, leads into a drum solo focusing on sound colour, and ends with a short reprise of the initial thematic motifs. It is a heterogeneous piece in which the parts are linked without any attempt to create a whole. The third piece is conventional in its framework (theme – improvisation – theme) and adventurous in its content. It opens with a typically angular Braxton theme in even (non-swinging) eighths and with a complex, wide intervallic structure, played by the horns in unison over an intricate rhythmic foundation laid out synchronically by bass and drums. Braxton's improvisation, in correspondence with the thematic material, is mostly in staccato, even eighths and seems purposefully to avoid any association with the rhythmic substance of conventional jazz.

The fourth piece shows the most stratified structural approach. It again starts with a unison line with dodecaphonic allusions, which develops peacefully over a second layer, a slow bass drone. The ensuing collective improvisations aim towards different goals: a gradual intensification and then reduction of rhythmic energy and structural density, and a constant change of register and instrumental sound colour. In the course of a few minutes Braxton moves from sopranino saxophone via B flat clarinet and flute to contrabass clarinet.

Five Pieces 1975 is an important album in Braxton's career. Although it by no means represents the vast scope of his musical world, this recording suitably demonstrates the possibilities of integrating the spontaneity of improvisation with structural processes of composition.

LP

***Five Pieces 1975*, Arista AL 4064 (USA)**

Anthony Braxton (as), Dave Holland (sb)
New York 1 July 1975 **You Stepped out of a Dream**

Braxton (as, sopranino s, cl, contrabass cl, fl, alto fl), Kenny Wheeler (tpt, flugelhorn), Holland (sb), Barry Altschul (d)
2 July 1975

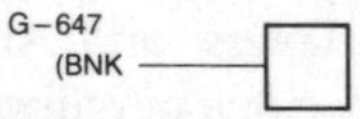

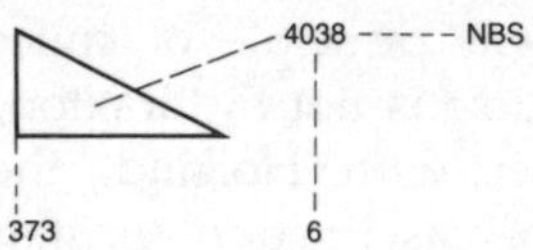

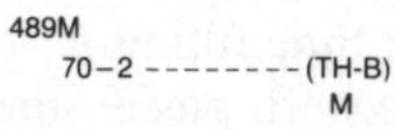

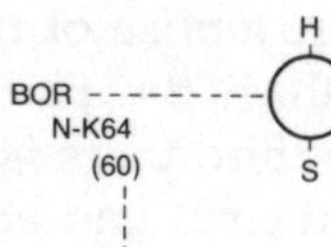

Alexander von Schlippenbach: *Globe Unity*

A united effort to imitate creative developments in the United States marks the history of jazz in Europe up to the middle of the 1960s. European musicians readily absorbed the changing aesthetics of Afro-American music, the development of new structural patterns and a gradual expansion of musical material. The closest possible imitation of the respective American original was a standard for musical quality. It was probably not only the lack of self-assurance concerning their own creative capacity that caused European musicians to produce such a decade of epigons and imitations; the range of expectations put up by audiences and jazz critics added to this development. To them, the prophet was esteemed in his own country only when interpreting the message sent by the American gods.

Towards the middle of the 1960s there was a gradual change in the way European musicians related to their American models. The development of American jazz itself may have caused this, but so may have the change in the way European musicians perceived themselves. Like their American models, they broke with the routine of harmonic-metrical schemes, dissolved the beat into an irregular series of accentuations and concentrated on musical sound instead of improvisations oriented towards melody. At the same time, however, they began to drift from the direct influence of American musicians. They created their own manners of expression and structural patterns, making these points central to their music. Thus, towards the end of the decade, a specific European type of free jazz found its way to the public.

What were the causes of this unexpected emancipation? At least two factors are worth mentioning, one inherent in the music itself, the other ideological or, if you will, political. The first is that, with the origin of free jazz, European musicians for the first time were confronted with a style that was not definite, not bound by a system of relatively limited standards, but comprising a variety of individual and group styles, one hardly comparing with the next. The development of a personal style within this conglomerate of styles called 'free jazz' was easier than ever before.

The second cause has much to do with the social and political atmosphere among young people during the late 1960s. The students' movement in Germany and France had come to a climax in 1968, and numerous young musicians sympathized with it. Above all two essential characteristics of this movement might have influenced the young free-jazz phalanx's self-perception: a distaste for any kind of authority and an underlying anti-Americanism which was intensified by the cruel consequences of the Vietnam War. For the first time since World

War II, the position of the USA as the 'lodestar' had been thoroughly questioned. Despite the common cliché of jazz musicians as romantic outsiders (of course there have been a few, such as Thelonious Monk), jazz musicians do not exist outside society, but are part of it. Certainly in the 1960s European jazz musicians were very much inside what was happening around them, and consequently these tendencies found shape in their perceptions of self and – in a mediated way – in their music.

One of the first and most important documents for the emancipation of European jazz is a recording by the Globe Unity Orchestra. Founded in 1966, the orchestra owes its existence to RIAS Berlin having requested Alexander von Schlippenbach to write a composition for the Jazzfest Berlin of that year. Schlippenbach successfully created a compositional framework that allowed for a great number of free-jazz players. Without falling back on old big-band clichés, he organized a structural variety while still leaving enough space for individual creative exertion and spontaneous interaction.

The nucleus of the Globe Unity Orchestra was made up of members of the Manfred Schoof quintet and the Peter Brötzmann trio, to whom were added five horn players and vibraphonist Karl Berger. Schlippenbach wrote two compositions of distinct character for the orchestra's performance and the recording sessions that followed: *Globe Unity* and *Sun*. *Globe Unity* is characterized by an intensive rhythmic power play, with parts for solos and collective ensemble organized according to given scalar material, clusters or tonally undefined chords. The basic conception shows similarities to Coltrane's *Ascension*, although a direct influence is unlikely. (Call-and-response patterns are a common way to organize orchestral free jazz.) Still, a comparison with *Ascension* is instructive. It reveals certain essential characteristics of European free jazz, already formed in this early phase of its existence. The basic rhythmic posture of *Globe Unity* – compared with the music of Afro-American musicians – is more hectic, nervous, at times violent. The improvisations presented by the horns concentrate more on sound and energy than on melodic continuity; they are consequently so anti-melodic that not even the 'screamers' in *Ascension* (Pharoah Sanders and Archie Shepp) can compare.

Even more impressive than the approach to composition and improvisation in *Globe Unity* is the systematic exploration of sound in *Sun*. Compared with *Globe Unity*, *Sun* is looser in its musical structure, more contemplative in its emotional substance and more concentrated on colour than on energetic power. The instrumentation emphasizes this. 'Little instruments', as the Art Ensemble of Chicago later dubbed them, such as rattles, triangles, lotus flutes, flexatones, etc., play a dominant role. Also, the way the horns are played shows a differentiated treatment of sound patterns, particularly in the trumpet solos by Claude Deron and Schoof; both solos involve undefined pitch (generated by the technique of half-valving, that is, depressing the pistons half way) and distorted sounds.

When the Globe Unity Orchestra's first production was presented to the public, it met strong resentment and caused many a misunderstanding. Newspaper headlines ran 'Odd men playing jokes at the Philharmonie' and 'A blend of jazz and chamber music'. Neither of these quotations underline the clear-sightedness of contemporary jazz critics. In any case, resentment against the Globe Unity's music and its classification as part of the hybrid 'third stream' had a result: public performances became rare. Only since 1972 has the ensemble performed on a regular basis, gradually stabilizing their musical language. This in no way diminishes the standing of the first Globe Unity Orchestra within the historical development of original European free jazz. It proved there was a musical substance in the making that could do without prefabricated patterns. It helped make clear that there was a growing potential for European musicians, in and apart from Globe Unity, to make this substance come alive.

LP

***Globe Unity*, Saba MPS SB 15109 (Germany)**

Claude Deron (tpt, lotus fl), Manfred Schoof (flugelhorn, triangle), Willie Lietzmann (tuba, marimba), Peter Brötzmann (as, gurke), Gerd Dudek (ts, duck call), Kris Wanders (bar, zorna as, lotus fl), Willem Breuker (bar, ss, ratchet), Gunter Hampel (bass cl, fl, pandeira), Buschi Niebergall (sb, siren), Peter Kowald (sb, bells), Jacki Liebezeit (d, per, darbuka), Mani Neumeier (d, gongs, per), Alexander von Schlippenbach (p, tam tam, clocks, gongs, knives, flexatone)

Cologne	6–7 Dec 1966	**Globe Unity**
add Karl Berger (vb)		**Sun**

* * *

Peter Brötzmann: *Machine Gun*

Since 1968 the mainstream of West German free jazz has been represented mainly by Brötzmann and Schlippenbach. There was a growing tendency towards working in large ensembles and an ever-increasing internationalization of the scene, involving principally English and Dutch musicians. 'In retrospect', Brötzmann stated in an interview with

Didier Pennequin ('Allemagne – Pays Bas', *Jazz magazine*, no.220, March 1974, 19–21), 'the year of 1968 was the year of big bands, where we met with friends to play like crazy.'

One of the most striking examples of the work of the large ensembles is Brötzmann's LP **Machine Gun**. (The title is not meant to express any military program; 'like a machine gun' was the way that Don Cherry described Brötzmann's playing, as reported in Bert Noglik: *Jazzwerkstatt International*, Berlin, 1981, p. 199.) **Machine Gun** may be seen as the product of what bassist Peter Kowald once called the 'kaputt-play' era: 'The main objective was to really and thoroughly tear apart the old values, this meaning: to omit any harmony and melody; and the result wasn't boring only because it was played with such high intensity... In a way, that 'kaputt-play' time has made anything 'playable', equally playable, that is possible in music... Today, for the first time, it becomes clear that our generation can do without the musical influence of most Americans' (Dirk Fröse: 'Freiheit wovon – Freiheit wozu? Peter Kowald Quintett,' *Jazz Podium*, xxi, Dec 1972, pp. 22–5). What kind of musical results were achieved in that period of 'kaputt-play', a period which not only Kowald considers to have been transitional? In the context of **Machine Gun** some general characteristics can be listed.

Composing is generally limited to a minimum. By and large without themes, the music presents riff-like attacks and interjections, at times directed only in their movement up or down. There is a tendency to use distorted thematic quotations. The players abandon definite pitch as a stable element of musical organization in favour of unstable sound patterns. Structural distinctions result mainly from collective variations of register, density and loudness. Developmental processes lead, somewhat inevitably, towards a limit where individual musical events cannot be strictly identified as such, but combine to become a diffuse, intensive totality. Sometimes homogeneous and low-pitched instrumentation, frequently used by Brötzmann's ensembles, supports this process. In general, the musicians have a restless attitude towards time. Even when density and intensity diminish and the structures open up, the basic tempo (not necessarily played, but felt) remains hectic. In fact, at that stage of development there is something like a standard tempo, probably on account of physiological reasons: a majority of recordings show an identical metrical basis, moving at 240 to 270 beats per minute. This means that a four-beat measure approximately corresponds to human pulsation, and thus the kind of free jazz we are dealing with here is body-related to a much higher degree than is generally assumed.

Not immediately touching upon the structural characteristics of this music, but upon its reception, is the problem of instrumental technique. From conversations, I have gathered that many listeners, especially those 'well-acquainted' with jazz, wonder whether those who make all that noise on stage just cannot play, whether they really do master their instruments. It seems relatively easy to dub it 'kaputt-play' as Kowald did, yet it is not that simple. Most musicians working in the ensembles of Brötzmann, Schlippenbach and Schoof had developed individual techniques enabling them not only to demolish conventions but also to develop, in a constructive way, new personal techniques. Someone who argues that Evan Parker's sound nuances, or Brötzmann's overblown sounds, have nothing to do with technique, someone arguing that Gerd Dudek's and Alan Skidmore's almost classical virtuosity is the sole acceptable quintessence of technique, simply reveals a narrow conception of technique. Technique in music means, at least to me, the ability to do what I want to do. Brötzmann expressed it more pointedly: 'I'm not what you would call a "good technician". To me, technique taught by conservatories is bullshit. To make a music like ours, you have to develop your own technique first and then make your own music. The objective of our music is not to play "right" or "wrong", that doesn't mean a thing. What really counts is to know what one's playing' (Pennequin, op. cit.).

CD

***Machine Gun*, FMP CD24 (Germany)**

Peter Brötzmann (ts, bar), Willem Breuker (ts, bass cl), Evan Parker (ts), Fred van Hove (p), Peter Kowald, Buschi Niebergall (sb), Han Bennink (d), Sven Johansson (d, per)

Bremen, West Germany	May 1968	**Machine Gun** **Responsible – for Jan De Ven** **Music for Han Bennink**

* * *

Music Improvisation Company: *The Music Improvisation Company 1968–1971*

During the early phase of its existence European free jazz developed a number of different schools or regional styles, and it was quite common to speak of German energy play, Dutch comical music or British sound research. This last is represented by the work of the

Music Improvisation Company (MIC), founded in 1968. The essence of its work lies in the idea of non-idiomatic music, as formulated by guitarist Derek Bailey. A freely improvised music, independent of all existing musical languages, would follow the individual techniques and preferences of the players exclusively.

Of course this idea is probably based on an illusion, for although the mere avoidance of any idiomatically fixed means of creation must not automatically result in a new musical idiom (it could, as with John Cage, lead into the dominion of chance), the practical results of the MIC's work make it quite clear that this music can easily be identified as a particular and unmistakable form of musical creation – in other words, as a music idiom. Obviously *style*, under certain preconditions, may be established when any associations with existing musical languages are forcefully avoided. One of the most important preconditions is that the improviser acts as a conscious ego and does not follow only the generative energy of chance. And this is obviously the case with the members of the MIC.

To describe the group's conceptual guidelines, it seems easier to identify features it does not exhibit rather than those it does: no tonality, no repetition, no melodic continuity, no periodicity, no system. On the other hand there is one feature obvious at first hearing: the emancipation of noise as an independent means of creation, 'noise' meaning sound with a dense structure of non-harmonic frequencies whose amplitudes and phases change randomly.

The most efficient noise-producer in the group, of course, is Hugh Davies. With his electronics he brings to the music a vast repertory of noise: static noise, like buzzing or humming, pulsating noise, like crackling or clapping, variable noise, like gliding frequency bands, etc. Also, guitarist Bailey uses his instrument to produce aperiodic sound structures by rubbing the strings with his fingers or other devices, and by working with variable string tension. And Parker finds a number of ways to produce non-harmonic and also percussive sounds on his saxophone. Thus the conscious manipulation of noise is one dominating feature of the MIC's work. The other is interaction. Because any written score or even verbal arrangements are taboo, the group relies exclusively on spontaneous actions and reactions among all four players. This interaction within the group converges most of the time, for although both Davies and Bailey speak of a tendency towards 'mutual subversion', meaning that one player might irritate the other by non-participation or contrary action, such situations occur only rarely, at least in the group's recordings. This form of agreement should not be confused with harmony and linear development, for the overall sound structure is predominantly dissonant and discontinuous.

LP

***The Music Improvisation Company 1968–1971*, Incus 17 (UK)**

Evan Parker (ss, electric autoharp), Hugh Davies (org, synthesizers), Derek Bailey (g), Jamie Muir (per)

London	4 July 1969	**Painting**
		Untitled 3
		Untitled 4
		Bedrest
	18 June 1970	**Its Tongue Trapped to the Rock by a Limpet, the Water Rat Succumbed to the Incoming Tide**
		In the Victim's Absence

* * *

Michel Portal: *Michel Portal Unit à Châteauvallon*

The French multi-instrumental reed player Michel Portal is an exceptional musician. Many listeners praise him as a brilliant interpreter of Mozart's Clarinet Concerto; others know him as an experimenter with sound who worked his way through Stockhausen's intuitive music as well as through Pierre Boulez's *Domaines*; still others saw him in the band that accompanied Edith Piaf at the staging of *Sheherazade*; and still others find him one of the most important improvisers in European contemporary jazz.

A musical chameleon? Although Portal's work is highly competent in all these areas, his main focus of interest – his love – is jazz: 'Jazz, for me, really offers the only possibility to be free, to float, to dream' (Philippe Carles and Francis Marmande: 'Michel Portal ou la parole au present', *Jazz magazine*, no.210, April 1973, 11–14, 32–6). In 1966 he was a member of the first French free-jazz group, led by pianist François Tusques. He worked with German pianist Joachim Kühn in 1969 and with English baritone saxophonist John Surman in 1970. In 1972 he appeared with his own group at the jazz festival at Châteauvallon. The concert was recorded and produced by the small French label Chant du Monde, and is, I believe, one of the most stimulating recordings to which European free jazz gave birth during the 1970s.

A cursory listening reveals a music that is as far away from American free jazz as from the diverse regional branches of the European *avant-garde*. The music at first gives the impression of being raw and unhewn, with sound complexes resembling square tones and rudimentary melodic contours resembling signals more than songs. There is no trace of French elegance and refinement. In fact the central creative dimensions of this music are to be found in neither melody nor harmony, but in rhythm and sound. That is, the structural and formal work of the group manifests itself essentially in a conscious stratification and junction of sound and rhythm and not in a sequence of melodic inventions or harmonic turns. One of the most important preconditions for the success of this work seems to lie in a distinct and collectively adapted sense for the significance of time and for the economy of material. In both respects the musicians, notwithstanding their drive towards ecstasy, show some quasi-bourgeois virtues: they are patient, in that they do not jump hectically from one event to another, but take their time to let processes and situations slowly grow; they are thrifty, in their concentration, over long stretches of time, on the exposure or variation of a rather narrowly confined repertory of sound structures, on certain forms of groundwork, on certain patterns or variations of intervallic constellations or phrases. All in all this is a collective enterprise of high sensibility, which, unfortunately, never found the acclaim that it deserved.

LP

***Michel Portal Unit à Châteauvallon*, Chant du Monde LDX 74526 (France)**

Bernard Vitet (c, tpt, vln), Michel Portal (bass cl, contrabass cl, as, ss, taragot), Léon Francioli, Beb Guérin (sb), Pierre Favre (per), Tamia (v)

Châteauvallon, France	22 Aug 1972	**No, No But it May Be**

CHAPTER 18

Fusion

Mark Gilbert

Fusion might be the youngest of jazz idioms, but it is not the first hybrid that jazz has produced. Jazz owes its very existence to a confluence of different elements, and almost every stage of its development has been marked by the absorption of some kind of alien influence. Nevertheless, in the early 1970s the term 'fusion' acquired a relatively specific meaning. Since then it has been used in the main to signify a union between jazz and rock or funk. However, there are exceptions, and a fully comprehensive definition remains elusive; even within the area described above, there are as many varieties of fusion as there are types of jazz.

The dominant form of fusion is most easily distinguished from mainstream jazz by its rhythms. Many fusion groups copied the heavily syncopated rhythmic patterns used by the bands which backed such soul artists as the Temptations, Sly Stone and James Brown in the 1960s. Herbie Hancock's Headhunters and the Brecker Brothers borrowed rhythm and much else from such bands; others, such as Bruford and the Mahavishnu Orchestra, had a closer similarity to white rock bands. Still others, like the Pat Metheny Group, Weather Report and Chick Corea's Return to Forever, employed rock and funk mannerisms but also made wide use of Latin American rhythms. However, one thing unified these different types of fusion: all were dominated by repetitive 'straight eighth' rhythms. Funk, rock and Latin music are based on an even division of the beat into two or four, which creates the firm march-like effect so typical of the fusion rhythm section. Swing and bop, on the other hand, divide the beat into three, and the result is a lighter, more flowing pulse. These are 'jazz eighth' rhythms. Funk, rock and Latin rhythms also tend to be more emphatic than swing and bop rhythms; the incisive sound of the snare drum, often produced by a synthesizer, became a hallmark of much 1980s funk-orientated fusion.

Along with the adoption of non-swing rhythms came the use of the instruments and sonorities found in 1960s rock and soul music. The highly amplified electric guitar, piano and bass became staple instruments in the fusion ensemble, as did the synthesizer once it became widely available in the early 1970s. Later, other wind and string instruments were amplified and played through signal processers such as the wa-wa pedal and the phase shifter. By the late 1980s, conventional instruments were able to interface with synthesizers. Many bands also carried Latin and African percussion.

Fusion received a mixed reaction from critics and consumers. Purists tended to see it as diluted jazz; others resented what they perceived as blatant commercialism. Indeed, the energetic marketing of much mediocre material helped to give good fusion a bad name. The genre's detractors dwelt on these artistic failures and ignored, or were ignorant of, the music's many triumphs. However, their cynicism was not shared by audiences – fusion is the most popular jazz form since swing and more than two decades after its emergence it continues to flourish and develop.

* * *

Miles Davis: *In a Silent Way*

A key figure in fusion's development was trumpeter Miles Davis, who worked in the idiom until his death in the 1991. Five of the nine record dates discussed in this chapter were led by Davis's ex-sidemen, and the first by Davis himself.

Davis had always shown a readiness to change direction, and during the 1960s, partly as a result of pressure from his record company, he became interested in rock and soul music. In February 1969 he recorded **In a Silent Way** and soon after abandoned the bop-derived style he had embraced since the mid-1940s.

In a Silent Way borrows extensively from rock music. One of the most important players on the recording is bassist Dave Holland, whose short, repetitive lines virtually define the structure of two of the three tracks and reflect Davis's interest in the sustained 'grooves' found in soul music. Except for a few brief variations, Holland plays the same two- or three-note figure throughout the entire 18 minutes of *Shhh/Peaceful*, while *It's About That Time* is built around two simple bass riffs. The second of these features a combination of notes which are characteristic of rhythm and blues, the music from which soul grew: major and minor thirds and a minor seventh. The bare frameworks of these pieces are also a reminder of Davis's modal work of the late 1950s, which, in reaction to the rapid chord changes of bop, featured tunes with as few as two chords.

Drummer Tony Williams is similarly economical. Except for a brief passage at the climax of *It's About That Time,* he confines himself to relentless, clock-like rhythms on snare drum and hi-hat. His playing here is rudimentary by comparison with his work in Davis's 1960 quintet, but no less dramatic.

In a Silent Way is dominated by haunting, dream-like moods. The playing is generally restrained, and the repetitive figures in the rhythm section combine with the floating textures produced by the three keyboard players to create a trance-like atmosphere which is disturbed only during the climaxes of *It's About That Time.* There were numerous precedents for this impressionist style in Davis's reflective work of the 1950s and in such of his 1960s quintet pieces as *Nefertiti,* and it was to find continued life in Weather Report, the fusion band formed in 1970 by Joe Zawinul and Wayne Shorter.

In typical jazz style, **In a Silent Way** was an impromptu session. Zawinul and guitarist John McLaughlin knew of the date only hours before, and Zawinul's *In a Silent Way* underwent radical revision in the studio. The spontaneity of the meeting can be sensed in the music, which often sounds as if it was arranged as it was performed. The arrangements, like the themes, have none of the complexity of later fusion, and, since the recording contains few preset harmonic progressions, the music often proceeds by other means. For example, *Shhh/Peaceful,* anchored throughout by a terse bass riff, progresses through simple variations of instrumental texture and moments of rest. However, the suspenseful bass motif begs for a resolution which never arrives, and leaves *Shhh/Peaceful* seeming like an unfinished blueprint for the more rounded *It's About That Time.*

The title track, which acts as a prelude to *It's About That Time,* illustrates Davis's attitude to music at that time. Keen to get away from complex chord changes and into groove-based playing, Davis took Zawinul's densely harmonized melody, discarded most of the chords and set it over a simple bowed bass drone and E major triad – the first sound heard from McLaughlin's guitar. The result is an elegiac tone poem which forms an effective contrast with the dark menace of *It's About That Time.*

It's About That Time is a masterpiece of dynamic control and development which inspires the best solos on the recording. It is built on two alternating bass figures, the first creating a sense of suspension which is both relieved and intensified by the increased mobility of the second. The first substantial solos are by McLaughlin, whose nervous, scurrying runs and brittle tone perfectly match the mood of the piece, and by

Wayne Shorter, who made his debut on soprano saxophone on this album. The brooding tension which has been mounting during the first part of the piece finally explodes during Davis's solo. Tony Williams, long restricted to urgent but restrained rim shots and hi-hat cymbal patterns, finds joyous liberation in splashing cymbals and cracking snare-drum accents before the recording draws to a peaceful conclusion with a literal repetition of the title track.

CD

***In a Silent Way*, Columbia Jazz Masterpieces CK 40580 (USA) and CBS Jazz Masterpieces 450982–2 (Europe)**

Miles Davis (tpt), Herbie Hancock, Chick Corea (elp), Joe Zawinul (org), Wayne Shorter (ss), Dave Holland (sb), John McLaughlin (elg), Tony Williams (d)

New York	18 Feb 1969	**Shhh/Peaceful**
	20 Feb 1969	**It's About That Time**
*as **It's About That Time**, but Zawinul (elp)*		**In a Silent Way**

* * *

Mahavishnu Orchestra: *The Inner Mounting Flame*

By the late 1960s, Miles Davis was a long-established and respected figure in the pre-rock jazz world, and his fusion experiments caused a considerable stir. However, while his high visibility meant that he became a focal point for the new movement, there is scant evidence to support the view that he founded it. He provided a platform for younger players who subsequently became leaders in the idiom, but in many cases these players had investigated rock and other non-jazz music before joining Davis. Furthermore, much of the music they produced after leaving Davis bore little resemblance to either **In a Silent Way** or its successor, **Bitches Brew**. Perhaps the most radical departures were made by one of the first of the **In a Silent Way** personnel to lead his own fusion band – John McLaughlin.

In his Mahavishnu Orchestra, McLaughlin sought to merge a wide range of influences, including rock, rhythm and blues, European concert music, Indian music and jazz. This was one of the most self-consciously eclectic and hard rocking of the early fusion bands. In fact, the group's 1971 debut album, **The Inner Mounting Flame**, seems not so much jazz–rock fusion as rock–classical, rock–raga, rock–folk or even rock–

rock fusion. Though many listeners have heard jazz elements in McLaughlin's guitar solos with the Mahavishnu Orchestra, and though, like drummer Billy Cobham, electric bass guitarist Rick Laird and keyboard player Jan Hammer, he had had experience with jazz, his sympathy with rock guitarists is stronger, and not just because he employs a distorted tone and such effects as wa-wa and flanging: the structure and harmonies of his compositions for the Mahavishnu Orchestra are generally more redolent of rock than jazz.

The Inner Mounting Flame reflects the heightened sense of spiritual awareness McLaughlin had developed while studying with the guru Sri Chimnoy in the months before he formed the Mahavishnu Orchestra. It was Chimnoy who had suggested the name Mahavishnu, meaning 'divine compassion, power and justice', for his disciple's new band. McLaughlin had long taken an interest in all aspects of Indian culture, including its music, and this is plainly audible in the sonorities and irregular metres of **The Inner Mounting Flame**. His choice of electric violinist Jerry Goodman as a second melody voice confirmed this interest, and also brought occasional touches of country and folk to the orchestra's music.

One of the most striking aspects of **The Inner Mounting Flame** is its relentless intensity. Tracks such as *Meetings of the Spirit, The Noonward Race* and *Awakening* have incredibly fast and varied thematic lines, the likes of which had never been heard before in jazz or rock. By today's standards the ensembles sound ragged, but at the time they represented a huge technical advance. Nowhere is this more apparent than in the work of Billy Cobham, whose mastery of irregular metres and fast tempos set the standard for jazz-rock drumming. *Awakening* provides an especially formidable example of his prowess: using the snare drum, he phrases along with a theme that moves at something around ten notes per second. This is somewhat faster than march tempo, but proves that Cobham's early years as a military bandsman were not wasted.

The players' virtuosity is further tested by the abrupt way in which new themes, time signatures and tempos are introduced. Precipitate transitions are especially apparent in *Dawn, Vital Transformation* and *The Dance of Maya*. In *Dawn*, an awkward double-time shift from $\substack{7\\4}$ to $\substack{14\\8}$ is accompanied by a radical change of key, with the only link between the two sections a dubiously pitched common tone from the guitar. *Vital Transformation* alternates without preparation between a lopsided $\substack{9\\8}$ and a slow waltz interlude, while *The Dance of Maya* butts a grotesque guitar theme in $\substack{20\\4}$ against an atrophied rhythm-and-blues shuffle in $\substack{17\\8}$. The last two are, however, finally woven into the kind of polytonal blend which might have delighted Charles Ives. Perhaps McLaughlin had some sort of cod surrealism in mind when he wrote these pieces, or perhaps he was recalling a particularly bizarre LSD experience, but it is hard to avoid the suspicion that they were formulated in a rather arbitrary manner. Instead of an evolution of logically related ideas, many of them present a series of unconnected episodes spliced into an uneasy montage.

McLaughlin takes a similar approach to improvising, particularly during up-tempo passages. His solos display a remarkable technical facility, but their turbulent energy does not disguise vagaries of pitching and timing and at best haphazard melodic development. They feature more repeated riffs than continuous melodies and closely mirror the harmony of the compositions, which are based chiefly on exotic minor and pentatonic scales. Apart from Jan Hammer's solo on *The Noonward Race* there is little evidence in **The Inner Mounting Flame** of the chromaticism found in modern jazz. Furthermore, for someone who is often classed as a jazz-rock player, McLaughlin the soloist makes surprisingly little use of the blues. Even in *The Noonward Race*, which opens with the funky dominant ninth chord beloved of soul musicians from James Brown (*Sex Machine*) to Prince (*Kiss*), McLaughlin's solo makes only the briefest of references to the blues.

The Mahavishnu Orchestra's fusion of disparate elements may be viewed as one which only partially coalesced. There are exceptions, as in the lyrical *A Lotus on Irish Streams* and *You Know You Know*, but variety is rarely balanced by unity in McLaughlin's writing. However, it should be remembered that **The Inner Mounting Flame** was the product of an era which placed a special value on experimentation. By that token, it is one of the most authentic – and most dated – of 1970s fusion albums.

CD

***The Inner Mounting Flame*, Columbia CK 31067 (USA)**

John McLaughlin (elg), Jan Hammer (elp), Rick Laird (elb), Billy Cobham (d), Jerry Goodman (vln)

New York 1971 — **Meetings of the Spirit**
Dawn
The Noonward Race

McLaughlin (g), Hammer (p), Goodman (vln) — **A Lotus on Irish Streams**

*as **Meetings of the Spirit*** — **Vital Transformation**
The Dance of Maya
You Know You Know
Awakening

* * *

Chick Corea and Return to Forever: *Hymn of the Seventh Galaxy*

The innovations of the Mahavishnu Orchestra were widely admired and imitated, not least by one of McLaughlin's fellow sidemen from **In a Silent Way**, Chick Corea, who gives more credit to Mahavishnu than to Miles Davis for inspiring his band Return to Forever. He debunked the myth of Davis's influence in conversation with Josef Woodward: 'that's Disneyland ... John's band, more than my experience with Miles, led me to want to turn the volume up and write music that was more dramatic' ('Chick Corea: Piano Dreams Come True', *Down Beat*, lv, September 1988, p. 19). There were other factors too. Around 1970 Corea had become involved with Scientology, the quasi-religious philosophical movement which, among its many tenets, holds that art should concern itself with communication rather than the pursuit of aesthetic perfection. He duly abandoned his explorations of free improvisation with the group Circle and assembled the first edition of Return to Forever, a mostly acoustic quartet which specialized in a gentle fusion of jazz and Brazilian music. His subsequent discovery of the Mahavishnu Orchestra encouraged him to regroup Return to Forever as an all-electric band.

Hymn of the Seventh Galaxy, the 1973 debut album by the new Return to Forever, contains many reminders of **The Inner Mounting Flame**, but also much that is new. Like the Mahavishnu Orchestra, Return to Forever featured high levels of amplification, intricate, rapidly executed themes and the sound of the overdriven electric guitar. It also used irregular time signatures (in *Hymn of the Seventh Galaxy* and the central section of *Theme to the Mothership*), but there the similarity ends. A constant tempo is maintained on all the tracks, and this not only makes them more accessible, but also illustrates Corea's concern with continuity. He had long admired the way in which Béla Bartók avoided the classical compositional formula of theme, development and recapitulation, and he applied similar methods to the construction of *Hymn of the Seventh Galaxy, Captain Señor Mouse, Theme to the Mothership, Space Circus part* 2 and *The Game Maker*. These pieces are all continuously developed, and although they feature only a limited degree of repetition they are highly unified. Even separate tracks are linked by suite-like connections. The electronic white noise which ends *Hymn of the Seventh Galaxy* is echoed by the gong which opens *After the Cosmic Rain*, and the two tracks use closely related keys and tempos. Similar links of key and mood unite the last three tracks, *Space Circus parts 1 and* 2 and *The Game Maker*.

Although Return to Forever inherited its thicker textures from the Mahavishnu Orchestra, much of Corea's writing reflects his interest in lighter weaves and sunny, optimistic moods. Where McLaughlin favours dour minor modes and airless arrangements, Corea is not averse to writing simple melodies in major keys, as in *Captain Señor Mouse* and *Theme to the Mothership*, or letting his music breathe, as in *After the Cosmic Rain, Space Circus parts 1 and 2* and *The Game Maker*. Even McLaughlin substitute Bill Connors cannot help but sound lyrical in such settings.

Hymn of the Seventh Galaxy is also marked by its use of Latin rhythms, which add to the buoyant, dancing quality of the music. Latin, or, to be more precise, Hispanic influences pervade most of Corea's work here, but especially his solos on *After the Cosmic Rain* and *Captain Señor Mouse*. The latter is built on a favourite of Corea's, the Phrygian mode, which has a characteristically Spanish flavour. Corea's long-standing involvement with jazz is also evident, both in the harmonic depth of his writing and in the extraordinary ideas expressed in his solo on *Theme to the Mothership*, where he appears to overdrive his amplifier in order to extract a singing, synthesizer-like tone from the Fender–Rhodes piano. Although he had yet to employ a synthesizer, Corea's interest in novel sonorities is further evident in the use of harpsichord on *Captain Señor Mouse* and the 'fuzz bass' solo on Stanley Clarke's *After the Cosmic Rain*.

The funk and soul side of popular music provided yet another influence upon this album. Clarke is responsible for the funky bass rhythms which underpin the central theme of *After the Cosmic Rain* and the long groove sections of *Theme to the Mothership* and *Space Circus part 2*, although he had yet to develop the slapping percussive attack which became his trademark. Corea has credited soul singers Sly Stone and Stevie Wonder as inspirations for his funkier passages, and his overdriven Rhodes is a forceful reminder of the clavinet sound heard in Wonder's *Superstition* from the 1972 album **Talking Book**.

CD

***Hymn of the Seventh Galaxy*, Polydor 825536–2 (USA)**

Chick Corea (org, elp, gongs), Bill Connors (elg), Stanley Clarke (elb), Lenny White (d, per)

New York	August 1973	**Hymn of the Seventh Galaxy**
add Clarke (fuzz bass, bell tree)		**After the Cosmic Rain**
*as **Hymn**, but add Corea (harpsichord)*		**Captain Señor Mouse**

*as **Hymn**, but Corea (elp)*	**Theme to the Mothership**
Corea (elp, p, org, harpsichord)	**Space Circus part 1**
*as **Hymn**, but Corea (elp)*	**Space Circus part 2**
*as **Hymn**, but Connors (g, elg)*	**The Game Maker**

* * *

Herbie Hancock: *Headhunters*

If Chick Corea was partially influenced by funk, his ex-Davis colleague Herbie Hancock adopted it wholesale. Although he came to international notice playing bop-based jazz in Davis's quintet of the mid-1960s, the pianist grew up in Chicago, surrounded by rhythm and blues. As early as 1963 he had had a pop hit with *Watermelon Man,* a naive gospel-flavoured tune which that year reached the Top 20 in a version by Mongo Santamaria and was later covered on record in more than 200 versions. After leaving Davis, Hancock formed an often esoteric sextet which was eventually dissolved due to poor record sales and Hancock's own misgivings about the material. His rhythm-and-blues muse was returning, and in 1972 he set about devising something like the music he had heard on James Brown's *Papa's Got a Brand New Bag,* Sly Stone's *Thank you falettinme be mice elf agin* and Stevie Wonder's **Talking Book**. The result was **Headhunters**, a million-seller and the archetypal jazz-funk album.

Hancock conceived **Headhunters** as a set of funk tunes directed at the charts, and, sure enough, the opening track, *Chameleon,* became a disco hit. However, in *Chameleon,* and in **Headhunters** as a whole, Hancock inadvertently produced something more than a model for much subsequent commercial funk writing: he created a musical masterpiece with enough substance to satisfy the most discriminating of jazz listeners.

Headhunters has its share of less than original elements, among them a predominance of $\frac{4}{4}$ dance metres, simple harmonic schemes (most of *Chameleon's* 15 minutes are occupied by two chords) and, unlike much of Return to Forever's **Hymn of the Seventh Galaxy**, the use of song structures in which the opening theme is repeated at the end. *Chameleon,* for all its modernity, has that feature in common with the Broadway and Tin Pan Alley songs which form the greater part of the swing and bop repertory.

However, two elements set Hancock's funk apart from its inspirations: one is its remarkably sophisticated rhythmic fabric, the other a wealth of jazz improvisation on the highest level. Regarding the former, Hancock told Bret Primack: 'In the popular forms of funk, which I've been trying to get into, the attention is on the interplay of rhythm between the different instruments. The part the Clavinet plays has to fit with the part the drums play and the line that the bass plays and the line that the guitar plays. It's almost like African drummers where seven drummers play different parts' ('Herbie Hancock: Chameleon in his Disco Phase', *Down Beat*, xlvi, 17 May 1979, p. 12). Nowhere is this principle better illustrated than in *Chameleon*, where the five elements that make up the rhythm section – an ARP synthesizer bass line, a guitar-like electric bass figure, drums and two keyboards – are introduced successively, gradually combining to form an artfully syncopated rhythmic counterpoint. Each part – basically a two-bar riff pattern – has its own space and rarely duplicates the movement of its neighbours; each remains individually audible in the ensemble. *Watermelon Man*, a funky re-working of the 1963 classic with a new eight-bar section and an array of exotic percussion, is similarly constructed. The two other tracks on the album, *Sly* and *Vein Melter*, both use funk rhythms, but feature less of the complex interplay found in *Chameleon*. The restful *Vein Melter* contains echoes of **In a Silent Way** in its atmospheric use of Fender–Rhodes electric piano and its repetitive bass line, although Hancock has said the tune was modelled on his composition *Maiden Voyage*, recorded in 1965.

Although the **Headhunters** band created some tightly arranged funk, it also jammed at length, with the result that the album contains more sustained improvisation than most of its contemporaries. *Chameleon* and *Sly* are built on mostly static harmony and thus provide ideal vehicles for extended modal improvisation. Keyboard solos from Hancock take up almost half of the 15-minute *Chameleon*. The first, on synthesizer, is unremarkable, perhaps because Hancock was feeling his way on the new instrument or was keen to sustain a populist flavour. However, a second, on Fender–Rhodes over a new bass figure, is full of jazz phrasing and ideas. The trio of Hancock, Paul Jackson and Harvey Mason produce three minutes of inventive Latin-flavoured jazz, and eventually, in the very best jazz manner, Hancock trades licks, not with another soloist but with a lyrical, synthesized string section that plays rapid chord changes in triple time; the effect is to throw the staccato funk sections into sharp relief. The clamorous Latin-funk rhythms of *Sly* prompt even wilder improvisations; seven of its ten minutes are filled with undiluted jazz from the Wayne Shorter-like soprano saxophonist Bennie Maupin and a ferociously creative Hancock.

CD

Headhunters, Columbia CK 32731 (USA) and CBS CD 69528 (Europe)

Bennie Maupin (ss, ts, saxello, bass cl, alto fl), Herbie Hancock (syn, clavinet, elp, pipes), Paul Jackson (elb, marimbula), Harvey Mason (d), Bill Summers (conga, shekere, balafon, agogo, cabasa, hindewho, tambourine, log drum, surdo, gankoqui, beer bottle)

San Francisco 1973

Chameleon
Watermelon Man
Sly
Vein Melter

* * *

Weather Report: *Heavy Weather*

As Hancock strove to produce highly structured funk arrangements, two others of his colleagues from **In a Silent Way**, Joe Zawinul and Wayne Shorter, were exploring the opposite extreme. The first two albums by their band Weather Report (formed in 1970 and so named by Shorter because of the ever-changing character of the music) were born largely of collective improvisation. In contrast to the repetitive funk bass lines, infectious riffs and hot solos of **Headhunters**, early Weather Report dealt in haunting, impressionistic textures and fierce, up-tempo interaction which often seemed like an extension of the early fusion experiments of Miles Davis. However, Zawinul's dominance of the band and appetite for larger audiences brought a marked move towards accessibility in the mid-1970s. Free improvisation was replaced by formal composition, often irregular time by imaginatively deployed Latin and funk rhythms, frequent atonality by lyrical melody. The culmination of this development, **Heavy Weather**, was recorded in 1976. It became the group's best-selling album and helped turn Weather Report into the most durable and influential of fusion bands. The new style was no better exemplified than by the celebratory *Birdland*, the disco hit which fuelled a thousand aerobics sessions.

Zawinul was inspired to write *Birdland* by hearing Count Basie's band at the New York club of the same name, and, apart from having many strikingly original features, the piece is a faithful tribute to the swing bandleader. Its rhythm – a crisp straight eight on the hi-hat cymbal – and much of its harmony are plainly of a later vintage, but the sustained use of bluesy riff figures is pure 1930s Kansas City jazz, while the bridge brings idiomatic swing-style chord changes. Zawinul was even able to mimic the warm sound of a big-band horn section by using his recently acquired Oberheim Polythonic synthesizer, an instrument which became central to the orchestral sound that typified Weather Report's music from this point on. (On the later album **8:30** the look back was carried still further in a live version of *Birdland* which replaces the straight eighth-note rhythm with a shuffle beat, though the older style beat does not work well for this piece.)

The full-time appointment of electric bass guitarist Jaco Pastorius (he had recorded only briefly on the preceding album, **Black Market**) not only enriched the orchestral resources of Weather Report but also transformed its sound and repertory. In Pastorius's hands, the electric bass became the complete instrument (as he had shown in *Portrait of Tracy* on **Jaco Pastorius**, his debut album as leader from the same year). He used it to play sustained pedal tones which had the depth and volume of a dozen double basses, traditional walking lines (though not on **Heavy Weather**), Latin and funk figures which had the complexity of an entire Latin American percussion ensemble, chords, and fluent high-register solos and front-line melodies (most conspicuously in the first theme of *Birdland*, where he uses harmonics and string bending like a guitarist). He did all this with a clarity and agility previously unknown on the electric bass.

Pastorius also drew on sound harmonic knowledge to enliven the most routine chord structures. His accompanying lines and fills in *Birdland* invigorate an already strong composition, as does his raw, penetrating tone, achieved by playing his fretless bass very close to the instrument's bridge. The fretless fingerboard also enabled him to play the kind of glissandi heard in the riff to *Palladium* and in *Harlequin*, where he slides an entire chord.

Pastorius contributed two compositions to **Heavy Weather**, both of which used the bass as a melody instrument and introduced a new rhythmic vitality to the band. The devices found in his solo on *Havona* are typical of much of his playing and were imitated by a generation of electric bassists. Indeed, although composition theoretically took precedence over improvisation in the new Weather Report, Pastorius became a major soloist. Even when he was accompanying, his lines were so forceful they often dominated the ensemble.

By contrast, Wayne Shorter's role as a soloist in Weather Report gradually diminished. However, a composition like *Palladium* shows that he had lost none of the writing skill which brought him recognition as one of the most original jazz composers of the 1960s.

CD

***Heavy Weather*, Columbia CK 34418 (USA), CBS CD 81775 (UK) and CBS 462525–2 (Europe)**

Wayne Shorter (ss, ts), Joe Zawinul (syn, p, v, melodica), Jaco Pastorius (elb, mandocello), Alex Acuña (d), Manolo Badrena (tambourine)
Hollywood 1976 **Birdland**

Shorter (ts), Zawinul (syn, elp), Pastorius (elb), Acuña (d)
A Remark You Made

Shorter (ss), Zawinul (syn, elp, melodica), Pastorius (elb), Acuña (d), Badrena (conga)
Teen Town

as ***Teen Town****, but Zawinul (syn, elp, p), Badrena (v)*
Harlequin

Acuña, Badrena (timbales, conga, tom-toms, v) **Rumba Mamá**

Shorter (ss, ts), Zawinul (syn, elp), Pastorius (elb, steel drums), Acuña (d), Badrena (conga, per)
Palladíum

Shorter (ss), Zawinul (syn, p, g, tabla), Pastorius (elb, mandocello), Acuña (d), Badrena (per)
The Juggler

Shorter (ss), Zawinul (syn, p), Pastorius (elb), Acuña (d)
Havona

* * *

Bill Bruford: *Feels Good to Me*

While American fusion was drawing explicitly from such pan-American popular idioms as funk, soul and Latin music, a somewhat different situation pertained across the Atlantic. Many budding young British fusion musicians absorbed the influence of soul music, but they took perhaps greater account of that peculiarly British phenomenon, art rock, as exemplified by such groups as Yes and King Crimson. Perhaps the most creative of British fusion bands was Bruford, led by a former member of both these groups, drummer Bill Bruford. At a time when much early fusion has dated badly, Bruford's 1977 début album, **Feels Good to Me**, remains a timeless masterpiece, its many achievements unsurpassed.

Bruford conceived **Feels Good to Me** as a rock album, notwithstanding its many virtues as a fusion recording. There is, however, a complexity of rhythm, harmony and form, not found in hard rock, which suggests borrowing from jazz and European concert music. There are funky elements, but no **Headhunter**-type grooves, and only passing reference to rhythm and blues and the blues; if ever there were a 'jazz–rock' as opposed to 'jazz–funk' fusion, this is it.

Feels Good to Me smoothly dovetails high velocity ensemble lines which have the harmonic and rhythmic complexity of bop (*Beelzebub* and *If You Can't Stand the Heat...*) with echoes of art rock (*Sample and Hold* and *Feels Good to Me*), jazz-inflected ballads (*Seems Like a Lifetime Ago* and *Either End of August*), heavy rock passages, a romantic piano and flugelhorn duet (*Springtime in Siberia*), Eastern folk flavours which long predate the 1980s world-music boom (the introduction of *Adios a la Pasada*) and impressionism reminiscent of **In a Silent Way** (passages in *Seems Like a Lifetime Ago* and *Sample and Hold*). Although Bruford told this writer that he 'felt like an amateur' when making the album, it is full of highly detailed arrangements, executed with astonishing precision. It displays a wide range of tone colour, mood, rhythm and metre (the first theme of *Beelzebub*, for example, is polymetric, using different metres for the rhythm section and lead instruments), but all the pieces evolve organically and virtually all are supported by a constant or at least regular pulse; there are none of the cut-and-paste arrangements found in the work of the Mahavishnu Orchestra.

Nobody in the band had a classical background; even Dave Stewart, the keyboard player who did much to flesh out the harmonies of Bruford's tunes, was largely self-taught. But, true to its art-rock antecedents, **Feels Good to Me** abounds in classical references. Several of the pieces are continuous suites rather than songs, and the themes to *Feels Good to Me, Either End of August* and *Springtime in Siberia* are all classically flavoured. On many tracks the sound of organ, synthesized brass and strings and the pure, uninflected tone of Kenny Wheeler's flugelhorn reinforce the impression; and on *Springtime in Siberia*, in his duet with Wheeler, Stewart supplies measured block chords which often recall Chopin or Debussy.

Jazz, meanwhile, is nowhere more apparent than in the highly chromatic playing of Allan Holdsworth, who since the early 1980s has been one of the most influential jazz-rock guitarists. A former reed player and disciple of Coltrane, Holdsworth employs the overdriven sound of the rock guitarist, but only because the sustained tones it generates allow him to emulate the phrasing of a saxophone. In pursuit of a reed-like sound, he has redrawn the boundaries of guitar technique and created a novel, unclichéd syntax for his instrument. Though much imitated, his agility, fluidity and lyricism have rarely been matched. **Feels Good to Me** contains some of his best playing, not least on *If You Can't Stand the Heat...*, where he makes uniquely expressive use of the guitar's vibrato bar.

Feels Good to Me also benefits from three appearances by singer Annette Peacock, whose mixture of suppressed hysteria and whispered passion is a delight, and from the bass playing of Jeff Berlin, who, while not as innovative as Pastorius or Stanley Clarke, matched both for virtuosity.

CD

***Feels Good to Me*, Editions EG CD 33 (USA)**

Dave Stewart (syn, org), Allan Holdsworth (elg), Jeff Berlin (elb), Bill Bruford (d, vb or xylophone)

London	August 1977	**Beelzebub**
add Annette Peacock (v)		**Back to the Beginning**

Kenny Wheeler (flugelhorn), Stewart (syn, elp), Holdsworth (elg), Berlin (elg), Bruford (d), Peacock (v)

	Seems Like a Lifetime Ago (part 1)
omit Wheeler; add Bruford (vb or xylophone)	**Seems Like a Lifetime Ago (part 2)**
omit Peacock; add Stewart (org, p)	**Sample and Hold**

Stewart (syn, org, p), Holdsworth, John Goodsall (elg), Berlin (elb), Bruford (d, tambourine)
Feels Good to Me

Wheeler (flugelhorn), Stewart (syn, p), Holdsworth (elg), Berlin (elb), Bruford (d, per)
Either End of August

*as **Beelzebub**, but Stewart (elp, p)*	**If You Can't Stand the Heat...**
Wheeler (flugelhorn), Stewart (p)	**Springtime in Siberia**

*as **Back to the Beginning**, but Stewart (syn, p), Bruford (d)*
Adios a la Pasada (Goodbye to the Past)

* * *

Brecker Brothers: *The Brecker Brothers Collection, volume one; The Brecker Brothers Collection, volume two*

If Bruford and the Mahavishnu Orchestra provide typical examples of jazz-rock, the Brecker Brothers, a band led by saxophonist Michael and trumpeter Randy Brecker between 1974 and 1982 and again since 1991, was the definitive jazz–funk fusion band. It used heavy rock amplification and wailing electric guitar, but its rhythms, all in $\frac{4}{4}$ time, followed the examples of James Brown and Motown. The brothers had been fascinated by funk and soul ever since arriving in New York in the late 1960s, although both had a solid background in jazz and toured and recorded with Horace Silver in the early 1970s. In 1969 they formed one of the first fusion bands, Dreams, a group which made much use of rhythm and blues. It recorded two albums but was only a modest commercial success, and the brothers moved into session work, eventually joining the studio elite. By the late 1980s Michael Brecker had played on more than 400 record dates, frequently supplying just brief eight-bar solos. However, in many instances he played astonishingly inventive, virtuosic full-length improvisations, and on the strength of this work he became probably the most widely imitated saxophonist of the 1980s.

The best of the band's early work is contained in the thoughtfully selected two-volume retrospective **The Brecker Brothers Collection**, a set largely free of the commercial inanities that stained the duo's character in the mid-1970s. There are pallid episodes, notably in the tracks from 1980–1 produced by George Duke, but nothing as spectacularly limp as *Oh My Stars*, *Finger Lickin' Good*, and *Lovely Lady*, three disco items whose only useful function can have been to satisfy Arista's accountants and highlight the sublimity of Randy Brecker's compositional triumphs.

The chief attraction of **The Collection** is its inclusion of the whole of the Brothers' mostly live album **Heavy Metal Bebop**. Such is the power of this set of six pieces that it is tempting to hear **The Collection** primarily as a reissue of that album, with such other choice items as *Rocks*, *Straphangin'* and *Jacknife* and studio versions of *Some Skunk Funk*, *Sponge*, and *Squids* as bonuses. Certainly **Heavy Metal Bebop** provided in its title the perfect summation of the sub-genre created by the Brothers and in its grooves the finest recorded performances of such pieces as *Some Skunk Funk*, *Sponge* and *Funky Sea, Funky Dew*.

The idea of synthesizing the aggression of heavy rock, the rhythmic strut of funk and the harmonic colour of post-bop jazz was not new, but no other band produced such a seamless and stunning interpretation of it as the Brecker Brothers. Perhaps no track better exemplifies this than the live version of *Some Skunk Funk*; in its apoplectic ensembles, delivered at a breakneck speed of 126 beats per minute (about eight notes – and not easy ones – each second), the Brothers' virtuosity, the harmonic sophistication of Randy's writing and the raw energy of rock-and-roll are perfectly integrated to devastating effect.

On top of all that is the soloing. The live setting of **Heavy Metal Bebop** seems to have inspired some of the siblings' best excursions. Randy, as well as demonstrating his mastery of rhythm-and-blues and a bop style that seems to owe something to Woody Shaw, intensified his improvisations with such electronic processing as harmonizer and wa-wa, the latter rendering his sound redolent of that of Miles Davis of the period. Mike debuted on harmonizer on **Heavy**

Metal Bebop, and his long, preaching cadenza on *Funky Sea, Funky Dew*, where he uses the device to produce rich chords reminiscent of a gospel choir, is one of the most compelling passages in an outstanding day's work.

CD

***The Brecker Brothers Collection, volume one*, Novus Series '70 3075–2 (USA) and ND 90442 (Europe); *The Brecker Brothers Collection, volume two*, Novus Series '70 3076–2 (USA) and ND 83076 (Europe)**

Randy Brecker (tpt, electric tpt, flugelhorn), Don Grolnick (tb), David Sanborn (as), Michael Brecker (ts), Bob Mann (elg), Will Lee (elb), Harvey Mason (d), Ralph MacDonald (per)

New York	Jan 1975	**Some Skunk Funk** **Sponge** **A Creature of Many Faces** **Rocks**

Randy Brecker (tpt), Michael Brecker (ts), Grolnick, Doug Riley (kbd), Steve Khan, Hiram Bullock (elg), Lee (elb), Steve Gadd (d), MacDonald (per)

New York	1977	**Funky Sea, Funky Dew**
Chris Parker (d) replaces Gadd		**Squids**

Randy Brecker (tpt), Michael Brecker (ts), Barry Finnerty (elg, guitorganizer), Neil Jason (elb), Terry Bozzio (d)

Roslyn, NY	1977	**Inside Out**
add Randy Brecker (kbd); omit (guitorganizer)		**Some Skunk Funk** **Sponge**
add Sammy Figueroa, Rafael Cruz (per)		**Funky Sea, Funky Dew** **Squids**

add Paul Schaeffer (elp), Alan Schwartzberg (d), Victoria (tambourine), Bob Clearmountain and others (handclaps), Kash Monet (v, per, handclaps), Jason, Jeff Schoen, Roy Herring (v)

New York	1978	**East River**

Randy Brecker (tpt), Michael Brecker (ts), Grolnick (elp), Jeff Mironov, David Spinozza (elg), Miller (elb), Gadd (d), MacDonald (per)

New York	1980	**Dream Theme**

Randy Brecker (tpt), Michael Brecker (ts), Mark Gray (elp), George Duke (syn), Bullock (elg), Jason (elb), Steve Jordan (d), Airto Moreira (per)

New York and and Los Angeles	1980	**Squish**

add Randy Brecker (flugelhorn)	**Baffled** **I Don't Know Either**

Randy Brecker (tpt, flugelhorn), Michael Brecker (ts), Gray (kbd), Finnerty (elg), Miller (elb), Richie Morales (d), Figueroa, Manolo Badrena (per)

New York	1981	**Straphangin'**
omit (per)		**Threesome**
add Figueroa, Badrena (per)		**Bathsheba** **Jacknife**
Don Alias (per) replaces Figueroa, Badrena		**Not Ethiopia**

* * *

John Scofield: *Still Warm*

The piquant combination of funk and post-bop harmony favoured by the Brecker Brothers is also evident in the work of guitarist John Scofield, a player who made his mark in both fusion and bop as early as the mid-1970s, but only came to widespread notice following a stint with Miles Davis in the mid-1980s. Like two earlier sidemen with Davis, Herbie Hancock and Chick Corea, Scofield had studied the great bop players, and his ability in this idiom is well documented on two recordings from the late 1970s which he made for the Enja label. But he also absorbed the rock and rhythm-and-blues sounds which were a part of his childhood in the 1960s, and these have taken their place in his style. An album from 1979, **Who's Who**, announced his interest in playing jazz in a rock and funk setting, and by the mid-1980s, thanks perhaps to his contact with Davis, his ideas in this area had acquired even stronger focus. The result was a series of electric albums recorded for Gramavision between 1984 and 1987, among which the 1985 **Still Warm** represented a peak of development. It confirmed the arrival of a composer and soloist of striking individuality.

Scofield's originality is most apparent in his improvisations. It was obvious enough in his earliest recordings, but it finds especially powerful expression in **Still Warm**. His special combination of blues, rock and post-bop elements has resulted in a new and highly idiosyncratic language not only for his instrument but for jazz at large. As far as bop goes, Scofield tends to avoid the continuous eighth-note lines which typify the playing of many bop guitarists, preferring to emulate the breath-punctuated phrasing of the horn player. From guitarists such as Otis Rush and Jimi Hendrix he has borrowed typical blues and rock techniques to produce such effects and sounds as note-bending, muting, harmonics and an overdriven tone. These are to be heard throughout **Still Warm**, but especially in *Rule of Thumb*.

However, rather more characteristic of Scofield the soloist than either personalized bop or blues licks is an extremely dissonant harmonic vocabulary, often expressed in wide intervallic leaps. This approach can be heard in the theme of *Protocol*, which also makes use of diminished scales. Towards the end of the piece, Scofield uses the blues technique of string bending but applies it to pairs of dissonant intervals rather than the usual blue notes. In the coda to *Rule of Thumb*, he takes risks which, in the hands of a lesser player, might result in gross errors. On one occasion he strikes, perhaps by accident, a highly dissonant interval, but makes it good by paraphrasing it a few moments later in a higher register. He then compounds the outrage by bending two highly dissonant and distinctly non-bluesy notes before resolving back into the home key.

Scofield has often been unreasonably modest about his abilities as a composer, claiming that he has only three or four ideas which are perpetually recycled. However, the handful of compositional formulas he reworks are distinctly his own, and often reflect the vocabulary found in his solos. **Still Warm** offers two tunes, *Techno* and *Protocol*, which are based on up-tempo funk dance rhythms. However, in this case 'funk' refers only to the powerful rhythmic groove set up by bassist Darryl Jones and drummer Omar Hakim. Harmonically and melodically, these pieces have the complexity of modern jazz, especially when Scofield solos. Another song type – slow with a lyrical melody – is heard in several pieces here, especially *High and Mighty* and *Rule of Thumb*. The latter in particular illustrates Scofield's idea about limited song types, since its mood and structure are highly reminiscent of *Holidays*, a piece from Scofield's trio album **Out Like a Light**, recorded in 1981. Along with *Techno* and *Protocol*, it is a highlight of **Still Warm**. At its centre is a simple 16-bar chord cycle over which Scofield builds an increasingly jubilant solo, creating a burgeoning sense of confirmation with the arrival of each new chorus.

CD

***Still Warm*, Gramavision R2 79401 (USA), 18–8508–2 (UK) and 971.028 (Germany)**

Don Grolnick (kbd), John Scofield (elg), Darryl Jones (elb), Omar Hakim (d, per)
New York June 1985 **Techno**

Still Warm
High and Mighty
Protocol
Rule of Thumb
Picks and Pans
Gil B643

* * *

Pat Metheny: *Still Life (Talking)*

If John Scofield is one indication of the continuing health and growth of fusion, his fellow guitarist Pat Metheny is another. Both were bop fanatics in their teens and both have developed distinctly individual voices. However, Scofield and Metheny's mature styles sit at opposite ends of the jazz spectrum. Where Scofield is preoccupied with angular, urban idioms and plays the blues in virtually everything, Metheny takes a markedly more lyrical, pastoral approach. Many listeners have discerned a country-and-western flavour in his music, and he has acknowledged the effect of a childhood near Kansas City in this respect. He has also shown an abiding fascination with another type of folk music – that of Latin America, in particular that of Brazil. Ornette Coleman's free jazz is yet another strong influence, and, although some observers have found it difficult to reconcile the typically smooth contours of Metheny's music with the angularity of much of Coleman's, Metheny has described the appeal of Coleman's music as being essentially melodic. Although the key elements of his style have been apparent since the late 1970s, Metheny's distinctive mix of North and South American vernaculars found particularly full expression in the Grammy Award-winning recording made in 1987, **Still Life (Talking)**.

Metheny had an early passion for the bossa novas of Antonio Carlos Jobim, and later for the work of Milton Nascimento, whom he credits as the inspiration for the wordless vocals which are heard throughout **Still Life (Talking)**. They are especially effective when carrying the soaring melodies of *(It's Just) Talk*. The explicit Latin rhythms which had been a novel feature of the group's previous album, **First Circle** (1984), are also revisited. These are not, however, the kind of rhythms associated with Machito or Tito Puente. These are muted, lightly dancing pulses rather than the strident grooves of the Cuban school.

A similarly muted quality distinguishes Metheny's guitar playing. Unlike Scofield, McLaughlin and other guitarists associated with fusion, he shows little evidence of a debt to rock or rhythm and blues, either in his writing or his playing. Among his early models were Wes Montgomery and Jim Hall, but Metheny's guitar sound is even darker than Montgomery's and further softened by the use of digital delay. Only a residue of his influences now remains; he has developed into a quite distinctive voice, recognizable after a few notes and much imitated by the late 1980s.

Still Life (Talking) marked the beginning of a return to extensive straight-ahead solo playing for Metheny – something which became fully apparent on the next album he made, in spring 1989, **Letter from Home**. Here, in 1987, he is particularly striking in *Third Wind*, where he takes a remarkable unaccompanied break and solo which recalls the example set by Charlie Parker's 1946 recordings of *Night in Tunisia*. This is an unequivocal bop solo, full of chromatic lines and delivered with enormous velocity and drive. His solo in the second section of this piece is played on a Roland guitar synthesizer, with the signature sound Metheny has made his own. He also takes a substantial guitar solo on *Minuano (Six Eight)*.

Metheny's partner of more than 15 years, keyboard player Lyle Mays, delivers solos which contrast dramatically with Metheny's. His considered piano outings on *So May it Secretly Begin* and *(It's Just) Talk* are masterpieces of understatement and appropriately recall Jobim's sparse piano solos. A similar subtlety is apparent in Mays's deployment of synthesizers, which are used mainly for unobtrusive string and horn sounds. Synthesized, almost funk-like horn riffs are heard towards the close of *(It's Just) Talk*, but these are virtually the only hint of rhythm and blues in the music of the Pat Metheny Group. The folky, banjo-like twang of Metheny's guitar synthesizer on *Last Train Home* says much more about the group's style.

CD

***Still Life (Talking)*, Geffen GHS 24145–2 (USA) and 924145–2 (UK)**

Lyle Mays (syn, p), Pat Metheny (g, elg, ?g syn), Steve Rodby (sb), Paul Wertico (d), Armando Marçal (per, v), David Blamires, Mark Ledford (v)

New York	March–April 1987	**Minuano (Six Eight)**
omit (g)		**So May it Secretly Begin**
*as **Minuano**, but Metheny (g syn), Rodby (?elb), omit (per)*		**Last Train Home**
*as **Minuano**, but Metheny (elg)*		**(It's Just) Talk**
*as **Minuano**, but Mays (syn), Metheny (g, g syn)*		**Third Wind**

Mays (syn), Marçal (per)	**Distance**
*as **Minuano**, but Metheny (g), omit (d), omit (v)*	**In her Family**

* * *

Gary Thomas and Seventh Quadrant: *By Any Means Necessary*

In 1987, when Miles Davis adopted the methods of Michael Jackson and Prince, his tenor saxophonist Gary Thomas left because he felt unable to oblige with the required funk licks. As Thomas's third album **By Any Means Necessary** shows, he was headed in a virtually diametrically-opposed direction. This seems a little ironic, since it is possible to imagine that Davis's singular 1984 album **Decoy** was an important influence on the M-BASE collective of which Thomas had been a satellite. Certainly **By Any Means Necessary** takes the mildly satanic cast of such pieces as Davis's title track *Decoy* and *What It Is* several steps further toward sonic hell.

The one thing Thomas's music does retain from Davis's band is a rather strictly observed backbeat; indeed the muscular but static drumming of Dennis Chambers is thrown into occasionally tedious relief by the restlessness of every other aspect of this music. Thomas, classically trained, had an early familiarity with irregular note-groupings, and although he sounds superficially like yet another Coltrane disciple, his admiration for the soloing of such players as Eddie Harris and Woody Shaw led him to develop an intervallic vocabulary rich in disturbingly dissonant fourths and seconds. Add to this a dense, Gothic conception of texture, a fierce, grainy saxophone tone, a fascination with sci-fi and its incidental music and a shopful of hi-tech instrumentation (the bass is the only acoustic instrument in an otherwise thoroughly plugged-in band – even Thomas's saxophone often interfaces with a synthesizer), and you have the ingredients for an apocalyptic soundscape that would serve perfectly as the jazz mix of the soundtrack to Terminator III.

This may sound like a recipe for indigestion, but Thomas's music exerts a grim fascination. The headlong energy, the long harmony and the powerhouse soloing of the leader and his guests John Scofield and Greg Osby add up to a gruelling but rewarding package. Thomas's tremendous virtuosity has been evident enough elsewhere in his fresh treatments of the standard repertoire, but his playing here is at the peak of expressiveness, inspired no doubt by a setting unlike any other in the genre.

CD

***By Any Means Necessary*, JMT 844432–2 (USA)**

Gary Thomas (ts, syn, fl), Tim Murphy (p, syn), John Scofield (elg), Anthony Cox (sb), Dennis Chambers (d), Nana Vasconcelos (per)

New York	May 1989	**By Any Means Necessary**
omit Scofield		**Continuum**
Thomas, Murphy, Scofield, Cox, Chambers		**You're Under Arrest**
add Geri Allen (p, syn), Vasconcelos		**Potential Hazard**
Thomas, Allen, Murphy, Cox, Chambers		**To the Vanishing Point**
Thomas, Murphy, Mick Goodrick (elg), Cox, Chambers, Vasconcelos		**Screen Gem**
Thomas, Greg Osby (as, syn), Allen, Vasconcelos		**Janala**
*as **By Any Means Necessary**, but add Goodrick (elg)*		**At Risk**
Thomas, Osby, Murphy, Cox, Chambers		**Out of Harm's Way**

CHAPTER 19

Avant-garde Jazz, Freebop, World Music and other Eclecticisms

Barry Kernfeld
(and Mark Gilbert on Keith Jarrett and M-BASE)

By the 1970s it had become apparent that John Coltrane's popular success in presenting an uncompromising brand of free jazz had been a complete anomaly. As it stood, the style attracted too few listeners to survive without some sort of modification. To be sure, European audiences for *avant-garde* art music recognized potential interconnections between that music and free jazz and consequently offered some opportunities for keeping the free jazz flame alive (as Steve Lacy has done in Paris). But this movement was never large, and its Eastern component collapsed with the fall of communism and the subsequent end of support for authorized free jazz groups. In the USA, the basic choices for musicians seemed to be to go on playing as before while scuffling along (as Cecil Taylor has done), to go on playing as before while securing a day job, perhaps even a connection to the academy, so that one's comfort would not depend entirely upon earnings from free jazz performance and recordings, or to modify the style, to make it accessible to a much larger audience.

The present chapter surveys some of the finest representatives of these modifications. Pointedly it surveys and does not summarize them, for the guiding principle of the past two decades – eclecticism – seems to go against the idea of a summary. This eclecticism may be historical and cross-cultural. It may draw from any style of jazz or from other musical genres, both popular and classical. It may incorporate aspects of literature and theatricality. The link to free jazz may remain strong, or the offshoot may transform a quality originating in free jazz into something quite distantly removed (as immediately below, in Oregon's brand of world music). These features may contrast with one another disc by disc, track by track, or even (and particularly for John Zorn) minute by minute. From the point of view of style, anything goes. And yet, as these selections demonstrate, an outlook that threatens to produce an eclectic stylistic hodgepodge may actually result in some very great jazz.

* * *

Keith Jarrett: *Expectations* (by Mark Gilbert)

The breadth of pianist Keith Jarrett's musical vision has often been remarked upon, but **Expectations**, a double LP reissued on one CD, is perhaps the most comprehensive single example of his eclecticism. His introspective musings, his classical aspirations, his performances of standards are all separately represented on various later albums for ECM, but in 1971 **Expectations** touched most of these bases, and others, at once.

The limitless pursuit of new juxtapositions that was typical of the era no doubt gave Jarrett's native catholicism an added impetus. This was a little over two years after Woodstock and a time when the term 'fusion' was still innocent of the specific and unflattering connotation it later acquired. Jarrett's 'fusion' was in any case immune from the commercial considerations that circumscribed so much music sold under that banner. The rambling excursions here into Ornette Coleman's territory (*Roussillon*, *Circular Letter*, and *Bring Back the Time When (if)*) see to that, as does the dark, classically-inflected epic *Nomads*, but even when Jarrett rollicks on a backbeat, as on the gospel vamps of *Common Mama* and *Take Me Back*, the few lingering Spyro Gyra fans are likely to be quickly dispersed by the music's raggedness.

That untidiness is part of a paradox that exemplifies the charm of **Expectations**. The music is full of seeming incongruities: the breathless, ecstatic pianism of *Common Mama* against Sam Brown's crude 'beat' guitar on *Take Me Back*, the simplicity and datedness of the gospel groove early in *There is a Road (God's River)* against the sophistication of the string passages that follow, the challenge of the Coleman take-offs *Roussillon* and *The Circular Letter* against the easy grooves of *Common Mama* and *Take Me Back*. Yet the loose, sometimes amateurish feeling engendered by the rhythm section and the superficial banality of some of the material helps illuminate a central tenet of Jarrett's philosophy: if the spirit is exulting, the rest will take care of itself, and here it does.

There is a curious little footnote to this collection: the American reissue on CD is identical in content to the original double LP, but the European reissue omits the 46-second-long track *Vision*, for piano and strings.

CD

***Expectations*, Columbia Jazz Contemporary Masters CK–46866 (USA) and 467902–2 (Europe)**

Keith Jarrett (p, org, sop, tambourine, per, arr), unidentified (strings), Charlie Haden (sb), Paul Motian (d)
New York 1971 **Expectations**

Jarrett (p, org, sop, tambourine, per, arr), Sam Brown (elg), Haden (sb), Motian (d), Airto Moreira (d, per)
Take Me Back

add Dewey Redman (ts, per) **The Circular Letter (for J-K)**
Sundance
Bring Back the Time When (if)

*as **Expectations*** **There is a Road (God's River)**

Jarrett (p), unidentified (strings) **Vision**

unidentified (brass and reeds), Redman, Jarrett, Haden, Motian, Moreira
Common Mama

Jarrett, Brown, Haden, Motian, Moreira **The Magician in You**

Redman, Jarrett, Haden, Motian **Rousillon**

unidentified (brass and reeds), Jarrett, Brown, Haden, Motian, Moreira
Nomads

* * *

Oregon: *Out of the Woods*

World music began to manifest itself in jazz in the mid- to late-1960s. Among many reasons, the civil rights movement encouraged an exploration of the musical heritage of American minorities; jazz musicians followed rock musicians in a search for spirituality in Eastern cultures; and free-jazz performers, seeking new timbral combinations, introduced non-Western instruments. A further development, with political origins in popular folk music, espoused a concern for the world's environment and generated, by extension of the idea that all the world is one, the idea that all the world's music might be one. Leading exponents were the Paul Winter Consort and Oregon, which was a politically less overbearing and musically more sophisticated quartet formed in 1970 by members of Winter's group: Paul McCandless, Ralph Towner, Glen Moore, and Collin Walcott.

Eight years later they recorded **Out of the Woods**, the finest example of this branch of world music. It expresses earnestness and sensitivity, hallmarks of environmentally concerned jazz. It draws the world together through a diverse melding of classical, folk, jazz, African, and Indian instruments and instrumental techniques. Yet it achieves its mood and diversity without sacrificing a firm base in the complexities of jazz harmony, rhythm, and improvisation. There are many original sounds, not all of them obvious. (Is that vibrating drone on *Fall 77* played on a jew's-harp? Is Moore clonking the body of the string bass as a drum in the middle of *Dance to the Morning Star*?). *Yellow Bell* has a haunting, metrically irregular theme, its melody played in unison by McCandless on oboe and Towner on piano. Delicate collective improvisations feature McCandless's oboe floating above rhythms driven by Walcott on tablā on *Cane Fields* and on thumb piano on *Dance to the Morning Star*, together with Towner's guitar and Moore's bass. On *Visions of a Dancer* the texture moves from collective improvisation in a ballad style, into a unison melody for oboe and sitar. And the inspirational song *Witchi-Tai-To* cohesively brings together the group's multi-instrumentalism: an introduction and theme on sitar and guitar, then joined by English horn and string bass; guitar, bass, and tablā; McCandless switching over to the oboe and Towner to piano, as Walcott takes up the ride cymbal and conga drum.

Owing to its soothing qualities, **Out of the Woods** became a model that jazz-tinged practitioners of the subsequent new age genre would imitate. At the same time it set a standard for substance that new age jazz musicians would never achieve.

CD

***Out of the Woods*, Discovery 71004 (USA)**

Paul McCandless (oboe), Ralph Towner (p), Glen Moore (sb), Collin Walcott (conga, ride cymbal)

New York	April 1978	**Yellow Bell**

McCandless (bass clarinet), Towner (flugelhorn), Moore, Walcott (tambourine); ?jew's-harp **Fall 77**

Towner (p) **Reprise**

McCandless (oboe), Towner (g), Moore (sb), Walcott (tablā) **Cane Fields**

McCandless (oboe), Towner (12-string g), Moore (sb), Walcott (thumb piano) **Dance to the Morning Star**

McCandless (oboe), Towner (p, 12-string g), Moore (sb), Walcott (sitar) **Vision of a Dancer**

Walcott (tablā) **Story Telling**

McCandless (oboe), Towner (g), Moore (sb), Walcott (tablā) **Waterwheel**

McCandless (English horn, oboe), Towner (p, g), Moore (sb), Walcott (sitar, tablā, conga, ride cymbal) **Witchi-Tai-To**

* * *

Pharoah Sanders: *Journey to the One*

As a participant in Coltrane's last groups, including the *ad hoc* orchestra that recorded *Ascension* in 1965, Pharoah Sanders was the most harshly violent of the free jazz tenor saxophonists. Indeed he played with such intensity that it often was possible to tell when he was soloing on an LP simply by looking for the most jagged grooves on the vinyl. After Coltrane's death in 1967 and with a then-strong interest in Asian philosophy affecting many jazz and popular musicians, Sanders planted his harsh playing into the larger context of a quiet, meditative, repetitive serenity that unfortunately seemed rather fluffy. Since the mid-1970s his stylistic realm has expanded as he has incorporated more conventional styles into his performances, and the philosophical fluffiness has become less central. An album from 1980, **Journey to the One**, provides a powerful representation of his wide-ranging creativity.

Greetings to Idris, Doctor Pitt, and *You've got to have freedom,* all composed by Sanders, show him at his most ecstatic level of inspiration. Each has a concise underlying theme: for *Greetings to Idris* and *You've got to have freedom,* loosely swinging, simple chord progressions; for *Doctor Pitt,* also a loosely swinging rhythmic feel, coupled to static harmony that moves slowly up and back, after the manner of Miles

Davis's *So What* and Coltrane's *Impressions*. Above these, Sanders utilizes a conventional approach to melody and a tone founded in Coltrane's tenor saxophone sound of the early 1960s, as well as radical melodic ideas and an intense, growling tone. He places these contrasting sounds into his solos with considerable variety, showing a sense of architecture that was lacking in the continuously shrieking (though none the less remarkable) blowouts that characterized his work in the 1960s.

Four tracks offer a summary and continuation of Coltrane's ballad style. *Easy to Remember* is a popular song by Rodgers and Hart, presented exactly as Coltrane would have done it. From this type of song, Coltrane began playing new and unconventional wordless ballads, including his *After the Rain*. Following in this manner, Sanders composed *Bedria* and *Kazuko (Peace Child)*. For all his dependence on Coltrane's innovations, on this last title, *Kazuko*, he actually outdoes Coltrane, offering an entirely original and starkly beautiful instrumental combination, with his tenor sax improvising smooth, airy lines and Paul Arslanian's harmonium and wind chimes providing a droning underpinning, as Yoko Ito Gates crisply and unpredictably plucks (and later, strums) the koto (a Japanese zither). World music also enters prominently into *Soledad*. Perhaps inspired by earlier performances by alto saxophonist John Handy (who, like Sanders, is based in San Francisco), Sanders incorporates his tenor sax improvisations into an Indian raga.

The principal sidemen include rhythm section members fluent in this continuation of Coltrane's musical legacy – pianist John Hicks (featured on *Yemenja*), bassist Ray Drummond and drummer Idris Muhammad – as well as trumpeter and flugelhorn player Eddie Henderson, whose melodic conception is strongly anchored in bop. When during Henderson's solo on *You've got to have freedom* Sanders is honking away in coordination with the singers, the flugelhornist seems out of touch with the tune. Sanders then takes over the spotlight and shows how it should be done.

CD

***Journey to the One*, Evidence ECD 22016–2 (USA)**

Pharoah Sanders (ts), John Hicks (p), Carl Lockett (elg), Ray Drummond (sb), Idris Muhammad (d)

San Francisco	1980	**Greetings to Idris**
add Eddie Henderson (tpt); omit (elg)		**Doctor Pitt**

Sanders (ts), Yoko Ito Gates (koto), Paul Arslanian (harmonium, wind chimes)
Kazuko (Peace Child)

Sanders (ts), Joe Bonner (p) **After the Rain**

Sanders (ts, tambura), Bedria Sanders (harmonium), James Pomerantz (sitar), Phil Ford (tablā) **Soledad**

Henderson (flugelhorn), Sanders (ts), Hicks (p), Drummond (b), Muhammad (d), Donna (Dee Dee) Dickerson, Bobby McFerrin, Vicki Randle, Ngoh Spencer (v)
You've Got to Have Freedom

Sanders, Hicks, Lockett, Drummond, Muhammad **Yemenja**

omit Lockett **Easy to Remember**

Sanders (ts, sleigh bells), Bonner (p, elp), Mark Isham (Oberheim synthesizer), Lockett (g), Joy Julks (sb), Randy Merritt (d), Claudette Allen (lead v), Dickerson, McFerrin, Spencer, Randle (v) **Think about the One**

Sanders (ts), Hicks (p), Chris Hayes (g), Drummond (sb), Muhammad (d)
Bedria

* * *

George Adams and Don Pullen: *Earth Beams*

In 1979 tenor saxophonist George Adams, pianist Don Pullen, string bassist Cameron Brown and drummer Dannie Richmond formed a quartet that remained intact until the drummer's death in 1988; Adams and Pullen continued to lead related groups, including Brown, until the saxophonist's death in 1992. Over the course of these 13 years the co-leaders made numerous fine recordings. **Earth Beams** offers great examples of their characteristic sound, drawn from soul jazz, modal jazz and free jazz.

Dionysus (with its gentle and simple riff pattern), *Sophisticated Alice* (founded on repetitions of a syncopated five-note rhythm associated with Bo Diddley) and *Saturday Nite in the Cosmos*, investigate the integration of dance music and free playing. In jazz there is typically only the loosest of relationships between titles and sound, but every once in a while someone manages to come up with a title that summarizes the music perfectly. *Saturday Nite in the Cosmos* is happy, gospel-derived, Saturday night party music, launched into space with copious amounts of free improvisation, and the whole dancing along in $\frac{5}{4}$ rather than common time.

Earth Beams, Magnetic Love Field (a duo by the co-leaders), and *More Flowers* are situated stylistically within the legacy of John Coltrane's music, particularly in the manner practiced contemporaneously in 1980 by Pharoah Sanders on selections discussed immediately above. Although he does not have the drumming technique of an Elvin Jones or an Idris Muhammad, Richmond does a respectable job of capturing an appropriately energetic and multi-faceted percussion style. *More Flowers* shows him to best advantage, adding tinkling bells to the quiet introduction, switching over to the cymbals for additional colouristic effects and then moving between swing and Latin rhythmic styles during the body of the piece. Brown is an authoritative bassist who participates equally in holding the band together and developing improvised lines. His solo on *Earth Beams* well displays his roaring tone and smartly differentiated melodic playing. Adams usually plays tenor sax with a hefty, broadly spread, bright tone (although he takes the harsh edge out of his sound at the beginning of *Dionysus*), and he blends heavily rhythmic funky gestures together with arhythmic free improvisation. Pullen takes the same approach to the piano, juxtaposing the formulas of soul jazz (he is also a soul jazz organist; see chapter 15) with anharmonic clusters, but additionally he contributes an original and idiosyncratic sound that makes his playing immediately identifiable. He has a manner of skating his fingers across the keyboard to achieve the illusion of continuously undifferentiated sliding sounds on an instrument that has 88 clearly differentiated pitches. To be sure, anyone can begin to reproduce this effect by thrashing along the white (or black) keys, but Pullen has developed it into a virtuosic technique, offering an astounding variety of such glissandos and using them as musical thought, rather than as a gimmick.

CD

***Earth Beams*, Timeless CDSPJ 147 (Netherlands)**

George Adams (ts), Don Pullen (p), Cameron Brown (sb), Dannie Richmond (d)

Loenen aan de Vecht, 3–5 Aug 1980 Netherlands	**Earth Beams**
Adams, Pullen	**Magnetic Love Field**
Adams, Pullen, Brown, Richmond	**Dionysus**
add Adams (fl)	**Saturday Nite in the Cosmos**
omit (fl)	**More Flowers**
	Sophisticated Alice

* * *

Carla Bley: *Social Studies*

The collaborative activities of composer and keyboard player Carla Bley and composer and trumpeter Mike Mantler have had a strong impact on jazz. Initially their focus was free jazz, with the formation of the Jazz Composer's Orchestra in 1964, the Jazz Composer's Orchestra Association, which from 1966 extended the group's performing activities into the realms of commissioning, producing, recording and distributing, and the New Music Distribution Service, which from 1968 was a pioneering outlet for albums and scores that were otherwise difficult to obtain. By decade's end 'free jazz' was a far too restrictive label for Bley's blossoming and expanding compositional style, as it took in elements of mainstream jazz styles, musical theatre, comedy, poetry, rock, pop, soul and world music. Bley and Mantler's subsequent recordings for their label Watt and their performances in a nine or ten-piece band under her leadership, became perfect representatives of the new eclecticism in jazz.

Probably the best of the resulting albums is **Social Studies**, recorded during the last part of 1980. It was Watt's eleventh issue and fittingly the first to be picked up by a major label, ECM; hence the amalgamated label name, ECM Watt. **Social Studies** is a spectacular record, perhaps her most serious one, offering six diverse compositions on which her fondness for silliness and shock effect is, although certainly not absent, none the less held in check and completely overshadowed by absolutely beautiful orchestral writing and meaty improvisation.

Revolutionary Tango (in Three Parts) is indeed a tango, with the persistent Argentinian dance rhythm underlying the entire performance. The three parts are broken by brief silences, but the entire track is a single unified piece featuring a tango theme that frames a succession of solos from electric bass guitarist Steve Swallow, trombonist Gary Valente, Mantler, tubaist Earl McIntyre, soprano saxophonist Carlos Ward, and Bley, playing organ. Outstanding passages include her luscious and idiomatic scoring for the brass instruments; Valente's solo, in which he fills a role previously taken by Roswell Rudd, laying out a splatty melody to assure that the music does not get too clean-cut; and the ending, with Swallow's improvised cadenza leading gracefully to the final low brass note. There is a nice touch of musical playfulness in the transition from Valente's to Mantler's solo, when Bley takes up an accompanimental line she had written for the saxophones and plays it on the piano, but twice as fast. There is also her one instance on this album of complete silliness, as McIntyre's tuba solo is interrupted by massed ensemble quotes of fragments of two renowned tangos: the *Habanera* from Georges Bizet's *Carmen* and

Hernando's Hideaway from the musical *The Pajama Game*. The joke works well, because it is not overdone.

Selecting the title *Copyright Royalties* is presumably Bley's way of asking the question: 'If I create a highly original, almost unrecognizable recomposition of *Mood Indigo*, why shouldn't copyright royalties come to me rather than to the estates of Duke Ellington, Irving Mills and Barney Bigard?' Borrowing existing structures, revising themes, retitling and then claiming composer credit is of course common practice in jazz, but no-one has ever put it so bluntly. Apart from her thematic revisions, Bley also uses the ensemble creatively: first the massed winds with drums only, the electric bass guitar and keyboards being omitted and the tuba functioning as the bass instrument; Tony Dagradi's clarinet solo accompanied by tuba and drums alone, with the remaining winds entering for his second chorus; Valente's characteristically splatty solo, accompanied by the rhythm section only; and finally, the full ensemble.

Útviklingssang (a Norwegian word meaning something like 'evolving song') again features Dagradi playing tenor saxophone rather than clarinet. This ballad is a study in orchestration, harmonization, and style, as Bley places a simple but majestic minor-key melody in varied jazz-rock settings, and then hands the piece over to Dagradi, whose improvisations add a jazz–soul flavour. *Valse Sinistre* is indeed a waltz. Modelled at first after the darkly moody orchestral style heard in Kurt Weill's *Three Penny Opera*, Bley's sinister waltz becomes a bop waltz during Valente's trombone solo, after which point the contrasting styles become amalgamated. *Floater*, perhaps the only weak track on this album, is a droning jazz-rock piece featuring Swallow's bass and once again Valente's trombone, for whom Bley inserts a zany passage of Latin rock in stoptime rhythms. The collection ends with *Walking Batteriewoman*, a completely wacked-out parody of formulaic soul-jazz organ combos. Odd-metred and irregularly-metred free jazz themes alternate with passages of conventional soul jazz, and Bley, who never has pretended to be an important jazz instrumentalist, finishes off the piece by delivering an unimaginably weird solo, the antithesis of funky organ playing.

CD

***Social Studies*, ECM Watt 831–831–2 (Germany)**

Michael Mantler (tpt), Gary Valente (tb), Joe Daley (euphonium), Earl McIntyre (tuba), Carlos Ward (as, ss), Tony Dagradi (ts, cl), Carla Bley (org, p), Steve Swallow (elb), D. Sharpe (d)

New York	Sept–Dec 1980	**Revolutionary Tango (in Three Parts)**

*as **Revolutionary Tango**, but Dagradi (cl)*	**Copyright Royalties**
*as **Revolutionary Tango**, but Dagradi (ts)*	**Útviklingssang** **Valse Sinistre** **Floater**
*as **Floater**, but Bley (org)*	**Walking Batteriewoman**

* * *

Anthony Davis, James Newton and Abdul Wadud: *I've Known Rivers*

In 1957 composer, conductor and musicologist Gunther Schuller launched Third Stream jazz, an attempt to bring together contemporary classical music and jazz. Little of consequence resulted, because of the incompatibility of contemporary classical music with the then-prevailing style, hard bop. Twenty years later, the situation had changed. Improvisation (operating under the name of aleatoric or chance playing) had become fashionable in Western art music; meanwhile free jazz had developed in directions that brought it stylistically into close proximity to the types of sounds prevailing in the academy. A number of musicians became comfortable playing in both genres and bringing the two genres together. Thus Schuller's idea came alive successfully, though perhaps in a rather different way than he had imagined.

Among the finest documents of this *avant-garde* jazz-classical fusion is **I've Known Rivers**, a predominantly serene album composed and performed by Anthony Davis, James Newton and Abdul Wadud. The instrumentation of their trio suggests in itself a strong step toward the classical mainstream: piano, flute and cello. Indeed Davis, the pianist, subsequently became quite well known on the 'other' side of the fence for having composed an opera based on the autobiography of Malcolm X, *X*, which was staged by the New York City Opera in 1986, four years after **I've Known Rivers** was recorded. Newton has spent a greater amount of time on the jazz side, and he ranks with Eric Dolphy and Roland Kirk at the top of the small list of those jazz musicians who have made this instrument work well. Wadud is lesser known and his instrument still uncommon in jazz.

Substantial portions of the performances on **I've Known Rivers** avoid a strong sense of rhythm or harmony, such avoidence being a shared characteristic of some types of free jazz and contemporary classical music. Additionally, the pamphlet notes take a cerebral approach that recalls formal concert programme notes, whereby the musicians describe their creations not only in emotional terms, but also with regard to concrete motivic relationships and structure, details of which therefore need not be repeated here. Counterbalancing these tendencies are elements of performance and composition firmly based in jazz, including (as Newton also points out in the notes) 'the rhythmic trust (swing)' [*sic*: thrust] of *Juneteenth* and the song form that guides the second half of his ballad *After You Said Yes*.

CD

***I've Known Rivers*, Gramavision R2 79427 (USA)**

James Newton (fl), Anthony Davis (p), Abdul Wadud (cello)

New York	April 1982	**Juneteenth**
		Still Waters
		After You Said Yes
		Tawaafa

* * *

Steve Lacy: *Morning Joy*

As a member of Cecil Taylor's group in the mid-1950s, soprano saxophonist Steve Lacy was involved in free jazz from its inception. In 1967 he moved to Rome and in 1970 settled in Paris, where he has held together a group devoted to bop and free jazz, the latter sometimes involving extra-musical elements of poetry and dance.

In his choice of repertory, Lacy has maintained a focus on either Thelonious Monk's music (which he has championed since the 1960s) or the leader's own compositions, and in this respect the CD **Morning Joy** is characteristic. Recorded in 1986, it presents two of Monk's pieces, *Epistrophy* and *In Walked Bud*, and four of Lacy's, all recorded live at the Sunset Club in Paris by a portion of his sextet: Lacy, alto and soprano saxophonist Steve Potts, string bassist Jean-Jacques Avenal and drummer Oliver Johnson. (His pianist Bobby Few and singer Irène Aebi were not hired for this job.) Lacy's compositions *Prospectus*, *Wickets* and the title track follow in the tradition of Ornette Coleman and Don Cherry's early collaborations. The themes are delivered in a loose rhythmic unison (Lacy and Potts together) and have no strict structural relationship to the ensuing improvisations. *Wickets* most clearly exemplifies this last quality, its fast and elusive theme proving to be nothing more than an introduction to extended improvisations on a slow-paced blues progression. Additionally, *Prospectus* and *Morning Joy* recall Coleman's manner of building a theme from several phrases of contrasting tempo and mood. Lacy's final contribution is rather different. Built on a jazz-rock beat, the performance of *As Usual* is tame by comparison to the version that Lacy would record four months later with his full sextet on the album **The Gleam** (Silkheart SHCD 102). Here within the quartet the saxophonists present Lacy's theme in a conventional manner. There, by means of horridly (and one presumes, intentionally) out-of-tune singing, the sextet convey the most nightmarish sort of drudgery implied in the phrase 'as usual'. Those who wish to experience Lacy's music in its most *avant-garde* posture are advised to seek out **The Gleam**.

In his prolific recording career, these thematic sources – Monk or Lacy himself – have sometimes carried over into performance, the bop and free jazz playing styles being kept distinct. But in **Morning Joy** they are integrated into what might be called, in jazz parlance, a freebop blowing session, with the emphasis on individual solos. There are some fine passages of improvised saxophone counterpoint on *Prospectus*, but the typical approach is for the two men to take turns in the spotlight, Potts going first. Whether playing alto or soprano sax, he generally invents impassioned solos, playing with a bright and harsh tone (the blues *Wickets* presents a mellower and moodier style), whereas Lacy's general method is to ruminate over little patches of motivic development while producing a hollow and dry tone on his soprano sax. Neither man is rigidly systematic about this. Their sounds overlap, and near the end of his segment on *Wickets* the normally restrained Lacy distorts tone and pitch drastically, so as virtually to speak through his instrument. The other featured soloist is Avenal, who pulls out the whole arsenal of string bass techniques – plucked, bowed, double-stops, harmonics – on *Wickets*. Since the days of Charles Mingus and Scott LaFaro, jazz bass playing has advanced so dramatically that a once remarkable virtuosity is now almost to be expected. This is said in admiration, not as an insult. Here is a bassist, largely unknown in the USA, playing as well as any jazz bassist whom you care to name.

CD

***Morning Joy*, hat Art CD 6014 (Switzerland)**

Steve Lacy (ss), Steve Potts (as), Jean-Jacques Avenel (sb), Oliver Johnson (d)

Paris	19 Feb 1986	**Epistrophy**
		Prospectus
		Wickets
		Morning Joy

Lacy, Potts (ss), Avenel (sb), Johnson (d) **In Walked Bud**

as ***Epistrophy****, but add ?Lacy (beaded shaker)* **As Usual**

* * *

John Zorn: *Spillane*

The eclecticism of the 1980s and 1990s, discussed so often in the present chapter, is carried furthest of all in the recordings of composer and saxophonist John Zorn, who has a wide and never lingering interest in just about any kind of music. In so far as jazz constitutes a portion of his creations, it may take the form of fairly rapidly changing stylistic collages. The title track of his CD **Spillane** is representative, leaping among rhythm-and-blues, bop, free jazz, latin jazz and fusion (with episodes of country rock music and urban blues thrown in as well), while all the while operating within the larger scope of a link among music, books and films inspired by author Mickey Spillane's well-known fictional detective, Mike Hammer.

As a means of assuring coherence within his careful and deliberate explorations of stark stylistic contrasts and within his interest in multi-media associations, Zorn bases *Spillane* on one of the most traditional and well-worn uses of jazz in films, namely its association with gangsters, death and sex. The death and sex themes carry over into the other two pieces of the CD. Zorn wrote *Two-Lane Highway* as a portrait of and feature for bluesman Albert Collins. For the most part it is a collage of straightforward amplified instrumental urban blues. Zorn composed *Forbidden Fruit* for the Kronos String Quartet plus voice and turntables (i.e., the record player manipulated manually to function as a musical instrument). It is a set of *avant-garde* theme and variations (complete with quotations from Beethoven's *Grosse fuge*). These two pieces are entirely outside the scope of this book, and consequently neither is detailed in the discography below. Yet as Zorn explains in his highly informative notes, such stylistic juxtapositions are the norm within the framework of his personal musical world, and listeners who pursue his creations further should have no expectation of pinning Zorn down within the world of jazz.

CD

Spillane**, Elektra Musician 9 79172–2 (USA)**

John Zorn (as, cl, arr), Jim Staley (tb), Anthony Coleman (p, org, celeste), David Weinstein (sampling keyboards, celeste), Bill Frisell (g), Carol Emanuel (harp), David

Hofstra (sb, tuba), Bob James (tapes, compact discs), John Lurie (voice of Mike Hammer), Robert Quine (voice of Mike Hammer's conscience)
New York June and August 1986 **Spillane**

* * *

Henry Threadgill: *You Know the Number*

In the mid-1980s, after having led the free jazz trio Air for over a decade, alto saxophonist and composer Henry Threadgill began to expand his orchestral palatte in new directions. He found his greatest success with his 'sextett', which offered a conventional front line of trumpet, trombone, and alto saxophone in combination with a rhythm section that was at least unusual, if not unique: cello, played by Diedre Murray (who together with Abdul Wadud pretty well cornered the American market for *avant-garde* jazz cellists); string bass, played by Fred Hopkins, Threadgill's longtime colleague in Air; and two drummers, including Pheroan Ak Laff, who had joined Air in the 1980s. The instruments add up to seven, not six, but Threadgill regarded the drums as one (and indeed they are not sharply differentiated on every track), hence the 'sextett'.

Their album **You Know the Number**, recorded in 1986, figured prominently in the then-new celebration of eclecticism in jazz. The stylistically wide-ranging array of compositions and arrangements are all Threadgill's own. Most striking of all is the hauntingly dissonant and beautiful ballad, *Silver and Gold, Baby, Silver and Gold*, in which the leader improvises on alto sax in a soulful, plaintive, Eric Dolphyesque manner against dissonant held tones, beneath which there emerges a current of slow, soft, but powerful swing. This is the sort of piece that many listeners will give up on immediately upon hearing its harsh and arhythmic opening. Give it a chance. Listen repeatedly, and see if its subtle beauty grows on you.

Threadgill's other ballad on this disc is *Paille Street*, which sounds as if it were a cyclically repeated exposition of possibilities for stretching out the harmonies in the opening motive of the popular song *April in Paris*. He plays bass flute on this track. (The disc notes also refer to his tenor saxophone, but it is not clear where that instrument sounds on this album.) *Bermuda Blues* is much like the sort of piece that was being played contemporaneously by the Dirty Dozen Brass Band: a harmonically static jazz-funk tune, weighted somewhat toward improvisational freedom but none the less requiring regular dance patterns from the bass and drums. *Those Who Eat Cookies* takes this freedom much further, with a wildly unpredictable syncopated theme surrounding a free jazz collective improvisation that offers the drummers considerable independence. *To Be Announced* is a free and dissonant collectively improvised calypso. *Theme from Thomas Cole* sounds like an amalgamation of jazz-funk rhythm and hard rock melody translated to free jazz instrumentation and dissonance. Finally, perhaps the strangest blend of all is heard on *Good Times*, which, owing to its rock beat and the character of the horn lines, recalls the sound of the pop group Chicago, modified by a cheery, gospel-derived chord progression and a looseness appropriate to Threadgill's *avant-garde* stance.

CD

***You Know the Number*, Novus 3013–2–N (USA)**

Rasul Sadik (tpt), Frank Lacy (tb), Henry Threadgill (as), Diedre Murray (cello), Fred Hopkins (sb), Pheeroan Ak Laff, Reggie Nicholson (d, per)

New York	12–13 Oct 1986	**Bermuda Blues**
		Silver and Gold, Baby, Silver and Gold
		Theme from Thomas Cole
		Good Times
		To Be Announced
as ***Bermuda Blues****, but Threadgill (bass fl)*		**Paille Street**
as ***Bermuda Blues***		**Those Who Eat Cookies**

* * *

John Carter: *Dance of the Love Ghosts*

The visit of his sons to Africa in 1973 inspired virtuoso *avant-garde* clarinettist John Carter to conceive of a grand programme of five suites depicting in music his personal vision of the history of West Africans becoming African-Americans. He recorded these suites between 1982 and 1989, the first for the Black Saint label and the remainder for Gramavision. Together they constitute one of the most ambitious, successful and compelling efforts at explicit storytelling in jazz. (Jazz is often felt to tell a story, but usually in a manner that is entirely personal and emotive, rather than explicitly programmatic.) This is serious music, not jazz party-time. In particular, Carter's fourth suite, **Fields**, recounts the drudgery and horror of slavery in a musical language that is at times terrifying. Hence newcomers might be advised to approach his grand work via the third suite, **Dance of the**

Love Ghosts, which despite the equally despairing programme (a father's disappearance from home, the journey in a slave ship, the rape of a slave) is extremely attractive musically in its combination of intensity and gentleness, representing not only the progression into slavery but also the future strength and achievements of African-Americans (including this very disc).

As has become common for those who once played in a hardcore free jazz style, Carter's music of the 1980s blends accessible elements into an *avant-garde* framework. *Dance of the Love Ghosts,* the last portion of *Journey* (featuring violinist Terry Jenoure) and the central portion *Moon Waltz* are high-energy free-jazz compositions and improvisations. The title track is tempered by a slightly bop- and blues-flavoured solo from Carter's longtime partner, cornetist Bobby Bradford. *The Silent Drum* brings in world music, specifically the Ghanaian Ashanti Drummers, whose spirit evokes from Andrew Cyrille a powerful solo of tom-tom drumming to end the piece. As if to represent the monotony and horror of the transoceanic trip, *Journey* brings in first a static funky bass pattern behind veteran trombonist Benny Powell (who fits in comfortably, showing complete independence from his years as a soloist in conventional big bands) and after that an unrelenting bop rhythm in support of bass clarinettist Marty Ehrlich. Among these various stylistic contrasts, the only incongruity involves the musical romanticism of *The Captain's Dilemma,* in which Jenoure sings the role of the rape victim. Finally, on *Moon Waltz* the free jazz segment is surrounded by a poignant collectively improvised theme that represents, as Carter's programme indicates, the birth of the blues.

The CD pamphlet details Carter's creative instrumentation, including his programmatic renaming of Jenoure's violin as a simulated masenqo (an Ethiopian single-stringed fiddle). A couple of details may be added to the description of the Ashanti Drummers. The dawuro is a clapperless Ghanaian bell. Kete is a generic name for the drum ensemble of the Akan people of Ghana, and it is not clear exactly what instrument is meant here. (For further commentary on the confusion that can result in trying to name and to identify African percussion, see the essay on the World Saxophone Quartet.)

CD

***Dance of the Love Ghosts,* Gramavision R2 79424 and 18–8704–2 (USA)**

Bobby Bradford (c), Benny Powell (tb, bass tb), John Carter (cl), Marty Ehrlich (bass cl, fl), Terry Jenoure (vln, v), Don Preston (synthesizer, electronics), Fred Hopkins (sb), Andrew Cyrille (dr)

New York	Nov 1986	**Dance of the Love Ghosts**

omit Jenoure (v); add Ashanti Drummers: Kwasi Badu (master drummer, v), Osei Assibey William (kete, v), Osei-Tutu Felix (dawuro, v)

The Silent Drum

omit Ashanti Drummers **Journey**

add Jenoure (v) **The Captain's Dilemma**

omit (v) **Moon Waltz**

* * *

Ornette Coleman: *In All Languages*

One of the most brilliant examples of eclecticism comes from alto saxophonist Ornette Coleman. His ongoing septet **Prime Time** had since its formation in 1974 presented a second generation fusion, in which an electric jazz–soul fusion style is fused with free jazz improvisation, as played by the leader together with two electric guitarists, two electric bass guitarists, and two drummers (including his son, Denardo). Coleman then carried this stylistic diversity further on **In All Languages** (1987). This linked and contrasting double album presents a reunion of his free jazz quartet of the late 1950s (discussed in chapter 16) and, separately, **Prime Time** (in which Coleman also plays trumpet), with seven of his compositions performed by both groups. The invited comparisons yield no losers here. Instead the performances are uniformly outstanding, the varied settings revealing the depth of his gifts as a writer, bandleader and performer.

As Jost has already described, a recurring quality of Coleman's music is the juxtaposition of contrasting themes and moods within individual titles. **In All Languages** offers free jazz and free-jazz–soul fusion interpretations of calypso (*Latin Genetics*); boogaloo (the quartet's *Feet Music*) updated to funk (the septet's *Feet Music*); rhythm and blues (portions of the title track); Coleman's distinctively personal soaring ballads (portions of *Mothers of the Veil*, *Space Church*, and the title track); and his equally distinctive skittering melodies (*Peace Warriors, Cloning*). In the quartet's improvisations on these diverse ideas, string bassist Charlie Haden and drummer Billy Higgins are accompanists to the partnership of Coleman and trumpeter Don Cherry. **Prime Time**'s collective improvisations have a much more unpredictable balance and variability. Sometimes the stylistic connection to jazz–soul fusion makes Coleman the star and his sidemen the accompanists, but this consideration also creates musical anarchy, whereby the drummers maintain a heavy dance beat independent of otherwise arhythmic elements. In general, the once revolutionary quartet seems polished, restrained and almost traditional by comparison with the zaniness of **Prime Time**, whose *Music News* (not performed by the quartet) sounds like James Brown freaking out.

It might be mentioned, just as a little item of curiosity, that the Caravan of Dreams (located in Coleman's home town Fort Worth, Texas) is the same organization that developed the ambitious, amusing and controversial Biosphere project, which lends its name to one of the tracks by **Prime Time**.

CD

***In All Languages*, Caravan of Dreams CD85008 (USA)**

Ornette Coleman (as), Don Cherry (pocket tpt), Charlie Haden (sb), Billy Higgins (d)
New York 1987 **Peace Warriors**

Coleman (ts), Cherry, Haden, Higgins **Feet Music**

as ***Peace Warriors*** **Africa is the Mirror of All Colors**
Word for Bird
Space Church
Latin Genetics
In All Languages
Sound Manual
Mother of the Veil
Cloning

Coleman (as), Charlie Ellerbe, Bern Nix (elg), Al MacDowell, Jamaaladeen Tacuma (elb), Denardo Coleman, Calvin Weston (d) **Music News**

add Coleman (tpt) **Mothers of the Veil**

omit (tpt) **The Art of Love is Happiness**
Latin Genetics
Today, Yesterday and Tomorrow
Listen Up
Feet Music
Space Church (Continuous Service)
Cloning
In All Languages
Biosphere
Story Tellers
Peace Warriors

* * *

Julius Hemphill: *Julius Hemphill Big Band*

In 1968 alto saxophonist Julius Hemphill began to participate in the free jazz scene in St Louis, where the Black Artists Group formed a lesser-known parallel to Chicago's Association for the Advancement of Creative Musicians. After coming to New York around 1974, he became a founding member of the World Saxophone Quartet, with which he remained from 1976 until 1990. During this period he figured prominently in the transition from hardcore free jazz to a more accessible pan-stylistic approach. One of the finest resultant documents is a collection of Hemphill's compositions and arrangements performed by an *ad hoc* group of New York musicians assembled for a recording entitled, simply, **Julius Hemphill Big Band**.

On this recording Hemphill inserts a brief passage of wild anharmonic collective improvisation into the ending of the opening track, *At Harmony* (perhaps as an ironic commentary on his title), but otherwise his general method of operation seems to be based on an updating and broadening of Eric Dolphy and Booker Little's demonstrations of playing 'outside': a copious use of pockets of textural denseness and harmonic dissonance, set against standard rhythms and forms (i.e., for the warped edge to be perceived as 'outside', it must operate against some sort of conventional 'inside'). Hence Hemphill's use of a fairly traditional big band instrumentation (although utilizing electric guitar rather than piano) and his incorporation of a pot-pourri of established stylistic contexts: modal jazz and hard bop on *At Harmony*; repeated oscillating chords on *Leora* (these chords borrowed from the opening of the second part of Igor Stravinsky's *The Rite of Spring*); funky blues, double-timed into a fast hard-bop blues on *C/Saw*; a romantic pop-orientated chord progression on *For Billie*; a pop-rock ballad, double-timed into a rhythm-and-blues shuffle on *Bordertown*; and the entire kitchen sink – a free–funk–bop–blues–rock–pop collage of jazz and poetry – on *Drunk on God*, Hemphill's setting of a surrealistic poem by K. Curtis Lyle. On this track the narrator, Lyle himself, unfortunately has a non-charismatic voice and little sense of musical pacing, and (perhaps intentionally on the part of the recording engineer, owing to these deficiencies) his speech is sometimes drowned out by the band, rendering the obscure poetry even more obscure.

Within this blend of 'out' and 'in', the ensemble and individual playing is sensational. The massed winds deliver Hemphill's skittering harmonized lines, drummer Ronnie Burrage kicks the band along, and a string of accomplished soloists step to the fore, including guitarists Jack Wilkins and Bill Frisell and saxophonists Marty Ehrlich, John Purcell and John Stubblefield. Hemphill himself is featured on most tracks.

Although his soprano saxophone work on *Bordertown* is unexceptional (the alto sax being his great strength), he is otherwise the outstanding soloist on the disc, particularly for his featured work on the ballads *Leora* and *For Billie*, on which he offers a sumptuous tone and a seemingly endless stream of creative melodies.

CD

***Julius Hemphill Big Band*, Elektra Musician 9 60831–2 (USA)**

David Hines, Rasul Siddik (tpt), Frank Lacy (tb), David Taylor (bass tb), Vincent Chancey, John Clark (french horn), Julius Hemphill (as, ss, arr), Marty Ehrlich (as, ss, fl), John Purcell, John Stubblefield (ts, ss, fl), J. D. Parran (bar, fl), Jack Wilkins, Bill Frisell (elg), Jerome Harris (elb), Ronnie Burrage (d), Gordon Gottlieb (per)

New York	Feb 1988	**At Harmony**
		Leora
		C/Saw
		For Billie
add K. Curtis Lyle (speech)		**Drunk on God**
omit Lyle		**Bordertown**

* * *

Dave Holland: *Triplicate*

The English string bassist Dave Holland came to the USA in 1968 and joined Miles Davis's pioneering jazz-rock group. The following year, drummer Jack DeJohnette joined Davis as well, replacing Tony Williams. Holland and DeJohnette were together again in the mid-1970s as sidemen in electric guitarist John Abercrombie's group. In 1988, after having individually established careers as bandleaders, they recorded **Triplicate** with alto saxophonist Steve Coleman, who had joined Holland's group earlier in the decade and by this time had established his own considerable independent reputation in association with M-BASE.

Probably the safest way to enter into Holland's brand of freebop is via a tune that Duke Ellington had recorded with John Coltrane, *Take the Coltrane*. This is a riff blues (musically unrelated to *Take the 'A' Train*, despite the pun in the title), and the trio stick to the 12-bar form throughout. There are solos from Coleman and Holland, followed by the conventional bop manner of trading phrases between alto sax and drums. But their blues style is as loose as it could possibly be, and

Coleman in particular is a master of playing bop-shaped melodic gestures that venture far from the presumed harmonies without losing touch with the underlying structure.

The final track, *Segment*, is a quintessential example of free-bop. Composed by Charlie Parker and also known as *Diverse*, *Segment* utilizes a 32-bar *aaba* popular song form with, unusually for Parker, a strong emphasis on minor-key harmonies. The trio follow this bop theme from beginning to end, but after the opening statement, Coleman and DeJohnette's respective harmonic and rhythmic treatment of it is so loose and disorienting that many listeners will not hear the performance in the context of this conventional background. Perhaps it will seem somewhat clearer during Holland's solo, a first-rate example of deft bop-orientated melodic improvisation on the string bass; during Holland's last chorus, Coleman plays a strange and quiet little riff on the *a* sections only, to reinforce the form. Then Coleman and DeJohnette launch into a freebop duo, and the esoteric approach resumes, before the leader returns to help finish off the piece.

Representing the Latin jazz component of bop, here translated into freebop, is Holland's composition *Triple Dance*, a samba. *Triple Dance* includes passages that slide into a bop rhythmic feeling, but for the most part Holland and DeJohnette set up the characteristic Brazilian bass and drum patterns. Soloing above these, Coleman pursues his characteristic manner of harmonic indeterminacy, which here may be recognized both in his own improvisational style and in his delivery of Holland's composed melody.

African Lullaby offers a taste of world music. According to the CD pamphlet notes, this is Holland's arrangement of a song of the Babezélé pygmies of West Africa. At the opening it sounds as if Holland has translated an idea from lamellophone (thumb piano) to the bass. Coleman's melody interlocks with, doubles and harmonizes Holland's ostinato, while DeJohnette focuses on tom-tom drum patterns and the occasional click of hi-hat cymbals, these elements of the drum set played in a manner that would fit equally as well with West Indian-influenced jazz as with an Africanized jazz rhythm.

Somewhat further down the line away from bop, is Holland's composition *Rivers Run*. It has four parts. In an unmetred collective improvisation, first Holland and then Coleman set up a sombre, obliquely defined tonal centre, and DeJohnette uses the drum set for colouristic effects rather than for timekeeping. Coleman solos over a quiet but funky rhythm defined by a not-quite-rigorously repeated bass pattern and DeJohnette's assorted swing rhythms. DeJohnette improvises alone, again in an unmetred and colouristic manner. Finally, a riff in rhythmic unison serves as a brief half-speed introduction and ending to a segment of fast freebop.

CD

***Triplicate*, ECM 1383 78118–21373–2 (USA)**

Steve Coleman (as), Dave Holland (sb), Jack DeJohnette (d)

New York March 1988

Games
Quiet Fire
Take the Coltrane
Rivers Run
Four Winds
Triple Dance
Blue
African Lullaby
Segment

* * *

Geri Allen: *The Nurturer*

Since the mid-1980s pianist Geri Allen has gradually become a prominent bandleader offering the now-typical stylistic expansion of the mainstream, in which bop provides a point of departure for diverse fusions. Her collection of pieces on **The Nurturer** is representative. Closest to Charlie Parker is *Batista's Groove,* offering a bop blues theme and alternating solos played by trumpeter Marcus Belgrave (a veteran of Ray Charles's bands) and alto saxophonist Kenny Garrett (a sideman in Miles Davis's last bands), but with a twist: while piano and bass lay out, Jeff Watts supplements the obligatory hard bop hi-hat backbeat rhythm (the cymbals snapping closed on beats 2 and 4) with syncopated snare and bass patterns of the sort heard in New Orleans brass bands. This nod toward New Orleans parade drumming testifies to the ongoing influence of the Marsalis brothers (with whom Watts has worked) and the Dirty Dozen Brass Band, whereby a previously specialized jazz percussion style has moved into the international mainstream. Watt's playing turns more (but not entirely) toward a standard hard bop drum style when Allen and bassist Robert Hurst join in. Other tracks, including *Night's Shadow, No.3* and *Silence and Song/The Nurturer,* introduce prominent elements of free jazz, particularly with regard to harmony, and they take a middle ground (freebop) in the complexity of the relationship between themes and solos. *Silence and Song/The Nurturer* and *Le Goo Wop* bring in a further element, jazz-funk, while *It's good to be home again, Night of Power* and Garrett's feature *Lullaby of Isfahn* are unabashedly romantic ballads.

Two footnotes on instrumentation are in order. The straight alto sax is an uncommon instrument. Perhaps it has a more nasal and splayed tone than the conventional instrument, as for example in the sound heard on *Night's Shadow*, if the comparison is anything like that between the straight and curved soprano saxophones. Yet this tone quality seems intrinsic to Garrett's musical conception, whatever saxophone he might have in his hands and mouth. Also, the CD notes credit Eli Fountain as percussionist, but it is not clear what he contributed. It sounds as if all the percussion sounds can have been played by Watts alone, except perhaps the quiet yet thick cymbal and bell sounds on Belgrave's feature, the free ballad *Night of Power*.

CD

***The Nurturer*, Blue Note CDP 7 95139 2 (USA)**

Marcus Belgrave (flugelhorn), Kenny Garrett (as and straight as), Geri Allen (p), Robert Hurst (sb), [Eli Fountain (per)?]

New York	5–6 Jan 1990	**Night's Shadow** **No.3** **It's good to be home again** (arr Gene Kee)
*as **Night's Shadow**, but Belgrave (tpt)*		**Batista's Groove**
omit Garrett		**Night of Power**
add Garrett		**Our Gang**
*as **Night's Shadow***		**Silence and Song/The Nurturer**
*as **Night's Shadow**, but Belgrave (tpt)*		**Le Goo Wop**
omit Belgrave		**Lullaby of Isfahn**

* * *

World Saxophone Quartet and African Percussion: *Metamorphosis*

The World Saxophone Quartet was formed by Oliver Lake, Julius Hemphill, David Murray and Hamiet Bluiett in 1976, but only with the making of this CD in 1990 (at which point Arthur Blythe replaced Hemphill) was the group able to resolve a discrepancy between its performance and its recordings. Heard live, the quartet had always been, and still is, consistently exciting. The experience of listening directly to musicians of this calibre is always special, and the ambience of a live performance adds variety to the sound. Yet in the comparatively antiseptic environment of the recording studio, the unvarying tone quality of the unaccompanied saxophone quartet grows tiresome, however great the musicians may be. This is especially true of the group's early recordings, in which a strong emphasis on free jazz techniques exacerbates the problem by adding sameness of texture to sameness of timbre. A partially satisfying solution came in the late 1980s, with the making of recordings devoted to rhythm and blues and to Ellington's music. By embracing traditional repertories, the quartet offered an additional textural element in the contrast between familiar tunes and wide-ranging improvisations. But the real solution came on **Metamorphosis** with the addition of a rhythm section (including electric bass guitar on three tracks) that provides the explicit beat for which the saxophonists' wonderfully rhythmic music cries out. In a brilliant stroke, the members chose not a conventional drum set, but African percussion, thus tapping into the ongoing interest in world music while also keeping the overall tone quality unusual and fresh. The plaintive singing and assertive chanting of percussionist Mor Thiam adds yet another element of variety to this achievement.

The asiko is a frame drum, and the signal drum is, well, a drum for signalling. The remaining percussion instruments listed in the CD pamphlet are difficult to identify. This is not surprising, given the galaxy of national names and variant spellings by which African percussion are known. In any event the sounds themselves are not at all obscure: various sizes of drum (hand-beaten), plus some sort of cowbell (struck) on *The Holy Men*, *Africa* and *Masai Warriors Dance*, some sort of beaded or sandpapered object (rubbed) on *Lullaby* and *Love Like Sisters* and some sort of rattle or gentle tambourine (hand-beaten or shaken) on *Su Mama Ah Zumu* and *Feed the People*.

The group's principal method is to set up repeated patterns for saxophones and percussion as a point of departure for launching into improvisations, some presenting soloists and others involving all the saxophones in uninhibited collective passages, on *The Holy Men*, *Lullaby* (with Lake playing flute), *Metamorphosis*, *Su Mama Ah Zumu*, *Africa* (with Murray on bass clarinet), *Masai Warriors Dance* and *Feed the People*. Also, Lake supplies his own feature *Love Like Sisters*, a pretty ballad that develops a subdued but funky, reggae-tinged flavour, reflecting one of his ongoing interests apart from jazz. And Murray supplies a *Ballad for the Black Man* and a gospel composition, *Lo Chi Lo*, with its reverent theme framing a fast and joyous improvised celebration.

Track by track identifications of soloists appear in the pamphlet, and one need only note the typo on the final track, the baritone saxophonist being Bluiett, not Murray. The soloists are sensational, yet even in this context of such consistently high quality playing, Murray stands out (as he does among all improvisers of his generation). *Ballad for the Black Man* provides a setting for his characteristically passionate stylistic package, in which he joins the soul of rhythm-and-blues tenor saxophone playing to the explorations of free jazz.

CD

***Metamorphosis*, Elektra Nonesuch 9 79258–2 (USA)**

Oliver Lake (ss), Arthur Blythe (as), David Murray (ts), Hamiett Bluiett (bar), Melvin Gibbs (elb), Mor Thiam, Chief Bey, Mar Gueye (per)

New York April 1990 **The Holy Men**

as ***The Holy Men****, but Lake (fl); add Thiam (v)* **Lullaby**

Lake (as), Blythe, Murray, Bluiett, Thiam, Bey, Gueye
Metamorphosis

add Thiam and group (v) **Su Mama Ah Zumu**

Lake, Blythe, Murray (bass cl), Bluiett, Gibbs, Thiam, Bey, Gueye; omit (v)
Africa

as ***Metamorphosis*** **Ballad for the Black Man**

as ***The Holy Man*** **Masai Warriors Dance**

as ***Metamorphosis*** **Love Like Sisters**
Lo Chi Lo
Feed the People

* * *

Sonny Sharrock: *Ask the Ages*

Having been inspired by the tenor saxophone and the newly emerging free jazz movement, Sonny Sharrock decided in 1959 that if asthma prevented him from blowing the tenor sax, he would instead take up electric guitar and learn to play it like a tenor sax. In 1964 he recorded as a member free-jazz tenor saxophonist Pharoah Sanders's group. In 1967 he received an offer for steadier work that placed his wildly innovative playing in the stylistically incongruous setting of pop-jazz flutist Herbie Mann's group. He remained a peripheral figure until the 1980s, when electric bass guitarist and producer Bill Laswell, recognizing Sharrock's originality and talent, began working with him. This led to several outstanding and stylistically varied albums embracing jazz, rock, blues, funk and folk. Among these discs is the particularly jazz-orientated disc **Ask the Ages**, released about four years before Sharrock's death from a heart attack in 1994.

The six tracks on **Ask the Ages**, all composed by Sharrock, exemplify his manner of bringing into jazz an array of timbres associated with hard rock, although evidently Sharrock developed this approach earlier and independently. His timbral palette includes the gritty but full-bodied, ringing and soaring sounds heard on a gentle ballad *Who does she hope to be?*, a bluesy riff tune *Little Rock* and the first half of a jazz-rock improvisation *Many Mansions* (while Sharrock accompanies Sanders's soprano saxophone solo). Sharrock also explores more intensely distorted sounds, both wailing and harsh, heard for example during his solos on *Promises Kept*, *As We Used to Sing*, and *Many Mansions*.

His devotion to Coltrane's tenor saxophone playing is highlighted by his choice of sidemen on this CD. String bassist Charnett Moffett ably follows in the path of Coltrane's bassist, the late Jimmy Garrison, by favouring steady droning patterns or rhythmically irregular improvised lines over a more conventional approach to jazz bass playing. Tenor and soprano saxophonist Sanders was a member of Coltrane's last groups and Sharrock's first employer; not surprisingly, Sharrock's manner of juxtaposing lyrical and wild melody mirrors Sanders's own. And Elvin Jones, Coltrane's drummer from 1960 to 1965, offers on **Ask the Ages** a quintessential document of his innovative and now widely imitated style. Jones takes several solos and is featured throughout the final track *Once Upon a Time*, on which he adds yet another tone colour to the disc by striking the set with mallets rather than sticks or brushes.

CD

***Ask the Ages*, Axiom 422–848 957–2 (USA)**

Pharoah Sanders (ts), Sonny Sharrock (elg), Charnett Moffett (sb), Elvin Jones (d)

New York?	*c.*1991	**Promises Kept**
Sanders (ss), Sharrock, Moffett, Jones		**Who does she hope to be?**
add (ts)		**Little Rock**

omit (ts)	**As We Used to Sing** **Many Mansions**
Sanders (ts), Sharrock, Moffett, Jones	**Once Upon a Time**

* * *

M-BASE Collective: *Anatomy of a Groove* (by Mark Gilbert)

In the late 1980s a group of musicians came together in Brooklyn to perform as M-BASE, an acronym for a slogan that typifies the collective's sub-Ph.d. pamphlet-note style: Macro Basic Array of Structured Extemporizations. Alto saxophonist Steve Coleman, a leading spokesman for M-BASE, suggests in the insert that its music is 'closely aligned' with Charlie Parker (whom he calls Charles Parker), Max Roach, John Coltrane, Thelonious Monk and others, but also influenced by the 'popular rhythm-based music' of the 1960s and 1970s. This might be taken to indicate that the sound of M-BASE is a not-too-distant cousin of the Brecker Brothers' heavy metal bebop (discussed in chapter 18). Little of the heavy metal component is heard here, save for one or two overdriven guitar solos, but there is an abundance of slapped electric bass, percussive single-coil guitar and crackling snare drum (in short, funk) over which are laid distinctly jazz-inspired solos: hence, jazz-funk.

It seems unlikely that the Collective would entertain so simple a definition of its music. Although heavily syncopated funky rhythmic patterns are intrinsic to the music of M-BASE, such patterns are typically skewed across irregular metres. Furthermore, M-BASE diverges from most earlier notions of funk-plus-jazz by drawing from the outer reaches of the jazz vocabulary. The collective sets great store on 'creative black music', a term that is probably a code for the jazz *avant-garde*, represented here by dislocated rhythms, saxophone ensembles rich in discordant tritones and minor seconds and solos that hang on to any underlying harmony by a thread. Whereas the Brecker Brothers' improvisations are based in an extension of conventional harmony, those of the principal soloists on **Anatomy of a Groove** – Coleman, his fellow alto saxophonist Greg Osby and electric guitarist David Gilmore – sound largely atonal. The resultant mix could be described as *avant-garde* funk, reminiscent at times of Ornette Coleman's Prime Time.

If the effect is rather severe, it is moderated by the contributions of

Cassandra Wilson, the most singular female jazz singer to emerge in recent years. As her performances on *Non-Fiction* and her own spiritual (in $\frac{13}{4}$ metre) *One Bright Morning* demonstrate, she draws from a wide emotional palette, by turns sensuous and chilling, sanguine and reproachful. Like her instrumental colleagues, she takes an individualistic view of harmony and melody. Newcomers to her singing are apt to remark on her eccentric pitching, forgetting perhaps that blues singers have forever been bending notes for effect. Wilson takes this procedure a few steps further, sometimes pushing whole phrases out of kilter. She can do this without fear of incoherence, since her music draws its form as much from rhythmic and timbral logic as from the organization of pitch, thus freeing up pitch variations for expressive purposes. Appetites whetted by Wilson's appearances here will find fuller satisfaction in her 1989 album **Jumpworld** (JMT 834434–2), a complete and as yet unsurpassed statement of her style.

Anatomy of a Groove may not be the most approachable of records, possibly because in attempting, as Coleman says, to produce 'the sum of our lives expressed in organized sound', M-BASE has created a musical analogue of the disaffection and alienation of a generation of urban African-Americans. There are times too, when the dissonance becomes relentless and the dynamic insufficiently varied, but the collective's complex blend of funky polyphony, austere harmony and spartan textures is probably the most striking non-revivalist jazz to emerge since the 1970s.

CD

***Anatomy of a Groove*, DIW 864 (Japan)**

Steve Coleman, Greg Osby (as), Andy Milne (kbd), David Gilmore (elg), Reggie Washington (elb), Marvin 'Smitty' Smith (d), Cassandra Wilson (v)

New York	Dec 1991–Jan 1992	**Cool Lou**
omit Wilson		**Teefah**
as ***Cool Lou***		**Anatomy of a Rhythm**

Coleman, Osby (as), Jimmy Cozier (bar), James Weidman (kbd), Gilmore (elg), Kevin 'Bruce' Harris, Washington (elb), Smith (d), Mark Ledford, Wilson (v)

		Nobody Told Me
omit Harris		**Non-Fiction**

Coleman, Osby, Cozier, Gilmore, Weidman, Washington, Smith

		Prism

Coleman, Osby, Cozier, Gilmore, Weidman, Harris, Washington, Smith, Wilson
Cycle of Change

omit Washington **One Bright Morning**

Graham Haynes (tpt), Coleman, Osby, Cozier, Gilmore, Weidman, Washington, Smith
Hormones

* * *

Jerry Granelli: *A Song I Thought I Heard Buddy Sing*

In 1977 Michael Ondaatje published his novel *Coming Through Slaughter*, based on the life of legendary cornetist Buddy Bolden and capturing the fantastic spirit and turmoil of the birth of jazz. The following year, in opposition to this literary path, Donald M. Marquis published *In Search of Buddy Bolden: First Man of Jazz*, in which through the careful examination of archival evidence and oral history, he aimed to demythologize Bolden's life. Now, 15 years later, drummer Jerry Granelli has revived the myth in a musical interpretation of Ondaatje's story.

As a writer I spend most of my time trying to get to the truth about the facts of jazz, but without ever forgetting that there is in jazz an irrational and a greater truth, more profound than facts and having to do with the interactions of music and God and humanity. So, never mind that even the title of Granelli's disc is misquoted and wrongly attributed. This is a spectacularly creative and moving performance, on the theme of jazz's greater truth.

The CD pamphlet consists mainly of excerpts from Ondaatje's novel, these serving as inspiration for the musical tracks, but Granelli mentions that the disc 'was also made from a fundamental desire to play the blues', which are at the heart of the music. *Wanderlust* is a slow blues first recorded by Johnny Hodges in 1938. Following the statement of the theme for the brilliant combination of alto sax, trombone, and electric guitar, saxophonist Kenny Garrett updates Hodges's role, improvising a relaxed, pretty melody with a tough boppish tone. This gives way to another brilliant passage of colour and contrast, in which a traditional, two-note blues riff played by Garrett and trombonist Julian Priester, supports Robben Ford's electric guitar blues solo, as Ford moves into a hard rock style. *Smoky Row* presents a moment of free funk. *The Oyster Dance* exemplifies one of Granelli's longstanding interests, odd metre, in this instance a mixed metre blues, with the drummer's funky rhythms guiding the band through an unusual 12-bar pattern of beats (7–7–7–7–5–5–7–7–5–7–4–4). *Billie's Bounce* is a bop blues closely identified with Charlie Parker (whose wild, tormented life warrants comparison with Bolden's); here as always Granelli purposefully re-composes the original by letting the horns rest, with the melody given instead to two guitars, these beginning in unison and then splaying out independently. Of the two, Bill Frisell is the first soloist, his instrument featuring a shimmering tone; Ford is next, beginning with a comparatively metallic and straight tone that then merges into a more distorted, heavy metal sound.

Coming Through Slaughter is a slow, free, bluesy original song composed by Granelli to represent the dilemma confronting Bolden as he is caught between jazz as God and jazz as the Devil. This theme continues into the following tracks, in which Bolden as an African-American Dr Faustus finds his musical soul torn between hymns and blues. *In that Number* ('...I want to be in that number, when the saints go marching in') evokes the New Orleans spirit with Granelli's parade-style drumming and the addition of a third horn player, Denny Goodhew, but again there is a deliberate twist to tradition, the front line of soprano sax, alto sax and trombone serving in place of the clichéd formation (trumpet, clarinet and trombone). Priester plays the melody of *When the Saints Go Marching In* as *In that Number* segues into *Prelude to Silence* (the two tracks overlapping), and Frisell briefly plays banjo, to reinforce the allusion to tradition. The horns again rest during a straight ballad interpretation of *I put a spell on you*, a rhythm-and-blues song composed by and closely associated with Screamin' Jay Hawkins (who transformed the theme of insanity into a personal comedy act). The suite ends with contrasting interpretations, rough and rhythmic, then gentle and loose, of Ornette Coleman's *Blues Connotation*. Bolden loses his battle.

CD

***A Song I Thought I Heard Buddy Sing,* Evidence ECD 22057–2 (USA)**

His World

Julian Priester (tb), Kenny Garrett (as), Robben Ford, Bill Frisell (elg), Anthony Cox (sb), Jerry Granelli (d)

Seattle	Jan–Feb 1992	**Wanderlust**
J. Granelli (elb) replaces Cox		**Smoky Row**
Cox replaces J. Granelli (d)		**The Oyster Dance**
omit Priester, Garrett, J. Granelli		**Billie's Bounce**

Buddy's Journey

add Priester, Garrett, J. Granelli — **Coming Through Slaughter**

add Denny Goodhew (as) — **In that Number**

Memories

omit Goodhew, J. Granelli; add Frisell (bj) — **Prelude to Silence**
(a) Shell Beach
(b) Lincoln Park

omit Priester, Garrett (bj) — **I put a spell on you**

add Priester, Garrett, J. Granelli — **Blues Connotation**

Epilogue

Blues Connotation (reprise)

Index to Names

Bold page numbers indicate main headings/principal selections.

Compiled by: INDEXING SPECIALISTS

Index to Titles

N.B. Bold entries indicate CDs and principal selections.

Compiled by: INDEXING SPECIALISTS